CONSUMER PROTECTION LAW

Markets and the Law

Series Editor:
Geraint Howells
Lancaster University, UK

Markets and the Law is concerned with the way the law interacts with the market through regulation, self-regulation and the impact of private law regimes. It looks at the impact of regional and international organizations (e.g. EC and WTO) and many of the works adopt a comparative approach and/or appeal to an international audience. Examples of subjects covered include trade laws, intellectual property, sales law, insurance, consumer law, banking, financial markets, labour law, environmental law and social regulation affecting the market as well as competition law. The series includes texts covering a broad area, monographs on focused issues, and collections of essays dealing with particular themes.

Other titles in the series

Consumer Protection Law
Second Edition

GERAINT HOWELLS
University of Lancaster, UK
STEPHEN WEATHERILL
University of Oxford, UK

ASHGATE

Published by
Ashgate Publishing Limited
Gower House
Croft Road
Aldershot
Hants GU11 3HR
England

Ashgate Publishing Company
Suite 420
101 Cherry Street
Burlington, VT 05401-4405
USA

Ashgate website: http://www.ashgate.com

British Library Cataloguing in Publication Data
Howells, Geraint G.
     Consumer protection law. - 2nd ed. - (Markets and the law)
     1. Consumer protection - Law and legislation - Great Britain
     2. Consumer protection - Great Britain
     I. Title II. Weatherill, Stephen, 1961-
     343.4'1071

Library of Congress Cataloging-in-Publication Data
Howells, Geraint G.
     Consumer protection law / Geraint G. Howells, Stephen Weatherill. -- 2nd ed.
          p. cm.
     Includes bibliographical references and index.
     ISBN 0-7546-2331-9
1. Consumer protection--Law and legislation--Great Britain. I. Weatherill, Stephen,
1961- II. Title.

     KD2204.H69 2005
     343.4107'1--dc22

                                                                            2004062390

ISBN (Hbk) 0 7546 2331 9
ISBN (Pbk) 0 7546 2338 6

Printed and bound in Great Britain by TJ International Ltd, Padstow, Cornwall

Contents

To Elizabeth with love from Geraint.
To Catherine with love from Steve.

Table of Cases

Table of Statutes and Statutory Instruments

Preface to the Second Edition

It is almost a decade since the first edition of this book was published. The gap between first and second edition was probably too long, but it has allowed us to refresh the approach of the book to a greater extent than if we had simply up-dated it from time to time.

A comparison of the contents list will show some of the changes. Thus food law is no longer treated as a separate topic; not because it is unimportant, but rather because it cannot adequately be dealt with in a generalist work. For similar reasons we have never covered financial services or utilities fully. Pressures of space have also caused us to delete the chapter on title and risk. Despite their obvious practical relevance we feel other courses will probably cover these topics and our central concern with the regulation of the consumer market can best be served by concentrating on other aspects. Some of the general discussion of private law and consumer protection have now been included in the chapter on quality of goods and services rather than being dealt with in a discrete chapter.

The first edition was published so long ago that we had a Conservative government. The change of political power has had an impact on consumer protection with the Labour government taking a more pro-active stance on consumer protection. It published a White Paper *Modern Markest: Confident Consumers* and made significant changes in the Enterprise Act 2002. Literally as this Preface was written the DTI published a Consultation paper on *Extending Competitive Markets: Empowered Consumers, Successful Business* suggesting that consumer policy will benefit from further initiatives in the near future.

One of the problems with this edition has been trying to keep pace with all the changes in this area and settling on a date when we have to accept that subsequent changes cannot be included or at least be no more than noted. We have aimed to state the law as at Easter 2004, but some late additions up to July were possible.

Some changes have resulted from continued developments at the European level. The adoption of a Directive on Unfair Commercial Practices is likely soon and this may have a significant impact in our fair trading laws, although less than might have been anticipated if it turns out to be a minimum harmonisation measure, rather that the maximum harmonisation measure first proposed. Likewise the implementation of the revised General Product Safety Directive has caused us problems, mainly due to the UK's failure to implement on time. Other areas like sale of goods, distance selling and e-commerce has also felt the impact of European legislation in the last decade. Domestically we are in the middle of a wide-ranging reform of consumer credit law and there have been major changes to access to justice and the organisation of enforcement. As always new cases have come along to test our understanding of the laws. Many of these changes have called for a complete restructuring of chapters. We hope the reader finds the new content to their liking.

Overall we feel that consumer protection is progressing. Policy is becoming more nuanced as policymakers try to liberalise the market and yet at the same time ensure strong consumer standards with practical enforcement. However, regulating something as dynamic as the consumer market is never easy and never dull, as we hope the reader will discover.

Geraint Howells
Stephen Weatherill

2005

Chapter 1

The Map of Consumer Protection Law

1.1 INTRODUCTION – THE NATURE OF THE LAW OF CONSUMER PROTECTION

1.1.1 Markets and Consumers

It may be useful to begin with a model of an economic system which is as alluring as it is unrealistic. Producers have to sell their goods to consumers in order to survive. They will only be able to sell to consumers what consumers want to buy. Consumer preference will dictate what is made available. Producers compete. Consumers choose. The 'invisible hand' of producers behaving in response to consumer preference organises the market. The survival instinct among producers which is instilled by the mechanism of competition will ensure an efficient allocation of resources. Given the stimulus of competition, resources will not be wasted. Production will stand in equilibrium with consumption. Viewed from this perspective, the market economy is a self-organising system.

A society based on this model of 'perfect competition' in the market should secure the best of all possible worlds for the consumer. The consumer, indeed, is dominant. He or she exercises the power of commercial life or death over suppliers in the shape of his or her purchasing decisions. The consumer will be supplied according to his or her preference and, for society generally, there will be no waste of resources. From the consumer standpoint, we might characterise a 'perfect' market as one where there is no such thing as an unsafe product or even a poor quality product. There are simply products of different types from which the consumer can choose. Increased demand will in theory lead to an increase in price, but a corresponding increase in supply will quickly restore equilibrium between supply and demand.

By contrast, in the absence of competition, inefficiency will prevail. Consumers will not be able to express their preference by sending messages via choice among competing products or services. Items may be produced which are not wanted, because the absence of competitive process obstructs the transmission of messages.

Competition in the market seems inherently desirable. That is a perception, however, which may serve as a starting point, but as no more than that.

1.1.2 Markets and their Practical Operation

It is easy to draw on individual experience to realise that this perfect system breaks down. Consumers have a voice which is much louder in theory than in practice. Consumers often simply do not know the nature of the products which are on offer. They want to buy the 'best' product, yet may be unable to make an informed choice. What does the consumer know about the qualities of the individual video or drug which is on offer? Even where relevant information is available it is common for consumers to misread it. Some risks are typically over-estimated, others under-estimated and consumer behaviour is in consequence wrenched away from what one might anticipate in a 'perfect' market.[1] In fact, the perfectly operating market system makes assumptions about informed stimuli delivered from the 'demand-side', the consumer, which are unrealistic and becoming ever more unrealistic in an era of bewildering technological advance. Such lack of information affects the message sent by consumer purchase to producer. It undermines faith in the ability of the unregulated market to operate as a perfect market which will deliver the best possible outcome for the consumer. Losing customers is the ultimate sanction against failure to meet consumer demand, yet the efficacy of that sanction is impaired in modern market conditions.

Nevertheless markets are flexible and may be capable of adjusting themselves. In a simple, small market lack of information might not prove a serious problem. Word will get around about variations between quality of products and the relative reliability of suppliers. In complex market conditions, however, this control over supplier behaviour becomes erratic, since information is transmitted haphazardly. For the average consumer, the purchase of expensive products which turn out not to meet consumer aspirations cannot simply be written off to experience. Nor is it comforting to expect that the seller of a dangerous drug or poisonous wine will not build up a loyal client base. At the other extreme, cheaper goods are typically sold by small traders, perhaps moving around markets or car boot sales, who will frequently be untraceable by consumers and who will not be concerned to build up repeat custom. True, markets for information may

---

[1]   Cf. J. Hanson and D. Kysar, 'Taking Behavioralism Seriously' (1999) 112 *Harvard LR* 1420; C. Sunstein (ed.), *Behavioral Law and Economics* (Cambridge University Press, 2000).

grow up alongside markets for products.[2] In the United Kingdom the obvious example lies in the Consumers Association's publication *Which?* Such support improves the consumer/supplier dialogue, but does not constitute a complete 'perfection' of the market. It cannot be comprehensive. In some markets, consumers are not even aware that they are under-informed, so the growth of a market for information provision will not readily help.

Absence of 'perfection' on the 'demand-side' may be accompanied by flaws on the 'supply-side'. In some markets, choice will be restricted by the existence of only a limited number of suppliers. The notion that rival suppliers must dance to the consumer's tune is false where the consumer's influence is thwarted because of a lack of competition. Such problems may arise because some or all of the relevant firms have decided to forego the unpredictable outcomes of competition in favour of collusion. Such a cartel will rob the free market of its defining competitive edge and deprive the consumer of choice. Some markets are structurally incapable of delivering competition. With a monopoly supplier, there is no competition at all and the consumer's position is grossly weakened.

More fundamental scepticism may exist as to whether the market system really is and can be in the consumer interest. The supplier/consumer relationship assumes a transfer of wealth, not its redistribution. Anyone can dine at the Ritz: but this notion of equality in the market is likely to cheer a rich consumer a great deal more than a poor consumer. If one wished to adjust the position of individuals in society rather than simply treat them as consumers within the economy, then it would not be deemed appropriate to leave the market to its own devices. Such an approach would prompt an interest in adjusting the nature of the market, or at least its outcomes. Wealth maximisation would be subordinated to wealth distribution and the consumer's needs would attract keener attention at the expense of the consumer's ability to pay.

Consumer demand is itself a controversial notion. Some observers doubt whether a defensible notion of demand can realistically exist in a modern economy which is so far removed from undistorted individual choice. For some commentators, firms are able to manipulate demand through strategies such as product promotion, on which much money is

---

2   For pathbreaking analysis, G. Stigler, 'The Economics of Information' (1961) 69 *Journal of Political Economy* 213. Cf. J. Stiglitz, 'The Contributions of the Economics of Information to Twentieth Century Economics' (2000) 115 *Quarterly Jnl of Economics* 1441.

invested in the modern economy.[3] The notion of 'false consciousness' describes a situation where consumers in the modern economy cannot really know what they want.[4]

A further feature of such radical dissatisfaction with the market as an organising model asks whether modern consumerism is compatible with good environmental practice. It is evident that an increasingly large group of consumers make purchasing decisions not simply on the basis of the tangible item they wish to acquire but also with reference to its mode of production. For example, has a piece of furniture been made in conditions which take account of the need to promote sustainable harvesting of timber? Labour standards may also affect some consumers' purchasing decisions. Has sports equipment been made in a jurisdiction notorious for low wages or use of child labour? For some consumers, choice and information may engage anxieties that transcend a simple market model of buying the product that best does the job.

This account has not yet drawn on the role of law. Markets can doubtless develop autonomously as a privately organised system. But today the pattern of the market can no longer be realistically assessed without taking account of the degree of intensity of public intervention. The modern market is characterised by centuries of State involvement which affects the simple process of private economic relations between supplier and consumer. This arises directly where the State takes on the role of supplier, as it has in many areas where mixed economies have developed. Moreover, outside such relationships, private economic arrangements are significantly affected by a mass of statutory interventions in the market which have accumulated over many years. The 'simple' consumer/supplier relationship cannot be pursued without reference to the place of the State in the market. At a rather straightforward level, it is assumed that legal consequences flow from a consumer transaction and that in the event of, for example, breach of promise, remedies in law are available. The State provides the framework for the vindication of such rights. This is uncontroversial. The modern debate is not about whether or not the State should have a role; the difficult questions revolve around the appropriate intensity of State participation in the economy and in society.

---

3   Cf. J.K. Galbraith, *The Affluent Society* (Deutsch, 1985); R. Unger, *False Necessity: Anti-Necessitarian Social Theory in the Service of Radical Democracy* (Cambridge University Press, 1987).

4   E.g. D. Kennedy, 'Distributive and Paternalist Motives in Contract and Tort Law, with special reference to Compulsory Terms and Unequal Bargaining Power' (1981–82) 41 *Maryland Law Rev* 563.

1.1.3 Law and Markets – The Scope of this Book

The law of the market economy has a wide scope. It covers law which sustains, promotes, curtails and adjusts the structure of a free market. In many cases it is based on political perceptions of the nature of the market economy. Within an overall political acceptance of the desirability of a market economy, there are many nuances of approach towards the way that market should be permitted to operate, with law used to achieve such adjustments. However, an accumulation of legal rules introduced by governments of different political complexions in the UK over many years has left the law of the economy in a patchwork state.

Consumer protection law can be understood only against such backgrounds. The consumer's place in the economy and in society attracts differing interpretations. Consumers are, after all, a heterogenous bunch and for most people it is probable that no theory feels intuitively completely correct or completely incorrect. Different perspectives contain their own truths. The law is affected by choices made about the identity of the consumer and the role he or she is supposed to play in the economy and in society. Consumer protection law has a range of possible rationales, some of which may conflict. The modern law has grown by accretion. The law now protects the consumer from a lot of different things in a lot of different ways and, as the law of market regulation has accumulated over the centuries since the days of the aleconner and obligatory cheap corn supply,[5] for a lot of different reasons. Consumer protection law is susceptible to neither neat nor narrow definition. Its scope is open-ended. It embraces both private law and public law; it requires appreciation of both national and transnational law. Consumer law sometimes appears self-contained – an example is provided by the EC's making of a distinctive consumer contract law – while elsewhere it forms part of broader commercial law. Defining the 'consumer' is an endemic problem in shaping the law which will be encountered on a number of occasions in the course of this book. Whether one chooses the label 'consumer law', 'trading law' or 'the law of trade practices' is not of central importance; it is however critical to appreciate that, irrespective of labels, the map of consumer protection law has fuzzy edges and one should know what lies beyond, including paths to other areas of law and the bridges to other academic disciplines such as economics, politics, sociology and psychology. This book tries to provide a full awareness of this breadth and ambiguity. Operating on the basis that the law of consumer protection is an aspect of the law of the economy, its objective is to show where the law of

---

5   A. Ogus, 'Regulatory law: some lessons from the past' (1992) 12 *Legal Studies* 1.

the economy which is not treated in depth within the confines of this book fits into the overall pattern. To some extent we present all law affecting the market as, directly or indirectly, law which affects the consumer interest, although choices have necessarily been made about the depth of the examination provided.

Accordingly the book examines the range of legal rules which offer support for the consumer, typically regarded as under informed and in a weaker position than the supplier. It seems that inequality of economic power between consumer and supplier is the key to scepticism about the modern unregulated market as an adequate defender of the consumer interest. The identification of inequality is but a starting point. It is, after all, an inequality which seems endemic to modern society. It cannot be removed. The shaping of consumer policy depends on pinning down the specific consequences of that inequality which are susceptible to legal control. It is critically important to appreciate that simply because some things go wrong for some consumers, nonetheless it is vital to examine precisely how and why the law might intervene in the market. Take the car boot sale, mentioned above. Should the consumer be protected from the risk of buying a faulty product? Not on one view, since the consumer who chooses to buy in such an environment ought to be alert to the risks. On the other hand, not all consumers *are* alert, leading one to consider a policy which assumes a rather high level of consumer gullibility. Thus the shaping of consumer policy may depend on what kind of consumer is being protected.[6] Then, the policy-maker needs to identify where the problem lies and how best it can be resolved. Is the issue the inadequacy of private law rights enjoyed by the consumer? If so, it may be appropriate to adjust the pattern of private law (Chapters 3–7). Inadequacy may refer to securing compensation for the consumer and/or to preventing a recurrence of the practices at issue. Is the problem that those rights cannot effectively be enforced? If so, questions of improving access to justice come to the fore (Chapter 14). If the matter is seen to require regulatory intervention separate from the private law relationships that comprise a consumer transaction, then varied techniques of public law require consideration (Chapters 8–11).

Both private law and public law contribute to this core aspect of consumer protection. Here, however, is an illustration of the open-ended nature of consumer protection law. If intervention follows from economic inequality, then it cannot be confined solely to the consumer/supplier relationship. There are similar reasons for intervening to protect the small trader dealing with a large trader. It will be seen that consumer protection

---

6   Cf. overview by T. Wilhelmsson, 'Consumer images in East and West', Chapter 3 in H-W. Micklitz (ed.), *Legal Unity or Legal Diversity* (Nomos, 1996).

law spills over into the wider field of trade practices law. This book also contains an examination of the law designed to address problems on the 'supply-side', usually termed 'competition law' but correctly included within the sphere of consumer law as a contribution to the better functioning of the market. Chapter 12 examines the problems caused by diminution in competition and in consumer choice on the supply-side. Legal measures are directed in some respects at curing such weaknesses on the supply-side, for example, by forbidding collaboration between competitors which restricts consumer choice, save in exceptional circumstances. In other respects the law acquiesces in such weaknesses but seeks to curtail their most damaging consequences. This may be observed in monopoly law, where the existence of economic dominance may be tolerated, but its exercise controlled.

The market in which the consumer is active today is not merely a national market. The process of market integration in the European Union has advanced rapidly over recent years so that the rules of the EC legal order serve as an increasingly important source of consumer protection law (Chapter 2). More widely still, international institutions, including the World Trade Organisation (WTO) and the United Nations,[7] have a role to play in the pattern of consumer protection. At a more subtle level, problems faced by consumers and markets have many similarities the world over. Discussion of the desirable scope and methods of consumer protection is improved by an awareness of comparative legal perspectives, which are also reflected in this book.

The book also draws in elements of the political debate. A perception of the false consciousness of the consumer leads to a legal response which is less than respectful of individual consumer freedoms expressed through market transactions. More broadly, if one believes that markets are not just, one will not be reluctant to interfere with them. This view locates the rationale for consumer protection beyond the economic sphere of mere market failure. At the other end of the political spectrum, the book does not neglect the argument that markets are or should be sacred and that limits must be placed on the capacity of the State to intervene in them and so undermine private economic freedom.

Ultimately this book is based on the belief that consumer law is not simply a matter of plugging a few gaps in the market system. Consumer

---

7   Cf. D.Harland, 'The United Nations Guidelines for Consumer Protection: Their Impact in the First Decade', Chapter 1 in I. Ramsay (ed.), *Consumer Law in the Global Economy: National and International Dimensions* (Dartmouth Publishing, 1997); S. Rachagan (ed.), *Consumer Protection in the WTO Era* (IACL, 1999).

law raises issues that are central to the determination of how our society views the citizen. This chapter draws the map.

1.2 THE PLACE OF PRIVATE LAW

The competitive free market allows the consumer to respond to a disappointing purchase by switching to another supplier. The law here has no role to play. However, such disappointment may be of a form that is capable of conversion into a legal remedy against the trader (whether or not the consumer also decides to use another supplier next time). Where what is supplied fails to conform to consumer expectation, English law may offer a remedy, whether in contract or in tort, enforced through the courts.

Contract protects consumer expectations engendered through the bargaining process. By providing a sanction in the event of failure to fulfil those expectations, the law acts to secure the enforceability of expressed consumer preference. Tort law operates beyond the realm of obligations agreed between producer and consumer. Even in the absence of agreement, tort imposes certain obligations on producers and distributors of goods.

The conferral of such individual legal rights on consumers offers a more direct protection of consumer demand than the more indirect and, in practice, greatly obscured sanction of commercial failure caused by withdrawal of custom. Failure to conform to agreed (contract) or required (tort) standards will result in legal liability. This protects the consumer and sharpens the message to the producer about the need to use resources in an efficient manner. Private law gives the consumer autonomy to act in the belief that he or she holds rights protected by law that can be asserted without the need to rely on an intermediary.

Current market practice assumes that private economic relations involve the possibility of State support, at the very least in the shape of providing for the enforcement of private law rights. These rights comprise, as a minimum, the obligations agreed between the parties. However, the consumer/supplier relationship under the private law today encompasses more than simple agreement, since both the courts and Parliament have extended the legal implications of the consumer/supplier relationship, and over the last 20 years this trend has been promoted and underpinned by legislative activity in the EC. Viewed from this perspective, the law provides a method of creating as well as fulfilling consumer expectations and of imposing liability on defaulting suppliers. This should support the trader's incentive to satisfy consumer preference and should improve the operation of the market.

The account that follows in parts 3 and 4 of this chapter surveys some modern developments in the scope of contract and tort law. Private law has been shaped and bolstered by the judges and by the (UK and EC) legislature to adjust the pattern of market relations and, sometimes directly, sometimes indirectly, to protect the consumer. This has done much to create a discernible framework of consumer protection law within the private law. However, it will be shown that some markets require public regulation, for reasons associated with the inadequacies of private law to achieve a free and fair market. This is examined in parts 7 to 9 of this chapter. It is a theme of this book, however, that the mixture of rationales and methods for intervention in consumer transactions today embraces such a range of (in places) conflicting aims that a simple objective account of what is at stake may misleadingly suggest that the development of the law has been a precise science. This is far from the truth. The rhythm of consumer protection in the UK has been discordant over the last thirty or so years, as the evolved regulatory assumptions of the 1960s and 1970s were sharply jolted by the sceptical attitudes of Conservative governments in power from 1979 to 1997 before embarking on a further process of change under Labour since 1997. Some of the key tensions that have moulded policy are tracked in part 1.9 of this chapter. In these unsettled circumstances, the best that can be done is to identify the several trends that comprise modern consumer protection law: trends such as identification of market failure and of, distinctively, a mistrust of the fairness of the market mechanism; also trends that embrace the fortification of consumer rights in private law and that move beyond the private law into the sphere of creating regulatory regimes directed at controlling practices likely to damage the consumer interest. Consumer lawyers must indeed possess a wide field of vision.

1.3 CONTRACT LAW AND ITS FUNCTION IN THE MARKET ECONOMY

1.3.1 The Function of the Law of Contract – Efficiency of Exchange

Put simply, contract law provides security for the recipient of a promise who has given something in return for that promise. However, the purpose of a contract in a market economy deserves closer scrutiny. In many respects, contracts are the lifeblood of a market economy. Simple one-off, over-the-table transactions are not the stuff of modern commerce, nor have they been since the Industrial Revolution. Rather, complex linked deals are the norm. Contracts allow long-term planning. Contract law provides security for those who act in reliance on the deals struck. Commerce revolves around promises made and promises fulfilled and, if not fulfilled, made good in other ways, backed by law.

The law has long enshrined a notion of the efficiency of exchange. Contract law seeks to promote bargains, because bargains constitute wealth-creating transfers. A simple example will help to make the point, although its apparent simplicity is unpicked below. If A has an item worth 100 to him, which is worth 200 to B, they will exchange it at 150 (assuming there are no other bidders) and both are better off as a result. Overall, society generally is better off as a result of a transaction beneficial to both A and B which prejudices no third party. The process of exchange ensures the efficient allocation of resources. This model makes a number of assumptions that are probed further below. However, it serves as a basic theoretical demonstration of the advantages of economic exchange. Indeed, on a theoretical model, it does not matter where initial entitlements to property lie. The market will secure the most efficient outcome; via a process of exchange, resources will reach the hands of the person who most values them – the so-called 'Coase Theorem'.[8]

Contract law enforces bargains and thereby induces parties to conclude contracts in the first place. Without law to back up promises and provide sanctions for reneging, deals would be short-term only. Firms would not be able to plan ahead, aware that default by their contracting parties will be remedied. Contract law facilitates the operation of the market economy. Indeed in a complex commercial world, where transactions typically relate one to another as part of a long-term pattern, contract law may be seen as the cement which holds the whole structure together.

At the commercial level, there is much to be said for the view that contract law should reflect business expectation. It should seek to achieve certainty and predictability in its operation. Litigation should not be a spin of the roulette wheel or else it will be needlessly encouraged, leading to waste of money and disruption of planning.

From this perspective, the function of contract and contract law is therefore to facilitate commercial exchange. Taken to a logical extreme, this seems to dictate that the law should unquestioningly serve the parties' wishes. Deals are struck to maximise both parties' wealth – why else? – and it is not the function of courts to interfere. Courts enforce contracts. The role of the judges is therefore rigidly confined to upholding contracts, as a reflection of the will of the parties and the interest of society in facilitating commerce. On this basis, the legislature too should maintain a strictly non-interventionist stance. This is the very core of 'freedom of contract'. The parties are free to deal; the role of law is not to interfere with that freedom, but simply to protect the deals struck.

---

8   R. Coase, 'The Problem of Social Cost' (1960) 3 *J Law & Econ* 1.

Most of the time, of course, contract law is a shadowy concept in the background once commercial relationships are afoot. Parties co-operate in the conduct of their commercial affairs, eager to avoid the costs, disruptions and potential harm to commercial reputation consequent on litigation.[9] In the words of an anonymous Wisconsin businessman; 'You can settle any dispute if you keep the lawyers and accountants out of it. They just do not understand the give-and-take needed in business'.[10] In practice contracts are adjusted during their lifecycle. Perhaps in response to such stimuli, some recent developments in English contract law manifest a greater readiness to uphold agreed contractual renegotiation than had previously been the norm.[11]

1.3.2 Limitations of the Law of Contract

The simple transaction between A and B mentioned above deserves closer scrutiny. The transaction seems efficient in the sense of wealth-creating; it seems appropriate to offer legal protection for the deal struck. However, some of the unstated assumptions require examination. The model assumes A and B are equally informed about the nature of the product and other background information relevant to the transaction. This will often not hold true. In an extreme case, informational imbalance may inhibit the conclusion of the deal. Legal intervention to ensure disclosure may be appropriate to improve the operation of the market. For example, in a market where goods of different quality are available at prices varying from 100 to 500, but where the consumer is completely unable to distinguish between goods on the basis of quality, the result will be consumer unwillingness to pay at the higher end of the price scale. As a result, sellers will simply withdraw better quality goods from that market. The process will continue; bad will drive out good. Legal intervention is

---

9   Famous empirical studies include S. Macaulay, 'Non-contractual relations in Business: A Preliminary Study' (1963) 28 *Am Soc Rev* 55; H. Beale and A. Dugdale, 'Contracts between Businessmen: Planning and the use of contractual remedies' (1975) 2 *Br J of Law and Soc* 45. Cf. I. Macneil, 'Contracts: Adjustment of Long-term Economic Relations under Classical, Neoclassical and Relational Contract Law' (1977–78) 72 *Northwestern Univ LR* 854.

10   Macaulay *op. cit.,* 61. Cf. D. Campbell and D. Harris, 'Flexibility in Long-term Contractual Relationships: the Role of Co-operation' (1993) 20 *JLS* 166; D. Campbell, H. Collins and J. Wightman, *Implicit Dimensions of Contract: Discrete, Relational and Network Contracts* (Hart Publishing, 2003).

11   E.g. *Williams v Roffey* [1991] 1 QB 1.

justified as a means of correcting problems caused by such intransparency.[12] This is an illustration of 'market failure' as a rationale for adding public intervention to the basic pattern of the market allied to private law.

On the A 100/B 200 model, if A is simply more skilled at negotiating than B (in general or because of special knowledge relevant to the transaction in question), A may be able to push the price above 150, which benefits both parties equally, towards 200, which then gives A the lion's share of the advantage. From the point of view of wealth maximisation, that may be irrelevant: as long as the transfer occurs, society is better off and it does not matter whether one party gains more than the other. We might also consider it proper to allow A to reap the rewards of his or her skill, which would dictate that, as a matter of policy, the law would not interfere. Such a non-interventionist stance might be further supported by the perception that A will have a reduced incentive to develop such skills unless allowed to profit from them; A's inhibited motivation might damage society's broader interests. However, depending on one's perception of the importance of fairness and the distribution of wealth, legal controls may be considered appropriate to protect B, the less skilled individual who is liable to be exploited. It might be judged that a pattern of wealth maximisation alone should be subordinated to a pattern of wealth distribution.

A further assumption underlying the A/B model is that the transaction does not affect third parties. That is unrealistic in most deals of any commercial significance. Transactions typically have implications affecting more than simply the contracting parties. Where A and B conclude a contract that will make both better off, but will prejudice a third party X, then the simple assumption that the deal is desirable and deserves non-interventionist legal respect requires more careful inquiry. From an economic perspective we might assume that, where A and B can compensate X and still ensure that everyone is better off, the deal is desirable judged against the overall interests of society and can and should proceed.[13] Achieving that compensatory transfer is problematic. For the lawyer, the introduction of X complicates the pattern, since the legal rights of X will frequently be difficult to identify. The simple suffering of economic harm caused by the conduct of others is not of itself a cause of

---

[12]   G. Akerlof, 'The Market for Lemons: Qualitative Uncertainty and the Market Mechanism' (1970) 84 *Q J Econ* 488.

[13]   In law and economics jargon, 'Kaldor-Hicks' efficiency refers to a situation where A/B/C *et al.*, are better off and, although X(s) are worse off, the aggregate losses of X(s) are smaller than the aggregate gains of A/B/C *et al.* This is in contrast to a situation where A/B/C are better off and no one is worse off, which is known as 'Pareto efficient'.

action at law. Tort law recognises only a more restricted range of liability. Moreover, even where X has a legal right, its effective vindication through legal proceedings or threat thereof will not be cost-free. The pattern becomes all the more complex and all the more prone to shelter A and B from accounting for the full costs of their actions where there are multiple X's. Where the impact of harm is diffused and the victims are not deemed sufficiently proximate to the actors, the chances of those suffering loss being able to establish the violation of a right under English tort law are reduced. Even if a legal right has been infringed, the smaller the loss suffered by individuals, the weaker the incentive to pursue the path of legal redress. 'Transaction costs' affect the process; in fact, the 'Coase Theorem'[14] operates in its pure form only in the absence of transaction costs, which will be rare indeed. A and B may therefore behave in a way that will benefit their own interests, but prejudice those of third parties, yet they may not bear the costs imposed on those third parties. Precisely the same observations may be made about the activities of a single person, C, which, equally, might benefit C while imposing costs on third parties for which C might not be held to account. The overall balance between A and B's (or C's) advantages and X's costs might still favour the former, in which case there might be reasons for simply allowing the deal or the activity (because of the maximisation of wealth that follows) or for allowing it but on terms which ensure that X has an opportunity to secure compensation from A and B or C (because of concern about the distribution of wealth). Where the overall balance shows that the advantages to the parties are outweighed by the disadvantages felt generally, then the market has failed to deliver an efficient outcome. Legal intervention to remedy this outcome might therefore be appropriate.[15] Specifically, A and B (or C) could be subjected to some form of control; they would then find limitations placed by law on their freedom to choose how to behave.[16]

Finally, the A/B contract may maximise wealth, but it assumes existing allocations of that wealth. G may value the item at 300; but if G can pay no more than 50, G will not be able to acquire the item. Contract law is not

---

14   Note 8 above.

15   For an attempt to identify criteria relevant in deciding whether to leave regulation of conduct to the private law or to introduce administrative control, see S. Shavell, 'Liability for Harm versus Regulation of Safety' (1984) 13 *J Legal Studies* 357; see also more recently P. Cane, 'Tort Law as Regulation' (2002) 31 *Common Law World Review* 305 and, in the UK context, B. Pontin, 'Tort Interacting with Regulatory Law' (2000) 51 *NILQ* 597.

16   See Chapter 1.8 below on the range of regulatory techniques.

involved in obligatory altruism. Through the application of other legal instruments, the State may involve itself more generally in such explicit wealth distribution. In this direction, and distinct from contract law, lie tax law and welfare law.[17]

This is by no means a comprehensive account of the limitations of the value of contractual freedom in the market nor of the types of legal response that may follow.[18] Its purpose is to illustrate the complexities of the ramifications of an apparently simple transaction in the modern economy. These nuances dictate a need for a rather sophisticated pattern of law, embracing both private and public law. At stake are elements of the correction of market failure and, additionally, the achievement of fairness to consumers (*inter alia*) as the economically weaker parties. Consumer protection law has a wide range of forms and objectives.

What follows is an exploration of the potential of the private law in this direction, followed by an examination of public intervention. It bears repetition that the patterns described below represent the incremental accumulation of centuries of activity and any peculiarities exposed should be assessed in that spirit.

1.3.3 Freedom of Contract

Freedom of contract was presented above as a cornerstone of wealth maximisation and, accordingly, as a notion demanding respect under the law. In its heyday, freedom of contract carried a flavour which transcended the economy. It is not uncommon to find powerful assertions by 19th-century English judges concerning the individualist nature of contract and the role of the law in protecting and enforcing such bargains once they were freely arrived at. Judges would not question the content of a bargain once it had met the required form for enforcement as a contract under English law. The judge would have no interest in whether the bargain seemed fair or unfair, as long as it represented an agreed exchange. Thus

---

[17] For descriptions and prescriptions of the role of contract law in wealth distribution, see A. Kronman, 'Contract Law and Distributive Justice' (1980) 89 *Yale Law J* 472; H. Collins, 'Distributive Justice through Contracts' [1992] *Current Legal Problems* 49; R. Brownsword, G. Howells and T. Wilhelmsson, *Welfarism in Contract Law* (Dartmouth, 1995).

[18] For treatment at more length and in more depth, see the (instructively varied) approaches taken by M. Trebilcock, *The Limits of Freedom of Contract* (Harvard University Press, 1993); H. Collins, *Regulating Contracts* (OUP, 1999); C. Sunstein, *Free Markets and Social Justice* (OUP, 1999); A. Hutchinson, 'Life after Shopping: From Consumers to Citizens', Chapter 3 in Ramsay (ed.), note 7 above.

deception would be a basis for judicial intervention, but plain foolishness would not, nor would an apparently remarkably low or high price. The consequence for parties contemplating entry into a contract was clear; they should take scrupulous care to look out for their own interests. They should satisfy themselves that the deal was beneficial to them because, once the contract was concluded, it would then be fruitless to ask a court to absolve them of any obligations for which they had lost enthusiasm or whose scope they had misperceived.[19] *Caveat emptor* – let the buyer beware – was an assertion of individual responsibility.

A famous high-water mark in the notion of judicial *laissez-faire* was the observation of Sir George Jessel MR in 1875 that:

> [I]f there is one thing which more than another public policy requires it is that men of full age and competent understanding shall have the utmost liberty of contracting, and that their contracts entered into freely and voluntarily shall be held sacred and shall be enforced by Courts of Justice.[20]

He resisted arguments that a contract assigning patents should be declared void on public policy grounds. He commented that the public policy doctrine controlled the enforceability of contracts to commit a crime or to perform immoral acts, but that he 'should be sorry to extend it much further'. He ruled in favour of the enforceability of the contract in question.

The religious imagery chosen by Sir George Jessel is a striking illustration of the belief that such notions transcend 'ordinary' law and are instead part of some higher set of norms which confer power on the individual citizen with which the State should not interfere.

The belief in individualism was a central tenet of the common law of contract during the 19th-century; as a corollary there was a suspicion of collectivism as a suppression of the freedom of the individual. A vivid manifestation of this stance is found in the common law's reluctance to recognise the collective nature and purpose of trade unions. Unions in the 19th-century were consistently seen through the lens of the restraint of trade doctrine as a distortion of the 'proper' individual contractual relationship, and not as a legitimate reaction to the relative impotence of individual workers in their relationships with employers.[21] The actions of

---

19 E.g. *Smith v Hughes* (1871) LR 6 QB 597.
20 *Printing and Numerical Registering Co v Sampson* (1875) LR 19 Eq. 462, 465.
21 For a critical account, see Lord Wedderburn, *The Worker and the Law* (Penguin Books, 1986), especially Chapters 1, 7.

unions and unionists were capable of incurring tortious liability, *inter alia*, where they interfered with contractual relationships, most notably between employer and employee and employer and supplier or customer. Present too were the perils of criminal liability. The intervention of statute was necessary to decriminalise the strike[22] and to protect the organisation of collective action from a liability at common law that would have wrecked the trade union as an institution.[23] The liability of individuals engaging in industrial action ebbed and flowed through the 20th-century. For most of its duration, common law liabilities were extended by the judiciary while until 1979 Parliament typically responded by extending statutory immunities. After 1979, however, the labour market policies of successive Conservative administrations, expressed through a series of Acts, brought a curtailment of the immunities enjoyed by both unions and individuals combined with the imposition of rigorous formal pre-conditions to the taking of lawful industrial action, such as obligatory ballots.[24] In this field the Labour government that assumed power in 1997 adjusted the scheme of regulation[25] but has not chosen to undo the core of the work undertaken by its Conservative predecessor.[26]

The labour market has similarities to the product market. Many of the reasons why individual employees cannot effectively bargain with employers can readily be transplanted to explain why consumers cannot effectively bargain with suppliers. However, consumers have not banded together in unions in the ways adopted by workers. The consumer interest is more diffuse than that of workers in the same factory or the same trade. The consumer 'strike' – a boycott – is very difficult to organise. It is not unknown – consider the fate of French goods in the USA in the wake of the invasion of Iraq in 2003, and the accusations of misuse of third world labour periodically aimed at Nike.[27] But do such tactics really work? And *should* they work – whose interests are being promoted by such campaigns? Even if successfully pursued, boycotts can generate tortious

---

22   This was (loosely) the effect achieved by the Conspiracy and Protection of Property Act 1875.

23   Most notably, the House of Lords ruling on union liability in *Taff Vale Railway Company v ASRS* [1901] AC 426, leading to the protection of the Trade Disputes Act 1906.

24   For discussion taking account of the historical context, see P. Davies and M. Freedland, *Labour Legislation and Public Policy* (Clarendon Press, 1993).

25   Employment Relations Act 1999.

26   For a detailed account see I. Smith and G. Thomas, *Smith and Wood's Industrial Law* (Butterworths, 8th ed., 2003).

27   Cf. M. Friedman, *Consumer Boycotts: Effecting Change through the Marketplace and Media* (Routledge, 1999).

liability for the participants, for which there is no statutory immunity. The law of defamation might also impede the pursuit of a consumer campaign against a particular trader. Consumer representative organisations play a role in expressing the voice of the consumer, but their political impact is limited and their membership relatively small. Furthermore, English law's preference for individuals surfaces at the procedural level, where individual actions are the norm and although collective or representative actions have increased in significance in recent years[28] they nevertheless remain very much the exception.[29] In many cases of consumer detriment, individual loss suffered will be small even though one producer may in aggregate have caused significant harm. The requirement that each individual consumer pursue his or her own claim separately operates severely to restrict consumer redress and the control of producers through the operation of the private law.

Accordingly there is no 'collective consumer law' which is analogous to the development of collective labour organisation and collective labour law. The impediments to creating such a pattern out of the diffuse interests of consumers provides a rationale for public intervention to achieve the protection for the consumer which cannot be achieved by the operation of the market. Discussion of such techniques follows in this chapter, beginning in part 1.7 below. However, further examination of the scope of the private law is called for. The analogy with labour law offers further illumination. The contract of employment remains the cornerstone of the employer/worker relationship, yet modern law has moved far beyond the 19th-century *laissez-faire* stance. Built into an essentially contractual relationship are elements such as an employee's right not to be unfairly dismissed and to be paid a minimum wage, established by statute,[30] and a right to be treated with respect by an employer, developed by the judiciary.[31] These rights are in principle enjoyed by a worker independently of the package that has been negotiated with the employer. The law of the contract of employment has distinctive features departing from the model of 'pure' contractual freedom in the direction of employee protection. Much the same has occurred in relation to the law of the consumer contract. The notion of respect for the parties' bargain as the sole

---

28   Consider 'super-complaints' under the Enterprise Act 2002, Chapter 12.3.5.2, and the EC's Injunctions Directive 98/27 and Part 8 of the Enterprise Act, Chapter 13.9.5.3.

29   Part 1.6 of this chapter.

30   Now contained in the Employment Rights Act 1996 and the National Minimum Wage Act 1998 respectively.

31   E.g. *Woods v W.M. Car Services* [1982] ICR 693; *Malik v Bank of Credit and Commerce International SA* [1998] AC 20.

source of legal rights and obligations has declined. In part this flows from a realisation that the notion of contractual freedom, which underpins judicial non-interventionism, is no longer necessarily realistic in the modern consumer transaction where the relationship between parties is typically economically imbalanced in favour of the supplier. Consumer contract law now embraces rights and obligations inserted into the relationship by judicial activism and by statutory intervention. There is considerably more to it than simply the parties' agreement.

1.3.4 The Decline of a Common Set of 'Contract Law' Principles

It would be misleading to assume that the connected themes of individualism, freedom of contract and judicial non-interventionism in the parties' bargain have lost their relevance to 20th-century commerce. The rationales which underpinned the 19th-century perspective largely hold true today in the commercial sphere, at least where the parties negotiate at arms length, sustained by more or less equal economic strength. In commercial transactions, the need to encourage and protect long-term planning continues to dictate a rigid law of contract, which enforces bargains and does not judge their merits.[32]

Moreover, the value of contract-as-exchange is still firmly part of the consumer perspective of the role of the market. Like commercial parties, a consumer choosing between two products can also use the law of contract to plan ahead by extracting guarantees about the durability of the product. The consumer does not know for sure which of two brands of washing machine will last the longer, since he or she is no expert. But he or she can buy the product plus a promise about durability, secure in the knowledge that the law will protect the promise bought in the event of default. The consumer will have a legal entitlement to compensation should the product fail to meet the promised standard of durability. In this manner the private law is in principle capable of filling the information gap which afflicts the consumer. It protects, and thereby induces, planning.

However, the overall picture of contract law as a means of establishing a long-term framework for a commercial relationship does not accord with the reality of many consumer transactions. For the consumer, deals will frequently lack the long-term relational flavour which characterises much commercial dealing. Nor will the terms have been settled as a result of often protracted arms-length negotiation between teams of sharp lawyers. Consumer purchases may be financially on a small-scale as far as the supplier is concerned, although they may loom large for the budget of an

---

32   Although even here legislative intervention has occurred; cf. Chapter 5.3 below.

individual consumer. Consumer purchases are frequently concluded on the basis of standard-form contracts, which the consumer will almost never have read nor will ever read. Negotiation on price or conditions is hardly typical of the average purchase of, for example, a video recorder or a train ticket.

Absence of effective negotiation and agreement may spur an instinctive readiness to intervene in such deals. However, the point should be taken that the mere fact that the context of the consumer transaction differs from that of the commercial transaction is not of itself a cause for criticism or intervention. The case of the standard-form contract is instructive. Such a contract might suggest itself as an instrument for the supplier to oppress the ill-informed consumer. That may occur. Yet the standard-form contract is not the irredeemable evil it is sometimes portrayed. It would be in the interest of neither consumer nor trader to sit down and hammer out terms for each and every transaction, quill pens doubtless in hand. The modern consumer economy is based on the standard-form contract because its use is efficient. It reduces time and money that would otherwise be spent on negotiating. Business can plan on the basis of its standard-terms and pass on cost savings via the price. The consumer stands to benefit from the use of standard-form contracts, although there are counterbalancing costs. The standard-form contract tends to enhance the power of the supplier who will have a greater awareness of the content of the contract. The consumer will typically be under informed and may 'accept' peculiarly disadvantageous terms. The notion that free will, a bargain and an agreement lie at the heart of a consumer contract is rather distorted by the prevalence of standard-form contracts which often go largely unread. This analysis suggests that the use of standard-form contracts may be desirable in principle, but that they might generate justifications for regulation where 'freedom of contract' has effectively converted big firms into legislators in the market.[33]

In modern economic conditions, the supplier/consumer relationship is typically imbalanced in favour of the supplier. The supplier knows more about the product or service. The more complex the subject matter, the less likely that the consumer will be capable of making any kind of informed judgement about quality or even safety. And even possession of relevant information may not help the consumer prone to assess risk inexpertly. By

---

[33] For a classic analysis see F. Kessler, 'Contracts of Adhesion – Some Thoughts About Freedom of Contract' (1943) 43 *Col L Rev* 629. Cf. the vigorous argument for intervention of D. Slawson, 'Standard Form Contracts and Democratic Control of Lawmaking Power' (1970–71) 84 *Harvard L Rev* 529. Cf. also the influential analysis of Arthur Leff, 'Contract as Thing' (1970) 19 *American Univ LR* 131.

contrast the supplier is more familiar with the nature of the transaction and the standard form involved; it is his or her job to conclude such transactions, whereas it may be an uncommon, even intimidating, experience for the consumer. The observation about imbalance need not form a point of criticism. It is simply an observation that there is little congruence between the large-scale commercial contract and the average consumer purchase. Contracts vary. They may have certain common features relating to the notion of an exchange between the two sides to a transaction, but there is an immense gulf in expectations between the major commercial deal and the small-scale consumer contract. Building the Channel Tunnel and buying a loaf of bread both involve 'contracts', but is it really useful to give them both the same label?

This throws up a central question in the modern law of contract: is it realistic or desirable to attempt to maintain a common set of contractual principles applicable to all bargains, or should one accept that different types of contract attract different types of legal response? If 'contracts' have infinite variety, then it may be unhelpful to think of a unified law of contract. Worse, it may be positively damaging to treat unlike contracts alike by seeking solutions drawn from some spurious set of common rules, whereas the variety of situations which may arise should instead be judged in the light of a more sensitive and nuanced legal structure. Simply put, is there a law of contract or a law of contracts? That is a question which invites a description of the modern law, but one must also adopt a prescriptive focus; *should* there be a fragmentation of the law of contract into discrete compartments? More fundamentally still, it is important to appreciate that contract law is simply part of the wider law of obligations, and that that wider law too varies in its application depending on the subject matter at issue. Some commentators have sought to describe and/or to prescribe a fresh (or, for some, rediscovered) approach to the basis of the law of obligations that no longer places significant weight on special legal rules arising from the defining fact of a bargain struck between the parties.[34]

It is possible to cast doubt on the viability or desirability of freedom of contract in the realm of consumer contracts. Such 'freedom' as may exist is greatly attenuated by the features of a mass production economy. The expectation in commercial contract law that the courts will do no more than act as conscientious protectors of the parties' negotiated bargain has

---

[34]   The flavour of the debate may be tasted in G. Gilmore and R. Collins, *The Death of Contract* (Ohio State University Press, 2nd ed., 1997); C. Fried, *Contract as Promise* (Harvard University Press, 1981). Cf. J. Gordley, *Philosophical Origins of Modern Contract Doctrine* (Oxford University Press, 1991); L. Niglia, *The Transformation of Contract in Europe* (Kluwer Law International, 2003).

no necessary place in the absence of such negotiation. That perception then provides an intellectual invitation to rethink the nature and purpose of the law in consumer contracts. It points towards the adoption of a legal approach which is more receptive to controlling the substance of deals rather than simply enforcing them once they display the requisite legal form. It suggests a possible role for the law in adjudicating on the 'fairness' of a deal, rather than simply regarding agreements as sacred and entitled to unquestioning legal protection.

At this point in our attempt to probe the intellectual case for choosing to shape a control function for the law of consumer contracts, it is appropriate to observe that the stumbling block of 19th-century judicial non-interventionism may not have been such a substantial obstacle after all. Sir George Jessel's dictum venerating contractual liberty as sacred provides a memorable 19th-century sound-bite, but the extent to which it faithfully represented the law even at that time has been questioned. Professor Atiyah, in particular, cogently demonstrated that the strength of the dam which supposedly held back interventionism had been exaggerated.[35] This thesis holds that it was the prevalent acceptance of the economic virtue of contractual freedom that shaped contract law theory throughout the 19th-century. Historical patterns were touched on by Lord Diplock in *Schroeder Music Publishing Co Ltd v Macaulay*.[36] He described the general 19th-century rule of non-interventionism in contracts, which permits only specific and exceptional instances of intervention, against a background of a pre-existing readiness to test contracts generally against a standard of unconscionability. He appears to envisage that theories about freedom of trade had been absorbed by the judiciary during the 19th-century and had caused a shift in the law. So the 'hands-off' judicial approach had not existed since time immemorial: it was a reflection of the times.

Throughout the large part of the 20th-century, incursions into contractual freedom grew, largely as the result of a perception that contractual freedom is neither reflective of nor desirable in the modern mixed economy. State interventionism in the market and in setting norms for private relationships and wide-ranging (if erratic) judicial activism have contributed enormously to this decline in the centrality of the autonomy of the parties. In the later part of the century, some developed the view that the wheel has turned full circle – or that the wheel should be turned full circle – and that individual autonomy should be reclaimed as part of an

---

35 Especially P. Atiyah, *The Rise and Fall of Freedom of Contract* (Oxford University Press, 1979). Cf. P. Atiyah, *Essays on Contract* (Oxford University Press, 1988).

36 [1974] 3 All ER 616, 623. The substance of the case is discussed below at 1.3.6.

insistence on free choice in the market. This trend is closely associated
with the Conservative administration that came to power under the
leadership of Mrs Thatcher in 1979. Reduction in interventionist
legislation refocused the law of contract on the parties' bargain; reduced
State participation in the market enhanced the importance and breadth of
dealings with private suppliers. Protection of tenants, employees and
consumers was curtailed; public monopoly supply of water and energy was
no longer to provide the norm. Some commentators followed. Atiyah,
having earlier made a vivid contribution to arresting assumptions that
freedom of contract was ideologically ingrained in English contract law,
had by the 1990s come to detect strong trends in favour of contractual
freedom as the dominant paradigm – and what is more, he heartily
approved.[37] It was left to others to develop exploration of contract law's
regulatory potential.[38] In any event the pattern followed by Conservative
governments from 1979 to 1997 was erratic. For example, in several areas
the influence of membership of the EU opposed these deregulatory policy
preferences. Control of unfair terms in consumer contracts in the UK is
stronger now than it was 20 years ago.[39] The election of a Labour
government in 1997 heralded a diminution in the rhetoric of dedication to
challenge the scope of public intervention in the economy. But the
administrations led by Mr Blair have been conspicuously anxious to insist
on their appreciation of the competitive advantages of markets, albeit that
they should be judiciously regulated. The 1999 White Paper entitled
Modern Markets: Confident Consumers[40] champions the market as an
institution in the service of the consumer. And for the public sector the
rhetorical emphasis has been on 'modernisation'.[41] Resuming public
intervention on the pre-Thatcher scale is remote from the agenda. Plainly
this story of incremental change in priorities attached to the nature,
purpose and form of market regulation has generated a profoundly complex
patchwork of legal intervention into private autonomy, and the current
cycle of government priorities is simply the latest chapter in the story. This
is further elaborated in part 1.9 of this chapter.

---

[37]   Cf. note 35 above: Atiyah has not written *The Rise and Fall and Rise of Freedom of
       Contract* but see in this vein *An Introduction to the Law of Contract* (Oxford
       University Press, 5th ed., 1995).

[38]   See part 1.3.8 of this chapter.

[39]   Chapter 5.

[40]   Cm. 4410 (1999). Available via http://www.dti.gov.uk/consumer/whitepaper/.

[41]   Cm. 4310 (1999), *Modernising Government*.

1.3.5 Control of Contracts – The Bargaining Phase

One approach to adjusting contract law in the light of the diminution in effective negotiation which characterises modern consumer contracts would involve a more sceptical examination of the process of decision making in consumer contracts. One need not deny that the law of contract is and should be uniformly based on an idea of individual autonomy. However one might be able to find elements in the supplier/consumer relationship which do not conform to that paradigm. The consumer is often not really negotiating freely or with full knowledge about the bargain. One could then seek to use the law to improve the transparency of the bargaining process and to control outcomes which are not deemed to be the product of proper contractual freedom.

In English law, both common law and statute display features which correspond to this perception. It is notorious that consumers will not read all the small-print on a document. This may be viewed as 'reality' departing from the 'theory' of free bargaining. Old cases show that the common law accepted, even perpetuated, the gulf between theory and practice. A brief consideration of case law is justified in order to elucidate these issues, although more specific discussion is provided in Chapter 5. *Thompson v London Midland and Scottish Railway Co*[42] arose out of an excursion taken by Mrs Thompson in Lancashire in the course of which she was injured as a result of the defendant's negligence as she was trying to disembark from a train. The ticket included a notice that it was issued subject to conditions shown in the company's timetables. In the timetable could be found a term excluding liability for injury 'however caused'. The timetables were not on display. They cost sixpence each. Mrs Thompson, moreover, could not read. The Court of Appeal held that, irrespective of whether any inquiries had actually been made by this consumer about the nature of the conditions in the timetable, she was bound under the contract by the conditions to which the ticket had laid a trail. The railway company had brought the conditions sufficiently to the notice of the consumer and was thereby protected from liability in damages.

Latterly the common law has responded more actively to the absence of negotiation about, agreement on, or even awareness of, terms in such situations. Decisions in recent years show that failure to bring unusually onerous clauses adequately to the attention of the consumer will result in their exclusion from the binding terms of the agreement. *Thornton v Shoe Lane Parking*[43] involved a claim for compensation for injury suffered in

---

[42]   [1930] 1 KB 41.
[43]   [1971] 2 QB 163.

the defendant's car park by Mr Thornton, 'a freelance trumpeter of the highest quality'.[44] The consumer received a ticket from an automatic machine on arrival at the car park. The ticket referred to conditions displayed on the premises, one of which excluded liability for such an event. The plaintiff knew nothing of this. The Court of Appeal decided that the defendants had not done enough to bring the clause to the attention of the consumer and that therefore it was not binding. The consumer's claim for damages succeeded. The approach in this case examines what the trader has or has not done with more rigour than was apparent in *Thompson* and takes more explicit and sympathetic account of the consumer's lack of knowledge. Lord Denning quite explicitly remarked on the 'fiction' of negotiation about such conditions, even in the days when an actual person may have supplied the ticket to a consumer. The perception of a 'fiction' applied with all the more force where a machine had dispensed the ticket.

An important recent case which emphasises transparency outwith the sphere of the exclusion clause and even outwith the consumer context is *Interfoto Picture Library Ltd v Stiletto Visual Programmes Ltd*.[45] The case concerned the enforceability of a clause included in printed conditions accompanying photographic transparencies owned by Interfoto and provided for the use of Stiletto. The clause in question required a fee to be paid in the event that the transparencies were retained longer than 14 days. Stiletto forgot they held the transparencies and were billed for £3,783.50 in accordance with the clause. This was an exorbitant rate, according to the judges of the Court of Appeal before whom Stiletto sought to show that the clause should not be held enforceable as part of the contract. Stiletto succeeded in defeating Interfoto's claim for the full sum apparently due under the clause. The Court of Appeal held that a particularly onerous or unusual contractual condition, which would not generally be known to the other party, would not be enforceable unless the party seeking to rely on that condition could show that it had fairly been brought to the other party's attention. This test was not met and Interfoto accordingly could not rely on the clause.

The modern trend exemplified by *Thornton v Shoe Lane Parking* and *Interfoto v Stiletto* appears to derive from judicial scepticism about the realistic nature of the 'agreement' struck, especially where a standard form is used. These decisions are not necessarily in conflict with the principle expressed several decades earlier in *Thompson*. It remains true that if the trader has done enough in the opinion of the court to bring the terms to the attention of the consumer, then those terms bind even if the consumer does

---

44   As we learn from the characteristically memorable first sentence of Lord Denning MR's judgment.

45   [1988] 2 WLR 615, [1988] 1 All ER 348.

not actually know of them. That issue is a question of fact to be determined on the facts of the individual case. However, a great deal more is now expected of the trader. It will be rarer for the consumer to be bound at common law by terms of which he or she is ignorant, especially when those terms are presented in standard form and *a fortiori* where those terms are out of the ordinary. In this sense, active disclosure of terms may be a precondition to their enforceability, thus motivating the supplier to adopt a more open strategy.

The common law has in this way been moulded to enhance the openness of negotiation. This ought to improve market transparency. Statutory intervention provides a number of examples of explicitly imposed requirements to disclose information. The use of defined forms is a favoured technique for alerting the consumer to the need to be aware of the nature and possible consequences of the transaction into which he or she is entering. English contract law normally leaves it to the parties to choose how they will record their agreement. Any document will do. Oral contracts are in principle enforceable. However, in defined circumstances, statutory rules stipulate the use of particular forms. Chapter 6, dealing with consumer credit, provides an account of the elaborate rituals that surround the conclusion of defined transactions in that field. Part of the objective of such intervention is to warn the consumer to be on his or her guard; another objective is to supply more specific and detailed information to the consumer of credit. Enhanced transparency is a prominent feature of the regulatory devices adopted by the UK and the EC to address the problem of unfair contract terms. This is examined in Chapter 5. The assumption is plainly that the private law, even stimulated by modern judicial activism, does not yield a market that is sufficiently transparent to permit informed, efficient decisions to be taken. And yet the policy-maker should be wary of assumptions that (some, perhaps most) consumers are capable of absorbing relevant disclosed information. Moreover, even the consumer who digests information may misperceive its significance. The capacity of disclosure rules and rules stipulating the use of particular forms to bridge the information gap and effectively to cure market failure is examined critically below in part 1.8.3 of this chapter.

1.3.6 Control of Contracts – The Substance

An objective of legal intervention in the bargaining phase, discussed above, is the improvement of transparency in order better to inform the consumer. A distinct technique may involve the acceptance of clauses as part of the contract, but their subjection to some broader check. Contracts, once entered into, might be reviewed more openly by the courts against some standard of fairness. This could be justified in pursuit of consumer protection as a reflection of the unfair imbalance which characterises the pre-contractual bargaining phase, especially, perhaps, where standard-term contracts are employed. Consumers might be thought in danger of exploitation. Plainly the nature of the control would require careful elaboration. However, the critical policy breakthrough would involve recognition that the bargain, once struck, is not then immune from intervention. It is an approach which involves public inquiry into the fairness of private decisions, not least on the basis that the private decision is reached only under distorted conditions.

English common law of contract has *not* taken this approach. The English judiciary has not been prepared to claim a general common law jurisdiction to inspect the fairness of bargains.[46] English law enforces promises once they have satisfied the 'tests of enforceability', traditionally the three requirements of agreement, consideration and the intention of the parties to create legal relations, and provided they are not affected by a fairly narrow range of vitiating factors, such as misrepresentation or duress. A 'fairness' check has no direct role to play.

There are isolated areas in which a species of fairness is employed to control a bargain. The restraint of trade doctrine, for example, involves control over employment and related contracts which is based on an assessment of fairness in the public interest and in the interest of the parties. In *A. Schroeder Music Publishing Co Ltd v Macaulay*[47] the House of Lords held that an agreement entered into by a young unknown song-writer on the standard-terms of a publishing company was unenforceable. Lord Reid doubted that the contract had been 'moulded by any pressure of negotiation'.[48] Had the economic imbalance between the parties not precluded the opportunity for real negotiation, his approach would have been significantly different and less prone to intervene.[49] There is nothing in the speeches in the House of Lords which disputes the competitive nature of the market. There were, presumably, a number of publishing

---

46   Lord Denning sought to develop such a doctrine in *Lloyds Bank v Bundy* [1975] QB
      326, at least where inequality of bargaining power is present, but this has not found
      favour in the House of Lords; cf. *National Westminster Bank v Morgan* [1985] AC
      686.

47   [1974] 3 All ER 616.

48   *Ibid.*, p. 622.

49   Macaulay, the composer of 'Love Grows where my Rosemary goes', was treated more
      favourably than George Michael, whose canon is rather better known and, partly for
      that reason, whose bargaining power is rather stronger. The contract in *Panayiotou v
      Sony Ltd* [1994] 1 All ER 755 was held enforceable.

companies willing to offer terms to young and unknown writers.[50] Yet all such deals would occur against a background of significant inequality of bargaining power. The decision seems to be based on the notion that it was not a *fair* market, at least from the perspective of the writer and, more broadly, the public interest in enjoying the fruits of the composer's work, and that the deal should therefore be controlled. The strictness and length of the restraint were judged unjustified. The publishers could, presumably, have concluded an enforceable contract with the composer, provided the terms were less restrictive, even in the absence of full negotiation. It seems, then, that there is some threshold to intervention in contracts in restraint of trade that the courts themselves fix.

Lord Diplock in *Schroeder v Macaulay* was careful to observe that the contract in question, one in restraint of trade, 'fell within one of those *limited* categories of contractual promises in respect of which the courts still retain the power to relieve the promisor of his legal duty to fulfil them'.[51] The common law asserts no *general* jurisdiction to set aside 'unfair' contracts. The sentiments of Sir George Jessel maintain their grip.[52] The typical consumer contract would be immune from the type of inquiry undertaken in a restraint of trade case such as *Schroeder v Macaulay*. To this extent, the common law seems to possess an inherent respect for agreements and for markets.

Statutory intervention has made some limited incursion into the notion that the law is simply the agreement of the parties. Consumer credit legislation confers powers on the courts to interfere with extortionate credit bargains.[53] The power is necessarily flexible, but it is also plainly intended that it should not be used lightly. This has proved to be the case and, in practice, very few instances of the reopening of agreements have occurred. Reasons for this infrequent interventionism doubtless lie in part in the narrow scope of the statutory rules, but probably also in the natural reluctance of a judge trained in the common law of contract to engage in assessment of the relative worth of the two sides to a bargain. This insight conditions one's assessment of the likely effect of reform proposals advanced in the 2003 White Paper *Fair, Clear and Competitive*[54] which propose the replacement of the notion of 'extortionate' by the lower threshold of intervention in an 'unfair' credit bargain.

---

50 For criticism of the decision from this and other perspectives, M. Trebilcock, 'The Doctrine of Inequality of Bargaining Power' (1976) 26 *Univ. Toronto LJ* 359.

51 623c, emphasis added.

52 See above Chapter 1.3.3.

53 Sections 137–140 Consumer Credit Act 1974. See Chapter 6.12 below.

54 Cm. 6040 (DTI, 2003). See further Chapter 6.12.3.

The Unfair Contract Terms Act 1977 invalidates some clauses absolutely and subjects others to a judicially applied test of reasonableness. The Act is of central importance to the assessment of the development of a distinctive law of consumer contracts. However, it also demonstrates the fuzzy edges of the law of consumer protection, for the Act is capable of controlling (some) terms in (some) commercial contracts.[55] In fact, the Unfair Contract Terms Act 1977, as all students quickly learn, is a statute burdened by a thoroughly misleading name. 'Unfairness' is an unsatisfactorily abbreviated summary of its control mechanism. Moreover, although contract terms are not its only concern (for it also applies to some non-contractual notices), not all contract terms are affected by it, only the limited category of exclusion and analogous clauses.[56] Nonetheless, the Unfair Contract Terms Act 1977 represents a significant statutory modification of the common law of contract in the direction of intervention in the bargain.

Cases such as *Thompson and Thornton* (see above) would be potentially affected by the Act. The issues of incorporation of terms would continue to be addressed in the same way. The common law of incorporation is not affected by the Act; if a term is not shown to be part of the contract, it cannot be enforced within the contract.[57] However, once an exclusion clause is shown to form part of the contract and to protect the party wishing to rely on it,[58] the Act ensures that there is still scope for legal inquiry into its enforceability. The clause will be void in defined circumstances. That in *Thompson*, which excluded liability for personal injury, would indeed now be void.[59] Other clauses are tested against a judicially applied test of reasonableness.[60]

The 1977 Act applies only to exclusion and cognate clauses. A broader control of unfair terms is exercised under the EC's Directive on Unfair Terms in Consumer Contracts.[61] All contract terms, not only exclusion clauses, are subject to control. A term covered by the Directive shall be regarded as unfair if, contrary to the requirement of good faith, it causes a significant imbalance in the parties' rights and obligations arising under the contract, to the detriment of the consumer. An Annex to the Directive

---

[55]   For more detailed discussion, see Chapter 5.
[56]   Chapter 5.6.3 below.
[57]   Chapter 5.2 below.
[58]   On interpretation, Chapter 5.2 below.
[59]   On special rules relating to transport, see *Chitty on Contracts* (Sweet and Maxwell, 1999).
[60]   Chapter 5.6.1 below.
[61]   Directive 93/13 OJ 1993 L95/29, Chapter 5 below.

provides an indicative and non-exhaustive list of the terms which may be regarded as unfair.

Although the Directive is broader than the 1977 Act in its coverage of all terms, not simply exclusion clauses, it is nonetheless narrower in applying only to terms that have not been individually negotiated. Individually negotiated terms are *not* controlled by the Directive, although it does not preclude their control under national law.[62] The thrust of the Directive is to regulate terms drafted in advance whose nature the consumer has been unable to influence. It seems to be assumed that in such deals the consumer will be less well informed than in others where he or she has been more actively involved in negotiation. Moreover, unlike the Unfair Contract Terms Act, the Directive is confined to consumer contracts alone. This aspect means that it constitutes a major development towards a distinctive law of consumer contracts. In fact, the EC's body of harmonisation measures governing consumer law operates as an important ingredient in the brewing of a consumer-specific brand of contract law.[63]

1.3.7 Implication of Terms into Contracts

Legislative intervention is not only concerned to eliminate (some) unfair terms from consumer contracts, but also to add terms into contracts independently of negotiation between the parties. Under the Sale of Goods Act 1979, for example, certain terms are implied into defined contracts. This protection is in places overlapped by and in others extended by more recent EC intervention in the field, the Directive on certain aspects of the sale of consumer goods and associated guarantees.[64] The terms mandated by law offer protection to the buyer quite independently of negotiation between the parties. Products must correspond to description; they must be of satisfactory quality; they must be fit for any purpose which has been agreed.[65] The supply of a defective product is effectively rendered a breach of contract by these requirements (which are examined at length in Chapter 4). Moreover, the legal rules serve to induce traders to provide consumers with better information – for example, on a product's proper

---

62   In fact, in the UK, the UCTA does exercise control over individually negotiated terms in defined circumstances, Chapter 5 below.

63   For fuller examination see Chapter 2.3.3.

64   Directive 99/44, OJ 1999 L171/12.

65   Sections 13, 14 Sale of Goods Act 1979.

mode of use – and in this sense they form part of the wider pattern of information disclosure as a feature of modern contract law.[66]

It might initially be felt that such terms are implied on the basis that they replicate what would have been agreed had the parties in the market actively negotiated on these matters. In the past, there may have been some validity in that interpretation. Its logical corollary would be that the parties could agree to exclude the terms should they see fit, which indeed was the position until 1973. However since 1973, the character of these terms as imposed by law (and not as the product anticipated to follow from bargaining) has been demonstrated by the legal rule that, in defined transactions, the terms cannot validly be excluded even if the parties agree on such exclusion.[67] These implied terms therefore reflect State-imposed minimum standards for the transaction, divorced from individual will. Consumers cannot bargain away such protection, wittingly or unwittingly.

The law governing the implication of terms has evidently moved the relationship between trader and consumer on to a more complex plane than a simple agreement, but the limitations of legal intervention should also be appreciated. Although the terms mentioned above are implied independently of agreement by the parties, there must be a contract in the first place to which the terms can attach. The implied terms under the Sale of Goods Act therefore apply only to the consumer/retailer relationship, which is contractual, and not to the consumer/manufacturer relationship which is not contractual, save in exceptional circumstances.[68] Yet it can cogently be submitted that in modern conditions it is really the manufacturer who is responsible for the quality of the product. The retailer is frequently a mere conduit. Legislative reform was mooted to adjust the common law to reflect more faithfully the practice of production and marketing. The Department of Trade and Industry (DTI) published a Consultative Document in 1992 which aired the possibility that legislation be introduced to render the implied terms enforceable outwith the contract of sale. The EC Commission published a 'Green Paper' in November 1993 which was similarly motivated. But the opportunity was lost. The EC's Directive as finally adopted is much more modest in its treatment of the relationship between the consumer and the manufacturer. It makes provision for the enforcement of a guarantee offered by a producer even in the absence of contractual status. But, this case of a voluntarily offered guarantee aside, it does not require that producers be made directly liable

---

66   Cf. S. Hedley, 'Quality of Goods, Information and the Death of Contract' [2001] *JBL* 114.

67   Initially the Supply of Goods (Implied Terms) Act 1973, now contained in s. 6 Unfair Contract Terms Act 1977; see Chapter 5 below.

68   Chapter 3.4 below.

to consumers for defects in their products. It merely instructs the Commission to prepare a report by July 2006 at the latest on the case for introducing such supplementary protection.[69]

1.3.8 Questions about the Modern Function of Consumer Contract Law

The Unfair Contract Terms Act 1977 and the Sale of Goods Act 1979, supplemented by the EC's consumer-specific Directives on unfair terms and sale of goods, are leading examples of modern pieces of legislation that put aside freedom of contract as an inadequate reflection of the reality of the circumstances in which the transaction is concluded. State regulation of the bargain is seen as an appropriate response to the economic imbalance between supplier and consumer. The market is affected by such legislative intervention. The message transmitted by consumers to supplier and producer is supplemented by a message added by the State, namely, that in contracts subject to these measures there are certain minimum quality levels which must be adhered to and certain standards of fairness which must be met, at least in the specific context of the types of clause controlled by the Unfair Contract Terms Act and now, more broadly, under the EC Directive on Unfair Terms in Consumer Contracts.

Beyond such relatively piecemeal massaging of the tradition of judicial non-interventionism, it might be possible to construct a much more radical stance which would disengage consumer contract law entirely from the notion of freedom of contract and instead present entry into and enforcement of (some) contracts as a type of 'privilege' available only on fulfilment of certain preconditions.[70] That involves substantial reconceptualisation of the law in this area and a deconstruction of the law of contract into a law of contracts which emphasises the regulatory function of the law pertaining to *some* contractual relations.

These interventions largely reflect the notion that it is not contracting *per se* which stimulates a need for legal control, but rather the presence of an imbalance between the parties which causes prejudice. The emphasis is thus on protection of consumers, not of business parties. Yet there are grey areas. Commercial relationships too can be profoundly imbalanced. The

---

69 Article 12, Directive 99/44.

70 Cf. some of the recategorisation of familiar material by H. Collins, *The Law of Contract* (Butterworths, 2003). Cf. also T. Wilhelmsson, *Critical studies in private law: a treatise on need-rational principles in modern law* (Kluwer, 1992); J. Adams and R. Brownsword, *Understanding Contract Law* (Fontana, 2000).

Unfair Contract Terms Act 1977 has limited application even to commercial deals;[71] the Sale of Goods Act 1979 does not operate exclusively in the area of consumer contracts.[72] The EC's Directives, by contrast, are confined to transactions between consumers and business parties. That the consumer transaction receives especially intensive control points to a fragmentation in the law of contract. Therefore it is a question of increasing importance whether this represents a patchwork of alterations to the core principle of freedom of contract or whether freedom of contract no longer reflects the nature of contract law applicable to the consumer. It has already been suggested in this account that one may doubt whether there are any 'general principles' of contract law at all.

Judicial and legislative intervention may be directed at the realisation of conceptions of social justice. Consumer protection is but part of this field of inquiry into the limitations of contractual freedom as a basis for delivering a fair distribution of resources, a perception that invites attempts to adapt the law to a more overt control function, rather than allocating that task exclusively to the tax and welfare systems. Other types of relationship provide further evidence of the fragmentation of the law of contract into a law of contracts. The law of landlord and tenant and the law of employee protection are nominally based on contract law and the core relationship at stake is contractual, but the legal techniques involved have drifted far from *laissez-faire* commercial contract law as normally understood. Independently of the content of the agreement, tenants and employees, like consumers, enjoy legal rights against landlords, employers and suppliers respectively.

This touches on contentious areas. Assessing the desirability of the development of rights for such groups, beyond the protection they are able to secure from the market, has been at the centre of political debate in recent years. The principal thematic concern of successive Conservative administrations from 1979 to 1997 was the damage done to market flexibility by such intervention. This perspective emphasises fears that protecting workers or tenants by law may deter the willingness of providers of jobs or accommodation to make them available in the first place. Setting minimum standards in consumer transactions deprives the consumer of choice. This prompted a rigorous scrutiny of such interventionist laws under a general policy umbrella of deregulation. At this end of the spectrum rests the view that the State should not interfere with the inherent freedom and self-operability of the market.[73] It is precisely here that some have identified the modern (re-)rise of individualist contract law, for in so

---

71   Chapter 5.
72   Chapter 3.
73   Chapter 1.9 below.

far as special legal protection is rolled back, what remains is what the market can deliver; what can be negotiated under a contract. But *should* this be so? Opposition to policies that prioritise private autonomy within a deregulated market takes several forms. Combat may be engaged on the basis of pursuit of economic efficiency. In so far as private actors take decisions based on irrational prejudice the economy is damaged, and there may be an economic case for the introduction of legal rules which suppress the inefficient conduct. From this perspective one might find a justification for rules prohibiting employers – and perhaps landlords and traders more generally – from discrimination on the basis of (*inter alia*) race or gender,[74] for such persistent prejudice exerts a damaging effect on the efficient allocation of resources in the markets concerned.[75] But it is plain that such legal regulation would also be capable of support from a standpoint that emphasises more general social concerns, rooted in equality and the protection of human dignity. In this sense denying the market a pre-eminent status as an organising mechanism for society reflects a belief that there is a core clutch of rights the protection of which transcends the rhetoric of economic efficiency. The Labour government that took power in the United Kingdom in 1997 has presented itself as devoted to the attempt to blend respect for the virtues of competitive markets with an anxiety to promote social justice. This quest is perfectly simple when expressed as a broad aspiration on paper, but fiendishly difficult to pursue in practice. In this vein the Human Rights Act 1998 is a landmark constitutional reform; it is examined more fully in part 1.9.3 of this chapter. In labour market policy, the introduction of a statutory minimum wage provides a good example of the tension between, on the one hand, private autonomy and market solutions and, on the other, regulating to cure perceived market failures and to achieve a degree of social justice.[76] In relation to the consumer, the 1999 White Paper provided the opportunity to articulate the contours of policy-making. Entitled *Modern Markets: Confident Consumers*[77] it champions the market as an institution in the service of the consumer, while accepting the possibility of market failure

---

74 For empirical evidence that this occurs see I. Ayres, 'Fair Driving: Gender and Race Discrimination in Retail Car Negotiations' (1991) 104 *Harvard Law Rev* 817.

75 For an illuminating clash of views, see R.A. Epstein and S. Deakin, *Equal Opportunity or More Opportunity* (Civitas, The Institute for the Study of Civil Society, 2002); cf. also C. Barnard, S. Deakin and C. Kilpatrick, 'Equality, non-discrimination and the labour market in the UK' (2002) 18 *International Journal of Comparative Labour Law and Industrial Relations* 129.

76 Note 30 above.

77 Cm. 4410 (1999). Available via http://www.dti.gov.uk/consumer/whitepaper/.

justifying public intervention.[78] The White Paper recognises that consumers are not a homogenous group. Some have special needs. 'A quarter of adults have difficulty in finding an entry in the Yellow Pages.... They are unlikely to understand complex contractual provisions.'[79] The White Paper is dedicated to the benefit of all consumers but declares a special focus on the needs of those with less developed consumer skills, those who are socially excluded and those on low incomes who can least afford to make a bad purchase. This final point amounts to an important recognition that inefficiencies should be assessed not simply in aggregate but also with an eye to their distributional consequences. However, the White Paper is rather light in concrete proposals to take account of vulnerable consumers in particular.

What is at stake here is the working out of one of the key themes of this book: that consumers are also citizens, and that consumer protection carries a necessary political dimension. These horizons are broader than contract law alone, but central to the debate is the extent to which contract law is regarded as requiring a regulatory supplement. Within this inquiry much rests on the type of contract at stake. The family of contracts is today enormously varied. So too is the family of contract law. It may be a matter of personal taste whether one views this as contract law in a phase of adjustment or whether the stretching of these 'principles' into wholly heterogeneous situations really means that discourse about contract law 'principles' now obscures the practical abandonment of common principles. For consumer law in particular, there remains no consensus on whether the topic is a discrete area of law with its own distinctive rationales or whether it is simply an assortment of existing principles of contract (and other) law defined as consumer law only because they happen to apply in some circumstances to consumers. There is a pressing need to establish coherence between the distinct rationales that offer themselves as bases for intervention.[80] The divergence of approach tends to surface where new initiatives designed to protect consumers as a group are proposed. For example, at EC level, some greeted the notion of special protection for consumers against unfair contractual terms as an alarming challenge to the integrity of private law; others welcomed such protection precisely because of its recognition that consumers need special

---

78   Part 1.9.2.3 of this chapter examines more fully the policy preferences articulated in the 1999 White Paper.

79   Section 3.31 White Paper.

80   Cf. in this direction G. Howells, 'Contract Law: The Challenge for the Critical Consumer Lawyer' in T. Wilhelmsson (ed.), *Perspectives of Critical Contract Law* (Dartmouth, 1993).

treatment.[81] Others again worried that consumers alone were offered protection that ought to have been extended to other economically weak parties.[82] The EC's subsequent intervention into sales law generated a further round of soul-searching. And, particularly in Germany, it provoked a major reform of domestic sales law which went far beyond the Directive's focus on the particular peculiarities of consumer sales law.[83] Contract law remains a dynamic field.

Whichever style of categorisation is preferred, modern consumer contract law operates in a manner quite distinct from the classic (and rather exaggerated) notions of individual freedom to contract and legal non-interventionism. Both judicial and legislative developments have combined to establish a pattern of control over the private supplier/consumer relationship.

1.4 TORT LAW AND THE CONSUMER

Tort law is largely the product of the judges, although a statutory overlay has recently increased in importance. Over the course of the last 100 years, the ability of the consumer to proceed in tort against traders with whom he or she has no contractual relationship has in many respects been enhanced. Tort law, whether judge made or statutorily developed, blurs further the simplicity of freedom of contract and the notion that private parties have autonomy to fix the limits of liability incurred for their actions.

The very existence of tort law is a recognition that obligations agreed between contracting parties are an inadequate expression of legal responsibility in modern society.[84] As a matter of policy, tort law imposes certain duties on individuals to compensate other individuals in the event that loss is suffered. This notion of 'fairness beyond the bargain' is already part of contract law in the shape of statutory intervention to place certain core implied terms in consumer (and other) contracts, but tort law takes the

---

81 Cf. Chapter 5.4.1 below; from the former perspective, see especially Brandner and Ulmer (1991) 28 *CMLRev* 647. For an explanation of what was at stake for the German lawyer, cf. N. Reich, 'Diverse Approaches to Consumer Protection Philosophy' (1991–92) 14 *JCP* 257, especially 264–7.

82 E.g. H. Collins, 'Good Faith in European Contract Law' (1994) 14 *Oxford JLS* 229.

83 Cf. H.-W. Micklitz, 'The New German Sales Law: Changing Patterns in the Regulation of Product Quality' (2002) 25 *JCP* 379; M. Krajewski, 'The new German Law of Obligations' [2003] *Euro Bus Law Rev* 201.

84 Cf. A Burrows, 'In defence of tort', Chapter 6 in his *Understanding the Law of Obligations* (Hart Publishing, 1998).

scope of such obligations beyond the contractual network. The ebb and flow of the imposition of liability in tort reflect shifting judicial conceptions of the appropriate place for loss to be borne in the absence of a pre-existing contractual arrangement agreeing allocation of responsibility. Study of those judicial choices is itself a fascinating field of inquiry.[85] The flexible and value-laden standards of negligence liability provide many insights into judicial conceptions of loss bearing in particular and fairness in society in general.[86] Choices made in courts about whose shoulders shall bear loss exert an intimate effect on decisions whether to purchase insurance cover and, more generally, they influence the whole climate of commercial activity. Tort law thus assumes an indirect regulatory function.

For the consumer, tort law offers some legal protection beyond the contractual network. It is the tort of negligence which has been most prominent. This allows the consumer to seek compensation outwith the narrow contractual relationship for loss suffered as a result of the supply of an unsafe product. Claims against a manufacturer are possible. The position of the consumer was strengthened still further by the extension of liability for the supply of a defective product secured by Part I of the Consumer Protection Act 1987, which implements the EC Product Liability Directive. As a corollary to the enhanced position of the consumer plaintiff, the defendant trader is exposed to wider potential liability and, in theory, should be induced to take more care to avoid causing loss to the consumer. The trader too will be induced to purchase insurance; part of the point is that he or she will be able to do so more cheaply than the individual consumer. Tort law affects the balance between trader and consumer; to some extent, tort law *is* the balance.

For the English tort lawyer, a Scottish case, *Donoghue v Stevenson*,[87] is the most famous breakthrough in favour of the consumer. It was held that a consumer could sue a manufacturer, with whom he or she had no contractual relationship, for compensation for physical injury or property damage suffered as a result of the negligent supply of a product. The manufacturer owes the consumer the famous 'duty of care' elaborated by Lord Atkin in this case. Subsequent case law has achieved a steady widening in the scope of this duty and potential liability, to the advantage of the consumer.[88]

---

[85] Cf. P. Cane, *The Anatomy of Tort Law* (Hart Publishing, 1997). For a critical account, see J. Conaghan and W. Mansell, *The Wrongs of Tort* (Pluto Press, 1999).

[86] E.g. P. Cane, *Atiyah's Accidents, Compensation and the Law* (Butterworths, 1999); P. Atiyah, *The Damages Lottery* (Hart Publishing, 1997).

[87] [1932] AC 562.

[88] Chapter 4.2.3.2.

Negligence liability is limited by the requirement that the plaintiff demonstrates fault on the part of the defendant trader. The requirement of 'fault' allows an element of judicial assessment of whether the risks of the conduct are outweighed by the potential benefits. Activities conferring benefits on society in general may be judged compatible with the standard required by negligence law, even where harm is foreseeably inflicted on an individual or individuals. 'The purpose to be served, if sufficiently important, justifies the assumption of abnormal risk.'[89] A consumer might be badly injured, even killed, by a drug; yet in negligence law this does not automatically mean that the supplier is a tortfeasor. A calculation of the countervailing benefits of the supply of the drug would be required under traditional negligence law. Here lies tort law's regulatory flavour; the law demands a cost-benefit analysis of particular types of conduct. Statute has intervened to impose additional potential liabilities on parties involved in the manufacture and supply of goods. Part I of the Consumer Protection Act 1987 was introduced to implement the EC's Product Liability Directive, a measure of legislative harmonisation. This is formally concerned with the equalisation of competitive conditions in the EU,[90] but by setting common rules on liability for the supply of defective products, its effect, in the UK at least, was to establish a significant new source of consumer protection. In implementation of the Directive, Part I of the Act introduced a regime which appeared to be a radical departure from standard negligence law and to offer a much more extensive protection to the consumer of unsafe goods. It seemed to impose liability for loss caused by products in a defective condition, irrespective of the conduct of the supplier. In fact, on closer inspection, the Act is notable in places for its obscurity. Defining 'defective' for these purposes is problematic,[91] while the availability of shelter from liability for unforeseeable defects dilutes the rigour of the legal standard to which commercial operators are subject.[92] However, Burton J's approach in *A v National Blood Authority*[93] illustrates the pro-consumer novelty of the new regime. In his inquiry into the defective nature of infected blood he actively excluded negligence-tainted assessment of the general benefit to society of supplying blood and the cost of taking precautions against the possibility of contamination. This

---

[89] Per Asquith LJ in *Daborn v Bath Tramways* [1946] 2 All ER 333, 336. Cf., for instance, *Watt v Hertfordshire CC* [1954] 1 WLR 835; *Bolam v Friern Hospital* [1957] 1 WLR 582.

[90] Chapter 2.3.3.

[91] Chapter 4.2.

[92] In more depth, Chapter 4.2.

[93] [2001] 3 All ER 289.

disinclination to take a broadly-based approach to the factors that govern 'defectiveness' shows the significance of this statutory extension beyond the negligence-dominated private law of consumer protection.[94]

The consumer who is injured by a product has opportunities to sue in tort which are broader than those available in contract. However, the consumer's ability to use the law of tort to secure compensation for loss suffered as a result of quality deficiencies in a product, rather than lack of safety, is much restricted. Quality failings are normally remedied through the law of contract, which provides only restricted opportunities for the consumer, especially in the light of the rules of privity that typically confine the consumer to a claim against the retailer alone.[95]

Tort law depends on judicial attitudes. In the tort of negligence, at least, liability in negligence for inflicting economic loss is imposed only exceptionally. The current judicial attitude in the UK is that the tort of negligence has a limited function to play in the area of economic loss; moreover, if advances in protection are to be put in place, it lies with Parliament not the judiciary to act. In 1990, Lord Oliver in *Murphy v Brentwood DC* declared that:

> ...I do not think that it is right for the courts not simply to expand existing principles but to create at large new principles in order to fulfil a social need in an area of consumer protection which has already been perceived by the legislature but for which, presumably advisedly, it has not thought it necessary to provide.[96]

Judicial activism ebbs and flows over time. There are wide variations in judicial readiness to 'adjust' the law, Lord Denning being the most famously innovative judge active in post War Britain. Lord Oliver's remarks suggested that negligence law in the hands of judges would enter a quiet period, at least in relation to economic loss. Even though much of the above description has been of judges reshaping the 19th-century law of commerce to match the 20th-century consumer society, it appears that the rise of statutory consumer protection is a factor in inducing respect for limits to the dynamic evolution of the common law.[97] More recent

---

[94]   See Chapter 4.2. For a discussion of the competing rationales for shaping legal rules in this area, see J. Stapleton, *Product Liability* (Butterworths, 1994). For a global comparative survey, see G. Howells, *Comparative Product Liability* (Dartmouth, 1993).

[95]   See Chapter 3 for limited reform in the area of Consumer Guarantees.

[96]   [1990] 2 All ER 908, 938.

[97]   See, generally and famously, on this issue, G. Calabresi, *A Common Law for the Age of Statutes* (Harvard University Press, 1982).

decisions of the House of Lords such as *Barrett v Enfield LBC*[98] and *Phelps v Hillingdon LBC*,[99] assert the importance of adopting a case-specific inquiry into the propriety of imposing liability, but they confirm a strong judicial reticence to allow recovery in tort for negligently-inflicted economic loss. One should be aware of the risk of overstating the coherence of the relationship developed by judges between liability arising in contract and in tort, but, in relation to economic loss at least, there is the suggestion of a recent resurgence in the importance of contract law and the acceptance of obligations by agreement; similarly, a decline in the importance of tort law and the readiness of judges to impose obligations inspired by a more general sense of (extra-contractual) social responsibility.

1.5 THE COSTS OF CONSUMER PROTECTION THROUGH PRIVATE LAW

1.5.1 Costs of Intervention in the Common Law of Contract

Whether contract or tort is involved, the imposition of obligations on traders to compensate consumers is not cost-free. For example, the requirement that goods are of satisfactory quality, violation of which permits a consumer claim for breach of contract, plainly sets minimum standards. These will be reflected in price. One can interpret the satisfactory quality requirement as a State-imposed restriction on the consumer's choice to buy at a lower price a product whose quality is less than 'satisfactory'. The restriction of consumer choice can be defended by reference to the perception that (most) consumers cannot really choose effectively in an unregulated market. Denying choice to buy a product of unsatisfactory quality is today uncontroversial, not least because this aspect of the Sale of Goods Act has been in force for fully a century, until 1994 in the guise of 'merchantable', rather than satisfactory, quality. However, it is always necessary and often much more controversial to test against a cost/benefit calculation more novel, deeper forms of intervention designed to protect the consumer.

The phenomenon of the exclusion clause is controlled by the Unfair Contract Terms Act 1977, now supplemented by the UK's Regulations which implement the EC's Directive on unfair terms in consumer

---

98   [2001] 2 AC 550.
99   [2001] 2 AC 619.

contracts.[100] It may initially seem inconceivable that there can be any benefit to a consumer in a clause which excludes the supplier's liability and causes loss to fall on the consumer. Yet the Act outlaws only a small number of exclusion clauses,[101] leaving others to be assessed against a reasonableness test. The consumer remains able to 'choose' to bear the loss. This is explicable when it is appreciated that exclusion clauses perform the very valuable function of allocating risk. A party who accepts a contractual term which, by excluding the other party's liability, makes it clear that he or she will bear that loss may plan accordingly. He or she may take out insurance against the loss at issue or may simply run the risk. The other party will need no insurance against that risk, nor need to plan to cover the cost of its occurrence. The result should be that the assumption of risk through the placement of the exclusion clause is reflected in the price. Put simply, you pay less if you are willing to exclude the other party from specified liability. This function of conscious, planned risk allocation via an exclusion clause dictates that, in the commercial sphere at least, courts should not interfere.[102]

In *Thompson*,[103] an element in the Court of Appeal's finding that the exclusion clause had been adequately brought to the notice of the consumer lay in the price of the excursion ticket, which was much lower than that of a standard ticket. This remains entirely valid as an observation on the function of exclusion clauses in favour of a supplier in offering the consumer the choice of a riskier journey at a lower price. It holds less water in a situation where the consumer was in fact unaware of the circumstances and was not making an informed choice. The Unfair Contract Terms Act 1977 permits control of exclusion clauses in (mainly) consumer contracts, but here too the apparent costs of exclusion clauses should be weighed against possible benefits. There are reasons in favour of permitting consumers to choose between protection from loss, for which a premium will doubtless be payable, and the risk of loss expressed in exclusion of supplier liability, for which a lower price should in theory be offered. The attempt to conserve consumer choice is reflected in the Unfair Contract Terms Act 1977. Schedule 2 contains a non-exhaustive list of guidelines to be employed in the application of the reasonableness test.[104] Account should be taken of 'alternative means by which the customer's

---

100 For detailed analysis see Chapter 5.
101 Chapter 5.5 below.
102 This is the very strong message of the House of Lords decision in *Photo Productions v Securicor*, Chapter 5.2 below, a case involving commercial parties.
103 Note 42 above.
104 Strictly Schedule 2 applies only to contracts controlled by ss. 6 and 7, but it has been used more broadly; see Chapter 5.6.1.1.

requirements could have been met'. Regard should be had to 'whether the customer knew or ought reasonably to have known of the existence and extent of the term'. The strong impression is that the further the situation departs from 'take it or leave it!' at the time of contracting, the more likely that the term will be thought reasonable. *Woodman v Photo Trade Processing*,[105] a decision which has gained more prominence than most County Court decisions, provides a valuable illustration of how the Act may operate in practice. The plaintiff took photographs of a friend's wedding to be developed by the defendant. They were ruined, but, in accordance with a notice displayed on the premises, the defendant offered Woodman only the cost of a new film as compensation. This limitation of liability was found to be unreasonable and Woodman was awarded £75. Subsequently it has become common practice for suppliers in this trade and others to offer varying ceilings of compensation for any damage caused, depending on the price paid by the consumer. The consumer can choose to buy more protection. Whether the terms are reasonable or not remains a question of fact, but the supplier is likely to be in a stronger position the greater the level of disclosure made and choice offered.[106] Similar comments may be made about the application of the control test established by the EC's Directive on unfair terms in consumer contracts, where the effect of the regime is also to encourage transparency.[107] As already observed,[108] the appeal of information-based techniques of consumer protection makes contestable assumptions about the adequacy of information transmitted and, in particular, about consumer ability to assess the risks at stake in a rational manner.

1.5.2 Costing Tort Law

Obligations imposed by tort law are not cost-free. A system which makes fault-free producers strictly liable for harm caused by the supply of unsafe products may seem determinedly pro-consumer. What if the consequence is that producers adopt a very cautious attitude to the marketing of new products for fear that innovation, which has unforeseen and unforeseeable

---

[105] *Which?* July 1981. Reprinted in C.J. Miller, B.W. Harvey and D.P. Parry, *Consumer and Trading Law, Text, Cases and Materials* (OUP, 1998) pp. 343–347.

[106] On implications of disclosure rules, see especially discussion of the work of George Priest in Chapter 3.

[107] See further Chapter 5.6 for discussion of whether the two systems of control are the same or merely similar.

[108] Cf. critique from the perspective of 'behaviouralism', note 1 above.

implications, may prove financially catastrophic? Consumers might then be protected at the cost of having innovation stifled. It may then be submitted that society would be better advised to permit producers protection from liability where they can show that they were pursuing innovation which unforeseeably went wrong. Such a calculation of rather intangible and hypothetical costs and benefits dogged the negotiation of the EC's Product Liability Directive, subsequently implemented in the UK by Part I of the Consumer Protection Act 1987.[109] It was a wrangle that was never satisfactorily resolved. The Directive, as adopted, allows States to choose whether or not to include a defence of this type, the so-called 'development risk' defence which, according to the Directive, protects a producer from liability where 'the state of technical and scientific knowledge at the time when he put the product into circulation was not such as to enable the existence of the defect to be discovered'.[110] The UK decided that it would opt to dilute strict liability in this way, and the same choice has been made by most other Member States.

Under a fault-based regime, a manufacturer of a new and, in the majority of cases, beneficial drug which has catastrophic but wholly unforeseeable side-effects will probably escape liability for the loss caused. There would be no fault. Those injured will have no claim at common law other than a contractual action against the retailer which will be of practical utility only where that retailer is sufficiently large. Worse, English law holds that there is no claim in contract at all where the drug has been supplied by the National Health Service.[111] Loss would lie where it fell, with the consumer. The replacement of fault-based liability by a strict liability system combined with the development risk defence would probably rarely have an impact on the outcome. The manufacturer will be protected by the defence; loss will lie where it falls. A 'pure' strict liability system, on the other hand, will allow a successful claim by any consumer able to show that the defendant has supplied the drug which caused the harm. Loss will be shifted on to the trader. This latter outcome may seem instinctively correct. The manufacturer took the profits and should bear the loss. A connected observation is that the manufacturer is in the best position to take precautions against the supply of unsafe goods and should therefore be given the strongest possible incentive so to do. Such arguments point in the direction of a strict liability system. Moreover, the manufacturer can buy insurance cover against liability, though this, of course, will be reflected in the price. In this way, loss suffered by a minority of unfortunate consumers will be compensated by a premium paid

---

[109]   Chapter 4.
[110]   Article 7(e) Directive.
[111]   *Pfizer v Ministry of Health* [1965] 1 All ER 450.

by all purchasers of the product. This may instinctively seem fair. Yet prices will rise, reducing consumer choice about risk-taking. Innovation may also be stifled by a rigid liability regime. Increasing insurance premiums and/or the costs of settling consumer claims may drive smaller firms out of the market, leaving supply in the hands of a few large firms and pushing the market structure towards oligopoly. In short, there are real choices to be made about the priorities of consumer protection and consumer choice in the market and the preceding description is only a simple framework. Where does society feel most comfortable about loss falling? That perception will then be translated into legal rules, whether devised by the judiciary or the legislature.

The choice between strict liability and fault-based liability may thus involve a cost benefit calculation containing many nuances. Some of the considerations are political, others economic, but all must be absorbed and balanced by anyone with an interest in shaping consumer policy.[112] Empirical evidence about how different liability systems actually work would help. However, data is often difficult to gather on a scale that is sufficiently comprehensive, and there is a risk that the debate proceeds according to assumption rather than demonstrated reality. Recent years have witnessed a ferocious debate in North America about what some have identified as a 'crisis' in product liability law. There have been perceptions of trends towards remarkably high awards in some areas and steep rises in the price of insurance. Some commentators have identified a declining commercial incentive to innovate and, as a result, impaired consumer choice. This has prompted proposals that the consumer interest would be served by a tort system that moves towards less, not more, generosity to plaintiffs. Such challenges to the intuition that consumers benefit from stricter forms of liability rule deserve careful attention but they are by no means free of their own questionable assumptions. First, it is less than the clear that the protests about rising levels of successful suits by consumers are supported by the evidence. Secondly, it is remarkably difficult to pin down the sort of empirical evidence that would help in drawing sensible conclusions about the effect of product liability rules. Evidence of the capacity of fault-based tort systems effectively to deter harm is equivocal.[113] Europe fares no better in the gathering of empirical evidence

---

[112] Cf. Stapleton, Howells note 94 above; J. Stapleton, 'Tort, Insurance and Ideology' (1995) 58 *MLR* 820.

[113] Cf. D. Dewees, D. Duff and M. Trebilcock, *Exploring the Domain of Accident Law: Taking the Facts Seriously* (OUP, 1996); M. Galanter, 'Real World Torts: an Antidote to Anecdotes' (1996) 55 *Maryland Law Rev* 1093; G.T. Schwartz, 'Empiricism and Tort Law' (2002) *University of Illinois Law Rev* 1067.

about how systems work. The debate in the early 1980s about the shaping of a product liability regime in the EC ranged those anxious lest a heavily pro-compensation system should depress the ready availability of insurance and thereby deter innovation against those who favoured the imposition of strict liability on producers of defective products in the belief that this would ultimately serve the consumer interest. The inclusion of the optional 'development risk' in the Directive, mentioned above and explored in more depth in Chapter 4, represented an unsatisfying compromise between these divergent attitudes to the consequences of choosing between liability rules, but it was promised that the matter would be re-visited in the light of experience. However, when the Commission published its first report on the Directive in 1995 it was able to do no more than observe briefly that on the basis of the limited available evidence there had been no increase either in the number of claims or in the level of insurance premiums.[114] Its second report, published in early 2001, proved equally unable to unearth much concrete information about problems and practice. It merely asserted that on the basis of the information available, it remained premature to propose any major changes to the existing regime.[115] The debate will be tracked more closely in Chapter 4, but for the present purposes it is sufficient to observe that implications of choices about which liability rule to adopt as a legal standard may be politically, economically and socially wide-ranging – but also hard to predict or even to measure.

The capacity of the tort system to provide an efficient and/or fair method for compensating injury has come under more fundamental attack in recent decades. Criticism has led to radical change in some parts of the world. The tort system generates some rather haphazard outcomes. A fault-based system can often mean that an unlucky few consumers bear loss through no fault of their own. On the other hand, strict liability places the loss indirectly on all consumers through higher prices, though even then the plaintiff must show that the product has caused his or her loss. Causation is always a problematic element in the consumer's claim in tort. Producer insolvency acts as a further potential hindrance to the consumer's claim. The result is that whichever brand of liability rule is preferred some instances of consumer loss will fall through the net and go uncompensated. Some observers have gone further and commented on how tort law protects only certain kinds of interests, certain types of loss. It certainly does not

---

[114]	COM (95) 617.

[115]	COM (2000) 893. The only amendment has been via Directive 99/34, which extends the material scope of the regime 'in the aftermath of the mad cow crisis', COM (2000) 893, p. 6.

operate as a comprehensive method for protecting the unfortunate in society.[116]

Consequently more direct State intervention has been proposed. In New Zealand, for example, it has not been possible to bring a tort action to secure compensation for most personal injuries since 1974.[117] There is instead a State-run benefits system. Accidental injury is compensated, irrespective of the identity of the party who has inflicted the loss, but the matter has been taken out of the private and into the public domain. To take the example of the supply of a drug with unforeseen side effects, the availability of an award of compensation to a victim would no longer hinge on the behaviour of the manufacturer or supplier or on the condition of the product. The State system would compensate the victim for the loss suffered. The system may appeal on grounds of fairness, but attracts criticism for the diminished incentives it creates for accident prevention (although, as mentioned above, evidence of the capacity of fault-based tort systems effectively to deter harm is in any event equivocal). Much more generally, it is possible to locate the range of activities of a modern Welfare State in a context which sees private law as inappropriate to the types of difficulties which may arise for the individual.

Critics of the perceived haphazard capacity of tort law in the United Kingdom to compensate injury and deter harmful activities have proposed the adoption of a replacement system along these lines. Atiyah, for example, has argued in favour of a no-fault road accident scheme combined with a system allowing individuals to choose to take out insurance to cover costs incurred by injuries suffered in other circumstances.[118] Orthodox claims in tort would no longer be available. In North America some commentators have aired proposals that exhibit similar scepticism about the value of adhering to a traditional fault-based model and which favour some brand of public compensation system.[119] The several possible models are by no means without their disadvantages – for example, Atiyah's insurance scheme is vulnerable to criticism based on

---

[116] Cf. J. Stapleton, *Disease and the Compensation Debate* (OUP, 1986).

[117] For an extended (and positive) account by a former Prime Minister of New Zealand, see Sir Geoffrey Palmer, 'New Zealand's Accident Compensation Scheme: Twenty Years On' (1994) XLIV *Univ of Toronto Law J* 223. For a briefer contrast with English law, see J. Miller, 'No-fault compensation in New Zealand' (1993) 3 *Consumer Policy Review* 73. Chapter 4 of this book explores these issues further.

[118] *The Damages Lottery* note 86 above.

[119] E.g. S. Sugarman, *Doing Away with Personal Injury Law* (Quorum, 1989); S. Sugarman, 'Quebec's Comprehensive Auto No-Fault Scheme and the Failure of Any of the United States to Follow' (1998) 39 *Les Cahiers de Droit* 303.

the inability of individuals to make an informed assessment of the worth of choosing to buy insurance which, moreover, might hurt socially and economically disadvantaged consumers to a disproportionately high degree. And even in New Zealand, political pressure has mounted in favour of a partial 're-privatisation' of the liability system, not least because of the costs of the State-run system.[120] The political appeal of radical reform of the law governing tort and compensation currently appears to be negligible and, for all the criticism it has received, the liability system survives in the UK as a key component of the law of consumer protection.

1.6 REDRESS AND ACCESS TO JUSTICE

Legislative adjustment of what might be termed the common law of consumer protection improves the position of the consumer and, in perhaps a rather imprecise way, helps to make more effective the market mechanism based on consumer/supplier dialogue. It helps to prevent the trader from escaping the brutal consequences of failing to satisfy the consumer. Yet there are gaps in that control. Common law contract and tort, even supplemented by legislative enhancement of rights, do not cover every instance of consumer loss. The result is that the market does not operate perfectly and resources may be wasted. This invites consideration of public regulation of the market divorced from the private supplier/consumer relationship. Study of this phenomenon begins below in part 1.7.

The case for public controls becomes all the stronger when account is taken of practical difficulties which confront consumers seeking to enforce legal rights, however generous those rights may seem on paper. Access to justice is examined at length in Chapter 14, but an overview of the issues is appropriate at this point. Such problems deepen our understanding that an effective consumer protection programme cannot be constructed from the operation of the private law alone.

Most fundamental of all is consumer ignorance of the law. Attractive though rights may look on paper, they will play a major role in the consumer/supplier relationship only where a sufficient number of consumers are aware of them. The retailer is liable for the quality of a product by virtue of the statutory terms implied in contracts concluded with the consumer. The manufacturer has no such contractual liability under the

---

[120] S. Todd, 'Privatization of Accident Compensation: Policy and Politics in New Zealand' (2000) 39 *Washburn Law Journal* 405.

implied terms.[121]Yet few consumers will not have been confronted by retailers who, at least as an opening gambit, suggest that the consumer's complaint should be directed elsewhere, higher up the supply chain. In fact, paradoxically, the more sophisticated and nuanced consumer protection law is on paper, the greater the risk that consumers will be confused by it and alienated from it in practice. Legal rights should be easy to grasp and to use. Lack of understanding of the law among consumers plainly defeats much of the purpose of the law. Moreover, it should not be left out of account that ignorance of and/or disinterest in the nuances of consumer law among practising lawyers, perhaps even combined with antipathy to consumer disputes as trivial complaints, constitute a yet further impediment to its practical impact.[122]

In part this leads to the charge that consumer protection law is, or has become, law for the middle class, at least (or especially) in its private law manifestations. The middle class complains about purchases, whereas poorer sections of society worry about being able to make purchases in the first place. It hardly matters whether a product is of satisfactory quality if you cannot afford it. The middle class understands the law and can either use it or threaten to use it; poorer sections of society are doubtful about its relevance to their needs. The allegation that consumer law is middle class law is not without foundation, though it would be churlish to hurl aside the accumulated body of legal protection on that under-articulated basis alone. However, if it is true that adjustment of the private law is of disproportionate assistance to already affluent members of society, then a stronger commitment to public law regulation may be appropriate.

Even where the consumer is aware, however dimly, that a legal point has arisen, it is a practical truth that literally the last thing that the typical disgruntled consumer will do is to initiate litigation against a trader. Court proceedings take time and cost money, even if they are ultimately successful. Naturally, if they are lost the consumer may be greatly out of pocket and obliged to pay his or her own costs and those of the other (winning) side. In practice, the cost of formal resort to law typically excludes the middle class as much as poorer members of society. Moreover, courts are intimidating to the average citizen. Consequently there will be a strong consumer preference to avoid legal proceedings. Frequently consumers write off loss to experience, occasionally perhaps after attempting to complain. The majority of consumers do nothing which

---

[121] Limited adjustment has been made in the particular context of Consumer Guarantees, see Chapter 3.

[122] Further discussed at Chapter 14.2.2 particularly in connection with the work of Macaulay.

will immediately affect the supplier's pocket. This is particularly likely to be the case in the event of small-scale loss incurred as a result of a disappointing purchase. The rational consumer will not invoke the law. This may provoke the reaction that, if the loss written off is small-scale, then the problem cannot be very serious and need not concern policy-makers. That may be complacent. An accumulation of a large number of small-scale losses all caused by the same supplier represents in aggregate a large problem. Yet the unrealistic expectation of the common law that each individual must pursue his or her own claim will conceal that large problem. This generates an inefficient market which is not subject to effective correction.

Where action is actively pursued by the consumer, informal settlement will be preferred, where feasible. This preference will to some extent be shared by the trader. The small trader, especially, will be almost as reluctant as the consumer to embark on the perilous seas of litigation from which it is notorious that lawyers normally emerge the main (and sometimes only) winners. Nonetheless the risk remains that traders, typically with more resources at their disposal than consumers, will be able to use consumer reluctance to litigate as a method for fobbing off the vindication of consumer rights.

The 1999 White Paper *Modern Markets: Confident Consumers* vividly asserts that markets work best when rivalry on the supply-side is accompanied by consumer behaviour which is bruisingly intolerant of failure to meet demand. It quotes Michael Porter, influential analyst of the conditions necessary for a nation to achieve international competitiveness: 'A stiff upper lip is not good for upgrading an economy'.[123] Consumers benefit from competitive markets, but they generate them too. Policy is therefore sensibly directed at improving consumer information and education, so that people are able to perform the role as demanding consumers which is a pre-condition to efficiently functioning markets. Better consumer education is identified in the White Paper as a pressing priority. This relates to education of both adults and schoolchildren. It also covers education about both the extent of protection guaranteed to consumers by law and also the ways to secure redress in the event that these rights are infringed. This is naturally a strategy that cannot be successful, nor even sensibly judged, in the short-term. A great deal more information on rights and their effective enforcement is today available through electronic sources,[124] but it is fair to conclude that improving

---

[123] Section 1.1 White Paper, note 77 above, citing M. Porter, *The Competitive Advantage of Nations* (1998). The White Paper is examined more fully below at 1.9.2.

[124] See e.g. the DTI's contribution:
http://www.consumer.gov.uk/consumer_web/index_v4.htm.

consumer education is as easy to acclaim on paper as it is hard to achieve in practice. Moreover, the better educated consumer also needs to become the more assertive consumer – a cultural shift towards a more complaining culture is desirable but hard to induce. The introduction of a 'You must complain more aggressively' bill into Parliament is as improbable a prospect as an Act of this type ever proving effective.

The capacity of the consumer to pursue an individual action could be enhanced by facilitating recourse to law. There is no need to abandon the effort to improve the structure of the private law; quite the contrary. Nor should one abandon attempts to improve consumer access to justice. Developments in the small claims procedure provide welcome examples of steps in this direction. More vigorous progress towards class/representative actions under English law would be valuable.[125] In the context of the internal market, attention also needs to be devoted to handling cross-border complaints.[126] Ultimately, however, the case for at least some public intervention in the market seems unanswerable. Indeed, this is accepted by the 1999 White Paper, albeit in a rather unspecific manner.[127] It is to these issues that the discussion now turns.

1.7 RATIONALES FOR PUBLIC INTERVENTION SUMMARISED

It is not difficult to construct a powerful argument that a legal system based exclusively on individual action by 'consumer' against 'trader' bears no useful relation to an economy of mass production and extended distribution and marketing chains. The pursuit of such distinct goals as the correction of market failure and fairness within a market order cannot be fully achieved under a system based purely on private law.

Contract and tort law both have limitations in sharpening the messages expressed by consumers about producer behaviour. The common law of contract is based on the doctrine of privity of contract. Accordingly, the consumer may sue the party to whom he or she paid money for the item – and no one else. As a corollary, the consumer who has not bought the product, for example the recipient of a gift, has no rights in contract at all. Since modern marketing typically puts the consumer at several removes from the manufacturer, the contractual claim brought by a consumer against the manufacturer of a faulty product is a rarity. Statutory reform –

---

125   Chapter 14.3.

126   Cf. the European Commission's cautious activity in the field of Access to Justice, considered in Chapter 14.9.3.

127   Section 7 White Paper. See Chapter 1.9.2 below.

in the shape of the Contracts (Rights of Third Parties) Act 1999 which provides a limited and defined route around the restrictions of contractual privity – is of little, if any, relevance to the typical consumer complaint. The EC's Sales Directive has improved the consumer's protection – but here too the reform, though valuable, is limited in scope.[128] Tort law partially fills these gaps. It takes legal responsibility for manufacture and marketing into wider realms than are recognised by the artificially confined law of contract. However, tort law too has limitations, its focus being on inadequate *safety*, not inadequate *quality*. Where a product fails to achieve suitable quality standards, the claim lies only in contract. Moreover, whereas liability for breach of contract is strict, negligence liability depends on fault on the part of the defendant. The fact that a consumer has been harmed is not of itself enough to ensure the success of a claim, although the Consumer Protection Act 1987 has improved the consumer's position.[129] Tort law protects only certain kinds of interest. Accordingly, contract and tort law offer protection to the consumer, but both have gaps in the framework of that protection. Inefficient behaviour may not be corrected.

Contract and tort are also limited in their capacity to deliver fair outcomes. Contract, classically, is in any event concerned with no such thing. It has latterly moved more in the direction of controls reflecting notions of fairness, but this aspect remains relatively unsophisticated and is in any event not undisputed.[130] Tort law is more allied with ideas of social fairness. However, as judge-made law, it remains erratic and unpredictable in its scope.

Such qualifications to the role of tort and contract in securing an efficient and fair market are greatly deepened by the practical problems of securing access to justice. The reluctance of consumers to go to court and the absence of effective recourse to representative actions together shelter producers from the consequences of their failure to fulfil consumer demand and expectation, while also denying consumers the practical enjoyment of legal rights. Consumers exhibit a cultural antipathy to vigorous pursuit of legal rights, and the gulf between the protection of the law in practice and its worth on paper may therefore be wide. From a comparative perspective this, in fact, may constitute a material difference between the European approach to consumer protection and that found in North America, where

---

[128] Directive 99/44. See Chapter 3.
[129] Chapter 1.4 above, Chapter 4 below.
[130] Chapter 1.3.4 above.

private consumer litigation is engaged with greater readiness and where accordingly public intervention may be judged a less pressing need.[131]

The perception that private law rights are often hazily understood by consumers and that their pursuit is frequently neglected sharpens the policy perception that an effective programme of consumer protection in the modern market must embrace public law too. For the benefit of consumers, for the benefit of fair and honest traders who find themselves exposed to dishonest competition, and in the public interest generally in an efficient market system, action to improve the operation of the market can be justified.

1.8 CHOICES BETWEEN FORMS OF PUBLIC REGULATION

It is immediately important to take care! The notion of 'public regulation' does not connote a homogenous category. Nor is there a simple or clear divide between private law and public law. Intervention may take many different forms. Regulation is a complex phenomenon.[132]

Moreover, the popularity of various forms of regulation has risen and fallen over time. Regulatory agencies may assume very different shapes, with diverse methods for securing accountability for decisions adopted. Rationales for interventions have varied. The distinctive notions of intervention to correct market failure and the non-economic motivation of fairness have enjoyed fluctuating levels of attraction. Political fashion has changed. After several decades in which the pattern of market regulation gradually intensified, a contrasting scepticism about the worth of the regulatory impulse was associated with the policies of successive Conservative governments led first by Mrs Thatcher, Prime Minister from 1979 to 1990, and then Mr Major (1990–1997). The Labour government headed by Mr Blair took office in 1997. It attempted to steer a new course which was shaken free of more traditional left/right political ideology, accepting that public regulation is in some circumstances justified but demanding careful assessment of how and why this might be so and, in

---

131 Cf. G. Howells and T. Wilhelmsson, 'EC and US Approaches to Consumer Protection – should the gap be bridged?' (1997) 17 *YEL* 207. Cf. also s. 4.20 of the 1999 White Paper, note 77 above, comparing UK consumers unfavourably with more assertive US consumers.

132 For investigation, see A. I. Ogus, *Regulation: Legal Form and Economic Theory* (OUP, 1994); R. Baldwin and M. Cave, *Understanding Regulation: Theory, Strategy and Practice* (OUP, 1999).

addition, reflecting a fresher readiness to re-think appropriate forms of public regulation.[133]

There is nothing new about the perception that policymakers should be aware that regulation may produce winners and losers, and that a cost-benefit calculation should be performed. The result of tensions from decade to decade associated with choosing priorities in the shaping of consumer policy is a patchwork of controls which must be assessed with an awareness of the melting pot of the history of consumer protection. Attempts to identify what individual initiatives are 'for' and how they fit coherently into a wider framework will, on occasion, aim at producing a master-plan that does not exist. Consumer protection law *is* a patchwork. However, this does not detract from the importance and value of attempting to construct a rigorous and transparent cost-benefit analysis to justify regulatory intervention – as long as one is aware, first, that quantification of costs and benefits may reflect subjective value judgements and, second, that it is perfectly possible and not uncommon to make the political judgement that justice requires that an overall cost be placed on society generally in support of a disadvantaged minority.

1.8.1 Quality Standards/Bans

An obvious intervention in the market is the imposition of minimum quality or safety standards, backed by bans on non-conforming products or services. Infringement of these standards could attract penalties in the form of fines or even, ultimately, imprisonment. Enforcement responsibilities would typically be placed in the hands of public authorities who would enjoy powers of investigation, prosecution and seizure of offending items. Such agencies tend to develop a flexible strategy for enforcement. Prosecution and conviction may be relatively easy to achieve, not least because regulatory offences arising in the field of consumer protection are typically strict liability offences. However, formal prosecution is often seen to serve a limited purpose and is commonly used only against rogue traders. If the objective is to achieve a basic quality or safety level, the enforcement officer will typically prefer to act by persuasion, guidance and co-operation. Where the officer considers that the trader wishes to comply, it is normal to devise an appropriate strategy so that there is no call to invoke costly formal proceedings. This co-operative pattern is underpinned in the UK by a tradition of local enforcement. Trading standards officers operating at local level get to know 'their' traders and establish a *modus vivendi*. It should also be pointed out that the nature of the standard which

---

[133] See part 1.9.2.3 of this chapter for a more extended discussion.

is legally required will also affect the climate of enforcement; very precise rules leave little room for doubt, whereas vaguer notions such as 'reasonable safety' invite flexibility.

The law of consumer protection provides several illustrations of this type of regulatory offence. It is formally a sub species of the criminal law, although the objective of correcting market failure lends it a flavour that is distinct from the normal run of the criminal law. The philosophy and practice of the regulatory offence are considered more fully in Chapter 11. Consumer safety law provides an example of this style of intervention: products must meet specified safety standards; supply of an unsafe product attracts penalties, normally fines, possibly imprisonment. Trading standards authorities possess a range of powers which may be exercised against traders and against the goods themselves.

Apart from incurring criminal liability, supply of an unsafe product will equally represent a breach of contractual terms, most pertinently the implied term of satisfactory quality under the Sale of Goods Act 1979. The consumer will be able to sue the retailer for any loss suffered. Tort law may also provide a potential course of action for the consumer. In this way precisely the same incident may attract both criminal and civil consequences. The purpose of the two regimes is distinct. The imposition of criminal liability is motivated by the perception that, first, informational imbalance impedes the capacity of the consumer to avoid unsafe products; and, secondly, that the private law cannot adequately secure the market from the supply of unsafe goods. The several reasons for this are suggested above, ranging from the consumer's potential difficulty in shaping a claim in contract or tort against the relevant defendant trader, to the consumer's reluctance even to bother with the pursuit of a legal action where costs appear capable of outweighing benefits. Any fine imposed is payable into public funds. By contrast, the consumer who pursues a private action, albeit supported by a statutorily implied term, is suing for compensation for his or her own loss. Damages are then directed into the pocket of the consumer.[134]

In some exceptional circumstances, statute may provide that a criminal offence also forms the basis for a liability in tort for breach of statutory duty. Section 41 of the Consumer Protection Act 1987 provides an example. This is additional to criminal liability arising and any separate claim in tort or contract. However, there is no evidence that the provision has yet exerted any significant practical impact.

---

[134] But compare the role of the compensation order in bridging the gap between criminal penalty and consumer compensation; Chapter 11.3.4.

The use of misleading trade descriptions has also led to the creation of the regulatory offence. The pattern of the Trade Descriptions Act 1968 has much in common with that of the law governing consumer safety (and is examined in Chapter 8). The application of a misleading trade description may similarly attract consequences on two levels, criminal and civil. The false claim may attract criminal liability under the Trade Descriptions Act 1968. Here too the perception is that the market plus the private law are inadequate to secure protection for consumers and for honest traders against parties dealing on a dishonest basis. The same mischief can also frequently be converted into an action for breach of contract and/or the basis for a claim in tort by an individual consumer who is misled, although the Act is not tied to the private law and may impose criminal liability where no contractual or tortious liability would be at stake.

The type of standard properly set by the law has come under close scrutiny in recent years. Whereas legal standards tended in the past to be detailed and prescriptive, it has become increasingly popular to prefer broadly phrased, target performance standards. This is particularly noticeable in the Consumer Protection Act 1987. In the field of consumer safety, the 1987 Act has shifted the focus of control towards a general standard requiring reasonable safety, which is applicable 'horizontally', across a whole range of products.[135] The general standard will be elaborated in individual product sectors as appropriate, *inter alia* by standards set by private bodies. This emphasis on the general duty has replaced the pre-1987 focus of the law which was directed at the regulation of individual product types in individual instruments, often in rather precise and detailed depth. Part III of the Consumer Protection Act 1987 introduces a general and flexible offence in the field of misleading pricing. This replaces the narrower offence contained in s. 11 of the Trade Descriptions Act 1968.[136] The application of the prohibition against misleading price indications is amplified by a Code of Practice. The notion of a general duty to trade fairly or its potentially more precise converse, a prohibition against unfair trading practices, has also come under consideration in recent years in the UK.[137] More recently, interest in developing such a regime has grown at EU level. In 2003 the European Commission published a draft Directive in this vein. This is examined in Chapter 8.7.3.

---

[135] Definitional issues arise; Chapter 10.5.1.

[136] Chapter 8.5.

[137] Cf. Sir Gordon Borrie, 'Trading Malpractices and Legislative Policy' (1991) 107 *LQR* 559; P. Circus, 'Should there be a general duty to trade fairly?' (1988) 6 *Trading Law* 238.

The motivations for this shift in regulatory policy towards broadly-based standards are several.[138] It allows more flexibility to enforcement agencies and to traders. Typically the amplification of the broadly-phrased legal standard is achieved by private standards-setting bodies which are likely to have more expertise than public agencies. The past practice of detailed standards attracted criticism for its tendency to ossify practice and deter innovation.

This is an aspect of regulatory technique where the approaches of the EC and the UK are complementary. The EC adopted a 'New Approach' on technical harmonisation in 1985,[139] which pledged that, as far as possible, the past (and notorious) tendency of EC measures to lay down detailed and rigid rules will be abandoned.[140] In its place comes a broader, more flexible type of harmonised standard. Manufacturers enjoy choice about how to achieve the stipulated level, thereby providing them with the opportunity and the incentive to innovate. The Toy Safety Directive,[141] a typical New Approach measure, establishes the requirement that toys shall be safe, which means that they shall comply with 'essential safety requirements' amplified in an Annex to the Directive. Conformity with European standards is one method of demonstrating conformity with these essential safety requirements. In this way the Community standard of safety is linked to private standards (although it remains the case that safety, as defined in the Directive, is the standard that must be met; the Community has not delegated the basic task of setting the legal standard to the private sector). A second method of demonstrating conformity involves securing type approval for a model which, although not complying with recognised standards, is nonetheless certified as safe. Since the legal requirement has been shorn of its rigidity, producers have leeway to innovate. In this way, the basic notion that the public authorities will set standards, rather than simply leaving them to the market, is preserved. Non-conforming products may not be sold. However, the type of standard at issue is significantly altered, as is the freedom of action of traders subjected to the legal regime.

---

[138] Cf. Ogus, note 132 above, Chapter 8; Baldwin and Cave, note 132 above, Chapters 4, 9.

[139] OJ 1985 C136/1.

[140] For an account of the New Approach in the light of the weaknesses which it addressed, see J. Pelkmans, 'The New Approach to Technical Harmonisation and Standardisation' (1987) 25 *JCMS* 249.

[141] Directive 88/378 OJ 1988 L187/1.

1.8.2 Regulating Traders

1.8.2.1 Registration and Licensing

Minimum standards plus a ban on non-conforming products comprise a relatively common form of public regulation, typically enforced *ex post facto*. In such circumstances, the sanction, most commonly a fine, is judged an adequate deterrence against the public being put at risk. Any trader is able to enter the field, but, once active, must comply with the regulatory standards. By contrast, in some sectors, it is considered inadvisable simply to permit all traders unrestricted access to the market, with only the back-up of sanctions in the event that the goods or services on offer fail to reach the statutory requirements. In such circumstances, regulatory controls may be directed at the trader him or herself.[142] The intensity of control may vary. Traders may be forced merely to register; they may require a licence; and/or they may be authorised to enter the market only after showing evidence of competence through some form of qualification. A supervisory agency will have to be established whose functions may vary from the mere maintenance of a register at one end of the regulatory spectrum to the imposition of training requirements and examination procedures at the other.

This type of control is more intrusive than simply setting a basic minimum standard for goods or services. Its benefits include the probability of greater security that goods or services below the required standard will not be released on to the market, because of the element of pre-authorization. The technique of registration and (a stricter control) licensing allows channels of supervision over a trade which can be exercised by public authorities. The public body is better placed to exercise control than in a system where standards are simply laid down and where any individual may, unannounced, choose to begin to trade. Typically, sanctions would be imposed for trading without a licence or without having registered, irrespective of evidence of any harm caused.

1.8.2.2 Costs of Regulation

However, more intrusive regulation involves costs. Endowing an agency with expertise may involve a substantial resource commitment. Furthermore, there is the less tangible damage done to the flexibility of the market. Rules such as these amount to barriers to market entry. They impede competition, for any would-be entrant must scale the barriers,

---

[142] Cf., Ogus, note 132 above, Chapter 10.

which may be rather low in the case of mere registration, but which can be much higher if the trader is required to hold qualifications. Those inside the system have an incentive to raise barriers to those outside, for example by persuading the licensing authority to impose entry qualifications. Setting standards may protect the consumer from unscrupulous traders, but those very standards also deprive the consumer of choice among traders adopting different practices. Of course, impeding competition is the very rationale for intervention: it has been determined that the market should not be a free-for-all. But it is always essential to analyse with care the benefits of securing a certain level of protection as against the costs of removing the possibility of (some) competition. This is a further expression of an endemic problem in consumer policy making: where does unfair competition which is liable to mislead shade into fair but fierce competition which maximises consumer choice?

Examples of the phenomenon of controlling market entry are numerous. The power to manufacture or to sell some products is controlled. Retailing alcoholic drinks on premises open to the public cannot be undertaken unless the individual concerned has first obtained a licence.[143] The manufacture and sale of drugs and medicines have been subjected to regulatory control for many centuries. Innovative research and development in this area are vital for society, but so is control over both the manufacture of products that may cause enormous harm to consumers and the availability of goods that may fall into the wrong hands. Part of the rationale for such close scrutiny lies in the perception that consumers are under informed and that supply decisions cannot be left to the unregulated market.

Examples of registration and licensing in specific sectors will be encountered in the course of this book. For instance, the Consumer Credit Act 1974, which requires that a licence be obtained to carry on a consumer credit, consumer hire or ancillary credit business, is examined at length in Chapter 11. Trading without a licence is a criminal offence. Numerically, this is a very significant control regime, since in a typical year well over 10,000 consumer credit licences are issued by the Office of Fair Trading (OFT). The power to refuse or revoke a licence permits the OFT, as the regulatory agency, to set standards of conduct expected of a trader in the sector in question.

The style of control varies. Within consumer credit licensing, there is continuing debate about the proper substantive and personal scope of the regime. This debate about intensity of regulation in this sector is tracked more closely in Chapter 9. It is probably not generally appreciated that

---

[143]   A justices' licence under the Licensing Act 1964.

estate agents are not required to hold a licence as a precondition to entering the market, although statutory powers exist whereby orders can forbid individuals from pursuing activities as an estate agent.[144] Licensing rules can vary in intensity. The benefits of market flexibility and open competition available as a result of the absence of prior licensing requirements must be judged alongside the cost of the risk that unscrupulous or incompetent traders may take advantage of unsupervised market entry to harm the unwary consumer.[145] In 2004 a market study conducted by the OFT[146] led to the conclusion that price competition among estate agents was weak and that some agents engaged in sharp practices such as failure to disclose a personal interest in a property, but the OFT did not consider that the introduction of a formal prior licensing system would be worthwhile.[147] Its recommendation in favour of better self-regulation and a campaign to improve consumer awareness of the virtues of shopping around was criticised by both the Consumers' Association and the National Association of Estate Agents, which called for tougher action against the minority of rogue traders.[148]

In a trade regulated by a licensing system, unacceptable performance, however defined, can ultimately result in the revocation of the licence. The State, through its appointed regulatory agency, thus directly determines the trader's commercial life or death. This confers very effective control powers on the regulator, able to revoke a licence or, more creatively, to improve standards by persuasion or veiled threat. It is possible to describe this system as an attempt to replicate the results that would be reached were the market operating 'perfectly', where inadequate performance would be commercially fatal and would necessarily cut short the survival of the supplier of unwanted goods or services. This description is partly accurate, although public intervention cannot properly mimic the market because it is fed by different stimuli: there is no invisible guiding hand. However, a pure market failure explanation seems inadequate to account for some modern manifestations of licensing requirements. Fairness is one element in the scope of consumer credit regulation, examined in Chapter 9. Unfair exploitation of poor consumers by suppliers of credit has stimulated

---

[144] Estate Agents Act 1979. See Chapter 8.4.

[145] Cf. research into the trade by M. Clarke, D. Smith and M. McConville, *Slippery Customers: Estate Agents, the Public and Regulation* (Blackstone, 1994). The slippery customers of the title are both estate agents and their customers.

[146] See Chapter 12.3.5.2 on the power to conduct market studies.

[147] *Estate Agency Market in England and Wales*, OFT 693 (March 2004).

[148] E.g. 'OFT inquiry accused of bottling out over rogue estate agents', *The Independent* 24 March 2004, p. 11.

intervention, even though one may also identify market failure rationales, such as under-information, at work in such circumstances.

1.8.2.3 Professions

Establishing regulatory agencies is costly. In many areas the State has been tempted to pass on the job to professional bodies and so reduce its direct costs. Another advantage is that the profession is likely to have a level of expertise and understanding of what is at stake that cannot be matched by a public agency without major expenditure. This is loosely described as self-regulation, a nuanced phenomenon requiring rather tighter definition (provided below at 1.8.4). Patterns vary according to the level of State control. The State may simply withdraw from the field and allow completely unrestricted market entry; alternatively, it may continue to require that market entrants meet specific qualification requirements, but delegate the task of devising and defining those thresholds to the industry itself. These are distinctive types of self-regulation/deregulation.

In fact, in a number of areas the activities of private bodies pre-date State interest. Many 'professions' have organised their own affairs over many years, even centuries, and the State may have come to endow their activities with statutory protection. The phenomenon of the profession deserves further, brief consideration. The term instinctively seems to imply a 'special' kind of job, to which entry is restricted by rigorous qualifications requirements. Remarkably, the lawyer can offer little that is more definitionally precise. There is no crisp dividing line between what can or should be termed a profession and what can or should not. The notion of 'professional' seems to involve an element of State recognition of and protection for the status achieved and the expertise provided, but the pattern varies. This is reflected in the sociological discussion of the phenomenon of the profession.[149] By common consent, doctors and lawyers are 'professionals'; refuse collection operatives and buskers probably are not. Yet all work for a living by providing a service to others. The distinguishing features seem to be qualification requirements which are prerequisites to market entry and standards of conduct post-entry, typically laid down and elaborated by the industry, but endowed with statutory effect. This leaves grey areas: plumbers? Rodent control officers? Taxi drivers?

The absence of precise legal categorisation of the professional means that each occupation must be treated individually in an appraisal of the

---

[149] E.g. T. Johnson, *Professions and Power* (Macmillan, 1972).

legal regime applying to those wishing to be active in it. 'Professional' status suggests State recognition; the professions have carved out a privileged place for their market in the State structure. In so far as that involves rules governing entry, a degree of inflexibility is the hallmark of the market for professional services. The perceived benefits of regulation – warranty of quality provided to the consumer and fair competition between suppliers – must be weighed against the costs. Precisely these issues have come increasingly to the fore in recent years as awareness of the anti-competitive effects of professional rules has risen. Sceptical State scrutiny of the insulation from open competition offered to the professions has intensified, in some areas drawing a response from professional bodies designed to maintain their sheltered position.[150] The consumer interest is plainly at stake in these wrangles, although the consumer voice is infrequently able to gain direct access to the dialogue.

In the UK, the reform of competition law, examined at length in Chapter 12 of this book, offers the latest example of the tendency towards more rigorous supervision of often long-standing professional rules. Arrangements between suppliers of professional services, even if struck within the framework of traditional guilds or societies, are capable of being regarded as restrictive of competition. Some may fix prices, others may pursue less overtly objectionable ends such as the setting of standards of ethical conduct. But, irrespective of the form chosen for these arrangements or their content, they typically constitute an expression of readiness to act in common made by parties who should in principle be expected to compete in the market. Their potential anti-competitive effect leaves them vulnerable to challenge as violations of the Competition Act 1998. The peculiar sensitivity of using this statute to exercise scrutiny over collectively agreed standards of professional behaviour and methods for securing their enforcement within the professions prompted the inclusion of a special power contained in Schedule 4 to the Competition Act. Pursuant to the Competition Act 1998 (Application for Designation of Professional Rules) Regulations[151] professional rules could be designated by the Secretary of State for Trade and Industry as falling outwith the prohibition against anti-competitive practices imposed by the Act. This was followed up by an OFT inquiry which led to the publication of a report in 2001 entitled *Competition in Professions*.[152] This was critical of a

---

[150] See e.g. R. Kerridge and G. Davis, 'Reform of the Legal Profession: An Alternative Way Ahead' (1999) 62 *MLR* 807. For a general survey of reforms pursued by the Conservative governments led by Mrs Thatcher, see A. Gamble, *The Free Economy and the Strong State* (Macmillan, 1994).

[151] S.I. 1999 No. 2546.

[152] OFT 328, 2001, available via http://www.oft.gov.uk.

number of restrictions favoured by professional bodies, including in particular barristers, accountants and architects. Among rules considered in the report are those pertaining to the status of QCs and to advertising of legal services. The government agreed with the critical assessment of the route to exclusion permitted by Schedule 4 of the Competition Act 1998 and repealed it in s. 207 of the Enterprise Act 2002. It is therefore entirely feasible that a range of traditional professional practices may come under sustained judicial scrutiny. The rules' claimed contribution to high standards of probity and transparency will be tested against their damaging impact on flexibility and consumer choice in the market.

The impact of European market integration has intensified the re-examination of the nature and purpose of professional rules, and developments that have already taken place at EU level are likely to inform the way the law is shaped in the UK. The expanding cross-border market for services has brought EC law of free movement into play as a means of challenging professional rules which act as entry barriers.[153] In *Commission v France, Italy, Greece*[154] the European Court found incompatible with Art. 49 (ex 59) EC national rules that made the provision of services by tourist guides subject to the possession of a licence, itself dependent on a particular qualification. Such rules tended to force visiting tour parties to use local guides (in practice the only people holding the required licence) rather than guides from their home State. The Court considered that in this case the competitive market was capable of serving consumer interests and that State-imposed entry barriers could not be justified. EC law supplies an increasingly significant deregulatory impulse. Nevertheless, EC law recognises certain interests which justify the maintenance of restrictive rules; it is not a charter for a deregulatory free-for-all. For example, it would not leave choice between doctors to the market, since qualification requirements are justified. As far as lawyers are concerned, the Court's decision in *Wouters* is of central importance in understanding that the context in which professional rules are applied is relevant to their legal assessment.[155] At stake were Dutch rules prohibiting multi-disciplinary partnerships between members of the Bar and accountants. This prevented the integrated supply of legal and accountancy services from a single source for which there would likely be consumer demand. Competition was restricted. The Court stated that 'account must

---

153   S. Weatherill and P. Beaumont, *EC Law* (Penguin Books, 1999), Chapter 19.
154   Cases C–154/89, C–180/89 and C–198/89 [1991] ECR I–659, 709, 727.
155   Case   C–309/99   *J.C.J.   Wouters,   J.W.   Savelbergh,   Price   Waterhouse Belastingadviseurs BV v Algemene Raad van de Nederlandse Orde van Advocaten* [2002] ECR I–1577.

first of all be taken of the overall context in which the decision of the association of undertakings was taken or produces its effects. More particularly, account must be taken of its objectives. It has then to be considered whether the consequential effects restrictive of competition are inherent in the pursuit of those objectives'. The point is that professional rules which at first glance appear to impede competition by forbidding particular commercial choices may be treated as lawful provided a broader assessment reveals that they have a beneficial effect on the market. The inquiry involves reference to the consumer interest, and in *Wouters* the Court acknowledged that any assessment of the Dutch rules must take account of their aim in securing the availability of legal services that are wholly independent of other commercial interests – including accountants – and dedicated to the client's interests.[156]

Areas of lawful restrictions to market integration have prompted the development of Community rules on professional qualifications – a classic instance of re-regulation at Community level designed to achieve the liberalisation of the Community-wide market. Following the 'New Approach' to technical harmonisation,[157] Community activity has shifted away from the establishment of rather rigid and typically rather limited profession-specific rules towards general 'horizontal' measures establishing looser common Community rules and laced with more mutual recognition.[158] Generally, this has projected into the Community legislative arena the central question of the function of rules of professional qualifications.[159]

---

[156] The 'Tourist Guides' cases arise under the law of free movement, while *Wouters* is a competition law case, but on the point of justifying restrictive trade rules the Treaty provisions are closely aligned: cf. K. Mortelmans, 'Towards Convergence in the Application of the Rules on Free Movement and on Competition?' (2001) 38 *CMLRev* 613.

[157] Chapter 1.8.1 above.

[158] Directive 89/48 on a general system for the recognition of higher-education diplomas OJ 1989 L19/16; Directive 92/51 on a second general system for the recognition of professional education and training OJ 1992 L209/25; Directive 99/42 on a mechanism for the recognition of qualifications, supplementing the general systems for the recognition of qualification OJ 1999 L201/77.

[159] For lawyers see Directive 98/5 OJ 1998 L77/36. A useful resource on mobility of lawyers within the EU is available via http://elixir.bham.ac.uk/.

1.8.3 Consumer Information

1.8.3.1 Policy

A further technique lies in intervention designed to improve consumer information.[160] The 1999 White Paper *Modern Markets: Confident Consumers*[161] places great weight on the virtue of generating a body of active consumers aware of what is available from suppliers and therefore able to use their power of informed choice to provoke efficiently functioning markets. Consumers should therefore have access to accurate, comprehensive and comprehensible information, in shops and through advertising media. For example, the White Paper welcomes the contribution of the EC's Directive which sets EU-wide standards for objective comparative advertising.[162] And it is observed that misleading descriptions are already controlled by the Trade Descriptions Act.[163]. Moreover, it should be remembered that, as demonstrated in part 1.3.5 above, the private law has been moulded to serve the interest of the consumer in greater transparency. However, the law can operate more positively. By *requiring* particular types of information to be made available to consumers, the law serves to bridge the information gap, permitting the consumer to choose between different types of product in an informed manner. The technique avoids the objection to the setting of minimum standards that the State is thereby taking away from the market the decision about what will and will not be available. Information disclosure addresses the market failings of informational imbalance, but then leaves the market to set its own quality levels. This technique is also usually cheaper to enforce.

The technique of information disclosure has become popular in recent years and is especially apparent at EC level. The notion that the consumer, duly informed and thereby protected, is able to participate fairly and effectively in the market has assumed the status of a guiding principle of

---

[160]   A. Ogus, note 132 above Chapter 7; G. Hadfield, R. Howse and M. Trebilcock, 'Information-Based Principles for Rethinking Consumer Protection Policy' (1998) 21 *JCP* 131; M. Trebilcock, 'Rethinking consumer protection policy', Chapter 4 in C. Rickett and T. Telfer (eds.), *International Perspectives on Consumers' Access to Justice* (CUP, 2003).

[161]   Cm. 4410 (1999). Available via http://www.dti.gov.uk/consumer/whitepaper/.

[162]   Section 3.15 White Paper. This is Directive 97/55: see further Chapter 8.6.3.

[163]   Section 3.18 White Paper. See further Chapter 8.6.1.

policy.[164] The European Court considers that the suppression of information to consumers may itself infringe Art. 28 (ex 30). In *GB-INNO v CCL*[165] the Court held that a Luxembourg law controlling the provision by a trader of information about prices was capable of impeding trade in goods from States where no such control was imposed. It declared that 'under Community law concerning consumer protection the provision of information to the consumer is considered one of the principal requirements'. The restrictive law was incompatible with Art. 28 (ex 30) EC.

EC rules in this area are in part motivated by the process of securing the integration of the market, and are examined more fully in that context elsewhere in this book.[166] For all systems, a powerful rationale for such intervention lies in the perception that consumer information reduces the imbalance of knowledge between consumer and trader which is the hallmark of the modern economy. The market is corrected by information disclosure in the sense that it becomes more efficient and competitive. Consumers are enabled to transmit messages to suppliers which reflect 'real' preferences, undistorted by the lack of transparency. Suppliers are thereby enabled to compete with each other more fairly and efficiently.

So described, the technique of information disclosure offers a seductively attractive method for avoiding heavy-handed interference with the supplier's choice about what to bring to market and consumer preference to buy from a range of available price and quality. It assumes the centrality of private autonomy in the market but aims to make that operate more perfectly. There is a dark side. It is necessary to investigate thoroughly whether consumers are capable of processing information that is disclosed to them. If empirical investigation casts serious doubt on the viability of information disclosure as a regulatory technique apt to deal with a problem in a particular sector, then presumed cures for market failure and/ or inequity will be illusory. The case for more intrusive intervention, such as the setting of product standards (1.8.1 above) or the licensing of traders (1.8.2 above), is correspondingly strengthened. A wealth of valuable research in recent years has exposed limitations in the cognitive capacity of consumers to process information and to act on it in a manner that is rational.[167] Any cost-benefit analysis of competing regulatory models must absorb such data or else risk under-protecting consumers. Informational intervention yields real benefits in the space it

---

[164] S. Weatherill, 'The Role of the Informed Consumer in European Community Law and Policy' (1994) 2 *Consum LJ* 49.

[165] Case C–362/88 [1990] ECR I–667.

[166] Chapter 2.

[167] Cf. note 1 and 108 above.

leaves for informed choice in the market and relatively low resource commitment to enforcement. But there are costs to be calculated in so far as the quest to mould a more alert, more questioning, more informed consumer is thwarted by the reality of everyday purchasing practice.

1.8.3.2 Examples of Informational Intervention

In the area of consumer credit, information disclosure has played a major role in the development of legal control of the market. This may be observed in both UK law and in the pattern of EC rules. Directive 87/102,[168] amended by Directives 90/88 and 98/7,[169] approximates national provisions concerning consumer credit. As Directives made as part of the programme of harmonisation of laws, market integration serves as their formal constitutional justification.[170] The Community measures take as their principal objective the maximisation of the consumer's awareness of the costs of credit. In this vein, the Preamble to the Directive declares that 'the consumer should receive adequate information on the conditions and cost of credit and on his obligations'. Article 3 is concerned to ensure that an advertisement displayed at business premises involving an offer of credit in which figures relating to costs are indicated shall include 'a statement of the annual percentage rate of charge'. Other provisions serve to improve the transparency of the transaction, though the measures leave the cost of credit largely unaffected. The substance of the bargain is thus largely untouched by this measure, but the process of making the bargain is controlled.

Existing law in the UK had already adopted the technique of information disclosure as a means of achieving consumer protection in this area. The Consumer Credit Act 1974 is also largely, but not exclusively, concerned with the transparency and fairness of the bargaining process, rather than the content of the bargain. Absorption of the EC rules was relatively unproblematic. The current pattern of the law is examined in more depth in Chapter 9. This also includes pertinent criticism of the limitations of a model premised on the virtues of information provision. The market for consumer credit offers fertile scope for reflection on how successful in practice the technique has been and can be once it is taken out of the regulatory laboratory and embedded in the consumer marketplace. In particular, it is plausible that some consumers are much

---

[168] OJ 1987 L42/48.

[169] OJ 1990 L61/14, OJ 1998 L101/17.

[170] Chapter 2.3.3.

better than others at processing and acting rationally in response to disclosed information, but that it is the group most in need of protection that is the least likely to be equipped to exploit it by performing the expected information-gathering exercise.

A further example of transparency lies in the requirement that a trader who advertises goods for sale must make it plain that those goods are being sold in the course of a business. The perceived mischief was that traders were pretending to be private sellers, for example, by advertising in classified columns of newspapers – a particularly popular trick amongst second-hand car dealers. Consumers might be induced to enter into a contract without being properly aware of its commercial nature. The intervention requires disclosure, so that consumers are put on their guard, without in any way directly affecting the content of any bargain that may be struck.[171] Equally, such intervention is a means of improving the market by promoting fair competition between traders, for, without such laws, open and honest trading would be undermined.

1.8.3.3 A Case Study – Upholstered Furniture

The regulation of upholstered furniture in the UK provides a useful illustration of the choices to be made. The perceived problem was not upholstered furniture as such, but the polyurethane foams they contained. Such foam is cheap, but relatively flammable in comparison with older types of stuffing and, once ignited, it gives off great heat and toxic fumes. Once a fire starts, the presence of the foam rapidly accelerates the process, making escape difficult and typically taking oxygen from the atmosphere with the result that victims die of asphyxia. Consideration of regulatory intervention was prompted in Parliament by regular pressure by a London Labour MP Ronald W. Brown, parliamentary adviser to the Furniture, Timber and Allied Trades Union.[172] Awareness of the degree of danger grew and was doubtless further stimulated by high profile disasters such as the Manchester Woolworths fire of May 1979 where ten people died in circumstances where burning foam acted as a contributory factor. Misperception of the risk by the under-informed consumer was likely to persist. The need for intervention in the market to set standards governing the flammability of upholstered furniture was accepted by the government.

---

[171] Business Advertisements (Disclosure) Order 1977 No.1918. It is of course necessary to determine the scope of acting 'in the course of a business' which on occasion has caused difficulties; cf. Chapters 3, 5.6.2.

[172] E.g. 859 H.C Deb. 2058–2070 (13 July 1973); 928 H.C. Deb. 494 (WQ) (22 March 1977).

However, it was not prepared to ban the foam altogether. No adequate alternative was available and a complete ban would have removed consumer opportunity to choose relatively cheap, albeit riskier, furniture. After a period of consultation, the regulations were made in May 1980 as the Upholstered Furniture (Safety) Regulations 1980.[173] The aim was to make furniture covering resistant to ignition in the home. Two tests were introduced, known as the cigarette test and the match test. Furniture was exposed to a heat source of the described type; if it underwent progressive combustion within a specific period, then it failed the test. After a transitional period, the rules were fixed in 1982 in a way that involved significantly different consequences depending on which of the two tests was failed. Failing the cigarette test meant that the furniture could not be marketed, but failing the match test meant only that the furniture had to have red-edged, triangular labels attached to it warning against the careless use of matches. The Minister, Sally Oppenheim, explained this to the House of Commons as a means of delivering 'reasonable protection of consumers against avoidable hazards, as well as against an unreasonable limitation of choice and an unacceptable rise in the price of furniture.'[174] The industry had pressed for mere self-regulation, whereas other sources had demanded stricter intervention. Strong comments were made in Parliament criticising the choice of minimum standards backed by a ban (the cigarette test) in one case and information disclosure (the match test) in the other.

Why was conformity with the cigarette test, but not the match test, made mandatory? The Minister stated that the insidious smouldering cigarette, which could cause a fire once the household had retired to bed, was a greater danger than the match, since any blaze it caused would be capable of immediate detection and extinction.[175] The Minister added the justification that technology was insufficiently advanced to provide an alternative, cheap fabric which would pass the match test. Resistance to a match flame is not as readily achievable as resistance to a smouldering cigarette. It appears that pressure from the furniture industry was a major element in diluting the consequences of failing the match test.[176] It is

---

[173] SI No 725.

[174] Debate at 985 H.C. Deb. 834–892 (22 May 1980); quote at 835.

[175] 983 H.C. Deb. 376 (WQ) 28 April 1980.

[176] Comments in this vein appear in the Parliamentary debates; and cf. Henry Swain, chief architect of Nottinghamshire County Council and closely involved with such furniture, *Architects Journal* May 1985, 'Fire: the Road from Fairfield'.

naturally common for an industry to devote large resources in order to influence regulatory decisions affecting its interests.[177]

Further regulations were made in 1983 – the Upholstered Furniture (Safety) (Amendment) Regulations 1983.[178] These provided that even furniture passing the test had to bear a (green-edged) label. Furniture failing the cigarette test continued to be banned. Furniture failing only the match test could be sold, but had to bear a warning label. The regulations also included specific and more stringent controls over children's furniture.[179] Here again there was fierce Commons debate about whether the proper balance had been struck.[180] The Minister at the time, Sir Gerard Vaughan, declared:

> Customer purchasing power is tremendously effective. I hope that customers will look out for furniture with a safety label and ask traders why they do not stock more of that furniture. In that way we shall increase the incentives for the industry to produce such furniture.[181]

This is a striking assertion of the role of information disclosure regulation in pushing the market towards a pattern where consumers can send messages to producers about their wants and thereby secure an efficient allocation of resources. Such comments assume a rather active consumer. They also assume a consumer who can process information rather skilfully, and act on it rationally and vigorously. If that does not happen, then the information imbalance is not cured; incentives to attend to desired levels of safety will not be transmitted to suppliers. The market will continue to fail.

For upholstered furniture, what was obviously at stake was a cost/benefit analysis, balancing the risks to consumers against the protection of traders, and embracing perceptions of the advantages of different forms of intervention. Consumer choice was a major consideration for the government. But passing the legislation was part of the hurly burly of the British political process, in which the choices and values at stake were not laid bare in a transparent, scientific manner. The issues were hotly disputed, predominantly along party political lines. In debate, it was argued that the speed of a fire caused by a match (rather than a cigarette) should require tighter, not looser, control; also that allowing

---

[177] Cf. part 1.9 below on agency capture and the broader critique of public choice.

[178] SI No. 519.

[179] Replacing the Children's Furniture (Safety) Order 1982 which, as required under the Consumer Safety Act, expired after 12 months; cf. Chapter 10.2 below on temporary measures in the field of consumer safety.

[180] 40 H.C. Debs. 306–319 (29 March 1983).

[181] *Ibid.*, 317–318.

the trade to avoid a mandatory match test because of the absence of adequate alternative technology hardly induced it to invest in a search for an alternative. And no scientific examination was conduced into whether consumers would really understand the implications of the several different types of label they would find attached to furniture in showrooms, nor, even if they would, whether they could make sensible risk assessments in selecting their purchases. In any event the government made its choice between regulatory techniques.[182]

The law is currently contained in the Furniture and Furnishings (Fire) (Safety) Regulations 1988 which revoke those of 1980 and 1983.[183] These Regulations adjust the detail of the pattern discussed above, but retain the technique of mandatory labelling as a means of informing the consumer.

This book takes as a thematic concern the appreciation that the technique of 'informational intervention' assumes the ability of consumers effectively to digest and act upon the information given. If the consumer is not competent to 'process' the information provided, then the intervention is ineffective as a means of market correction. This comment applies to warnings designed to inform about safety risks; it applies equally to accumulations of small print designed to alert consumers to threats to their economic interests. Information provision must be carefully judged. Warning labels must neither under inform nor (less often considered) over inform.[184] Worse, such laws, if effective on paper but not in practice, are open to criticism as a mere sham designed to legitimate the continued supply of unsafe goods or unfair practices against which consumers are not able to take proper precautions. A further twist is that informational intervention will typically inform some consumers but not all. What of consumers who cannot read? What of consumers who cannot read English? Choices have to be made about whether the provision of information is satisfactory. Scepticism about the value of information disclosure in curing market failure and in protecting the consumer would induce one to pause briefly to consider improving the delivery of the message before moving on (if still unsatisfied and if willing to accept curtailment of consumer choice) to the imposition of minimum standards and a ban on products that do not comply.

---

182 On the US experience, cf. P. Linneman, 'The Effects of Consumer Safety Standards: the 1973 Mattress Flammability Standard' (1980) 23 *Jnl Law and Econ* 461.

183 S.I. No.1324.

184 The furniture industry criticised the labels originally proposed as 'too frightening and would lead to people who had started to buy furniture to pay instead for a package holiday'; debate of 22 May 1980, note 145 above, col. 838.

1.8.3.4 Doorstep Selling

'Doorstep selling' provides a final, useful case study in choices between regulatory techniques. Such choices are in some circumstances complementary, but in others competing. 'Doorstep selling' refers to sales methods which involve the seller arriving on the doorstep and them trying to persuade the consumer to buy a product or a service. The discussion may be instigated by the trader without any invitation by the consumer. It typically takes place away from business premises. In some circumstances it may be that the practice is beneficial to consumers, particularly, for example, if they are geographically isolated. However, the perceived risk is that the consumer may be caught unawares and may enter into a contract to which he or she would not have agreed in a 'normal' business environment. Doorstep sellers have accumulated a rather bad reputation for deceitful, pressure tactics; the familiar sign, 'No Hawkers!' is a legacy of such days. Many jurisdictions have developed controls over this selling technique. In 1974 the UK introduced statutory requirements that doorstep callers selling on credit must possess a licence; it also banned unsolicited doorstep selling of money loans. Furthermore consumers were given a 'cooling off' period after the conclusion of defined agreements involving the supply of credit, within which a right of cancellation could be exercised. More general protection is now available as a result of EC Directive 85/577, the 'Doorstep Selling' Directive, which addresses the legal protection of 'the consumer in respect of contracts negotiated away from business premises'.[185] It too requires a 'cooling off' period, giving the consumer a minimum of seven days in which to withdraw from a contract concluded in the circumstances defined by the Directive.[186] Other provisions in the Directive oblige traders to provide consumers with notice in writing of their right of cancellation. It is very much a device of consumer information. The transaction may be concluded and enforced on whatever terms the parties may agree, but the consumer is to be supported in the pre- and post-bargaining phase. This is consumer choice in the free market, but with account taken of the 'surprise element' in such deals, as the Directive's Preamble describes it.[187] In fact, several EC Directives adopt a comparable approach to the protection of the consumer, by requiring pre-contractual information disclosure and a post-contractual

---

[185] OJ 1985 L372/31. See Chapter 7.
[186] Articles 1–3.
[187] Italy's failure to implement this Directive gave rise to the European Court's regrettable decision that consumers derive no directly effective rights under an unimplemented Directive against private suppliers: Case C–91/92 *Dori v Recreb*: Chapter 2.4.3.

'cooling off' period, although some, such as that dealing with distance selling,[188] go much further than the Doorstep Selling Directive. The Commission itself concedes that variation in the precise detail of the rules measure by measure is regrettable,[189] and a more coherent basis for assessing the virtue of the cooling-off period might usefully be sought.[190]

It is important to appreciate that Community law does not forbid doorstep selling. It recognises the potential harm to the consumer interest that may result from its use, but chooses to regulate it by supporting the informed consumer. Consumer choice is maintained, but the law attempts to secure transparency in that choice.[191] National contract law is affected by the Directive; contracts covered are enforceable, but the consumer receives support in the pre-contractual phase and the opportunity to escape from the deal for seven days after the agreement which, under the normal English common law of contract, would be regarded as the conclusive moment of contract formation.

The Directive is built on the assumption that the selling technique in question need not be forbidden completely, but it recognises that an alternative view may be taken. Article 8 states that the Directive 'shall not prevent Member States from adopting or maintaining more favourable provisions to protect consumers in the field which it covers'. It is therefore open to Member States to choose to intervene in the market with a ban rather than the more limited EC preference for informational intervention. On this model of minimum harmonisation, regulatory diversity within the EC is tolerated, notwithstanding the obstruction this represents to the pursuit of a uniform cross-border marketing campaign.[192]

In the UK the Directive was duly implemented in the Consumer Protection (Cancellation of Contracts Concluded away from Business Premises) Regulations 1987.[193] Contracts are unenforceable unless they

---

[188] Directive 97/7, considered in Chapter 7.

[189] European Commission Communication on Contract Law, COM (2001) 398, 11 July 2001.

[190] Cf. P. Rekaiti and R. Van den Bergh, 'Cooling-off periods in the Consumer Laws of the EC Member States: a Comparative Law and Economics Approach' (2000) 23 *JCP* 371.

[191] Cf. discussion of the work of Ison in Chapter 6.8, doubting whether effective consumer protection can be achieved short of a ban on the practice.

[192] The European Court found that a French rule banning such practices was compatible with EC law given its contribution to consumer protection: Case 329/87 *Buet v Ministere Public* [1989] ECR 1235. However, see Chapter 2.2.5 for discussion of the compatibility of this decision with more recent rulings of the Court.

[193] S.I. No. 2117, subsequently amended. See Chapter 7.

provide written notice of the right to cancel within seven days. These Regulations follow the Directive and do not impose stricter rules. As a matter of law, the Regulations must be interpreted to conform to the Directive in the event of ambiguity,[194] but no problems of interpretation have arisen in the UK.

Doorstep selling is examined in more detail in Chapter 7. It will be appreciated that some of the concerns about the capacity of the technique to induce consumers to enter into deals without adequate information apply with all the more force to traders relying on modern technological advances to sell goods or services without any physical contact with the consumer. Mailshots, fax, telephone and television are all part of modern marketing and selling. Such practices are not limited to national markets. Indeed they are peculiarly suited to cross-border trade. Regulation of such 'distant selling' is also examined in more detail in Chapter 7.

1.8.4 Self-regulation, Codes of Practice and Benchmarking

Public regulation is costly not only in the inflexibility it may bring to markets, in the reduction in consumer choice and the inefficiency it may induce among those sheltering behind regulatory barriers, but also in the cost of establishing institutions and buying the expertise to devise appropriate standards. From the perspective of reducing costs, there is accordingly an incentive to prefer methods that draw more heavily on the expertise of those directly engaged in the relevant industry.

Self-regulation is a phrase which may encompass a range of distinctive techniques. It is possible to eliminate State involvement entirely in the conduct of trade. Any regulation that then occurs is purely private, perhaps the product of the activities of a trade association. The market order reigns, subject to the possibility that rules agreed between firms may attract the interest of the competition authorities.[195] Such State withdrawal may occur on the explicit or implicit understanding that, if the market generally or the industry's own self-regulation in particular proves ineffective (however this is judged), then the State will intervene. There are other types of 'self-regulation' which do not involve such a decisive State withdrawal.[196] In recent years interest in exploiting the combination of the best efforts of private and public actors in order to craft a viable and sensitive system of

---

[194]   Case 14/83 *Von Colson* [1984] ECR 1891; Case C–106/89 *Marleasing* [1990] ECR I–4135. Chapter 2.4.2.

[195]   Chapter 12, especially 12.2 on cartels and restrictive practices.

[196]   For a survey of forms and consequences for legal control, see J. Black, 'Constitutionalising Self-Regulation' (1996) 59 *MLR* 24.

regulation has grown. The State may set standards, but leave it to the industry itself to police compliance. Alternatively, the State may require that standards be set by the industry, then check the adequacy of those standards, and leave policing compliance to the industry. In so far as both the State and the regulated industry have common interests in settling on a regulatory design that is suitable to meet their particular needs, there is much to be said in favour of a model that strives to achieve a co-operative scheme.

Where rule-setting and/or policing is performed through a trade association, costs are incurred by the industry not by the State. If the system is well respected within the industry, it will be observed with a minimum of fuss. A co-operative atmosphere generates willing and argument-free adherence. Compliance rates in such situations may be higher than in a system imposed from outside involving confrontational enforcement, where co-operation may be patchy or grudging.[197]

In several sectors, privately generated Codes of Practice have assumed a significant role in consumer protection. Codes of Practice are typically an expression of the industry's own commitments, not necessarily driven by State compulsion. Codes may establish levels of best practice which extend beyond legal requirements. For example, there is no common law obligation for a supplier to repair a defective product. The standard remedies are rejection of the goods and/or damages, and it is only very recently, in the implementation of the EC's Directive on sales of consumer goods, that English law has been able to accommodate a remedy of compulsory repair.[198] Codes have typically provided for repair in a number of sectors for many years. Such commitments are doubtless useful marketing ploys. As such they may engage the contractual responsibility of parties to the Code towards buyers. If in the shape of guarantees, their status too may be up-graded above that envisaged by the common law as a result of the EC Sales Directive.[199] However, the creation of formal legal enforceability is normally neither the purpose nor the principal perceived role of codes. They are intended to operate primarily on an informal basis, and frequently are designed to induce a consumer to buy from a trader who subscribes to a Code rather than one preferring to operate without a promise to abide by the provisions of a Code. This is simply an aspect of competition in the market. In so far as they offer effective protection of

---

[197] Cf. I. Ayres and J. Braithwaite, *Responsive Regulation: Transcending the Deregulation Debate* (OUP, 1992); A. Ogus, 'Rethinking Self-Regulation' (1995) 15 *OxJLS* 97; Baldwin and Cave note 132 above Chapter 10.

[198] Directive 99/44. See Chapter 3.6.

[199] Chapter 3.2, 3.7.

existing rights and, indeed, the promise of enhanced rights, Codes of Practice are also very much to the benefit of the consumer.

Arbitration procedures in the event of dispute are common features of Codes. It may be in the interest of trader and consumer to resolve disagreement through quick and cheap arbitration cures. Nonetheless there is a risk that a consumer may feel dissatisfied about his or her treatment at the hands of the industry. This suggests that access to the ordinary courts ought to remain open even where the consumer has agreed to waive such recourse. The Consumer Arbitration Agreements Act 1988 secured this protection for the consumer, but regrettably this was curtailed by the Arbitration Act 1996. The agreed waiver is unfair and not binding for the purposes of the Unfair Terms in Consumer Contracts Regulations 1994 so far as it relates to a claim which does not exceed an amount specified by order, currently set at £5000.[200] But above that threshold the agreed waiver will be disapplied only where it contravenes the statutory test of unfairness. One would hope that it would routinely be disapplied as a case of an under-informed consumer being saddled with serious detriment, but the loss of the unambiguous rule stipulated by the 1988 Act is unfortunate.[201]

The costs of self-regulation are in some ways the reverse of the benefits. If independent scrutiny is lacking, there is a risk that checking compliance may be less than rigorous. Even subconsciously, the industry may come to regard the Code as a cosy arrangement, largely for its own benefit rather than that of consumers. It is also possible that Codes may breed anti-competitive cartels.[202] Moreover, there is no effective method of securing enforcement of a Code against those who choose not to join the body through which supervision is practised or, indeed, against traders expelled from that body. The Code is not automatically applicable throughout the industry: rogue traders can opt out or cheerfully accept exclusion.

Such problems may lead to a recognition that some statutory overlay to a purely private Code is required. Membership of a private body may be made mandatory by the State, while the detailed arrangements for admission and conduct are left in the hands of the private body. This pushes private industry arrangements into a twilight world between market and State – as was previously observed in relation to the connected phenomenon of professional qualifications.[203] This method may be a

---

[200] The Unfair Arbitration Agreements (Specified Amount) Order, S.I. 1999 No. 2167.
[201] See further Chapter 14.
[202] See Chapter 12.2.
[203] Section 1.8.2.3 above. Cf. also the increasing list of Ombuds, considered in Chapter 14.

means of ensuring the delivery of common standards across the board. It also confers on those within the industry an immunity from competition. There are ambiguous consequences for the consumer, torn between State protection and choice in the market.

The EC has played a part in the shift from 'pure' self-regulation to administrative support. For example, in the UK advertising was regulated for many years by the industry itself. Initiatives at EC level brought change. Since the majority of Member States could not accept that public controls over misleading advertising should be entirely excluded, the Directive on Misleading Advertising required the insertion of a role for public authorities.[204] This was implemented into the UK's system by giving a power to the Director-General of Fair Trading, now vested in the OFT, to take action against misleading advertising.[205]

The 1999 White Paper entitled *Modern Markets: Confident Consumers*[206] exhibits a close interest in forms of regulation that blend the contributions of both public and private actors. This reflects a thematic emphasis by the Labour government that took power in 1997 on liberating thinking from orthodox public or private compartments. The White Paper places an emphasis on making wider use of codes of practice. The Government proposed to give the OFT powers to approve and publicise codes which meet defined core principles. This has been implemented in the Enterprise Act 2002. The code sponsor is expected to promise to comply with the published core criteria and then the OFT must be persuaded that the criteria are met in practice. The OFT's approval may be communicated to consumers by use of a code logo. This device, examined more fully in Chapter 13, is designed to improve transparency in the market. The perception is that a partnership of sorts may be struck between private parties and public bodies. At stake is neither self-regulation in its unconditional form nor a total assumption of rule-making competence by the State. Expertise is shared within a framework of 'co-regulation' that establishes core principles of good practice while retaining a degree of organisational flexibility for each particular sector. The role of the State in promoting good business practice is developed further in the White Paper's embrace of the fashionable notion of 'benchmarking'.[207] Businesses are encouraged to benchmark their performance against leading market players so as to learn and absorb how best to meet consumer demand. It is a deeply appealing notion. Good practice generates a wave of more good practice

---

[204] Directive 84/450.

[205] Enforcement powers have lately been extended: see Chapter 8.6.

[206] Cm. 4410 (1999). Available via http://www.dti.gov.uk/consumer/whitepaper/.

[207] Sections 4.20–4.22 White Paper.

within a sector in which benchmarking takes a grip. The State does not set the rules. It simply facilitates exchange of high-quality know-how. The potential flaw lies in the risk of market failure. If consumers are deprived of adequate information about the relative merits of particular suppliers, then incentives to upgrade quality of performance are stifled. In such circumstances bad will drive out good.[208] And it is also possible that benchmarking may come to be seen as a disturbingly close relative of practices which unlawfully substitute co-operation for competition.[209]

1.9 STATE REGULATION AND INDIVIDUAL FREEDOM

1.9.1 The Costs and Benefits of Regulation

It bears repetition that in all these circumstances regulation cannot be costless.

> If considerations of cost and business practicability did not play a part in determining what employers carrying on such businesses could reasonably be expected to do to prevent the commission of an offence under the Act, the price to the public of the protection afforded to a minority of consumers might well be an increase in the cost of goods and services to consumers generally.

This was said by Lord Diplock in *Tesco Supermarkets Ltd v Nattrass*[210] in examining the scope of the defence that reasonable precautions have been taken, available to a trader accused of a criminal offence under the Trade Descriptions Act 1968.[211] The dictum represents an unusually clear judicial statement of the key theme that regulation may produce winners and losers, and that a cost-benefit calculation should be performed. The general question of how to calculate the relative costs and benefits of regulatory intervention taxes all those involved in the shaping of consumer protection law. And it always has.

Where the State chooses to set standards of any type, it is interfering with the 'pure' market system based on supplier and consumer dialogue. Costs involved in setting minimum standards, for example, involve higher prices, depressed consumer choice and the erection of entry barriers which circumscribe market flexibility. Honest traders might rightly claim

---

208 Part 1.3.2 above.
209 Chapter 12.2.
210 [1971] 2 All ER 127, 151h.
211 For deeper discussion, see Chapter 11.2.

protection from dishonest rivals, but there is less justification in claiming protection from fair, if fierce, competition. Techniques such as minimum standards and licensing may all be attacked from these perspectives. Moreover, in all these instances there will be a need to establish regulatory agencies which determine where minima should be fixed and how unfair competition should be distinguished from its fair but fierce cousin. Regulatory institutions are expensive and their judgements will rarely prove controversy-free. Studies suggest a risk that agencies may be 'captured' and deliver decisions reflective of the interests being regulated rather than the broader public interest they are designed to serve.[212] Beyond the more limited notion of capture, 'public choice' analysis is devoted to the idea that impartial and efficient decision-making cannot be delivered by public agencies. The State is a corporate enterprise, 'selling' laws to buyers (whether it recognises it or not).[213] Powerful interest groups will be able to manipulate the process in order to secure regulation that suits their interests at the expense of less effectively represented groups, of which consumers may be a prime example.[214] The messages of such analysis include an insistence on suspicion of the motivation for law-making and an awareness that regulatory failure should be taken every bit as seriously as market failure.[215]

This is not to concede that State decisions are not justifiable or worthwhile on a cost/benefit analysis. Many of the preceding pages have been devoted to a demonstration of rationales for intervention. The market is far from 'perfect'; perfection is unobtainable and, in some circumstances, undesirable. The law has a range of functions in achieving adjustments dedicated to improving the operation of the market and addressing questions of fairness. However, some of the severe economic and political critiques of regulation over recent years have had the salutary effect of forcing some hard looks at rationales for intervention. Perhaps there had been a tendency to assume that the costs of market failure justify intervention, without an adequate appreciation that intervention too may bring costs. After the onslaught of public choice analysis and the sustained

---

212 E.g. A. Peacock (ed.), *The Regulation Game* (Blackwell, 1984).

213 A major influence is J. Buchanan, see e.g. *Liberty, Markets and State* (Brighton, 1986).

214 Cf. M. Trebilcock, 'Winners and Losers in the Modern Regulatory System: Must the Consumer always lose?' (1975) 13 *Osgoode Hall LJ* 618.

215 Further, P. Farber and P. Frickey, *Law and Public Choice: A Critical Introduction* (1991); M. Stearns, *Public Choice and Public Law* (1997); Ogus note 132 above, Chapter 4; Baldwin and Cave note 132 above, Chapter 3.

deregulatory rhetoric and, to a lesser degree, deregulatory practice of some recent British governments, such comfortable assumptions are long buried.

1.9.2 Political Perspectives and Recent British Practice

Some analysts have endeavoured to adopt a constitutional perspective in addressing the cost/benefit assessment relevant to intervention. Consumer choice is a political matter. State intervention can be viewed as hostile to individual freedom. At a rather simple level this has been plain in political observations about the superiority of the Western free market over the State-run economies of Eastern Europe. Competition was able to do what the State could not. 'Socialism collapsed because it literally could not produce the goods' according to Peter Lilley, then Conservative Secretary of State for Trade and Industry, in a June 1991 speech. Free competition and minimal State intervention has a flavour of not only economic efficiency, but also individual rights and democratic freedom. Discussion of competitive markets and non-intervention by the State thus inevitably invites consideration of political ideology, which may be reflected in legal rules.

1.9.2.1 Regulation, Freedom and Fairness

The quest to create a framework for testing the democratic and constitutional legitimacy of legal intervention in the market deserves brief inspection. Hayek, an economist with legal and political bents, emphasises the efficiency of spontaneous order in the market.[216] The market has an inherent capacity for self-correction and will deliver outcomes superior to a programme of public intervention. This is not to advocate a law-free market; quite the contrary. Hayek is an enthusiastic supporter of the common law, believing it to incorporate tendencies of flexibility and self-correction comparable to the virtues which he attributes to the market mechanism more generally. His criticism is directed at State intervention to 'adjust' the operation of the market in the (alleged) public interest. Such legislation cannot be as 'informed' as the directions chosen by the market system and must therefore yield inferior results. Intervention, with an appeal to social justice, is no more than an attempt by the few, able to

---

[216] Naturally, it is difficult (and unfair) to seek to distil the essence of extensive writing into a few short paragraphs. Hayek's principal insights are contained in his three volume work *Law, Legislation and Liberty* (Routledge and Kegan Paul, 1973, 1976, 1979).

exercise transient power, to wrest extra benefits for themselves at the expense of wealth maximisation for the whole of Society.[217] Such views are firmly rooted in an agenda designed to maximise individual freedom in society by limiting the role of the State.[218] On this model, constitutional limitations would be set on the role of the State both in the market and in society; as a corollary, individual freedoms in the market and in society would be constitutionally protected from State interference.[219] Recent years have witnessed a rise in scholarship that, for all its distinctive points of emphasis, is loosely connected by a shared antipathy to State intervention in the market. The public choice school is marked by the special vitriol it reserves for the motivations that underpin law-making and law-makers. In the competition/anti-trust law field, the Chicago School has developed related perceptions of the damage done by an interventionist policy which intrudes on private decisions guided by the order of the market. The Chicago School has accordingly called for a retreat in the application of competition law and has succeeded to a significant degree in its quest to emphasise the primacy of market decisions in the US.[220] Competition law has comprised only one, albeit high-profile, area of debate. In North America, too, Hayek's approval of the efficiency of the common law, combined with distrust of public intrusion into private rights, has been matched by the branch of the Law-and-Economics school associated with, among others, Richard Posner, who has written that 'Statutory or constitutional as distinct from common law fields are less likely to promote efficiency'.[221] Atiyah, among other critics, has questioned precisely what is envisaged in this context by the common law, which is after all hardly a monolith.[222] Others have accepted the value of the analytical framework demanded by this branch of the Law-and-

---

217 Hence the chosen title of Volume Two of Hayek's three volumes, *The Mirage of Social Justice*.

218 Cf. *inter alia* R. Nozick, *Anarchy, State and Utopia* (Blackwell, 1974); M. Friedman, *Capitalism and Freedom* (University of Chicago Press, 1962). The pathway back to John Stuart Mill's 1859 work *On Liberty* (Routledge, 1991) does not deviate significantly.

219 For general discussion, see M. Loughlin, *Public Law and Political Theory* (Clarendon Press, 1992); on Hayek especially, pp. 84–104. Cf. also A. Ogus, 'Law and Spontaneous Order: Hayek's Contribution to Legal Theory' (1989) 16 *Jnl Law and Society* 393.

220 Cf. e.g. R. Bork, *The Antitrust Paradox* (Basic Books, 1978).

221 R. Posner, *Economic Analysis of Law* (Little, Brown and Co, 1986), p. 21. Cf. R. Epstein, *Simple Rules for a Complex World* (Harvard U.P., 1995).

222 Cf. Chapter 7 in his *Essays on Contract* (OUP, 1988).

Economics school, but shudder to adopt its prescriptions without the leavening influence of other insights into the role of law in society.[223] Even within the discipline of Law-and-Economics itself the debate has moved on and broadened. The function of institutional arrangements in dictating patterns of conduct today attracts attention as a necessary corrective to earlier more limited emphasis on the power of the individual.[224] Moreover, the bounded rationality of participants has come to play a more prominent role in investigation of what markets are likely to deliver.[225] The intellectual terrain is rich, and it is here that this book takes its stand, proud to accept the wide range of influences in the melting pot of consumer law and practice.

1.9.2.2 Conservative Government in the UK, 1979–1997

In Europe, it may be thought an irony that the Hayek thesis and its cousins have had their deepest influence in the UK where legal tradition does not readily accommodate the process of constitutionalisation elaborated by Hayek. The policies of the Conservative administrations in power from 1979 to 1997, initially under the leadership of Margaret Thatcher and later under John Major, were transparently shaped by an awareness of the Hayek description of the ills of intervention and his prescription of the virtue of removing regulation.[226] In the light of the pressures and compromises that characterise modern politics and law-making, it would certainly be unrealistic to suppose that a precise match between the Hayek analysis and the record of the Thatcher administrations could be demonstrated. Nonetheless the influence of thinking that intervention in the

---

[223] For an entertaining overview, see J. Ziegel, 'What can the Economic Analysis of Law teach Commercial and Consumer Law Scholars?', Chapter 12 in R. Cranston and R. Goode (eds.), *Commercial and Consumer Law: National and International Dimensions* (OUP, 1993).

[224] Cf. e.g. J. March and J. Olsen. 'The New Institutionalism: Organizational Factors in Political Life' (1984) 78 *American Political Science Review* 734; J. Elster, 'Rational Choice History: A Case of Excessive Ambition' (2000) 94 *American Political Science Review* 685; J. Bendor, T. Moe and K. Shotts, 'Recycling the Garbage Can: An Assessment of the Research Program' (2001) 95 *American Political Science Review* 169.

[225] Cf. the 'behavioralism' scholarship mentioned in note 1 above; also M. Richardson and G. Douglas, *The Second Wave of Law and Economics* (Federation Press, 1999); Hadfield, Howe and Trebilcock note 160 above. For an overview see Baldwin and Cave note 132 above, Chapter 3.

[226] Loughlin note 219 above provides a great deal of relevant material.

market is damaging to its efficient operation and to the liberty of the individual was splashed over a range of policies.

This is to an extent simply history. A fuller account may be inspected in the first edition of this book.[227] But the policies towards regulation of the market devised during 18 years of Conservative government from 1979 to 1997 will reverberate for some time to come in the UK and beyond. A summary is therefore appropriate. In legal terms they appear piecemeal. Inevitably so. Given the absence of a written constitution in the UK, reform was achieved through specific legislative and administrative initiatives rather than any formal restructuring of the constitution. Indeed, the very absence of explicit constitutional constraint facilitated the execution of a remarkably radical policy. Nonetheless, some commentators identified in these shifts a broader pattern which amounts in aggregate to a change in the relationship between private and public sectors in the UK which was of a dimension of constitutional significance.[228]

Part of the policy was directed at closer scrutiny of regulatory intervention in the economy. The flavour of the programme is readily judged by the titles chosen for a White Paper of 1985, 'Lifting the Burden'[229] and a further White Paper in 1986, 'Building Businesses... Not Barriers'.[230] It became part of governmental policy that assessment of the costs of compliance should accompany all proposals for new measures.[231] The Deregulation and Contracting Out Act was passed in late 1994 amid rhetorical insistence on the battle against 'red tape'. Specific instances of deregulation within the Act were rather esoteric. They included procedural aspects of competition investigations, betting on Sundays (which was liberalised) and control of knackers' yards.[232] The true potential lay in Chapter 1 of Part 1 of the Act. This conferred a power on Ministers to make orders to amend or repeal enactments that impose a burden[233] affecting any person in the carrying on of any trade, business or profession.

---

[227]   Pages 69–76.

[228]   C. Graham and T. Prosser, *Privatising public enterprises: constitutions, the state and regulation in comparative perspective* (OUP, 1991). For comparative work, see M. Moran and T. Prosser (eds.), *Privatisation and Regulatory Change in Europe* (OUP, 1994). See also T. Daintith and M. Sah, 'Privatisation and the Economic Neutrality of the Constitution' [1993] *Public Law* 465.

[229]   Cm. 9571.

[230]   Cm. 9794.

[231]   Cf. Ogus note 132 above, pp. 162–5, revealing US origins; similarly Baldwin and Cave note 132 above, Chapter 7.

[232]   Sections 7–12, 20, 31 respectively.

[233]   That word again! Cf. text at note 229 above.

The Act was drafted in order to provide a basis for future adjustment of the regulatory climate in a wide range of fields without the need for the government to plan specific primary legislation. But, despite the ostentatious creation of a Deregulation Task Force, remarkably little was in fact achieved pursuant to this legislation. Few deregulating orders were introduced while across the sweep of government activity many new regulatory initiatives were advanced. Meanwhile, the UK had some success in exporting the procedure of compliance cost assessment to the EC, although it was never clear whether in Brussels the same relative values were put on costs and benefits in the substantive application of compliance cost testing.[234]

The phrase 'Victorian values' was bandied around with some lack of discrimination in the political discourse of the 1980s and 1990s. It was used both as praise and as criticism. However, in embracing the virtue of contractual freedom in the market (and the connected value of individual responsibility in society), there was a reassertion of much of the flavour of 19th-century *laissez-faire* commercial law. Some deregulation was achieved; probably more significantly, new initiatives to regulate were regarded with scepticism and some were blocked.

The debate about regulatory reform is by no means new, but rather an old debate reinvigorated. It has long been perceived that a policy raising legal requirements for entry to and/or performance in markets may have ambiguous consequences for consumers. Supply may be choked off or may grow outside the law (in black markets) as traders seek to evade costs and consumers seek to maximise choice.[235] The key to the policy shift in the UK after 1979 was greater readiness to find that the costs of intervention outweigh the benefits. For all the insistence on the use of cost-benefit analysis, the strong impression persists that market solutions were viewed as inherently preferable. The consequences of this should be fully appreciated; they bridge the gap between the initial discussion in this chapter of the private law and the ensuing examination of public law. In so far as public controls are eliminated, the law of consumer protection shifts back towards the law of contract and tort. Atiyah, writing in 1979, made this point powerfully in the following terms:

---

[234]   For comparative research into compliance cost assessment, see J. Froud, R. Boden, A. Ogus and P. Stubbs (eds.), *Controlling the Regulators* (Macmillan, 1998). See also Baldwin and Cave note 132 above, Chapter 12.

[235]   Cf. the work of Cayne and Trebilcock, published in 1973, in relation to regulation of the supply of consumer credit, referred to in Chapter 6.3. Technological development (e.g. 'e-shopping') plays a part in challenging the viability of restrictions on market access.

Freedom of contract naturally suits the strong, and is disadvantageous to the weak. When there is a return to free collective bargaining, then the result will usually be an increase in earnings differentials... though American political thinkers may argue that greater economic equality cannot be merely assumed to be a principle of justice, but needs to be justified,[236] there is little sign that this is an acceptable position in England.[237]

There is no need to labour the point, for it will be immediately apparent that this invites consideration of the extent to which the shifts of the period from 1979 to 1997 in the political map of the UK have affected the roles of the private and public law of consumer protection and, therefore, the position of the consumer in society. As already mentioned, they affected Atiyah's own perceptions.[238] Probably not high on Atiyah's 1979 agenda were the implications of the EC for freedom of contract. This source has exerted an increasing influence on the domestic scene, in a number of areas operating in a quite different way from that which would likely have been chosen by the British government acting alone. Chapter 5, dealing with Unfair Terms, provides a particularly revealing illustration of the role of the EC in challenging notions of freedom of contract in a more radical fashion than has been the norm in the UK. In other areas the Conservative government itself was willing to reform and strengthen regulation in defence of the consumer. Control of misleading price indications under the Consumer Protection Act 1987, examined in Chapter 8, provides an example. The story is not one of unrelenting deregulation.

A further aspect of the UK's policy involved a reduction in State ownership. The policy of selling assets in the public sector to the private sector is normally but loosely described as 'privatisation'. Like deregulation and self-regulation, privatisation is best seen as an umbrella term embracing several distinctive elements of policy.[239] The programme of transfer of assets from State to private sector was part of the process. This embraced, for example, telecommunications, gas and water supply.[240] In budgetary terms alone, this was highly significant, with the government

---

[236] A footnote reference is here made, *inter alia*, to Nozick note 218 above, pp. 232–3.

[237] In *The Rise and Fall of Freedom of Contract* note 35 above, pp. 648–9.

[238] Cf. P. Atiyah, *Introduction to the Law of Contract* (OUP, 1995), and part 1.3.4. above.

[239] Summarised in Ogus note 132 above, pp. 287–94. Cf. D. Bos, 'Privatisation in Europe: A Comparison of Approaches' (1993) 9 *Oxford Rev of Economic Policy* 95.

[240] For a collection of essays surveying several sectors, M. Bishop, J. Kay and C. Mayer, *Privatisation and Economic Performance* (OUP, 1994).

receiving tens of billions of pounds as a result of such sales. In part, the programme was motivated by economic expectations of realising greater efficiency in the private sector, which ought to operate to the advantage of the consumer. This economic assumption was plainly accompanied by the political perception that the State ought to withdraw from the market and offer enhanced freedom to private actors. Here again is an area where private contractual freedom, with all its limitations, has regained a prominence previously buried under the prevalence of State supply.

Privatisation as such does not necessarily yield a more competitive market. Where a monopoly is transferred from public into private hands, the same considerations discussed in Chapter 12.3 damage consumer welfare. In some circumstances attempts were made to inject competition into the market. In others, rightly or wrongly, the Government deemed the fostering of competition to be impossible or undesirable. Accordingly, a feature of the privatisation programme was the creation of new agencies designed to supervise the privatised utility. These assumed a bewildering number of guises. Transparency was little helped by the proliferation of odd acronyms designating these agencies – OFGEM, OFTEL, OFWAT and so on.[241] Price control and quality standards have been imposed by the regulator, in part as compensation for the absence of competition which in theory would have ensured such controls.[242] The perception of the reforms was that the consumer had been ill-served by the State as provider, but the establishment of these new regulatory institutions revealed that simply exposing the consumer to a market order would not be tolerated either. In some circumstances this was because of the perception that consumers were confused and consequently found themselves ill-prepared to make an informed choice. But an additional consideration holds that some such services are in any event most efficiently supplied under conditions of monopoly which may permit unfair exploitation.[243]

Even in areas that in principle remained within the province of the public sector, fresh emphasis was placed on the contractual nature of supply relationships. 'Contracting-out' of public services became highly

---

[241] Supervising the gas and electricity, telecommunications and water industries respectively. See the Competition and Service (Utilities) Act 1992. For valuable legal perspectives see Baldwin and Cave note 132 above, Chapters 14–23; T. Prosser, *Law and the Regulators* (OUP, 1997); C. Graham, *Regulating Public Utilities* (Hart Publishing, 2000); J. Black, P. Muchlinski, and P. Walker, *Commercial Regulation and Judicial Review* (Hart Publishing, 1998); C. McCrudden (ed.), *Regulation and Deregulation: Policy and Practice in the Utilities and Financial Services Industries* (Clarendon Press, 1998).

[242] Cf. Chapter 12.

[243] Cf. D. Helm and T. Jenkinson, *Competition in Regulated Industries* (OUP, 1998).

voguish. This policy was developed in Part II of the Deregulation and Contracting Out Act 1994. In the National Health Service, an 'internal market' was created within which the distinct functions of buyers and sellers were supposed to be disentangled from the pre-existing bureaucratic maze. Such re-shaping of the governance of the public services was fiercely controversial, with objection taken to the basic notion that a market could or should be instituted for the supply of such services.[244] A significant degree of legal and institutional rethinking was required.[245]. The supposed rise of consumers' private market freedoms was conspicuously associated with the rhetoric surrounding the Citizens' Charter, in which John Major invested much political capital.[246] In residual areas of public ownership too, consumer choice in a market order was to prevail – or, at least, that was to be the chosen presentational focus.

1.9.2.3 Labour Government in the UK from 1997

The Labour government that took power in 1997 under the leadership of Tony Blair had its own distinct political philosophies. It would be unwise to aim to portray its conduct as driven by a single coherent and enduring ideology. No modern government is permitted the luxury to bathe in such pure milk. But if the two decades of Conservative government were characterised by, in short, a vigorous scepticism about the virtues of State intervention in the market and State provision of services, then the 'New Labour' administrations in power since 1997 have been more evidently concerned, in short, to take a more open-minded approach to the assessment of the competing merits of market solutions and public intervention and, where appropriate, to blend the two. Policy priorities of the Conservative years, including deregulation, privatisation and contracting-out, were not actively maintained, but nor were they rigidly discarded. Instead an aspiration to avoid the simple public/private cleavage was evident.

---

244 See R. Flynn and G. Williams (eds.), *Contracting for Health: Quasi-Markets and the National Health Service*. (OUP, 1997).

245 Cf. e.g. I. Harden, *The Contracting State* (Open University, 1992); M. Freedland, 'Government by Contract and Public Law' [1994] *Public Law* 86; P. Vincent-Jones, 'Contractual Governance: Institutional and Organisational Analysis' (2000) 20 *OxJLS* 317; A. Davies, *Accountability: a Public Law Analysis of Government by Contract* (OUP, 2001).

246 Cm. 1599 (1991). Cf. A. Barron and C. Scott, 'The Citizens Charter Programme' (1992) 55 *MLR* 526.

Influential authors such as Anthony Giddens developed the notion of a 'third way' which has become grossly cheapened by political over-use and ultimately abuse but which, in its original manifestation, made a case for setting aside assumptions that political choices are confined to either embracing the cosy comforts of State care and provision or engaging in the sturdy struggle for success through the exploitation of opportunities provided in the free market.[247] The 'third way' insists that these stark alternatives should not exhaust the political imagination. Instead both approaches may contain their verities and policy should be crafted without preconceptions as to whether State or market is 'best'. Achieving goals such as effective labour market regulation, the creation of jobs and the successful delivery of health, education and social welfare services should not be imprisoned by choices between the politically traditional right or left – between the market or the State.

Conspicuous is the subordination of any explicit commitment to active wealth distribution engineered by the State to the preference to promote open and competitive markets. The third way does not neglect the value of social solidarity, but has been criticised for lacking viable proposals for doing much to promote it.[248] This is some distance from traditional socialist thinking. It is designed to be exactly that, and much of the rhythm of party politics in the UK in recent years has followed the Labour Party's successful capture of the centre ground. In this sense the adoption of an approach inspired by the 'third way' has been a spectacular political success. Quite what it means to the detail of policy, *inter alia* in the field of consumer protection, is another question again. The absence of concrete prescriptions constitutes a prominent point of criticism for those unpersuaded that the 'third way' is more than a skilful sound-bite, at least when it is transferred from thinkers of the stature of Giddens into the grubbier hands of politicians.

In the mishmash of political slogans that have gained prominence in recent years 'modernisation' is perhaps the one that has been most closely associated with 'New Labour'. *Modernising Government* is (*inter alia*) the title of a White Paper published in 1999.[249] The precise meaning of modernisation is admittedly not easy to grasp. However, it appears to be intended to convey an attitude to the delivery public services which is not conditioned by political dogma, but which instead adopts an open-minded and flexible approach to selecting the framework that is most effective to

---

[247] A. Giddens, *The Third Way* (Polity, 1998) and *The Third Way and its Critics* (Polity, 2000). Cf. A. Etzioni, *The Third Way to a Good Society* (Demos, 2000).

[248] E.g. S. Hall, 'The Great Moving Nowhere Show' *Marxism Today* November-December 1998, 9. Cf. C. Hay, *The Political Economy of New Labour* (MUP, 1999).

[249] Cm. 4310 (1999), *Modernising Government*.

achieve the policy ends in view. The point is not simply that location of point of delivery in the public sector is not assumed to be the superior of location in the private sector (or *vice versa*). The point is that there is no necessary bright line between the two. Nor should there be. For 'third wayers' both State and market are part of the solution and they should be employed in a co-operative style.

The 1999 White Paper entitled *Modern Markets: Confident Consumers*[250] acts as a complement to the White Paper on *Modernising Government*. The two are distinct in the sense that the former is targeted at the functioning of private supply markets, while the latter deals with public services. But part of the prevailing political ideology is that such distinctions are in any event elusive and ripe for deconstruction.

Modern Markets: Confident Consumers champions the market as an institution in the service of the consumer. The linkage suggested in the document's title is expressed slightly more fully in the Executive Summary which declares that 'Confident consumers, making informed decisions in modern, competitive markets, promote the development of innovative and good value products. And better performance in business in turn benefits consumers'. This approach, which thematically binds together the White Paper's agenda, reveals a number of assumptions about the appropriate trajectory for public intervention in the name of consumer protection. As a starting point the White Paper accepts that markets benefit consumers but the markets must be competitive, and they must be populated by consumers who are confident and capable of making informed decisions. So policy should be directed at fostering competition. Innovation and producer competition in price and quality should follow. And consumer satisfaction should follow from that.

The White Paper calls for re-invigoration of competition policy in order to root out inefficient practices on the supply-side. In defence of the competitive process, cartels must be tackled, monopolies controlled, mergers scrutinised for potential anti-competitive implications. In the light of the fact that the first edition of this book published in 1995 made a strong case for the recognition of competition policy as an ingredient in any coherent understanding of the scope of the public dimension of consumer protection, the 1999 White Paper's embrace of this view can only be warmly welcomed. The details are examined more fully in Chapter 12. The White Paper also makes a strong case in favour of the virtues of informed, well-educated consumers who do not tolerate a quality of

---

[250]   Cm. 4410 (1999). Available via http://www.dti.gov.uk/consumer/whitepaper/.

production or service that falls below their expectations. The policy implications of this perception are also examined more fully elsewhere.[251]

What more? *Modern Markets: Confident Consumers* asserts that 'Consumer legislation is already well developed and needs little extension. Risk, cost and alternative ways of achieving the desired result will always be considered before regulation'.[252] The DTI's 2003 report entitled *Comparative Report on Consumer Policy Régimes*[253] airs the possibility of adopting a more general control over unfair trading practices[254] and improving the structure of enforcement in the UK,[255] but here too radical extension in the body of consumer protection laws is plainly not envisaged; nor is radical curtailment. In the 1999 White Paper, simplification is promised as part of the process of improving the regulatory climate. Rules accumulate over the years and even if judged desirable in principle, the thicket of provisions can sometimes usefully be thinned out by adoption of a more approachable consolidated regime. Weights and measures legislation is mentioned in this vein by the White Paper; so too consumer credit and the control of unfair terms.[256] However, the White Paper includes an express commitment to protect the public from *inter alia* serious trading malpractice and unsafe products. For all the virtue of markets freed in whole or in part from public control it remains recognised that they may fail and that this may constitute a justification for public intervention.

The climate of receptivity to deregulation has clear echoes of the policy emphasis preferred by previous Conservative administrations, although those engaged in the New Labour project would doubtless wish to emphasise their ideologically distinct concern to examine the case for and against regulation without preconception. The White Paper, while protective of the principle that public regulation of markets may be required in some circumstances, carries an explicit concern not to impose undue regulatory burdens. Such excess does not merely harm business. It harms consumers by reducing choice and raising prices.[257] Fine words. No government has yet introduced new regulation by greeting it as foolish or unnecessary. And, from the perspective of private industry, it is common, for example, for the Confederation of British Industry to apply its whip to the government's flanks by seizing easy publicity through complaints about

---

251   On education and access to justice see Chapter 14.
252   Executive Summary; see also ss. 6.1–6.3.
253   http:// www.dti.gov.uk/ccp/topics1/pdf1/benchmain.pdf (October 2003).
254   Chapter 8.7.
255   Chapter 13.
256   Sections 6.11, 6.12, 6.15 White Paper. See Chapters 9, 6 and 5 of this book.
257   Section 6.4 White Paper.

damage to British industry's competitiveness. Consumer laws are part of this political circus. The government's decision to inject criminal sanctions into competition law in the Enterprise Act 2002 provides an example of regulation bitterly criticised as unduly heavy-handed.[258] The debate about regulation of the financial services market too offers examples of this type of discourse, which is especially acute at times of revealed scandal. Everyone agrees that necessary regulation should be adopted and that unnecessary regulation should not, so what matters at bottom is how one judges the necessity of regulation. The White Paper promises a regulatory impact assessment that will take full account of the consumer interest. The key to making such a policy coherent is to make transparent the nature of the assessment of the value of proposed regulatory initiatives.

The vehicle used most prominently to take forward this process has been the government's *Better Regulation* Task Force, established in 1997 as an independent body including consumer representation and entrusted with an advisory function.[259] It is, of course, perennially delicious that inquiry into the nature and purpose of regulation always begins with the establishment of a regulatory body, but the label *Better Regulation* was evidently intended to convey a more open-minded spirit than the preference for explicitly *deregulatory* initiatives pursued by the previous government.[260]

The Task Force's five published principles of Good Regulation are proportionality, accountability, consistency, transparency and targeting. Who could disagree? What matters is practice. Within the walls of government a key role is played by the Regulatory Impact Unit (RIU), located within the Cabinet Office.[261] This is charged with the responsibility of overseeing the patterns according to which regulation and deregulation develop in the UK. Its mission is ensure that the enduringly elusive balance between necessary protection and unnecessary burdens is struck. Its main statutory weapon is the Regulatory Reform Act 2001, which for these purposes replaces the Deregulation and Contracting Out Act 1994. This provides Ministers with a wide power to make statutory instruments in order to reform primary legislation. It is 'law which imposes burdens' which is the explicit target of s. 1. After years of rhetorical

---

258 Chapter 12.2.4.4.

259 Further information is available via http://www.brtf.gov.uk.

260 Cf. P. Cartwright, 'Better Regulation in the UK? The Better Regulation Task Force Review of Consumer Affairs' [1998] *Consum L.J.* 485. See more generally Baldwin and Cave note 132 above, Chapter 6 of which is entitled *What is 'Good' Regulation?*; Froud, Boden, Ogus and Stubbs (eds.), note 234 above.

261 Further information is available via http://www.cabinet-office.gov.uk/regulation/.

condemnation of 'burdens',[262] s. 2 goes so far as to provide a statutory definition of a burden for these purposes, albeit that it is broad and non-exhaustive. The Act allows action against 'a restriction, requirement or condition (including one requiring the payment of fees or preventing the incurring of expenditure) or any sanction (whether criminal or otherwise) for failure to observe a restriction or to comply with a requirement or condition, and any limit on the statutory powers of any person (including a limit preventing the charging of fees or the incurring of expenditure)'. Section 3(1)(a) forbids the making of an order if the Minister is of the opinion that it would remove any 'necessary protection'. Section 3(2)(a) provides that an order may create a burden only if the Minister is of the opinion that its provisions taken as a whole 'strike a fair balance between the public interest and the interests of the persons affected by the burden being created' and that its is desirable that the order be made on account of its reduction of (other) burdens.

Governmental rhetoric at the time of the Act's entry into force was heavily geared to the anticipated cost savings for business. So far, it is hard not to conclude that the policy is remarkably close in its motivation to that pursued by the Conservatives in the early to mid-1990's, and the real test will be whether, unlike the Conservative initiative, there emerges regulatory reform that is real. The RIU's *Better Policy Making: A Guide to Regulatory Impact Assessment* was published in January 2003 and is available electronically.[263] The RIU is also responsible for liasing with the European Commission, which in 2002 adopted its own Action Plan for Better Regulation, which emphasises the need for assessment in advance of the impact of proposed measures coupled to consultation with affected parties.[264] This is part of the Commission's broader concern to improve the quality of Europe's regulatory environment.[265]

The calculation of the costs and benefits of regulation remains politically salient. In January 2004, Michael Howard, in one of his most high-profile political acts after assuming the leadership of the Conservative Party (in opposition) in Autumn 2003, published a statement of principles which included the belief that 'red tape, bureaucracy, inspectorates, commissions, quangos, czars, units and targets came to help and protect us,

---

[262]   Notes 229, 233 above.

[263]   Via http://www.cabinet-office.gov.uk/regulation/ria-guidance.

[264]   Relevant material may be inspected via:
        http://europa.eu.int/comm/governance/suivi_lb_en.htm.

[265]   *European Governance: a White Paper*, COM (2001) 428. Cf. D. Wincott, 'The Governance White Paper, the Commission and the Search for Legitimacy', Chapter 22 in A Arnull and D. Wincott, *Accountability and Legitimacy in the European Union* (Oxford, 2002).

but now we need protection from them'. This is evidently motivated by a political desire to draw a distinction with Labour policies depicted as driven by a more heavy-handed State role. Underpinning any such discussion at the level of practical policy-making, rather than high politics, must be clear-sighted calculation of precisely what 'red tape' achieves.

Deregulation is one aspect of modern thinking about regulatory strategy. The scope of public service provision is another. The Labour government in power since 1997 has not pursued a policy of rolling back privatisation by re-asserting State ownership across a range of sectors. Not only would that have demanded an enormous financial commitment, it would also have contradicted the 'third way' principle that a more dispassionate examination should be made of the relative worth of the private and public sectors. The 1999 White Paper *Modern Markets: Confident Consumers* made this observation:

> The previous Government put utility services in the private sector. But the competition between companies was initially often limited and insufficient attention was given to consumer interests. As soon as it came into power, the Government initiated a review of utility regulation. More competition is now being introduced to bring the maximum benefits for consumers. The Government has decided that the utility regulators should be given a new primary duty to protect consumers. This will shift the balance of economic regulation in favour of the consumer. Wherever possible and appropriate, this will be done by promoting or facilitating competition. In some sectors, effective competition will take time to achieve. In these areas, the Government will ensure regulation is tough and targeted at the interests of consumers.

A mixed pattern of competitive markets and regulated provision is envisaged – with the consumer interest to the rhetorical forefront.[266]

If one were to identify the distinctive nature of 'New Labour' when compared with previous Labour governments it would lie in its readier rhetorical embrace of competitive markets as a generator of wealth. Public intervention is accepted as appropriate in circumstances in which it can be justified, but there is no routine assumption in its favour. The White Paper is concerned to avoid pre-conceptions about how to regulate to protect the consumer. And, as mentioned above,[267] the field of consumer protection

---

266 Cf. C. Scott, 'Analysing Regulatory Space' [2001] *Public Law* 329. See also note 241 above, and on recent practice P. Birkinshaw, *European Public Law* (Butterworths, 2003), Chapter 12, especially pp. 534 *et seq.*

267 Chapter 1.3.8.

continues to offers an illuminating insight of the endeavour to ally this policy preference with aspects of social justice. The White Paper is dedicated to the benefit of all consumers but declares a special focus on the needs of those with less developed consumer skills, those who are socially excluded and those on low incomes who can least afford to make a bad purchase. However, in this context the White Paper is rather thin on detail.[268] For those of a critical mindset, this is the 'third way' in its classic form.

1.9.3 Constitutional Limitations on Regulation

1.9.3.1 In the UK

What of the specific role of law? The advisability of restricting consumer choice through legal intervention in the market should be a matter of interest to anyone involved in consumer policy. However until recently orthodox British legal thinking would typically assume that the basic decision to intervene or not ultimately forms part of the assessment made by the policy-maker on whom legislative competence has been conferred by statute. Constructing a framework to test the constitutional validity and permissible scope of State intervention to curtail economic freedoms would form the analytical starting point for consumer lawyers in some European jurisdictions and in some quarters in North America. For the orthodox British observer that is plainly a point of comparative legal interest, but not one that will instinctively suggest itself as fertile material for litigation strategies.

No longer. The Human Rights Act 1998 is a landmark statute in the UK. It requires that the judiciary read and give effect to legislation in a way which is compatible with rights set out in the European Convention, to which the Act cross-refers. This interpretative obligation is designed to rescue provisions that might otherwise be condemned as infringements of human rights and it may permissibly involve the judiciary in straining language in order to achieve compatibility between the provision in question and Convention rights. Ultimately, if even after vigorous judicial attempts to follow the interpretative route a statute is deemed incapable of being read in a manner that is compatible with Convention rights, the judiciary is empowered to issue a 'declaration of incompatibility'. This will be a 'last resort'.[269] According to this model the measure in question

---

[268] Cf. G. Howells, 'United Kingdom's Consumer Policy White Paper – A Step in the Right Direction?' [2000] *Consum L.J.* 181.

[269] *R v A* [2001] 3 All ER 1 (per Lord Steyn).

is not invalidated by judicial decision. Remedying incompatible primary legislation is a task belonging not in the judicial but in the political sphere. The assumption is that Parliament will respond to the declaration of incompatibility by repealing the offending measure or, at least, that if it declines to do so, the magnitude of such a political refusal to comply with human rights will have been highlighted by the judicial decision.

One might reasonably have anticipated that the Human Rights Act would be of potential relevance to the sphere of consumer protection. Regulation of the market in favour of the consumer interest carries with it the potential for interference with commercial rights and freedoms, which may be of a type protected by the human rights régime. Nevertheless, even the most perceptive consumer lawyer would have been surprised by what actually transpired. In 2001 a provision in a consumer protection statute achieved the notable historical distinction of attracting the first-ever judicial declaration of incompatibility.

In *Wilson* v *First County Trust*[270] the Court of Appeal concluded that s. 127 of the Consumer Credit Act 1974 was incompatible with the protection extended by the Human Rights Act to traders. Mrs Wilson did not repay a loan of £5,000 advanced by First County Trust, pawnbrokers. She claimed instead the loan agreement did not include certain required terms and that accordingly, pursuant to s. 127, the agreement, not having been properly executed, could not be enforced nor could the security be retained by the pawnbrokers. The argument was accepted. But the question then arose whether s. 127's statutory bar against recovery by the creditor in such circumstances violated protected property rights and rights of access to a court held by the trader. It did, according to the Court of Appeal. The court objected to the inflexible nature of the provision. This was an unnecessarily severe means to achieve the policy aim of the system for regulating the consumer credit market. Sir Andrew Morrit observed that 'There is no reason why that aim should not be achieved through judicial control; by empowering the court to do what is just in the circumstances of the particular case'.[271] The Court of Appeal found no way to rescue the unambiguously worded s. 127 by interpreting it in a manner compatible with Convention Rights and it therefore granted a declaration of incompatibility. This is an alarming decision which nourishes a general anxiety that the discourse of human rights is apt to prioritise individual interests while demonstrating an under-appreciation of broader objectives

---

[270] [2001] 3 All ER 229.
[271] Note 270 above, 245a.

achieved in the public interest by frameworks of market regulation.[272] If the matter in hand truly led to a violation of the trader's human rights, it would be difficult to defend any regulatory system that operates on the basis of bright-line rules. Instead a case-specific inquiry would have to be conducted on each occasion that a matter fell within the relevant regime. That would generate huge unpredictability, it would be enormously costly and it would reduce the incentives of traders to comply faithfully with the stipulated provisions of consumer protection. Gratifyingly the House of Lords decided that the Court of Appeal was wrong. On appeal in *Wilson v First County Trust*[273] it discharged the declaration. The attachment of formal statutory requirements to the manner of concluding an agreement, coupled to a sanction of unenforceability of the agreement in the event of non-compliance, is capable of being treated as a proportionate response to a perceived social ill. Money-lending of the type at stake in the case is precisely the sort of transaction that has for centuries given rise to serious problems of exploitation of ill-informed and/or needy consumers. Its rigorous control under the Consumer Credit Act does not infringe Convention rights, even though – as their Lordships freely accepted – the chosen statutory regime may generate results that seem harsh on particular traders. Parliament's anxiety to protect particularly vulnerable consumers was therefore allowed to stand untainted by a finding of incompatibility with Convention Rights.

The lesson of the litigation in *Wilson* is that public regulation undertaken in the consumer interest must be 'human rights proof', but that, as the House of Lords has made clear, the regulatory value associated with the adoption of bright line rules is part of the currency for assessing the compatibility with the Act of provisions that may in some individual cases cause hardship to traders. Their Lordships took explicit account of the superiority of a general rule over a requirement of case-specific assessment as a device to secure deterrence of malpractice and effective protection of vulnerable consumers.[274] It was noted *obiter* that the further the legal sanction contained in the general rule departs from clarity and absence of ambiguity, the more likely that it will be successfully challenged:[275] but s. 127 survived its test. Tough on traders? They can protect themselves by complying with the statutory rules. More generally, *Wilson* is but one

---

272 See generally T. Campbell, K. Ewing and A. Tompkins (eds.), *Sceptical Essays on Human Rights* (OUP, 2001).

273 [2003] 4 All ER 97. The case is also significant for its treatment of the scope of the Act's retrospective effect.

274 Note 273 above, Lord Nicholls 121a-f, Lord Hobhouse 138b-f, Lord Scott 146c-f.

275 Note 273 above; Lord Nicholls 121g-j. Changing the statutory threshold may also affect the assessment: see Chapter 6.5.4.

manifestation of a broader trend within which the senior judiciary have been quick to dampen assumptions that the Human Rights Act is a charter for wresting control from the institutions of representative democracy acting in the general interest into the hands of aggressively interventionist judges fed by litigants seeking to cure individual woes.[276]

The novelty of the Human Rights Act should not be over-estimated. It is admittedly bringing judicially-enforced 'rights protection' firmly into the mainstream of domestic law. But the influence of the EU has already generated an incremental process of constitutional review of not only administrative action but also legislative choices. EU law is supreme in the event of conflict with the law of the Member States, and it is in addition directly effective before the courts of those States. Consequently judges in the UK have been equipped with a power to disapply domestic rules in cases with an EC dimension ever since the UK joined in 1973. EC law imports a form of constitutional review unfamiliar to the traditions of constitutional law centred on Parliamentary sovereignty, and may be fairly regarded as a catalyst to the embrace of the brand of judicial review of State action now envisaged by the Human Rights Act. So, prior to the Human Rights Act, the House of Lords had already begun to decide cases that manifested acceptance of obligations derived from EC law to review laws duly passed by Parliament. For example, in *EOC v Secretary of State for Employment* threshold provisions of the Employment Protection (Consolidation) Act 1978 were declared incompatible with EC equality law.[277] In making an order in such terms, their Lordships denied that this was a case of domestic judges explicitly declaring the UK in breach of the EC Treaty; however, constitutional sensitivity notwithstanding, this was the practical effect.

1.9.3.2 In the EU

The EC legislature, unlike Westminster, cannot claim a sovereign power to enact laws in all areas. Its powers are limited by the system's founding Treaties. So the European Court is empowered to annul acts that are not validly based on the (limited) competences attributed to the EC by the Treaties. This famously occurred in *Tobacco Advertising*, where Germany

---

[276] See especially *Brown v Stott* [2001] 2 All ER 97; *R (Alconbury Ltd) v Environment Secretary* [2001] 2 WLR 1389.

[277] [1994] 1 All ER 910, applying the *Factortame* rulings.

successfully sought the annulment of a measure of harmonisation.[278] Constitutional review of EC rules is not confined to the question whether competence exists. The valid exercise of competence is conditional on compliance with general principles protected by the legal order. EC law imposes restrictions on regulatory competence based on principles that include proportionality, protection of legitimate expectations and protection of fundamental rights.[279] These principles control both EC acts and national acts within the sphere of EC law. Pursuant to Art. 5(2) EC the principle of subsidiarity also controls the exercise of legislative competence.[280] Furthermore, EC law enshrines a notion of freedom of expression which may be capable of conversion into a legal instrument for challenging national and EC laws that impede commercial free speech – notably, advertising. In *ERT v Dimotiki* the Court interpreted the scope of the freedom to provide services 'in the light of the general principle of freedom of expression embodied in Art. 10 of the European Convention on Human Rights'.[281] In that case State restrictions on broadcasting had to be justified with reference to the Convention mediated through the 'general principles' of Community law. No adequate justification was forthcoming. As far as challenge to EC rules is concerned, Germany advanced submissions in *Tobacco Advertising* to the effect that the harmonisation Directive, which envisaged an almost total ban on advertising of tobacco products throughout the territory of the EU, violated principles of freedom of expression. The Court had no need to address the point, since the Directive was in any event found to lack a valid legal basis. But it is possible that future challenges to more constitutionally sturdy measures may elucidate the scope of the principle of freedom of expression when invoked by commercial parties as a basis for limiting public intervention in the market. This is an intriguing prospect. Moreover, it is notable that both the EC system and the UK's Human Rights Act are powerfully driven by the practice of the European Convention, and one may therefore expect to see regular cross-references between different jurisdictions charged with similar tasks of supervising the exercise of public power.[282] Experience from outside Europe may prove relevant too, albeit probably less directly

---

[278] Case C–376/98 *Germany v Parliament and Council*, examined at more length in Chapter 2.3.5.

[279] S. Weatherill and P. Beaumont, *EC Law* (Penguin Books, 1999) Chapter 8; T. Tridimas, *The General Principles of EC Law* (OUP, 1999).

[280] See Chapter 2.3.6.

[281] Case C–260/89 [1991] ECR I–2925.

[282] For broader discussion of the evolution of connections between systems, see C. McCrudden, 'A Common Law of Human Rights? Transnational Judicial Conversations on Constitutional Rights' (2000) 20 *OxJLS* 499.

influential as a result of contextual differences.[283] But this is by no means a charter for automatic de-regulation and the dominance of market freedom. Article 10 of the European Convention on Human Rights (and therefore, indirectly, the EC and UK legal orders) envisages limitations on freedom of expression in accordance with what is 'necessary in a democratic society'. It is perfectly conceivable that advertising restrictions may be treated as validly imposed pursuant to this concession. The EC measure introduced in response to the annulment of the Tobacco Advertising Directive scrupulously claims in its Preamble to respect the fundamental right of freedom of expression while subjecting certain types of advertising to legal restriction.[284] Its validity has not been tested in court.

However, for present purposes, it suffices to make the point that constitutional review of market regulatory laws in the UK and in the EU may become more prominent in coming years. To this extent, the application of the theories of regulation discussed here may come to form part of the armoury of even the practising English commercial lawyer.[285]

1.9.4 Consumers and Society

Questioning the place of the State in the market has been a fertile field for theorists in recent years, although examining the operational utility of some of the theories espoused remains an underdeveloped aspect of the debate. We believe, in writing this book, that the construction of theoretical underpinnings is vital in drawing the map of consumer protection. A great many social and political assumptions are embedded in the choice between these different forms of intervention. 'Consumer choice' may be taken as a slogan of freedom from the unduly interventionist State; by contrast, it may

---

[283] Cf. treatment of the constitutionality of regulation of tobacco advertising in Canada, *RJR Macdonald Inc et al v Canada* [1995] 3 SCR 199 (Supreme Court).

[284] Directive 2003/33 OJ 2003 L152/16.

[285] German commentators, in particular, are more accustomed to such notions of (loosely) economic constitutional law and are already well advanced in developing frameworks of analysis at EC level. For a valuable survey of what this may involve, see C. Joerges, 'European Economic Law, the Nation-State and the Maastricht Treaty' in R. Dehousse (ed.), *Europe After Maastricht* (Law Books in Europe, 1994). For historical background, see D. Gerber, 'Constitutionalising the Economy: German Neo-liberalism, Competition Law and the "New" Europe' (1994) 42 *Amer J Comp Law* 25. Cf. on a broader geographical scale S. Bottomley and D. Kinley (eds.), *Commercial Law and Human Rights* (Ashgate, 2001).

be taken as the abandonment of the bewildered consumer to the uncaring mass market. More subtly, consumer choice may free *some* consumers from unwanted mollycoddling, while subjecting others to exploitation. We welcome the recent emphasis on rigour in analysis of costs and benefits. We are saddened by the impression that it is no longer politically fashionable to concede that wealth maximisation might cheerfully be subordinated to wealth distribution in the cause of contributing by legal regulation to a more just market and a more harmonious society. Consumer law, we repeat,[286] is part of shaping a society.

---

286   Chapter 1.1 above.

Chapter 2

European Union Consumer Policy

2.1 THE DEVELOPMENT OF THE EUROPEAN UNION AND ITS LEGAL ORDER

2.1.1 National and International Markets

Much of the discussion presented in Chapter 1 of this book has examined the operation of markets and evaluated their capacity to deliver effective consumer protection. Discussion of the limitations of markets can be pursued in relation to the legal regulation of any market. Problems of the type exposed in Chapter 1 affect the operation of all markets whatever their territorial scope. Accordingly, legal intervention may be considered at national level, but also at transnational level. As the process of market integration in Europe develops, it is increasingly to Europe that one must look for a layer of consumer policy-making which is additional to national law-making.

The European Union, of which the longer established European Community forms part, is an international organisation which has evolved into a uniquely sophisticated and complex system for securing peaceful and prosperous co-existence among (most of) the States of Europe. It lies far beyond the scope of this chapter to provide an examination of the modern European Union that is remotely comprehensive. For those in need of background information, other sources must be consulted for a deeper examination of the history of the process of European integration,[1] its institutional architecture[2] and the contribution of the new legal order to its evolution.[3] Assuming here that the reader is familiar with the basic

---

[1] J. Pinder, *The Building of the European Union* (OUP, 1999); D. Dinan, *Ever Closer Union?* (Macmillan, 1999); B. Rosamund, *Theories of European Integration,* (Macmillan, 2000).

[2] E. Bomberg and A. Stubb, *The European Union – How Does it Work?* (OUP, 2002); A. Warleigh, *Understanding European Union Institutions* (Routledge, 2002).

[3] P. Craig and G. de Burca, *Text, Cases and Materials on EU Law* (OUP, 2002); S. Weatherill and P. Beaumont, *EU Law* (Penguin, 1999); S. Weatherill, *Cases and Materials on EU Law* (OUP, 2003); D. Wyatt and A. Dashwood, *European Community Law* (Sweet and Maxwell, 2000); A. Arnull, *The European Union and its Court of Justice* (Oxford, 1999).

constitutional and institutional building blocks of the Union, there follows an exposition from the consumer perspective of the pattern of development of, first, the European Community and, more recently, the European Union of which the European Community now forms part.

2.1.2 The European Community Prior to the Creation of the European Union

As an international organisation, the European Union's formal source of legal authority lies in its founding Treaties, which have been periodically revised. The Treaty of Paris led to the founding in 1952 of the first of the three European Communities, the European Coal and Steel Community. In 1958, the Treaties of Rome created the European Economic Community (EEC) and EURATOM (the European Atomic Energy Community). The original six Member States were France, Germany, Italy, Belgium, the Netherlands and Luxembourg. The breadth of the EEC ensured that it was by far the most important of the three Communities. It was concerned with economic integration across all sectors, but in no small measure was also motivated by the desire to achieve a political restructuring of the European continent. To give effect to its ambitions it was built on a Treaty which contained clearly expressed legal rules designed to achieve integration and regulation. It possessed its own institutions which were competent to adopt legislation in those areas where power had been transferred to it from national level by the Treaties. Economic integration was to be achieved through the application of legal rules.

The text of the original Treaty of Rome remained unamended in any significant respects until 1987 when the Single European Act came into force. That amending Treaty added several new competences to the Community's armoury and also made important institutional adjustments, notably in the raising of the Parliament's profile. Of prime importance was the insertion of a new provision into the Treaty which permitted the adoption by qualified majority vote of measures required to secure the completion of the internal market by the end of 1992. This emphasised the commitment of the Member States to deepen yet further the process of integration, explicitly at the economic level, but inevitably also involving a political dimension.

2.1.3 From European Community to European Union

By the start of the 1990s, the original six Member States had been joined by six more – the United Kingdom, Ireland and Denmark, which became members at the beginning of 1973, Greece (1981) and Spain and Portugal

(1986). In December 1991, the 12 Member States agreed a major revision to the structure of the system. This was contained in the Treaty on European Union agreed at Maastricht in the Netherlands. Aspects of this next stage were rather ambitious and were fiercely opposed by some shades of opinion in most Member States. However, ratification was secured in all 12 Member States after almost two years of vigorous debate and the Treaty came into force on 1 November 1993. The Maastricht Treaty amended important aspects of what was the EEC Treaty and renamed the EEC the 'EC', the European Community. The Maastricht Treaty also introduced two new areas outside the parameters of existing EC integration where the Member States committed themselves to work in co-operation: Foreign and Security Policy, and Justice and Home Affairs. There was now a European Union built on three 'pillars'. The pre-Maastricht pattern of the European Communities (comprising the E(E)C, the Coal and Steel Community and EURATOM) represents only one of these three pillars. The EC retains its institutionally and constitutionally distinctive character. The two new pillars, Foreign and Security Policy and Justice and Home Affairs, are essentially intergovernmental in character. They do not yield directly effective or supreme laws, nor are they marked by the institutional sophistication of the EC. In this sense there is a European Union – but the European Community is only part of it. And there is EU law – but EU law serves as an 'umbrella' term referring to the diverse legal phenomena that occur under the three pillars. EC law is part of EU law, but EC law is not co-terminous with EU law. This chapter and this book will on occasion step outside the EC pillar of the EU – hence the reference to the 'EU' in the chapter title – but it will be primarily focused on EC law, and that will be the normally employed label.

The European Community post-Maastricht was altered in shape in a number of substantial respects: there was an enhancement of the Community's competences, including in the field of consumer protection (2.3.4 below); the status of Citizenship of the Union was created; and adjustments were made to the legislative procedure which strengthened the position of the Parliament. Perhaps the centrepiece was the insertion into the EC Treaty of detailed provisions designed to lead to Economic and Monetary Union. The single currency, the *euro*, became a reality at the start of 1999, as envisaged by the Treaty, although as yet not all Member States participate. The United Kingdom was granted an 'opt-out' in a Protocol to the Maastricht Treaty and it has not chosen to surrender the right to stand aside and retain the pound.

2.1.4 Treaty Revision after Maastricht: Amsterdam and Nice

Since the Maastricht Treaty entered into force in 1993 the pattern of regular Treaty revision and regular geographical enlargement has continued to mark the Union's lifecycle. The Treaty of Amsterdam was agreed in October 1997. It secured ratification according to domestic constitutional procedures in the Member States while attracting noticeably less opposition than the Maastricht Treaty and it duly entered into force on 1 May 1999. The Amsterdam changes to the Treaties were incremental. They did not disturb the basic existence of the three-pillar structure of the European Union. They did, however, shift material between the pillars. Legal provisions relevant to the free movement of people within the Union were moved from the third pillar to the first pillar, the EC. The third, formerly dealing with Justice and Home Affairs, is now re-worked and re-styled *Provisions on Police and Judicial Co-operation in Criminal Matters*.

The Amsterdam Treaty also re-numbers the whole of both the EC and the EU Treaties from start to finish. This means that it is critical to be fully aware that legal texts pre-Amsterdam may be using a different numerical 'currency' from those published after the Amsterdam Treaty's entry into force on 1 May 1999. This is, of course, a vicious trap for the unwary! To avoid confusion it is normal practice to refer to Treaty articles by their current number, with their former number appended in brackets – for example, Art. 28 (ex 30) on the free movement of goods and Art. 95 (ex 100a) governing the harmonisation of laws.

The next round of Treaty revision was agreed in December 2000 at Nice. The Nice Treaty, like the Amsterdam Treaty before it, maintains the three-pillar structure of the Union, while making detailed adjustments to each of the pillars. Nice, like Amsterdam, causes only incremental change. Its core aim was to adjust the Union's institutional architecture in order to make it fit to meet the challenge of planned enlargement into central and eastern Europe. It suffered a turbulent passage through the ratification procedures in the Member States, but the Nice Treaty eventually entered into force on 1 February 2003.

2.1.5 Enlargement and the 'Future of Europe'

The original group of six Member States, which had become a group of 12 by the time of the Maastricht Treaty, had expanded again to 15 at the start of 1995 when Austria, Finland and Sweden joined. But the next and most recent round of accessions is not simply the largest influx, it also represents a major statement of the changing face of Europe since the demise of the Soviet Union in 1989. Ten countries joined the Union on 1

May 2004: Cyprus, the Czech Republic, Estonia, Hungary, Latvia, Lithuania, Malta, Poland, Slovakia and Slovenia. Outside the EU's core 25 lies a further ring. The European Economic Area (EEA) came into being at the start of 1994 and now comprises the EU's 25 Member States plus Iceland, Liechtenstein and Norway. The EEA is based on a body of law that is in many respects comparable to, though not so ambitious as, the EU's system. Switzerland co-operates with the EU according to bilateral arrangements, but has no present intention to apply to join, while several countries in eastern Europe, such as Bulgaria and Romania, have applied for membership. The *European* Union is still a slightly misleading name, for it is not entitled to claim authority from the Atlantic to the Urals – but its influence is now felt throughout the continent.

Although the Nice Treaty made the necessary detailed adjustments to the institutional architecture to prepare the Union for enlargement to a family of 25, a desire to perform more radical surgery on its anatomy took hold. In December 2001 the European Council in Laeken agreed to convene a Convention on the 'Future of Europe'. It held its inaugural session under the Chairmanship of Valery Giscard d'Estaing in February 2002. Representatives of Heads of State and government were joined by representatives of the Parliament and the Commission and of national Parliaments. The aim was to follow a debating procedure that would be far more transparent than previous practice with a view to producing a draft 'constitutional Treaty' that would equip the Union with an efficient and comprehensible working method for the future. Even informed citizens can barely grasp the current rules of the Union's game, given the messy incrementally adjusted set of Treaties, and it was hoped that the Convention's text, agreed and released in July 2003, would serve the Union and its citizens better.[4] It proposes *inter alia* the elimination of the three-pillar structure in favour of a more coherent European Union. However, the intergovernmental conference that convened in the autumn of 2003 was unable to agree to the proposed text, nor to any amended version. At Brussels in December 2003 the Heads of State and Government found themselves locked in a disagreement about, in particular, voting power in the Council which they could not resolve. It is likely that the text prepared by the Convention on the 'Future of Europe' will remain on the table as a future basis for reshaping the structure of the EU, but some hard political negotiation will be required to achieve consensus. Once a text is agreed it will come into force only once it is ratified in all 25 Member States.

---

[4] Texts may be inspected at:
http://Europeanconvention.eu.int/bienvenue.asp?lang=EN&Content=.

2.1.6 The Nature of Economic Integration

The integration movement was powered in the early post-war years by individuals with a political commitment to a species of federal Europe.[5] Explicit political integration was, however, largely eschewed in the original Treaty in favour of economic integration. The lack of clarity in the precise location of the balance between the Union's political and economic ambitions remains its major flashpoint. In any event, according to Art. 2 of the EC Treaty, the Community aims to establish a '"common market" involving the free circulation of the factors of production'. In the EC it is customary to regard the 'four freedoms' as the cornerstone of the notion of the common market; that is, the free movement of goods, persons, services and capital. Free movement is achieved by dismantling impediments to internal trade within the area. Additionally, in common markets States lose independence over trade policy at their external borders. There will be a common external commercial policy and also a degree of common policy-making for the internal area.

Economic theory suggests that there is a 'virtuous circle' in economic integration.[6] As borders are removed there is increased competition, yielding wider consumer choice. There should be higher quality goods and services available; producers must achieve this in order to survive in the fiercer competitive environment. Integration should also permit firms to realise economies of scale. Their production runs will be longer, which allows more efficient use to be made of plant. This should yield lower prices which will be passed on to the consumer by producers eager for the business which will ensure survival. The market will be reshaped for and by businesses that are able to restructure operations to the European level, for example through the conclusion of distribution deals or, more radically, through merger or takeover.

Common market theory places the consumer as the ultimate beneficiary of the whole process, albeit as a passive recipient of the advantages of cross-border commercial activity. From this perspective, economic integration in Europe is in itself a form of consumer policy.

2.1.7 From Common Market to Internal Market

The development of the common market in Europe had considerable momentum in the early years, but progress had become very sluggish by the early 1980s. Much trade was free, but there were significant impediments to the completion of a common market. Consequently the

---

5   E.g. Jean Monnet, Robert Schuman, Paul-Henri Spaak. Cf. Pinder note 1 above.

6   See e.g. M. Artis and F. Nixson, *The Economics of the European Union* (OUP, 2001).

Commission imaginatively sought to reinvigorate the whole process by establishing the '1992' programme – the task of securing the completion of the Community's internal market by the end of 1992.

The 1992 project was first explained in detail in the Commission's White Paper of 1985;[7] this covers the economic and political advantages of completing the internal market and sets out a programme of legislative action required to achieve that end. In paragraph 12 it declared that:

> The reason for getting rid entirely of physical and other controls between Member States is not one of theology or appearance, but the hard practical fact that the maintenance of any internal frontier controls will perpetuate the costs and disadvantages of a divided market....

Legally, the project was defined in a provision newly inserted into the Treaty in 1987 by the Single European Act. This is now found in Art. 14 EC. It provides that:

> The Community shall adopt measures with the aim of progressively establishing the internal market over a period expiring on 31 December 1992... The internal market shall comprise an area without internal frontiers in which the free movement of goods, persons, services and capital is ensured in accordance with the provisions of this Treaty.

The completion of this 'area without internal frontiers' was closely tied to the Treaty amendments of the Single European Act. Article 95 (ex 100a) was also introduced by the Single European Act with effect from 1987. Its purpose was to give a very practical thrust to the legislative programme through the removal of the national veto over Community legislative action in the field of harmonisation of laws. This shift in Council voting rules to qualified majority was required so that the political expression of commitment to deepening the integrative process could take practical effect.

Many of the economic virtues identified as resulting from the completion of the internal market are no different from those expected to flow from the creation of a common market. It has always been a moot point precisely how much less ambitious the internal market is than the common market. Does the internal market policy, for example, abandon the commitment to Community-wide regulatory strategies that has long been associated with the common market, or does it simply readjust short-term

---

[7]   COM (85) 310. See R. Bieber, R. Dehousse, J. Pinder, J. Weiler (eds.), *1992: One European Market?* (Nomos Verlagsgesellschaft, 1988).

priorities? The Single European Act does not purport to answer this question; nor has it been addressed in any subsequent constitutional act. However, in the internal market, as in the common market, the consumer is envisaged as the ultimate beneficiary of the more efficiently functioning market.

2.1.8 'Beyond 1992'

At the end of 1992, it was vividly apparent that the consumer was in a better position. The completion of the internal market in accordance with the Treaty had in principle established the right of private consumers to move freely across borders and to return home with whatever they pleased for their private consumption. Although in the past consumers had typically been regarded as the passive beneficiaries of free trade through enhanced choice, they are increasingly able actively to enjoy the benefits of an integrated market. The Court too has made plain its view that the consumer has the right to treat the Community as border-free and to 'travel freely to the territory of another Member State to shop under the same conditions as the local population'.[8] Some of the possible legal implications of using Community policy to encourage active cross-border shopping are discussed below.[9]

Since the end of 1992 the process of market-making has not come to an end. Instead the priorities pursued by the Commission, in particular, have shifted. It is more overtly concerned to emphasise the need for the effective application of the existing rules of the internal market rather than to pursue significant new legislative initiatives. This process of managing the internal market is directed at promoting belief that its rules are respected in practice as well as on paper. In 2003 the Commission declared that:

> Free movement of goods (and services) in the Internal Market is above all based on confidence. Confidence of businesses that they can sell their products on the basis of a clear and predictable regulatory framework. Confidence of Member States' administrations that the rules are respected in practice throughout the EU and that the competent authorities in other Member States will take appropriate action when this is not the case. And, of course, consumers' confidence in their rights and that the products they buy are safe and respect the environment.... [10]

---

8   Case C–362/88 *GB-INNO-BM v Confederation du Commerce Luxembourgeois* [1990] ECR I–667.

9   Section 2.3.5. below.

10   Commission Communication of May 2003, Internal Market Strategy, Priorities 2003 – 2006, COM (2003) 238 final.

2.1.9 The Role of the European Court of Justice

Critical to the rapid development of the integrative process has been the contribution of the European Court of Justice. Its interpretation of the Treaty injected enormous vitality into the whole process. The Court was not prepared to regard the Treaty as 'traditional' international law, with the result that the EC legal order quickly developed a character of its own. In 1991 the Court acclaimed what is in many respects its own creation as the 'constitutional charter of a Community based on the rule of law'.[11] The legal rules governing integration were interpreted actively in accordance with what the European Court viewed as the spirit of the Treaty. The waning of national economies and the growth of a European economy were accelerated by the Court's frequent preference, in cases of doubt, to interpret the law in a manner conducive to integration. The *Cassis de Dijon* decision, examined below at 2.2.2, provides a classic illustration of this jurisprudential trend. On the constitutional plane, the Court insisted that EC law could be enforced at national level – the principle of direct effect[12] – and that it must be applied by national courts in preference to any conflicting national law – the principle of supremacy.[13] The Court reasoned that, without such principles, the system envisaged by the Treaty simply would not work. In consequence the prosecution of the integrative process did not simply rest with the relevant Community institution, the Commission, challenging defaulting Member States before the European Court. The enforcement of the law was additionally put in the hands of individuals who were able to enforce rights to enjoy the fruits of integration by challenging public authorities in national courts. In this sense, the conferral of individual rights through the notion of direct effect had both a policing and a democratising function. The Art. 234 (ex 177) preliminary reference procedure allowed the European Court to oversee and guide the development of the law at national level. In effect it co-opted national courts to the job of enhancing the objectives of the EC.

---

[11]   *Opinion 1/91* [1991] ECR I–6079.
[12]   Case 26/62 *Van Gend en Loos* [1963] ECR 1.
[13]   Case 6/64 *Costa v ENEL* [1964] ECR 585.

2.2 COMMUNITY TRADE LAW

2.2.1 'Negative Law' and the Consumer Interest

The pursuit of economic integration through law requires a framework for controlling and, where appropriate, prohibiting national rules which obstruct free trade. Several core provisions of the EC Treaty operate as a restriction on national measures which may have an effect hostile to cross-border trade. These provisions are termed 'negative' in that their effect is to strike down national measures where they conflict with the 'greater good' of market integration, subject only to narrowly defined exceptions.

Article 28 (ex 30) is the principal provision designed to achieve the free movement of goods. It provides that:

> Quantitative restrictions on imports and all measures having equivalent effect shall, without prejudice to the following provisions, be prohibited between Member States.

More helpfully and more broadly, Art. 28 (ex 30) has been interpreted by the Court to prohibit:

> all trading rules enacted by Member States which are capable of hindering, directly or indirectly, actually or potentially, intra-Community trade.[14]

This is the renowned *Dassonville* formula, the key to its application being the *effect* of a measure. Once a measure is shown to affect trade between Member States, it is susceptible to challenge via Art. 28 (ex 30). It is the breadth of the formula which is remarkable although, in its November 1993 ruling in *Keck*, the Court curtailed its outer margins in ruling that there is no actual or potential, direct or indirect, barrier to inter-State trade such as would allow the invocation of Art. 28 (ex 30) where national laws apply to all traders active on the national territory and affect in the same way in law and in fact the marketing of national products and those originating in other Member States.[15]

The Treaty contains a narrow list of exceptions to Art. 28 (ex 30) in Art. 30 (ex 36). This envisages trade barriers 'justified on grounds of public morality, public policy or public security; the protection of health

---

14   Case 8/74 *Dassonville* [1974] ECR 837.
15   Cases C–267 and 268/91 *Keck and Mithouard* [1993] ECR I–6097. For discussion of the impact of *Keck* see N. Nic Shuibhne, 'The free movement of goods and Article 28 EC: an evolving framework' (2002) 27 *ELRev* 408; C. Barnard, 'Fitting the remaining pieces into the goods and persons jigsaw' (2001) 26 *ELRev* 35.

and life of humans, animals or plants...'. Article 30 (ex 36) adds that '[s]uch prohibitions or restrictions shall not, however, constitute a means of arbitrary discrimination or a disguised restriction on trade between Member States.' The Court has followed a consistent line whereby the scope of derogation from the basic principle of free movement is construed narrowly. This approach serves to advance the overall cause of welding national markets into a single European market.

Article 28 (ex 30)'s application in the area of goods has a parallel in Art. 49 (ex 59) in the area of services. Article 49 (ex 59) has also been interpreted by the European Court as an instrument for controlling national measures that inhibit suppliers of services from treating the wider market as integrated.

The economic advantages of the free movement of goods and services are the advantages of the common/internal market as a whole.[16] The process should deepen competition among producers and suppliers and thereby enhance consumer choice. The application of Community 'negative law' to sweep away obstructive national law serves the consumer interest in the sense that it contributes to the integrative process of which the consumer is theoretically the ultimate beneficiary. There is a consumer interest in free trade and in deregulating national markets within the wider European market.

In summary, national rules which impede consumer choice in the integrating market are in jeopardy. The Court has condemned national laws which 'crystallise given consumer habits so as to consolidate an advantage acquired by national industries concerned to comply with them'.[17] Laws which protect domestic producers from competition confine consumer choice in a manner hostile to the basic expectations of market integration.

2.2.2 The Ruling in *Cassis de Dijon*

The '*Dassonville* formula' plainly applies to border controls and discrimination against imported goods, but it is much broader and is also capable of catching national technical rules and standards. Such measures do not discriminate against imports and in many cases were introduced long before the EC came into existence and were not designed to interfere with cross-border trade at all. However, it is their *effect* which is critical. Litigation involving Cassis de Dijon, a French blackcurrant liqueur,

---

16 Section 2.1.4 above.

17 Case 170/78 *Commission v United Kingdom* [1980] ECR 417; Case 178/84 *Commission v Germany* [1987] ECR 1227.

provided the Court with the opportunity to establish how Art. 28 (ex 30) applies to national technical rules which do not discriminate according to nationality, but which nevertheless have an effect hostile to market integration.[18]

The Court's ruling concerning the importation of French Cassis de Dijon into Germany provides a famous example of the application of Art. 28 (ex 30) to open up the market to secure enhanced consumer choice. German law imposed restrictions on the marketing of weak alcoholic drink, supposedly as an aspect of consumer health protection. The Court was unable to identify in this measure any coherent policy serving the consumer interest. The German measure simply denied the German consumer the opportunity to try a product made according to a different tradition. The national rule fell foul of Art. 28 (ex 30) as unlawful State suppression of consumer choice.

It should be fully appreciated that in the Cassis de Dijon ruling the Court was dealing with two competing aspects of the consumer interest. On the one hand, Art. 28 (ex 30) represented the consumer interest in market integration and enhanced choice. On the other hand, the challenged German measure was itself presented as a means of consumer protection; it therefore represented the consumer interest in regulation at national level. The Court was choosing in effect between different perceptions of where the consumer interest lay. In *Cassis de Dijon* itself, the resolution was quite straightforward because the German law was a thoroughly unmeritorious method of (alleged) consumer protection. In fact, the real protection enjoyed under the German law was that of German producers able to monopolise consumer choice. In other cases, the balance between consumer choice in the wider market and consumer protection at national level may be finer. This balancing task projects EC trade law into the realms of difficult decisions about what is best for the consumer; decisions that some have viewed as involving a risk that choices made in the context of free trade law may undermine national standards of consumer protection. This is a key issue in assessing the scope of EC law and policy and is discussed further below.[19]

The *Cassis de Dijon* ruling provides a strong impetus in favour of free trade between Member States in traditional products. It enshrines a principle of 'mutual recognition'. This holds that if a product is fit for the market of one Member State, then it should be considered fit for the markets of all other Member States. Only exceptionally may products which are satisfactory in their country of origin be excluded from the

---

18   *Cassis de Dijon* is more formally known as Case 120/78 *Rewe Zentrale v Bundesmonopolverwaltung für Branntwein* [1979] ECR 649.

19   Comparable issues arise in international trade law. See e.g. G. De Burca and J. Scott (eds.), *The EU and the WTO: Legal and Constitutional Aspects* (Hart, 2001).

market of the State to which they are exported. This exceptional restriction on free trade was explained by the Court in *Cassis de Dijon* in the following terms;

> [o]bstacles to movement in the Community resulting from disparities between the national laws in question must be accepted in so far as those provisions may be recognised as being necessary in order to satisfy mandatory requirements relating in particular to the effectiveness of fiscal supervision, the protection of public health, the fairness of commercial transactions and the defence of the consumer.

The final phrase in this observation draws attention to the point that consumer protection is explicitly recognised as a 'mandatory requirement' which may be successfully advanced as a reason for maintaining a national law which inhibits cross-border trade. However, the impetus towards free trade is strong and powerful reasons must be shown by the State to justify rules which subordinate consumer choice and free trade to national 'mandatory requirements'. Germany failed to defend its law in the *Cassis* case itself.

2.2.3 *Cassis de Dijon* – the Subsequent Case Law

In a large body of case law the *Cassis de Dijon* principle has been employed to sweep away national rules which hinder the free movement of goods, resulting in wider consumer choice. Not infrequently, as in *Cassis* itself, the national rule found to be incompatible with EC law has ostensibly been a measure of consumer protection.

Walter Rau v De Smedt provides a good example of the application of the '*Cassis* principle'.[20] The case concerned the compatibility with Art. 28 (ex 30) of a Belgian law requiring margarine to be marketed in cube-shaped blocks. The Court accepted that such a rule impeded the importation into Belgium of margarine marketed in different ways in other Member States. Consumer choice in Belgium was hampered and, as the Court observed and as economic theory dictates, margarine cost more in Belgium under this regime than in neighbouring States. The Belgian law was presented as a measure of consumer protection: the packaging requirement allegedly made margarine readily identifiable on the shelf and distinct from butter. The Court was unpersuaded that this consideration should override the consumer interest in a competitive cross-border market

---

[20]   Case 261/81 [1982] ECR 3961.

and enhanced choice. It did not exclude the possibility of national initiatives taken to protect consumers, but the rule at issue was too rigid:

> It cannot be reasonably denied that in principle legislation designed to prevent butter and margarine from being confused in the mind of the consumer is justified. However... Consumers may in fact be protected just as effectively by other measures, for example by rules on labelling, which hinder the free movement of goods less.

It is fairly common for the Court to find a restrictive national rule to be incompatible with Art. 28 (ex 30) because it represents a disproportionate intervention in the market. The Court has frequently held unlawful stricter measures which suppress products where information provision might have sufficed to achieve consumer protection. These are cases which demonstrate the principle that even where the *end* of consumer protection may provide a justification for a trade-restrictive measure, the *means* employed must be the least restrictive of trade still capable of meeting the end in view. States must regulate with an eye to the wider demands of an integrated market. In the famous 'Beer Purity' case, *Commission v Germany*,[21] the Court ruled against German regulations which had the effect of excluding from the German market beers brewed according to different styles in other Member States. This application of Art. 28 (ex 30) enhanced the choice of the German drinker. The Court was quite explicit in its view of the availability of consumer information as a regulatory technique which is less restrictive of trade than rules that stipulate permitted and non-permitted ingredients. The Court commented that 'even where... beers are sold on draught' information may be provided 'on the casks or the beer taps'. The intended result is that the (informed) consumer is then enabled to exercise choice in accordance with his or her own (informed) preferences, rather than have that choice confined by governmental intervention.

Suppression of information may itself be found to violate the requirements of EC law. In *GB-INNO v CCL*[22] the Court held that a Luxembourg law controlling the provision by a trader of information about prices was capable of impeding trade in goods from States where no such control was imposed. This was incompatible with Art. 28 EC.

The same formula has been increasingly applied by the Court to Art. 49 (ex 59) where similar economic issues arise and where it has accordingly developed a similar legal formula involving a trade off between the advantages of market integration and the merits of the challenged national rule. For example, it has held that tourists should be

---

21   Case 178/84 [1987] ECR 1227.
22   Case C–362/88 note 8 above.

able to choose guides who know their needs and their language instead of being supplied only with guides licensed by the host State.[23] As explained in Chapter 1, this is part of a process whereby EC law serves to deregulate national markets made rigid by (often long standing) technical rules.[24]

2.2.4 The Scope for Defending National Rules that Obstruct Trade

National rules which do not impede cross-border trade within the meaning of the *Dassonville/Keck* test[25] are not susceptible to challenge under EC trade law. However, even where the rule exerts an impact on cross-border trade adequate in principle to trigger Arts. 28 (ex 30) or 49 (ex 59), the rule is not automatically unlawful. In a minority of cases, national rules have been found to meet the 'mandatory requirements' test. In such circumstances, free trade and consumer choice do not prevail over national choices concerning market regulation.

National rules which restricted the marketing of strong alcoholic drink were ruled compatible with Art. 28 (ex 30) in *Aragonesa de Publicidad Exterior SA (APESA) v Departamento de Sanidad y Seguridad Social de la Generalitat de Cataluna (DSSC).*[26] Even though such rules affected the sales of such drink from other Member States, the Court was persuaded that the benefits of consumer choice should not prevail over the consumer interest in public health protection set by the regulating body at national level. Thus EC law does not create a wholly deregulated 'free for all' in the market. This ruling provides a neat contrast to the Court's entirely understandable scepticism in the *Cassis de Dijon* case that controlling the supply of *weak* alcoholic drink could form part of a coherent policy of public health protection.

In the services sector, the Court has similarly found that Art. 49 (ex 59) EC does not provide a means for eliminating *all* national rules shown to obstruct trade. It remains open to Member States to show justification, provided that it is recognised by Community law. *Customs and Excise Commissioners v Schindler*[27] involved a challenge to restrictions imposed by British authorities on invitations to participate in German lotteries posted from the Netherlands to British residents. The European Court

---

23 Cases C–154/89, C–180/89 and C–198/89 *Commission v France, Italy, Greece* [1991] ECR I–659, 709, 727.

24 Chapter 1.8.2.3.

25 Chapter 2.2.1 above.

26 Cases C–1, C–176/90 [1991] ECR I–4151.

27 Case C–275/92 [1994] ECR I–1039.

found this to be an obstruction to the integration of the market for such services. However, it was prepared to accept that such national rules are capable of justification. The UK explained that its rules were designed to prevent crime, to ensure honest treatment of gamblers and to avoid the stimulation of demand in the gambling sector which may have damaging social consequences if taken to excess. The European Court conceded that the law governing the free movement of services does not preclude such national rules 'in view of the concerns of social policy and of the prevention of fraud'.[28] Such rules must be apt to achieve such worthy objectives.[29] The ruling in *Alpine Investments v Minister van Financiën*[30] offers the reminder that market regulation may pursue the objective of consumer protection at the same time as establishing standards of proper conduct in order to forestall rogue traders undermining the reputation of the majority of participants in the market. Dutch rules restricted the practice of 'cold calling' potential consumers of financial services. This acted as an impediment to Dutch suppliers of services seeking to drum up business in other Member States. The Court did not think it proper to allow the Netherlands to justify its practices as contributions to the protection of consumers in other States, for such concerns were, in short, not its business. But it reached a result that respected the Dutch authorities' competence to regulate the market even where market fragmentation followed by holding that the protection of the reputation of Dutch firms in the sector could count as a justification for the rules.

In sum, the Court's formula is not dedicated to an unqualified model of commercial freedom in Europe. Local regulatory autonomy is respected if it does not impede cross-border trade (*Keck*) and, even if restrictive of trade, it is respected if shown to be justified (*Cassis de Dijon, Alpine Investments*). In relation to the free movement of both goods and services the Court has insisted that 'the fact that one Member State imposes less strict rules than another Member State does not mean that the latter's rules are disproportionate and hence incompatible with Community law'.[31] However, this statement of principle should be situated in its true context – in most of the cases that have reached Luxembourg it is plain that the regulating authority has failed to persuade the Court that its rules are justified.

---

28   Paragraph [63] of the ruling.

29   Cf. Case C–243/01 *Gambelli* judgment of 6 November 2003, in which the Court, dealing with a particular restriction, remarked on more general Italian initiatives to *increase* gambling.

30   Case C–384/93 [1995] ECR I–1141.

31   In connection with the free movement of goods, Case C–294/00 *Deutsche Paracelsus Schulen* [2002] ECR I–6515, and in connection with the free movement of services, Case C–3/95 *Reisebüro Broede v Gerd Sanker* [1996] ECR I–6511.

2.2.5 The Sensitivity of the Court's Role in Shaping the Consumer Interest in EC Law

There are cases which lie very close to the dividing line between lawful and unlawful national measures. In settling these 'hard cases', the Court is obliged to develop its own conception of how far national authorities should be permitted to intervene in the market to protect the consumer where that intervention will affect the broader interests of market integration. The Court finds itself forced to judge the legitimacy of distinctive national philosophies of consumer protection in an integrating market.[32] This is especially apparent where national measures designed to protect the economic interests of consumers are at stake.

Where the Court prefers free trade over national consumer protection, it exposes itself to the criticism that it is using the law of market integration to diminish national standards of protection. That risk, however, is inherent in the *Cassis de Dijon* formula. The crucial point rests in the scope of the national justifications that the Court is prepared to acknowledge as capable of overriding the impetus of integration through law.

National rules designed to protect consumers' economic interests, such as those which address deceptive marketing practices, may impede trade where they differ State by State. The impediment arises where the use of a technique employed in State A is forbidden in State B, which forces the trader to pursue a different strategy especially for State B. Where that happens, the importer into State B is forced to adapt and is therefore at a disadvantage compared to State B's own traders. This is sufficient to trigger Art. 28 (ex 30) in accordance with the *Dassonville* formula, refined in *Keck*.[33] The obstructive effect on trade requires the Court to scrutinise the national rules from the perspective of the *Cassis de Dijon* formula and to balance the consumer interest in an integrated market against the consumer interest in protection at national level. National rules are based on notions of deception which may be relative: 'hard sell' in one State may be 'unfair sell' in another. The Court's jurisprudence provides a window on distinct national views on the methods which traders should and should

---

[32] See e.g. S. Weatherill, 'Recent case law concerning the free movement of goods: mapping the frontiers of market deregulation' (1999) 36 *CMLRev* 51; M. Poiares Maduro, 'Striking the elusive balance between economic freedom and social rights in the EU', Chapter 13 in P. Alston (ed.), *The EU and Human Rights* (Oxford, 1999); C. MacMaolain, 'Free movement of foodstuffs, quality requirements and consumer protection: have the Court and Commission both got it wrong?' (2001) 26 *ELRev* 413.

[33] Chapter 2.2.1 above.

not be allowed to use in seeking to drum up business. The Court must then evaluate what level of protection may be provided at national level consistently with the demands of the law of market integration.

Schutzverband gegen Unwesen in der Wirtschaft v Y. Rocher GmbH[34] displays a policy preference in favour of a free market in information allied to a free market in goods. German law prohibited advertisements in which individual prices were compared, except where the comparison was not eye-catching. Rocher showed that the rule inhibited its ability to construct an integrated marketing strategy because it could not export to Germany techniques used elsewhere in States with more liberal laws. The European Court focused on the fact that German law controlled eye-catching advertisements whether or not they were true. The law thus suppressed the supply of accurate information to the consumer. The Court's ruling leaves no room for doubt that such a restriction cannot find justification under Community law. German law will have to be liberalised.

Verband Sozialer Wettbewerb eV v Clinique Laboratories SNC[35] involved a challenge to a German law that prohibited the use of the name 'Clinique' for cosmetics, because of an alleged risk that consumers would be misled into believing the products had medicinal properties. This rule was held to impede trade in goods marketed in other Member States under the 'Clinique' name. Article 28 (ex 30) was thus relevant; the *Keck* threshold was crossed. It fell to Germany to show justification for the rule. Germany was unable to do this to the Court's satisfaction. The Court was not persuaded that there was sufficient likelihood of consumer confusion for a barrier to trade to be justified.

The decisions in *Rocher* and in *Clinique* relax the grip of national laws which seem to regard consumers as more gullible than the European Court will acknowledge. Similarly in *Verein gegen Unwesen in Handel und Gewerbe Köln eV v Mars GmbH*[36] the Court, asked to consider a German order suppressing 'flash' advertising on product packaging, was nothing short of brutal in ruling that the marketing practice would not mislead a 'reasonably circumspect' consumer and that it therefore could not be forbidden. Yet other cases suggest a greater readiness on the part of the Court to accept that a free flow of marketing practices may not be achieved by virtue of the application of Art. 28 (ex 30).

Oosthoek's Uitgeversmaatschappij[37] involved rules imposed in the Netherlands which controlled the offer of free gifts as an inducement to purchase encyclopaedias. Sellers from outside the Netherlands who were accustomed to using such marketing methods were forced to alter their

---

34   Case C–126/91 [1993] ECR I–2361.
35   Case C–315/92 [1994] ECR I–317.
36   Case C–470/93 [1995] ECR I–1923.
37   Case 286/81 [1982] ECR 4575.

strategy for the Dutch market, thus impeding integration.[38] The Court conceded that the banned marketing techniques could result in consumers being misled. It ruled that it was accordingly possible to justify the Dutch rules as measures necessary to prevent deception and to enhance consumer protection and fair-trading. Similarly, in *Buet v Ministere Public*[39] the Court held that a French law which prohibited 'doorstep selling' of educational material was not incompatible with Art. 28 (ex 30) in view of its contribution to the protection of consumers from pressure selling tactics.[40] More generally, the Court in *Estee Lauder Cosmetics*[41] hinted at receptivity to a nuanced appreciation of what may be treated by national authorities as 'misleading' and therefore susceptible to suppression when it accepted that 'social, cultural or linguistic factors' may justify special local anxiety about particular practices tolerated elsewhere.

By way of a concluding example, the controversial nature of the Court's use of the *Cassis de Dijon* formula is memorably encapsulated in a single case where Court and Advocate-General adopted diametrically opposed views on the desirability of achieving consumer choice through the abolition of national regulatory measures. In *Drei Glocken v Centro-Sud* the Court followed its *Cassis* approach in holding unlawful Italian technical rules governing the composition of pasta.[42] It held that it was incompatible with Art. 28 (ex 30) to prohibit the sale in Italy of imported pasta made from common wheat or from a mixture of common wheat and durum wheat. The result was market integration and consumer choice; the Italian consumer did not *have* to buy unfamiliar imported types of pasta, but could do so if he or she chose.

However, the Advocate-General in the case reached precisely the opposite conclusion. He would have held the Italian law lawful and would thus have perpetuated market segregation. He was concerned that the Italian consumer would be confused by the appearance on the market of unfamiliar pasta products. He presented a vigorous view that labelling products would not have been enough to provide adequate information to

---

38   This seems enough to cross the *Keck* threshold for the invocation of Art. 28 (ex 30), 2.2.1 above, especially in light of the *Clinique* ruling. See especially [15] of the ruling in *Oosthoek*.

39   Case 328/87 [1989] ECR 1235.

40   Nor was the legislation pre-empted by the 'Doorstep Selling' Directive (Directive 85/577 OJ 1985 L372/31 on the protection of the consumer in respect of contracts negotiated away from business premises), for that Directive is 'minimum' in character. See further Chapter 1.8.3.4, and, on the detailed law of doorstep selling, Chapter 7.

41   Case C–220/98 [2000] ECR I–117.

42   Case 407/85 [1988] ECR 4233.

the consumer steeped in the history and culture of pasta. The Advocate-General would thus have ruled out market liberalisation until the Community had introduced legislation to clarify the area.

It is rare for an Advocate-General's Opinion to find absolutely no favour with the Court, which subsequently delivers the authoritative ruling in the case. This emphasises how sensitive and delicate the balance may be between free trade and national market regulation in Art. 28 (ex 30) cases.

2.2.6 From Negative to Positive

The Advocate-General's Opinion in *Drei Glocken v Centro-Sud* that legislation was needed to harmonise national laws and to open up the market was rejected by the Court. However, the disagreement highlights the need to discuss the function of Community legislation as a supplement to primary Treaty provisions in the development of EC consumer policy.

Some national laws, although not many and not those in *Cassis de Dijon* or in *Drei Glocken*, will survive the application of 'negative law' under Arts. 28 (ex 30) and 49 (ex 59) and persist in obstructing market integration. The classic constitutional response of the EC to areas where 'negative law' is insufficient to integrate the market is harmonisation; that is, 'positive' action by the Community to introduce its own regulatory rules applicable throughout the Community. Positive Community action may be required in order to advance market integration. Common Community rules may be needed to replace national rules obstructive of trade where those national rules are held lawful when tested against the Treaty provisions governing free movement. Harmonisation therefore serves as a legislative supplement to the judicial contribution to market-making. More generally, a large integrated market may require an integrated structure of regulation. At European level too one may be confronted by market failure,[43] and this prompts a search for appropriate regulatory responses. However, the following section examines the difficulties which confront the translation of this notion of a need for 'positive' Community consumer policy-making into a practical set of legal rules. It is necessary to appreciate the *constitutional* context of European consumer policy.

---

[43]   Chapter 1.

2.3 THE SHAPING OF EU CONSUMER POLICY UNDER THE TREATY

2.3.1 The Principle of 'Attributed Competence' Under the Treaty

Economic theory holds that market integration is itself ultimately in the consumer interest. The intensification of competition should serve the consumer by increasing the available choice of goods and services, thereby inducing improvements in their quality and reduction in their price. As explained, EC 'negative law' is an indirect form of consumer policy in its capacity to remove national impediments to integration.

When one turns to consider the scope of 'positive law' enacted at European level to promote the interests of the consumer one immediately confronts the difference between the European Union, as an international organisation, and a State as normally understood. At national level the shaping of consumer policy is ideally conducted according to a careful examination of priorities and policy preferences. But, by contrast, Art. 5(1) EC declares that 'The Community shall act within the limits of the powers conferred upon it by this Treaty and of the objectives assigned to it therein'. This is the so-called principle of 'attributed powers' and it means, in short, that the EC may only act in so far as its Treaty provides it with an adequate authorisation. A particular policy may be thought eminently desirable but if its pursuit would extend beyond the grant of competence made by the Treaty then, constitutionally, it is off-limits the EC.

So the first question that must be asked when devising a 'positive' contribution by the EC to consumer policy is: what does the Treaty have to say about the matter? And the answer is different depending on the date. 1 November 1993, the entry into force of the Maastricht Treaty (s. 2.1.3 above), is the critical date in the evolution of EC consumer policy.

One would look in vain in the Treaty as it existed prior to 1 November 1993 for a direct expression of the consumer interest. The consumer was mentioned only in five of the original Treaty Articles and each of those references was tangential only.[44] In contrast to competition policy, for example, which was elaborated within the Treaty,[45] consumer policy lacked independent identity. It was simply assumed to lie in the general notion that the consumer will benefit from the process of market integration. The programme of legislative harmonisation admittedly

---

[44] The original Arts. 39, 40, 85(3), 86 and 100a; each has now been re-numbered by the Amsterdam Treaty (s. 2.1.4 above) and some have been amended.

[45] Chapter 12.

affected the interests of consumers, but its primary constitutional focus was on the construction of an internal market.

The constitutional deficiencies in Community consumer policy were addressed by the Maastricht Treaty which entered into force on 1 November 1993. From this moment consumer protection was recognised explicitly within Art. 3 EC as a Community activity. But even this breakthrough must be examined with a careful awareness of the fundamental principle of 'attributed competence'. The relevant provision authorising the Community to legislate to achieve defined ends of consumer protection, which is now Art. 153 EC, does not grant an unlimited legislative competence. It places the EC in a position subordinate to the Member States (see 2.3.5 below).

It might be tempting to suppose that the creation of an integrated European market would require the sort of European-wide regulation which is needed to support any market, whatever its territorial scope. However, constitutionally, the EC cannot claim any general regulatory competence. The limited grant made by the Treaty represents a severe impediment to the possibility of moving beyond 'negative' law to a comprehensive 'positive' Community consumer policy.

There are three strands to the evolution of the EC's 'positive' consumer law, and each must be viewed against the constitutional background made specific by Art. 5(1) EC's principle of 'attributed competence'. The first and second strands, 'soft law' (see 2.3.2 below) and the programme of legislative harmonisation (see 2.3.3 below), reach back before the explicit recognition at Maastricht of the place of consumer protection in the Treaty. The third, the explicit recognition of a limited legislative competence to advance consumer interests at European level, is a creation of Maastricht and is now to be found in Art. 153 (see 2.3.4 below).

2.3.2 The Development of Programmes of Action and Soft Law

The starting point in the evolution of a Community consumer protection policy is found in the Council Resolution of 14 April 1975 on a preliminary programme for a Community consumer protection and information policy.[46] This was the first attempt to provide a systematic framework for the development of Community consumer policy, although it was necessarily undertaken against the constitutional background of an absence of specific legal base authorising legislation explicitly dedicated to the consumer interest. The Annex to the Resolution, a 'Preliminary Programme of the European Economic Community for a Consumer

---

[46]   OJ 1975 C92/1.

Protection and Information Policy', offered at Point 3 a statement of five basic rights:

(a) the right to protection of health and safety,
(b) the right to protection of economic interests,
(c) the right of redress,
(d) the right to information and education,
(e) the right of representation (the right to be heard).

The Annex observed that in the modern market economy the balance has shifted away from the consumer in favour of the supplier. This imbalance has deepened the need to improve information about rights among consumers and to provide information to support freer choice.

The first Resolution was followed in 1981 by a second along largely the same lines.[47] The third programme was presented in 1986 by which time the Community had fixed its goal of completing the internal market by the end of 1992,[48] a policy objective which heavily influenced the document. The 1992 internal market policy also informed the next document, the Council Resolution of 9 November 1989 on future priorities for re-launching consumer protection policy.[49]

On 3 May 1990 the Commission published a Three Year Action Plan of Consumer Policy in the EEC (1990–92).[50] This initiated a regular programme of Action Plans designed to provide a coherent framework for the articulation of policy. There were four main areas of focus selected 'because of their importance in building the consumer confidence necessary to support the implementation of the internal market': consumer representation, consumer information, consumer safety and consumer transactions.

In June 1992, the Council agreed a Resolution on future priorities for the development of consumer protection policy.[51] The second Three Year Action Plan followed in July 1993 under the subtitle 'Placing the Single Market at the service of European consumers'.[52] This plan was located in the context of the completion of the internal market. By contrast the next document in the sequence, the Commission's Priorities for Consumer

---

[47] OJ 1981 C133/1.
[48] OJ 1986 C167/1.
[49] OJ 1989 C 294/1.
[50] COM (90) 98.
[51] OJ 1992 C186/1.
[52] COM (93) 378.

Policy covering 1996–1998,[53] adopted a conspicuously broader focus than the building and maintenance of the internal market. It made specific reference to matters such as the supply of essential public utility services, the consumer interest in the information society, and practical encouragement of sustainable consumption. It also broadened the geographical horizons. Assistance for the development of consumer policies in Central and Eastern Europe was added to the agenda; so too review of consumer policy in developing countries.

Decision 283/99 of the Parliament and Council established a general framework for Community activities in favour of consumers for 1999–2003.[54] The Commission continued to plan on a three-year cycle, issuing its Consumer Policy Action Plan for 1999–2001.[55] Subsequently it published a report on both this Action Plan and on the General Framework.[56]

The mostly recently released documents are the Commission's Consumer Policy Strategy for 2002–2006, communicated to the Parliament and the Council in 2002,[57] which provoked an approving Council Resolution of December 2002.[58] Ambitious breadth remains evident. Three priorities are identified in the work programme: a high common level of consumer protection, effective enforcement (including administrative co-operation and redress), and the involvement of consumer organisations in EU policies.

Such resolutions, action plans and strategy documents are of importance in setting out a coherent programme for the EU as an actor with responsibilities in the field of consumer protection. But they do not constitute binding Community legal acts. Nor do they compensate for constitutional deficiencies rooted in the Treaty. No matter how sophisticated the paperwork, these soft law sources are incapable of subverting the fundamental constitutional point asserted by Art. 5(1) EC that in principle the EC's *legislative* authority in the consumer field reaches no further than is allowed by the Treaty.

2.3.3 Legislative Harmonisation Relevant to the Consumer

The 'soft law' programmes examined in the previous sub-section assert a political commitment to consumer protection at European level. This was

---

53   COM (95) 519.
54   OJ 1999 L34/1.
55   COM (98) 696.
56   COM (2001) 486.
57   OJ 2002 C137/2.
58   OJ 2003 C11/1.

first agreed by the Heads of State and government of the Member States at the 'Paris Summit' in 1972. The peculiarity in this is constitutional in nature. For until 1993, the date of entry into force of the Maastricht Treaty, the Treaty was barren of any explicit grant of a legislative competence in the field of consumer protection. There was consequently for two decades a mismatch between the political commitment to consumer protection and the Treaty's explicit recognition of an EC legislative competence in the field. Nonetheless legislation of significant interest to the consumer was adopted, and continues to be adopted, in the name of harmonisation. Article 5(1) EC asserts that the EC is competent only where so provided by its Treaty, but the competence to harmonise laws has always been part of its armoury. Where laws differ State-by-State, the creation of an integrated market is impeded. Some such disparities between national laws will be unlawful, as in the landmark *Cassis de Dijon* ruling and many others subsequently. Some national laws will nevertheless be justifiable and remain in place as lawful trade barriers.[59] The classic EC response is the harmonisation of such laws in order to establish a common Community rule. In this way Community laws come into existence in order to integrate the market, although their incidental effect is additionally to regulate it. And in so far as the national rules subjected to the discipline of harmonisation are rules of consumer protection, the end product is a form of 'Europeanised' consumer protection. Community 'consumer policy' of this type has been developed indirectly, driven by the process of market integration, not market regulation. But it has generated a significant body of rules all the same.

The original Treaty of Rome empowered the Community to pursue legislation designed to approximate national provisions which directly affect the establishment or functioning of the common market. This was found in Art. 100, now re-numbered as Art. 94[60]. As explained above, a further provision was inserted into the Treaty by the Single European Act in 1987 in order to accelerate the process of law-making needed to achieve a completed internal market by the end of 1992. This was Art. 100a, now amended and re-numbered as Art. 95. This permits the adoption of harmonisation legislation in the areas to which it refers by qualified majority voting in Council. States may be outvoted and bound by legislation with which they disagree.[61]

---

[59]   Cf. cases at note s 26, 27 and 30 above.

[60]   The Amsterdam Treaty is responsible for this re-numbering; see section 2.1.4 above.

[61]   Article 95(4) *et seq* envisages the possibility of an application to the Commission for permission to apply non-conforming rules.

Divergences in national consumer protection laws have been treated as exerting a detrimental effect on market integration. Accordingly the Community has in several areas acted to put in place its own consumer protection laws. Such laws contribute to the equalisation of competitive conditions in the market. These are then implemented at national level and become part of the fabric of consumer protection in the Community generally and in each individual Member State.

The body of what can indirectly be termed EC consumer protection legislation touches both private law and public law. It covers both protection of the safety of consumers and their economic interests. The following list identifies the most high-profile measures adopted under the programme of legislative harmonisation and provides a representative cross-section of Community activity;

1. Council Directive 85/374 of 25 July 1985 on the approximation of the laws, regulations and administrative provisions of the Member States concerning liability for defective products; Directive 99/34 of the European Parliament and of the Council of 10 May 1999 amending Council Directive 85/374/EEC on the approximation of the laws, regulations and administrative provisions of the Member States concerning liability for defective products.[62]
2. Council Directive 90/314 of 23 June 1990 on package travel, package holidays and package tours.[63]
3. Council Directive 93/13 of 5 April 1993 on unfair terms in consumer contracts.[64]
4. Council Directive 88/378 of 3 May 1988 on the approximation of the laws of the Members States concerning the safety of toys.[65]
5. Directive 2001/95 of the European Parliament and of the Council of 3 December 2001 on general product safety.[66]
6. Council Directive 84/450 of 10 September 1984 relating to the approximation of the laws regulations and administrative provisions of the Members States concerning misleading advertising; Directive 97/55 of the European Parliament and of the Council of 6 October 1997 amending Directive 84/450/EEC concerning misleading advertising so as to include comparative advertising.[67]

---

[62] Directive 85/374 OJ 1985 L210/29, Directive 99/34 OJ 1999 L141/20. See Chapter 4.
[63] Directive 90/314 OJ 1990 L158/59. Implemented in the UK by the Package Travel, Package Holidays and Package Tours Regulations 1992, S.I 1992/3288.
[64] Directive 93/13 OJ 1993 L95/29. See Chapter 5.
[65] Directive 88/378 OJ 1988 L187/1. See Chapter 10.
[66] Directive 2001/95 OJ 2002 L11/4. See Chapter 10.
[67] Directive 84/450 OJ 1984 L250/17, Directive 97/55 OJ 1997 L290/18. See Chapter 8.

7. Council Directive 85/577 of 20 December 1985 to protect the consumer in respect of contracts negotiated away from business premises.[68]
8. Council Directive 87/102 of 22 December 1986 for the approximation of the laws, regulations and administrative provision of the Members States concerning consumer credit; Council Directive 90/88 of 22 February 1990 amending Directive 87/102 for the approximation of the laws, regulations and administrative provisions of the Member States concerning consumer credit; Directive 98/7 of the European Parliament and of the Council of 16 February 1998 amending Directive 87/102 for the approximation of the laws, regulations and administrative provisions of the Member States concerning consumer credit. [69]
9. Directive 94/47 of the Parliament and Council of 26 October 1994 on the protection of purchasers in respect of certain aspects of contracts relating to the purchase of the right to use immovable properties on a timeshare basis.[70]
10. Directive 97/7 of the European Parliament and of the Council of 20 May 1997 on the protection of consumers in respect of distance contracts.[71]
11. Directive 99/44 of the European Parliament and of the Council of 25 May 1999 on certain aspects of the sale of consumer goods and associated guarantees.[72]
12. Directive 98/27 of the European Parliament and of the Council of 19 May 1998 on injunctions for the protection of consumers' interests.[73]
13. Directive 2000/31 of the European Parliament and of the Council of 8 June 2000 on certain legal aspects of information society services, in particular electronic commerce, in the Internal Market ('Directive on electronic commerce').[74]
14. Directive 2002/65 of the European Parliament and of the Council of 23 September 2002 concerning the distance marketing of consumer

---

[68] Directive 85/577 OJ 1985 L372/31. See Chapter 7.
[69] Directive 87/102 OJ L 42/48; Directive 90/88 OJ 1990 L61/14; Directive 98/7 OJ 1998 L101/17. See Chapter 6.
[70] Directive 94/47 OJ 1994 L280/83.
[71] Directive 97/7 OJ 1997 L144/19.
[72] Directive 99/44 OJ 1999 L171/12. See Chapter 3.
[73] Directive 98/27 OJ 1998 L166/51.
[74] Directive 2000/31 OJ 2000 L178/1.

financial services and amending Council Directive 90/619/EEC and Directives 97/7/EC and 98/27/EC.[75]

All these measures significantly affect national consumer law and most are examined at length at appropriate points in this book. As is plain from the list, most of the older measures were adopted by the Council alone, while the more recent measures have been adopted under the Art. 251 'co-decision' procedure which has become the normal method of legislating in the EC and which involves both Parliament and Council. But all are measures of harmonisation. Directive 85/577, for example, seventh on the list above, states in its Preamble that the practice of doorstep selling is the subject of different rules in different Member States, and that 'any disparity between such legislation may directly affect the functioning of the common market'. Accordingly harmonised rules are introduced to regulate the practice at European level.

The Member States of the EC are under an obligation to implement these Directives in their domestic legal orders.[76] The EC Treaty envisages that Directives will become part of national law through national implementing measures. The UK has done this in respect of all the above measures.[77] Each is part of domestic law, although the national implementing measures do not stand alone; they must be interpreted in the light of the Directives.[78] Accordingly, the pattern of EC law is part of the pattern of law in the UK. EC law is part of English law by virtue (on the traditional model) of the European Communities Act 1972. EC law must not be placed in a setting external to domestic law. The controls over the market exercised as a result of these EC initiatives have been discussed several times in Chapter 1 at the level of policy and will be seen to permeate the book's treatment of the substantive law of consumer protection.

In practice, the constitutional genesis of Community consumer protection law is not of immediate importance in the application of laws in the UK. These laws, initially in the shape of Directives, become domestic consumer protection law and must be enforced as effectively as law emanating from a purely domestic source. The fact that a Directive is formally designed to integrate the market does not lessen its impact, often profound, on the relevant domestic law of consumer protection. Directive 85/374, the Product Liability Directive,[79] is concerned with harmonisation

---

[75] Directive 2002/65 OJ 2002 L271/16.

[76] Articles 10 (ex 5) and 249 (ex 189) EC.

[77] Although not always in line with the deadline set by the Directive: see Chapter 10 on the late implementation of Directive 2001/95.

[78] The *Marleasing* principle; see 2.4.2 below.

[79] Note 62 above.

of national laws. Because Art. 1 provides that 'the producer shall be liable for damage caused by a defect in his product' it improves the position of the injured consumer in the UK where liability rules have been based on the fault of the producer rather than the defectiveness of the product.[80]

2.3.4 The Title on Consumer Protection in the Treaty

As mentioned in the above commentary, the pattern of Community consumer protection policy was altered by the entry into force of the Maastricht Treaty on 1 November 1993. The prevailing enforced constitutional connection between consumer protection and market integration, via the Treaty Articles governing harmonisation, remains significant, but post-Maastricht it is no longer the only legislative game in town. For the first time EC competence in the area of consumer protection is established independently of the process of market integration through harmonisation pursuant to Arts. 94 (ex 100) and 95 (ex 100a).[81] The relevant provision introduced at Maastricht was a new Art. 129a EC, but this was re-numbered and significantly amended at Amsterdam. A debate has begun to take shape about whether the legal infrastructure to promote active consumer participation in the market has now been adequately constructed; and, if not, what more may be required.[82] Underpinning that debate is the heart of the EC Treaty's explicit commitment to consumer protection, which is now located in Art. 153 EC. It reads as follows:

1. In order to promote the interests of consumers and to ensure a high level of consumer protection, the Community shall contribute to protecting the health, safety and economic interests of consumers, as well as to promoting their right to information, education and to organise themselves in order to safeguard their interests.
2. Consumer protection requirements shall be taken into account in defining and implementing other Community policies and activities.
3. The Community shall contribute to the attainment of the objectives referred to in paragraph 1 through: (a) measures adopted pursuant to

---

[80] For further details of this regime, see Chapter 4.

[81] For commentary at the time see H.-W. Micklitz and S. Weatherill, 'Consumer Policy in the European Community: Before and After Maastricht' (1993) 16 *JCP* 285.

[82] Cf. the rather different perspectives adopted by J. Stuyck, 'European Consumer Law after the Treaty of Amsterdam: Consumer Policy in or beyond the internal market?' (2000) 37 *CMLRev* 367; and G. Howells and T. Wilhelmsson, 'EC consumer law: has it come of age?' (2003) 28 *ELRev* 370.

<blockquote>
Article 95 [ex 100a] in the context of the completion of the internal market; (b) measures which support, supplement and monitor the policy pursued by the Member States.

4.   The Council, acting in accordance with the procedure referred to in Article 251 [ex 189b] and after consulting the Economic and Social Committee, shall adopt the measures referred to in paragraph 3(b).

5.   Measures adopted pursuant to paragraph 4 shall not prevent any Member State from maintaining or introducing more stringent protective measures. Such measures must be compatible with this Treaty. The Commission shall be notified of them.
</blockquote>

The elevation of consumer protection to the status of a Community common policy was confirmed at Maastricht by an addition to Art. 3 which now provides that 'the activities of the Community shall include... a contribution to the strengthening of consumer protection'. Article 153(2) buttresses this statement by dictating the 'horizontal' application of consumer protection requirements across the sweep of the EC's business. Moreover, the EU Charter of Fundamental Rights, proclaimed in December 2000, states in Art. 38 that 'Union policies shall ensure a high level of consumer protection'. This carries political rather than legal weight, for the Charter is not binding. Treaty revision may in future alter this.[83]

It is plain from the third paragraph of Art. 153 that two routes to law-making are envisaged.[84] The first, pursued *via* Art. 153(3)(a), cross-refers to the well-established competence to harmonise laws – although Art. 153(1) is firmer in its commitment to high levels of consumer protection than is Art. 95(3), most of all in engaging the Community, not simply individual institutions. The second, pursued *via* Art. 153(3)(b), is the innovation inserted into the Treaty by the Maastricht Treaty with effect from 1993. Its character suggests a subordinate role for EC action. European consumer legislation adopted under Art. 153(3)(b) seeks to improve the quality of national consumer policy and not at all to replace it. In fact, few such measures have been adopted. One might mention a Decision on the establishment of a system of information on home and leisure accidents[85] and a Directive on the indication of prices offered to consumers.[86] One would have to confess that this is not an exciting track record. Although, as a general comment, Art. 153 has created an opportunity to develop a role for the EC as a generator of consumer

---

83   Among the proposals of the Convention on the Future of Europe, Chapter 2.1.5 above, is to endow the Charter with binding legal force.

84   In Case C–183/00 *González Sánchez* [2002] ECR I–3901 the Court carefully distinguishes between Arts. 153(3)(a) and (b).

85   Decision 3092/94 OJ 1994 L331/1, amended by Decision 95/184 OJ 1995 L120/36.

86   Directive 98/6 OJ 1998 L80/27.

protection law which is autonomous of the law of market integration,[87] the dominant source of laws relevant to the consumer has even since Maastricht remained the programme of legislative harmonisation. More recently, however, the constitutional limits of this source have become more visible.

2.3.5 Rules Governing the Existence of Competence

Legislative harmonisation has made and continues to make a substantial contribution to shaping an EC consumer policy, even if only indirectly in the sense that harmonisation's principal focus is on market-making. The indissociable linkage between harmonisation as a tool of market integration and harmonisation as an exercise in selecting the appropriate technique for regulating the European market is recognised in Art. 95(3). This provides that 'The Commission, in its proposals envisaged in paragraph 1 concerning health, safety, environmental protection and consumer protection, will take as a base a high level of protection, taking account in particular of any new development based on scientific facts. Within their respective powers, the European Parliament and the Council will also seek to achieve this objective'. Moreover Art. 153(2), set out above, states that 'Consumer protection requirements shall be taken into account in defining and implementing other Community policies and activities'. Therefore internal market law and consumer protection do not exist in isolation from each other.

Nevertheless, it must be conceded that some measures of legislative harmonisation make little visible contribution to market-making. Directive 85/577,[88] for example, states in its Preamble that the practice of doorstep selling is the subject of different rules in different Member States, and that 'any disparity between such legislation may directly affect the functioning of the common market'. It is hard to believe this laconically stated claim. The measure's dominant concern appears to be consumer protection not market integration, and its Preamble cheerfully refers to the political importance of developing a consumer policy for the EC which is manifest in the 'soft law' instruments mentioned above.[89] In truth the Member States, acting unanimously in Council, had 'borrowed' the competence to harmonise in the Treaty in order to advance consumer protection at EC

---

[87] Cf. Chapter 14 dealing with Access to Justice.
[88] Directive 85/577 note 68 above.
[89] Chapter 2.3.2.

level, even though at the time this was not explicitly authorised by the Treaty.

More recently this politically ambitious reading of the reach of the EC's competence has come under closer scrutiny. In *Germany v Parliament and Council*[90] the Court annulled Directive 98/43 on the advertising of tobacco products on the application of Germany (which had been outvoted in the Council). The measure had been adopted as part of the harmonisation programme.[91] The Court was unimpressed. It insisted that harmonisation measures 'are intended to improve the conditions for the establishment and functioning of the internal market'. The Directive in question went far beyond the permitted limits. It prohibited the advertising of tobacco products in circumstances remote from the imperatives of market-making – for example, on ashtrays and parasols used on streets cafés. This was, in effect, public health policy, for which the Community possesses a competence: but the relevant provision, Art. 152, expressly forbids harmonisation. In declaring that the Community legislature does not enjoy 'a general power to regulate the internal market' the Court gave practical force to the constitutionally fundamental principle of attributed competence found in Art. 5(1) EC. The implication of *Tobacco Advertising* for consumer policy-making is that Art. 95 should not be used for measures which do not actually contribute to eliminating obstacles to free movement or to removing distortions of competition. Article 153(3)(b) is available instead to support consumer protection that cannot be tied to market-making in this fashion – but the textual limits of Art. 153, discussed above (2.3.4), must be respected.

This does not deny the connection between market-making and consumer protection. Quite the reverse. In both *Tobacco Advertising* and the subsequent decision in *R v Secretary of State for Health ex parte British American Tobacco (Investments) Ltd and Imperial Tobacco Ltd*[92] the Court accepts that protective concerns should play a central role in fixing the content of harmonising measures. This policy association is guaranteed by the EC Treaty in Arts. 95(3), 152(1) and 153(2). The Court's point is only that the threshold demand that a measure adequately contribute to improving the conditions for the establishment and functioning of the internal market must be crossed before any question

---

[90] Case C–376–98 [2000] ECR I–8419. See T. Hervey, 'Community and National Competence in Health after Tobacco Advertising' (2001) 38 *CMLRev* 1421; J. Usher, 'Annotation' (2001) 38 *CMLRev* 1519; G. Howells, 'Federalism in USA and EC – the scope for harmonized legislative activity compared' (2002) 10 *Euro Rev Private Law* 601.

[91] Pursuant to Art. 100a, now Art. 95, and also Arts. 57(2) and 66, now Arts. 47(2) and 55, governing the services sector.

[92] Case C–491/01 [2002] ECR I–11453.

about the *quality* of the European-level protective regime may be addressed.

Some older measures of harmonisation are today vulnerable to challenge. The 'Doorstep Selling' Directive,[93] for example, was largely motivated by the political consensus in favour of EC consumer protection and its Preamble pays only lip-service to the perspective of market-making. Awareness that the limits of EC competence must be taken seriously pervades some recent policy documents. The Commission's 2001 Communication on European Contract Law initiated a debate about how best to shape a European dimension to contract law[94] and this was followed up by a 2003 Action Plan on a more coherent European Contract Law.[95] In the 2001 Communication the Commission declares that it is actively seeking to uncover areas in which the internal market is malfunctioning because of deficiencies in the existing bloc of harmonised contract law; and that these are likely to be the areas in which future harmonisation will be focused. The shadow of the *Tobacco Advertising* judgment looms large.

The precise dimensions of that shadow are not yet known. Some more recent harmonisation measures affecting the consumer assert in their Preambles a concern to introduce common rules not simply to cure competitive distortion affecting sellers but also to strengthen consumer confidence.[96] This suggests a more active role for legislative harmonisation designed to promote the consumer interest than is suggested by *Tobacco Advertising*. It remains to be seen how this more ambitious rationale rooted in the generation of consumer confidence will fare if tested before the Court.[97]

Were the draft Constitutional Treaty prepared by the Convention to enter into force (2.1.5 above) it would not clear the air. Article III–65 provides that the legislature '...shall establish measures for the approximation of the provisions laid down by law, regulation or administrative action in Member States which have as their object the

---

[93] Directive 85/577 note 68 above. See Chapter 7.

[94] COM (2001) 398. See D. Staudenmayer, 'The Commission Communication on European Contract law and the Future Prospects' (2002) 51 *ICLQ* 673.

[95] COM (2003) 68. See J. Karsten and A. Sinai, 'The Action Plan on European Contract Law: Perspectives for the Future' (2003) 26 *JCP* 159; M. Kenny, 'The 2003 Action Plan on European Contract Law: is the Commission running wild?' (2003) 28 *ELRev* 538.

[96] E.g. Directive 93/13 note 64 above, Directive 99/44 note 72 above.

[97] S. Weatherill, 'The Commission's Options for Developing EC Consumer Protection and Contract Law: Assessing the Constitutional Basis' (2002) 13 *Euro Bus L Rev* 497.

establishment and functioning of the internal market...'. The precise meaning and scope of this competence is not amplified further.

2.3.6 Subsidiarity and the Exercise of Competence

Article 5(1) EC insists that the EC may not legislate unless its Treaty confers competence on it in the relevant area. But even if competence exists, Treaty rules condition its exercise. Article 5(2) sets out the principle of subsidiarity. According to this the Community shall take action 'only if and in so far as the objectives of the proposed action cannot be sufficiently achieved by the Member States and can therefore, by reason of the scale or effects of the proposed action, be better achieved by the Community'.[98]

Subsidiarity, a creature of the Maastricht Treaty, serves as a slogan for a politically complex debate about how the European market is most efficiently regulated. The core meaning of Art. 5(2) is elusive. This is primarily because this formulation simply reflects the problem of dividing competences between Community and Member States, instead of attempting directly to address it. Sir Leon Brittan described it as a method for identifying the 'best level' for regulatory activity in the Community.[99] This rendition is important and helpful, because it brings out the point that subsidiarity is not based on preconceptions about centralisation or decentralisation. Instead it is a matter of *efficiency* – problematic though such a test must doubtless prove in practical application, whether by politicians or by judges.

A Protocol was attached to the Amsterdam Treaty. Its aim was to put flesh on subsidiarity's skeletal bones. It insists *inter alia* that 'Subsidiarity is a dynamic concept and should be applied in the light of the objectives set out in the Treaty. It allows Community action within the limits of its powers to be expanded where circumstances so require, and conversely, to be restricted or discontinued where it is no longer justified'. A helpful illustration is provided by the market for cross-border financial transactions. A lack of transparency promoted the adoption of a non-binding EC Resolution.[100] But this proved ineffective and, in the light of this experience of the failings of a market lacking EC rules, binding legislation was duly proposed and adopted.[101] Subsidiarity, frequently touted as a basis for rebuffing EC intervention, may in appropriate

---

[98] Article 5(2) does not apply to areas of exclusive EC competence, but areas relevant to consumer protection are not of an exclusive nature; see Case C–491/01 note 92 above.

[99] [1993] *Public Law* 567, 574.

[100] Recital 90/109 on the transparency of banking conditions relating to cross-border financial transactions, OJ 1990 L67/39.

[101] Directive 97/5 on cross-border credit transfers, OJ 1997 L43/25.

circumstances serve to justify it. However in other circumstances subsidiarity operates more feebly. Directive 2000/31 on electronic commerce[102] includes in its Preamble the glib statement that 'by dealing only with certain specific matters which give rise to problems for the internal market, this Directive is fully consistent with the need to respect the principle of subsidiarity'. This is mere lip-service and suggests subsidiarity, a vague slogan, exerts a negligible practical constraint over political readiness to exercise the Community's legislative competence.

As a legal principle subsidiarity is of limited value in checking the exercise of Community legislative competence. The Court's most revealing decision is *R v Secretary of State for Health, ex parte British American Tobacco and Imperial Tobacco*.[103] Faced with the submission that a Directive establishing harmonised rules governing warnings on tobacco packaging violated the principle of subsidiarity, the Court simply asked itself whether the objective of the proposed action could be better achieved at Community level. Since the objective was the elimination of trade barriers caused by existing legal diversity among the Member States, the matter was resolved there and then. Only the Community can do this. Accordingly judicial review of the validity of measures of harmonisation is of real significance pursuant to Art. 5(1) EC, as is made plain in *Tobacco Advertising*, but of little practical weight pursuant to Art. 5(2).

2.3.7 The Risk that EC Legislation may Depress Standards

Concern has been expressed from time to time about the potential risk that EC legislative initiatives may set standards below those prevailing at national level. Were this to happen, free trade would be achieved at the expense of consumer protection. This fear exists alongside the risk (commented on above in 2.2.2) that Community negative law may sweep away national choices concerning market regulation and consumer protection. The allegation that positive Community rules have depressed existing standards is difficult conclusively to rebut or to sustain. Individual sectors must be assessed. A related concern is that, even where standards are not lower, their effective enforcement is severely impeded by the unchecked flow of goods across borders throughout the extensive territory of the Community. This may make it difficult to track down goods that are unsafe, an aspect which raises questions about appropriate strategies of

---

[102] Note 74 above.
[103] Case C–491/01 note 92 above.

enforcement practice in the internal market.[104] At this stage, the reader should simply be aware that these are real and recurrent points of concern in appraising the impact of EC rules on consumer protection.[105]

Constitutionally, attempts have been made to alleviate such fears. Market-making *via* the harmonisation of laws is explicitly tied in the Treaty to the quality of protection achieved under the common rule. Article 95(3) was mentioned above (section 2.3.5). It directs that the Commission, Parliament and Council shall be concerned to take into account a high level of protection of health, safety, the environment and the consumer. Article 153(2), mentioned above (section 2.3.4), is also significant for its instruction that consumer protection requirements shall be taken into account in defining and implementing other Community policies and activities. The practical vigour of these commitments to consumer protection may be doubted: much depends on the depth to which the consumer interest is embedded into the institutional culture of the Community, and that is difficult to track. However, at the very least, Arts. 95(3) and 153(2) demonstrates sensitivity to the charge that the EC's legislative activity might choose as its benchmark the lowest common denominator of regulatory protection among the Member States.

The accusation that the EC tends to depress regulatory standards invites consideration not only of the content of EC rules but also of their impact on national competence. Even if the EC legislates at a level inferior to the protective standard preferred by a particular jurisdiction, damage is limited if the regulator remains free to opt to maintain or introduce stricter rules. Article 153(5) (see section 2.3.4) envisages exactly this. Legislation adopted by the EC pursuant to Art. 153(3)(b) operates as a minimum standard. Member States must offer that minimum level of protection but they are free to regulate more intensively in the field in question, subject only to the requirement of compliance with the Treaty itself (most obviously the rules governing the free movement of goods and services). This is 'minimum' rule-making and the Treaty stipulates it is the norm not only for consumer protection under Art. 153(3)(b) but also *inter alia* for environmental protection (Art. 176 EC). Norbert Reich vividly captures this phenomenon of shared regulatory competence: 'the more competences the Community is acquiring, the less exclusive will be its jurisdiction'.[106]

---

[104] Cf. Chapter 10.6.

[105] See further S. Weatherill, 'Pre-emption, harmonisation and the distribution of competence to regulate the internal market', Chapter 2 in J. Scott and C. Barnard (eds.), *The Legal Foundations of the Internal Market* (Oxford: Hart Publishing, 2002).

[106] 'Competition between Legal Orders: A New Paradigm of EC Law' (1992) 29 *CMLRev* 861, 895.

What of harmonisation pursuant to Art. 95? An express procedure is located in Art. 95(4) *et seq* which permits an application to be made to the Commission according to defined criteria for authorisation to apply standards which are stricter than the agreed harmonised rule. The grant of such an authorisation would upset the integrated market and is therefore to be treated as exceptional,[107] although the procedure is no dead letter.[108] A more difficult question is whether, in the absence of a successful application to the Commission made pursuant to Art. 95(4) *et seq*, a State may apply stricter standards than are fixed in the measure of legislative harmonisation. Here the law is in a state of flux. Legislative practice is clear. Fears that standards may be lowered by EC intervention have been addressed by the frequent use of the 'minimum harmonisation' formula even in measures adopted pursuant to Arts. 94 (ex 100) and 95 (ex 100a). On this model, EC legislative intervention does not totally pre-empt national choices; free trade is placed alongside, not above, national market regulation and consumer protection. It is common in measures harmonising rules protecting the economic interests of consumers. For example, the Directive on Unfair Terms in Consumer Contracts[109] is minimum in character and therefore does not preclude the application of stricter control of unfair terms under national law.[110] The 'Doorstep Selling' Directive is similarly explicitly stated to be 'minimum' in character and in *Buet v Ministere Public*[111] the Court held that this proviso meant that it did not exclude the possibility of France choosing to go so far as to prohibit the practice entirely – subject only to compliance with Art. 28.[112]

This practice seems to acknowledge the viability of a model of 'minimum harmonisation'. A 'pure' model of an integrated market is sacrificed to the possibility of local preference to set stricter rules of market regulation. But harmonisation, albeit of a minimum nature, goes part of the way to levelling the commercial playing field, while also respecting a limited space for the expression of local regulatory autonomy, provided it is justified under the Community's rules governing free movement.

---

[107] Case C–41/93 *France v Commission* [1994] ECR I–1829; Case C–319/97 *Antoine Kortas* 1999] ECR I–3143.

[108] E.g. Case C–3/00 *Denmark v Commission* [2003] ECR I–2643 (Commission refusal of authorisation annulled by the Court).

[109] Directive 93/13 note 64 above.

[110] Chapter 5.

[111] Case 328/87 [1989] ECR 1235.

[112] This was demonstrated to the Court's satisfaction, see section 2.2.5 above.

More recent case law suggests a new intolerance by the Court of this compromise model. In *Tobacco Advertising*[113] one element of the Court's objection to the challenged measure was that it included no clause guaranteeing that products conforming to the harmonised standards would be entitled to access to export markets throughout the territory of the EU. In *British American Tobacco*[114] it was commented with approval that the measure upheld in that case by the Court *did* include such a 'market access' clause. The implication is that it is a condition of the validity of a measure of harmonisation that it excludes the possibility of States making stricter demands of imports than are envisaged by the EC act itself. A State must resort to the relatively narrow authorisation procedure in Art. 95(4) *et seq* in order to secure a basis for such an impediment to trade. This unquestionably strengthens the capacity of legislative harmonisation to integrate markets. Perhaps that is the intent of Art. 95. But it is hard to reconcile with past practice, both legislative and judicial. The impression that the Court has embarked on a newly vigorous campaign to interpret the legal provisions governing harmonisation in a fashion devoted to market integration and potentially harmful to local regulatory diversity also emerges from *María Victoria González Sánchez v Medicina Asturiana,* which concerns Directive 85/374 the 'Product Liability' Directive.[115] This measure is a product of Art. 100, now 94, rather than the post-Single European Act base supplied by Art. 95 (ex 100a). The Court took the opportunity to include in its reasoning the observation that 'unlike, for example, Council Directive 93/13... on unfair terms in consumer contracts... the Directive contains no provision expressly authorising the Member States to adopt or to maintain more stringent provisions in matters in respect of which it makes provision, in order to secure a higher level of consumer protection'. It ruled out the possibility of Spain retaining a more generous régime of consumer protection for fear of competitive distortion within the European market. It remains to be seen how this line of case law will develop, and how it will influence legislative practice.[116] It is notable that the Commission's legislative proposals in the field of unfair

---

113   Case C–376/98 note 90 above, paras. 101–105.
114   Case C–491/01 note 92 above, paras. 74–75 of the judgment.
115   Case C–183/00 note 84 above. See also two other cases decided on the same day, Case C–52/00 *Commission v France* [2002] ECR I–3827, Case C–154/00 *Commission v Greece* [2002] ECR I–3879. See further Chapter 4.
116   Cf. G. Howells and T. Wilhelmsson, 'EC consumer law: has it come of age?' (2003) 28 *ELRev* 370; M. Dougan, 'Vive La Différence? Exploring the Legal Framework for Reflexive Harmonisation within the Single European Market' (2002) 1 *Annual of German and European Law* 113; P. Rott, 'Minimum Harmonization for the Completion of the Internal Market? The Example of Consumer Sales Law' (2003) 40 *CMLRev* 1107.

commercial practices, examined in Chapter 8.7.3, envisage no scope for national measures that are stricter than the harmonised rule. It is at least arguable that under the Court's current interpretative stance, in so far as any legislative concession to States to set stricter rules than a harmonised standard serves to impede cross-border trade, the validity of reliance on Arts. 94 or 95 EC is called into question.

2.4 EUROPEAN UNION LAW WITHIN THE NATIONAL SYSTEM[117]

2.4.1 The Pattern of EC Law within the National Legal System

It was explained above (see section 2.1.3) that EC law is part of EU law, but not co-terminous with it. The vast majority of rules mentioned in this chapter and in this book are the product of the EC rather than the wider non-EC EU, and it is in relation to EC law alone that the European Court has embarked on its quest to shape a system suitable for achieving the objectives mapped out in the Treaty. The account that follows is concerned with the impact of EC law alone within the national legal orders of the Member States.

It is commonplace that EC law forms part of the national legal order of the participating Member States. However, although EC law is national law, not a severable body of law, Community measures and their application at national level raise some special problems of their own, all of which will be observed in this book. Their potential overlap with existing domestic law requires careful attention in implementation and application. The existence of relevant Community law is capable of affecting future domestic initiatives. For instance, any national law measure which is likely to impede trade may need to be tested against the requirements of Community trade law, inviting consideration of the scope of 'negative law' examined earlier in this chapter. Similarly, any national law likely to impinge on an area already occupied by Community legislation may be legally pre-empted by the Community norm and therefore be unenforceable. Minimum rule-making, whereby Community measures require States to put in place minimum requirements but also permit them to set more protective standards, is increasingly in vogue in Community consumer policy-making, but, as described above (see section 2.3.7), its application under Art. 153 EC is guaranteed by the Treaty while

---

[117] The major textbooks mentioned at note 3 above provide comprehensive treatment of these constitutional issues.

its role under Arts. 94 and 95 is more questionable. The issue of the extent to which national competence to act in a field survives EC legislative intervention will be addressed in a number of areas covered by this book.[118]

Measures with a Community origin cannot be interpreted within a purely domestic context. It may be appropriate to seek interpretative assistance from the European Court through the Art. 234 (ex 177) preliminary reference procedure. Moreover, measures with a Community origin cannot be enforced within a purely domestic context. The development of Community-wide patterns of consumer protection places demands on enforcement authorities to set up cross-border administrative structures and channels for information sharing. There is a certain logic in the development of Community-wide regulatory strategies in parallel with Community-wide marketing strategies pursued by traders, although the practical details of that process will only evolve fully over time.[119]

2.4.2 The Effect of Directives at National Level

EC law is part of the pattern of domestic law. There is, however, one important constitutional limitation on the impact of EC law at national level which may diminish the vitality of EC consumer protection initiatives. This limitation applies to Directives, which are the most fertile source of EC consumer protection law. According to Art. 249 (ex 189) EC, a Directive:

> shall be binding, as to the result to be achieved, upon each Member State to which it is addressed, but shall leave to the national authorities the choice of form and methods.

It is a Treaty violation for a Member State to fail to implement a Directive; such default may lead to proceedings brought by the Commission under Art. 226 (ex 169) EC against the State before the European Court in Luxembourg. However, the formulation in Art. 249 (ex 189) EC appears to mean that where a Member State fails to implement a Directive properly, the protection envisaged under the Directive is unavailable to the individual before a national court until such time as the appropriate implementing measures are put in place. Such a gap in legal protection would severely weaken the impact of the EC Directive as a legal instrument, especially given that wilful non-implementation or simply

---

[118] Cf. e.g. Chapters 4, 5, 8 and 10.

[119] Cf. Chapters 8.7.3 and 10.6 for more detailed exploration of practice.

delayed implementation, whilst not the norm, nonetheless remains regrettably common.

Mindful of the precariousness of the Directive as a source of rights, the European Court has developed its jurisprudence in order to enhance the impact at national level of unimplemented Directives. There are three major elements in the Court's campaign.

First, in the absence of proper implementation, a Directive couched in sufficiently clear terms is capable of being applied directly by national courts against the State. The rationale for this direct effect of Directives lies in the inequity which would follow from permitting a State to plead its own wrongful default in order to escape obligations envisaged under a Directive. Therefore an individual who acts in conformity with a Directive after its deadline for implementation will be able to rely on that Directive before national courts in order successfully to defend a criminal charge based on existing law which has improperly not been amended in the light of the Directive.[120] A State employee who is the victim of discrimination on grounds of sex forbidden by an unimplemented Directive, but not unlawful under national law, is able to rely on the Directive before national courts in proceedings brought against the State as employer.[121] This route is rendered all the more vigorous by the European Court's insistence on a wide definition of 'State' for these purposes.[122] However, its limits lie in the Court's refusal to accept that Directives can be enforced in this way against private parties. According to the Court's ruling in *Marshall*, the private sector employee discriminated against on grounds of sex cannot rely on the Directive in an action before national courts against his or her employer.[123]

Second, in the absence of implementation, national courts are expected to fulfil an obligation to interpret existing national law in order to conform with Community law. Article 10 (ex 5) EC imposes on national authorities, including courts, a duty of fidelity towards the Community. As part of this remarkably flexible obligation, the Court observed in *Marleasing SA v La Comercial Internacional de Alimentacion SA*[124] that:

> ...in applying national law, whether the provisions in question were adopted before or after the directive, the national court called upon to

---

[120] Case 148/78 *Pubblico Ministero v Ratti* [1979] ECR 1629.

[121] Case 152/84 *Marshall v Southampton Area Health Authority* [1986] ECR 723.

[122] E.g. Case C–188/89 *Foster v British Gas* [1990] ECR I–3133.

[123] Case 152/84 note 121 above; in fact, in this case, the plaintiff was able to rely on the unimplemented Directive because she *was* employed by the State, widely defined.

[124] Case C–106/89 [1990] ECR I–4135.

interpret it is required to do so, as far as possible, in the light of the wording and the purpose of the directive in order to achieve the result pursued by the latter and thereby comply with the third paragraph of Article [249 (ex 189)] of the Treaty.[125]

This formula deepens the penetration of Directives into the national legal order even in the absence of implementation. As a form of 'indirect effect', it may be used to reshape national law in the light of a Directive even in proceedings between private parties. The Court has subsequently added that it imposes obligations on national courts in the event of incorrect *application* of the rules at national level even if the act of implementation itself is accurate. 'Consequently, the adoption of national measures correctly implementing a directive does not exhaust the effects of the directive.'[126] The Court has also included 'settled domestic case law' within the scope of national law that must be interpreted with reference to a relevant Directive.[127] The limitations of the *Marleasing* principle lie in the demands which it makes on the ingenuity of national judges. The route will be effective especially, and perhaps only, in circumstances where national law exists which is capable of an interpretation consistent with the unimplemented Directive. The principle dictates only that the national court asked to repair the failings of the national legislature should go 'as far as possible' in interpreting the law in the light of the Directive.

Third, failure to implement a Directive may result in the liability of the State to compensate individuals who have suffered loss caused by such non-implementation. The recognition that EC law may require the availability of such a remedy in national legal orders came in the landmark decision in *Francovich and Others v Italian State*.[128] In this case, Italy had failed to implement Directive 80/987, which requires States to set up guarantee funds to compensate workers in the event of employers' insolvency. Lack of clarity in identifying the institutions responsible for payment precluded a finding that the Directive was capable of direct effect. Yet the Court declared that:

> ...the full effectiveness of Community provisions would be affected and the protection of the rights they recognise undermined if individuals were not able to recover damages when their rights were infringed by a breach of Community law attributable to a Member State.

---

[125] The third paragraph of Art. 249 (ex 189), referring to the Directive, is extracted above.

[126] Case C–62/00 *Marks and Spencer plc v Commissioners of Customs and Excise* [2002] ECR I–6325.

[127] Case C–456/98 *Centrosteel Srl v Adipol GmbH* [2000] ECR I–6007.

[128] Cases C–6 & C–9/90 [1991] ECR I–5357.

The Court stipulated three requirements that must be met before the State will incur liability. First, the result prescribed must involve the conferral of rights on individuals. Second, the content of the rights must be capable of identification on the basis of Directive. Third, a causal link between the Treaty violation and damage suffered by an individual must be demonstrated.

The *Francovich* ruling has the potential to bypass the complex questions about the scope of the direct effect of Directives. It shifts the focus of the individual's claim away from the identity of the party (private or public) against which rights under the Directive are envisaged towards the State as the party responsible for putting rights in place in the national legal order. In this sense a *Francovich* claim is more direct, although claims based on the direct and indirect effect of Directives are not precluded. *Francovich* extends the protection available to the individual prejudiced by non-implementation of a Directive.

It is immediately apparent that the financial consequences could be enormous, calling to mind the spectre of liability in an indeterminate amount to an indeterminate number of plaintiffs. Such fears have led to close confinement of liability for economic loss in English law and in other systems, at least where the harm is not caused deliberately or maliciously.[129] The Italian State's infraction in *Francovich* was plain and had indeed already been recorded in a judgment of the European Court.[130] Subsequent rulings have provided the European Court with the opportunity to refine the principles of liability in cases of less glaring infraction. In *Brasserie du Pêcheur*,[131] in which the Court made explicit that liability may arise for violation of primary Treaty provisions, not simply mishandling of Directives, it was held that a right to reparation arises only where a breach of EC law is sufficiently serious. The wider the discretion permitted to the State, the less likely that the condition will be satisfied. In the field of consumer protection, failure to implement a Directive is likely to be the most relevant State infraction, and this is a matter where discretion has no role to play. Implementation is simply obligatory. Therefore one might have confidence that in principle a *Francovich* action would succeed if the State has done nothing, as in *Francovich* itself,[132]

---

129 Cf. Chapter 1.4.

130 Case 22/87 *Commission v Italy* [1989] ECR 143.

131 Joined Cases C–46/93 & C–48/93 *Brasserie du Pêcheur SA v Germany and R v Secretary of State for Transport, ex parte Factortame Ltd and others* [1996] ECR I–1029.

132 See also Case C–178/94 *E. Dillenkofer v Bundesminister der Justiz* [1996] ECR I–4845, concerning Directive 90/314 on package travel, note 63 above.

although the State that has made a genuine attempt to implement a Directive but has excusably misinterpreted its intent may be sheltered from liability under this model.[133]

A fundamental practical weakness in the value of the *Francovich* claim lies in its inappropriateness to the 'small-scale' claimant. The individual envisaged as the recipient of rights under a Directive (whether in the field of employment or consumer protection), but whose enjoyment of those rights is thwarted by non-implementation of the Directive, would ideally prefer simply to vindicate those rights in a relatively straightforward action against employer or trader. This, however, is not possible where that employer or trader is not part of the 'State'. The *Francovich* claim for compensation is then a useful second best, but, as explained, recent case law discloses that State violation which is not sufficiently serious is not a basis for a successful claim. Moreover, the practical obstacles confronting a private consumer or employee wishing to sue the State are high.

2.4.3 Absence of Horizontal Direct Effect

The gap in constitutional protection lies in the Court's refusal to acknowledge that wrongfully unimplemented Directives are capable of horizontal direct effect; that is, that they cannot be employed by one private party against another private party, but rather only against the State. Both 'indirect effect' and *Francovich* liability offer limited scope for avoiding the worst consequences for the individual of that gap in enforceability of rights envisaged under a Directive. However, they cannot alter the basic point of the *Marshall* ruling[134] that one private individual cannot rely on a Directive as such in proceedings at national level against another private party.

This is rather damaging for the consumer's interest. In most situations the consumer will wish to rely on rights under a Directive against another private party, usually a trader. If the Directive has been implemented, the consumer can rely on the national implementing measures, which should be interpreted in the light of the Directive. If it has not been implemented, the consumer is denied the protection envisaged under Community law. The consumer may attempt to persuade the national court to interpret existing national law, if any exists, to accord with the Directive. This is a rather uncertain route and depends on national judicial capability and willingness. The consumer may sue the State for compensation. This will be unrealistic in most situations of small-scale individual loss. In practical

---

133   E.g. Case C–392/93 *R v H.M. Treasury, ex parte British Telecommunications* [1996] ECR I–1631.

134   Note 121 above.

terms, the consumer's effective protection lies in reliance on the Directive in litigation with the trader, whether as plaintiff or as defendant, yet it is precisely this 'horizontal direct effect' which the European Court is not prepared to admit.

In *Paola Faccini Dori v Recreb srl*, a decision of July 1994,[135] the European Court confirmed its *Marshall* ruling. The litigation in *Dori* arose in the consumer field. The ruling maintains that there is a gap in protection for the consumer wishing to rely on a right envisaged under a Directive against a private party, such as a supplier, where that Directive has not been implemented. Italy had failed to implement the Doorstep Selling Directive in time.[136] On Milan Railway Station, Ms Dori was lured into a contract covered by the Directive by a seller of educational material. Under the Directive, she should have been entitled to claim a right to withdraw from the deal and, having 'cooled-off', she decided that she wished to exercise that right. Under Italian law no such right existed. She was thus bound to the deal unless she was able to plead the Directive before the Italian courts against the supplier, a private party. The matter was referred to the European Court under the Art. 234 (ex 177) procedure. The Court adhered to the *Marshall* ruling and held that the Directive could not be directly effective in such circumstances. In maintaining this constitutional barrier to the impact of EC Directives at national level, the Court conformed to the wishes of the majority of Member States whose strong submissions to the Court in *Dori* against horizontal direct effect testified to the sensitivity of this area of law.

That Ms Dori was denied a right which she was supposed to enjoy under a Directive seems to weaken the vigour of EC consumer protection law. The rationale for the Court's stance can be traced back to its reasons for accepting that Directives are capable of direct effect against the State in the first place. Where the State has improperly failed to implement, it should not be able to benefit therefrom; accordingly, Directives may be enforced against it directly before a national court. By contrast, the private trader or employer is not at fault for the absence of implementation and may indeed have no knowledge of the lack of conformity of national law with a Directive. On this reasoning it might seem unfair to allow a private party such as an employee or a consumer to invoke an unimplemented Directive before a national court against another private party. Neither private party is 'at fault'; the State is the culprit for the flawed legal position at national level. This is a strong reason for welcoming the decision in *Francovich* for turning the focus on to the defaulting State.

---

[135] Case C–91/92 [1994] ECR I–3325.
[136] Note 68 above; more fully, Chapter 7.

In refusing to accept that the consumer could enforce the terms of the Directive against her supplier, the Court mentioned the availability to Dori of an action against the State based on *Francovich* principles. This is welcome in theory, but in practice seems rather unrealistic. The prospect of pursuing an action against the Italian State would probably be sufficiently daunting to dissuade the vast majority of consumers from making use of *Francovich*. Consumer rights would go unvindicated; State default would not be penalised.[137] A consumer in such circumstances simply wishes to exercise a right to withdraw from a contract, involving, if necessary, a suitable defence to a claim for breach of contract where he or she refuses to pay sums due under the contract from which withdrawal has occurred. This is the effective method of protecting consumer rights; it is the effective method of securing observance of Directives throughout the territory of the Community; and the effective method of securing the equality of the individual before Community law, irrespective of nationality. Drawing on such perceptions, horizontal direct effect was powerfully urged upon the Court in *Dori* by its Advocate-General, Herr Lenz. However, such recognition of the horizontal direct effect of Directives was rejected by the Court in 1986 in *Marshall* and that rejection was confirmed in *Dori*. The impression that in *Dori* the Court had closed the matter for some time to come has been confirmed. In the decade since the *Dori* decision there has been no judicial wavering on this point. The harm done to the consumer interest is vividly demonstrated by the point that some of the subsequent case law has, like *Dori*, involved disappointed consumers.[138] But the Court's view remains clear. Directives remain incapable of horizontal direct effect in the national legal orders.

None of these constitutional problems arise provided that the State complies with its obligation to implement Directives within the national legal order. Gratifyingly, the UK's record of implementation of Directives in general and consumer protection Directives in particular is commendable, though not flawless.[139]

---

137 Cf. pre-*Dori* but clearly aware of its imminence, A.G. Jacobs in Case C–316/93 *Vaneetveld v SA Le Foyer* Opinion of 27 January 1994: 'the possibility for the individual, under *Francovich*, to claim damages against the Member State where a directive has not been correctly implemented is not, in my view, an adequate substitute for the direct enforcement of the directive. It would often require the plaintiff to bring two separate sets of legal proceedings, either simultaneously or successively, one against the private defendant and the other against the public authorities, which would hardly be compatible with the requirements of an effective remedy'. This point was not tackled in the Court's ruling of 3 March 1994 in Case C–316/93, [1994] ECR I–763.

138 E.g. Case C–192/94 *El Corte Ingles v Cristina Blazquez Rivero* [1996] ECR I–1281, concerning Directive 87/102 note 69 above.

139 See Chapter 10 for the maltreatment of Directive 2001/95.

Chapter 3

The Quality of
Goods and Services

3.1 INTRODUCTION

Rules on the safety of products and making producers responsible for the harm caused by their products are justifiable in terms of public policy relating to health and safety. Although there are some debates as to whether the right balance is being struck, few people doubt that such laws have a legitimate place in a modern market economy. The position as regards laws regulating the quality rather than the safety of products might be thought to be more controversial. After all the consequences are usually less serious and many might consider that consumers should be given more freedom to decide whether products and services provide the quality they desire. In truth there are few laws that mandate quality standards. Those that come to mind exist in the food area where the temptation of pass off inferior products in ways that are hard to detect by, for example, reducing the content of meat in sausages, is evident and of long pedigree.[1] Standard setting otherwise tends to be related to tangential matters such as ecological factors, rather than imposing minimum quality standards as such. Of course there are numerous voluntary standards, such as BS standards, that could be made express terms of contracts and can be taken into account in assessing whether goods are satisfactory.[2]

Historically the common law approach was to place the onus on the buyer to look out for his own interests. This principle of *caveat emptor* is still reflected in s. 14(1) of the Sale of Goods Act 1979 which states there is no implied term about the quality of fitness for purpose. However, this is made subject to major exceptions set out in that and the succeeding section or the Act and in other enactments. Lord Steyn has commented that the principle of *caveat emptor* has become the principle of *caveat venditor*.[3] Why then has the implication of minimum contractual standards such as those requiring all goods sold to consumers to be of satisfactory quality and fit for purpose come to be accepted as such a commonplace in our law?

---

[1]   Assize of Bread and Ale 1266 is an early example.

[2]   *Britvic Soft Drinks v Messer* [2002] 1 Lloyd's Rep 20 and on appeal [2002] 2 Lloyd's Rep 368.

[3]   *Slater v Finning* [1997] AC 473 at 486.

One obvious explanation is the familiar theme running through consumer protection of the information asymmetries which place the consumer at a disadvantage. The trader is better placed than the consumer to know the quality of the goods and services. Of course the producer is really the one who knows about the product, but as we shall see concerning quality defects the private law places the obligations on the seller. Nevertheless it is not unrealistic to suggest that a trader who sells products has a greater obligation to inform himself of their quality than a consumer who is simply purchasing them to fulfil a particular need. Indeed in a world in which consumers purchase an ever widening range of products and the diversity within product categories is become ever greater, it is harder to expect the consumer to look after his own interests: mobile phones and computers are just two now everyday products which present a labyrinth of perplexing choices for many.

A distinction has been drawn between 'search' goods whose attributes can be determined before purchase,[4] such as the printer speed of a printer and 'experience' goods which can only appreciated during use. A meal is an obvious example of experience goods, but other products such as savings and pension policies can only assessed once one has experienced how they perform. Even with 'search' goods merely discovering the attributes of a product may not be sufficient to assess its quality. All this tells you is how well it is supposed to perform. You might also be able to assess the quality of its appearance and finish, but other important factors can only be discovered after purchase. Factors relating to reliability, durability and how well it performs can only be experienced.[5] Where products are low value and purchased repeatedly one might still argue that the market is the best mechanism as few consumers will continue to buy goods they find unsatisfactory and word-of-mouth will soon spread. However, where purchases are one-off or only occasional such as a car then there is a need to ensure the consumer is guaranteed a minimum quality. This need of course increases with the value of the goods where a wrong purchase can significantly affect the welfare of the consumer, but the law does not make such distinctions and imposes the same obligations as regards quality on all goods.[6]

If the issue is one of information one might suggest that the answer is to provide more information. This approach has been adopted with regard to additional guarantees offered[7] and there have been some attempts to

---

4   G. Hadfield, R. Howse and M. Trebilcock, 'Information-Based Principles for Rethinking Consumer Protection Policy' (1998) 21 *Journal of Consumer Policy* 131.

5   C. Twigg-Flesner, *Consumer Product Guarantees*, (Ashgate, 2003) at p. 4.

6   Although that standard is applied more rigorously in the case of more expensive goods, see Chapter 3.5.6.3(ii).

7   See Chapter 3.7.

develop logos to reflect assurances of quality.[8] The basic quality standards implied by law remain a minimum mandatory requirement. It assures the consumer that all products must meet certain minimum quality standards to participate in the UK market place and if they fail to do so the consumer can seek redress. Economics dictates that goods and services will meet these minimum standards as traders will suffer economically if they have to compensate consumers where those minimum expectations have not been reached. It is a societal view that it is not in the interests of consumers to be given the opportunity to purchase products failing to meet such standards. Although this might be seen as potentially disadvantaging the poor by preventing them access to poorer quality, but cheaper products, this is not really a danger for as we shall see the standard is a flexible one that can be modified by how the trader presents the products and by drawing defects to the consumer's attention.

As well as protecting the consumer, the minimum quality standards can also be seen as having a function in promoting the interest of high quality producers and also the general market confidence. This is because of what Akerloff has described as the 'lemon' effect.[9] If consumers are unable to identify which are the high quality products there is little incentive for producers to invest to making their products high quality; indeed if they did so they would be forced out of the market by producers who produced inferior products which the consumer could not differentiate. The imposition of minimum quality standards at least produces a level below which the race to the bottom cannot fall. If producers were to continue to produce below this level they would have to suffer the economic consequences of claims by consumers.

An important change was made to the implied quality terms in 1973 by the Supply of Goods (Implied Terms) Act. Previously the implied terms had been default rules. They were implied unless the parties agreed otherwise. This left the notion of freedom of contract and party autonomy intact in theory. In reality this initial allocation of rights might affect the contractual balance if traders failed to exclude them through inertia or because they did not want openly to refuse to agree to what were generally accepted minimum quality standards. Even if they did exclude them at least one could argue transparency was increased as consumers would be dealing with someone, they knew would not offer these minimum guarantees of quality. The move in 1973 to make these implied terms non-excludable in consumer contracts was part of the general move to control unfair terms. Clearly excluding minimum guarantees of quality would have been viewed as one of the most obviously unfair contractual provisions and

---

8   This is usually in connection with codes of practice: see Section 13.9.5.2.

9   G. Akerloff, 'The market for "Lemons": Quality, Uncertainty and the Market Mechanism' (1970) 84 *Journal of Law and Economics* 488.

have been an obvious target of regulatory activity. The motivations for such regulation would have been a mixture of concern about the consumer's inequality of bargaining power and the possibility that this is exploited by the trader; the danger of consumers being unfairly surprised by terms hidden in standard form contracts; and a normative desire on the part of some to create what they perceive to be fairer standards in the market place.

The issues surrounding controls on exclusion clauses are explored more fully in Chapter 5. Nevertheless the fact that implied terms are non-excludable makes the question of their content more crucial. If the standard is pitched too high then criticisms that the law restricts choice and can be anti-competitive might have more force, whilst if it is too low one might question whether it serves any useful purpose. It also raises questions about the relationship between the legal guarantees and the voluntary guarantees offered by retailers and producers (which we will call 'consumer guarantees'). If the legal guarantees are pitched at a high level, then there might be less need to control the consumer guarantees as the law would provide adequate protection. Where, however, the legal guarantees are less extensive there might be more justification in regulating the way consumer guarantees are offered because they need to be relied on more as a source of protection. In some legal systems the distinction between legal and consumer guarantees becomes blurred when consumer guarantees are required for some products[10] and their content even regulated by law.[11]

3.2 THE IMPACT OF EUROPE

The English law of sales has become more complicated since the first edition of this book. This is due to the adoption by the EC of Directive 1999/44/EC on certain aspects of the sale of consumer goods and associated guarantees.[12] Europe signalled its interest in the topic when in November 1993 the European Commission issued a *Green Paper on Guarantees for Consumer Goods and After-Sales Services*.[13] Provisions on this matter had previously been included in drafts of the Unfair Terms in Consumer Contracts Directive. The Council, however, saw the issues of

---

10   Spain has traditionally required guarantees to be provided for durable goods.

11   This is the tradition in Eastern Europe where the standardisation bodies typically specified the content of guarantees and often enforced compliance See G. Howells and H.-W. Micklitz, *Consumer Guarantees in Central and Eastern Europe – Approximation, Harmonisation and Compatibility with European Union Law* (Centre de droit de la Consommation, 2000).

12   OJ 1999 L171/12.

13   COM (93) 509.

unfair contract terms and guarantees as distinct and asked the Commission to consider whether harmonisation of national legislation in this area was needed. The *Green Paper* included a thorough survey of national laws on this subject. The diversities highlighted by that study were seen to justify the need for Community action. The Directive's recitals justify it in terms both of ensuring consumers are free to purchase in other states confident that they have the benefit of a uniform minimum set of fair rules and thereby act as a motor for the internal market and as means of preventing distortions in competition.

The Directive's emphasis on internal market thinking was explicable because its legal basis was linked to the internal market.[14] Yet it is surprising that concrete measures which might have really promoted consumer confidence in shopping in other member states by giving them an increased chance of finding a defendant in their home jurisdiction, were excluded. Recital 13 to the Directive does recommend that producers of consumer goods list one contact address in every state where their products are marketed. But this is only a recommendation and otherwise the Directive merely states there shall be a review of the case for introducing producer's direct liability by 7 July 2006 and even the more limited possibility of imposing liability on members of selective distribution networks was not taken up.[15] Under EC competition law members of such networks have to honour guarantees purchased through such networks, but not outside the official distribution network.[16]

The way confidence has been increased is to ensure that consumer sales law meets minimum standards throughout Europe. No longer can a consumer be defeated by the defence in Germany that the defect came to light more than six months after the sale or that a defect in Italy had not been reported to the seller within eight days.[17] It introduces a European wide consensus on the standards goods must meet if they are presumed to be in conformity with the contract and introduces a range of remedies available across Europe. In some countries this has produced great improvements in their level of consumer protection. Indeed in Germany it has been the impetus for a fundamental reform of their sales law in general.[18] In the United Kingdom there have been a few marginal improvements, but as our protection was quite high in any event the most

---

[14] Article 95 EC Treaty.

[15] Article 12.

[16] *Hasselblad (GB) Limited v Commission*, C–86/82 [1984] ECR 883 and *Metro ZSB-Großmärkte Gmbh & Co KG v Cartier SA*, C–376/92 [1994] ECR I–15.

[17] Article 5(2) now requires that any notification period be of a minimum of two months. The notification obligation is not included in UK law.

[18] H.-W. Micklitz, 'The New German Sales Law: Changing Patterns in the Regulation of Product Quality' (2002) 25 *Journal of Consumer Policy* 379.

notable feature has been that the law has become more complex. In part this was because the new regime, although integrated into existing legislation was placed on top of our existing regime in order not to reduce the level of protection afforded consumers. The method of implementation has also meant that consumer sales are now subject to a regime distinct from that applying to commercial sales, albeit that the existing implied terms remain at the heart of both systems. Looked from a purely UK perspective the Directive might well be viewed as a mixed blessing, but it is clear that Europe wide it has improved the lot of the consumer. The most important provisions of the Directive are those related to legal guarantees. The new rules on consumer guarantees are quite modest; whilst the possibility of regulating after-sales service, considered by the Green Paper, has not been acted upon.

3.3 CLASSIFICATION OF CONSUMER TRANSACTIONS

It is important to differentiate the various legal forms of consumer transactions in order to determine which legislation governs the transaction at hand. These laws are important for regulation of the quality of goods and services because they imply terms about quality. The importance of the distinctions between types of transactions has diminished as the statutory protection afforded consumers in sale transactions has been extended to other categories of transactions. The distinction nevertheless, remains important because, *inter alia*, a different standard is applied to contracts for services than to contracts for goods; only the Sale of Goods Act 1979 contains a detailed scheme covering the passing of property; the right to reject is lost in different circumstances in sale contracts than under other contracts, sale of goods contracts have special rules on mistake and frustration and there are some differences in the rules relating to exclusion clauses. The reader may wish to reflect whether it is sensible to maintain these different regimes, or whether the rules might not usefully be harmonised as part of a codification exercise to remove or at least reduce the differences.

3.3.1 Sale

During the 19th-century a considerable body of case law developed around the buyer/seller relationship. Sir Mackenzie Chalmers was given the task of drafting Sale of Goods legislation which codified the common law position and the Sale of Goods Act appeared on the statute book in 1893. The Act was amended by the Supply of Goods (Implied Terms) Act 1973, and these and other changes were consolidated in the Sale of Goods Act 1979.[19] This in turn has been amended by the Sale and Supply of Goods Act 1994 and most recently the Sale and Supply of Goods to Consumers Regulations 2002.[20]

Section 2(1), Sale of Goods Act 1979 defines a contract of sale as 'a contract by which the seller transfers or agrees to transfer the property in goods to the buyer for a money consideration, called the price'. The two key elements of the definition are the commitment to transfer ownership and the requirement for a money consideration.

The requirement that there must be a commitment to transfer ownership explains why a hire-purchase agreement is not a sale. A hire-purchase agreement involves a hire contract with an option to purchase. Although the option is usually a mere technicality the possibility remains that the consumer could meet his hire obligations and then decide not to exercise his option to purchase and simply return the goods to their owner. By contrast a 'credit sale' is a straightforward sale, with the buyer simply being given time to pay the price. A 'conditional sale' is more like a hire-purchase agreement, since it provides for the payment of the price by instalments, with an agreement that the property will be transferred at some future time, usually when all the instalments have been paid. However, conditional sales remain within the scope of the Sale of Goods Act since there is a commitment to sell and are known as 'agreements to sell'; however, they have been assimilated to hire-purchase contracts for certain purposes.[21]

If the contract is not for a money consideration, it will be one of barter or exchange which is now governed by the Supply of Goods and Services Act 1982. We discuss below the difficult matter of how part-exchange contracts should be classified. The lack of a money consideration also means that the Sale of Goods Act 1979 does not cover gifts which are again within the scope of the 1982 Act.[22]

Section 61(1), Sale of Goods Act 1979 defines goods as including 'all personal chattels other than things in action and money...; and in particular "goods" includes emblements, industrial growing crops, and things

---

[19] The Law Reform (Enforcement of Contracts) Act 1954 removed the rule which rendered unenforceable contracts for the sale of goods valued at more than ten pounds which had not been evidenced in writing.

[20] S.I. 2002/3045.

[21] See e.g. s. 25(2), Sale of Goods Act 1979 and s. 14, Supply of Goods (Implied Terms) Act 1973.

[22] The Unsolicited Goods and Services Acts 1971 and 1975 allow a consumer to treat as an unconditional gift goods which are sent to him unsolicited where the sender does not recover them within six months or within 30 days of having a notice served on him by the recipient.

attached to or forming part of the land which are agreed to be severed before sale or under the contract of sale'. An interesting point is whether blood comes within the definition of goods. This has become particularly acute in recent times with a number of scares involving blood or blood products contaminated with the HIV virus. In the US the dominant trend is to treat the supply of blood as a service and hence subject to negligence rather than strict liability standards.[23] We shall see that such cases have been treated in the UK as product liability cases.[24] There are also debates concerning whether software programmes are goods, although a distinction seems to be developing between 'off-the-shelf discs' which are treated as goods and programmes devised or adapted for a specific purpose which are more readily viewed as having a sizeable service element.

3.3.2 Hire-purchase

Section 15, Supply of Goods (Implied Terms) Act 1973, and s. 189(1), Consumer Credit Act 1974, both provide a definition of a hire-purchase agreement which requires (a) that the goods are bailed in return for periodic payments, and (b) that the property in the goods will pass if the terms of the agreement are complied with and one of the following occurs: (i) an option to purchase is exercised, (ii) a specified act is performed by a party to the agreement, or (iii) any other specified event happens.

In part the development of hire-purchase was a response to the legal regime which used to exist. The use of hire-purchase side-stepped the requirement, which existed until 1954, that contracts for goods valued at more than ten pounds had to be evidenced in writing; it also avoided the statutory scheme which had been put into place by the Sale of Goods Act 1893. The value to traders of using hire-purchase contracts was greatly enhanced by two decisions at the end of the last century. In *Helby v Matthews*[25] a hirer was held not to be a person who had bought or agreed to buy goods and so could not pass a good title on to a third party by virtue of s. 25(1), Sale of Goods Act 1979. *McEntire v Crossley Bros.*[26] decided that a hire-purchase contract did not need to be registered under the Bill of Sales Acts 1878 and 1882 as the hirer has no property over which to grant security.

---

23   See *Hyland Therapeutics v Superior Court* 175 Cal. App. 3d 509, 220 Cal Rptr. 590
     (1985): and see discussion in A. Clark, *Product Liability,* (Sweet & Maxwell, 1989) at
     pp. 61–2.
24   See Section 4.2.4.3.
25   [1895] AC 471.
26   [1895] AC 457.

The common law had implied terms into hire-purchase contracts similar to those implied into sale contracts; these were placed on a statutory footing by the Supply of Goods (Implied Terms) Act 1973. When we consider consumer credit we shall note that various aspects of the credit element of hire-purchase transactions were covered by the Hire-Purchase Acts of 1938 and, particularly, of 1964. This regulation by form caused some creditors to chose other less well regulated forms of credit provision before the Consumer Credit Act 1974 provided a comprehensive regime for regulating consumer credit based on the substance and not the form of the transaction.

3.3.3 Barter or Exchange

An important requirement for there to be a sale of goods is a money consideration. Where instead goods are transferred for other goods, there is a contract of barter and exchange.[27] Part 1 of the Supply of Goods and Services Act 1982 implies terms regarding title, description, quality and fitness into contracts 'for the transfer of goods'. This covers contracts under which a person agrees to transfer the property in goods other than excepted contracts.[28] Excepted contracts include (1) those covered by similar legislation (such as sale, hire-purchase and trading stamps),[29] (2) transfers made by deed, without any consideration other than the presumed consideration imported by the deed, and (3) contracts involving mortgages, pledges, charges or other security.[30]

Esso Petroleum Ltd v Commissioners of Customs and Excise[31] involved a promotion in which coins bearing likenesses of the 1970 English football World Cup squad were given away with every four gallons of petrol. In a case brought by the Customs and Excise to determine whether purchase tax was payable on the coins, the House of Lords held that the coins were not supplied under a contract for the sale of goods since the consideration was not money but the collateral contract of buying the petrol. Professor Atiyah has argued that this was a wrong interpretation because the four gallons of petrol had to be paid for by means of a cash consideration.[32] Much of the significance of this distinction has now been

---

27 Of course money is sometimes transferred, not for its value as a unit of currency, but for its own collector's value, in which case it could form the basis of a contract of exchange; see *Moss v Hancock* [1899] 2 QB 111.

28 Section 1(1), Supply of Goods and Services Act 1982.

29 See Trading Stamps Act 1964.

30 Section 1(2), Supply of Goods and Services Act 1982.

31 [1976] 1 All ER 117.

32 P.S. Atiyah (1976) 39 *MLR* 335.

removed by the enactment of the Supply of Goods and Services Act 1982, but it remains significant because some differences persist, for instance the question of when property passes.

The time of property passing was the crucial issue in the Irish case of *Flynn v Mackin and Mahon*,[33] which raised the interesting question of whether a part-exchange deal was a sale or barter. This involved the purchase of a new car for the buyer's old car and £250. The transaction was held to be one of barter, but it seemed clear that if the parties had fixed a price for the old car then it would have been a sale. In *Aldridge v Johnson*[34] a transfer of barley for bullocks with money covering the difference was held to be a sale as a money value had been given to them. *Bull v Parker*[35] involved the exchange of new riding equipment for old and £2; here no value had been fixed, but the court accepted the value of the new equipment as being £4. If a sale can be found where either the parties have fixed a value on the goods or the value can be readily ascertained, then most consumer part-exchanges will be sales since the price of new consumer durables are fairly standard and the value of the exchanged item can be assumed to be the price of the new item minus the cash element.[36] However, it may be possible to see the part-exchange deal as involving two contracts: a sale of the new goods and an exchange of the part-exchanged goods.

3.3.4 Work and Materials

Whenever goods are supplied, one is in a sense paying for both the raw materials and the skill of the designer and manufacturers of the finished product. In some instances, however, the skill element becomes dominant so that, as was said in *Watson v Buckley Osborne & Co*, the contract 'is really half the rendering of services and in a sense, half the supply of goods'.[37] That case involved a hairdresser applying hair dye, with the consequence that strict liability for (the then) merchantable quality was applied to the goods element. One test used is whether the court considers the delivery of a product is the main element of the contract (a contract for the sale of goods) or whether the skill and labour are the main element and

---

33   [1974] IR 101: see C. Canton, (1976) 39 *MLR* 589.
34   (1857) 7 E&B 883.
35   (1842) 2 Dowling N.S. 345.
36   Cf. s. 73, Consumer Credit Act 1974 which provides, that where a credit contract is cancelled and goods have been taken in part-exchange, then they should be returned or a part-exchange allowance paid equal to the sum agreed or, failing that, such sum as it would have been reasonable to allow in respect of the part-exchanged goods.
37   [1940] 1 All ER 174 at 180.

the passing of the article is ancillary (a contract for work and materials). An alternative approach is to consider that all contracts should be viewed as contracts of sale where the purpose is to transfer goods to a consumer which he or she did not previously own.[38] This latter approach seemed to dominant, but the former may have been reintroduced by courts which have rephrased the question to ask what is the substance of the contract, rather than what is the more substantive component in the product ultimately delivered.[39] These tests are of course somewhat arbitrary and one has to agree with the editors of *Benjamin* that 'It has yet to be appreciated that a decision of this problem can be reached only by adopting one or the other of these equally arbitrary rules'.[40] The practical consequences of the classification have been much reduced of late, although the distinction retains some residual relevance. Also it should be mentioned that the courts have become more flexible and no longer require that a contract should categorically be classified under one heading or the other. Thus in *Hyundai Heavy Industries Ltd v Papadopoulos*[41] a contract to build a ship was held to be a contract of sale, but it was recognised that it also had some of the characteristics of a building contract.

Again the significance of the distinction between contracts for the sale of goods and other contracts has decreased. The Law Reform (Enforcement of Contracts) Act 1954 removed the requirement that contracts for the sale of goods valued at £10 or more had to be evidenced in writing. Also the implied terms in sale of goods contracts have been extended to the goods element of a contract for work and materials, first by case law[42] and then by statute in the Supply of Goods and Services Act 1982. However the distinction is still relevant in determining the consumer's right to reject goods and terminate the contract, in determining the time when property passes and possibly also in the recovery of advance payments by a consumer who defaults. In a contract for work and materials the goods element is governed by Part I and the service element by Part II, Supply of Goods and Services Act 1982.

3.3.5 Hire

Section 6(1), Supply of Goods and Services Act 1982 provides that 'a contract for the hire of goods' means a contract under which one person

---

[38] *Lee v Griffin* (1861) 1 B and S 272. In this case the Court in fact adopted a different approach.

[39] *Robinson v Graves* [1935] 1 KB 579.

[40] Benjamin's *Sale of Goods*, (6th ed.) (Sweet & Maxwell, 2002), at p. 38.

[41] [1980] 2 All ER 29.

[42] See notably *Young & Marten Ltd v McManus Childs Ltd* [1969] 1 AC 454.

bails or agrees to bail goods to another by way of hire, other than an excepted contract'. Consumers may sometimes prefer to hire than to buy for several reasons. Generally the repairing obligation under a hire contract remains with the owner. Thus when televisions were first marketed and were less reliable in performance than their modern counterparts, many consumers preferred to hire and leave the repairing obligation on the rental company. This is a less common reason for renting nowadays, not only because of improved product standards, but also because firms prefer to sell goods and then offer insurance cover against breakdown. These insurance policies also raise important consumer protection issues, with reports that some stores push their own policies rather than the cheaper cover offered by some manufacturers.[43] Renting is also useful when goods are rapidly developing in sophistication. Renters usually have far greater flexibility in upgrading to a newer model than do owners. Also renting may be a cheaper option for a consumer than buying, especially where the goods are only wanted for a short period. Of course hirers of goods have the same interest as buyers in the quality of goods and Part I, Supply of Goods and Services Act 1982 implies similar terms to those provided for under the Sale of Goods Act 1979.

3.3.6 Service

Too frequently consumer lawyers concentrate on sale of goods law and neglect the large amount of consumer contracts which concern services. Some of these relate to the consumer's health and safety and are therefore of vital importance, although medical negligence has expanded to such an extent that it has now become a topic in its own right. Other service contracts are vital to the consumer's economic interest, such as insurance and banking law. It is important to note that the financial services sectors have often managed to exempt themselves from general consumer protection measures.[44] Again these are areas which merit book length consideration in their own right. There remain, however, a large number of mainstream consumer service contracts covering, for example, hairdressers, car repairers, plumbers, decorators, electricians and gas-fitters. Generally these types of contracts are unregulated, with self-regulatory controls varying in effectiveness from sector to sector. Some,

---

[43]   See Chapter 3.8.

[44]   For instance, they were excluded from the Unfair Contract Terms Act 1977, but are subject to Unfair Terms in Consumer Contracts Regulations 1999.

such as estate agents, travel agents and tour operators, have proved especially troublesome and have been subjected to special regulation.[45]

Section 12, Supply of Goods and Services Act 1982 defines a 'contract for the supply of a service' as being one under which a supplier agrees to carry out a service. Part II of the Act implies terms into service contracts, though these are generally less demanding than for goods. For instance, a supplier is only under the implied obligation to carry out the service with reasonable care and skill. Contracts of service and apprenticeships are excluded, but a contract is a contract for the supply of a service, whether or not it also relates to the transfer, bailment or hire of goods. As noted, the goods element is covered by Part I, Supply of Goods and Services Act 1982.

3.4 MISREPRESENTATION AND EXPRESS TERMS

When seeking redress for poor quality goods and services the consumer lawyer instinctively looks to the statutory implied terms as the source of protection. This is often the easiest route and we will devote a great deal of attention to these terms as they not only have great practical significance, but also at a legal policy level are indicative of how the legal system approaches the special needs of consumer protection.

Nevertheless it is important not to forget other contractual rules.[46] In many cases the starting point will be what was actually said between the parties and what the contract expressly stated. Statements made by sellers may either be misrepresentations or terms of the contract. Relevant factors in determining whether they are misrepresentations or terms are (i) the stage when the statement was made (the nearer to the contract the more likely it is to be held to be a term); (ii) the importance of the statement; and (iii) the respective knowledge, skill or expertise of the parties. The courts are more likely to construe statements to be terms in consumer contracts.[47] Such an approach has been facilitated in recent times by an acceptance that the parol evidence rule is only a presumption and the written contract may not be the whole of the agreement.

For misrepresentations it is possible to seek rescission[48] and where the statement was made fraudulently or negligently damages are available.

---

45   . Estate Agents Act 1979 and Package Travel, Package Holidays and Package Tours Regulations, S.I. 1992/3288.

46   A useful summary is found in C. Willett, 'The Role of Contract Law in Product Liability' in *Product Liability*, G. Howells (ed.) (Butterworths, 2001).

47   See, *Oscar Chess Ltd v Williams* [1965] 1 WLR 623.

48   Damages can be awarded in lieu of rescission where the statement was made otherwise than fraudulently: s. 2(2) Misrepresentation Act 1965.

Where the negligent misrepresentations preceded a contract the consumer does not need to rely on the common law doctrine of *Hedley Byrne v Heller*,[49] but can rely on s. 2(1) of the Misrepresentation Act 1965 which places the burden on the party making the statement to prove he had reasonable grounds to believe and did believe the facts represented to be true.

Once a statement becomes a term of the contract it has to be classified as a condition, warranty or innominate term. Breach of a condition gives rise to the right to repudiate the contract and claim damages; only damages can be claimed for breach of warranty; whereas whether breach of an innominate terms allows repudiation depends upon how serious the consequences of the breach are. Owing to the serious consequences of breaching a condition the courts will be slow to hold a term to be such and a party desiring to ensure they can terminate the contract for breach of a term should specify it is a condition in this strict sense in the clearest possible terms.[50] It is possible that some express terms will make precise statements about the quality of the goods. A recent case considered whether such terms related to the quality of goods at the moment of their delivery or whether there was a continuing warranty.[51] This was relevant for limitation purposes. Although much will turn on the precise wording of the term it seems usually such terms will refer to the condition of the goods on delivery and hence limitations periods will run from that moment.

However, many pre-contractual statements may have no legal significance as they will be 'mere puffs', too loosely worded or obviously exorbitant to be expected to have legal consequences. Furthermore most advertisements will not have contractual significance as they are classed as invitations to treat and thus form no more than the impetus for contractual agreement which starts in earnest when the consumer makes an offer in response to the advertisement and this is accepted by the trader. In this way traders can protect themselves from potentially serious mistakes where prices are mislabelled. If incorrect prices on websites, for example, were treated as offers then a trader could find himself committed to thousands of disadvantageous contracts before the mistake was realised and the offer withdrawn.[52]

---

49 [1964] AC 465.

50 Even describing it as a condition may not be enough to ensure the courts treat it as a condition in this strict sense: *Schuler v Wickman* [1974] AC 235.

51 *VAI Industries v Bostock* [2003] BLR 359, noted by C. Twigg-Flesner (2004) 120 *LQR* 214.

52 For example, Dixons sent e-mails offering laptops for 99p instead of £900 and Amazon's UK site advertised iPaq Pocket PC's for £7.32 instead of the normal price of £300.

There are times when advertisements can be framed in such specific terms that consumers can rely on them. The classic example is *Carlill v Carbollic Smoke Ball*,[53] which as all first year law students know involved a company being bound by its advertisement to compensate individuals catching influenza after using the smoke balls. Equally, Hoover famously found themselves committed to offering customers who had bought their products free holidays in America. Also sometimes pre-contractual statements of producers can lay the foundation for a claim based on collateral warranty.[54]

However, instances of contractual liability in such situations remain the exceptions rather than the rule. Moreover, it is difficult for common law contract doctrines to impose liability for pre-contractual statements in advertising or elsewhere where they are typically made the manufacturer, and yet the contract is concluded with the retailer. One impact of the recent changes to sales law brought about by implementation of the Directive has been to address this problem to some extent.[55]

In the UK such liability as has been imposed on manufacturers has been through the manipulation of contract rules, such as those relating to collateral warranties Some countries have addressed this problem through tort liability. American law has generally found manufacturers liable in tort where there has been an express warranty in the absence of privity, even for pure economic losses.[56] In Australia and New Zealand statutory reforms have held manufacturers liable for their promotional material.[57] Recovery in English law is more limited for, under *Hedley Byrne v Heller*[58] economic losses resulting from negligent misstatements require the parties to be in a special relationship.[59] In *Lambert v Lewis*[60] Stephenson LJ said: 'We cannot regard the manufacturer and supplier of an article as putting himself into a special relationship with every distributor who obtains his product and reads what he says or prints about it and so owing him a duty to take reasonable care to give him true information or

---

[53] [1893] 1 QB 256.

[54] *Shanklin Pier Ltd v Detel Products* [1951] 2 KB 854.

[55] See Section 3.5.6.3.

[56] *Randy Knitwear Inc v American Cyanamid Co* 181 NE 2d 399 (1962); *Seely v White Motor Company* 403 P 2d 145 (1965): see generally J. Phillips, 'Misrepresentation and Products Liability' (1990) 20 *Anglo-Am LR* 327.

[57] See J. Goldring, L. Maher and J. McKeough, *Consumer Protection Law*, (Federation Press, 1993); S. Todd, 'Consumer Law Reform in New Zealand: the Consumer Guarantees Act 1993' (1994) 2 *Consum LJ* 100.

[58] [1964] AC 465.

[59] See generally R. Bradgate, 'Misrepresentation and Product Liability in English Law', (1990) 20 *Anglo-Am LR* 334.

[60] [1982] AC 225 at 264.

good advice'. Recent developments relating to the concept of duty of care in the general law of negligence, such as *Caparo Industries Ltd v Dickman*[61] and *Murphy v Brentwood DC*,[62] support this restrictive approach.

Given the lack of a tortious remedy in the United Kingdom, a fundamental problem with relying on contract to deal with pre-contractual statements is that contractual obligations are only enforceable by consumers against the party contracted with.[63] Producers, who do not sell their products directly to the consumer, do not have any legal responsibility to the consumer for the quality of the goods, save where they cause damage covered by product liability laws.[64] The recent EC Directive ducked the issue of making producers directly liable for the quality of goods and instead proposed this issue be reviewed in the future. From a European perspective it would be helpful to have producer liability as this might improve access to redress for goods brought in another member state if the producer has representatives across Europe. In terms of justice it might also be thought natural that the person responsible for producing the poor quality product should be liable.[65] Of course there would also be a number of issues to be resolved, such as how producers could be protected for liability resulting from the actions or representations of sellers and also how any damages might be calculated as the producer would doubtless have sold his product for less than the consumer paid. For the time being, however, liability for quality defects in English law rests solely on the person who contracted with the consumer. The EC Directive does give the final seller the right of redress against the person responsible higher up the contractual chain. The UK has done nothing to implement this and it is uncertain whether the existing contract rules comply as they would permit reasonable exclusion clauses in the commercial contracts between links in the supply chain.

---

[61]   [1990] 1 All ER 568.

[62]   [1990] 2 All ER 908.

[63]   In limited circumstances the Contracts (Rights of Third Parties) Act 1999 might assist, but will rarely be invoked in typical consumer situations.

[64]   See Chapter 4.

[65]   R. Bradgate and C. Twigg-Flesner 'Expanding the boundaries of liability for quality defects' (2002) 25 *Journal of Consumer Policy* 345 and *Consultation Document on Consumer Guarantees* (DTI, 1992).

3.5 IMPLIED TERMS

3.5.1 Background

The Sale of Goods Act 1979 (and analogous legislation covering other supply contracts) imply terms governing the quality of goods supplied.[66] Services are also dealt with in the Supply of Goods and Services Act 1982.

The 1979 Act is based on the provisions of the Sale of Goods Act 1893 and these were themselves merely a codification of the common law principles. This common law origin has for a long time been an important influence on how the law has been interpreted. Indeed we shall note a conservative approach to interpretation was adopted which referred back to the common law origin of rules, even when for instance a modern statutory definition of merchantable quality was introduced. Only recently does the law seem to be taking a more modern approach signalled by the change in terminology to satisfactory rather than merchantable quality and hopefully underlined by the introduction of new rules originating in Europe which cannot simply be interpreted in the typical common law tradition.

3.5.2 Classification of Terms

The legislation implies terms requiring that goods correspond with their description, are fit for their purpose and are of satisfactory (formerly merchantable) quality.[67] The implied quality terms for goods are classed as conditions.[68] Breach of a condition even to a minor extent, gives the buyer the right to reject the goods and/or claim damages, although restrictions have recently been placed on the non-consumer buyer's right to reject. There is strict liability for breach of these terms; in other words, a seller cannot claim that it was not his or her fault that the term was breached or even that it was impossible for him to prevent the term being breached.[69]

This strict liability in relation to the quality of goods should be contrasted with the position in relation to services, where suppliers are

---

[66]　Reference will be made mainly to sale contracts in the following text, but also where appropriate to corresponding provisions in other statutes. For a discussion of which Acts correspond to which transactions, see Chapter 3.3.

[67]　There are also terms implied relating to sale by sample, but we will not consider these save to note the general principle that goods must correspond with both their description and any sample; see, for instance, s. 15, Sale of Goods Act 1979. In the consumer context this may be relevant, for instance, in the sale of carpets.

[68]　Section 14(6) Sale of Goods Act 1979: this allows rejection of the goods and repudiation of the contract for their breach.

[69]　*Frost v Aylesbury Dairy Co* [1905] 1 KB 608.

only required to carry out the service with reasonable skill and care.[70] Also this is not a condition and so whether breach gives rise to a right to terminate the contract will depend upon the seriousness of the breach.

3.5.3 Implied Terms and the Conformity Principle

The implied term is a technique of the common law. Other countries laid down minimum quality standards often with very similar objectives, but using different legal mechanisms. When enacting the Consumer Sales Directive the European legislator was struggling for an umbrella term to blend the different traditions and decided upon the rule that the seller must supply goods which are 'in conformity with the contract of sale'.[71] It then lists a number of factors which if the goods comply with they should be viewed as being in conformity with the contract.[72] These could map quite easily on to the implied terms to be considered below as they govern, compliance with description, sample or model, fitness for particular purpose, fitness for normal purposes and having normal quality and performance. The UK has indeed in the implementing law, the Sale and Supply of Goods to Consumers Regulations 2002,[73] relied heavily upon its existing implied terms, modified to take account of the new requirement to consider public statements by the retailer, producer or his representative. Although it has introduced a new remedies regime predicated on goods not conforming to the contract, this concept is merely defined as breach of an express term or a term implied by s. 13–15 Sale of Goods Act 1979.[74]

This seems an acceptable method of implementation. Although it creates a bifurcated standard for consumer and non-consumer sales it does at least maintain the traditional English law concepts.[75] Directives are intended to give member states some freedom over the manner of implementation, but it is a fine line between justified national deviations and non-implementation, particularly as the European Court has at times been rather strict in requiring transparency of implementation.[76] Some doubts have been raised as to whether the Directive fully implements the Directive although our hunch is that given the generally high level of

---

[70] Section 13, Supply of Goods and Services Act 1982. See 3.5.8.

[71] Article 2(1).

[72] Article 2(2).

[73] S.I. 2002/3045.

[74] Section 48F, Sale of Goods Act 1979.

[75] In the longer term there may be some sense in looking at the need for separate consumer and non-consumer sales regimes: see M. Bridge, 'What is to be done about Sale of Goods?' (2003) 119 LQR 173.

[76] *Commission v Netherlands*, C–144/99 [2001] ECR I–3541.

protection afforded to consumers by sales law the Commission will not see bringing infringement proceedings against the UK as a priority.

The following discrepancies have been noted by Bradgate and Twigg-Flesner:[77] (i) description in the Directive is not limited to essential characteristics as it is in s. 13, Sale of Goods Act 1979; (ii) the rules on sale by sample in s. 15 Sale of Goods Act 1979 are more limited than those on reference to sample in the Directive; (iii) the Directive refers to the purposes for which goods are 'normally' supplied, which some suggest may be broader than the phrased 'commonly' supplied in the Sale of Goods Act 1979, (iv) there is no reference in English law to the 'performance' which is normal in goods of the same type; (iv) the rules relating to non-conformity due to incorrect installation do not provide for strict liability as they are implemented by reference to the reasonable skill and care standard of s. 13, Supply of Goods and Services Act 1982. Some of these such as whether performance needs to be stated and whether there is a difference between normally and commonly could easily be seen as legitimate national variations; the others (especially the negligence standard for installations) perhaps raise more legitimate concerns. Bradgate and Twigg-Flesner also raise concerns about whether the new remedies regime is too generous to traders, by allowing them too wide a choice of alternative remedies to repair or replacement.[78] This however arises out of ambiguity in the Directive itself.

A potentially significant practical impact of the Directive is that where the buyer deals as a consumer there is a presumption that the goods did not conform at the date of delivery to the contract of sale, if the non-conformity came to light within six months of delivery.[79] However this presumption is only a presumption and so does not apply if it is established that the goods did conform at the date of delivery. Equally it does not apply where it is incompatible with the nature of the goods or the nature or the lack or conformity. Thus one would not expect soft fruit to remain in a satisfactory condition for six months! Equally if a glass is smashed, the most likely explanation is that it was dropped and not due to a quality defect.

---

[77] R. Bradgate and C. Twigg-Flesner, *Blackstone's Guide to Consumer Sales and Associated Guarantees*, (OUP, 2003). In their careful analysis they also note several other possible inconsistencies. See also C. Willett, M. Morgan-Taylor and A. Naidoo, 'The Sale and Supply of Goods to Consumers Regulations' [2004] JBL 94.

[78] See Chapter 3.6.7.

[79] Section 48A(3)–(4), Sale of Goods Act 1979; s. 11M(3)–(4) Supply of Goods and Services Act 1982.

3.5.4 Correspondence with Description[80]

In comparison with the implied terms, which mandate minimum quality standards, the requirement that goods comply with their description might appear rather weak. It can, however, be an important source of consumer protection since it is implied in all sales contracts, not merely those where the sale is in the course of a business which is a requirement for the quality conditions to be implied. Also it can apply where the goods fail to conform to the description, even if they are of proper quality and perform the task expected of them. For instance, it would provide redress where a suit described as being 'all wool' is partly synthetic. The description condition can also relate to the quality of goods supplied. Thus an aspect of quality can be made an element of the description itself; the presence of extraneous material may then breach the description condition.[81] In addition, whether goods are fit for their usual purposes may help decide whether they comply with their description.[82]

Section 13(1) makes the implication of the term that goods comply with their description dependent on there being a 'contract for the sale of goods by description'. Where the contract concerns future or unascertained goods, it will always be one by description. However, it is more problematic to apply this to contracts of specific goods (i.e. where the contract relates to particular goods, not goods of a particular kind). Case law originally gave a liberal interpretation to this phrase, as shown by Lord Wright in *Grant v Australian Knitting Mills*[83] stating:

> there is a sale by description even though the buyer is buying something displayed before him on the counter: a thing is sold by description, though it is specific, so long as it is sold not merely as a specific thing, but as a thing corresponding to a description.

---

[80] Section 13, Sale of Goods Act 1979; ss. 3 and 8, Supply of Goods and Services Act 1982; s. 9 Supply of Goods (Implied Terms) Act 1973.

[81] In *Pinnock Bros v Lewis and Peat Ltd* [1923] 1 KB 690, copra cake was not held to be properly so described because of the presence of castor beans; but cf. *Ashington Piggeries v Christopher Hill* [1972] AC 441 where the House of Lords found that herring meal was properly so described despite the presence of dimethylnitrosamine which rendered it unfit for use as mink food.

[82] Thus Davies LJ in the Court of Appeal in *Christopher Hill v Ashington Piggeries* [1969] 3 All ER 1496 gave the example of oysters which he suggested may not properly be described as such if they were not fit for human consumption. Similarly in *Toepfer v Continental Grain Co* [1974] Lloyd LR 11 the example of 'new-laid eggs' was used to show that a description of goods can include a statement of their quality.

[83] [1936] AC 85 at 100.

This generous interpretation was probably given because, at that time, there had to be a sale by description for the merchantable quality condition (as it then was) to be implied. This is no longer the case, but case law has been confirmed by s. 13(3), Sale of Goods Act 1979 which provides 'a sale of goods is not prevented from being a sale by description by reason only that, the goods being exposed for sale or hire, are selected by the buyer'. This is of course the position with regard to supermarket purchases.

Section 13 might be considered remarkable for it appears to state that express terms of the contract will also be implied terms. The danger is that too many representations about the product are elevated to the status of terms in reliance on s. 13, so that the distinction between contractual terms and representations is obliterated.[84] This is especially dangerous as some of the decisions, although admittedly in commercial contexts, have found the condition breached and rejection possible for very minor breaches of description.[85] The modern approach is to limit the elements of the description covered by the implied condition, with other aspects of the description being treated as warranties or innominate terms. Thus Lord Diplock in *Ashington Piggeries v Christopher Hill*[86] stated:

> The description by which unascertained goods are sold is... confined to those words in the contract which were intended by the parties to identify the kinds of goods supplied.

More recently, in *Harlingdon & Leinster Enterprises v Christopher Hull Fine Art*,[87] this trend was reinforced when it was said that there could be no sale by description unless that description was so influential as to become an essential term of the contract.

3.5.5 Quality Conditions – Some Common Features

The common law principle of *caveat emptor* (buyer beware) is still to be found in the Sale of Goods Act 1979, s. 14(1) providing that:

---

[84] See *Beale v Taylor* [1967] 1 WLR 1193.

[85] *Arcos Ltd v Ronaasen & Son* [1933] AC 470 (order of half-inch thick staves to make cement barrels was rejected as only five per cent met specification although nearly all the rest were good to within one tenth of an inch); *Re Moore & Co and Landauer & Co Ltd* [1921] 2 KB 519 (involved the delivery of the correct number of tins of canned fruit (3000); but rejection allowed as half the cases contained 24 instead of the prescribed 30 tins, despite an arbitrator's finding that the value was unaffected).

[86] [1972] AC 441 at 503.

[87] [1990] 1 All ER 737.

> Except as provided by this section and s. 15 below and subject to any other enactment, there is no implied term about the quality or fitness for any particular purpose of goods supplied under a contract of sale.

However, this basic statement of the *caveat emptor* principle has in modern times been highly qualified by the existence of implied terms relating to the fitness and quality of goods. Of central importance are the implied conditions of merchantable quality and fitness for purpose. Before examining the particular features of these two implied quality conditions certain features common to both terms will be considered.

3.5.5.1 Limitation to Business Activity

In the 1893 Act the merchantable quality condition was made contingent on the seller dealing in goods of that description, whilst the fitness for purpose condition was implied into contracts where the goods were of a description which it was in the course of the seller's business to supply. These provisions could have been quite narrowly interpreted to exclude sales which were not part of the essential functions of the business, for example, sales by a petrol station which sold cuddly toys as a special promotion might have been excluded. The Supply of Goods (Implied Terms) Act 1973 implemented the recommendations of the Law Commission[88] so that the quality conditions were implied wherever there was a sale 'in the course of a business'.

There is a danger that if the narrow interpretation given by courts in other contexts to the phrase 'in the course of a business' is applied to sale of goods legislation then the position could be similar to that prior to the 1973 amendments. Some sales of goods by businesses might not attract the protection of the implied terms if they do not form an essential element of the business. This narrow interpretation is present in trade description and unfair contract terms legislation, where the courts have only held sales to be in the course of a business if they were an integral part of the business.[89] In those contexts, such an interpretation may have policy justifications – namely not imposing criminal liability for false trade descriptions on private individuals, and extending the absolute ban on the use of certain exclusion clauses to small businesses when making purchases not connected with their own trade or profession. A similar

---

88   Law Com 24 and Scot Law Com 12, Exemption Clauses in Contracts First Report: Amendments to the Sale of Goods Act 1893 (1969).

89   On trade descriptions see *Davies v Sumner* (1984) 1 WLR 1301(discussed at Chapter 8.2.2). See Chs. 9 and 10 and on unfair terms see *R & B Custom Brokers Co Ltd v United Dominions Trust Ltd* (1988) 1 WLR 321 (discussed at Chapter 5.6.2).

narrow interpretation in the present context would pose a serious threat to consumer protection. Such an approach seemed unlikely, especially given the view of Lord Wilberforce in *Ashington Piggeries v Christopher Hill*[90] when he said:

> I cannot comprehend the rationale of holding that the subsections do not apply if the seller is dealing in the particular goods for the first time... what the Act had in mind was something quite simple and rational: to limit the implied conditions of fitness or quality to persons in the way of business as distinct from private persons.

This has been strongly confirmed by the Court of Appeal in *Stevenson v Rogers*[91] where a sale by a fisherman of his only boat in order to replace it was held to be a sale in the course of business. The Court looked at Hansard and the Law Commission reports and noted there had been a deliberate change of wording in 1973 and there was no evidence this had intended to be changed when the laws were consolidated in 1979. The result was that there was no requirement for regularity of dealings and it was sufficient that the sale was not made by a private individual. Decisions which had in other contexts read a requirement of regularity of dealing in that type of goods were viewed as limited to their particular contexts.

The provision would therefore seem to catch a broader category of transactions than the position pre-1973, but some grey areas still remain as to what counts as a business. The only assistance to interpretation given in the Act is that business includes 'a profession and the activities of any government department (including a Northern Ireland department) or local or public authority'.[92] It is still a matter of speculation whether charities are to be treated as businesses, although one might expect that when charities operate on a commercial basis the provisions would apply to them. It is also uncertain whether the provisions catch the 'amateur entrepreneur', for example, someone who makes jewellery and sells it at car boot sales to supplement their normal income.

3.5.5.2 'Goods Supplied'

The implied terms of fitness for purpose and satisfactory quality relate to goods supplied under the contract. The phrase 'goods supplied' has been interpreted widely to include (i) extraneous goods supplied with the goods contracted for, such as the detonator which was included in the supply of

---

[90] [1972] AC 441 at 494.
[91] (1999) 2 WLR 1064.
[92] Section 61, Sale of Goods Act 1979.

coalite in *Wilson v Rickett Cockerell & Co Ltd*,[93] and also (ii) the packaging and containers in which goods are supplied, like the returnable mineral water bottle in *Geddling v Marsh*.[94]

3.5.6 Satisfactory Quality[95]

The implied term that goods comply with their description and the term requiring goods to be fit for a purpose made known by the buyer to the seller (considered below at 3.5.2) are relatively uncontroversial. Everyone can agree that goods should be as described and fit for their purpose, especially where it is clear that the seller know of the purpose and that their skill or judgment is being relied upon by the buyer. It is more difficult to agree what general standard should be expected of all goods.

Imposing mandatory standards regulating the quality of goods can be criticised as infringing the consumer's freedom to bargain for a reduced price in return for a reduced quality product, or at least an assumption of responsibility for any defects which occur. However, the law has long recognised the desirability of imposing such a right to minimum quality. The common law implied a term that goods should be of 'merchantable quality' and this was codified in the Sale of Goods Act 1893. Merchantable quality was also to be found in the Sale of Goods Act 1979 and analogous legislation for other supply contracts, before the Sale and Supply of Goods Act 1994 reformed the implied term to one of 'satisfactory quality'.

So long as the term was implied only to the extent that the parties had not excluded or modified it, it could be said not to infringe the doctrine of freedom of contract. It could be taken as reflecting the minimum quality condition which would have applied had the parties been forced to agree a term acceptable to both. However, we have noted that since 1973 the term has been non-excludable in consumer contracts.[96] It cannot be denied that freedom of contract has been restricted, but such restrictions are justified since a seller who supplies goods without basic assurances as to their quality can be assumed to be exploiting the consumer's weak bargaining position or vulnerability, since no right-thinking person would buy goods without such a minimum assurance.

The imposition of this standard should not mean that poor consumers will be unable to purchase some goods due to the high minimum standards pricing them out of their range. Price is a relevant factor in determining the appropriate standard and it is accepted that different levels of quality will

---

93   [1954] 1 QB 598.
94   [1920] 1 KB 688.
95   See W.C.H. Ervine, 'Satisfactory Quality: What Does it Mean?' [2004] JBL 684.
96   See now s. 6, Unfair Contract Terms Act 1977: discussed in Chapter 5.

exist for many goods. Rather the law seeks to prevent poor consumers (and others) making bargains which worsen their position. When one agrees the price for goods, it must be assumed that one has certain expectations about their quality which are reflected in the price paid. If the goods fail to reach those minimum standards, then the bargain will unfairly reduce the wealth of the consumer who would have paid too much for the product in terms of the bargain he or she believed they had struck.

A distinction should be drawn between the legally prescribed minimum standards and the higher standards which may be guaranteed, usually by the manufacturer, in separate consumer guarantees, offered as additional protection to that provided by the law. However, statements made in order to promote a product may be relevant in raising the required legal minimum quality expected of it, if they cause the consumer to expect higher quality.

3.5.6.1 From Merchantable to Satisfactory Quality

The 'merchantable quality' definition was criticised for being unsuitable for consumer transactions since it was based on whether the goods were saleable; goods might still be saleable even if they did not meet consumer expectations. It was also argued that the term simply did not make sense to the general public and, as interpreted, had come to concentrate too heavily on the functional aspects of goods.[97] The sting of some of the criticisms had perhaps already been removed by a number of more pro-consumer interpretations of the term 'merchantable quality', notably in *Rogers v Parish (Scarborough) Ltd*[98] where the court took notice of the consumer's interest in having a car which not merely functioned, but also met his other legitimate expectations concerning its appearance. However, the problems which consumers frequently complain about – such as minor defects, aesthetic flaws and lack of durability – were still only implicit in the definition. The major advantage of the 1994 reforms may prove to be, not the switch from merchantable to satisfactory quality, but rather the clarification of the relevant factors to be taken into account in determining whether that standard has been breached.

In its 1987 *Sale and Supply of Goods*[99] report, the Law Commission considered the merchantable quality condition should be replaced by a new term having two elements: the first part would set out the basic principle; the second would list specific aspects of quality. Three standards were canvassed for the first element (i) a qualitative standard (such as, 'good

---

97 See Law Com 160, Scot Law Com 104, *Sale and Supply of Goods*, (1987) at para. 2.9.
98 [1987] 2 All ER 232.
99 Law Com 160, Scot Law Com 104 *op. cit.,* at 3.1–3.61.

quality'), (ii) a neutral standard (for instance, 'proper quality') or (iii) a 'full acceptability' standard. In opting for a full acceptability standard, the Law Commission recognised that it was moving away from both the usability test (as laid down by Lord Reid in *Kendall v Lillico*) and the prevailing statutory definition, in favour of the approach of Dixon J in *Australian Knitting Mills v Grant* (these are considered below at 3.5.6.2). Regarding the list of specific aspects of quality, the Law Commission wanted to include fitness for purpose, but to give it less prominence and to include other relevant aspects such as appearance and finish, freedom from minor defects, safety and durability.

Reforms along the lines proposed by the Law Commission form the basis of the amendments made by the Sale and Supply of Goods Act 1994[100] to the Sale of Goods Act 1979 and analogous legislation; subject to one significant alteration. The DTI preferred to use the term 'satisfactory' rather than 'acceptable' quality. 'Satisfactory quality' was considered to be more demanding and favourable to the consumer. It also avoided any possible ambiguity arising from 'acceptable' being used to define the quality demanded and 'acceptance' also being used to determine when the right to reject was lost.[101]

It is hard to assess the significance of the change in terminology. It must be hoped that the courts appreciate that this change is intended to underpin moves to increase consumer protection but, until case law is built up, no one can be sure. Indeed, one of the arguments against change is that the consumer will suffer from uncertainty as the new rules are litigated. Many of those critical of the change also suggest that the pre-existing law had already developed in the consumer's favour to the position where, in practice, the new rules will have no appreciable impact on the level of protection afforded. A distinction might, however, be drawn here between the law in books and the law in practice. Most consumer complaints get nowhere near the appellate courts, or even the county courts, but rather are settled over the shop counter or by exchange of letters. At this level, even if consumers were aware of their right to have goods of merchantable quality, they might not have been able to comprehend the level of quality that referred to, or might have been easily wrong footed by sellers who put forward their own favourable interpretation of the law. The same possibility exists under the amended law, but consumers may feel more confident that their view of what constitutes 'satisfactory quality' is just as valid as that of the seller.

The problem is that satisfactory is a vague term; more like the qualitative standard which the Law Commission rejected; nevertheless the

---

[100] On this see G. Howells, *Consumer Contract Legislation – The New Law*, (Blackstone, 1995) Chapter 2.

[101] See Chapter 3.6.3.

Law Commission talked about goods having to be of 'good' or 'sound quality' which seems more demanding than merely having to be 'satisfactory'. Satisfactory goods might mean those of quite a good quality; on the other hand the adjective might be applied to goods which only just make the grade. For these reasons it is hard to say whether satisfactory is a more demanding standard than acceptable. On the one hand it could be argued that no one would accept goods which were not satisfactory; but sometimes it is known that some consumers do sometimes accept goods they are not satisfied with, or at least not entirely satisfied with.

The new term refers to goods which a reasonable person would regard as satisfactory. A criticism of the old definition of merchantable quality had been that, by only requiring goods to be as fit 'as it is reasonable to expect', the standard 'expected' could be decreased as quality standards declined and consumers came to expect faults in goods.[102] This reading may have been pessimistic, for whilst one may have differing expectations of the performance of goods, generally one could reasonably expect goods to be produced to the correct specification, so that sellers would, at least, be liable for manufacturing defects. By referring to the objective standard of the reasonable person and by removing the reference to expectation, the new definition should remove any such doubts.

3.5.6.2 Relevance of Cases on Merchantable Quality

Before considering the new term of satisfactory quality in some detail, it is necessary to consider whether the old cases on merchantable quality retain any value. Commercial lawyers, who have mastered the nuances of the intricate case law in this area, appear reluctant to disregard it, so that the old case law is likely to be used by way of analogy. A good example of this desire to hang on to the past is the way in which the courts treated the 1973 amendment, which defined merchantable quality, and became s. 14(6), Sale of Goods Act 1979. Prior to this the case law had shown two trends: one favoured a definition of merchantable quality based on 'acceptability' the other on 'usability'. However, it is fair to say that the two approaches overlapped and that some judges approved both approaches, failing to realise that they were based on different foundations. Representative of the 'acceptability' approach is the dicta of Dixon J in the High Court of Australia in *Australian Knitting Mills Ltd v Grant*[103] where he stated that goods:

---

[102] See Law Com 160, Scot Law Com 104, *op. cit.*, at para. 2.11.
[103] (1933) 50 CLR 387 at 418.

should be in such an actual state that a buyer fully acquainted with the facts and, therefore, knowing what hidden defects exist and not being limited to their apparent condition would buy them without abatement of the price obtainable for such goods if in reasonably sound order and condition and without special terms.

The alternative 'usability' approach is encapsulated in Lord Reid's view expressed in *Kendall v Lillico & Sons Ltd*[104] that lack of merchantable quality meant:

that the goods in the form in which they were tendered were of no use for any purpose for which goods which complied with the description under which these goods were sold would normally be used, and hence were not saleable under that description.

The usability standard came to be viewed as most suitable in the business context, whilst the acceptability test was viewed as more consumer friendly. This is perhaps ironic given the latter derived from dicta concerned with the saleability of goods and hence reflected the mercantile ancestry of the term. Back in 1969 the Law Commission had proposed a statutory definition of merchantable quality based on the concept of acceptability[105] but this was criticised, resulting in the definition introduced in 1973 being weighted towards the usability approach. Thus the definition provided that:

Goods of any kind are of merchantable quality within the meaning of subsection (2) above if they are as fit for the purpose or purposes for which goods of that kind are commonly bought as it is reasonable to expect having regard to any description applied to them, the price (if relevant) and all other relevant circumstances.

One might have thought that once a statutory definition had been provided the old case law could be discarded. This was indeed the view of Mustill LJ in *Rogers v Parish (Scarborough) Ltd*[106] who rejected the notion that parliamentary draftsmen had simply reproduced 'in more felicitous and economical terms the gist of the speeches and judgments previously delivered'. He further stated that the new definition, being 'clear and free from technicality', should be able to solve the majority of cases without reference to the prior intricate case law. By contrast, Lloyd LJ in *Aswan*

---

104   [1969] 2 AC 31 at 77.
105   Law Com 24, Scot Law Com 12, *op. cit.,* at para. 43.
106   [1987] 2 All ER 232.

Engineering v Lupdine[107] took the view that the statutory definition was 'as accurate a representation of Lord Reid's speech in *Kendall v Lillico* as it is possible to compress into one sentence' and relied on previous case law.

It may be harder for judges to interpret the 1994 reforms in this way for it is not a matter of applying a definition to an existing term, but rather of replacing the old term with a new term. This change has perhaps been further underlined by the fact that the implied terms also now have to be viewed in the context of the European Directive and the principle of conformity to the contract. Thus all the old chestnuts (such as the application of the term to minor defects and durability) will have to be looked at afresh. One suspects that, as the essential question remains the same – what is the minimum standard expected of goods? – judges (and advocates) will still seek to rely on existing case law, although perhaps in a more indirect, inspiration seeking way than in the past. However, in the final analysis there are limits to the assistance the case law can give for as the Sheriff Principal in *Thain v Anniesland Trade Centre*[108] noted questions of quality ultimately turn on their facts.

3.5.6.3 Satisfactory Quality – The New Term

It may be useful to set out the implied term of satisfactory quality found in the amended s. 14, Sale of Goods Act 1979:[109]

> (2) Where the seller sells goods in the course of a business, there is an implied term that the goods supplied under the contract are of satisfactory quality.
>
> (2A) For the purposes of this Act, goods are of satisfactory quality if they meet the standard that a reasonable person would regard as satisfactory, taking account of any description of the goods, the price (if relevant) and all the other relevant circumstances.
>
> (2B) For the purposes of this Act, the quality of goods includes their state and condition and the following (among others) are in appropriate cases aspects of the quality of goods –
>
>   (a) fitness for all the purposes for which goods of the kind in question are commonly supplied,
>
>   (b) appearance and finish,
>
>   (c) freedom from minor defects,

---

[107] [1987] 1 All ER 135.

[108] [1997] SLT 102.

[109] Cf. ss. 4(2), 9(2) Supply of Goods and Services Act 1982, and s. 10(2), Supply of Goods (Implied Terms) Act 1973.

(d)   safety,

(e)   durability.

Some of the factors are the same as those which applied under the old law (description, price and the state and condition of the goods);[110] some are amended (such as which purposes the goods should relate to), while others make explicit what was probably implicit within the old law (appearance and finish, freedom from minor defects, safety and durability). The description of the goods should always be considered when assessing their satisfactory quality, but the other factors are only to be considered if relevant or in appropriate cases. The factors discussed may not be the only relevant factors, but they are the ones which give most cause for debate and so will be considered in more detail. For the reasons discussed above, many cases decided under the old law will be considered because similar factors were raised under the old law. Nevertheless, great care should be taken when drawing any conclusions from the old case law since the courts were applying these factors against a different standard – 'merchantable' rather than 'satisfactory' quality.

   This core definition of satisfactory quality applies to both consumer and non-consumer sales, but a potentially significant (at least in terms of contract theory) additional relevant circumstance was added in the case of consumer sales by the Sale and Supply of Goods to Consumers Regulations 2002.[111] This introduced three new subsections into s. 14:

(2D) If the buyer deals as consumer... the relevant circumstances mentioned in subsection (2A) above include any public statements on the specific characteristics of the goods made about them by the seller, the producer or his representative, particularly in advertising or on labelling.

(2E) A public statement is not by virtue of subsection (2D) above a relevant circumstance for the purpose of subsection 2(A) above in the case of a contract of sale, if the seller shows that –

(iii) at the time the contract was made, he was not, and could not reasonably have been aware of the statement;

(iv) before the contract was made, the statement has been withdrawn in public or to the extent that it contained anything which was incorrect or misleading, it had been corrected in public, or;

---

110   State and condition were also previously considered as aspects of quality, but had not previously been stated as part of the definition of merchantable quality. They were located in s. 61(1) Sale of Goods Act 1979.

111   S.I. 2002/3045.

(v) the decision to buy the goods could not have been influenced by the statement.

This new factor is also considered below.

(i) Description

The description is clearly relevant in assessing what would amount to satisfactory quality. If goods were described as 'shop-soiled' or second-hand, they would still have to be of satisfactory quality, but the consumer would be expected to put up with some defects which would not be satisfactory if found in perfect new goods. Cases of second-hand goods give rise to particular difficulties in ascertaining the appropriate standard.[112] The purposes for which goods are used also interrelates with the description applied to them. Compare mahogany wood and chipboard. The purchaser of chipboard could not complain because it was unsuitable for making a dining room suite, whereas the purchaser of high-grade mahogany would rightly be dissatisfied if the wood was not of sufficient quality to be used to make furniture. Sometimes it may be the case that goods are described by reference to certain standards which can be taken into account as part of the goods' description.[113]

The inclusion of description as a factor relevant to the assessment of satisfactory quality leads to the possibility that some aspects of the product's description, which are not sufficiently central to be included within the description for the purposes of s. 13, might nevertheless lead to liability for lack of satisfactory quality. In *Harlingdon Ltd & Leinster Enterprises v Christopher Hull Fine Art Ltd*,[114] Slade LJ was keen not to allow plaintiffs in at the back door (through s. 14) when the front door (s. 13) was closed to them. That case involved a sale between art dealers of a painting which was attributed erroneously to 'Münter'. The reason for not extending liability to such cases is clearly expressed by Nourse LJ who took the view that, because art dealers accepted that the attribution of paintings was an imprecise science, the principle *caveat emptor* should

---

112 Cf. *Bartlett v Sidney Marcus* [1965] 2 All 753 (buyer of a second-hand car, which was usable, could not complain about a defect in the clutch, even if it was more serious than had been thought by the parties at the time of sale); *Thain v Anniesland Trade Centre* [1997] SLT 102 (five year old car with 80,000 miles developing a droning noise after two weeks was not unsatisfactory), but in *Crowther v Shannon Motors* [1975] 1 All ER 139 an eight year old Jaguar sold with a clapped out engine was held to be unmerchantable.

113 *Britvic Soft Drinks v Messer* [2002] 1 Lloyd's Rep 20 and on appeal [2002] 2 Lloyd's Rep 368.

114 [1990] 1 All ER 737.

rule; this was especially so as the plaintiffs were in fact experts in German expressionists whilst the defendants were not. That reasoning can be criticised since the satisfactory quality term is implied, even if there was no reliance on the part of the buyer. The dissenting opinion of Stuart-Smith LJ that the merchantable quality term was breached by the description may well prove to be the view which holds sway in the consumer context. It is noteworthy that he applied the words of Mustill LJ in *Rogers v Parish (Scarborough) Ltd*[115] who said 'the description "Range Rover" would conjure up a particular set of expectations'.

(ii) Price

The role of price is quite complex, though it should be noted that the statute requires it to be taken into account only *if relevant*. Clearly the fact that goods are reduced in price or are in a sale should not lead one to expect lower quality. Equally, the fact goods are cheap does not excuse their shoddiness. On the other hand, what is satisfactory for economy goods may well be unsatisfactory for superior goods. In other words the issue of price should generally serve to raise expectations above those generally held about that type of product, but should not reduce them. If a seller wants to reduce his liability in return for supplying a product of lower quality, he should do so by adding a description such as 'damaged goods' or 'shop-soiled' or by pointing out the defects. The price mechanism should not be used a medium for conveying messages about defects in the product quality, as the consumer may fail to appreciate these; however, price can be used to convey messages about superior quality. The consumer who finds cheap goods may consider him or herself fortunate to have discovered good quality goods at bargain prices; those who pay high prices expect to receive quality goods above the ordinary.

Thus in *Rogers v Parish (Scarborough) Ltd*[116] Mustill LJ said of a Range Rover: 'The factor of price was also significant. At more than £16,000 this vehicle was, if not at the top end of the scale, well above the level of an ordinary family saloon. The buyer was entitled to value for his money'. Similarly in *Shine v General Guarantee Corp,*[117] a case involving a second-hand Fiat X-19, Bush J considered it relevant that the buyer had thought he was purchasing an enthusiast's car, of the mileage shown, at the sort of price cars of that age and condition could expect to fetch. In fact he was buying a car which had been submerged in water for 24 hours, an insurance write-off, which 'no member of the public, knowing the facts,

---

[115] [1987] 2 All ER 232.
[116] [1987] 2 All ER 232.
[117] [1988] 1 All ER 911.

would touch with a barge pole unless they could get a substantially reduced price to reflect the risk they were taking'.

(iii) Fitness for Purpose

Whereas the fitness for particular purpose implied term covers specific, perhaps unusual purposes, which the buyer has made the seller aware of, by contrast the satisfactory quality term covers fitness for *all* the purposes for which goods of the kind in question are commonly supplied. This is an improvement on previous interpretations of the law and follows the Law Commission's recommendations. There had been debate over whether, to be merchantable, goods had to be fit for all their common purposes or whether it was sufficient that they were fit for one purpose. The statutory definition had referred to goods having to be 'fit for the *purpose or purposes* for which goods of that kind are commonly bought'. One might have been forgiven for thinking that the reference to purposes in the plural meant that goods had to be fit for all their common purposes. However, in *Aswan Engineering v Lupdine*[118] it was held that goods only had to be fit for one purpose; references to purposes in the plural was to cover goods of high quality which are expected to be fit for purposes over and above those of lower quality goods.

Whatever the rights and wrongs of the position under the old law, that has now changed. What may have been appropriate when goods simply had to be merchantable (and goods fit for *a* purpose would certainly find a buyer) does not necessarily apply when they have to be satisfactory. This may be one area where the change of terminology bites – but note it is a change in terminology supported by a change in the list of relevant factors. Nothing necessarily hangs on the change from merchantable to satisfactory quality. It may even be the case that, on the facts of *Aswan*, the goods would be found to be of satisfactory quality, since they only have to be fit for the purposes for which the goods are *commonly* supplied. *Aswan* involved plastic pails which could not stand the extreme Kuwaiti heat; it may still be found, as a matter of fact, that exposure to Kuwaiti heat was not one of the purposes for which the pails were commonly supplied.

(iv) Appearance, Finish and Freedom from Minor Defects

The Law Commission proposed that the new definition of quality should refer to appearance and finish and freedom from minor defects. It also made the point that these were separate elements. Appearance and finish refer to aesthetic aspects; minor defects refer to minor functional elements. The 1994 amendments do list these aspects separately, but it is useful to

---

118 [1987] 1 All ER 135.

consider them jointly for they raise similar issues. Part of the problem with including these as aspects of quality is that, if the goods are found to have breached the implied term, then the potential remedy of rejection of the goods and repudiation of the contract may appear too severe. This may explain why in the past courts have not found minor defects to render goods unmerchantable where the buyer was seeking rejection,[119] which in turn meant that there was no remedy at all for these defects. The prior law had in fact made progress in recognising these aspects as relevant in determining the quality of goods supplied. Mustill LJ in *Rogers v Parish (Scarborough) Ltd*[120] stated that:

> the purpose for which "goods of that kind" are commonly bought.... would include in respect of any passenger vehicle not merely the buyer's purpose of driving the car from one place to another but of doing so with the appropriate degree of comfort, ease of handling and reliability and, one might add, of pride in the vehicle's outward and interior appearance.

The 1994 amendments clarify that appearance and finish and freedom from minor defects are relevant factors, but note that the presence of such a defect will not necessarily render the goods unsatisfactory as they are only to be considered in appropriate cases as part of the overall assessment of the goods' quality. It may well be that an accumulation of minor defects renders a product unsatisfactory. The defect might be so minor as to render it *de minimis*. Thus on the facts of *Millars of Falkirk v Turpie*,[121] a minor defect in a new car, which could cheaply and easily be remedied, might still be found not to render the car unsatisfactory. Equally, a scratch on a kitchen sink might breach the implied term, but a similar scratch on a rain bucket intended for use in the garden might not.

A reviewer of the first edition of this work considered this analysis unduly pessimistic, but we stand by it.[122] Consider the example of a new car perfect in everyway, except that the cigarette lighter does not work. Would a judge really hold the car was unsatisfactory and allow it to be rejected because of the presence of this minor defect? We doubt it. But this does raise intriguing questions of whether the United Kingdom has satisfactorily implemented the EC Sale of Consumer Goods Directive. Its principle of conformity with the contract would seem to include minor non-conformities, because it expressly states the remedy of rescission

---

119   See *Millars of Falkirk Ltd v Turpie* 1976 S.L.T. 66, where the complaint involved a leakage from a power steering unit which would cost at most £25 to repair.

120   [1987] 2 All ER 232 at 237.

121   1976 S.L.T. 66.

122   C. Ervine, [1997] 5 *Consum. Law J.* 62.

should not be available where the non-conformity is only minor.[123] The Directive's remedies regime is well suited to deal with minor defects as usually the remedy will be repair. The United Kingdom has chosen to put in place the Directive's remedies alongside the existing Sale of Goods Act remedies, but since there must first be a breach of the implied conditions, minor defects may not be properly covered. This then leads on to the question of whether when interpreting satisfactory quality the courts will be able to give indirect effect to the Directive's principle of non-conformity, by extending its scope to cover minor defects. One suspects they will be willing to do so long as they are able to avoid the remedy of rejection where this seems disproportionate.

(v) Durability

Like appearance, finish and freedom from minor defects, the question mark over whether durability was a relevant aspect of quality seems to have arisen, not so much from disagreement about the need for goods to be durable, but rather from concern about the remedies which are available should they prove not to be durable. In particular, there was concern not to give a long-term right to reject. As we shall see, in sale contracts this risk does not exist since the right to reject is lost after goods have been retained for a reasonable period of time, but it is a possible risk in other contracts where the right to reject is only lost after the buyer has learned of the defect and has affirmed the contract.

There is a theoretical debate as to whether the defect must have been present at the time the goods were delivered or whether there can be liability on the basis that the goods simply did not last as long as they should have done. In practice, if goods wear out too quickly, this will be treated as being due to some defect that must have existed when they were supplied.

The inclusion of durability was a moot point under the previous law, with much of the debate actually arising in the context of fitness for purpose and whether, to be fit for their purpose, goods had to last for a reasonable time. Nevertheless, the comments have obvious relevance to the debate on satisfactory quality where fitness for purpose is a relevant factor. In *Crowther v Shannon Motors Co*[124] Lord Denning seemed to cast doubt on the judge at first instance's statement that the car had to go for a reasonable time; whereas in *Lambert v Lewis*,[125] Lord Diplock did not doubt that there 'is a continuing warranty that the goods will continue to be fit for that purpose for a reasonable time after delivery'. What a reasonable

---

[123] Article 3(6).
[124] [1975] 1 All ER 139.
[125] [1981] 1 All ER 1185.

period of time is of course depends on the nature of the product. Thus the inclusion of durability as a relevant factor removes any uncertainty. It is appropriate to note that there is no obligation in English law for manufacturers and retailers to stock spare parts or provide servicing facilities, although provisions along these lines are found in various codes of practice.

(vi) Safety

It is inconceivable that dangerous goods would be held to be satisfactory, but the inclusion in the statutory list of relevant factors is a useful clarification. A number of cases, often involving motor vehicles, make it clear that goods that cannot be used safely will not be merchantable.[126]

(vii) Public Statements

We have already commented on how making the seller liable for public statements was considered a radical departure from traditional contract law principles. The significance is not in relation to the seller's statements. This merely clarifies that statements of the seller even if not forming terms of the contact can nevertheless be taken into account. Rather it is in imposing liability on the seller for statements made by the producer or his representative. This seems to breach the sanctity of contract whereby parties are only liable for obligations they have agreed to take on. Here contractual obligations are imposed for statements the seller has no direct responsibility for. Surprisingly no explanation for this policy is found in the recitals to the Directive, but it must be based in part on the recognition that retailers do seek to taken advantage of the marketing by producers and also on the idea that as they are in the market to make a profit from the selling of a product they have a responsibility to keep abreast of how the product is marketed. Again this can be seen as more onerous for small traders, but as we shall see its application should allow for fair treatment.

The extent of the obligation is indeed limited by some of the limitations found within s. 14(2E). A retailer will not be liable of statements he did not and could not reasonably have been aware of. So retailers need only be reasonably vigilant in monitoring market developments. Major retailers might be expected to follow the statements of producers more closely than small traders. A market trader in England could hardly be expected to know of advertisements in the Italian press, unless by chance he was an Italian or had just visited there on holiday. Equally he might not be expected to check the producer's website, but he could be expected to have knowledge of national and local advertising

---

[126] E.g. *Bernstein v Pamson Motors (Golders Green) Ltd* [1987] 2 ALL ER 220.

campaigns. Larger retailers will be expected to have more systematic methods for collecting data on producer's statements; the exact extent depending on the particular context. There will also be no liability if the statement was withdrawn or the error publicly corrected. There will be no liability if the decision to buy the goods could not have been influenced by the statement. The scope of this exclusion in unclear. It would certainly cover the situation where it can be proven the buyer had not seen the statement. It may also be extended to situations where the misstatement was so insignificant that it could not seriously have influenced the decision, but there may be some factors which individuals find important although most consumers would not and it is hard to know how to apply this provision in such situations.

It should also be noted that the liability only applies to statements about specific characteristics. Thus a claim that a car had a specific fuel efficiency would be caught, but not more general claims about products. Even a false statement that the car had been voted 'best in its class' might not be caught as this statement is probably not related to a specific characteristic of the goods. The provision says that it particularly includes such statements made in advertising and on labelling. However, it is not limited to such circumstances: announcements on websites, press releases and even public statements made to regulatory agencies are other examples of public statements that could be the basis of liability.

(viii) Other Issues

Some more general points can be made about the satisfactory quality term. Like its predecessor, it is independent of any consumer guarantee offered by manufacturers and retailers; thus a defect cannot be disregarded simply because it can be repaired under a consumer guarantee. As Mustill LJ noted in *Rogers v Parish (Scarborough) Ltd*,[127] the consumer guarantee was 'an addition to the buyer's rights, not a subtraction from them, and it may be noted, only a circumscribed addition since it lasts for a limited period and does not compensate the buyer for consequential loss and inconvenience'.

Equally the goods will not fail to be satisfactory if something has to be done to them before use, so long as the buyer can be assumed to know of this requirement. Thus in *Heil v Hedges*,[128] pork chops infected with trichinae were held to be merchantable as they were safe when cooked. In contrast, in *Grant v Australian Knitting Mills Ltd*,[129] underpants with traces of sulphites which caused dermatitis were unmerchantable; although

---

[127] [1987] 2 All ER 232.
[128] [1951] 1 TLR 512.
[129] [1936] AC 85.

they would have been safe if washed before wearing, one cannot be expected to wash one's underpants before putting them on for the first time! One suspects that goods could be rendered of unsatisfactory quality by the instructions supplied with them, although there is no direct authority on this point since the case where the issue was raised restricted its discussion to whether instructions could render goods unfit for a particular purpose.[130]

The satisfactory quality term is implied regardless of whether the buyer relied on the seller's skill and judgment; thus the term is of wider application than the fitness for purpose term. It also applies to latent defects, so long as they were present at the time the goods were delivered. As was graphically stated by Lord Ellenborough in *Gardiner v Gray*:[131] 'The purchaser cannot be supposed to buy goods to lay them on a dunghill'. However, s. 14(2)(C), Sale of Goods Act 1979 makes it clear that the satisfactory quality term,

> does not extend to any matter making the quality of goods unsatisfactory-
> (a)   which is specifically drawn to the buyer's attention before the contract is made;
> (b)   where the buyer examines the goods before the contract is made, which that examination ought to reveal, or
> (c)   in the case of a contract for sale by sample, which would have been apparent on a reasonable examination of the sample.

Section 14(2)(c)(a) could easily be used as a way of reducing expectations of standards. The point has been well made that the courts should be vigilant to ensure both that the consumers are aware of the nature of the defect and the consequences flowing from it, before they allow this avenue of escape for sellers.[132]

As regards inspections the important point to note is that there is no obligation on a consumer to make an inspection. If the consumer chooses to inspect the goods, liability will only be excused for defects which *that* examination ought to have revealed.[133] Thus if the consumer examined the

---

130   Cf. *Wormell v RHM Agriculture (East) Ltd* [1987] 3 All ER 75.
131   (1815) 4 Camp 144.
132   C. Twigg-Flesner, 'Information disclosure about the quality of goods – duty or encouragement?' in G. Howells, A. Janssen and R. Schulze (eds.), *Information Rights and Obligations: A Challenge for Party Autonomy and Transactional Fairness* (Ashgate, forthcoming).
133   Note that this was an amendment from the original wording which had referred to *such* rather than *that* examination and had been interpreted to catch a consumer who had only looked at the outside of barrels although he had been offered the opportunity

bodywork of the car, this would not prevent the car being held unsatisfactory because of mechanical faults. The effect of any expertise of the consumer on whether defects ought to have been revealed is problematic. If the expert consumer undertakes an examination which would not have revealed a defect to the ordinary consumer, but ought to have been revealed to someone with his or her particular expertise, the position is unclear. Is the standard that of the reasonable average consumer, or is the expertise of the consumer to be taken into account so that what ought to be revealed relates to that particular examination, i.e. an expert examination?

A potential trap for the unwary consumer was highlighted by the facts of *R & B Customs Brokers v UDT*.[134] This involved the purchase of a car on conditional sale. There was an interlude between the consumer taking possession and the contract being concluded by the finance company signing the agreement. During this time the purchaser became aware that the roof of the car leaked. Did this mean that he was barred from complaining about the defect, given that the relevant date for assessing what examination had been made was the time of contract? In *R & B Custom Brokers Ltd v UDT* the Court of Appeal did not find it necessary to answer this question. The matter is potentially unfair to consumers since when a finance company signs the forms is a factor outside their control; they are only likely to know the contract has been concluded after the event. The general position of consumers has been improved by the 2002 Regulations, which provides in consumer sales, that goods remain at the seller's risk until delivered to the consumer.[135] However, this particular trap remains.

3.5.7 Fitness for Purpose

Section 14(3), Sale of Goods Act 1979[136] implies a term that goods will be fit for any particular purpose made known by the buyer to the seller:

> Where the seller sells goods in the course of a business and the buyer, expressly or by implication, makes known –
> (a)   to the seller, or

---

to undertake a more thorough examination; see *Thornett & Fehr v Beers* [1919] 1 KB 486.

[134]   [1988] 1 All ER 847.
[135]   Section 20(4) Sales of Goods Act 1979.
[136]   Cf. ss. 4(4) and 9(4), Supply of Goods and Services Act 1982 and s. 10(3), Supply of Goods (Implied Terms) Act 1973.

(b)   where the purchase price or part of it is payable by instalments and the goods were previously sold by a credit-broker to the seller, to that credit-broker, any particular purpose for which goods are being bought, there is an implied condition that the goods supplied under the contract are reasonably fit for that purpose, whether or not that is a purpose for which such goods are commonly supplied, except where the circumstances show that the buyer does not rely on the skill or judgment of the seller or credit-broker.

Whereas the satisfactory quality condition governs the general expectations of quality, the fitness for purpose condition provides protection for the consumer who has particular demands of the goods which he makes known to the seller and who relies on the seller's skill and judgment to ensure that the goods possess those qualities. The result of case law and the statutory amendments to the implied condition, which were effected by the Supply of Goods (Implied Terms) Act 1973, have ensured that fitness for purpose does not cover only very specialised particular purposes which were directly brought to the seller's attention, but rather overlaps to a large extent with the satisfactory quality condition.[137] There may be benefit to consumers in this. Judges may be reticent to hold that a product is unsatisfactory, perhaps because they are reluctant to give a wholesale condemnation of it, especially as they may be uncertain as to what standard to expect of various products. By contrast finding a product is unfit for a particular purpose does not require a judgment of the product as a whole, but simply its ability to perform a particular function. In this case the standard expected of the goods (i.e. the particular purpose to be achieved), has been agreed by the parties and therefore does not need to be imposed by the judge, who simply has to assess whether the purpose can be fulfilled by the goods.

The provision has not been limited to very narrow particular purposes. The particular purpose can be very general, for instance driving a car. This example also illustrates that it can cover the goods usual purposes. Also the condition has been applied to goods with only one purpose: for instance, the hot water bottle in *Priest v Last.*[138]

Difficulties sometimes surround the application of the section to situations where the goods are adequate for the general population, but something renders them unfit in relation to a particular purchaser. Generally the seller will not be liable for any particular sensitivities of the purchaser unless they are brought to his attention. This explains why the

---

[137]   This overlap was considered of no moment by the Law Commission: Law Com 160, Scot Law Com 104, *op. cit.,* at para. 2.19.

[138]   [1903] 2 KB 148.

defendant in *Griffiths v Peter Conway*[139] was not liable when the Harris Tweed coat purchased by the plaintiff caused her to contract dermatitis due to her unusually sensitive skin. Also there was no liability in *Slater v Finning*[140] where the failure of a camshaft was due to external factors the suppliers had not been informed about. By contrast in *Manchester Shipping Lines v Rea*,[141] a coal merchant was held to have breached the fitness for purpose condition by supplying coal which was unsuitable for a particular ship. As there is no standard ship, the merchant ought to have checked that the consignment was suitable for that ship. This shows that, while sellers will not be liable for abnormal sensitivities of which they were not aware, they will be liable for supplying goods unsuitable for people with obvious special conditions. For example, a woman who is obviously pregnant should not be given drugs that are dangerous for someone in that condition. In some circumstances where there are different grades of goods, the seller can be expected to make enquiries as to the appropriate product to be supplied. For example, if someone drives to a garage and asks the attendant to fill up their car, which only runs on unleaded petrol, then leaded petrol would be unfit for the purpose. It does not seem unreasonable to suggest that either the attendant should know the correct grade of petrol for that make of car or should make enquiries of the consumer.

For the fitness for purpose condition to be implied, the buyer must have made known the purpose for which he or she wants the goods. However, this can be made known implicitly by virtue of the circumstances surrounding the transaction. The purchaser must also have relied upon the seller's skill and judgment. However, the courts realise that, in the consumer context, such reliance will seldom be explicit. Rather there will be an implicit expectation 'that the tradesman has selected his stock with skill and judgment'.[142] It is clear from the revised wording of s. 14(3) that the burden is on the seller to show that there was no reliance. However, it would still be possible for a seller to argue that it was unreasonable in the circumstances for the buyer to have relied upon him.[143] This might be the case where the seller had refused to vouch for the goods, but had expressed an opinion 'for what it is worth'. Given the restrictions on the use of exclusion clauses, such a possibility would appear desirable, but would not necessarily be immune from attack as an exclusion clause.[144] In any event

---

[139] [1939] 1 All ER 685.

[140] [1997] AC 473.

[141] [1922] 2 AC 74.

[142] Per Lord Wright in *Grant v Australian Knitting Mills* [1936] AC 85.

[143] *Jewson Ltd v Boyhan* [2003] EWCA Civ 1030.

[144] Cf. *Smith v Eric Bush* [1989] 2 All ER 514, but see discussion at Law Com 24 and Scot Law Com 12, *op. cit.*, at para. 37.

it should be noted that the buyer will be held to have relied upon the seller's skill and judgment even if the reliance is only partial. Thus if a customer specifies the desired qualities of the goods, but leaves the seller some freedom in the selection of materials, then the fitness for purpose condition is implied.

Where the seller can only supply one particular brand or where the buyer specifically requests a particular brand, it is sometimes suggested that there can be no reliance on the seller's skill and judgment. Thus in *Wren v Holt*,[145] where a customer purchased ale from a tied house, there was considered to be a basis for a finding that he could not have relied upon the seller's skill and judgment. Hopefully a different decision would be reached nowadays, as the burden is clearly on the seller to establish that the buyer did not rely upon him. Where the seller only sells one brand of goods, one may be entitled to expect that he has selected a brand which is fit for its purpose. Where a particular brand is requested, there may be a more arguable case that the buyer relied upon the producer's publicity and marketing, rather than on the seller's skill and judgment in the selection of the product. There may nevertheless be aspects of a product about which the buyer continues to rely on the seller. For instance, when purchasing a glass of beer in a free house, a customer may rely upon his or her own general preference as to which brewery's beer to select, but nevertheless may continue to rely on the landlord to serve it in a proper condition. This partial reliance would seem to bring into play the full scope of the implied condition that the goods are fit for their purpose. Our example may be exceptional in that most goods are pre-packaged, with no opportunity for the retailer to affect their quality. In appropriate circumstances therefore, the request for a particular brand may be evidence that a seller could put forward to persuade the court that the buyer had not relied on his skill and judgment.

It is worth reiterating that breach of the implied conditions is a matter of strict liability. Thus in *Kendall v Lillico*,[146] Lord Reid, whilst noting the illogicality of his own position, nevertheless found that 'an assurance that the goods will be reasonably fit for his purpose covers not only defects which the seller ought to have detected but also defects which are latent in the sense that not even the utmost skill and judgment on the part of the seller would have detected them'. However, the standard does not require goods to perform their functions perfectly: rather they have to be *reasonably* fit for their purpose. In determining the appropriate standard 'the rarity of the unsuitability would be weighed against the gravity of its consequences'.[147] There is also flexibility built into the determination of

---

[145]   [1903] 1 KB 610.

[146]   [1969] 2 AC 31 at 84.

[147]   Per Lord Pearce in *Kendall v Lillico* [1969] 2 AC 31 at 115.

what the particular purpose of the goods is. Thus clearly whilst a family saloon, sports car, minibus and truck are all bought to be driven, they also have different purposes in relation to their optimum speed, the number of passengers they can carry and the weight they can bear. The Court of Appeal has accepted the principle that goods can be rendered unfit by the provision of inadequate or misleading instructions (and presumably by the failure to supply any instructions), although, on the facts of the case it was held that the instructions were not misleading.[148]

3.5.8 Services

Contracts for the supply of services are governed by Part II of the Supply of Goods and Services Act 1982. This includes terms that unless otherwise agreed such contracts will be performed within a reasonable time[149] or charged at a reasonable rate.[150] However the term we are concerned with is the implied term that, where a supplier is acting in the course of a business, the service will be carried out with reasonable skill and care.[151] This standard applies to the service element regardless of whether goods are also transferred, bailer or hired, in which case quality conditions relating to the goods may also be relevant.[152]

This negligence standard for services contrasts with the strict liability standard for goods. This is justified because in services it is not always possible to guarantee outcomes. There are too many variables as the service provider interacts with products, humans and nature over which he may not have full control. Of course a service provider can contract to deliver a certain outcome and then would be liable if it did not materialise. The standard is similar to negligence. Reasonable care does not require the best service possible, but the supplier must comply with standards common to persons in his or her profession. If he holds himself out as having a special skill then it is justifiable to assume that what is reasonable will be judged accordingly.

The EC Sales Directive requires that defects from installation be treated as equivalent to a lack of conformity. When implementing this the UK was content to leave installation to be dealt with under the reasonable skill and care standard of the 1982 Act and it might be doubted whether this is proper implementation.

---

[148] *Wormell v RHM Agriculture (East) Ltd* [1987] 3 All ER 75.
[149] Section 14, Supply of Goods and Services Act 1982.
[150] Section 15, Supply of Goods and Services Act 1982.
[151] Section 13, Supply of Goods and Services Act 1982.
[152] Section 12(3), Supply of Goods and Services Act 1982.

There are two further differences reflecting the more lenient approach to services than goods. First, s. 13 is simply a term and is not classed as a condition. This means repudiation of the contract will only be available if the consequences of breach are serious. We shall see that in consumer contracts repudiation is available for any breach of the quality conditions however minor. Second, whereas the quality conditions in sale of goods contracts are non-excludable, the implied term in s. 13 can be excluded. However, this is expressly subject to the Unfair Terms in Consumer Contracts Act 1977[153] and presumably now also the Unfair Terms in Consumer Contracts Regulations 1999. Moreover an express term does not negative the implied term unless inconsistent with it.[154]

3.6 REMEDIES

3.6.1 Traditional Remedies

Contract terms can be divided into three categories. Conditions give the right to repudiate the contract and/or claim damages. Warranties only ever give rise to a claim in damages, whilst breach of innominate terms (otherwise known as intermediate stipulations) may permit repudiation depending upon the seriousness of the consequences of breach. The implied quality terms in relation to goods are classed as conditions giving the consumer the right to reject the goods and/or claim damages.[155] The remedies in non-consumer sales contracts have been restricted so that rejection is not possible where this is unreasonable,[156] but in consumer sales the automatic remedies of rejection and/or damages remain. *Clegg v Olle Andersson (T/A Nordic Marine)*[157] Hale LJ (as she then was) defended this right even when the seller has behaved reasonably and rejection might seem disproportionate. However, we shall see that in relation to sales contracts the drawback is the ease with which the right to reject the goods can be lost.

A curious feature of English sales law was that there was no legal recognition of the remedies of repair or replacement, despite these remedies being widely used in practice and commonly provided for in the voluntary guarantees issued by manufacturers. The debate surrounding whether a right to cure should be introduced into UK law was often confused because of uncertainty over whether what was being proposed

---

153   Section 16(1), Supply of Goods and Services Act 1982.
154   Section 16(2), Supply of Goods and Services Act 1982.
155   See Schedule 2, Sale and Supply of Goods Act 1994.
156   See, s. 15A, Sale of Goods Act 1979.
157   (2003) 1 All ER (Comm) 721.

was the right of consumers to opt for cure or their being forced to accept cure. More subtle fears were expressed as to whether even if the strong right of rejection was retained, the mere presence of cure remedies might be misrepresented by traders to consumers as requiring them to accept attempts at cure before rejection.

The unfettered right of consumers to reject defective goods is an important weapon in the consumer's hand, which many argued should not be diluted. However, it had been suggested that sellers should be allowed to opt to cure, rather than be forced to accept the consumer's rejection of the goods and repudiation of the contract, where this is reasonable (for example, in the case of a minor and easily repairable defect). At first glance this seems attractive, but in reality few consumers would seek rejection and repudiation for a minor defect. A party normally relies on a minor infraction to withdraw from a contract in the commercial context, where the real reason for wanting to escape is external to the contract itself, for example, commodity price fluctuations. It is sometimes suggested that rejection may be too serious a remedy for minor defects; indeed there is evidence that the courts failed to find the merchantability condition breached where the remedy being sought for a minor defect is rejection of the goods.[158]

For commercial contracts the problem of bad faith rejection of goods on the pretext of a minor defect has been addressed by statutory amendment.[159] In the consumer context, however, one must ask why a consumer is rejecting for an apparently minor defect? It is very likely that what appears to the outsider as a minor defect in fact has a major impact on the consumer, undermining his or her confidence in the goods. Given that the value of goods, such as a new car, may represent a considerable amount of the consumer's wealth, his or her interest in feeling secure in the purchase deserves protection. Take the facts of *Millars of Falkirk Ltd v Turpie* which concerned a new Ford Granada – an up-market car (even presumably by the standards of solicitors from whose ranks the purchaser came). The defect was a leak in the power steering box, in itself a minor problem only costing £25 (in 1973) to put right. Yet the sellers had attempted repair once – unsuccessfully – and the purchaser, fearing he had a 'lemon', repudiated the contract. Did he overreact? If so, it should not have been beyond the wit of the court to find the car unmerchantable – since presumably we would want the seller to take some responsibility for this defect – and yet find technical reasons (of which we shall see there are several possibilities) for finding the right to reject lost, leaving the purchaser with a claim in damages. Restricting the right to reject may thus look attractive in theoretical terms, but undermining the clear right to reject

---

[158] See *Millars of Falkirk Ltd v Turpie* 1976 SLT 66.
[159] Section 15A, Sale of Goods Act 1979.

will be damaging in the real world everyday practice of enforcing consumer rights, since traders will be able to exploit ambiguity in the definition of what amounts to a minor defect. Of course there is the separate issue as to whether minor defects will always amount to lack of satisfactory quality under English law.[160]

In its 1983 Working Paper, the Law Commission had suggested that the seller be given the statutory right to cure where refusal would be unreasonable.[161] Yet it had changed its mind by the time of its Final Report in 1987, believing this to be inappropriate in many commercial transactions[162] and fearing it might weaken the rights of consumers.

There is not the same danger in providing consumers with the right to demand cure. Admittedly, unscrupulous traders could deliberately misrepresent the law so that a right to demand cure comes to be treated as a duty to accept cure, but the answer is to educate the public and use fair trading laws to bring errant traders to heel, rather than allowing the fear of law breaking to stunt the proper development of the law. There are reasons why consumers may want a right of cure: they may be happy with the goods and want them repaired or they may be happy with the deal they struck and simply wish the defective goods supplied to be replaced by goods of the proper agreed standard. The difficulty is to know how to make the remedy effective in the sense that, if a seller refuses to cure, the consumer is left with a claim for damages and is no better off than at present.

One of the most important consequences of implementing the Consumer Sales Directive has been to give the UK consumer a new suite of remedies: repair, replacement, price reduction and rescission. All are now potentially available. We will consider the detail of these new remedies below, but it is important to stress that these are additional to the rights under the Sale of Goods Acts and analogous legislation. So a consumer with defective goods can still choose to reject them under the Sale of Goods Act 1979. Alternatively he could rely on the new remedies regime to seek to cure the defect. The danger of the consumer being confused by the new regime has already been noted. There will be a need to consider the education of consumers and monitoring of trader conduct. The relationship between the two remedies regime also needs to be clear. It would be unfair, for instance, for a consumer to ask for goods to be repaired and then shortly afterwards seek to reject the goods and terminate

---

[160] See 3.5.6.3(iv).

[161] Law Com WP No. 85 and Scot Law Com Con Memo No. 58, *Sale and Supply of Goods* (1983) at 4.26–4.62.

[162] But it did, of course, propose to restrict the right to reject in non-consumer sales to situations where it is reasonable to do so: see Law Com 160, Scot Law Com 104, *op. cit.*, Chapter 4.

the contracts. This is achieved by requiring the seller to be given a reasonable time to repair or replace the goods before rejecting them and terminating the contract.[163]

3.6.2 Rejection

Section 11(3), Sale of Goods Act 1979 sets out the remedies for breach of conditions and warranties, but in a rather convoluted manner. Thus a breach of warranty is said to give rise to a claim for damages, but not a right to reject the goods and treat the contract as repudiated. It does not say expressly that breach of condition does give the right to reject the goods and treat the contract as repudiated, but this can be implied from the obvious contrast drawn between the remedies for breach of warranty and breach of condition. Section 48D, Sale of Goods Act 1979 talks about the buyer rejecting the goods and terminating (rather that repudiating) the contract.

From this it appears that every rejection gives the consumer the right to treat the contract as repudiated or terminated depending upon one's preferred terminology. Of course it would be open to the consumer to reject the goods, but keep the contract alive by accepting an offer to cure. Yet one interpretation of the wording of an earlier part of s. 11(3) is more equivocal as it states that breach of a condition *may* give rise to a right to treat the contract as repudiated. Some commentators have drawn the conclusion that English law already knew a right of cure since rejection of the goods need not repudiate the contract; the defect could be remedied by repairing specific goods or replacing goods which were unascertained when the contract was made.[164] However, the case often relied on to support this proposition, *Borrowman, Phillips & Co v Free and Holes*,[165] (and other similar cases) have all involved rejection and re-tender of documents under documentary sales. Any right of cure is unlikely to apply where the goods themselves had been rejected. Certainly any right to re-tender would have to take place before the time for delivery, since buyers can refuse to accept late delivery.[166] In the consumer context, the courts are likely to treat the remedies of rejection and repudiation as inseparable (unless voluntarily separated by the consumer) since the breach of the

---

[163] Section 48D, Sale of Goods Act 1979, s. 11Q Supply of Goods and Services Act 1982.

[164] Goode, *Commercial Law* (Penguin, 1999) pp. 363–5.

[165] (1878) 4 QBD 500.

[166] The time for delivery will be that set by the contract or failing that delivery must take place within a reasonable time: see standard commercial law textbooks for more detailed treatment, e.g. P. Atiyah, *Sale of Goods* (Pitman, 2001) Chapter 10.

implied term will be seen as destroying the consumer's confidence in the bargain.[167]

The seller may be able indirectly to persuade the consumer to accept an offer to cure in the knowledge that an unreasonable refusal of that offer may be treated as a failure to mitigate and be reflected in a lower award of damages. However, where the nature of the breach is such that the consumer has lost confidence in the seller, then one can anticipate that the courts will be slow to treat such a consumer as having unreasonably turned down an offer to cure.

It may be that only part of a consignment of goods is defective. Can a buyer reject the defective part and retain the remainder? The position used to be that where a buyer accepted all the goods or part of them then, unless the contract was severable, the right to reject had been lost.[168] The one exception to this was provided by s. 30(4), Sale of Goods Act 1979 which had allowed a buyer to reject goods which did not correspond with the contract description and retain those that did.[169] The Law Commission recommended that a similar right of partial rejection be introduced where part of a consignment was defective,[170] and this has been implemented by the Sale and Supply of Goods Act 1994. This provides for a new s. 35A, Sale of Goods Act 1979 which, subject to any contrary intention in the contract, allows a buyer to reject goods which are not in conformity with the contract, whilst retaining others which are unaffected by the breach. However, it also provides that, where the sale is of one or more 'commercial units', then a buyer accepting goods which form part of such a commercial unit is deemed to have accepted all the goods making up the unit.[171] A 'commercial unit' is identified as a unit division of which would materially impair the value of the goods or the character of the unit. Thus if the goods supplied were a lamp set, comprising a matching base and shade, one of the parts could not be accepted and the other rejected.

3.6.3 Acceptance

Section 11(4), Sale of Goods Act 1979 provides that:

---

[167] R. Bradgate and F. White, 'Rejection and Termination in Contracts for the Sale of Goods' in *Termination of Contracts*, J. Birds, R. Bradgate and C. Villiers (eds.), (Chancery, 1995).

[168] Section 11(4), Sale of Goods Act 1979.

[169] This has now been repealed: see s. 3(3), Sale and Supply of Goods Act 1994.

[170] Law Com 160, Scot Law Com 104, *op. cit.*, at para. 6.9.

[171] Section 35(7), Sale of Goods Act 1979.

> Where a contract of sale is not severable and the buyer has accepted the goods or part of them, the breach of a condition to be fulfilled by the seller can only be treated as a breach of warranty, and not as a ground for rejecting the goods and treating the contract as repudiated, unless there is an express or implied term of the contract to that effect.

The loss of the right to reject on acceptance can be particularly severe because of the wide range of circumstances in which s. 35, Sale of Goods Act 1979 provides that the buyer is deemed to have accepted the goods. The harshness of this rule has been mitigated by statutory amendments introduced in 1994 and subsequent case law. There is no equivalent of this rule in legislation governing other types of supply contracts where the loss of the right to reject is governed by the common law concept of affirmation. The rejection remedy is generally kept alive for longer in those other contracts than is the case in sale contracts.

However, the rule that acceptance bars rejection does not apply to severable contracts. Thus where goods are delivered in instalments or even if they are delivered at the same time, but can be treated as independent elements, the buyer will be free to accept the fit goods and reject the defective instalments. Indeed, in appropriate circumstances, the consumer may be able to argue that there is not one contract, be it severable or otherwise, but rather a series of individual contracts. The contract itself may also expressly or impliedly allow rejection after acceptance.

Section 35, Sale of Goods Act 1979 provides for three circumstances in which goods are deemed to have been accepted:

(i) *when the buyer intimates to the seller that he has accepted them.*[172] This intimation may be express or implied. Of particular concern in the consumer context are delivery notes, which consumers are often asked to sign to indicate that they accept the goods. Typically the goods are delivered in a form that prevents the consumer from immediately inspecting their quality and yet an appropriately worded delivery note might have the effect of removing the consumer's right to reject the goods.[173] This was more clearly the case prior to the 1994 amendment to the Sale of Goods Act 1979, since this form of acceptance was not treated as being subject to the proviso in s. 34 of the Act that goods cannot be accepted until there has been a reasonable opportunity to examine them. Since the 1994 amendments, acceptance will no longer occur by intimation unless the buyer has had a reasonable opportunity to examine the goods.

---

[172] Section 35(1)(a), Sale of Goods Act 1979.

[173] It is possible that such a note would be caught by s. 13, Unfair Contract Terms Act 1979, which controls exclusions or restrictions on rules of evidence.

(ii) *when the goods have been delivered and the buyer does any act in relation to them which is inconsistent with the ownership of the seller.*[174] This is a confusing provision, since if the buyer has bought the goods, then why should the buyer not behave in a manner inconsistent with the seller's ownership? To make sense of it, one must treat the seller's ownership as being a conditional form of ownership based on the residual interest in the return of goods properly rejected. An example often given of an act which was inconsistent with the seller's ownership is a sub-sale. Even prior to the 1994 amendments, acceptance could not be deemed in this circumstance until there had been a reasonable opportunity to examine the goods. Thus, even if goods pass directly to a sub-buyer, rejection would be possible if, on examination, they were found to be defective. The amended Act provides that goods are not deemed to be accepted merely because they are delivered to another under a disposition or sub-sale.[175] This does not state that such a sub-sale or disposition cannot be an act inconsistent with the seller's ownership, but seems to emphasise the point that mere re-sale is not enough and that the actions of the parties must be considered in determining whether acceptance has occurred. The types of situations where acceptance is properly deemed to have occurred on this basis are those where the buyer is unable to return the goods because they have been incorporated into other goods in a way which prevents them from being easily removed[176] or where it would be unfair to allow rejection as the buyer has used them for longer than necessary for the purpose of testing.[177]

Repairing defective goods could clearly be viewed as an act inconsistent with the seller's ownership when the repair was effected either by the buyer or someone other than the seller. Where the seller is allowed to repair the goods, it is hard to see how this could be inconsistent with his ownership and yet this possibility has been alleged.[178] Clearly a consumer could preserve the right to reject the goods, should an attempted repair by the seller prove to be ineffective, by expressly stating such a reservation. However, it seems wrong to make consumer rights depend upon the consumer having the knowledge and foresight to negotiate with the seller over the intricacies of sales law. Thus, following the recommendations of the

---

[174] Section 35(1)(b), Sale of Goods Act 1979.
[175] Section 35(6)(b), Sale of Goods Act 1979.
[176] *Mechan & Sons Ltd v Bow, McLachlan & Co Ltd* (1910) SC 785.
[177] *Heilbutt v Hickson* (1872) LR 7 CP 438.
[178] See Law Com WP No. 85 and Scot Law Com Con Memo No. 58, *op. cit.,* at para. 2.56.

Law Commission, the 1994 amendments provide that a buyer is not deemed to have accepted goods merely because he asks for, or agrees to, their repair by or under an arrangement with the seller.[179]

(iii) *when the buyer retains the goods after the lapse of a reasonable time without intimating that he has rejected them.*[180] This is the most controversial of the various forms of deemed acceptance, in part because the case law has on occasions construed a reasonable time unduly strictly. Thus in *Bernstein v Pamson Motors*,[181] for instance, a reasonable period of time was held to have elapsed after three weeks, during which the consumer had been ill and had only driven the car 142 miles. Rougier J held that the statute removed the right to reject after the goods had been retained for a reasonable period of time, noting that there was no qualification that the period of time should be reasonable in relation to the opportunity to discover the defect. Somewhat contradictorily, he then went on to suggest that what is a reasonable time depends upon the facts of the case. He was clearly concerned to promote the 'commercial desirability of [allowing] the seller to close his ledger reasonably soon after the transaction is complete'. However, he also noted the need to consider the nature of the goods and their function from the buyer's point of view, stating that 'the complexity of the intended function is clearly of prime consideration here. What is a reasonable time in relation to a bicycle would hardly suffice for a nuclear submarine'. The difference between the complex and the simple product lies in the time needed to discover defects; the judge was in fact doing what he denied was relevant – taking the possibility of examination into account, albeit (on the facts of the case) not very generously. The amended Sale of Goods Act 1979 now makes it clear that, in determining whether a reasonable time has elapsed, the question of whether a buyer has had a reasonable opportunity to examine the goods is a material factor.[182] Although note that there is no requirement that there must have been an opportunity to examine the goods before the goods can be deemed to have been accepted.

The Court of Appeal in *Clegg v Olle Andersson (T/A Nordic Marine)*[183] has now held – in a decision which is to be welcomed by consumers – that *Bernstein v Pamson Motors* is no longer good law following the statutory amendments. This case involved a purchase of a yacht. When it was delivered in August 2000 the seller informed the

---

[179] Section 35(6)(a), Sale of Goods Act 1979.
[180] Section 35(4), Sale of Goods Act 1979.
[181] [1987] 2 All ER 220.
[182] Section 35(5).
[183] (2003) 1 All ER (Comm) 721.

buyer that its keel was substantially heavier than in the manufacturer's specifications. Rejection only occurred by letter of 6 March 2001, but the Court held this was acceptable. The parties had been negotiating about the possibility of modification and repair and the buyer had only received answers to their requests for information on 15 February 2001.

Bradgate notes that the effect of prior case law has been that, where there is a latent defect, the right to reject is lost before the buyer is aware of the defect.[184] This would still be the case after the 1994 amendments since, even if a buyer is given a reasonable opportunity to examine the goods, latent defects would not be discovered. This does not conflict with the notion that satisfactory quality (as it then was) requires goods to be reasonably durable. However, what it actually does is to admit that durability is a concern, but that rejection is not an appropriate remedy for this manifestation of lack of satisfactory quality. This approach was supported by the Law Commission in its 1987 report, but might perhaps be questioned. In other supply contracts the right to reject is only lost once the buyer is aware of the defect and affirms the contract. Allowance should then be made for any use and enjoyment the consumer has derived from the goods prior to their rejection, although the law might not always make this possible. This is preferable to relying on damages to ensure justice. Injustice could arise if the goods retain some residual worth even after the durability defect emerges and consumers have to retain goods they are not satisfied with. This is because, in calculating damages, allowance will be made not only for the satisfactory performance the consumer has enjoyed prior to the defect materialising, but also for the subsequent limited utility the consumer can derive from the goods. The burden of making use of the residual utility in the goods should be placed on the seller rather than the consumer: the seller is the one who caused the future performance to be lower than anticipated and can more easily find someone willing to buy goods with reduced performance. The consumer should not be forced to accept goods which are unsatisfactory even if he or she is partially compensated.

3.6.4 Affirmation

The rules which provide for the loss of the right to reject on acceptance only apply to contracts of sale. They do not apply to contracts of barter or

---

[184] R. Bradgate, *Commercial Law* (Butterworth, 2000) at p. 319.

exchange, contracts for work and materials, hire, nor hire-purchase and (by statute) they do not apply to conditional sales.[185]

In contracts other than sale contracts, the right to reject is only lost where the buyer has affirmed the contract, waived the breach or is estopped from relying on his or her right to terminate. Most commonly the courts will look to see if the contract has been affirmed. The important point to note is that affirmation can only take place once the buyer is aware of the defect. Thus, there is in effect a long-term right to reject.[186]

In sale contracts, rejection of goods will lead to recovery of the full price paid on the basis that there has been a total failure of consideration. Where the contract is for hire or hire-purchase and the goods have been used for some time prior to rejection, there will not have been a total failure of consideration: therefore, rather than permitting the recovery of the full price, damages will equal the cost of hiring a replacement less the value of the use the hirer has enjoyed.[187] Where the defect is serious and arose early in the hire period this may result in a hirer recovering all, or almost all, of his money. Indeed in *Farnworth Finance Facilities v Attryde*,[188] Lord Denning suggested that the value of the use of the motorcycle for 4,000 miles was offset by the trouble the consumer had suffered. Because of this discretion to do justice by fixing the level of damages so as to take into account the value the buyer received from his or her use of the goods prior to rejection, these rules seem preferable to the rule in sales law that acceptance bars rejection. It is unfortunate that the Law Commission came out against any change in the law.[189] The position of contracts for the supply of goods which do not involve an element of hire, but which are nevertheless not subject to the rule that acceptance bars the right to reject (such as conditional sale, barter and exchange and work and materials contracts) is unclear. If goods rejected as unsatisfactory due to lack of durability are treated as giving rise to a total failure of consideration, then injustice could occur. Allowance should be made in appropriate cases for the use and enjoyment the consumer has had of the goods.

---

[185] Section 14, Supply of Goods (Implied Terms) Act 1973. It is the law's policy to treat hire-purchase and conditional sale transactions in a similar manner.

[186] *Farnworth Finance Facilities v Attryde* [1970] 1 WLR 1053.

[187] *Charterhouse Credit Ltd v Tolley* [1963] 2 QB 683.

[188] [1970] 1 WLR 1053.

[189] Law Com 160, Scot Law Com 104, *op. cit.*, at 5.1–5.13.

3.6.5 Damages

The measure of damages for breach of the implied quality conditions is the contractual one of seeking to put the consumer into the position he or she would have occupied had the contract been performed properly. Section 53(2), Sale of Goods Act 1979 provides:

> the measure of damages for breach of warranty is the estimated loss directly and naturally resulting, in the ordinary course of events, from the breach of warranty.

This is similar to the common law test in *Hadley v Baxendale*.[190] Section 53(3) goes on to state that:

> In the case of breach of warranty of quality such loss is prima facie the difference between the value of the goods at the time of delivery to the buyer and the value they would have had if they had fulfilled the warranty.

It is important to note that damages are not restricted merely to the intrinsic reduction in quality of the goods, but also cover consequential losses such as loss of profits which would have been generated from the intended use of the goods and more significantly in the consumer context, any personal injury damages.

From the consumer perspective the problem with damages as a remedy is that although they may seem to compensate consumers fully for the difference in value between goods of proper and defective quality, they nevertheless often fail to take into account the incidental costs incurred and the distress and inconvenience caused to consumers. In this respect the judgment in *Bernstein v Pamson Motors Ltd*[191] is enlightened for, although the remedy of rejection was refused, the damages awarded included the plaintiff's cost of making his way home on the day of the breakdown, the loss of a full tank of petrol, £150 for a 'totally spoilt day, comprising nothing but vexation' and compensation for being without a car (until such time as he unreasonably refused a substitute). The problem is that few such cases get to court and settlements rarely take account of these elements; nor indeed are consumers likely always to find so sympathetic a judge. Even this relatively generous calculation of damages fails to allow for the disappointment in having made a bad bargain, since no allowance was made for the fact that the consumer had been deprived of the feelings of pride and enjoyment in his new purchase. Damages for loss of enjoyment have been awarded in a few cases, but these have involved

---

[190]   (1854) 9 Exch. 341.
[191]   [1987] 2 All ER 220.

contracts whose purpose was for the consumers to enjoy themselves. Thus damages for loss of enjoyment have been awarded for breach of holiday contracts[192] or a contract to take wedding pictures,[193] but the courts have been reluctant to extend this to other contracts where the disappointment resulted simply from the failure to perform the contractual obligations.[194]

3.6.6 The New Remedies

It was always foreseen that the EC Consumer Sales Directive would afford the consumer four remedies: repair, replacement, price reduction and rescission. Initially the Commission had proposed that the consumer be allowed the free choice of the remedies, although rescission would not be available for minor defects. As the Directive progressed through the political process, one of the concessions the business community obtained was the introduction of a hierarchy in the remedies regime, with the consumer first having to allow the trader the opportunity to cure the defect. Although it was possible to show how the free choice regime could be applied without unduly prejudicing the trader,[195] the hierarchy is nevertheless aimed at ensuring the remedy is proportionate to the nature of the quality defect presenting itself. However, if this had replaced the existing United Kingdom law the level of protection would have been reduced, because the automatic right to reject goods breaching the implied quality conditions would have been lost. The Government's commitment not to reduce protection as a result of the implementation of the Directive explains why the United Kingdom has a dual remedies regime.

The new remedies regime only applies when the buyer deals as a consumer and the goods do not conform to the contract of sale.[196] In these situations the consumer also benefits from the presumption of non-conformity with regard to defects coming to light within six months of delivery.

---

[192] *Jarvis v Swans Tours Ltd* [1973] QB 233, *Jackson v Horizon Holidays Ltd* [1975] 1 WLR 1468.

[193] *Diesen v Samson* [1971] SLT 49.

[194] *Woodar Investment Development v Wimpey Construction UK* [1980] 1 WLR 277.

[195] H. Beale and G. Howells, 'EC Harmonisation of Consumer Sales Law – A Missed Opportunity? ' (1997) 12 *Journal of Contract Law* 21.

[196] Section 48A, Sale of Goods act 1979. Parallel rules are found in s. 11M-S Supply of Goods and Services Act 1982.

3.6.7 Repair or Replacement

If a consumer is seeking to rely upon the new remedies he/she must first require the seller to repair or replace the faulty goods. Any repair or replacement must be must undertaken within a reasonable time without causing significant inconvenience to the buyer and the seller must bear any necessary costs incurred in doing so (including labour, materials or postage).[197] In this regime questions relating to what is a reasonable time or significant inconvenience are determined by reference to the nature of the goods and the purpose for which the goods were acquired.[198]

In principle the consumer can choose between the remedies of repair or replacement. However, if one is impossible or disproportionate it cannot be required.[199] Repair might be impossible because spare parts are no longer available. Replacement might be impossible if the trader cannot access further supplies. In the case of individually crafted goods or second-hand goods it might be difficult to require replacement where each product has slightly different characteristics. Although some second-hand markets are fairly standardised, such as the second-hand car market where cars fit into easily recognisable price categories, nevertheless variations in their condition and lack of control over their supply would make it difficult to require that replacements be provided.

A buyer can also refuse to repair or replace the goods if this would be disproportionate. A remedy will be disproportionate in comparison to another if it imposes unreasonable costs taking into account the value of the goods if they had been in conformity with the contract, the significance of the lack of conformity and whether the other remedy could be effected without significant inconvenience to the buyer.[200] A controversial aspect of the implementation is that the disproportionateness of the requested remedy is not judged solely as between repair and replacement, but the requested remedy can also be judged against price reduction and rescission.[201] There is an ambiguity in the wording of the Directive. It could be read as entitling the consumer to either repair or replacement unless both were impossible. The only choice for the trader being to refuse the requested repair or replacement in favour of the alternative if one was disproportionate. However, this might lead to the seller having to perform a very onerous repair, for instance, out of all proportion to the value of the goods. The alternative interpretation is not very appealing from a consumer protection standpoint. It views repair and replacement as merely options

---

[197] Section 48B(2), Sale of Goods Act 1979.
[198] Section 48B(5), Sale of Goods Act 1979.
[199] Section 48B(35), Sale of Goods Act 1979.
[200] Section 48B(4), Sale of Goods Act 1979.
[201] See R. Bradgate and C. Twigg-Flesner, *op cit.*, at p. 119.

for the seller rather than the consumer. It brings all four remedies into the equation and allows the seller to choose the one that is least costly. This may be justifiable on economic efficiency grounds, but can easily lead to consumers being given redress in a form they are dissatisfied with. If this is the case one might wonder why the law does not simply list the four remedies and allow the trader to select which he offers. However, the law is in fact not quite so extreme and does allow the consumer to choose where remedies do not impose disproportionate burdens, but in the first instance that choice must be between repair and replacement. The cards are very much stacked in favour of the seller and this emphasises why the United Kingdom was keen to maintain its existing remedies regime with the clear right to reject.

Where repair and replacement is available the new law has taken the bold step of making specific performance available.[202]

3.6.8 Price Reduction and Rescission

The remedies of price reduction and rescission come into play where either the buyer cannot require repair or replacement or has failed to effect cure within a reasonable period of time and without significant inconvenience to the buyer.[203] Price reduction is a novel remedy in English law, although known to continental systems. It will often have the same result as damages, but has a different underlying rational. Rather than looking at what consequences flow from the breach, presumably the rational will be to see what price reduction is needed to reflect the value of the goods actually received by the consumer.

Rescission is the most drastic remedy and the Directive had restricted this by not allowing it for minor defects.[204] This restriction is not found in the implementing law, but usually fairness will be achieved by the court ordering another remedy. Rescission is conceptually distinct from repudiation which is the traditional remedy for breach of a condition. Rescission treats the contract as if it had never existed, whereas repudiation brings the contract to an end from the moment of repudiation. Rescission was the terminology used in the Directive and it has been understandably copied in the implementing law. However, although one should perhaps presume it has its traditional common law meaning, one must be conscious that as a European concept it will be interpreted by the European Court of Justice so as to give an autonomous European meaning which will be inspired by the traditions common to the member states and

---

[202] Section 48E(2), Sale of Goods Act 1979.
[203] Section 48C(2), Sale of Goods Act 1979.
[204] Article 3(6).

therefore may not be identical with the English understanding of rescission. Certainly where rescission occurs any reimbursement may be reduced to take account of the use the consumer has had of the goods.[205] Presumably the right to rescission would be available even where the right to reject has been lost by acceptance.[206]

A puzzling feature of the Directive is that while it weighed the disproportionate burden of repair and replacement against each other and arguably against all the other remedies, there is no similar test for refusing price reduction or rescission on the basis that the other is the less burdensome. One can easily imagine situations where price reduction was the most appropriate option, for instance where a product could not be replaced or would be expensive to repair and yet the defect was relatively insignificant. The Sale of Goods Act 1979 gets around this problem by giving the courts wide powers to replace the remedy required by the consumer with the one it considers appropriate.[207] Again, on a strict reading this appears to breach the Directive, but can be supported by looking at its scheme and the underlying logic of preventing disproportionate burdens being placed on traders.[208]

3.7 CONSUMER GUARANTEES

So far we have considered the quality obligations which are imposed by law on suppliers of goods and services. These can be seen as premised on an 'exploitative' theory, under which suppliers are assumed to be capable and (in some cases) willing to exploit their position to impose unfair terms on consumers and in particular to restrict their obligations in such a way that they do not satisfy the legitimate expectations of consumers. We now turn our attention to the express warranties given with goods. These are the additional warranties voluntarily given, usually by manufacturers, but occasionally by retailers. They typically come as part of the overall package of goods and are thus not paid for directly; rather the cost of the guarantee is included in the price of the goods. Occasionally these are very generous 'satisfaction' guarantees that simply allow you to return the product if you are unhappy with it. However, we will concentrate on the more typical guarantee which usually offers to put things right should the product fail within a specified period.

---

205   Section 48C(3), Sale of Goods Act 1979.
206   See, Bridge, *op. cit.*
207   Section 48E(3)(4).
208   See Recital 11.

3.7.1 Rationales for Regulation

Early regulation of consumer guarantees may have been based on an 'exploitative' theory which tried to prevent manufacturers from using guarantees as a medium to restrict their own obligations, rather than giving additional rights. There may have been some justification for this approach. For instance, the leading US product liability case of *Henningsen v Bloomfield Motors*[209] involved a guarantee for a new car under which the manufacturer agreed to replace defective parts for a short period (90 days or 4,000 miles), but only 'if the part is sent to the factory, transportation charges are prepaid, and if the examination discloses to its satisfaction that the part is defective'. As the Court itself said, it is hard to imagine a greater burden on the consumer or a less satisfactory remedy. The OFT in 1986 felt that 'All too often... it seems that guarantees are used merely as a marketing ploy, a source of additional revenue for the supplier, or even a means of diverting consumers' attention from their legal rights'.[210] These problems have largely been overcome through the development of better commercial practice prompted by (i) regulators, (ii) s. 5, Unfair Contract Terms Act 1977, which prohibits terms in consumer guarantees excluding loss or damage arising from the fact the goods are defective due to the negligence of someone involved in the manufacture or distribution of the goods,[211] and (iii) Regulation 4 of the Consumer Transactions (Restrictions on Statements) Order 1976[212] which requires guarantees to carry a notice that the consumer's statutory rights are unaffected. This latter provision also serves the useful ancillary function of bringing the existence of the statutory rights to the buyer's attention.

Consumer guarantees are voluntary in the sense that the manufacturer can decide whether or not to offer such a guarantee.[213] George Priest has argued that there are dangers in mandating too high a level of guarantee.[214] His criticisms are most relevant to legal guarantees which are mandatory, but also apply in a limited way to consumer guarantees, as it is sometimes suggested that where such guarantees are offered they should have a

---

[209] (1960) 161 A 2d 69.

[210] Office of Fair Trading, *Consumer Guarantees* (OFT, 1986) at p. 27. More recent findings of the OFT suggest consumer guarantees are less of a problem.

[211] There is no similar provision relating to services.

[212] S.I. 1976/1813.

[213] In some countries, such as Greece, there is a requirement that all consumer durables be accompanied by a guarantee, whilst in France a standard (NFX 5002) is mandated for electrical household appliances and audiovisual equipment.

[214] G. Priest, 'A Theory of the Consumer Product Warranty' (1981) 90 *Yale LJ* 1297; cf. W. Whitford, 'Comment on a Theory of the Consumer Product Warranty' (1982) 91 *Yale LJ* 1371.

mandatory minimum content. He argues that his 'investment theory' largely both explains and justifies the limitations which are found in consumer guarantees. His argument is that the best level of cover should be fixed by the market rather than be mandatorily imposed. If this level is too high, then there will be little incentive for consumers to allocate resources to avoid defects arising: thus the number of defects will increase and the generality of consumers will be forced to pay for those who either overuse or misuse their products.

Priest's theory might well explain why there are certain exclusions in consumer guarantees, such as those relating to unusual uses or non-consumer uses of goods, and why there are sometimes shorter guarantee periods for product parts which might be subject to greater intensity of use by consumers. Yet this free market philosophy only works in a market characterised by perfect information. A third theory in relation to guarantees is the 'signal' theory. This is premised on the idea that a 'guarantee' sends certain signals to consumers about a product's quality. Thus most suppliers would wish to have product guarantees that at least reflected the general level of such guarantees, so as to encourage confidence in their product. However, there are dangers. Manufacturers may realise that consumers are only interested in the central aspects of the guarantee and thus take the opportunity to restrict the application of its less important elements. Even more dangerous is the fact that manufacturers can seek to benefit from the confidence the granting of a guarantee engenders in the consumer, whilst in fact giving nothing or very little beyond what is required by law. This is the thinking behind laws such as the US Magnuson-Moss Warranty – Federal Trade Commission Improvement Act 1975.[215]

The Magnuson-Moss Act requires a clear and conspicuous designation of warranties as either 'full' or 'limited'. Full warranties must meet specified standards. For instance, the guarantee must contain specified information such as, identifying the warrantor, including his address; providing a statement of the products or parts covered and what the warrantor will do in the event of a defect, when and at whose expense; stating the duration of the warranty; providing details of how the warranty can be invoked and of informal dispute machinery, as well as a statement as to whether this machinery has to be invoked before going to court.[216]

---

215   15 US Code 2301. See Twigg-Flesner, *op cit.*, Chapter 6.

216   In an attempt to reduce consumer enforcement costs, consumers can be required to use informal dispute settlement procedures prior to the courts if those procedures meet the standards imposed by the Federal Trade Commission. That these standards are very strict may be part of the explanation as to why few manufacturers have established such schemes: see I. Ramsay, *Consumer Protection* (Weidenfeld and Nicolson, 1989) at p. 451.

Such warranties must not affect the implied warranties and as a minimum must provide for remedy i.e. repair within a reasonable time and without charge if a consumer product has a defect, if it malfunctions or fails to conform to the written warranty. There is also a so-called 'lemon' provision whereby, after a reasonable number of attempts[217] to remedy defects or malfunctions, the warrantor must allow the consumer to elect either a refund or replacement (without charge) of the product or part; if the replacement of a part is involved, there shall be no charge for its installation.

Such provisions help to increase the information provided to consumers as they ensure that the guarantee has some content. However, to be effective there must be either a pre-vetting system, so that warrantors seek permission to use certain words or perhaps display a certain standard mark (although there is a danger of a profusion of such marks) or else protection of designated terms under trade description law. The advantage of such a scheme is that consumers can be educated about the value of looking for products carrying such guarantees and this can stimulate competition. One could even imagine a system of graduated designations depending on just how superior to the legal minimum the guarantee was, though an over complicated system must be avoided.[218]

It has been argued that consumer guarantees actually have a far more practical role in providing a mechanism through which informal dispute resolution can be facilitated.[219] Even some of those who doubt whether guarantees act as effective signals of quality nevertheless support the encouragement of guarantees because of this redress function.[220]

3.7.2 Legal Problems Surrounding the Consumer Guarantee and Reform Proposals[221]

The legal problems posed by consumer guarantees include: the need to ensure they do not undermine the legal minimum protection provided by mandatory law, perhaps by creating confusion as to which applies; concerns over their legal enforceability; and, ensuring consumers have

---

[217] The Federal Trade Commission can produce rules specifying what constitutes a reasonable number of attempts by the warrantor to remedy a defect or malfunction under different circumstances.

[218] See G. Howells and C. Bryant, 'Consumer Guarantees: Competition or Regulation?' (1993) 1 *Consum LJ* 3.

[219] J. Braucher, 'An informal resolution model of consumer product warranty law' (1985) *Wisconsin Law Review* 1405.

[220] Twigg-Flesner, *op. cit.*

[221] See generally G. Howells and C. Bryant, *op. cit.*

proper information about the content of the guarantees. English law now addresses these issues in a far more satisfactory manner, although despite flirting with the idea it has failed to ensure that when used terms like guarantee can be assumed to have a core content, as under the Magnuson-Moss Act in the US.

In 1986, the OFT found the position relating to consumer guarantees to be unsatisfactory, but saw its role as being the use of persuasion to improve the position.[222] It was working towards greater transparency and whilst recommending that the number of expressions used should be limited did not seek to impose any standardised meaning on the use of such terms. The National Consumer Council's report, *Competing in Quality*[223] went further and proposed that the term 'guarantee' be restricted to promises given free of charge. These would have to be labelled as 'total guarantees', 'retailers' total guarantees' (where granted by the retailer) or 'limited guarantees'. The influence of the Magnuson-Moss Act was apparent. The proposals respected the voluntary nature of consumer guarantees, but would have required a statement to be made as to whether cars and specified consumer durables carried a 'total guarantee' and, if so, its duration. Although 'limited guarantees' could be given, they would have to be clearly marked as such. The National Consumer Council proposals took the provision of consumer information seriously. Consumers can be educated to look for 'total guarantees' and be informed of their meaning, whilst they will be quizzical of a product or service which offers only a 'limited guarantee'. In 1990, a Private Member's Consumer Guarantees Bill sought to implement these proposals, as well as those of the Law Commission to reform the implied quality conditions,[224] but the proposals on guarantees were unacceptable to the Government and the Bill failed to reach the statute book.[225]

The matter of consumer guarantees was again raised in the *Department of Trade and Industry Consultation Document on Consumer Guarantees*.[226] The Department rejected the notion of using legislation to require that guarantees be given or to establish the minimum content of guarantees. It preferred to leave the matter to be resolved by market competition. It did, however, have a few positive proposals to resolve some

---

[222] Consumer Guarantees – A Report.

[223] NCC (1989).

[224] The Bill would have replaced merchantable quality with a test of 'satisfactory quality' (instead of 'acceptable quality' as favoured by the Law Commission) and the problem of defining defect in the consumer guarantee provisions would also have been resolved by relating it to the standard of 'satisfactory quality'.

[225] See C. Willett, 'The Unacceptable Face of the Consumer Guarantees Bill', (1991) 54 *MLR* 552.

[226] DTI (February 1992).

of the legal problems surrounding consumer guarantees. Thus, it proposed that manufacturers should be civilly liable for the performance of their guarantee to the consumer and that in cases where the manufacturer is based outside the UK the manufacturer's guarantee would be enforceable against the importer.[227]

More dramatic, perhaps, was the proposal that retailers should be jointly and severally liable with the manufacturer for the manufacturer's guarantee. In principle, an increased number of defendants is desirable so that insolvency and other chance events do not prevent the consumer from recovering. The law of contribution and the negotiation of contracts can then determine how the losses fall within the commercial chain. Nevertheless there may be some problems with holding retailers jointly liable with manufacturers, particularly for small retailers. Part of the problem is that retailers will not be able to control the guarantees given by manufacturers and may even be unaware of their content. If they are to be made liable for them, then there might have to be a provision (as exists under Irish sales of goods legislation) for retailers to disclaim liability for manufacturers' guarantees. Certainly the retailer could not be expected to carry out all the terms of the guarantee; for instance, repairing obligations must be interchangeable with monetary compensation since, apart from the very large electrical outlets and department stores, retailers do not, and cannot be expected to, keep service departments.

Reform of English law in this area has however finally come about because of the Consumer Sales Directive. In its Green Paper the Commission had been keen to promote the use of 'European' guarantees, by which it meant the common application of guarantee conditions for all goods of the same type and brand throughout the Community and the real possibility of implementing the guarantee wherever the goods are purchase. The Commission suggested a term such as 'Euro-guarantee' which should be a protected label or designation. These plans were dropped, which is a shame as it is unfortunate that companies can continue to supply products with differing guarantees within the same common market place. However, the legal problems surrounding consumer guarantee have been largely resolved.

3.7.3 Link with Minimum Legal Protection

In some European legal systems there is a requirement that consumer guarantees must give something over and above the minimum legal requirement. Although desirable in principle, there are various practical

---

[227] The fact that the importer is the importer into the United Kingdom and not the importer into the European Union might cause some problems under European Law.

problems with giving effect to such a requirement. Often guarantees are given by manufacturers rather than retailers on whom the legal requirements are placed: is that enough in itself to satisfy this requirement? Usually it would be possible to show how in some respects the guarantee is more protective than the law requires even if overall it is less protective. Would such a guarantee satisfy the requirement? This requirement has not become part of the Directive.

A more serious risk is the danger that consumer guarantees fail to make consumers aware of their legal rights or worse still represent that the consumer has to rely on the guarantee rather than those rights. This is addressed by the Directive, but did not need to be implemented as the Consumer Restrictions on Statements Order 1976[228] requires all guarantees to contain a statement that such rights do not or will not affect the statutory rights of the consumer. The Directive might be thought to require more than this negative statement, since it says the guarantee shall state the consumer has legal rights under applicable national legislation. However, it must be implicit in a statement that your statutory rights are not affected that you have such rights and there is no obligation to provide a summary of those rights.

3.7.4 Enforceability

The remaining elements of enforceability and content are dealt with in the Sale and Supply of Goods to Consumers Regulations 2002.[229] These define a consumer guarantee as 'any undertaking to a consumer by a person acting in the course of his business, given without extra charge, to reimburse the price paid or to replace, repair or handle consumer goods in any way if they do not meet the specifications set out in the guarantee statement or in relevant advertising'. The guarantor is 'the person who offers a consumer guarantee to a consumer'.[230]

Regulation 15(1) makes it clear that consumer guarantees take effect at the time the goods are delivered as a contractual obligation owed by the guarantor under the conditions set out in the guarantee statement. This is a useful clarification of the law. Although they raised few practical problems, there were theoretical difficulties sometimes in demonstrating that consumer guarantees were enforceable. This may have been because if the consumer had not known about them before contracting they might not be found to form part of the bargain; or more significantly where they were offered by someone other that the seller there would be problems because

---

[228] S.I. 1976/1813, Regulation 4.
[229] S.I. 2002/3045.
[230] Regulation 2.

of the lack of privity. Courts in the past might have needed to be imaginative in using techniques like the collateral contract to make a consumer guarantee binding. Often this might have been premised on the return of a guarantee card. Such techniques are no longer necessary.

However, privity still poses some problems which have not been resolved. In other words subsequent owners of the goods, be they donees or purchasers, do not have any contractual rights against the guarantor, even assuming the original purchaser can assert such rights. Where goods are bought by someone at the express request of another, the courts might circumvent the privity rule by the use of agency and might even on appropriate facts be able to find the donor of goods to have acted as the agent of the donee. In any event, such analyses would not assist the subsequent purchaser.

3.7.5 Content

The Directive did not try to control the content of guarantees by imposing minimum content rules. Neither did it adopt the intermediate position of having default rules that apply unless the guarantee provides otherwise. Instead it restricted itself to requiring that certain information be provided. Guarantees must set out in 'plain intelligible language'[231] their contents and the essential particulars for making claims, notably the duration and territorial scope of the guarantee as well as the name and address of the guarantor.[232] If offered within the United Kingdom they must be in English.[233]

The consumer can request from the guarantor or anyone who offers the goods that the guarantee be made available in writing or in another durable medium.[234] This is intended to encourage consumers to shop around and compare guarantees before buying. However, it is a rather symbolic provision for one should not expect many consumers to take advantage of it.

---

[231] Cf. discussion of this phrase in Unfair Terms in Consumer Contracts Regulations, see Section 5.6.1.2.

[232] Regulation 15(2).

[233] Regulation 15(5).

[234] For discussion of writing and durable medium, see Section 7.4.4.

3.8 EXTENDED WARRANTIES

There has been a trend for manufacturers and particularly retailers to offer extended warranties purchasable by the consumer.[235] These usually cover breakdown of the product, but some also extend to accidental damage and theft. The cost of such extended warranties has been the subject of debate, due to the allegation that some retailers push their own policies even if they are not the best available and leave the consumer ignorant of cheaper contracts offered by manufacturers. The OFT reported concerns on this topic in 1994.[236] In 2002 it reported again and found continued evidence that the market was uncompetitive.[237] It found consumers face information imbalances about the reliability of electrical products and retailers exploit their point of sale advantage over other possible competitors. The policies make excessive profits because of their low claims ratios and their pricing does not seem to reflect differing failure rates for differing products. It is particularly unfortunate that low income and vulnerable consumers are more likely to take out such extended warranties.

The OFT referred the matter to the Competition Commission, which found that indeed there was a complex monopoly situation in the market for extended warranties sold at the point of sale.[238] The majority recommended that the price of extended warranties be displayed alongside electrical goods and in advertisements. There should be a right to cancel warranties within 45 days with a full refund. Written quotations should be available for 30 days on the same terms including any offer of a discount. Information should be provided on statutory rights, the availability of extended warranties from other organisations, possible relevance of household insurance, cancellation rights and the nature of the warranty. A minority recommendation would restrict point of sale warranties to one year leaving the market to compete for extensions beyond that.

In theory this two tier guarantee level – normal guarantee and extended guarantee – should be applauded as it allows consumers to select the level of cover desired, but does not force all consumers to pay for long-term guarantees. The danger is that the additional cover is both overpriced and provides only what consumers had come to expect under the normal guarantee. There is also a related issue, namely that consumers may feel bound to take on the extended warranties because the cost of after-sales service is priced artificially high.

---

235 See C. Twigg-Flesner, *op. cit.*, 46–50.

236 See OFT, *Extended Warranties on Electrical Goods*, (OFT, 1994) which complained of a lack of transparency and competition and questionable selling practices.

237 OFT, Extended Warranties on Domestic Electrical Goods – A Report on an OFT investigation.

238 Competition Commission, Extended warranties on domestic electrical goods, (2003).

3.9 REFLECTIONS ON THE LAW RELATING TO QUALITY

The rules relating to quality are of great practical significance to consumers. They also provide useful material with which to consider many issues that are central to the study of consumer law. It is a good illustration of the rather patchwork and *ad hoc* development of consumer law. Common law rules have been put into statutory form at different times and with different results depending upon the form of contract. European regulation has added another layer of complexity and caused a separate regime for consumer sales to be developed. The case for harmonisation and possibly codification clearly needs to be considered.

Regarding the substance of the law, we have followed the debate over the extent to which mandatory minimum quality conditions should be laid down or whether businesses should be left free to compete in the marketplace by offering a range of levels of guarantee. There is also the connected question of the extent to which information provisions can be relied on to inform consumers of the quality of the product or guarantee they are purchasing and the form in which that information should be provided.

Recently, there has been recognition that the law in this area must be modernised to take on board the consumer perspective. Traditional legal rules, such as the privity rule, have been viewed as problematic in the modern economy in which the consumers more often look to the manufacturer than the retailer for redress when goods are defective. New solutions have started to be addressed, but producer liability is still not fully on the agenda.

Europe has once again been the engine for reform in this area. Whether it has produced the right reforms is a matter for debate. Certainly it has increased the complexity of English consumer sales law. Bizarrely the Directive seems to have failed to address the real issues that might improve cross-border consumer sales; namely, enhancing the prospects of the consumer having a defendant in his own state by developing producer or network liability in the case of exclusive distribution networks. What it has done it ensure that all European states have a common modern approach to sales law. European Community law is at the heart of sales law which is itself the cornerstone of private law. This has given impetus to the development of European Private Law as a subject and debates about whether Europe should have a Civil Code. Also whereas traditionally sales law was developed with the paradigm business to business transaction in mind, increasingly rules are being developed in the consumer context which are 'influencing' of 'infecting' (depending on your viewpoint) commercial law.

Chapter 4

Product and Service Liability

4.1 THE NATURE OF THE DEBATE

4.1.1 What is Product and Service Liability?

Product and service liability are concerned with the damage which products or services cause to persons or property (other than the defective product itself). Product and service liability are traditionally seen as being concerned with tort liability, where the duty of care has imposed obligations on businesses to protect consumers from physical damage to their person or property. By contrast, the purpose of contract law is to protect the economic interests of the consumer; as such, it is more concerned with defects in the quality of the product or service itself. The boundaries, however, are not clear-cut. Indeed one of the debates in modern product liability law is the extent to which the defectiveness standard should be based around consumer expectation rather than risk:utility. The consumer expectations standard has its origins in contract law principles where the transaction gives rise to expectations.

4.1.2 Product and Service Liability Distinguished

Although concerned with essentially the same problems – how to raise consumer safety standards and how to compensate consumers who have suffered accidents – product and service liability have tended to be treated separately. There has been a greater willingness to move towards imposing strict liability for products than services. This bifurcation is unfortunate. Many accidents arise out of the provision of products in the course of a service, and sometimes it is unclear whether an accident has arisen because of a fault in the product or the way the service provider has used the product. Take a car repair. There may be a dispute as to whether an accident has been caused by the replacement part or the way it was installed, particularly if the manufacturer complains that the product was used inappropriately. It is by no means self-evident that a lower standard should apply to service providers than to the supplier of goods.[1]

The general justification for subjecting services to a lower standard of liability than products is that outcomes cannot be guaranteed where services are concerned. Thus whilst service providers can be expected to take care to try to achieve the desired result, a successful outcome cannot be assured.[2] For instance, where the service involves an interrelationship between the service provider and the subject of the service, the outcome often cannot be predicted. Certainly those who provide medical or health care services are aware that individuals react differently to treatment. Equally it is understood that garments can sometimes react idiosyncratically to chemicals applied to clean or treat them, while car mechanics and domestic engineers warn that very occasionally their repair may not work depending upon the response of the particular product to the attempted repair.

To reject strict liability for services may be to misunderstand the debate. Since many services are now automated, a certain consistency of outcome can be predicted and expected. Strict liability does not necessarily mean blaming the service provider and imposing liability every time a service fails to produce the desired result. For instance, the simple failure of a technique would not attract liability (other than possible contractual liability) unless it had caused actual damage. Where services do cause damage, either due to some error or for reasons unknown, then the same risk-spreading rationales can be invoked to justify liability as have been used in the context of products. To take a medical example, whether a patient is treated with drugs or operated on may be a matter of patient or doctor preference. It seems absurd that the law can protect the patient against unknown risks associated with the drug, but not the unknown risks

---

1   See J. Stapleton, *Product Liability* (Butterworths, 1994) pp. 323–36.

2   A service provider could however guarantee the outcome and attract liability in contract for that promise. This was alleged in *Thake v Maurice* [1986] 1 All ER 497 where it was claimed that the doctor had guaranteed the permanent sterilisation of Mr Thake, a railwayman who already had five children. However the majority of the Court of Appeal held this was not the effect of their conversations with the doctor since 'in medical science all things, or nearly all things, are uncertain... that knowledge is part of the general experience of mankind'. Mr Thake had become fertile again by the process known as 'spontaneous recanalisation' and the doctor was held liable in tort for his failure to warn of this possibility. However in *Greaves & Co (Contractors) Ltd v Baynham Meikle & Partners* [1975] 1 WLR 1095, engineers were found to have warranted that a warehouse would be fit for its intended purpose. Lane LJ stressed that this did not mean that all professionals would be taken to warrant the successful outcome of their endeavours, merely that the facts of the case justified the implication of a warranty.

associated with the operation. The operation does not have to cure the patient, but it should not make his position worse (except, possibly, to the extent of risks which were accepted as inherent within the procedure).

Much of the controversy surrounding service liability stems from the fact that it includes high-risk areas such as medical negligence. Not only does this mean that powerful pressure groups campaign against extensions of service liability, but also that courts and legislatures are hesitant to impose what may turn out to be a potentially wide and burdensome liability. Hard cases such as medical negligence, and its counterpart in the products sphere – pharmaceutical liability – point up the problems of using the private law to strike an appropriate balance between compensation for those injured and the sensible development of activities which are clearly socially justifiable and economically useful. The danger is that, if these areas are treated as special cases and dealt with separately under administrative or insurance based schemes then, rather than heralding a more general reform of the law, the excuse will be made that, as the most serious problems have been solved, little need be done in other areas.

We shall see in the area of consumer safety law that the public law controls introduced by the General Product Safety Directive have been clarified to make it clear that they apply to products supplied in the context of service.[3] The EC is also considering regulating service safety.[4] However, as regards civil liability until recently there have no moves to impose more than a standard of due care for services, and attempts to introduce a directive reversing the burden of proof were rejected.[5] The Commission has recently commissioned a study on civil liability of services.

4.1.3 The Move towards Strict Liability

The trend to impose stricter standards in the area of products liability will become evident. Thus it is often stated that the European Product Liability Directive[6] introduced 'strict liability' into Europe. This followed the lead given by the US, which had known strict products liability since at least 1963.[7] However, the term 'strict liability' is often misunderstood. It does not equate with absolute liability. Most of the strict liability tests are formulated using a defectiveness standard that places some of the risks on

3   See Section 10.3.4.
4   *Ibid.*
5   OJ 1991 C12/8, see Chapter 4.3.3.
6   374/85/EEC, OJ 1985 L210/29.
7   See the decision in *Greenman v Yuba Power Products* 377 P 2d 897 (1963) (Supreme Court of California) and s. 402A Restatement (Second) of Torts (1965).

to the product/service user. Thus imposing strict liability does not necessarily make the producer the insurer of all harm caused by the product. Moreover, even if liability is imposed in principle some defences are normally available to the trader.

The term 'strict liability' covers a range of liability systems of varying degrees of strictness. In theory, whereas fault-based systems judge the behaviour of producers and suppliers against some objective standard of what should reasonably be expected of them, strict liability judges the end product (or service) against objective criteria. It is not a sufficient excuse that the failure to meet the objective standard can be explained away on reasonable grounds. The objective criteria are usually based on a consumer expectation or risk:utility analysis.

The EC Product Liability Directive essentially adopts a consumer expectation standard. This can be seen as less objective than a risk:utility analysis, since it turns on the subjective appreciations of consumers as a body. Broadly, however, the two standards can be seen as being fairly similar as consumer expectations tend to be based on a rough-and-ready balancing of risks and benefits. Equally these standards need not produce results very different from those arrived at in negligence, for both consumer expectations and the risk:utility calculations seem to take into account what can be expected of producers. Thus it was stated in the Supreme Court of Washington that: 'In considering the reasonable expectations of the ordinary consumer, a number of factors must be considered including the relative cost of the product, the gravity of the potential harm from the claimed defect and the cost and feasibility of eliminating or minimising the risk'.[8] The extent to which the English High Court decision in *A v National Blood Authority*[9] signals a different stricter approach by deciding not to take into account the avoidability of harm will be discussed below.

What, then, is the difference between a negligence and a strict liability regime? The answer is, partly, that under the former one judges the actions of the various agents in the light of circumstances appertaining at the time the action occurred. Under the latter one *usually* judges the product by the standards existing at the time of the accident or possibly even at the time of trial. Thus, the time frame of the assessment is the essential element in a strict liability regime. However, the word usually is emphasised for strict liability regimes can also contain 'state of the art' or 'development risks' defences which undermine this principle.[10]

---

[8]   *Seattle First National Bank v Tabert* 542 P 2d 774 at 779 (1975).

[9]   [2001] 3 All ER 289.

[10] See C. Newdick, 'The future of Negligence in Product Liability' (1987) *LQR* 288, 'The Development Risks Defence of the Consumer Protection Act 1987' (1988) *Camb*

The terms 'state of the art' and 'development risks' are often used interchangeably, but we prefer to distinguish them as being two separate though related defences. We understand the 'state of the art' defence to refer to the plea that the product should not be found defective since it offered the level of safety considered adequate at the time it was marketed, albeit that standards have subsequently improved. Thus, whereas a car without front seat belts might be considered defective today, a car so produced in the 1950's would not be held defective for failing to include a safety device which had not become standard, or even common, at that date. Though known of at the time of sale, the danger was accepted.

'Development risks', on the other hand, are risks which were not known of at the time of marketing. If they had been known about they would have prevented the product from being marketed according to the standards of safety current at the time of marketing. For example, the drug diethylstilbestrol (DES) gave rise to vaginal, cervical and genital cancer in the offspring of mothers who ingested the drug as a miscarriage preventative. This unfortunate side effect had a latency period of ten to twenty years. Clearly the risk was not known of when the product was marketed; equally it was a risk which would never have been considered acceptable judged against the standards in place at the time of marketing. Where producers are not held liable for such risks, the defence is known as the 'development risks defence'. The inclusion of these defences often provokes criticism from consumer groups for they can be viewed as undermining the rationales of risk spreading and loss distribution which underpin strict product liability. However, these defences do provide mechanisms through which legal systems can fine-tune the degree of 'strictness' within a liability regime and hence determine the exact manner in which risks are allocated between producer and consumer.[11]

Another hallmark of strict liability regimes is that they tend to channel liability towards the person best placed to control the product and insure the risk involved. In most cases[12] this is the producer. This is recognition that in modern conditions where mass produced, pre-packaged goods are the norm, the consumer looks to the producer (rather than the retailer) for guarantees regarding the safety of goods. This contrasts with the position both under the law of contract, which traditionally has imposed liabilities only on contracting parties, and with the law of tort, which imposes

---

LJ 455 and 'Risk, Uncertainty and Knowledge in the Development Risks Defence' (1991) 20 *Anglo-Am L Rev* 309.

[11] See N. Terry, 'State of the Art Evidence: From Logical Construct to Judicial Retrenchment', (1991) 20 *Anglo-Am Law Rev* 285.

[12] In the European Product Liability Directive other policies dictated the additional placing of liability on 'own-branders' and importers into the Community, with lesser obligations being placed on suppliers.

liability on the party at fault regardless of their place in the production chain. In the area of service liability, no similar move has occurred to trace liability back to the person who develops dangerous ways of providing services rather than the actual provider of the service. Thus when the European Commission issued a draft European Service Liability Directive (since withdrawn) imposing liability on the 'supplier of services', the one and only extension was that, in some circumstances franchisors would have been jointly and severally liable with their franchisees. Of course, the network of links in the service sector is different in nature from that in the retail goods sector, as services are not physically passed between the parties in the same way. On the other hand, intellectual property rights are owned in techniques and processes used in the provision of services. It is therefore interesting to note that, outside the specific area of franchising, no attempt has been made to bring those who may be the true source of the danger within specific service liability regimes, although they may, of course, be subject to negligence liability.

4.1.4 The Nature of Defects

4.1.4.1 Categories of Product Defects

In relation to products, eight possible types of defect/damage can be isolated – a categorisation offered simply to help elucidate the issues involved in this complicated area. There may well be overlaps between the categories, as for example when a design defect also involves a development risks defect.

(i)   Manufacturing defects concern defects caused by an error in the production process or by the use of defective raw materials. Courts are more likely to impose liabilities for this type of defect than any other. This is partly because it is easier for them when an objective standard exists against which the defective product can be judged (the perfect product), and also because it can be presumed that the flaw arose from somewhere within the production and distribution chain. Moreover the consequences of imposing liability can be less severe, since there is no question of requiring the product to be redesigned or permanently withdrawn from the market. The faulty product or batch must simply be withdrawn and any damage remedied.

(ii) Design defects are the most serious of all since defective design threatens the continued existence of a product, at least in the form in which it is currently marketed. Courts are understandably hesitant about condemning the design of products, because choices over design raise 'polycentric' issues and a number of factors may inter-react.[13] Many of these cases involve a complicated balance of risks and benefits – safety versus access to innovative/useful/attractive consumer products and pharmaceuticals. An added complication is that the more safety features that are built into the design, the higher the cost of the product. This can penalise lower-income consumers, who lose access to goods in order that higher-income consumers can buy themselves greater safety.

(iii) Warning defects are closely related to design defects. While the product design itself may not be inherently defective, the product can be rendered defective by the lack of a warning. Warning defects arise where a product contains an acceptable risk, but is rendered defective by the failure of the producer to inform the consumer of that risk. Courts may be more willing to find a product defective on the grounds of failure to warn than for defective design, since this is less judgmental. The danger is that, if too many warnings are given, their impact is lost, either because the more important warnings are obscured amongst the others or because warnings become so commonplace that they are not taken seriously. The behavioural economics literature shows us how for many reasons consumer may fail to react 'rationally' to warnings.[14] They may be unable to process them properly or discount the likelihood that misfortune will affect them.

(iv) Instruction defects are similar to warning defects in that they concern the information provided to the consumer, but differ in that the defect is not a failure to warn of an inherent danger in the product. Instead the defect involves the creation of danger by the failure to inform the consumer of how to use a product safely. The mutually exclusive nature of warning and instruction defects is well illustrated by an example borrowed from Dillard and Hart[15] who describe a new toothpaste which permanently discolours teeth if used more than twice a day. They suggest that an instruction such as 'For Best Results Use Twice Daily' or even 'Do Not Use More Than Twice Daily' would not be sufficient to avoid liability. There is a need both for instructions on to how to use the product and for a warning of the dangers involved if these instructions are not complied with.

(v) Development risks defects are those which only come to light after the product has been marketed. Whether these defects are covered by the

---

13   J. Henderson, 'Judicial Review of Manufacturers' Conscious Design Choices: The Limits of Adjudication' (1973) 73 *Columbia LR* 1531.

14   See Chapter 1.1.2.

15   H.C. Dillard and H. Hart, 'Product Liability; Directions for Use and Failure to Warn' (1955) 41 *Virginia LR* 145.

liability regime is a touchstone by which to test how 'strict' liability is under any particular regime.

(vi) State of the art defects are elements of a product which, although acceptable when marketed, have subsequently become less acceptable. This is not because they now pose any greater danger, but rather because safer alternatives or replacements have emerged or because the need for the product has been reduced in some other way. Liability is not typically imposed for state of the art defects.

(vii) Post-marketing defects concern not so much the product per se but the failure to warn of dangers, to recall products or to take other remedial action once a danger has been discovered. Even fault-based systems can use this as a means of compensating for development risks if the producer does not act responsibly once such risks are discovered. What is required will of course depend upon the nature and extent of the danger concerned.

(viii)   System damage, a term coined by Børge Dahl,[16] covers risks which are inherent within a product, whose marketing is nevertheless considered justifiable. Examples might be the risk of being cut by a sharp knife or, more contentiously, the risk of contracting cancer from smoking cigarettes. Since the product is of an acceptable standard, we call this 'system damage' rather than 'system defect'. If liability is imposed for system damage, then the legal regime will be approaching the position where the producer becomes the insurer of his products.

4.1.4.2 The Manufacturing/Design Defect Distinction

The distinction between manufacturing defects and design defects is controversial. This is driven by US debates where there is a move to restrict true strict liability to manufacturing defects.[17] Those who oppose this point out that it is hard to demarcate some manufacturing defects from design defects. For instance, it a screw gives way on an isolated occasion this might be put down to it being a weak screw, but the more frequent the incidents the more likely it is to be viewed as a design error for failing to select an appropriate type of screw.[18]

When an English judge, Mr Justice Burton in *A and Others v National Blood Authority*,[19] reviewed this debate he preferred to distinguish between standard and non-standard products. Non-standard products refer

---

[16] B. Dahl, 'Product Liability in Denmark' in *Product Liability in Europe* (Kluwer-Harrap, 1975).

[17] See Chapter 4.2.2.

[18] J. Vargo, '2(b) or not 2(b), that is the question' [1998] *Consum. L.J.* 144.

[19] [2001] 3 All ER 289.

to either one-off manufacturing defects or design defects resulting from the way the production system was designed. Maybe this terminology will become more common in the United Kingdom, but as it is well known in the international literature we will continue to refer to manufacturing and design defects for the time being. Although this may seem a rather dry terminological debate in fact it represents a battleground at the heart of the product liability debate. It connects to the debate about whether strict product liability was intended to be merely a tidying up exercise and a means of addressing evidential problems or represented a more fundamental shift in liability regimes.

4.1.4.3 Service Defects

The types of product damage find their counterparts in relation to services, though some of the terms might be expressed differently. Thus instead of manufacturing defects, one might talk in terms of service component defects. These would cover the use of defective materials or even incompetent staff. Rather than design defects one would talk of process defects, where the complaint would relate to the actual technique or process used. Of course there are some cases which straddle the boundary of service component and process defects. For example, damage caused by the decision of a service supplier to use a particular technique or process in a particular case may either be put down to an error by the individual concerned (service component defect) or be blamed on the actual process (process defect) depending on just how maverick the individual's judgement is considered to be. Warning defects are commonplace in the service sector, where consumers frequently complain that they were not told of relevant dangers, for example, of the risks associated with an operation or with a dry-cleaning process that can damage sensitive materials. Information defects are not usually related to a failure to inform the consumer on how to perform the service, for this is normally done by the professional concerned. The information defect will arise from a failure to tell the consumer how to behave after the service has been performed, for example the need to watch out for danger signs that a repair has not worked properly, or to use the product at less than full capacity for a certain period of time after repair. Development risk, state of the art and post-marketing defects can equally apply to services as to products. System damage also results from services, for example, the risk that an attempted repair could actually damage the object being repaired or the risk of side effects from operations.

4.1.5 Rationales for Strict Liability

There are several justifications for imposing strict liability.[20] Indeed one of the problems in this whole area is a lack of articulation of the rationale underlying the adoption of strict liability.

For some minimalists it is indeed merely a rationalisation of the law. They note that, particularly, in the United States the privity principle was being stretched to make producers liable for harm their products caused. Making the producer's directly liable in tort, rather than indirectly liable in contract, was merely removing an anomaly in jurisdictions where contract doctrines had been manipulated to provide redress. Elsewhere it prevented unnecessarily circuitous litigation where sellers had to be sued and then have producers and other links in the supply chain joined. Equally it was also seen as a means of assisting consumers overcome an evidential imbalance. This is most evident in relation to manufacturing defects where the manufacturer is obviously better place to demonstrate whether things went wrong during the manufacturing process. The manufacturer should, however, also be better placed to know the alternative design choices that were available. In a review of the reform debates which gave rise to strict product liability in the Restatement (Second) of Torts (1965) it has been convincingly argued that these modest objectives were what the reformers had in mind.[21]

Product liability has both compensation and deterrence functions. In terms of compensation it is viewed as a means of spreading the risks attached to the use of a product or service across all users, rather than letting the risk lie where it falls on the unfortunate victims. So in a sense strict liability imposes a compulsory form of insurance, with the premium being borne by the producer. In theory the producer should be able to reflect this cost in the price of the product. The threat of having to pay compensation is the deterrent effect. Obviously the higher the likelihood of being sued and the greater the compensation the bigger the deterrent threat. Deterrence is probably a greater motivation for product liability in the US than Europe. Product liability litigation is more common in the US and damages higher, especially if punitive damages are brought into the equation. In many ways this is symptomatic of the US and EC approaches to consumer protection.[22] The US prefers to rely on private law, whereas Europe still believes the state can control the marketplace. Also there is

---

20   See J. Montgomery and D. Owen, 'Reflections on the Theory and Administration of Strict Tort Liability for Defective Products' (1976) 27 *SCLRev* 803; also see Chapter 1.5.2.

21   G. Priest 'Strict Products Liability the Original Intent' (1989) 10 *Cardozo LR* 2301.

22   G. Howells and T Wilhelmsson, 'EC and US Approaches to Consumer Protection – Should the Gap be Bridged?' *Yearbook of European Law 1997*, 207

probably still less mistrust of corporations in Europe, or at least a reluctance to believe that they would expose consumers to harm solely to increase profits. On the other hand the US prefers to trust trial lawyers – motivated by punitive damages and contingent fees – to monitor and control wrongdoing. Tobacco is a case in point, for the combination of whistleblowers and aggressive plaintiff lawyers in the US taking advantage of generous disclosure rules have led to increased knowledge about what tobacco companies knew and how they presented their product to the public.[23] One question is whether in the age of multi-national corporations, the wrongdoing exposed in the US is only carried out there or whether similar practices are remaining unexposed in Europe.

Strict liability places liability on a person because of their relationship to a product, usually as its producer, and not necessarily because of any fault on their part in relation to the product. This affronts some commentators sense of fairness. They believe it threatens the liberty and autonomy of commercial agents to hold them liable for damage where they are not at fault.[24] Why should the producer be singled out to be the channel for insurance? Placing the risk on the producer, even in the absence of fault, has been justified on the basis that the producer is involved in a profit-making venture and should be responsible for damage resulting therefrom.[25]

An economic analysis of the law can be taken to favour either negligence or strict liability. Negligence can be seen as the most efficient as it encourages the producer to invest as much as necessary to reduce all foreseeable risks.[26] Stricter standards which force the producer to try to reduce risks further are arguably inefficient as how can a producer do more to reduce unforeseeable risks? Of course imposing stricter standards does not force someone to take more than reasonable precautions, but simply requires them to pay compensation (often through the vehicle of insurance) notwithstanding that they have taken reasonable care. This leads to full internalisation of the harm caused by the product. If these cost are not borne by the producer the price of the product would not reflect its full cost and following the laws of supply and demand more of the product would be consumed than is desirable.

---

23   G. Kelder and R. Daynard, 'The Role of Litigation in the Effective Control of the Sale and Use of Tobacco' (1997) 8 *Stan L and Policy Review* 63.

24   See D. Owen, 'Products Liability Principles of Justice' (1991) 20 *Anglo-Am L Rev* 238.

25   See, D. Beyleveld and R. Brownsword, 'Impossibility, Irrationality and Strict Product Liability' (1991) 20 *Anglo-Am L Rev* 257 and J. Stapleton, *op. cit.*, Chapter 8. T. Honoré, 'Responsibility and Luck: The Moral Basis of Strict Liability' (1988) 104 LQR 530.

26   See R. Posner, *Economic Analysis of Law* (Aspen, 2002).

There are also practical advantages to placing liability on the producer. The producer is often the person best placed to obtain insurance. It will be certainly be cheapest for him as he can control the risks best. Few individuals are likely voluntarily to take out first-party insurance, while some high-risk individuals may have difficulty finding insurers willing to write policies to cover them. This assumes, however, one has some sort of social welfare function for product liability. In an age when the inability of the welfare state to meet the needs of the injured is becoming ever more apparent one can only predict the demands for product liability will become more strident. Indeed the state is likely increasingly to look to tortfeasors to compensate it for the health care costs caused by harm caused by them and their products.[27]

Thus even if the initial impetus for strict liability was simply the tidying up of doctrine many have since seen it as having more social welfare objectives. The problem is that even many of those who accept the social welfare rationale for strict liability are sometimes reluctant to apply the principle when faced with a concrete case involving an innocent defendant. This, perhaps, partially explains why state of the art or development risks defences seem inevitably to 'sneak' into product liability regimes. Also the system is not explicit in merely treating the producer as a channel for insurance. The need to find a defect inevitably causes producers to feel their product is being condemned. All this leads to 'unstable' product liability regimes where the failure to set out clearly what the objectives are has left the courts having to interpret ambiguous legislation with little guidance.

4.2 PRODUCT LIABILITY

4.2.1 General Trends

Before considering the product liability law of the UK, it is instructive to note the general trend in Western legal systems towards strict products liability. It is worthwhile studying US law because it has influenced the adoption of similar principles elsewhere. Also the number and size of awards to victims of product related accidents in the US brought into sharp focus the debate on how far liability rules could be relied upon to perform the social function of compensating accident victims, without threatening the viability of manufacturing industry. A brief consideration of other European legal systems will illustrate that the introduction of strict liability

---

27   See discussion in Law Commission Consultation Paper, *Damages For Personal Injury: Medical, Nursing and Other Expenses*, Law Com. No. 144.

in the European Product Liability Directive was not a bolt out of the blue, but rather reflected a general trend within European civil law.

4.2.2 United States[28]

The need for strict product liability is arguably greatest in countries, such as the US, where there is minimal public health provision and where sizeable portions of the population are without health insurance. Here it performs the very basic function of at least ensuring that the victim's medical costs are recovered. Certainly from an early time the US courts were receptive to arguments extending liability for defective products. Manufacturers were held liable for breach of express[29] and implied warranties,[30] even in the absence of privity. Finally, however, in *Greenman v Yuba Power Products*[31] the courts developed a tort of strict liability for product defects independent of contract. Section 402A of the Restatement (Second) of Torts (1965)[32] stated:

> (1) One who sells any product in a defective condition unreasonably dangerous to the user or consumer or to his property is subject to liability for physical harm thereby caused to the ultimate user or consumer, or to his property...

In order to avoid placing too great a burden on high-risk socially desirable products, comment K to the section provides that, in the case of an unavoidably unsafe product, 'such a product, properly prepared and accompanied by proper directions and warning, is not defective, nor is it unreasonably dangerous'.

The Restatement left open the question of how defect should be defined. Some courts have adopted a consumer expectation test, but others

---

28 For a summary of the early development, see G. Howells, *Comparative Product Liability* (Dartmouth, 1993) Chapters 12–13. Of course it should be remembered that there is no such thing as one US law on products liability because each state has its own rules, as do the Federal courts. Indeed in 1987 Michigan, North Carolina, Virginia and the District of Columbia were reported not to recognise strict product liability actions: see R. Bieman, 'Strict Products Liability: An Overview of State Law' (1987) 10 *J Prod Liab* 111.

29 *Baxter v Ford Motor Co* 12 P 2d 409 (1932) (Supreme Court of Washington).

30 *Henningsen v Bloomfield Motors* 161 A 2d 69 (1960) (Supreme Court of New Jersey).

31 377 P 2d 897 (1963) (Supreme Court of California).

32 This is a non-binding, but highly influential, text of the American Law Institute which tries to reflect court practice throughout the states.

preferred a risk:utility analysis[33] or at least a two pronged test, such as that proposed in *Barker v Lull Engineering Co Ltd*.[34] In *Barker* it was stated that a plaintiff would win his case if he demonstrated either that the product:

> failed to perform as safely as an ordinary consumer would expect when used in an intended or reasonably foreseeable manner or... if the plaintiff proves that the product's design proximately caused his injury and the defendant fails to prove... that on balance the benefits of the challenged design outweigh the risk of danger inherent in such design.[35]

During the 1970s and 1980s many commentators talked in terms of the United States experiencing product liability crises, with insurance cover for high-risk products becoming outrageously expensive or simply unobtainable. It may be questioned whether such crises really occurred. A few cases caught the headlines when firms were forced into bankruptcy, but they had involved the marketing of very dangerous and clearly defective products.[36] Equally, whilst the US tends to award higher damages than most other countries, and in particular has strong punitive damage laws, most of the $1M+ awards were for very seriously injured consumers. The Presidential Task Force set up to consider the problem came to no firm conclusions on whether tort law was contributing to the perceived crisis. It did however find that the tort system created uncertainty which caused insurers to 'panic-price' their premiums to cover themselves against the uncertainties in the law.[37] It additionally found that high premiums were also due to poor manufacturing practices and to insurers trying to compensate for poor returns on their investments during times of low interest rates.

The US experience was used by some to argue against Europe placing similar burdens on its industry through the adoption of strict liability, or at least to argue that the development risks defence should be included. However, comparisons with the US can be misleading. First, American

---

33   In *Phillips v Kimwood Machine Co* 525 P 2d 1033 (1974) (Supreme Court of Oregon) it was said that: 'A dangerously defective article would be one which a reasonable person would not put into the stream of commerce if he had knowledge of its harmful character. The test therefore is whether the seller would be negligent if he sold the article knowing of the risk involved'.

34   573 P 2d 443 (1978) (Supreme Court of California).

35   *Ibid.*, at 452.

36   E.g. A.H. Robins filed for bankruptcy following litigation over the Dalkon intrauterine device.

37   Final Report, Interagency Task Force on Product Liability (Department of Commerce, 1977).

consumers tend to be more litigious than their counterparts in the UK. This is explained, in part, by the greater access to the courts because of the contingency fee system (where clients pay no fee, but the lawyer obtains a percentage of any award of damages); and perhaps more importantly by there being no liability on the part of the plaintiff to pay the other side's costs if the case is lost. Second, damages in the US are higher than in the UK. There are various possible reasons for this – the high cost of health care, the greater availability of punitive damages and, perhaps most importantly, the fact that (unlike in the UK), damages are awarded by a jury which can be swayed by emotional arguments to award victims large amounts. A jury may also be tempted to take into account that up to 40 per cent of the damages may go to the lawyer by way of contingency fees. This has also been said to explain why the US does not tend to be worried by instances of double recovery through damages and other compensations systems.[38] Third, courts in the US have also relaxed causation rules. Thus even if a plaintiff cannot identify the exact brand of a product which injured him or her, he or she can sue any producer of the same product and recover damages in proportion to that manufacturer's share of the market.[39]

However, it has been possible to discern a turn in the tide in favour of defendants. At the doctrinal level this was illustrated some time ago by the debate played out in the Supreme Court of New Jersey, which eventually decided that the unknowability of the defect was a factor to be taken into account in assessing whether a product was defective – in other words the development risk defence was accepted.[40] Empirical evidence also suggested that in recent years plaintiffs are faring less well at the trial court level.[41] In addition, whereas attempts to legislate for limits on tort liability at the Federal level have been unsuccessful, at state level many reforms have been introduced.

---

[38] B. Markesinis, 'Binding Legal Cultures' (1993) 27 *Israeli Law Review* 363.

[39] See *Sindell v Abbott Laboratories* 607 P 2d 924. There are of course some limitations to this rule, notably that a substantial share of the market must be joined as defendants. Defendants can also escape liability if they prove that their product could not have been the one which caused the damage, e.g. if it was not sold in the plaintiff's locality or was of a different appearance to that remembered by the plaintiff.

[40] *Feldman v Lederle Laboratories* 479 A 2d 374 (1974) (Supreme Court of New Jersey), disagreeing in this respect with the decision in *Beshada v John-Mansville Products Corp* 447 A 2d 539 (1982) (Supreme Court of New Jersey).

[41] J. Henderson and T. Eisenberg, 'The Quiet Revolution in Products Liability: an Empirical Study of Legal Change' (1990) 36 UCLA 479.

The American Law Institute (ALI) has also reformed its model product liability law so that there is a negligence standard for design defects.[42] The Restatement (Third) of Torts: Product Liability now provides:

> § 2. Categories of Product Defect
>
> A product is defective when, at the time of sale or distribution, it contains a manufacturing defect, is defective in design, or is defective because of inadequate instructions or warnings. A product:
>
> (a) contains a manufacturing defect when the product departs from its intended design even though all possible care was exercised in the preparation and marketing of the product;
>
> (b) is defective in design when the foreseeable risks of harm posed by the product could have been reduced or avoided by the adoption of a reasonable alternative design by the seller or other distributor, or a predecessor in the commercial chain of distribution, and the omission of the alternative design renders the product not reasonably safe;
>
> (c) is defective because of inadequate instructions or warnings when the foreseeable risks of harm posed by the product could have been reduced or avoided by the provision of reasonable instructions or warnings by the seller or other distributor, or a predecessor in the commercial chain of distribution, and the omission of the instructions or warnings renders the product not reasonably safe.

The debate around the Restatement was very heated. The ALI Restatements are intended to restate the consensus of state court practice. The 1965 reforms were a departure from this as the introduction of strict liability was recognised as being a break with traditional doctrines. The reporters for the ALI on this most recent occasion suggested that the court practice was favourable to the defence,[43] but this has been ferociously denied.[44] The contentious issues are the drawing of a distinction between manufacturing and design defects and the need for the plaintiff to establish a reasonable alternative design. Some who favour the reforms even argue it is misleading not to admit a negligence standard is being applied to design

---

[42] See K. Ross and H. Bowbeer, 'American Product Liability Law Undergoing Revision' (1994) 2 *Consum LJ* 96.

[43] For an article written by the authors of the Restatement see J. Henderson and A. Twerski, 'Achieving Consensus on Defective Product Design' (1998) 83 *Cornell Law Review* 867.

[44] J. Vargo, 'The Emperor's New Clothes: The American Law Institute Adorns a "New Cloth" for Section 402A Products Liability Design Defects – A Survey the States Reveals a Different Weave' (1996) *Univ. of Memphis Law Rev* 493.

defects.[45] Indeed it could be argued that in comparison with the Third Restatement the position in Europe under the Directive is more protective.[46] However, the Restatements are not binding and can only influence state courts in the hope of creating greater uniformity.[47] Currently the position is unsettled as there is no agreement on whether the Restatement should be adopted with the state legal systems all developing their own approaches. There will be a certain tendency for them to retain their existing jurisprudence.

4.2.3 Europe

Many European legal systems were developing stricter product liability laws even before the 1985 Directive. This trend was not limited to the specific area of pharmaceuticals, although this was one of the first areas for law reform. The Scandinavian countries had developed insurance-based solutions to the product liability problem and Germany had introduced a specific regime in its Medicines Act 1976. In Spain, the Consumer Protection Act 1984 was passed in response to a disaster involving contaminated cooking oil. This extended a form of strict liability to a range of products including pharmaceuticals, but also covering foodstuffs, hygiene and cleaning products, cosmetics, health, gas and electricity services, home appliances, lifts, means of transport, motor vehicles, toys and other products for children.

The general civil law had also been developing to meet the problem posed by individuals injured by defective products. This is perhaps most clearly seen in countries such as France, Belgium and Luxembourg where problems of privity were sidestepped by the creation of an 'action directe' between the consumer purchaser and higher links in the distribution chain.[48] Consequential damages caused by hidden defects (vice cachée) were allowed to be recovered, by presuming the seller of a defective product to have known of the defect and hence to have acted in bad faith, with the result that consequential damages were available and exclusion

---

45   D. Owen, 'Defectiveness Restated: Exploding the "Strict" Products Liability Myth' (1996) 3 *Univ of Illinois L Rev* 743.

46   G. Howells and M. Mildred 'Is European Product Liability More Protective than the Restatement (Third) of Torts: Product Liability?' (1998) 65 *Tennessee Law Review* 985–1030.

47   For an example of how US courts use the Restatements see, *Delaney v Deere & Co*, P 2d 930 (Kan, 2000).

48   See G. Howells, *op. cit.*, Chapter 7.

clauses rendered void.[49] In Austria, contract law has been developed to protect consumers by accepting the notion of contracts having protective effects for third parties.[50]

Equally, however, the inclination of many countries was to reject contract as a way of resolving product liability disputes in favour of tort laws. This underlines the law's increasing recognition that the person responsible for the quality and safety of products is the producer, rather than the retailer with whom the consumer has a contractual nexus. A good example of tort law aimed explicitly at the manufacturer is the French case law based on Art. 1384.1 of the Civil Code which, *inter alia*, makes a person liable for things in their keeping. Goldman was concerned that the product user was being unfairly made the insurer of the product's quality.[51] He therefore drew a distinction, which has been accepted by the courts, between 'garde de la structure' (the product's design) and 'garde du comportement' (how the product is used). Whilst the user was responsible for damage caused by the latter, the manufacturer remained liable for the 'garde de la structure'.

Germany is the country which has most strongly rejected an extension of contract in product liability in favour of stronger tort laws.[52] The so-called 'chicken-pest' case saw a reversal of the burden of proof being introduced for manufacturing defects, which was later extended to design defects and recently to warning defects (but not to post-marketing warnings). Germany was seriously affected by the Thalidomide (or Contergan as it was known in Germany) tragedy and as a result passed the Medicines Act 1976, which arguably introduced a form of strict liability for drugs by making pharmaceutical companies liable for harmful effects which go beyond a measure defensible according to medical science and for damage which occurred as a consequence of labelling or instructions for use not corresponding to the findings of medical science.

4.2.4 United Kingdom

4.2.4.1 Product Liability and Contract Law

In the UK contractual claims can be significant in product liability actions since consequential damages are recoverable. Also a claim in contract has

---

49 In France this is an irrebuttable presumption, but in Belgium there are limited grounds on which a defendant can rebut this presumption.

50 This was based on academic writings such as that of F. Bydlinski, 'Vertragliche Sorgfaltspflichten zugunsten Dritter' (1960) 82 *JB* 359.

51 *La détermination de gardien responsable du fait des choses inanimées* (Sirey, 1947).

52 See G. Howells, *op. cit.*, Chapter 8.

the advantage over a claim in negligence that liability is strict – if a term is breached, it is no defence that the person in default exercised all reasonable care not to break the contract (unless of course the term was phrased to require only the exercise of reasonable care). Also in contracts for the sale or supply of goods, the consumer benefits, *inter alia*, from the terms of satisfactory quality and fitness for purpose being implied. Thus the consumer's contractual rights remain a powerful weapon if the other party to the contract is worth suing. They are of course no use if someone other than the injured party bought the defective goods or if the supplier cannot be sued, e.g. is not traceable or is bankrupt.

The UK has, however, failed to break free from the shackles of the privity doctrine in the manner achieved by the US and French courts. Thus in *Daniels and Daniels v White and Tabard*,[53] Mr. Daniels purchased lemonade from a publican for his wife and himself. The lemonade contained carbolic acid. Whilst Mr. Daniels could sue the publican in contract, his wife had no contractual remedies as she was not party to the contract (there was also found to be no breach by the manufacturer of its duty of care in negligence). Thus only one consumer could recover, and only against the publican and not the manufacturers who had been the source of the contamination. Of course, the manufacturer could eventually be held liable in contract by virtue of the parties in the distribution chain suing back up the distribution line, a process, however, that is circuitous and wasteful in terms of litigation costs. Moreover, where the risk falls will, to some extent, be arbitrary depending upon the terms of the supply contracts between the links in the chain and whether a link is broken, for example, by the bankruptcy of a distributor.

There have been several attempts to circumvent privity which we discussed in relation to liability for sub-standard goods.[54] Of course it is rare that a manufacturer will make specific claims about the safety of his products. One novel case where liability was imposed on the manufacturer for a false safety claim arose in Denmark and involved a 'Trumf' pressure cooker. The advertisement offered a 5,000 Kroner reward to the first person succeeding in exploding a 'Trumf' pressure cooker which incorporated a fully automatic safety device. Rather ironically, the advertisement had earlier stated that the 70,000 housewives using the 'Trumf' could take comfort in the fact that the pressure cooker which had exploded the week before was not a 'Trumf'.[55] Absent such explicit claims, we have seen that it is still difficult to impose contractual liability on the manufacturer. This is of course less significant in the context of

---

[53] [1938] 4 All ER 258.

[54] See Chapter 3.4.

[55] See G. Howells, *op. cit.*, pp. 162–163.

product liability claims because tortious liability is available for damage to person and property.

4.2.4.2 Negligence

Every law student knows of the infamous case of *Donoghue v Stevenson*,[56] involving the snail in a ginger beer bottle. Not only was the judgment of Lord Atkin in that case later to be regarded as laying down a general test for establishing negligence, at least where physical damage is concerned, but it was also a product liability case which established that:

> a manufacturer of products, which he sell in such a form as to show that he intended them to reach the ultimate consumer in the form in which they left him with no reasonable possibility of intermediate examination, and with the knowledge that the absence of reasonable care in the preparation or putting up of the products will result in an injury to the consumer's life or property, owes a duty of care to the consumer to take that reasonable care.[57]

Thus manufacturers could be liable in tort for defective products, but only if they were at fault.[58] The fault requirement would seem to exclude system damage and state of the art or development risk defects from the scope of negligence liability. This is because there is no liability for acceptable risks and because the actions of the producer are judged at the time of marketing, with no hindsight knowledge being imputed.[59]

It is with regard to manufacturing defects that the negligence standard has been most effective in imposing liability on producers. This was not always true. For instance, in *Daniels and Daniels v White Ltd and Tabard*[60] there was no finding of negligence because the manufacturers were held to have fulfilled their duty of care by providing a good system of work and adequate supervision: it was not their negligence which had caused the carbolic acid to get into the lemonade bottle! A more consumer friendly approach seems to have been taken by the Court of Appeal in *Hill*

---

[56] [1932] AC 562.

[57] *Ibid.*, at 599.

[58] However, other links in the distribution chain can be held liable if their failure to take reasonable care caused injury: see the liability of the retailer in *Fisher v Harrods Ltd* [1966] Lloyd's Rep 500.

[59] However, we will see that the courts have been quite stringent in their consideration of what knowledge can be expected of the defendant.

[60] [1938] 4 All ER 258.

v James Crowe (Cases) Ltd[61] where it was decided either that the manufacturer's system was deficient or that an employee, for whom the manufacturer was vicariously liable, had failed to implement the system properly. Of course, the accident could have arisen without anyone being at fault, but the courts have created an almost automatic presumption that manufacturing defects are the result of the fault of someone within the scope of the manufacturer's control. The injured party is unlikely to be able to pinpoint the exact cause of the defect, however, as all the relevant activity took place within the privacy of the defendant's factory. To counter this information inequality, consumers are greatly assisted by the dictum of Lord Wright in *Grant v Australian Knitting Mills*[62] that the injured party 'is not required to lay his finger on the exact person in all the chain who was responsible, or to specify what he did wrong'. Negligence is found as a matter of inference from the existence of the defect taken in conjunction with all known circumstances.

Design defects are the most complex cases. They involve the court assessing the producer's conduct in the light of the dangers posed by the product and the benefits it brings to society. Of course this assessment is objective so that a producer cannot claim his inexperience as an excuse; equally, specialist producers are held to the standard of expertise they profess to possess.[63] The key feature which distinguishes assessment of design in negligence and strict liability is the time-frame within which the assessment is made. In negligence, producer's actions are judged by the standard to be expected at the time the product was marketed. However, the courts have shown themselves to be quite demanding, requiring that manufacturers establish efficient procedures to monitor developments in scientific knowledge[64] and that, once knowledge is in their domain, they utilise it to the fullest extent.[65]

If a product breaches safety regulations there may be a civil action for breach of statutory duty, though these rarely occur in practice.[66] Non-compliance with industry standards will normally be evidence of negligence, although an occasional departure from a standard practice may

---

[61]   [1978] 1 All ER 812.

[62]   [1936] AC 85 at 101.

[63]   See *Stokes v GKN (Bolts and Nuts) Ltd* [1968] 1 WLR 1778 at 1783.

[64]   *Vacwell v B.D.H. Chemicals Ltd* [1971] 1 QB 88 (liability for failure to take account of the explosive qualities of boron tribromide when it comes into contact with water – even though this was not mentioned in the four modern texts which the defendants had consulted, including the standard work on the industrial hazards of chemicals).

[65]   *IBA v EMI (Electric) Ltd and BIIC Construction Ltd* (1981) 14 BLR 1 (liability for failure to take account of the effects of accumulations of ice on steel television masts).

[66]   Section 41(1), Consumer Protection Act 1987.

be justified.[67] Conversely, compliance with a regulatory standard will generally be evidence that a defendant behaved reasonably so long as the standard is a well-respected one.[68]

In *Wright v Dunlop Rubber Co Ltd*[69] manufacturers were held liable for continuing to supply an antioxidant even after discovering that it had carcinogenic properties and for failing to warn of the danger to customers who had already bought the chemical. A duty to warn existing purchasers was also found in *Walton and Walton v British Leyland UK Ltd*[70] where British Leyland had decided not to recall its Allegro cars to make an adjustment to the wheels, but rather preferred to avoid adverse publicity by waiting until the cars were being serviced to make the adjustment. This was considered to be an inadequate response and the company was held liable for the death and serious injuries caused by a wheel coming off. This post-marketing liability can still be highly relevant for even if a product is not found to be defective under the Consumer Protection Act 1987 (perhaps because of a development risks defence) it may be possible to find fault with the producer's response to problems.

4.2.4.3 Consumer Protection Act 1987[71]

The UK had the honour of being the first Member State to implement the Product Liability Directive. However, some aspects of the implementing legislation can be criticised for not conforming to the wording of the Directive, and thus giving UK consumers less protection than they ought to enjoy. The European Court of Justice has reviewed the wording of the development risks defence in the Consumer Protection Act 1987 and held the Commission had not satisfied the relevant burden of proof to establish an infringement. This does not mean the wording was necessarily in line with the Directive, although we shall see the tenor of the judgment was sympathetic to the UK position. Nevertheless, the consumer may still be able to invoke EC law to obtain the level of protection which should have

---

67   *Brown v Rolls Royce* [1960] 1 All ER 577.
68   *Albery & Budden v BP Oil Ltd & Shell UK Ltd* (1980) 124 *SJ* 376.
69   (1972) 13 KIR 255.
70   12 July 1978, unreported.
71   See G. Howells, *op. cit.*, Chapter 6; A. Clark, *Product Liability* (Sweet & Maxwell, 1989) and J. Stapleton, *op. cit.* Reform proposals along these lines had been proposed by the Law Commission in Law Com 82, Scot Law Com 45, *Report on Liability for Defective Products* (Cmnd 6831, 1977) and by Pearson, *Royal Commission on Civil Liability and Compensation for Personal Injury* (Cmnd 7054, 1978). It is interesting to note that both these reports came out against the inclusion of the development risks defence.

been afforded under the Directive.[72] This task may be assisted by s. 1, Consumer Protection Act 1987 which states that its provisions should be construed so as to comply with the Product Liability Directive.[73] Indeed in a High Court case the judge simply by-passed the wording of the Act and relied directly on the Directive.[74]

Before considering the detail of the Consumer Protection Act 1987, it is important to remember that Art. 13 of the Directive expressly states that it shall be without prejudice to contractual or non-contractual liability or special liability schemes existing in member states when the Directive was notified.[75] In the UK it is likely that the implied quality conditions will continue to be invoked where a contractual nexus exists between the injured party and the supplier of the defective product. In fact, many practitioners believe that 'strict liability' will simply be used as an additional action to those which already exist in contract and negligence.[76]

The European Court of Justice has held that the Directive is a maximal harmonisation directive, meaning that except where the Directive specifically grants members states options it cannot be more protective than the Directive. Both Greece and France were condemned for removing the 500 Euro threshold on property damage.[77] This seems petty since one of the major sources of distortions arises from the vastly differing approaches to pain and suffering damages across Europe which are not harmonised at all by the Directive. France was also condemned for extending strict liability to sellers. Although possibly this decision is justified as France made this extension in a new law implementing the Directive, the reality is that this was the position under existing French law which should not be affected by the Directive. Some French commentators consider their existing jurisprudence has to be reworked in the light of this decision, but this would seem wrong and lead to the conclusion that the Directive would also affect how in the UK the implied quality conditions had to be interpreted.[78] Similarly whilst the European Court of Justice was right to say that Spanish consumers could no longer rely on their Consumer Protection Act 1984, once it had been repealed by a law implementing the

---

[72] See Chapter 2.4.2.

[73] This reflects the jurisprudence of the European Court of Justice, see Chapter 2.4.2.

[74] *A v National Blood Authority*, [2001] 3 All ER 289.

[75] Article 13.

[76] See I. Dodds-Smith, 'The Impact of Product Liability on Pharmaceutical Companies' in *Product Liability, Insurance and the Pharmaceutical Industry*, G. Howells (ed.) (MUP, 1991).

[77] *Commission v France*, C–52/00, [2002] ECR I–3827 and *Commission v Greece*, C–154/00 [2002] ECR I–3879.

[78] G. Howells in 'Product Liability – A History of Harmonisation' in *Towards a European Civil Code* (3rd ed.), (forthcoming).

Directive, it is harder to justify their view that Spain would not have been entitled to keep this law in place.[79] The European Court of Justice seems to think that only special liability schemes linked to specific sectors, like the German Medicines Act, are protected by Art. 13.

(a) Product

The scope of Part I of the Consumer Protection Act 1987, which implements the Product Liability Directive, is delineated by reference to the definition of a 'product'. Product is defined as meaning any goods or electricity, including products comprised in other products either as components, raw materials or otherwise.[80] At one time there was an express exclusion for game or other agricultural produce which has not undergone an industrial process, but this has now been removed.[81] The reason for the exemption was probably due to the politically powerful farming lobby. The justifications for the exclusion probably did not pass muster, but its repeal was not related to any logical debate, but was rather a political response at the European level to the 'mad-cow disease' problem. It is hard to imagine how any victim would be able to trace their illness to a product supplied by a particular producer in order to take advantage of the Directive.

Product also seems to cover blood and body parts despite the objections that such things are not produced. Their inclusion probably reflects the business activity which surrounds most supplies of such products. One reference to the European Court of Justice concerned a kidney which could not be used for a transplant because of the condition solution used to prepare it.[82]

Difficult questions also surround whether intellectual products should be included.[83] It seems likely that where software is included in a final product then there should be liability and equally where an 'off-the-peg' programme is involved a case can be made out for liability. But it will be necessary to show how this is different from say dangerous information in a book, which would not be covered. Where a programme is tailored to the individual needs of a client, then any dangers seem better dealt with in the field of professional liability.

---

[79] *González Sanchez v Medicina Asturiana SA* Case C–183/00, [2002] ECR I–3901.

[80] Directive 1(2), Consumer Protection Act 1987.

[81] By Directive 1999/34/EC: OJ 1999 L141/20.

[82] *Henning Veedfald v Århus Amtskommune*, C–203/99, [2001] ECR I–3569, see note G. Howells (2002) 6 *European Review of Private Law* 847

[83] S. Whittaker, 'European Product Liability and Intellectual Products' (1989) 105 *LQR* 125.

(b) Persons Liable

The Act channels liability primarily towards three economic agents: producers, own-branders and importers. Producers are persons who manufacture products, or win or abstract a substance. Where the product has not been manufactured, won or abstracted, but its essential elements are attributable to an industrial or other process, then producers are persons who carry out that process.[84] There remains a potential gap. Whilst primary agricultural produce is within the definition of product it is hard to see how the farmer can be brought within the definition of producer. Channelling liability towards producers is a recognition that, because they are usually larger in size and more likely to be able to control the quality of the product than retailers, they are therefore better able to insure against the product liability risk.

Own-branders are persons who, by putting their name on the product or by using a trademark or other distinguishing mark, have held themselves out to be the producer.[85] Own-brand names are increasingly common amongst large retailers. Extending liability to them recognises, both that they will generally have a substantial influence over the quality of goods they receive from their suppliers, and also that they will often be large enough concerns to carry the product liability burden. It is uncertain whether own-branders are singled out as a target of liability because of their economic strength, or simply because they may disguise the fact that the goods were manufactured by someone else. An interesting question is whether chains which 'own-brand' products can escape liability by expressly stating on the packaging that they did not produce it, i.e. this product has been selected for X Supermarket. In such circumstances it could be argued that they have not held themselves out to be the producer of the product. However, it could equally be argued that placing their name on or using a trademark or other distinguishing mark in relation to the product is evidence that they do hold themselves out as the producer. However, it is probably the case that own-branders can avoid liability by in this manner. However, if it is permitted, one would hope that any exculpatory statement would have to be given due prominence to be effective, so that the sensible policy of equating the economically powerful own-brander with the producer is not undermined too easily.

The right to sue may be illusory for consumers if it can only be exercised against some distant foreign entity. Therefore the Directive provides for the right to sue the importer of goods into the single market. Provision for this is also found in s. 2(2)(c) of the Consumer Protection Act 1987. However, it is important to note that the right can only be exercised

---

[84] Sections 2(2)(a) and 1(2), Consumer Protection Act 1987.
[85] Section 2(2)(b), Consumer Protection Act 1987.

against the first importer into a Member State, who may not be the actual importer into the UK. Such a rule makes sense to European legislators concerned to promote the concept of a single market, but it may still leave British consumers having to litigate overseas, albeit with the assistance of the Brussels Regulation on Jurisdiction and the Enforcement of Judgements in Civil and Commercial Matters.[86]

Although primary liability falls on the above-mentioned persons, suppliers can be liable in certain circumstances. The Act defines 'supplier' widely, to cover not only the supplier to the injured party, but also others in the supply chain, including those who supplied defective component parts.[87] A supplier will be liable if the injured person requests assistance to identify one or more of the individuals having primary liability and the supplier fails within a reasonable period to comply with that request or to identify his or her own supplier. The request must be made within a reasonable period of the damage having occurred[88] and at a time when it was not practicable for the injured person to identify all those persons with primary liability.

(c) Liability

Section 2, Consumer Protection Act 1987 imposes liability for damage caused wholly or partly by a defect in a product. Whilst the requirement to prove negligence no longer exists, the claimant must still establish that the product was defective and that the defect caused his or her injury and that damage recoverable under the Act was suffered.

(d) Causation

Causation is likely to remain a major stumbling block in product liability cases. Defendants may not wish to rely on technical defences relating to whether their product was or was not defective, but may prefer to deny that their product was the cause of the injury. Particularly where the product is alleged to have caused the claimant to contract a disease, it may be difficult for the claimant to show that the illness was caused by the product rather than other genetic or environmental factors. The suggestion in *McGhee v National Coal Board*[89] that the plaintiff could be assisted in such cases by the burden of proof being reversed and placed on the defendants was emphatically rejected in *Wilsher v Essex Area Health Authority*.[90] It awaits

---

[86]   See Chapter 14.9.2.
[87]   Section 2(3), Consumer Protection Act 1987.
[88]   This restriction does not appear in the Directive.
[89]   [1973] 1 WLR 1.
[90]   [1988] 2 WLR 557.

to be seen what the impact on product liability claims will be of the House of Lords' decision in *Fairchild v Glenhaven Funeral Services*[91] that in some circumstances liability can be imposed despite being unable to pinpoint which tortfeasor caused the harm. It is uncertain how far this decision can be applied outside the particular facts of the case. Certainly in *Gregg v Scott*[92] the majority in Court of Appeal seemed content to confine it within strict limits.

Causation was a crucial issue in *X v Schering*[93] where the claimants conceded they had to show that the risk of thrombosis from the third generation contraceptive pill was twice as great as from the alternatives, before liability could be established. Establishing causation between the MMR vaccine and autism is of course highly contentious and the difficulties and cost of establishing such a link were no doubt a significant factor in public funding for those cases being dropped.

An interesting issue is whether as causation appears in the Directive it is to be given an autonomous European interpretation. It is improbable that serious thought was given to this possibility as the measure worked its way through the legislative process, but as a matter of EC law the fact that causation rules fall within the scope of a Directive means that in principle it falls to the European Court to offer authoritative interpretation. One may well expect the Court to be cautious should it be invited to answer preliminary references made by national courts on questions of causation, but, as may be observed in connection with procedural matters arising under the Directive on unfair terms[94] it is occasionally capable of adopting a surprisingly assertive position with regard to the 'Europeanisation' of legal matters that are treated differently within the Member States' legal order but have been placed under a regime of harmonisation.

(e) Defect

The choice of defectiveness standard is a key issue in any liability regime. Section 3(1), Consumer Protection Act 1987 provides:

> there is a defect in a product... if the safety of the product is not such as persons generally are entitled to expect; and for those purposes 'safety' in relation to a product, shall include safety with respect to products comprised in that product and safety in the context of risk of damage to property, as well as in the context of risks of death or personal injury.

---

[91] [2003] 1 AC 32.

[92] [2003] Lloyds Rep Med 105.

[93] (2003) 70 BMLR 88.

[94] See *Oceano GroupEditorial v Quintero*, C240/98 [2000] ECR I 4941: discussed at Section 5.6.1.5.

Section 3(2) continues to provide that:

> in determining... what persons generally are entitled to expect in relation
> to a product all the circumstances shall be taken into account, including –
> (a) the manner in which, and purposes for which, the product has been
>   marketed, its get-up, the use of any mark in relation to the product
>   and any instructions for or warnings with respect to, doing or
>   refraining from doing anything with or in relation to the product,
> (b) what might reasonably be expected to be done with or in relation to
>   the product; and
> (c) the time when the product was supplied by its producer to another,
>   and nothing in this section shall require a defect to be inferred from
>   the fact alone that the safety of a product which is supplied after that
>   time is greater than the safety of the product in question.

(f) Conceptual difference from negligence

The difference between strict liability and negligence is often said to be
that instead of having to establish unreasonable conduct (negligence), one
has to establish the defective condition of the product (strict liability).
However, it could be argued that defective condition should not be limited
to situations where an actual physical defect exists in the product. Products
might be defective because they had been represented to be safer than they
were; equally and more controversially products might be defective
because they posed a risk of harm, even if it could not be established
whether the specific product would cause harm (for example, where a non-
identifiable percentage of blood carried a long term risk of infection or
pace-makers inserted in patients that carried a higher than acceptable risk
of failure).[95]

It is generally accepted that for manufacturing defects strict liability
will always lead to liability. However, we saw that this was generally the
case under negligence regimes in any event. Although it could be
questioned whether this approach is justified, given that manufacturing
defects may be unavoidable in mass production, it certainly seems to be the
position. More debateable is whether as regards design defects strict
liability is any more than a form of 'super-negligence'. Given that
negligence was applied strictly to producers there may be little difference
in practice.

---

[95] G. Howells 'Defect in English Law – Lessons for the Harmonisation of European
      Product Liability' in Duncan Fairgrieve (ed.), *Product Liability in Comparative
      Perspective* (CUP, forthcoming).

(g) The case law

Three of the early cases seemed to suggest that strict liability would have little impact. In *Worsley v Tambrands Ltd*[96] the Court rejected the argument that a tampon packet was defective for providing inadequate warnings of the risk of toxic shock syndrome. It was accepted as adequate to place the risk of toxic shock on the box with an insert leaflet providing full details. It was not relevant that this was less explicit that the leaflet in the US. This could be explained by the UK leaflets being multi-lingual. As well as emphasising how defectiveness claims can be countered by effective warnings this case also underlines the general point that defect does not require the ultimate level of safety. Products will not be defective so long as they meet a minimum standard fixed by the defectiveness standard, regardless of whether the product could have been made safer in some way.

A claim for compensation for a pregnancy caused by a condom breaking again underlined that defectiveness did not lead to liability every time a product failed.[97] The judge noted that whilst the users' expectations were that the condom would not fail, there were no claims that they would never fail and people understood that no method of contraception was 100 per cent, especially as in this case the product had to be 'user friendly'. Moreover that case is another illustration of the continuing impact of causation as there was a debate as to whether the condom was damaged by ozone contamination in the factory or when it was left exposed for a couple of weeks after intercourse.

The two cases just discussed seem instinctively to be correctly decided, but *Foster v Biosil*[98] gives more cause for concern. This involved a breast implant that leaked. There was no negligence found on the part of the surgeon, but the judge suggested that not only did the claimant have to establish a defect, but also the cause of the defect. The need to remove from claimants the need to prove how defects arose is a widely accepted rationale for strict liability. This decision was unfortunate, but as it was only at the county court level it carries no precedent value, but is perhaps indicative of the difficulty some lawyers have in understanding the concept of strict liability. The next two decisions, one by the Court of Appeal and an important High Court case on contaminated blood, did suggest that the legal system was prepared to ensure there was a marked difference between negligence and defectiveness.

---

96   [2000] PIQR P95.
97   *Richardson v LRC Products Ltd*, [2000] PIQR P164, (2001) 59 BMLR 185
98   (2001) 59 BMLR 178.

In *Abouzaid v Mothercare (UK) Ltd*[99] the Court of Appeal upheld a finding that a 'Cosy-toes' fleece-lined liner was defective. This was attached to a pram by means of elasticated straps, which had light metal buckles at their end that sprang back and struck the eye of a twelve year old who was tying it for his sibling. Defectiveness was said to be based on the expectations of the public as determined by the Court. The judges stressed that the case would not have been successful in negligence, but the fact no-one could have been expected to recognise the risk in 1990, when the accident happened, or that the danger had not been considered in standards committees were irrelevant considerations to the assessment of defectiveness. If the strap posed an unacceptable risk today, it must have also been unacceptable in 1990 and moreover the development risks defence did not apply. The case of *A v National Blood Authority*[100] will be considered in more detail below, because – in the course of holding the National Blood Authority liable for blood contaminated with Hepatitis C – Mr Justice Burton gave the most detailed judicial analysis of strict liability in Europe to date. However, the floodgates are not open US style as evidenced by the subsequent decision that McDonald's were not liable for serving coffee and tea that was too hot and in inadequate cups.[101]

(h) A consumer expectation standard

The European defectiveness standard is a variant on the consumer expectation standard, which has been widely rejected in the US. One problem that has arisen with this standard is as to how it could be applied to obvious dangers, for surely (it is argued) consumers cannot expect an obviously dangerous product to be safe? More generally, it can be criticised for being an essentially norm-reflecting standard, which simply

---

[99]   *The Times*, 20 Feb. 2001. See E. Deards and C. Twigg-Flesner, 'The Consumer Protection Act 1987: Proof at last that it is protecting consumers?' (2001) 10 *Nott. LJ.* 1.

[100] [2001] 3 All ER 289. G. Howells and M. Mildred, 'Infected Blood: Defect and Discoverability: A First Exposition of the EC Product Liability Directive' (2002) 65 *Modern Law Review* 95, C. Hodges, 'Compensating Patients' (2001) 117 LQR 528.

[101] *Sam B and others v McDonalds' Restaurants Ltd*, decision of the High Court 27 March 2002. In a US decision from New Mexico, *Stella Liebeck v McDonald's Restaurants*, the plaintiff successfully sued McDonald's for scalds from hot coffee, She was awarded £2.7M punitive damages (reduced to $480,000 on appeal) and settled for an unspecified amount before a further appeal. Fun is often poked at such decisions, but defenders of the US system would argue these criticisms are unjust for the case turned on the US jury finding that McDonalds had made a calculated decision to make their coffee hotter to improve aroma and reduce complaints about lukewarm coffee and ignored 700 complaints about the temperature of their coffee.

forces consumers to accept the prevailing expectations of safety without imposing any more demanding standards. The level of safety which consumers expect is to some extent psychologically conditioned. Consumers tend to be concerned about short-term gains (such as increased speed or lower prices) and frequently view consider safety as a more remote concern. This is encouraged by the typical, and understandable, human desire to believe that someone other than ourselves will be the unfortunate victim of an accident. Consumers also tend to overvalue large risks (like the possibility a plane might crash) and undervalue smaller long-term risks (such as consumption of high cholesterol foods).[102]

A more realistic interpretation is that the standard is not actually based on what consumers actually expect, but rather on what they should be entitled to expect. This can be higher or lower than their actual expectations. This seems to be the approach of the UK courts as we saw in the Court of Appeal decision in *Abouzaid* and most notably by Mr Justice Burton's view in *A v National Blood* that the court should act as an informed representative of the public at large. Indeed in a strong judgment he held that issues of avoidability; the impracticability, cost of difficulty of taking measures; and the benefit to society or utility of the product were not relevant when determining defectiveness. In a bold interpretation he construed the Act's requirement to take all circumstances into account to be limited to all relevant circumstances and was keen to prevent any elements of negligence from creeping into the statutory regime.

This was an important decision in which liability was imposed for blood supplied infected with Hepatitis C.[103] The judge rejected the US distinction between manufacturing and design defects and preferred to draw a distinction between non-standard and standard products, although in truth there may be little more than semantics behind the differing terminology. Non-standard products could either be one-off manufacturing defects or design defects resulting from the way the production system was designed. The judge considered the blood that was contaminated to be non-standard products.

The judge rejected, as too philosophical, the argument that the blood could be a standard product, with the risk of it being contaminated the possible defect. The judge obviously felt easier when he was able to point to the allegedly defective blood having a harmful characteristic that was not present in the majority of bags. However, his analysis has the benefit of hindsight, for at the time of supply it could not be known which of the bags

---

102 See F.P. Hubbard, 'Reasonable Human Expectations: A Normative Model for Imposing Strict Liability for Defective Products' (1978) 29 *Mercer L Rev* 465 and D. Burley, 'Risk Assessment and Responsibility for Injuries Associated with Medicines' in G. Howells (ed.), *op. cit.*

103 Albeit the eventual levels of damages awarded were modest.

was contaminated. Although it was known some blood was infected there was no test to detect it.

For non-standard products the judge's approach was to consider whether the harmful characteristic was accepted by the public.[104] In this case he held that it was not because although the medical profession knew of the risks, the general public did not. Although it was not possible to have supplied blood screened for Hepatitis C, Burton J argued that the public were only not entitled to expect the unattainable if they had been informed that it was unattainable. If they had not been informed of the risk, the product did not provide the safety they were entitled to expect. It had been suggested that the National Blood Authority had done enough by informing the medical professions, but this 'learned intermediary' defence was rejected.[105] However, one wonders what more the National Blood Authority could have done to inform consumers? Would use of the web and media be sufficient?

Also one might question whether this seemingly pro-claimant decision might not amount to an illusory pot of gold over the rainbow for claimants, if in the end it provides an escape route for producers so long as they do adequately warn of risks. Although the judge noted the tension between warnings that might limit liability and exclusions of liability that are not allowed, it is not clear how these issues inter-relate.[106]

The presence of the development risks defence was another factor persuading the judge that he was justified in applying a strict construction of defectiveness. Equally one might argue that if the defence was removed the defectiveness standard could be applied in such a way as to protect legitimate products.[107] However, the judge was also clear that the development risks defence did not apply: the risk of Hepatitis C was known about, it was not undiscoverable. What was not possible was its detection, but that was not within the scope of the defence.

---

[104] Although the approach to standard products was not dealt with in as much detail, it is clear a similar, but modified, approach would be adopted. The distinction between standard and non-standard products was recognised as not being absolute.

[105] For criticism of this see Hodges, *op. cit.*

[106] G. Howells, 'Information and Product Liability – a game of Russian Roulette' in G. Howells, A. Janssen and R. Schulze (eds.), *Information Rights and Obligations: A Challenge for Party Autonomy and Transactional Fairness* (Ashgate, forthcoming).

[107] Cf. G. Howells and M. Mildred 'Is European Product Liability More Protective than the Restatement (Third) of Torts: Product Liability?' (1998) 65 *Tennessee Law Review* 985.

(i) Other issues arising from the adoption of a consumer expectation standard

With such an open textured defectiveness standard, much is left to judicial interpretation – a particular problem in a standard applied throughout the European Union. There is an obvious danger that courts in different legal systems will apply the test in an inconsistent manner as a result of their various legal traditions and the socio economic conditions which influence their expectations of safety. In particular there is a difference in judicial philosophy. Continental judges are used to applying broad principles in their Civil Codes and see individual decisions as simply judicial application of the written law. English judges have more of a tradition of having to give detailed reasons for their chosen application. This is evidenced by the lengths Mr Justice Burton felt he had to go to explain his decision in the *A v National Blood Authority*. It has been noted that French courts seem to take a different approach to applying the defect standard.[108] They seem to demonstrate a greater willingness simply to impute a defect and this may come from the function of the French (and many continental judges) as merely the appliers of the written law. English judges have a different role and feel bound to justify fully their application of the law.

There is also the problem of knowing how the standard is to be applied to vulnerable groups such as children, old people and the handicapped. Presumably the Court will take into account the manner and purposes for which the product was marketed, so that if it is clearly targeted at vulnerable groups, it will have to be rendered safe for their uses. Persons generally would expect this, even if they themselves did not require the same protection.

A common problem in product liability cases is the extent to which producers are liable when the product has been misused in a foreseeable manner. By taking into account what might reasonably be expected to be done with or in relation to a product, the Act seems to strike a balance. Blatant misuses (such as drying a cat in a microwave) could not reasonably be expected, but the product might be expected to be put to some uses other than those for which the product was specifically marketed. There is regrettably no express reference to children or other vulnerable groups, but all the circumstance must be taken into account. Thus if erasers were marketed which looked and smelled like fruit, then it should be possible to argue that they were defective: producers might reasonably expect that small children might put them in their mouths and attempt to eat them.

---

108 *Product Liability in the European Union* (Lovells, 2003) at 15.

(j) State of art

The 'state of the art defence'[109] is actually contained within the definition of defect itself, for by taking into account the time at which the product was supplied, the court must judge the product against the standard of safety which would have been expected at that time. This is reinforced when the section goes on to say that a defect should not be inferred simply because a safer product was subsequently supplied. This accords with the existing position under negligence law, but it does not mean that the fact that a product is subsequently modified to make it safer cannot be used as evidence that such modifications could have been made at the time it was originally supplied. It simply provides that defectiveness cannot be inferred from the mere fact that modifications have subsequently taken place.

(k) Development risks

The Act also contains a 'development risks' defence.[110] The Directive gave Member States the option of removing this defence, but only Luxembourg and Finland have taken this up. The Spanish because of their tradition following the Colza cooking oil scandal and the Consumer Protection Act 1984 have removed the defence for high risks products (which ironically are the very products one would usually have assumed it would have been introduced to protect). Some development risks may also be caught by the special pharmaceutical liability regime which applies in Germany.

Grave doubts had been expressed as to whether the UK's version of the defence correctly implements the Directive. Section 4(1)(e), Consumer Protection Act 1987 provides that it is a defence for the producer to show:

> that the state of scientific and technical knowledge at the relevant time was not such that a producer of products of the same description as the product in question might be expected to have discovered the defect if it had existed in his products while they were under his control.

Article 7(e) of the Directive had provided a defence if the producer proved:

> that the state of scientific and technical knowledge at the time when he put the product into circulation was not such as to enable the existence of the defect to be discovered.

---

[109] See Chapter 4.1.3 for an explanation of how we differentiate the state of the art and development risks defence.

[110] Generally, see M. Mildred 'Development Risks Defence' in Duncan Fairgrieve (ed.), *Product Liability in Comparative Perspective* (CUP, forthcoming).

In fact the House of Lords had passed an amendment to bring the defence into line with the wording of the Directive. Under the Lords' amendment, the defence would have applied if 'the state of scientific and technical knowledge at the relevant time was not such as to enable the existence of the defect to be discovered'. However, during the passage of the Bill the 1987 General Election was called and their Lordships were forced to accept the reinstatement of the original Government wording as the price for not seeing the Bill fail for lack of time before the dissolution of Parliament.

There were at least two respects in which the UK's development risks defence appeared to be more generous to producers than that contained in the Directive. First, it introduced the concept of expectancy, whereas the Directive is concerned with 'the plain unvarnished concept of discoverability'.[111] Second, it did not test discoverability against stringent objective criteria, but rather judged producers by the standards of producers of similar products – implying that there are different standards to be expected of different producers. This seemed to smack of a very weak negligence type liability.

In many ways the defence sits uneasily within a strict liability regime, for it introduces issues of foreseeability and reasonableness more resonant of negligence than strict liability. The European Commission recognised this and did not want the defence, but had to accept it because otherwise a number of member states would have resisted the introduction of strict liability. In these circumstances the Commission drafted a very narrow defence, which only seemed to exclude those risks which are unable to be discovered. The problem was to know how far this could be taken. Would the defence be defeated, for instance, because information had been available which if looked at from a different perspective or connected to other information could have revealed the defect although that step had not been taken. Some commentators argued that the UK had correctly implemented the defence, as sense can only be made of the defence if reasonable expectations are taken into account.[112] The problem is whether logic should have a role to play in interpreting a defence which in principle has no logical place in a strict liability regime and is simply the result of political compromise.

The question of whether the United Kingdom had correctly implemented the defence was eventually taken to the European Court of Justice. In *Commission v United Kingdom*[113] the Court clearly had some

---

111   See Baroness Burton of Coventry, HL Debs. Vol. 485, Col. 849, 9 March 1987.

112   See C. Newdick, 'The Development Risks Defence of the Consumer Protection Act 1987' (1988) *Camb LJ* 455 and 'Risk, Uncertainty and Knowledge in the Development Risks Defence' (1991) 20 *Anglo-Am L Rev* 309.

113   C–300/95, [1997] ECR I–2649

sympathy for the United Kingdom's interpretation. It found the Commission had not satisfied it according to the necessary standard of proof that the United Kingdom had failed to implement the defence as required by the Directive. The Court took a strict view of what amounted to knowledge and equated it with the best available knowledge. Knowledge accumulates over time and as science develops so does its view of truth. An opinion which is in the minority one day, would still seem to amount to knowledge to defeat the defence if it later becomes accepted. However, it was sympathetic to the United Kingdom and producer arguments by deciding that only knowledge that was accessible to the producer was relevant to defeat the defence. This requirement of accessibility is not found in the Directive.[114] The Court gave the example of European producers not being expected to know of research in a Manchurian journal; but this begs the question of whether British producers would find a Greek journal any more accessible than a Manchurian. In fact modern data base searches can be multi-lingual, Indeed Burton J in *A v National Blood Authority* commented that if Manchuria was noted for the product then you would indeed be expected to research its journals. He gave as an example of inaccessible knowledge unpublished possibly in-house laboratory experiments.

We have already seen that the judge held the defence did not apply to protect defects which were known about, but with respect to which the state of science and technology did not permit their discovery. He also commented on the German Supreme Court decision that held the defence could not apply to manufacturing defects and commented that for his non-standard category the defence might possibly work on one occasion only before the risk was known about. With respect to both these last two conclusions it might be commented that this interpretation is quite harsh to defendants since the defence refers not to whether the risk can be discovered, but rather whether the defect can be discovered. If the state of science and technology cannot permit a defect to be detected in individual products or during production quality control why should the defence not apply? The counter argument is that this is too much like negligence and under a strict liability regime once a risk is known of the producer should insure against its materialising and/or invest to enable it to be detected.

(l) Defect stricter than negligence

Given the choice of a consumer expectation standard, the inclusion of state of the art and (a broad) development risks defence, it might be argued that the new strict liability standard differs little from the previous negligence

---

114   Howells and Mildred (2002), *op. cit.*

liability regime.[115] Perhaps the most significant change has been with regard to the burden of proof. Whereas in a negligence liability regime the burden was on the claimant to show that the producer had behaved unreasonably in marketing a defective product, under the new product liability law the burden is placed on the defendant to establish that the state of scientific and technical knowledge affords him a defence. Given the consumer's probable lack of scientific and technical knowledge and the cost of obtaining it, this may be a significant reform. On the other hand producers may find it fairly easy to put forward some evidence to suggest that they could not have had the relevant knowledge and thus effectively force the injured party to disprove their expert evidence. It may be that the courts should be allowed to appoint an expert or automatically grant legal aid whenever the development risks defence is invoked.

A touchstone test often used to determine whether the strict product liability regime is actually stricter than negligence is to assess how it would impact on thalidomide. It will be remembered this drug was one of the triggers for product liability reform when it caused deformities in the off-spring of mothers who ingested it. At the time there would have been no liability in negligence because it was thought that a drug that was not toxic for the mother would also not be toxic for the foetus; moreover the placenta was assumed to filter out most harmful substances and research was not undertaken on the effects of drugs on the foetus. Indeed once research began it took some considerable time before an animal – the white rabbit – was discovered that displayed the same effects. Given the presence of the development risks defence it is likely that thalidomide would not be labelled defective because the state and scientific knowledge would not have revealed the defect. The difference perhaps lies in the fact that once someone had suggested this was a defect liability could have arisen in strict liability, but in negligence it would only arise when that opinion than become so widely held that it would be unreasonable to ignore it.

(m) Defences

In addition to the development risks defence there are several other defences specifically provided for in the Consumer Protection Act 1987. For all of them it is important to remember that the burden is on the defendant to establish the defence.

---

[115] See J. Stapleton, 'Products Liability Reform – Real or Illusory' (1986) 6 *OJLS* 392; C. Newdick, 'The Future of Negligence in Product Liability' (1987) 104 *LQR* 288.

(n) Compliance with mandatory requirements

It is a defence to establish that the defect is attributable to compliance with any requirement imposed by or under any enactment or with any Community obligation.[116] This defence is actually narrower than it might at first appear since it only relates to statutory standards; compliance with voluntary standards, such as those of the BSI, would not be an automatic defence. Also for the defence to apply, there must have been no way in which the defect could have been avoided and the enactment complied with. As most standards seek to promote safety, this will rarely be the case. Equally, most standards do not require that the product must conform to a specific form, but rather leave an element of discretion to the producer by providing for a range of criteria within which the product must fall. For instance, regulations might provide for maximum and minimum tolerations of substances or temperatures. Only if no way exists for a safe product to be made within that range can the defence apply.

(o) No supply

It is also a defence for the defendant to show that he or she never supplied the product.[117] This would protect defendants who have goods stolen from them, as well as ensuring that producers are not responsible for counterfeit goods. It would not, however, protect a producer who, knowing goods are defective, decides not to market them, but finds that they have subsequently been marketed in error by his employees.

(p) No business supply

Defendants will also be able to raise a defence if the only supply of the product to another was otherwise than in the course of a business and without a view to profit.[118] It would, however, not exempt goods supplied free as part of a promotional campaign. Like all attempts to exclude non-business liability such exclusions raise problems in borderline cases, such as, for instance, whether or not charities are included. The European Court of Justice has held that public hospitals are not allowed to invoke this defence in a case involving a kidney that was damaged when being prepared for a transplant.[119]

---

116 Section 4(1)(a), Consumer Protection Act 1987.
117 Section 4(1)(b), Consumer Protection Act 1987.
118 Section 4(1)(c), Consumer Protection Act 1987.
119 *Henning Veedfald v Århus Amtskommune*, C–203/99, [2001] ECR I–3569, see note G, Howells (2002) 6 *European Review of Private Law* 847.

(q) Defect did not exist at time of supply

There is no liability if the defect did not exist at the time the product was supplied.[120] Thus producers are not liable for subsequent deterioration due to poor storage. They are, however, liable for defects which materialise after supply, so long as they existed at the time of supply. The reversal of the burden of proof may be a significant factor when applying this defence.

(r) Component parts

There is also a specific defence for producers of component parts. Such producers can raise a defence if the defect constituted a defect in a subsequent product and was attributable to the design of the subsequent product or to compliance with instructions provided by the producer of the subsequent product.[121]

(s) Contributory negligence, volenti, limitations

There are several other possible defences. Thus a defendant can plead contributory negligence[122] and probably *volenti non fit injuria*, although there is a prohibition on exclusions of liability under the Act.[123]

(t) Limitations

The Act also provides for a three-year limitation period from the date the action accrued or, if later, the date of knowledge, i.e. the date the claimant (or someone in whom the right of action had previously been vested) should have known that he had a right of action worth pursuing against an identifiable defendant.[124] There is also a longstop barring actions ten years after the product was supplied by a producer, own-brander or importer.[125] Whilst such a long-stop may have been acceptable as a trade-off for the inclusion of the development risks, it is less acceptable when a development risk defence is permitted. It does, however, provide a limit to the period for which product records need to be kept. Finally, it should be

---

120 Section 4(1)(d), Consumer Protection Act 1987.
121 Section 4(1)(f), Consumer Protection Act 1987.
122 Section 6(4), Consumer Protection Act 1987.
123 Section 7, Consumer Protection Act 1987.
124 Section 11A, Limitation Act 1980.
125 Section 11(A)(3) Limitation Act 1980: the longstop was circumvented in *Horne Roberts v SmithKline Beecham plc*, [2002] 1 WLR 1662 where because of a construction of the Limitation Act 1980 a substitute defendant was allowed to be added outside the ten year period where the wrong defendant had been sued in error.

remembered that the Act's provisions only came into force on 1 March 1988 and so do not apply to products supplied before that date.

(u) Damages

Injured parties can claim damages for personal injury and death under the same heads as apply in negligence actions. Thus damages can be claimed for both economic losses (like loss of wages) and non-economic losses (such as pain and suffering and loss of amenity). The Directive allowed Member States the option of placing a limit on damages resulting from personal injury and death caused by identical items with the same defect of not less than 70M Euro. This option has been invoked by countries which traditionally combine strict liability with a ceiling on damages (countries such as Germany, Spain and Portugal), but was not taken advantage of by the UK, where such limitations would run counter to the common law tradition.

There are some limitations on the type of property damage recoverable. First, the property damage must exceed £275.[126] The preamble to the Directive states that the aim of this limitation is to avoid litigation in an excessive number of cases. In the UK if that figure is exceeded, then the whole amount of property damage is recoverable. This is different from the position adopted in other European countries where the £275 (or equivalent) is treated like an insurance policy excess and deducted from any claim. The UK approach seems preferable, for otherwise small amounts of property damage could be litigated (i.e. if £276 of damage was suffered, a claim could be brought for £1). Once litigation takes place then there would seem to be no reason not to allow full recovery. To take more cases out of the scope of the Directive, a better approach would be to raise the threshold, rather than making litigation less attractive by making the amounts recoverable smaller.

Second, the Directive does not apply to loss or damage to the product itself or to the whole or any part of any product which has been supplied with the product comprised in it.[127] It could be objected that this restriction is drawn too widely. The Directive talks of 'damage to, or destruction of, any item of property other than the defective product itself'. It might be suggested that, as a component part is a product in its own right then any damage it causes to the end product could be recovered under the Directive, although it is clearly not recoverable under the Act. This argumentation smacks of the complex structure theory which has been rejected in negligence,[128] and has also not been included within the scope

---

[126] Section 5(4), Consumer Protection Act 1987.
[127] Section 5(2), Consumer Protection Act 1987.
[128] See *Murphy v Brentwood District Council* [1990] 2 All ER 908.

of implementing laws in other European countries. It would, however, make sense to permit such recovery. At present when a car is damaged by a defective component, the recovery of damages depends upon whether the component is the original or a replacement: only in the latter instance can the damage be recovered from the producer of the component part.

Third, the damaged property (note that this restriction does not apply to the defective product which caused the damage) must have been ordinarily intended for private use, occupation or consumption and also actually have been intended by the claimant for his or her own private use, occupation or consumption.[129]

It is unclear which test of remoteness of damage would apply. One would imagine that in torts of strict liability, the defendant would be liable for all direct consequences of his tortious actions, without there being any requirement of foreseeability. However, in *Cambridge Water Co Ltd v Eastern Counties Leather Plc*,[130] a case of liability in nuisance and *Rylands v Fletcher*, the House of Lords imposed a foreseeability test of remoteness in respect of torts of strict liability. One suspects that, especially given the inclusion of the development risks defence, the courts will be tempted to apply the test of reasonable foreseeability to liability under the Consumer Protection Act 1987. Matters of foreseeability, which cannot be used as a defence to an allegation of defectiveness under the Act, might then be invoked to avoid liability on the basis that the damage was too remote. This would further undermine the strictness of the product liability regime under the Consumer Protection Act 1987.

4.2.5 Reform

The European Commission has issued a Green Paper on reforming the Product Liability Directive.[131] It also commissioned a study.[132] However, despite many ideas being floated in the Green Paper there is little sign of significant reforms being forthcoming. The idea had been floated of making the Directive the sole source of protection for those injured by defective products, but this does not seem to have much support despite the current trend favouring maximal harmonisation. Since the 'father' of the Directive, Dr. Taschner left the Commission there seems less enthusiasm

---

[129] Section 5(3), Consumer Protection Act 1987.

[130] [1994] 1 All ER 53. This was in fact a case of historic pollution which could not have been predicted as being classed as pollution at the time it occurred i.e. a development risk.

[131] COM (1999) 396 and second report at COM (2000) 893.

[132] *Product Liability in the European Union* (Lovells, 2003).

for activity in this area. Equally it may be salient that the Directive is the responsibility of DG Markt rather than DG SANCO.

4.3 SERVICE LIABILITY

4.3.1 Negligence

Whilst the notion (if not the reality) of strict liability has become commonplace in products liability discussions, the same cannot be said of service liability where the legal mind set is still firmly wedded to the principle of fault liability. In tort, suppliers of services will typically be held to be under a duty of care to protect the safety of their customers and to ensure that they do not damage the goods they perform their services on. However the standard of care is only the negligence standard of taking reasonable care.

The standard of care was classically expounded by McNair J in *Bolam v Friern Hospital Management Committee*[133] where the learned judge stated:

> The test is the standard of the ordinary skilled man exercising and professing to have that special skill. A man need not possess the highest expert skill... it is sufficient if he exercises the ordinary skill of a competent man exercising that particular art.[134]

The judge went on to consider the relevance of common practice when assessing a professional's conduct:

> A doctor is not guilty of negligence if he has acted in accordance with a practice accepted as proper by a responsible body of medical men skilled in that particular art.... Putting it the other way round, a doctor is not negligent, if he is acting in accordance with such a practice, merely because there is a body of opinion that takes the contrary view. At the same time, that does not mean that a medical man can obstinately and pig-headedly carry on with some old technique if it has been proved to be contrary to what is really substantially the whole of informed medical opinion.[135]

---

[133] [1957] 2 All ER 118.
[134] *Ibid.* at 121.
[135] *Ibid.* at 122.

The standard reflecting test applied in cases of professional negligence can be criticised from a consumer perspective.[136] The courts have always been more willing to challenge doctors' views as to whether patients should have been more fully informed of the risks associated with their treatment.[137] Thus was taken a step further in *Bolitho v City and Hackney Health Authority*[138] when the House of Lords said that it would not be a defence to negligence to simply lead expert evidence supporting a practice if there is no logical basis to the opinion. However it would be rare for the courts to find genuinely held medical beliefs to be so unreasonable. However, nevertheless it must be welcomed that the courts are willing on appropriate occasions to be critical and not simply accept every common practice as acceptable.

Moreover someone who 'professes to exercise a special skill must exercise the ordinary skill of his speciality'.[139] Indeed the judges will assess the reasonableness of an actor's conduct in the light of the post he or she holds rather than by the qualities of the individual concerned.[140]

Once negligence is established, the claimant still needs to prove that the negligence caused the damage complained of. As with product liability, the requirement to prove causation is likely to be a real problem for consumers. The objection is not that causation should not have to be proven, but rather that the present rules are too restrictive and formalistic to allow claimants a fair chance. Causation must be proven on the balance of probabilities and this is taken to mean that there was a 51 per cent chance that the defendant caused the damage. Yet in many cases there are several possible explanations for a claimant's injuries, with the defendant's negligence being just one. The defendant is more likely than the claimant to be able to explain the actual cause of the damage, as he or she would have controlled the process which caused the injury; yet the burden is placed on the claimant. This seems wrong given that the claimant is innocent and the defendant is at fault.

---

[136] For an interesting and lively critique of how the courts deal with professionals, see M. Joseph, *Lawyers Can Seriously Damage Your Health* (Michael Joseph, 1984).

[137] In *Sidaway v Bethlem Royal Hospital Governors* [1985] 1 All ER 643 at 663 Lord Bridge said: 'But, even in a case where, as here, no expert witness in the relevant medical field condemns the non-disclosure as being in conflict with accepted and responsible medical practice, I am of opinion that the judge might in certain circumstances come to the conclusion that disclosure of a particular risk was so obviously necessary to an informed choice on the part of the patient that no reasonably prudent medical man would fail to make it'.

[138] [1997] 4 All ER 771

[139] *Maynard v West Midlands Regional Area Health Authority* [1985] 1 All ER 635.

[140] *Wilsher v Essex Area Health Authority* [1986] 3 All ER 801.

4.3.2 Supply of Goods and Services Act 1982[141]

The Supply of Goods and Services Act 1982 implies into contracts for the supply of a service (which includes contracts where goods are also supplied) a term 'that the supplier will carry out the service with reasonable care and skill'.[142] The section only implies this term when the supplier is acting in the course of a business. Also this is not a condition in the strict sense, so whether a breach justifies termination of the contract will depend upon the seriousness of the consequences of the breach.

The implied term seems to be a codification of the common law position and also imports into the contractual context the negligence case law concerning what amounts to reasonable care and skill.[143] From a consumer perspective, the term may be less favourable than similar terms implied into consumer contracts in Australia (by s. 74, Federal Trade Practices Act 1974[144]) and in Ireland (by s. 39 of the Irish Sale of Goods and Supply of Services Act 1980). Section 74 of the Australian Act talks about 'due skill and care' while s. 39(b) of the Irish Act provides for 'due skill, care and diligence'. 'Due skill' might be considered more demanding than 'reasonable care and skill'.

The Irish law also implies a term 'that the supplier has the necessary skill to render the service', whereas under English law if a consumer discovers that a supplier lacks the necessary skills to perform the task he or she will probably have to wait to see if the task is actually performed negligently. There is unlikely to be a term implied that the supplier possesses the necessary skills, especially given the possibility that the supplier might subcontract the work to a competent person. One exception to this may be where a supplier must possess a licence or other qualifications. Where the supplier falsely represents him or herself as having a special status (for example, being a member of a trade association), then the contract could be rescinded, and damages claimed, for misrepresentation.

Under the Australian Act, where the consumer makes known the 'particular purpose for which the services are required or the result that he desires the services to achieve', there is then 'an implied warranty that the services supplied... will be reasonably fit for that purpose and are of such a nature and quality that they might reasonably be expected to achieve that result'. We have noted earlier in this chapter that in English contract law, while it is possible to promise that a service will achieve a particular

---

141 See G. Woodroffe, *Goods and Services – The New Law* (Sweet & Maxwell, 1982).

142 Section 13, Supply of Goods and Services Act 1982.

143 See Woodroffe, *op. cit.*, at p. 104.

144 See N. Palmer and F. Rose, 'Implied Terms in Consumer Transactions – The Australian Approach' (1977) 26 *ICLQ* 169 at 185–190.

outcome, this will only be found to be so where an intention to give such an express promise can be established.[145]

The Supply of Goods and Services Act 1982 clearly stopped short of making the suppliers of services strictly liable. Would that have been such a drastic step? Surely dry-cleaners can be held liable for clothes they damage, even if negligence cannot be shown. Even in the most contentious area of medical negligence, which probably would have to be subject to a specific regime, strict liability would not make doctors liable for the failure of medical treatment. Liability would only be imposed where the doctor's actions made a patient worse, for example, through failure to diagnose or improper performance of the treatment, the difference being that the doctor need not be found to be at fault. The move away from a system which requires one party to blame the other should help in the process of achieving settlements, if professionals can be made to feel that their professional conduct is not being questioned. After all, there may be many explanations for why things go wrong besides professional error.

4.3.3 Draft Directive on the Liability of Suppliers of Services[146]

The European Commission published a draft Directive on Service Liability in 1991. The project has been abandoned. Why did this happen? The Commission is notoriously more cautious in relation to services than products, in part because the single market justifications for European legislative activity in this area are less obvious. The draft Service Liability Directive was a victim of the current vogue of invoking subsidiarity as a ground for not legislating at the European level. There were also powerful pressure groups in the service sector countering suggestions that legislation was needed in respect of services. In particular, the medical and architectural professions lobbied hard to be removed from the scope of any Service Liability Directive. The Commission concluded that the 'proposal stands no chance of being adopted without sweeping changes which would risk voiding it of much of its substance'.[147]

The key features of the now obsolete draft Directive are nevertheless worth mentioning in outline. They illustrate the more hesitant approach of legislators to services than products – even by those who wish to do something to help consumers in this area. The draft Directive was based on fault liability. However, the injured party would have been assisted by a

---

145 See note 3.
146 OJ 1991 C 12/8. See Th. Bourgoignie, 'Liability of Suppliers of Services in the European Community: the Draft Council Directive' [1991] *E Consum LJ* 3.
147 *Commission Communication on new directions on the liability of suppliers of services:* COM (94) 260.

reversal of the burden of proof and by the fact that, when assessing fault, account would have been taken of the behaviour of the supplier of the service, who 'in normal and reasonably foreseeable conditions, shall ensure the safety which may reasonably be expected'.[148] This would seem to be a rather limited obligation to ensure safety, as emphasised by the fact that a party was not at fault merely because 'a better service existed or might have existed at the moment of performance or subsequently'.[149] The reversal of the burden of proof would have assisted consumers, but might have been undermined by Art. 5 of the draft Directive which required the injured person to prove damage as well as the causal relationship between that damage and the performance of the service. In order to establish such a causal relationship, the injured party would doubtless have had to show what exactly in the performance of the service had caused the damage. In practice, this might have amounted to having to prove how the supplier was at fault in the provision of the service – the very element for which the draft Directive had intended to place the burden of proof on the defendant.

Europe is now considering how to address service safety.[150] Its focus remains, however, on regulatory tools rather than civil liability. Although it has recently commissioned a study on liability for services, so some developments might arise in the future.

4.4 ALTERNATIVES

Improving the substantive rules may only be a partial solution to the question of accident compensation for consumers. Most solutions fail to address the basic problem that private litigation is a very expensive way of providing compensation. It is also very arbitrary since it requires the consumer to bring him or herself within what are sometimes technical and narrow grounds for recovery. Not only must there be a ground for recovery, but in addition the consumer must have evidence to establish the claim and also be fortunate in having a readily suable and solvent defendant. Some countries have sought to avoid the dangers of the private litigation system.

---

[148]   Article 1(3) COM (93) 378 final.
[149]   Article 1(4) COM (93) 378 final.
[150]   See 10.3.4.

4.4.1 Scandinavia[151]

Scandinavian countries have adopted an insurance-based solution. In Sweden, for example, there are insurance-based schemes covering injuries caused both by pharmaceuticals and medical accidents. Although these schemes are alternatives to the court, in practice they are more generous, making private law largely redundant within the area of their operation. The theory behind the schemes is to base liability on causation rather than proof of fault or defectiveness, with the advantage that defendants can admit liability without having to concede culpability. Causation is also given a more relaxed interpretation than under the general law. However, much of the schemes' success might be due to the fact that businesses only have to meet moderate costs for financing them. With the nation's social insurance covering a large proportion of the injured person's economic losses, the insurance schemes only have to provide a top-up element.

4.4.2 New Zealand[152]

The most radical reform has been in New Zealand, where the Accident Compensation Act 1982 essentially abolished common law actions for death or personal injury. Instead those who suffer 'personal injury by accident' in New Zealand recover economic losses in the form of periodic payments of up to 80 per cent of the person's previous salary, subject to a maximum ceiling which is pitched at a fairly high level. Non-economic losses are paid as a lump sum. Despite criticisms[153] the New Zealand scheme remains a model of what a sensible cost efficient accident compensation scheme might look like. However, in recent times there have also been warnings about the dangers of giving up private redress in favour of state benefits. The benefits under the New Zealand scheme have been seriously reduced over the years. This has caused many to wonder whether they were right to trade off civil liability for administrative compensation[154] and lawyers have tried to push wider open the few remaining avenues for private law redress, such as where punitive damages can be claimed.

In any event it would be a significant challenge to introduce a similar scheme in a larger country with a less homogenous society than exists in

---

[151] G. Howells, *op. cit.*, Chapter 9.

[152] G. Howells, *op. cit.*, Chapter 16.

[153] See R. Miller, 'The Future of New Zealand's Accident Compensation Scheme' (1989) 11 *U Hawaii Law Rev* 1.

[154] S. Todd, 'Privatization of Accident Compensation: Policy and Politics in New Zealand' (2000) 39 *Washburn* LR 404.

New Zealand. This is unlikely to happen because of the number of powerful interest groups which have a vested interest in keeping the present system in place – lawyers, insurers, expert witnesses and also possibly those with a privileged position under the existing regime (for example, workers who benefit from workers' compensation schemes and also possibly now consumers who benefit from strict liability regimes).

4.5 PERSPECTIVES FOR THE FUTURE

The role of the private law is likely to remain strong in British law. In the present litigation culture it is perhaps surprising that product liability cases are not more abundant. The contrast with the numerous cases in the US is very striking. Often the reason is that cases which would be litigated as product liability in the US are dealt with in other ways in the United Kingdom. Workplace accidents involving dangerous products would be health and safety cases in the United Kingdom, for instance. Partly of course this is because the incentives in terms of lawyers' contingent fees and damages are not the same on this side of the Atlantic. Again lawyers' ignorance of the Consumer Protection Act 1987 must be a factor as they either think it only covers consumer products or prefer to deal with cases on the basis of familiar negligence principles. However, private remedies for product and service related injuries look likely to be a permanent and increasingly important part of the litigation landscape. The *A v National Blood Authority* decision has placed strict liability at the forefront of litigators' minds and marked out the differences between it and negligence. The impact of that decision is still to be discerned and the speed with which its scope is tested may well depend upon the willingness of the Legal Services Commission to fund test cases in this area.[155]

---

[155] In that respect the omens are not good for claimants as funding has stopped in the MMR vaccine litigation. An appeal was also not funded in the McDonald's coffee case. The Legal Services Commission uses a test which assesses the costs of bringing the action against the likelihood of success and the gains if successful.

Chapter 5

Unfair Terms

5.1 RATIONALES FOR CONTROLLING UNFAIR TERMS

In the theoretical caricature of the perfect market, there can be no such thing as a contract term that is unfair. Freely negotiated terms represent the parties' wishes. A term is a term – it cannot be unfair. Both parties have gained from the deal; why else would they have concluded it? To impose legal control over 'unfair' terms involves some value-judgement about the content of a bargain that is divorced from the parties' own perceptions at the time of contracting. Such legal intervention finds its rationale in the imperfections of the market. Realistically, negotiation over terms is not simply a matter of contractual freedom. Many factors obscure the 'purity' of the individual bargain and contribute to the parties' inability to make informed choices.

This suggests that the principal rationale for controlling terms that are 'unfair' lies in the imbalance between supplier and consumer. The capacity of the consumer to bargain over terms which he or she perceives as not being in his or her interest is attenuated in modern economic conditions. Some situations offer the consumer the choice of 'take it or leave it'. More fundamentally still, the consumer may not even know of some conditions. The use of the standard form contract, in particular, may obscure from the consumer the nature of the bargain, especially where terms are buried in small print. In some circumstances, the consumer may be referred for further information about contractual terms to a separate document which is not readily available. This is common practice in the case of tickets.

It remains a theme of this book that the identification of inequality is but a starting point. After all, the inequality at stake here seems incapable of elimination in modern market conditions. The elaboration of a legal response depends on deciding on the specific consequences of inequality which call for control.

However, the shaper of legal policy must be sophisticated. It was explained in Chapter 1 that the initial impression that the standard form contract prevents the consumer from participating actively in contract negotiation may be only part of the picture.[1] Often individual negotiation will be time-consuming and costly, and thus in the interests of neither

---

1   Chapter 1.3.4.

trader nor consumer. Standard form contracts accelerate the process. In a competitive market, at least, such contracts ought to allow traders to cut costs which should then be passed on to consumers through lower prices. There may be costs and benefits to intervening in standard form contracts and the law needs to be shaped accordingly.

Should the law catch negotiated contracts too? On the one hand, one might suppose that the presence of negotiation establishes the reality of a freely concluded bargain and that intervention is not required. On the other hand, if one assumes an endemic power imbalance, the fact that the contract was not drawn up in advance, but instead settled between those parties, does not mean that it is truly a reflection of wishes. Negotiation may simply provide the supplier with greater opportunity to exploit his or her superior economic strength. The law must choose its scope for intervention.

The type of term which in English law has aroused most attention is the exclusion clause. Typically, such a term excludes the liability of the supplier for things that go wrong. Consumers may find that they have no effective redress under a contract when they do not get what they expected. The perception is that the exclusion clause requires legal control because the consumer may be unaware of the claims he or she is surrendering by 'agreeing' to a contract containing the clause. As a general perception, it may indeed be true that the phenomenon of exclusion clauses has the capacity to damage the consumer interest. However, exclusion clauses have a function to play which may help the consumer. They help to allocate risk. If a supplier knows where the loss will fall, the price can be fixed accordingly. A consumer prepared to assume risk under a contract may be offered a lower price. Exclusion clauses allocate risk and permit the parties to decide in advance where they will stand if things go wrong. Typically the party bearing the risk can then decide on insurance cover; without an exclusion clause both parties would wastefully need to seek protection. Exclusion clauses may simply be bought and sold; to outlaw them would be to diminish consumer choice. This positive view of the function of the exclusion clause depends on the consumer being adequately informed about the process, which will frequently not be the case. This suggests a need for a legal intervention that is nuanced and, if possible, attuned to the level of information that a consumer has about the clauses on offer.[2]

---

2   Cf. H. Collins, *Regulating Contracts* (OUP, 1999), Chapter 11, 'Unfair Contracts'.

5.2 JUDICIAL INTERVENTION

In English law, the judicial response to unfair terms has been indirect. The English judiciary has shunned a general jurisdiction to pronounce on the fairness of bargains. Lord Denning's attempt to move the law in such a direction in *Lloyds Bank v Bundy*,[3] at least in situations of inequality of bargaining power, has been resisted by the higher courts, not least because of the perception that it is for Parliament, not the courts, to decide where such intervention is proper and what form it should take.[4] This judicial reluctance is to a large extent the corollary of the notion of freedom of contract. The parties determine the bargain; the courts enforce those choices. On this model, fairness is not a matter for the courts. English contract law enforces promises where they represent an agreement, are supported by consideration and where the parties have the intention to create legal relations. Once the deal falls within these parameters, it is enforceable as a contract, unless vitiated, for example, by a misrepresentation or the influence of duress. These are the bounds of the judicial role and they are not necessarily congruent with notions of fairness.

However, elements of fairness may infiltrate judge-made contract law. Chapter 1 of this book demonstrates that the 'hands-off' judicial role is no longer an adequate depiction of modern contract law, in the consumer sphere at least. Elements of fairness permeate the law, even though it is controversial whether these elements are sensibly put together to form a coherent general requirement of fairness as a prerequisite to contracting.[5] The determination of whether a contract has been formed, on what terms and whether it is vitiated may allow an indirect reference to notions adjacent to fairness. The doctrine of economic duress has connections with notions of fairness in dealing. Where an agreement is procured as a result of pressure, the party subjected to that pressure may be able to have it set aside. The problem is the identification of where the margin lies between undue pressure and acceptably tough commercial tactics.[6] It would be unusual to find such issues arising in the context of a consumer transaction. The consumer's problems are more likely to lie in inadequate information

---

3 [1975] QB 326.

4 E.g. Lord Scarman in *National Westminster Bank v Morgan* [1985] AC 686. For discussion see S. Thal, 'The Inequality of Bargaining Power Doctrine' (1988) 8 *Oxford JLS* 17.

5 See further Chapter 1.3 above.

6 Cf. *Pau On v Lau Yiu Long* [1980] AC 614; *Atlas Express Ltd v Kafko Ltd* [1989] QB 833; *Williams v Roffey Bros and Nicholls (Contractors) Ltd* [1990] 2 WLR 1153.

and limited choice caused by the nature of the modern market, rather than in duress inflicted by an individual supplier. For similar reasons the role of equitable protection against undue influence[7] has a role to play that lies outside the scope of this book.

The rules of incorporation of terms are capable of being moulded into an indirect method of expressing a view of fairness in the negotiating process. It is possible for judges to exclude 'unfair terms' by use of the rules of incorporation, although one would not expect to see an explicit recognition that this is what was happening. So a term will be part of the contract and enforceable as a term only where sufficient has been done to bring it to the attention of the party against whom it is to be enforced. This seems to occur especially where the judge is of the view that real negotiation and freedom of contract are missing. This may be especially appropriate in relation to standard form contracts and is evident in the robust approach of Lord Denning MR in *Thornton v Shoe Lane Parking*.[8] The more unusual or onerous the term, the more active the steps that are expected of a supplier, on pain of denying enforceability to the term. The most potent recent illustration of this technique in the UK came in *Interfoto v Stiletto*[9] The Court of Appeal held that a 'particularly onerous or unusual'[10] contractual condition, which would not generally be known to the other party, would not be enforceable unless the party seeking to rely on that condition could show that it had fairly been brought to the other party's attention. This test was not met and Interfoto accordingly could not rely on the clause. The case involved business parties. It is probable that in the consumer context the judiciary would be all the more tempted to adopt such rigorous scrutiny of the enforceability of clauses that are out of the ordinary and/or onerous.[11] But they must cross that threshold. *O'Brien v Mirror Group Newspapers*[12] was, for Hale LJ, a reminder of her pedigree as a legal academic.[13] The case, she said, 'would make an excellent

---

7   Cf. *National Westminster Bank plc v Morgan* [1985] AC 686; *Barclays Bank plc v O'Brien* [1993] 4 All ER 417; *CIBC Mortgages plc v Pitt* [1993] 4 All ER 433; *Royal Bank of Scotland v Etridge (No 2)* [2002] AC 773.

8   Chapter 1.3.5.

9   [1988] 2 WLR 615, [1988] 1 All ER 348, Chapter 1.3.5 above.

10   Per Dillon LJ WLR 620e, All ER 352f. Note that a condition need not be both onerous *and* unusual; a condition that is usual in the trade, but onerous, would still require elucidation in so far as the other party would not generally be aware of it.

11   Cf. Chapter 1.3 above on the deeper interventionism of consumer contract law in comparison with commercial contract law.

12   [2002] CLC 33; *The Times*, 8 August 2001.

13   Dame Brenda Hale, now a Law Lord, was a full-time member of the Law Faculty of Manchester University from 1966 to 1984, when she became a Law Commissioner.

question in an undergraduate contract law seminar'. It was less enjoyable for the consumer. He thought he had won £50,000 on a scratch-card game launched by the *Daily Mirror*. But there had been an error. The newspaper had printed many more winning cards than planned. In offering the consumer just £34 it relied on a rule which stated that 'Should more prizes be claimed than are available in any prize category for any reason, a simple draw will take place for the prize'. The rules were not printed on the scratch-card. The card simply invited readers to inspect the newspaper for the rules, though it did not refer to a particular page and in any event the rules did not appear in every edition. The consumer denied the rule was incorporated into the contract. The claim for £50,000 nevertheless failed. The Court of Appeal decided that the clear reference to the rules on the card, coupled to their discoverability from back issues of the *Mirror*, was enough to secure their incorporation. *Interfoto v Stiletto* was distinguished on the basis that the term in the present case was *not* onerous, nor even unexpected. The term merely deprived the consumer of a windfall for which he had done little in return. The newspaper was protected under the contract.

Evidently there is a limit to what judges can do with such rules and there is a limit to what they are prepared to do. Much depends on the facts of particular cases. In any event this is not a direct check on the fairness of the substance of a bargain, so that although this method may be sufficient to exclude a minor term that is not properly incorporated, it will be useless to tackle a wickedly imbalanced clause which is plainly part of the contract on the rules of incorporation.

A further judicial device used indirectly to control terms, especially exclusion clauses and cognate terms, lies in the insistence that, even where such terms are incorporated, any ambiguity is construed against the party wishing to rely on them. This is the *contra proferentem* rule. For example in *Hollier v Rambler Motors Ltd*[14] a clause excluding liability for 'damage caused by fire to customers' cars on the premises' was held to be ineffective to exclude liability for negligently inflicted fire damage in the absence of explicit reference to negligence. This decision comes close to finding ambiguity where none exists, rather than construing ambiguity in a manner favourable to the party against whom the clause is being enforced.[15] It comes close to rewriting the contract in what the court perceives to be a fairer manner. This trend of intervention disguised as interpretation reached its zenith in the determination of the courts to deny

---

[14] [1972] 2 QB 71.
[15] Cf. E. Barendt (1972) 85 *MLR* 644 for an insight into thinking prior to legislative intervention.

effect even to clearly worded exemption clauses where the result would be to rob the other party of the essence of what he or she was supposed to be receiving under the contract.[16] The *contra proferentem* approach is still a part of English law, but the contortions adopted by the judiciary are now much less marked. Indeed there is explicit recognition that the advent of legislative control renders judicial activism on this scale inappropriate. The courts now feel that they should not strain the process of interpretation of contractual terms in order to avoid what might seem to them to be odd results. *Photo Productions v Securicor* represents a strong statement of judicial deference to the parties' bargain. Lord Diplock commented that 'the reports are full of cases in which what would appear to be very strained constructions have been placed upon exclusion clauses, mainly in what today would be called consumer contracts and contracts of adhesion. ...[A]ny need for this kind of judicial distortion of the English language has been banished by Parliament's having made these kinds of contracts subject to the Unfair Contract Terms Act 1977'.[17] Over twenty years later, in *Bank of Credit and Commerce International v Ali*,[18] a case involving the interpretation of an employee's release agreement, Lord Hoffman chose to draw lessons from the development of the law governing exemption clauses. He similarly set his face against 'judicial creativity, bordering on judicial legislation'. The norm is use of 'ordinary principles of construction'.[19]

The litigation in *Photo Productions v Securicor* involved commercial parties and the House of Lords declined to strain the interpretation of clear words which were 'fairly susceptible of one meaning only'.[20] So the fact that one of Securicor's employees had burned down Photo Productions' factory did not deprive Securicor of the shelter of an appropriately worded exclusion clause. The failure of Photo Productions' claim for over £600,000 in damages does not seem peculiar once one appreciates that the exclusion clause represented the parties' chosen risk allocation, on which depended contract price and purchase of insurance cover. Without the clause, Securicor would have charged more and bought insurance. It was more efficient to let Photo Productions use its intimate knowledge of the condition of its factory to determine how much insurance to buy. The fact

---

16   The so-called fundamental breach doctrine exemplified by *Karsales v Wallis* [1956] 1 WLR 936.

17   [1980] AC 827, 851; cf. Lord Wilberforce 843.

18   [2001] 2 *WLR* 735.

19   Lord Hoffman dissented, but his disagreement with his brethren was not on this point.

20   Lord Diplock, *ibid*. In similar vein, *Ailsa Craig Fishing Co Ltd v Malvern Fishing Co Ltd* [1983] 1 WLR 964; *George Mitchell (Chesterhall) Ltd v Finney Lock Seeds Ltd* [1983] 3 WLR 163.

of employing Securicor would doubtless have led to a reduction in the cost of that insurance greater than the price paid to Securicor for its services. A decision which disallowed Securicor the protection of the exclusion clause would have defeated the parties' intention at time of contracting.

Absent statutory intervention, the temptation to adopt an activist judicial approach in the consumer sphere might on first impression seem likely to remain on foot, given that full negotiation and openness are less likely to prevail than in the commercial setting. However, as is indicated by the remarks of Lord Diplock in *Photo Productions v Securicor*, echoed by Lord Hoffman in *Bank of Credit and Commerce International v Ali*, the advent of the Unfair Contract Terms Act 1977 renders it improbable that judges will ever again resort to the past extremes of interpretation. Legislative intervention has reduced the perceived need and, for some, has also cast doubt on the legitimacy of judicial creativity in the field. Nevertheless, it still holds true that instances of genuine ambiguity will be resolved against the party seeking to rely on an exclusion or cognate clause, which will normally operate in the consumer's favour.

5.3 PUBLIC INTERVENTION TO CONTROL UNFAIR TERMS

The common law's indirect methods of controlling unfair terms remain in place. They retain relevance. An unincorporated clause is ineffective and, unfair or not, it will not bind as part of the contract. Therefore consideration of the common law rules logically precedes application of the statutory controls. However, with regard to exclusion clauses, the focus of English law for over 25 years has been on a direct form of control of unfairness exercised by the Unfair Contract Terms Act 1977 (commonly known as UCTA). This Act envisages a direct challenge to terms which are indisputably part of the contract between the parties and places in the hands of the judiciary the power to rule (some) terms unenforceable.[21] The availability of this power has reduced the judicial motivation to use indirect routes to attack clauses perceived to be unfair.

The 1977 Act is one of two sources of direct control over unfair terms in English law. The second source lies in the Unfair Terms in Consumer Contracts Regulations 1999.[22]

The 1999 Regulations, an adjusted version replacing Regulations made in 1994,[23] represent the United Kingdom's implementation of the EC's

---

[21]   There are some other specific statutory controls scattered throughout the law. On consumer credit see Chapter 6.12.

[22]   S.I. 1999 No. 2083.

Directive on Unfair Terms in Consumer Contracts,[24] adopted in March 1993 and the deadline for implementation of which fell at the end of 1994. The Directive applies to all relevant contracts concluded after 31 December 1994. This harmonising measure is made under *what was* Art. 100a EC, and *is now* (after amendment) Art. 95 EC, which links it to the process of establishing the Community's internal market.[25] Its Preamble explains that disparity between national laws distorts competition between suppliers in the market and that ignorance of the law in other Member States deters consumers from making direct purchases in them. The Directive attempts to distil acceptable common principles from diverse national backgrounds and its character as a minimum measure,[26] permitting stricter national rules, is a realistic reflection of that diversity.

As a matter of Community law, the UK's implementing Regulations must be interpreted in order to conform to the Directive.[27] This includes a requirement that the day-to-day application of the Regulations comply with the requirements of the Directive, because the European Court has made clear that implementation of a Directive constitutes a continuing obligation which is not exhausted by proper implementation on paper.[28] Accordingly the Regulations cannot be viewed in isolation from the parent Directive. The description below reflects this constitutional relationship by referring where necessary to the Directive in discussing the Regulations in order to emphasise the necessary association between the two. Reference is made to the Directive alone, rather than to the implementing Regulations, where comment is directed at its broad structure and policy objectives.

The two sources of control over unfair terms in English law are not coextensive. In some respects the Unfair Contract Terms Act is the more extensive. In other respects the Regulations implementing the Directive exercise a broader control than the Act. This means that the implementation of the Directive in the UK has significantly extended the scope of legal intervention. The criteria for control under the Act and the Regulations have much in common, but they are not identical. This partial duplication creates a rather unhappy pattern, causing confusion among

---

23   The Unfair Terms in Consumer Contracts Regulations 1994, S.I. No. 3159. The 1999 regulations differ from the 1994 version primarily by adopting an approach more closely aligned with the text of the directive itself (5.6.1.2 below) and by extending the scope of enforcement (5.8 below). See S. Bright, 'Winning the battle against unfair contract terms' (2000) 20 *Legal Studies* 331.

24   Directive 93/13 OJ 1993 L95/29.

25   Chapter 2.3.3.

26   Article 8, Directive 93/13.

27   Chapter 2.4.2.

28   Case C–62/00 *Marks and Spencer plc v Commissioners of Customs and Excise* [2002] ECR I–6325, Chapter 2.4.2.

both commercial parties and consumers. It also adds to the costs of
compliance by requiring firms to take additional legal advice. The deeper
the divergence between the controls envisaged by the two regimes, the
trickier the handling of the law will prove to be. The desirable route would
be the consolidation of both regimes into a single statute that would reflect
the current state of the law controlling unfair contract terms. However,
pressures on Parliamentary time have thus far precluded this option in the
UK. Preparing proposals for future consolidation has, however, been part
of the recent work programme of the Law Commission. In 2002
consultation papers were issued by both the English and Scottish Law
Commissions.[29] The proposals are sketched in section 5.4.4 below.
Pending any such reform, the law governing unfair terms continues to run
in two streams, sometimes flowing in the same channel but sometimes
flowing separately and with different levels of vigour.

Constitutionally, the result of this double control is as follows. In some
areas the Act alone applies. In other areas the Regulations based on the
Directive alone apply. In areas where both the Act and the Regulations
implementing the Directive apply, both controls coexist. The Regulations
apply, but so too does the Act. Any controls under the Act that are more
stringent or more extensive than the Regulations may be enforced,
provided only that that neither frustrates the achievement of the objectives
of the Directive nor conflicts with rules of primary Community law such as
those governing the free movement of goods under Art. 28 (ex 30) EC.[30]
The Directive, a minimum measure, does not pre-empt national initiatives
which offer more stringent protection,[31] nor does it affect national
measures outwith its scope. So, for example, although the Directive does
not address individually negotiated terms, it offers no objection to national
rules which extend control into that area. Such extended control exists
under the Act and is not affected by the implementation of the Directive.
Where the scope of the Act and the Regulations overlaps, but the latter
apply a stricter control, the national controls are correspondingly
strengthened. However, it is not clear whether the Regulations

---

29 Law Commission Joint Consultation Paper on *Unfair Terms in Contracts* (Law Comm
    Consultation Paper No 166, Scottish Law Comm Discussion Paper No 119), August
    2002. This is recommended reading: included is a very full account of the current law.
    For comment see E. MacDonald, 'Unifying Unfair Terms Legislation' (2004) 67 *MLR*
    69.

30 The ruling in C–267 and C–268/91 *Keck and Mithouard* renders it highly improbable
    that Art. 28 would affect such even-handed national laws; Chapter 2.2 above.

31 Article 8 Directive Contrast the General Product Safety Directive which is not
    minimum and does pre-empt national rules; Chapter 10.

implementing the Directive *do* envisage a stricter control test than the Act.[32]

5.4 THE SCOPE OF THE UK AND EC INTERVENTIONS COMPARED AND CONTRASTED

The principal differences between the two regimes lie in three areas. These are explained in this section in advance of a more detailed account of the scope of the law, presented in section 5.5 below.

5.4.1 Types of Contract Covered

The Regulations based on the Directive catch only unfair terms in contracts 'concluded between a seller or supplier and a consumer'.[33] The Act catches some contracts which are not consumer contracts. On this point, the implementation of the Directive has buttressed English law, but English law is already more ambitious in the scope of contracts covered.

The Act's extension into commercial contracts may readily be explained if one accepts that the primary motivation for control is the fact of economic imbalance. That may apply to the supplier/consumer relationship, but also to the relationship between large and small firms. One would nonetheless expect to see a different type of control over commercial contracts as opposed to consumer contracts, and this is reflected in the Act.[34] The Regulations by contrast do not intrude into the commercial sphere. This does not mean that the rationales for controlling (some) business bargains have been considered but rejected at Community level. In fact the limited scope of the Directive is largely a reflection of its development in the European Commission's Consumer Policy Service, which enjoyed limited practical opportunity to move beyond the consumer sphere.[35] Moreover, the ambitions of the Directive dwindled in the face of the political pressures which for a decade delayed the final adoption of a measure affecting only terms in consumer contracts that have not been individually negotiated.[36]

---

[32] Section 5.6.1.3 below explores the potential in this direction.

[33] Regulation 3(1)/Art. 1(1) Directive.

[34] Cf. Chapter 5.6 below.

[35] The relevant actor within the Commission is now Directorate-General 'SANCO', the Directorate-General for Health and Consumer Protection.

[36] The Parliament called for a Directive in the field in 1980 (OJ 1980 C291/35); in 1984 the Commission published a discussion paper (COM (84) 55); in September 1990, the

5.4.2 Types of Term Covered

The Regulations based on the Directive catch only terms that have not been individually negotiated. Terms that have been individually negotiated are untouched. Earlier drafts of the Directive had proposed a wider control, but criticism of intervention into terms individually agreed by the parties resulted in the more modest reach of the Directive as finally adopted.[37] The Unfair Contract Terms Act is more ambitious, being capable of catching even negotiated terms. The Act is also broader than the Regulations because it catches non-contractual notices, not simply contractual terms to which the Regulations are confined.

With regard to the substance of the term, rather than the manner of its negotiation, the Act is more restricted, being limited to exclusion and cognate terms in contracts. The careful definitions found in the Act of terms caught are absent from the Regulations. The Regulations catch all terms in consumer contracts that have not been individually negotiated. The sole exception is found in Regulation 6(2). This provides that:

> In so far as it is in plain intelligible language, the assessment of fairness of a term shall not relate:
> (a) to the definition of the main subject matter of the contract, or
> (b) to the adequacy of the price or remuneration, as against the goods or services supplied in exchange.

This is designed to implement Art. 4 of the Directive. In fact, the original 1994 implementing Regulations attempted to re-work these notions in order to clarify them,[38] but in the light of the risk that this may generate divergence between UK approaches and the European Court's view of the scope of the régime the text was adjusted by the 1999 Regulations which adhere more faithfully to the text of the Directive. Nonetheless Regulation 6(2) – or, to identify the true villain, Art. 4(2) of the Directive – is a regrettably obscure provision. The core point appears to be that unfairness

---

Commission published a proposal (OJ 1990 C243/2), revised in March 1992 (OJ 1992 C73/7). Final adoption was in March 1993. H. Brandner and P. Ulmer offer critical comment on the 1990 draft at (1991) 28 *CMLRev* 647, which is illuminating especially in the light of subsequent changes made before adoption. Cf. also Note: Reich, 'From Contract to Trade Practices Law: Protection of Consumers' Economic Interests by the EC' in T. Wilhelmsson (ed.), *Perspectives of Critical Contract Law* (Dartmouth, 1993); M. Tenreiro, 'The Community Directive on Unfair Terms and National Legal Systems' [1995] *European Review of Private Law* 273.

[37] Cf. note 36 above; especially critical comments by H. Brandner and P. Ulmer.
[38] Note 23 above.

does not arise simply where goods or services are overpriced, provided the relevant terms are in plain intelligible language. This represents an important limitation to the regime's scope for checking the fairness of the substance of a bargain.

Even allowing for this sole exclusion, the Regulations are considerably more ambitious than pre-existing controls under English law in the type of term subject to control. This pattern creates odd overlaps and odd loopholes. A clause such as that held unincorporated in *Interfoto v Stiletto*[39] would, had it been held today to have contractual force, be unassailable under the Act and the Regulations. The Act would not touch it because it was not an exclusion clause. The Regulations would not touch it because it did not appear in a consumer contract.

5.4.3 The Control Test

The Unfair Contract Terms Act 1977 invalidates some clauses absolutely and subjects others to a judicially applied test of reasonableness. The Regulations do not invalidate any clauses automatically – there is no 'blacklist'.[40] A term covered by the Regulations shall be regarded as unfair if it is a term which 'contrary to the requirement of good faith causes a significant imbalance in the parties' rights and obligations arising under the contract, to the detriment of the consumer'.

A question of critical importance is how closely aligned the tests of reasonableness under the Act and unfairness under the Regulations will prove to be. They are certainly not far apart. This similarity is emphasised in the only opportunity taken by the House of Lords to explore this matter in *Director-General of Fair Trading v First National Bank plc* which is examined more fully below.[41] Both control tests invite consideration of similar aspects of the bargain, such as any imbalance in knowledge between the parties. However, the role of good faith may steer the control originating in the Directive away from the notion of reasonableness. Although the latter is familiar to the English lawyer, the former is foreign.[42] Good faith has a developed meaning in continental European systems, which may come to influence its interpretation under the Directive, which then must transmit into the English legal system. For it should be appreciated that it is not a task for English judges alone to resolve the relationship between the Act's test of reasonableness and the

---

[39] Note 9 above.
[40] Earlier drafts of the Directive *did* contain such a blacklist; cf. note 36 above.
[41] [2002] 1 All ER 97. See 5.6.1.3 below.
[42] Although it has a developed meaning in the specialist area of insurance contracts.

Directive's notion of unfairness. The authoritative source of interpretation for the Directive is the European Court, via the Art. 234 (ex 177) preliminary reference procedure. If the European Court develops a distinctive interpretative approach to the control test, any consequent gulf between the Act and the Regulations implementing the Directive will require closing by careful handling at domestic level.[43] Implementation is a continuing process. The Regulations cannot be divorced from the Directive.[44] The same admonition must, of course, be directed at all the Member States as they develop the law in the area affected by Directive 93/13.

5.4.4 The Current Complexity, Possible Reform and Consolidation

There follows a more detailed examination of the scope of legal control over unfair terms. This requires an elaboration of both the 1977 Act and the 1999 Regulations implementing the Directive. The explanation is necessarily rendered complicated by the lack of integration between the two systems. It was explained in Chapter 1 that the less straightforward and accessible consumer protection law becomes on paper, the weaker its practical impact in helping the average consumer. The fact that there are two régimes and a lack of precision within both means that, regrettably, control of unfair terms in the UK is a prime candidate for assessment from that dispiriting perspective. Therefore the preparation of proposals by the Law Commissions for England and Wales and for Scotland which are aimed at securing a consolidated and more coherent régime is to be welcomed.[45]

The stated provisional aim of the exercise undertaken by the Law Commissions is to replace the 1977 Act and the 1999 Regulations with a single measure. This would maintain the level of protection for consumers currently provided by the Act and Regulations in (confusing) combination. The Directive must remain implemented in full, but the extra protection furnished by the Act is not to be sliced away. For example it is intended that terms 'black-listed' under the Act will remain beyond the pale even though the Directive requires no more than that they be subjected to a test of fairness. The control over terms in business-to-business contracts, a matter currently dealt with only by the Act and confined thereunder to exclusion and limitation clauses, would be rationalised so as to cover all

---

43 Further below, Section 5.6.1.3.
44 See especially Case C–62/00 note 28 above; Chapter 2.4.2.
45 Note 29 above.

terms that have not been negotiated. This would extend public control beyond the Act. The application of a reasonableness test to judge terms would depend *inter alia* on the relative size of the parties: one would expect intervention to be uncommon where contracting business parties possess comparable economic strength. Moreover, it is proposed that the whole package be re-written in a more transparent manner. Few legal tasks are tougher than 'simplifying' statutory material but, if the quest is successful, improved consumer protection will be the welcome result. But this lies in the future.

5.5 THE SCOPE OF CONTROL

5.5.1 Exclusion of Liability for Negligence

Section 2 of the Unfair Contract Terms Act (UCTA) deals with attempts to exclude liability for negligence.[46] It catches not only contract terms, but also other notices[47] too. Section 2(1) declares that '[a] person cannot by reference to any contract term or to a notice given to persons generally or to particular persons exclude or restrict his liability for death or personal injury resulting from negligence'. In s. 2(2) a more nuanced control is created over exclusion of liability for negligence resulting in other types of harm. Section 2(2) provides that 'In the case of other loss or damage, a person cannot so exclude or restrict his liability for negligence except in so far as the term or notice satisfies the requirement of reasonableness'.

Section 2, like ss. 3–7 of the Act, applies only to business liability; private sales are excluded.[48] Business liability is defined in ss. 1(3) and 14. The key notions are that it covers liability for breach of obligations or duties arising from things done or to be done by a person in the course of a business (whether his or her own business or another's);[49] or from the occupation of premises used for business purposes of the occupier. For the purposes of s. 2, it matters not what status the other party holds. Both business and consumer parties may benefit. By contrast, it will be seen below that in ss. 3–7, the status of the other party is critical to the scope of protection; the consumer is more favourably treated than the business person.

The Regulations implementing the Directive operate differently. A term in a contract caught by the régime – that is, a term in a consumer

---

46 Defined in s. 1(1).
47 Defined in s. 14.
48 Subject to one exception in s. 6(4), Section 5.5.5 below.
49 See Section 5.6.2 below on 'course of a business'.

contract that has not been individually negotiated – which excludes liability for negligence is then tested against the notion of unfairness. This is amplified in Schedule 3 to the Regulations, drawn from an Annex to the Directive, which acts as a 'grey list'. In this list for guidance one finds, *inter alia*, precisely the sorts of clauses controlled by s. 2 of the Act. The very first term in the list compares with that invalidated by s. 2(1) UCTA. No clause is automatically invalidated by the Regulations based on the Directive, in contrast to s. 2(1) of the Act. Probably most, if not all, courts called on to apply the control envisaged by the Regulations would find such an exclusion unfair and unenforceable. However, for English law purposes, because the Directive does not pre-empt more stringent measures of national protection, s. 2(1)'s rule of invalidity continues properly to be applied, notwithstanding the Community intervention.

5.5.2 Exclusion of Liability for Breach of Contract

Section 3 of the Unfair Contract Terms Act imposes a reasonableness test over terms that exclude or restrict a party's liability when in breach of contract. The same reasonableness test is applied to terms that are the basis of an entitlement to render a contractual performance substantially different from that which was reasonably expected or to render no performance at all. A term allowing a holiday company to switch a tourist booked for Spain to Scunthorpe would be controlled by s. 3.

Via the Regulations that implement the Directive, such terms are subjected to the unfairness test, provided they appear in consumer contracts and have not been individually negotiated. Several of the terms mentioned in the Schedule to the Regulations would also fall comfortably within the scope of s. 3 of the Act.[50] However, the Regulations are wider and catch terms that would escape s. 3.

The s. 3 control is exercised over a party falling within the defined sphere of business liability who wishes to enforce a term against another contracting party who deals as consumer (defined, 5.6.2 below) or on the other's written standard terms of business (which goes undefined). Here is a hybrid control. Consumer contracts are caught, whether or not they are individually negotiated. Commercial deals are caught,[51] but only where written standard terms of business are concerned. The Act here exercises a broader control than the Regulations, going beyond the consumer sphere.

---

[50] E.g. (b), (c), (j), (k).
[51] Subject to an exception for international supply contracts, as defined in s. 26.

Even commercial contract law is not unscathed by regulatory intervention.[52]

5.5.3 Indemnity Clauses

Section 4 of the Unfair Contract Terms Act subjects to the reasonableness test terms concerning the enforcement of indemnity clauses by a person with business liability against a person dealing as consumer. This covers indemnification of 'another person (whether a party to the contract or not) in respect of liability that may be incurred by the other for negligence or breach of contract'. The Regulations subject such standard form terms arising in consumer contracts to the unfairness test.

5.5.4 Guarantees

Section 5 of the Unfair Contract Terms Act invalidates terms, rather than simply putting them to scrutiny against the test of reasonableness. Section 5 covers 'guarantee' of consumer goods and is deliberately widely drawn.[53] 'In the case of goods of a type ordinarily supplied for private use or consumption, where loss or damage arises from the goods proving defective while in consumer use[54] and results from the negligence of a person concerned in the manufacture or distribution of the goods, liability for the loss or damage cannot be excluded or restricted by reference to any contract term or notice contained in or operating by reference to a guarantee of the goods.' Section 5(3) provides that s. 5 does not apply as between parties to a contract under or in pursuance of which possession or ownership of the goods passed; in such circumstances other sections, such as ss. 2 and 6, would apply. Section 5's main target is the manufacturer's guarantee.

Section 5 is a rather broad provision and is designed to do away with the old habit of presenting the consumer with an apparently attractive 'Guarantee' which, on closer inspection, actually grossly undermines contractual or other rights. It is phrased to catch guarantees whether contractual or not. The Regulations, by contrast, catch contract terms alone.

---

[52] Cf. Chapter 1, esp. 1.3.

[53] On guarantee, s. 5(2)(b).

[54] Widely defined s. 5(2)(a).

5.5.5 Exclusion of Statutorily Implied Terms

Section 6(1) invalidates terms excluding or restricting liability for breach of obligations arising from s. 12 of the Sale of Goods Act 1979 and s. 8 of the Supply of Goods (Implied Terms) Act 1973.[55] These are the implied undertakings as to title. Section 6(1) operates in all types of transaction, consumer or business. Section 6(2) is narrower in its scope, benefiting only a person dealing as a consumer (defined, 5.6.2 below). It invalidates terms excluding or restricting liability for breach of obligations arising from ss. 13, 14 or 15 of the Sale of Goods Act 1979 and the corresponding sections of the Supply of Goods (Implied Terms) Act 1973, which are ss. 9, 10 or 11. Then, according to s. 6(3), exclusion or restriction of precisely these same liabilities is subjected to the reasonableness test where applied against a person dealing otherwise than as a consumer. The distinction between ss. 6(2) and 6(3) shows that the consumer receives more extensive shelter from exclusion clauses than the commercial party, but that the Act does not address consumer protection alone. In commercial contracts, one might anticipate that the closer to equality the economic relationship, the more likely that the reasonableness test will be satisfied.[56] This permits account to be taken of the nuances of economic imbalance on a case-by-case basis.

A final twist to s. 6 is that it applies not simply to business liabilities within s. 1(3), but also to those arising under any contract of sale of goods or hire-purchase agreement.[57] Private sales are caught, although the use of exclusion clauses in such transactions is doubtless uncommon; in any event the statutorily implied terms have a limited role to play in private transactions.[58]

The Regulations based on the Directive do not catch the commercial contracts over which the Act exercises control because of the EC régime's limitation to consumer contracts. The Regulations would control such terms where they appear in consumer contracts and have not been individually negotiated with reference to the unfairness test. As explained, in so far as the Act is stricter and broader than the Regulations, its continued application is not called into question by virtue of the

---

[55] Exclusion clauses in contracts under which goods pass, but which are not governed by the law of sale of goods or hire purchase, are controlled under s. 7 UCTA. Section 8 of the Act also inserts a new s. 3 into the Misrepresentation Act 1967 dealing with exclusion of liability for misrepresentation.

[56] See further on the reasonableness test, Section 5.6.1.1 below.

[57] Section 6(4) UCTA 1977.

[58] Chapter 3.

Directive's minimum formulation. The invalidation of exclusion clauses achieved by ss. 6(1) and 6(2) remains secure.

5.6 DEFINITIONAL ISSUES

At least three critically important definitional points arise, which in the Unfair Contract Terms Act 1977 are delayed until later sections. First, what is at stake in the application of the apparently vague 'reasonableness' test? Second, who deals as a consumer? Third, what is a clause that 'excludes or restricts liability'? The first two questions have parallels in the Regulations, although the third does not have a precise equivalent, because all terms, not simply exclusion clauses, are in principle capable of being caught by the Regulations.

5.6.1 The Control Test

5.6.1.1 The Unfair Contract Terms Act 1977

Section 11 of the Act amplifies the 'reasonableness' test. It is open-ended. The essence of the test is that it depends on the circumstances at the time of contracting. It is for a party claiming that the term or notice satisfies the test to show that it does; this is normally likely to be advantageous to the consumer as the party against whom the term is typically enforced.[59]

Regrettably, the Act chooses not simply to sketch an all-embracing reasonableness test. Section 11 splits up the control. In relation to a contract term, the term 'shall have been a fair and reasonable one to be included having regard to the circumstances which were, or ought reasonably to have been, known to or in the contemplation of the parties when the contract was made'. In the application of the reasonableness test under ss. 6 or 7 (only), 'regard shall be had in particular to the matters specified in Schedule 2'. Then, in relation to a notice without contractual effect, s. 11 directs that it 'should be fair and reasonable to allow reliance on it, having regard to all the circumstances obtaining when the liability arose or (but for the notice) would have arisen'. Under s. 11(4), it is provided that in applying the reasonableness test to a restriction of liability to a specified sum of money, regard shall be had, *inter alia*, to the resources available to the party seeking restriction to meet the liability should it arise and how far it was open to cover himself by insurance.

---

59   Section 11(5).

It is doubtful whether anything useful is served by preferring this set of three rambling subsections[60] over a single, broadly-phrased depiction of reasonableness.[61] Such scepticism seems to be shared by the courts. Section 11(2) of the Act restricts the use of the guidelines in Schedule 2 in making a reasonableness assessment to the control exercised by ss. 6 and 7, but in practice their impact has been felt more generally.[62] The guidelines for the application of the reasonableness test contained in Schedule 2 are as follows:

(a) the strength of the bargaining position of the parties relative to each other, taking into account (among other things) alternative means by which the customer's requirements could have been met;
(b) whether the customer received an inducement to agree to the term, or in accepting it had an opportunity of entering into a similar contract with other persons, but without having to accept a similar term;
(c) whether the customer knew or ought reasonably to have known of the existence and extent of the term (having regard, among other things, to any custom of the trade and any previous course of dealing between the parties);
(d) where the term excludes or restricts any relevant liability if some condition is not complied with, whether it was reasonable at the time of the contract to expect that compliance with that condition would be practicable;
(e) whether the goods were manufactured, processed or adapted to the special order of the customer.

The courts have a wide jurisdiction to make their assessment. These guidelines are not exhaustive. It seems plain that the scope of consumer choice is a central element in the assessment. Suppliers are induced to offer a range of prices. One would suppose that the tighter the exclusion, the lower the price – in a competitive market, at least. Provided a genuine and transparent choice is made available, a supplier is entitled to expect that such marketing techniques will push a court towards a finding that the clauses are reasonable.[63] Guideline (c) also pushes in the direction of

---

60 Sections 11(1)–11(3).
61 The disjointed pattern is largely attributable to the accretion of legal controls statute-by-statute; UCTA was not the first adventure in this field, although it is the widest-ranging.
62 Cf. dicta of Slade LJ in *Phillips Products Ltd v Hyland* [1987] 2 All ER 620, 628.
63 Absence of choice was a factor in the finding of unreasonableness in *Woodman*, 1.5.1 above.

greater transparency. The rules of incorporation already dictate a need for openness;[64] even where the term is incorporated on this test, an even greater level of openness may be required by the Act on pain of finding a term unreasonable and unenforceable.

In *Smith v Eric S Bush*, Lord Griffiths commented on the impossibility of drawing up an exhaustive list of relevant factors.[65] This indicates that it is inappropriate to accumulate case law as binding precedent. Abstract points of law are not at stake and the role of the appellate courts is limited.[66] Individual contracts and the circumstances in which they are made vary. However, Lord Griffiths provided a list of matters which should 'always be considered'. These cover comparison of bargaining power; practical opportunity to seek alternative advice; difficulty of the task undertaken in respect of which exclusion of liability is sought; and the practical consequences of the decision on the question of reasonableness. The final factor strongly suggests that the implications of a decision on the cost of insurance should play a part in the reasoning, beyond the specific reference to insurance in s. 11(4) in the context of limitation of liability.[67] Plainly the application of the test demands a balancing of several factors and one would seldom find a case in which the pointers are all in one direction.[68]

5.6.1.2 The Regulations Implementing the Directive

The control test in the Regulations provides that a term covered by the regime shall be regarded as unfair if 'contrary to the requirement of good faith [it] causes a significant imbalance in the parties' rights and obligations arising under the contract, to the detriment of the consumer'.[69]

Schedule 2 to the UK's Regulations, reflecting an Annex to the Directive, provides an indicative and non-exhaustive list of the terms which may be regarded as unfair. This, then, is neither a black nor white but a grey list. Courts may use it as interpretative aid and it is clearly of real practical importance. Inspection of the list reveals that features that are

---

64 Especially *Interfoto v Stiletto* 1.3.5 above.

65 [1990] 1 AC 831.

66 Cf. Lord Bridge in *George Mitchell v Finney Lock* note 20 above; applied by the C.A. in *Phillips Products Ltd v Hyland* [1987] 2 All ER 620.

67 See above in this sub-section, 5.6.1.1.

68 For illustrations of the practical application of the test, see e.g. *RW Green v Cade Bros Farms* [1978] 1 Lloyd's Rep 602; *Singer Co Ltd v Tees and Hartlepool Port Authority* [1988] 2 Lloyd's Rep 164; *Smith v Eric S Bush* note 65 above.

69 Regulation 5(1), Art. 3(1) Directive.

especially likely to trigger unfavourable scrutiny include granting to traders ill-defined discretionary powers,[70] especially where no equivalent protection is extended to consumers,[71] imposing disproportionately heavy burdens on consumers[72] and protecting the trader from claims that the consumer would ordinarily expect to be able to make.[73]

Regulation 6(1) provides that unfairness shall be assessed 'taking into account the nature of the goods or services for which the contract was concluded and by referring, at the time of conclusion of the contract, to all the circumstances attending the conclusion of the contract and to all the other terms of the contract or of another contract on which it is dependent'.

Regulation 7, drawn from Art. 5, provides that any written term of a contract shall be expressed in plain, intelligible language. Where there is doubt about the meaning of a term, the interpretation most favourable to the consumer shall prevail. Regulation 7 seems close to the *contra proferentem* rule of interpretation in English law.[74] It remains to be seen whether it is stronger.

5.6.1.3 The Tests Compared and Contrasted

How close is the unfairness test in the Regulations, drawn from the Directive, to the test of reasonableness in the 1977 Act? It is first useful to point out why any divergence is of practical significance. The consequences of any gulf are small where the Act is stricter than or as strict as the Regulations. It is permissible for English law to apply a control tighter than that under the Directive, for the latter sets only a minimum Community-wide standard. However, the position is different where the Regulations are seen to be tighter than the Act. It is then necessary to apply that stricter control to terms within the scope of the Regulations. Control of such terms will accordingly be stricter than that currently exercised under UCTA. If this occurs, the oddity of the bifurcated English mechanism for controlling unfair terms will be sharply exposed. With this practical point in mind, it is appropriate to consider whether the two regimes are indeed distinct. Comment is necessarily tentative, for more than a decade of experience under the Directive has scarcely begun to unravel the intriguing complexity at stake in shaping a 'Europeanised' notion of unfairness.

---

70 Schedule 2(1) to the Regulations, terms (g), (j), (k), (m).
71 Schedule 2(1) to the Regulations, terms (c), (d), (f), (l), (o).
72 Schedule 2(1) to the Regulations, terms (e), (h).
73 Schedule 2(1) to the Regulations, terms (a), (b), (n), (q).
74 Chapter 5.2 above.

The initial assumption among UK officials was that reasonableness under the Act and unfairness under the Regulations implementing the Directive would frequently yield the same result.[75] Indeed the influence of the Act may be observed in the Directive. It is no coincidence that some of the Act's terminology finds its way into the Directive, especially its Preamble. Both invite an appraisal of the bargaining environment as an aspect in assessing substantive fairness. But, as academic commentators observed,[76] there is scope for divergence. Perhaps the key point to appreciate is that the authoritative source of interpretation for the Directive is the European Court. It would be a mistake for a national court simply to assimilate the national rules that implement the Directive to existing domestic law. Rather, they must be applied with an eye to their European derivation. Points of interpretative difficulty should be resolved by the European Court, whose authoritative rulings act as a method of securing a common Community-wide approach to the application of the Directive.

5.6.1.4 A Contribution from the House of Lords

As yet there is no directly relevant judgment of the European Court. The House of Lords took the opportunity to explore the matter in *Director-General of Fair Trading v First National Bank plc*.[77] The term at issue appeared in the bank's standard form regulated credit agreement. It provided that interest should be chargeable until payment of the borrower's outstanding balance 'after as well as before any judgment, such obligation to be independent of and not to merge with the judgment'. This was

---

[75] This view is expressed in the DTI Consultation Document on Implementation of October 1993, where it is added that similarity will reduce problems of overlap between Act and Regulations/Directive. However, the DTI's Further Consultation Document of September 1994 is more cautious and explicitly accepts that 'the two tests are not the same' (p. 3).

[76] Cf. R. Brownsword and G. Howells, 'The Implementation of the EC Directive on Unfair Terms in Consumer Contracts – Some Unresolved Questions' [1995] *JBL* 243; E. Macdonald, 'Mapping the Unfair Contract Terms Act 1977 and the Directive on Unfair Terms in Consumer Contracts' [1994] *JBL* 441.

[77] [2001] 3 *WLR* 1297, [2002] 1 *All ER* 97. For comment see S. Whittaker, 'Assessing the Fairness of Contract Terms: The Parties' Essential Bargain, its Regulatory Context and the Significance of the Requirement of Good Faith' [2004] *Zeitschrift für Europäisches Privatrecht* 75; E. Macdonald, 'Scope and Fairness of the Unfair Terms in Consumer Contracts Regulatuions' (2002) 65 *MLR* 763. The case is decided against the background of the 1994 Regulations, note 23 above, rather than the 1999 Regulations, but this appears to make no difference of substance.

designed to protect the bank. Under the relevant statutory regime,[78] it would enjoy only a more qualified entitlement to interest in the event of default by the borrower leading to legal proceedings and judgment against him or her. The result is that a defaulting borrower might find him or her self obliged to pay under an instalment order made by a court, and yet also remain contractually bound to pay interest which, pursuant to the statutory regime, is not taken into account in calculating the pattern of instalments.

Evans-Lombe J had held in favour of the bank[79] but his order was reversed by the Court of Appeal.[80] The House of Lords allowed the bank's appeal. Lord Bingham accepted that the borrower might be 'disagreeably surprised' to find the interest payable mounting pursuant to the challenged term even after a court judgment of more limited effect, but their Lordships did not consider it unfair. Lord Bingham found no significant imbalance in the parties' contractual rights and obligations to the detriment of the consumer. He considered that the term was an element in the balance of the bargain struck between lender and borrower.[81] He added that in the absence of the term the contract would be unbalanced to the detriment of the lender. Lord Millett took the view that the term ensured the bank would secure repayment of all that was due to it under the contract and that this was no more and no less than a borrower would expect.

It is unfortunate that the first review of the Regulations by the House of Lords took place in such a quirky case. The term's inclusion in the contract was attributable to the bank's desire to supplement its protection in circumstances where the statutory regime was of limited effect. The consumer who defaults and finds him or her self subject to legal proceedings would likely be confused on discovering the gap between the contract and the statutory regime, and might even think that gulf unfair. But this is not the normal case of tackling a term as 'unfair' *per se*. All the same, the case is significant for judicial pronouncement on the nature of the control exercised by the Regulations. Lord Bingham observed that matters listed as relevant under the Regulations also appear in the guidelines for the application of the reasonableness test laid down by the Unfair Contract Terms Act 1977, 'suggesting that some similarity of

---

[78] The Consumer Credit Act 1974 and the County Courts (Interest on Judgment Debts) Order 1991 (SI 1991/1184).

[79] [2000]1 *WLR* 98.

[80] [2000] *QB* 672.

[81] Though it was not treated as excluded from review as the main subject matter of the contract, see Regulation 6(2)/Art. 4 Directive, s. 5.4.2 above.

approach in applying the two tests may be appropriate'.[82] He also described the requirement of good faith as 'one of fair and open dealing'. Lord Steyn agreed, explicitly referring to *Interfoto* v *Stiletto*.[83] Terms should be given appropriate prominence if capable of prejudicing the consumer. Good faith 'looks to good standards of commercial morality and practice', in the view of Lord Bingham.

There is, of course, no ill-advised attempt to assume an exact parallel between the Act and the Regulations. The speeches fully and correctly accept that the Regulations fall to be construed in the light of the EC Directive. However, the impression in *First National Bank* is of an ambition to accommodate the test in the Regulations within existing English law assumptions. It is to the European Court in Luxembourg that one must turn for the authoritative interpretation of provisions found in a Directive. It is arguable that in the case the House of Lords should have made use of the Art. 234 (ex 177) preliminary reference procedure in order to exploit the Court's ability to offer a common European interpretation of notions of fairness under the Directive. Lord Bingham considered the matter sufficiently free from doubt to be capable of application without the involvement of the European Court, which is surprising given that the House of Lords was, after all, taking a view different from the Court of Appeal.[84] But, pending further judicial exploration, the ruling in *First National Bank* emphasises the importance of providing information to the consumer in the assessment of fairness. In similar vein the OFT tells consumers that 'Good faith means that traders must deal fairly and openly with you'.[85] This chapter has shown a thematic connection between consumer protection and transparency, and this is central to legal regulation in this area.[86] A trader who does nothing to alert the consumer to the inclusion of a clause causing a significant imbalance in the parties' rights and obligations arising under the contract to the detriment of the

---

[82] The 1994 Regulations on the basis of which the case was decided, included these matters, but they are deleted from the 1999 Regulations: however, they are found in the Directive's Preamble so Lord Bingham's point retains pertinence.

[83] Note 9 above.

[84] This point is made with reference to the diversity of meanings of good faith in European legal systems in comments on the case by S. Whittaker note 77 above; M. Dean (2002) 65 *MLR* 773; see also P. Nebbia (2003) 40 *CMLRev* 983.

[85] http://www.oft.gov.uk/Consumer/Unfair+terms+in+contracts/default.htm.

[86] M. Wolf, 'Party Autonomy and Information in the Unfair Contract Terms Directive', Chapter 16 in S. Grundmann, W. Kerber and S. Weatherill (eds.), *Party Autonomy and the Role of Information in the Internal Market* (De Gruyter, 2001); F. Brunetta d'Usseaux, 'Formal and substantive aspects of the transparency principle in European private law' [1998] *Consum LJ* 320.

consumer will surely face a finding of unfairness even if the clause is judged incorporated into the contract. However, it is submitted that it is wrong to assume that terms are to be treated as fair provided the trader has informed the consumer of their presence. 'Good faith' is but part of the test. Some terms may be so damaging to the consumer interest that they are unfair no matter how assiduous the trader in drawing the consumer's attention to them.[87]

5.6.1.5 A Contribution from the European Court?

Notwithstanding the accommodating approach taken in *First National Bank*, the possibility of significant divergence between the European Court's approach and that of the English courts should not be under estimated. The phrase 'good faith', in particular, lacks definition for English lawyers. True, English law may conceivably possess differently labelled principles that work similar magic to a control based on 'good faith'. These represent piecemeal solutions[88] and it may be helpful to treat English law's chief target as the suppression of bad faith rather than the promotion of good faith.[89] In any event it is plain that 'good faith' has a much more developed (albeit far from uniform) meaning in continental legal systems.[90] The European Court is likely to draw on established national traditions and, perhaps, autonomous Community notions in developing what is meant by good faith, which may lead to unfamiliar notions penetrating English law via the medium of the Directive. It is of central importance to appreciate that simple application of the reasonableness test familiar from over two decades of the Unfair Contract Terms Act would be inappropriate in the light of the capacity of the

---

[87] Cf. the exploration of this issue in the Law Commission Consultation Paper, note 29 above, pp. 39–53.

[88] Cf. Bingham LJ (as he then was) in *Interfoto v Stiletto* note 9.

[89] E. McKendrick, *Contract Law* (Macmillan, 2003), esp. Chapters 12, 17. See also J.F. O'Connor, *Good Faith in English Law* (Dartmouth, 1990).

[90] H. Collins, 'Good Faith in European Contract Law' (1994) 14 *Oxford JLS* 229; J. Beatson and D. Friedman (eds.), *Good Faith and Fault in Contract Law* (Oxford, 1995); R. Brownsword, NOTE Hird and G. Howells (eds.), *Good Faith in Contract: Concept and Context* (Ashgate, 1999); R. Zimmermann and S. Whittaker, *Good Faith in European Contract Law* (Cambridge, 2000); F. Martinez Sanz, 'Good Faith of the Parties', pp. 127–138 in H. Schulte-Noelke and R. Schulze, *European Contract Law in Community Law* (Bundesanzeiger, 2002).

European Court to push the Directive's control test in different and, for English lawyers, unfamiliar directions.

It should also be appreciated that the legal base of the Directive is *what was* Art. 100a and *is now* (after amendment) Art. 95.[91] In formal constitutional terms, this is not a measure of consumer protection, but a measure designed to contribute to the process of market integration by equalising competitive conditions. And yet it is clear that the European Court is prepared to provide an interpretation of the Directive which is influenced by the connection between the programme of legislative harmonisation and consumer protection (Chapter 2.3). In *Oceano Grupo Editorial SA v Rocio Murciano Quintero*[92] the Court was asked by a Spanish court whether a court is empowered to consider of its own motion whether a term is unfair within the meaning of the Directive. The Court could have placidly ruled that this is a procedural matter falling for determination according to national law alone, but it did not do so. In pursuit of the achievement of the objectives of the Directive, it was more ambitious. It stated that 'the system of protection introduced by the Directive is based on the idea that the consumer is in a weak position *vis-á-vis* the seller or supplier, as regards both his bargaining power and his level of knowledge'. A consumer may be ignorant of available legal protection and this prompted the conclusion that 'effective protection of the consumer may be attained only if the national court acknowledges that it has power to evaluate terms of this kind of its own motion'. The Court also used the Directive as a springboard to interpret rules of civil procedure relevant to the vindication of consumer rights in *Cofidis SA*.[93] The preliminary reference concerned a procedural rule prohibiting the national court, on expiry of a limitation period, from finding a term to be unfair. Here too the Court could conceivably have left this within the autonomy of the legal order of the Member States; but here too it judged that the Directive demanded more. In proceedings in which consumers are defendants, it ruled the imposition of such a limitation period was incompatible with the protection intended to be conferred on them by the Directive.

These rulings do not touch directly the notions of good faith or unfairness. But they suggest the Court, if provided with an appropriate opportunity, would interpret these notions in a conspicuously pro-consumer manner.[94] It is at least possible that the European Court will feel

---

91   Chapter 2.3.3.

92   Cases C–240/98 to C–244/98 [2000] ECR I–4941. Annotation by J. Stuyck (2001) 38 *CMLRev* 719.

93   Case C–473/00 [2002] ECR I–10875.

94   Cf. its interpretation of 'compensation' under Directive 90/314 on package travel (Chapter 2.3.3) in Case C–168/00 *Simone Leitner* [2002] ECR I–2631.

motivated to take the Directive's control test into different areas from those which domestic courts have chosen in applying the reasonableness test and in applying local rules adopted to implement the Directive. And were the control required under the Directive to prove more rigorous than that currently applied under English law, then the pattern of domestic control of unfair terms will alter significantly in the areas covered by the Regulations and, perhaps, by a kind of legal osmosis, in areas outwith the reach of the new regime as well.[95]

5.6.2 Dealing as a Consumer

Section 12 of the Unfair Contract Terms Act defines the notion of 'dealing as consumer'. This is the trigger to the control exercised under several sections of the Act (including ss. 3, 4 and 6(2)), although it has already been explained in section 5 of this chapter that the Act has some, though more limited, application even where neither party deals as consumer.

A party to a contract deals as consumer in relation to another party if:

(a) he neither makes the contract in the course of a business nor holds himself out as doing so; and
(b) the other party does make the contract in the course of a business; and
(c) in the case of a contract governed by the law of sale of goods or hire-purchase, or by s. 7 of this Act, the goods passing under or in pursuance of the contract are of a type ordinarily supplied for private use or consumption.

The section concludes by declaring that, on a sale by auction or by competitive tender the buyer is not in any circumstances to be regarded as dealing as consumer.[96] Subject to this, it is for those claiming that a party does not deal as consumer to show that he or she does not.[97] This is a valuable protection for the consumer, for it should ensure that 'grey areas', especially likely to arise in determining what is the 'course of a business',[98] are resolved in his or her favour. It is buttressed by the Court of Appeal ruling in *R & B Customs Brokers Co Ltd v United Dominions Trust* which took a surprisingly narrow view of when something occurs in

---

[95] On the possibilities and limitations of such 'Europeanisation' of private law, see L. Niglia, *The Transformation of Contract in Europe* (Kluwer Law International, 2003).
[96] Section 12(2).
[97] Section 12(3).
[98] Cf. Chapter 3.5.5.

the course of a business.[99] This pushes situations where one party clearly acts commercially, while the other is on the cusp between private and commercial activity, into the sphere of the more intrusive statutory control over business/consumer contracts rather than leaving it subject to the more limited control exercised over business/business contracts.[100] The corollary is less favourable to the advocate of broadly based consumer protection. It also means that where one party clearly acts in a private capacity, while the other is on the cusp between private and commercial activity, the matter is likely to escape classification as a business/consumer contract and, as a private deal, it will not be subject to control at all.[101]

The Directive is briefer, in the style of drafting typical of Community measures, and this is reflected in the implementing Regulations. Regulation 4 provides that the regime controls contracts between sellers or suppliers and consumers, although it is only terms that have not been individually negotiated that are caught. Regulation 3, drawn from Art. 2 of the Directive, provides that consumer means 'any natural person who, in contracts covered by these Regulations, is acting for purposes which are outside his trade, business or profession'. A legal person falls outside this definition of the 'consumer'.[102] Regulation 3 provides that seller or supplier means 'any natural or legal person who, in contracts covered by these Regulations, is acting for purposes relating to his trade, business or profession, whether publicly owned or privately owned'.

This notion of 'consumer' appears more limited than the English approach, especially in the light of the decision in *R & B Customs Brokers Co Ltd v United Dominions Trust*.[103] Moreover, in contrast to the Act, the Directive and the implementing Regulations are silent on the burden of proof.[104] Nonetheless, the character of the Directive does not preclude national law from choosing to exercise control over situations which are not consumer transactions within the Directive.[105] As explained, UCTA does this.

---

[99]   [1988] 1 All ER 847.

[100] See further Chapter 8.2.2.3, in relation to trade descriptions law.

[101] Cf. E. MacDonald, 'In the course of a business – a fresh examination' (1999) *Web Law Journal*, accessible via http://webjcli.ncl.ac.uk/1999/issue3/macdonald3.html.

[102] Case C–541/99 *Cape Snc v Idealservice Srl* [2001] ECR I–9049.

[103] Note 99 above.

[104] For an argument that it should be interpreted to favour the consumer, see S. Weatherill, 'Prospects for the development of European private law through 'Europeanisation' in the European Court – the case of the Directive on unfair terms in consumer contracts' (1995) 3/2 *European Review of Private Law* 135.

[105] Cf. French law at issue in Case C–369/89 *Ministère Public v di Pinto* [1991] ECR I–1189.

5.6.3 Types of Term

Although the Act, in contrast to the Regulations implementing the Directive, does not catch all contract terms, s. 13 is important in providing a wide scope to the types of terms that are caught.[106] Terms that exclude or restrict liability are controlled, but by virtue of s. 13 so too are:

(a)   making the liability or its enforcement subject to restrictive or onerous conditions;
(b)   excluding or restricting any right or remedy in respect of the liability, or subjecting a person to any prejudice in consequence of his pursuing any such right or remedy;
(c)   excluding or restricting rules of evidence or procedure.

It is also provided that ss. 2 and 5 to 7 control exclusion or restriction of liability by reference to terms and notices which exclude or restrict the relevant obligation or duty. This brings within the scope of the Act an attempt, for example, to deny the existence in the first place of a duty, as opposed to a mere attempted curtailment of that duty.[107] On one view, this extension plugs a potential gap in the Act that could otherwise have been exploited by astute drafting. On another view, it reveals a failure to come to terms with the fundamental question of whether exclusion clauses restrict liability for breach of a duty or define the scope of that duty.[108] The judicial and statutory preference is for the former view,[109] but further litigation may yet be called for in elucidation of this issue.[110]

The application of the Regulations to all types of term means that they require no definition of which terms are and are not caught.[111] The types of term that are conspicuous in the grey list in the Regulations' Schedule 2,

---

[106]   See e.g. *Stewart Gill Ltd v Horatio Myer & Co Ltd* [1992] 2 All ER 257.

[107]   Cf. *Smith v Eric S Bush* [1990] 1 AC 831, [1989] 2 All ER 514; *Phillips Products Ltd v Hyland* [1987] 2 All ER 620.

[108]   See B. Coote, *Exception Clauses* (Sweet and Maxwell, 1964).

[109]   Especially the House of Lords in *Smith v Eric S. Bush* note 65 above.

[110]   Contrast *Phillips v Hyland* note 80 above with *Thompson v T. Lohan Ltd* [1987] 2 All ER 631. Cf. Note: Palmer, 'Clarifying the Unfair Contract Terms Act 1977' [1986] *Business Law Review* 57; E. Macdonald, 'Mapping the Unfair Contract Terms Act 1977 and the Directive on Unfair Terms in Consumer Contracts' [1994] *JBL* 441.

[111]   Subject only to the exclusion under Art. 1(2) of the Directive of 'The contractual terms which reflect mandatory statutory or regulatory provisions and the provisions or principles of international conventions to which the Member States or the Community are party, particularly in the transport area'. This appears in Regulation 4(2).

drawn from the Directive's Annex, include those that confer unilateral decision-making powers on the supplier and those that envisage the imposition of obligations on consumers where no corresponding obligations are borne by suppliers. Bringing such terms within the control of UCTA would be difficult, although it might be possible to stretch s. 3 in such directions.[112] It is plain that all the terms covered by s. 13 of the Unfair Contract Terms Act are capable of falling within the Regulations, provided they appear in consumer contracts and have not been individually negotiated, but all other types of term are also included. By way of specific example of the broader scope of the Regulations, s. 13(2) of the Act cautions that 'an agreement in writing to submit present or future differences to arbitration' is not to be treated as subject to control,[113] whereas such an agreement would fall within the Regulations.[114] A term 'requiring any consumer who fails to fulfil his obligation to pay a disproportionately high sum in compensation' is explicitly mentioned in Schedule 2 to the Regulations,[115] but would escape control under the Act.[116] However, it should be recalled that terms which describe the main subject matter of the contract are not to be tested for unfairness under the Regulations.[117] Therein lies further fertile ground for the debate about whether clauses restrict liability or define duties.[118]

The Regulations require a definition of individual negotiation, for they control only contractual terms which have not been individually negotiated. This notion is explained further in Regulation 5(2), reflecting Art. 3(2) of the Directive. A term shall always be regarded as not individually negotiated (and therefore within the scope of the regime) 'where it has been drafted in advance and the consumer has therefore not been able to influence the substance of the term.' Individual negotiation of a term does not preclude the application of the control to the rest of the contract if an overall assessment indicates that it is nevertheless a pre-formulated standard contract (Regulation 5(3)). It rests with the seller or supplier who claims that a term has been individually negotiated to prove this (Regulation 5(5)).

---

112 Chapter 5.5.2 above.
113 Which is not to say that it may not be subject to separate statutory control; Chapter 14.x on the Consumer Arbitration Act.
114 Cf. Schedule 2/Annex, term (q).
115 Term (e).
116 Although it may be the subject of separate control under English law as a penalty clause.
117 Chapter 5.4.2 above.
118 For discussion in this direction, see Brownsword and Howells note 76 above. See also the Law Commission Consultation Paper, note 29 above, pp. 23–33.

5.7 INSURANCE AND EMPLOYMENT CONTRACTS

The position of the insurance industry is complex and influenced by its determined efforts to isolate itself from control of unfair contract terms. The industry was largely successful in achieving that objective in the Unfair Contract Terms Act, but less so at European level. According to Schedule 1 of the Unfair Contract Terms Act, ss. 2 to 4 of the Act do not extend to any contract of insurance.[119] The Directive offers no such exclusion. However, as explained above, the Directive does not envisage any direct control over the fairness of the price paid for goods or services. The recitals to the Directive explicitly add that this means that, in insurance contracts, 'the terms which clearly define or circumscribe the insured risk and the insurer's liability shall not be subject to such assessment since these restrictions are taken into account in calculating the premium paid by the consumer'. The October 1993 DTI Consultation Document on Implementation of the Directive proposed the insertion of this provision into the implementing Regulations' Schedule of Exclusions. However, the DTI's Further Consultation Document of September 1994 abandoned this idea, explaining that it added nothing to the basic point that the regime does not address the relationship of price to substance, reflected in Regulation 6(2). Accordingly there is no special provision made for the insurance industry in the Regulations.

The Act provides that ss. 2(1) and 2(2) of the Act do not extend to a contract of employment, except in favour of the employee.[120] Otherwise the Act is capable of application to employment contracts. In *Bridgen v American Express Ltd*[121] the High Court applied the normal test under s. 12[122] and concluded that s. 3 of the Act is in principle capable of application in favour of an employee, although on the facts the term did not fall within the scope of s. 3(2) and therefore fell beyond the reach of statutory control. The limitation of the scope of the Directive to consumer

---

[119] Schedule 1 provides for other exceptions. Briefly summarised, these deal with contracts so far as they relate to the creation or transfer of an interest in land or intellectual property rights, contracts so far as they relate to the formation or dissolution of a company or its constitution, and contracts so far as they relate to the creation or transfer of securities. Terms in such contracts are capable of being caught by the Regulations/Directive, subject to the probability that the Directive applies only to contracts for the supply of goods and services (so not touching the creation or issue of financial securities).

[120] Schedule 1 of the Act.

[121] [2000] *IRLR* 94.

[122] Section 5.6.2 above.

contracts means that employment contracts are wholly outwith its scope. This was made explicit in the 1994 Regulations but is omitted from the 1999 Regulations. The exclusion of employment contracts is nevertheless made plain in the Directive's Preamble, which serves an interpretative aid to the Directive itself and consequently also to the Regulations.

5.8 ENFORCEMENT

The Unfair Contract Terms Act operates on the basis of private enforcement in the sense that it is for individual consumers, as plaintiffs or defendants, to make use of it in private contractual disputes. Even though the Act places some burdens of proof on traders, to the consumer advantage, nevertheless the pattern is open to criticism for its obscurity and practical ineffectiveness. This is part of the wider picture of the consumer difficulty in securing effective access to justice, examined in Chapter 14. There is only a small element of public control. The Consumer Transactions (Restrictions on Statements) Order 1976[123] makes it an offence to display certain terms that are void under the Unfair Contract Terms Act. This Order is now subject to the enforcement procedures crafted under Part 8 of the Enterprise Act 2002.[124]

Article 6 of the Directive requires Member States to provide that unfair terms shall not bind the consumer. The contract shall continue to bind the parties if capable of remaining on foot without the unfair terms. Implemented in Regulation 8, this conforms to the pattern under the 1977 Act and poses no difficulty for English law. It remains to be seen how the European Court's readiness to interpret the Directive in a manner that influences rules of civil procedure will be absorbed in the United Kingdom. It is arguable that the decision in *Oceano Grupo*[125] leads to the conclusion that the Directive requires, rather than simply empowers, judges to scrutinise the fairness of terms of their own motion.[126]

Public control is also envisaged. Article 7 of the Directive provides that 'Member States shall ensure that, in the interests of consumers and of competitors adequate and effective means exist to prevent the continued use of unfair terms in contracts concluded with consumers by sellers or suppliers'. It is further provided in Art. 7(2) that the 'means' referred to shall include 'provisions whereby persons or organisations, having a

---

[123] SI 1976/1813, as amended by SI 1978/27.
[124] See Chapter 13.9.5.3.
[125] Note 92 above.
[126] S. Whittaker, 'Judicial Interventionism and Consumer Contracts' (2001) 117 *LQR* 215.

legitimate interest under national law in protecting consumers, may take action according to the national law concerned before the courts or before competent administrative bodies for a decision as to whether contractual terms drawn up for general use are unfair, so that they can apply appropriate and effective means to prevent the continued use of such terms'.

For the UK, the DTI initially proposed a minimalist response based on leaving control in the hands of private litigants before the ordinary courts.[127] Remarkably, with regard to Art. 7(2), it was declared that 'UK law at present contains no general provision for representative actions; only a party to a contract may sue under that contract. Thus according to the national law concerned (i.e. that applying in the UK) this provision can have no effect'. This was fiercely and effectively attacked for its failure to provide the effective control required by the Directive.[128] The DTI then had a change of heart.[129] The Regulations initially imposed a duty on the Director-General of Fair Trading to consider complaints and the power to seek a court injunction against persons using unfair terms in contracts concluded with consumers. This was the basis of the proceedings considered above in *Director-General of Fair Trading v First National Bank*.[130] The terminology is already dated: by virtue of the Enterprise Act 2002 these powers are now treated as vested in the OFT, not the Director-General, whose office is abolished. In fact, notwithstanding the applicable nomenclature, resort to judicial proceedings has been rare. Although only a court can formally determine whether a term is fair, the OFT carries out the large majority of its enforcement work on an informal basis by approaching traders and persuading them to abandon or alter terms. The availability of recourse to the courts as a 'back-up' tends to induce compliance by traders without the need for that formal step to be taken.[131] The regular bulletins issued by the OFT provide a vivid insight into the type of practices which have commonly been withdrawn in the shadow of this legal regime.[132] It is conspicuous that some sectors have attracted particular attention. In 2002, for example, the OFT issued a report into health and fitness club membership contracts, warning consumers to watch out *inter alia* for clauses committing them to automatic renewal and stating

---

[127] Consultation Document of October 1993.
[128] E.g. R. Bragg (1994) 2 *Consum LJ* 29, 36–37.
[129] Further Consultation Document, September 1994.
[130] Section 5.6.1.4 above.
[131] S. Bright, 'Winning the battle against unfair contract terms' (2000) 20 *Legal Studies* 331.
[132] They are available electronically: http://www.oft.gov.uk/Consumer/default.htm.

the OFT's view that such clauses may be unfair and therefore unenforceable.

The now-revoked 1994 implementing Regulations[133] went no further than this. They conferred no special status on consumer organisations as enforcement agencies. This contrasted with practice in several other Member States and was arguably incompatible with the requirements imposed by the Directive. Litigation by the Consumers' Association was commenced but not concluded[134] because the argument was won on the political plane once a Labour government took office in 1997. The current implementing Regulations, introduced in 1999,[135] altered the position by equipping bodies other than the OFT with the competence to take preemptive action. A 'qualifying body' is empowered to institute court proceedings in cases involving perceived use of unfair terms. The identity of this mysterious monitor is elucidated in Schedule 1 to the Regulations: qualifying bodies include several sectoral regulators, such as the Director-General of Gas Supply and of Water Services, and the Financial Services Authority was added to the list in 2001.[136] Of particular pertinence to consumer protection, included in the list are all local authorities and the Consumers' Association. The only limitation on the standing of these qualifying bodies is set out in Regulation 12(2). It is incumbent on such bodies to notify the OFT of an intention to apply for an order at least fourteen days beforehand. The Regulations envisage co-ordination between the several bodies charged with the responsibility to enforce these rules and this has been strengthened by agreements struck between the OFT and the qualifying bodies. It remains to be seen whether litigation will become more common now that access to the courts has been extended beyond the OFT.

This reinvigorated pattern of enforcement in the field of unfair terms should be viewed against the background of more general emphasis on strengthened public enforcement of consumer protection laws manifest in particular in the procedure created by Part 8 of the Enterprise Act 2002. This envisages action against practices that harm the collective interests of consumers and is examined more fully in its broader context in Chapter 13.

---

[133] Note 23 above.
[134] Case C–82/96 *R v Secretary of State for Trade and Industry, ex parte Consumers' Association* was withdrawn in 1997.
[135] Note 23 above.
[136] The Unfair Terms in Consumer Contracts (Amendment) Regulations 2001 S.I. No. 1186.

Chapter 6

Consumer Credit: Private Law

6.1 INTRODUCTION

The consumer credit industry is an important sector of the economy and one which has a strong impact on the economic health of the nation.[1] Until the early 1970's consumer credit regulation had two explicit aims – to protect consumers and ensure the amount of consumer credit did not have deleterious effects on the general economic health of the nation.[2] Strands of this latter policy remained until 1982, when the practices of requiring minimum down-payments and maximum repayment periods were discontinued.[3] Whilst no longer an explicit policy of the law, the link between consumer credit regulation and the wider economy remains. Lenders can either be too cautious and dampen down economic activity or too willing to lend stoking up the economy, especially the housing market. The current discussion about introducing a responsible lending principle suggests that most concern is nowadays with lenders' eagerness to lend.

The White Paper, *Fair, Clear and Competitive*,[4] reported that seven per cent of households were over-indebted judged by the criteria used for the Household Survey, whereas 20 per cent of those approached admitted to having financial difficulties.[5] Unsurprisingly this was linked to low income and financial and social exclusion. For instance, the percentage of over-indebted households rose to 14 per cent where weekly income was between £150–200. Common causes of falling into debt are major life events such as separation from a partner, having a child, falling ill or becoming disabled, or changes in circumstances such as loss of

---

[1] See I. Ramsay, 'Credit, Class and the Normalisation of Debt Default' in *Aspects of Credit and Debt*, G. Howells, I. Crow and M. Moroney (eds.), (Sweet & Maxwell, 1993) at p. 64 and Crowther, *Consumer Credit* (Cmnd 4596, 1971).

[2] This latter function was performed by Control Orders made by the Board of Trade under the Emergency Laws (Re-enactments and Repeals) Act 1964. These laid down minimum deposits for credit contracts and minimum advance payments under hire contracts and in that way allowed consumer expenditure to be controlled.

[3] Control of Hiring and Hire-Purchase and Credit Sale Agreements (Revocation) Order 1982 No. 1034.

[4] Cm 6040 (DTI, 2003); hereafter White Paper.

[5] *Ibid.*, Chapter 5.

employment. However, one in seven people cited long-term low income as a cause. The White Paper dwelt on the costs of over-indebtedness and in particular the impact on the heath and prospects for debtors and on the costs to the state of picking up the pieces of debtors who are stressed, ill and potentially vulnerable to lose their home, jobs and future access to credit. One aspect of the current reforms is to make consumers more aware of their commitments when entering into credit contracts. However, in the White Paper the Government is keen that these legal reforms are backed up by supporting policies to promote financial literacy, improve debt advice and promote affordable credit options, such as social fund loans and credit unions.

Consumer credit laws should also be viewed in the context of personal bankruptcy law. This was reformed in the Enterprise Act 2002 so that first time bankrupts at least could be rehabilitated within a few months, although stronger sanctions would be reserved for those who persistently used bankruptcy proceedings. This is part of a general trend across Europe to move away from restrictive bankruptcy rules under which the bankrupt was viewed as being at fault and either should pay his or her debts or at least not enjoy relief for many years.[6] Instead the US model is being adopted, under which the debtor is stereotypically viewed as being a victim of circumstances and indeed possibly a valued risk-taker, who should be integrated back into the credit market as soon as possible. Ironically this is happening at the very time US laws are themselves being made less liberal. However, this chapter will concentrate upon the consumer protection aspects of consumer credit and, more particularly, upon the private law remedies available to consumers. Chapter 9 considers the public law regulatory controls on consumer credit.

Consumer credit law is today based around the Consumer Credit Act 1974 ('CCA 1974'), which resulted from the Crowther Royal Commission on Consumer Credit.[7] That is a large and complicated piece of legislation, which seeks to regulate the substance and not the form of the agreements by imposing a complex legal framework dependent upon terminology which it created itself. Clarke LJ recently made 'a plea for simplification of what has become an area of law of extraordinary complexity, even though it is intended to protect the ordinary consumer'.[8] Reform is certainly on the agenda. Some aspects like advertising regulation and licensing might be simplified, but the basic structure is likely to remain unchanged. Therefore, there will continue to be a need to grapple with the basic concepts and

---

6   See, J. Niemi-Kiesilainen, I. Ramsay and W. Whitford, *Consumer Bankruptcy in Global Perspective* (Hart, 2004).

7   See Crowther, *op. cit.*

8   *McGinn v Grangewood Securities Ltd* [2002] EWCA Civ. 522.

structure of the Act before the substantive provisions can be understood and applied.

In 2001 the DTI issued a Consultation Document *Tackling loan sharks – and more* which set out five main drivers for reform: (i) implementing the government's manifesto commitment to tackle loan sharks; (ii) the need to improve the consumer credit licensing regime, (iii) the knock-on effects of the Financial Services Authority regulating mortgages: (iv) the EC consultation on reforming the Consumer Credit Directive, and (v) building on the Task Force Report on tackling over-indebtedness. Priority areas for reform were said to be (a) increasing/removing the financial limits, (b) making the early settlement regulations fairer, (c) enabling consumers to conclude credit agreements on line, (d) reforming the licensing regime, (e) making extortionate credit bargain provisions more effective, (f) simplifying the advertising regulations, including regulations on APR's, and (g) simplifying the rules on multiple agreements. You may not yet be conversant with these issues, but they are considered in more detail below. They are mentioned now simply to give you an idea of the nature of current reform debates. A series of consultation documents dealing with topics (a)-(e) were produced during 2002–3. The Government's conclusions are found in the White Paper, *Fair, Clear and Competitive*, published at the end of 2003, which also considers other issues such as advertising and multiple agreements. Alongside this was published a consultation document, *Establishing a Transparent Market*, which dealt with early settlement, advertising, form and content of credit agreements, APRs on credit cards and on-line agreements. It included draft regulations. Although the current law will be presented in this chapter, where relevant the likely direction of future reform will also be indicated.[9] Where this is possible by secondary legislation this can be anticipated to be introduced in the near future, but where primary legislation is needed time will need to be found in the legislative calendar, which is never easy for consumer matters which have a relatively low political priority.[10]

Mention has been made of the EC Consumer Credit Directive as a driver for reform. When in 1987 the EC enacted a Directive approximating the laws, regulations and administrative provisions concerning consumer

---

[9] Just as this book was going to press the following Regulations were laid before Parliament: Consumer Credit (Advertisements) Regulations 2004, Consumer Credit (Agreements) (Amendment) Regulations 2004, Consumer Credit (Early Settlement) Regulations 2004 and Consumer Credit (Disclosure of Information) Regulations 2004. It has not been possible to deal with them in the text but the broad contours of reform are explained.

[10] An excellent commentary on current reform debates is provided by E. Lomnicka, 'The Future of Consumer Credit Regulation' in *Contemporary Issues in Law* (forthcoming).

credit[11] it was fairly modest and did not require major amendments to the UK law. The Directive placed an emphasis on information provisions, but also contains, *inter alia*, rules requiring the supervision of creditors, restricting creditor remedies, allowing for a rebate if credit is repaid ahead of time and introducing a limited form of connected lender liability for the quality of goods supplied. As the Directive is a minimal harmonisation directive, there was no need to repeal more stringent provisions contained in the CCA 1974.[12] The Directive has been amended to introduce a common method of calculating the APR,[13] but in 2002 a far more ambitious reform was proposed.[14] In many respect the proposed directive covers familiar ground for those conversant with the CCA 1974. There are some novel features such as the creation of a central database of defaulters, the introduction of the principle of responsible lending and a rule which would have prevented the problem of endowment policies not being sufficient to repay capital – which many British consumers might have wished had been introduced a couple of decades ago, but obviously restricts the freedom of the market. At the time of writing the future of the draft directive is uncertain. It is an ambitious proposal with measures which will disturb some in the credit industry and at the same time, as in most respects it seeks total harmonisation, consumer groups and national governments will be nervous lest their consumers are exposed to unfair or harmful practices they cannot regulate.

6.2 HISTORY OF CONSUMER CREDIT[15]

Some form of credit has probably always had (and always will have) a place in human society: some of the oldest records which survive from Mesopotamia are of credit transactions. Of course usury was for a long time condemned by religion and hence the state. However, over time as society became more complex and credit became a necessary lubricant for the consumer market, controls on lending were relaxed. The earliest forms of consumer credit seem to be tradesman's credit, pawn-broking and money-lending. Tradesman's credit from the shopkeeper or the itinerant

---

11 87/102/EEC OJ 1987 L 42/48. This was amended by Directive 90/88/EEC OJ 1990 L 61/14, which introduced a common method for calculating the annual percentage rate (APR), see 7.4.5. Member States which already had a method of calculating the APR can retain their national systems during a transitional period. Harmonisation of the method of calculating the APR is a particular problem for France.

12 For discussion of minimal harmonisation see Chapter 2.3.7.

13 Directive 90/88/EEC OJ 1990 L 61/14.

14 COM (2002) 443.

15 See Crowther, *op. cit.*, at pp. 31–49.

peddler grew in the 17th- and 18th-centuries, when economic reality dictated that sellers had goods to sell but consumers did not have the money to pay for them (at least not immediately). Pawn-broking became an important form of credit in late 16th-century London. It was widely used by the poor, with clothing being a common item to pawn.[16] By contrast professional money-lending, as opposed to casual lending between friends and families, seems to have been the source of credit used by impecunious middle and upper-class consumers.

Pawn-broking was first regulated in 1603 and a comprehensive consolidating statute was passed in 1872, which remained in force with minor amendments until replaced by the CCA 1974. The Bills of Sale Acts from 1854 to 1891 regulated money-lending which involved chattel mortgages,[17] but it was not until the 1900 and 1927 Moneylenders Acts that a comprehensive system of regulation of money-lending was established, with exemption given to those 'bona fide carrying on the business of banking'. This caused many businesses to apply for certificates to be banks in order to be exempted from the Moneylenders Acts. That many of these businesses were not banks in the accepted sense highlights a problem endemic in attempts to regulate any business activity: the ability of businesses to alter their legal form or the nature of their trading activities in order to circumvent regulation.

Various types of credit also evolved to meet the needs of particular times. Thus the advent of expensive, but popular, consumer durables gave birth to the hire-purchase transaction, initiated in the 1860's by the Singer Sewing Machine Company. Later it became commonplace to buy expensive consumer goods such as cars on hire-purchase. Hire-purchase was encouraged by two judicial decisions that increased its appeal to lenders. *Helby v Matthews*[18] decided that, as the hirer under a hire-purchase agreement had not bought or agreed to buy goods, he could not pass a perfect title to a third party by virtue of (what became) s. 25(2), Sale of Goods Act 1979. *McEntire v Crossley Bros*[19] held that hire-purchase contracts did not fall foul of the Bills of Sale Acts requirement to register security interests, as the hirer had no property over which to grant security. Various malpractices involving hire-purchase contracts soon became apparent. Most notable was the practice of 'snatching back' goods, whereby the agreement was terminated and the goods repossessed on the

---

[16]   In 1572 a bill was drafted which would have set up state-financed pawnshops loaning at six per cent to prevent the poor from being exploited. Similar systems operated on the continent, such as the *mont de piété* in France: see G. Howells and M. Moroney, 'Social Lending in Europe' in G. Howells *et al., op. cit.*

[17]   The Bills of Sales Acts 1878–1882 (as amended) remain in force.

[18]   [1895] AC 471.

[19]   [1895] AC 457.

pretext of a minor irregularity when perhaps almost all the instalments had been paid. Hire-purchase contracts thus came to be highly regulated. First, by the Hire-Purchase Act 1938 and later by the Hire-Purchase Acts 1954 and 1964 (which were consolidated in the Hire-Purchase Act 1965) and the Advertisements (Hire-Purchase) Act 1967. The increased regulation of hire-purchase contracts caused some companies to change to rental agreements as a means of circumventing regulation.[20] This resulted in the Crowther Committee recommending that hire contracts be brought within the scope of credit legislation.

There is an interesting contrast between the regulation of hire-purchase transactions and money-lending. Whereas the scope of money-lending legislation was defined by the nature of the lender, hire-purchase legislation referred to the nature of the agreement. However, both approaches were easily circumvented, by either changing the status of the lender or the form of the agreement. One of the great advances made in the CCA 1974 was to regulate according to the substance of the agreement, albeit at the expense of creating a complex regime.

There has always been a certain amount of self-help credit. Indeed in earlier times building societies had their origins as self-help associations. Recently the credit union, a financial co-operative, has seen something of a resurgence, but remains a marginal player.[21] Several forms of commercial consumer credit grew out of the self-help movement. Thus check clubs[22] gave way to check trading companies, under which traders gave consumers checks they could cash at specified shops and pay for by instalments to their door-to-door collector. Akin to this was the 'Scotch Drapery' or tallyman system, where itinerant traders would supply goods such as clothing and bedding on instalment credit that they would collect on the doorstep. Check and tally trading have always been most common in the North of England, where they remain an important source of working class credit. A 1994 study showed the continued importance of weekly doorstep

---

20   This was commented upon by Mr. Justice Sachs in *Galbraith v Mitchenall Estates Ltd* [1964] 2 All ER 653 at 659.

21   See R. Berthoud and T. Hinton, *Credit Unions in the United Kingdom* (Policy Studies Institute, 1989); G. Howells and G. Griffiths, 'Britain's Best Kept Secret – An Analysis of Credit Unions as an Alternative Source of Credit', (1991) *JCP* 443; G. Howells and G. Griffiths, 'Slumbering Giant or White Elephant – Do Credit Unions have a Role in the United Kingdom Credit Market', (1991) 42 *NILQ* 199; G. Griffiths and G. Howells, 'Credit Unions in the United Kingdom and Possible Legislative Reforms to the Credit Unions Act 1979' in G. Howells *et al.*, *op. cit.*

22   Members would save periodic amounts and make withdrawals in turn until they had received their share of the total money.

collected credit to the working class economy[23] and this form of lending continues to thrive. Another important source of consumer credit, widely but not exclusively used by the working classes, are mail order catalogues.[24]

Given the prominence of the High Street banks in today's consumer credit market, it may perhaps come as a surprise to learn that for a long time banks were reluctant to enter the personal finance market, preferring merely to provide overdrafts to those more affluent members of society who had bank accounts. It was as late as 1958 when the banks entered the personal finance market with the Midland Bank leading the way with a Personal Loans Scheme. More recent times have seen banks achieve a deeper penetration of the consumer market.[25] There is a heated debate today about the need for banks to offer a universal service including a basic bank account, but this would not necessarily include the right to credit.[26]

The credit card has become an important source of consumer credit. The White Paper notes that in 1971 there was only one credit card, now there are 1,300. Today over £49bn is owed on credit cards, compared to £32m thirty years ago.[27] There is often much debate about the costs of credit cards. Currently there is concern about the practices of credit card companies including the offering of introductory rates, but not explaining to consumers fully how such schemes work.[28] The OFT has also referred store cards, which typically have higher rates than credit cards issued directly by banks and finance companies, to the Competition Commission.

---

23 See K. Rowlingson, *Moneylenders and their Clients* (Policy Studies Institute, 1994). This study showed the importance of both money loans and loans connected with purchases from the trader.

24 Crowther had some concerns about how mail order catalogues should be regulated in relation to price disclosure. Conducting most of their business on credit they did not have, or advertise, cash prices; *Crowther, op. cit.*, pp. 96–9 and 266–7. As with interest-free credit offers, the problem is that consumers who do not take advantage of the credit offer are penalised. Crowther recommended that a prominent statement should be made that no discount is given for cash.

25 The Policy Studies Institute estimates that 8 out of 10 adults have a current account with a bank or building society: R. Berthoud and E. Kempson, *Credit and Debt: The PSI Report* (Policy Studies Institute, 1992). This was confirmed in a subsequent study of debtors; see I. Crow, G. Howells, M. Moroney, 'Credit and Debt: Choices for Poorer Consumers' in G. Howells *et al., op. cit.* at p. 31.

26 P. Cartwright, *Banks, Consumers and Regulation*, (Hart, forthcoming) Chapter 8. The Post Office may have an important role to play in relation to such accounts.

27 *Op. cit.*, at 4.

28 See Treasury Select Committee First Report, *Transparency of Credit Card Charges*, HC 125 Session 2003–4.

Banks also issue cards known as EFTPOS[29] cards, which in many respects provide (absent the credit facility) the same function as credit cards and give rise to similar consumer protection problems. Yet they are not treated as instances of connected lending between the card issuer and the supplier and so escape some of the consumer protection provisions contained in the CCA 1974.[30]

6.3 LAW REFORM IN THE 1970s

A distinction can be drawn between two types of credit: credit for need and credit for convenience. Typically lower waged people borrow to make ends meet, whilst the more affluent borrow to increase their purchasing power of consumer durables. However, whilst there may be two basic reasons for borrowing, there are – as the preceding brief history of consumer credit law illustrates – multifarious forms of credit. Traditionally the law has drawn a distinction between a money loan and the provision of goods and services with the assistance of credit. Equally the law has differentiated between renting and buying on credit. Whilst these divisions make sense for some purposes, they frequently have more to do with chance and the choice of legal form than with any fundamental economic distinctions relating to the nature of the transaction being entered into. This is the important insight which the Crowther Committee provided in its 1971 critique of the law. The Committee found seven broad types of defects in the law:

(i)   Regulation of transactions according to their form instead of according to their substance and function.
(ii)   The failure to distinguish consumer from commercial transactions.
(iii) The artificial separation of the law relating to lending from the law relating to security for loans.
(iv)   The absence of any rational policy in relation to third party rights.
(v)   Excessive technicality.
(vi)   Lack of consistent policy in relation to sanctions for breach of statutory provisions.
(vii) Overall, the irrelevance of credit law to present day requirements, and the resultant failure to provide just solutions to common problems.

---

[29]   This stands for 'Electronic Fund Transfer at Point of Sale'.
[30]   Section 187(3A), CCA 1974. This means that the card issuer is not jointly liable with the supplier of goods for their quality; see Chapter 7.11. Also if the card cannot be used for credit and hence is not a credit-token, the consumer will not benefit from the protection the Act affords consumers when credit-tokens are lost or misused; see Chapter 7.16.

Crowther recommended the enactment of a Lending and Security Act to provide for a proper and fair means of granting and enforcing chattel mortgages and to deal with those credit practices which need to be regulated for both commercial and consumer transactions. Consumer protection measures would be contained in a Consumer Sale and Loan Act. In its White Paper, *Reform of the Law on Consumer Credit*,[31] the Government accepted the need for a Consumer Credit Bill, but was not convinced of the need for a radical reform of the law relating to security interests. The CCA 1974 was the result.[32] The issue of security in chattels was examined in a report by Professor Diamond[33] and has recently been subject of much activity at the Law Commission.[34]

At one level the CCA 1974 should be judged by how well it deals with the technical problem of regulating a complex and fast changing industry in a manner which is comprehensible to the industry and consumer advisers and which also prevents the creation of loopholes in consumer protection. However, a substantive evaluation of the legislation requires some understanding of what its functions ought to be. Crowther saw three primary tasks for consumer credit legislation:[35]

(i) Redressing bargaining inequality by means such as disclosure requirements, prohibiting false and misleading information, providing a floor of consumer rights and controlling harsh terms.
(ii) Controlling trading malpractices through a licensing system and criminal and civil sanctions.
(iii) Regulating the remedies for default.[36]

These goals should be borne in mind when considering the success of the CCA 1974. It is also of interest to note Crowther's views on the balance that should be achieved in consumer protection measures. Thus whilst

---

[31] (Cmnd. 5427, 1973).

[32] Limitations of space prevent the text going into fine detail on the CCA 1974, in particular it should be noted there is no discussion of the rules on security or pawn-broking. For a more detailed discussion by one of the present authors, see G. Howells, *Consumer Debt* (Sweet & Maxwell, 1993).

[33] This has recently been re-examined by Professor Diamond, but again no action has been forthcoming: see A. Diamond, 'A Review of Security Interests in Property' (HMSO, 1989).

[34] See, *Registration of Security Interests: Company Charges and Property other than Land* (Consultation Paper 164).

[35] *Op. cit.*, at pp. 234–5.

[36] It should perhaps be noted that the Government considered that another purpose of the reform was 'to release the credit industry from existing outdated restrictions': *Reform of the Law on Consumer Credit, op. cit.*, at p. 6.

advocating loss spreading (by placing the loss on the business where there are two relatively innocent parties), Crowther thought this policy should be tempered by (i) the realisation that if this went too far, then good consumers would end up subsidising bad consumers, and (ii) the probability that if creditor remedies were restricted too much they would resort to extrajudicial (perhaps illegal) measures of self-help. This argument finds echoes in the work of Cayne and Trebilcock, who argue that consumer protection laws can be exclusionary (with lenders refusing to supply credit) or degenerative (leading to the creation of black markets).[37] This light regulatory philosophy was supported by Sir Bryan Carsberg, when Director-General of Fair Trading, who applauded the essentially non-interventionist form of the consumer credit legislation, stating:

> Perhaps the greatest strength of the Act is that it does not seek to meet its objectives through interventionist action such as interest rate-capping or direct control of the substance of contracts. Rather, it explicitly endorses freedom of contract within a framework of rules designed to ensure openness: consumer protection is attained in large part through measures to ensure that full and truthful information about credit contracts is available to consumers.[38]

This is still the main thrust of Government policy. Although it wants some greater controls on extortionate credit bargains, it is not keen on the idea of interest rate ceilings. Equally, whilst continuing to favour information strategies as a method of debtor protection, it appreciates they have to be more sophisticated than simply providing as lot of information to the consumer and hoping they can understand and use it.

6.4 STRUCTURE OF THE CCA 1974

To understand consumer credit law one needs a firm grasp of the terminology and structure of the CCA 1974. The Act has two features which can help users to comprehend what is necessarily a complex piece of legislation. Section 189 gathers together all the relevant definitions. It is in effect an index for the Act. Schedule 2 provides examples and descriptions

---

37   D. Cayne and M. Trebilcock, 'Market Considerations in the Formulation of Consumer Protection Policy' (1973) 23 *UTLJ* 396.

38   *Consumer Credit Deregulation* (OFT, 1994) at p. 6.

of how the draftsmen considered the Act should apply in particular circumstances.[39]

6.4.1 Credit

6.4.1.1 What is Credit?

There has been a good deal of recent litigation surrounding what amounts to credit. Usually this has been because one of the parties is seeking to argue that the agreement was a regulated agreement and unenforceable because it was not in the prescribed form. In *Dimond v Lovell*[40] the question before the House of Lords was whether credit had been granted at all. It concerned accident hire companies that allowed the innocent victims of car accidents to hire replacement cars and defer payment until the firm had recovered the costs on the hirer's behalf. The firms made money from charging rates higher than might be paid on the open market and through the costs of recovering the sums owed. Insurers were concerned that this practice was inflating the costs of accidents and argued that the agreement with the hire company was a regulated agreement that was unenforceable against the consumer as it was not in the correct form. The House of Lords held that the agreements were indeed for the provision of credit; otherwise the hire company would have been able to recover hire fees during or at the end of the hire agreement. The agreement was therefore unenforceable and damages could not be recovered in respect of it. It remains possible, however, to draft contracts that are exempt from the CCA 1974 and hence enforceable despite not complying with the Act's requirements. For this reasons most such agreements require repayment in less than four instalments within a year.[41]

---

[39] It has been alleged that Example 21 is erroneous in describing a cheque guarantee card as providing credit. Dobson argues that the mistake lies in describing the consumer as being 'free' to withdraw the whole balance and then use the cheque card again in a transaction which the bank is bound to honour. Dobson correctly notes that the consumer may be physically – but not legally – free to do so; see P. Dobson, 'The Cheque Card as a Consumer Credit Agreement' [1987] *JBL* 126. Professor Goode has raised similar doubts about Examples 16 and 18 which relate to the complicated definitions of multiple agreements; see R. Goode, *Consumer Credit Law* (Butterworths, 1989) at pp. 155–6. Although regrettable, such inconsistencies should not pose a problem for s. 188(3), CCA 1974 clearly states that, in the case of a conflict between Schedule 2 and any other provisions of the Act, the latter shall prevail.

[40] [2002] 1 AC 384.

[41] See, *Thew v Cole, King v Daltry*, (2003) EWCA Civ. 1828.

By contrast in another case it was found that after the event insurance taken out by a claimant to insure legal costs and not payable until the conclusion of the case was not the provision of credit.[42] Similarly a credit allocation to gamble on stock market fluctuations did not fall within the Act's definition of credit.[43] Also a wage advance to a solicitor against future commission based on profit costs generated was not credit.[44] Usually these cases have arisen as one party is seeking to argue there was a grant of credit in order to claim the formalities had not been properly complied with and hence the agreement was unenforceable. These cases show that knowledge of consumer credit law is valuable in many contexts where it might not at first seem obviously relevant. It also illustrates how the detailed rules on formalities can have a dramatic impact out of all recognition with their turgid nature.

6.4.1.2 How Much of the Advance is Credit?

Another difficult question has been to ascertain whether a payment forms part of the 'credit' or part of the 'total charge for credit' as defined by the Consumer Credit (Total Charge for Credit) Regulations 1980.[45] How sums are classified can be important in order to determine whether an agreement is within the financial limit of £25,000 and therefore regulated. It also affects the rate of interest. If, for instance, a document fee is part of the credit, rather than the total charge for credit, the interest will be lower as the charge for credit will be lower and the amount borrowed higher than if it were treated as part of the charge for credit.

Recently, much interest has centred on such question because if creditors make a mistake as to whether something is credit or part of the charge for credit, they will have failed properly to state a prescribed term and the agreement will be totally unenforceable. We shall see how in *Wilson v First County*[46] the failure to treat a document fee as part of the charge for credit rendered the whole agreement unenforceable. Mrs Wilson kept her £5,000 loan, did not have to make any repayments and got back the BMW she had pledged.

Another grey area has involved money used to pay off arrears when a new loan is taken out and whether the repayment was credit as part of a new loan or formed part of the total charge for credit as it was a cost associated with the new advance. In *Watchtower Investments Ltd v*

---

42   *Tilby v Perfect Pizza Ltd*, 2002, Lawtel.
43   *Nejad v City Index Ltd*, 1999 Lawtel.
44   *McWillan Williams v Range*, [2004] EWCA Civ. 294.
45   S.I. 1980/51.
46   [2003] 3 WLR 568.

Payne[47] the payment of arrears was correctly treated as credit as the loan had been expressly 'to clear arrears'. In *McGinn v Grangewood Securities Ltd*[48] the creditor had simply taken it upon himself to repay the arrears and should have treated it as part of the total charge for credit. This error rendered the agreement unenforceable. These examples serve to illustrate how complex consumer credit law is and how understandable mistakes can render agreements unenforceable.

6.4.2 Regulated Agreements

The CCA 1974 only applies to regulated agreements, save for the extortionate credit bargain provisions that apply to all credit bargains. For an agreement to be regulated, the debtor or hirer[49] must be an individual. This therefore means that the scope of the Act extends beyond private consumers to partnerships, but not to corporations (which have a separate corporate legal personality). The intention was to bring small businesses within the scope of the Act, but this test works rather arbitrarily: whether or not a small business is incorporated does not necessarily reflect the need of the trader for protection. The test can, however, be justified on the basis that, where a trader is not trading as a body corporate it is difficult for the other trader to know in what capacity, private or professional, the person is contracting. Therefore it may be better to extend the requirements and protection of the CCA 1974 to all such individuals.

Regulated agreements cover both 'consumer credit agreements' and 'consumer hire agreements'. A consumer credit agreement is a 'personal credit agreement' for credit not exceeding £25,000.[50] The notion of a threshold, which can be changed by statutory instrument, was introduced because it was felt that if the amount of credit granted exceeded a certain figure, consumers were in less need of protection. This policy might be questioned. Borrowing large amounts may simply reflect greater need. In some ways the policy of the former hire-purchase legislation was more sensible in linking regulation to the total price of the goods purchased, rather than the amount of credit extended. Take the example of two consumers buying a £30,000 car. The richer of the two is able to put down a sizeable deposit of £10,000 and thus bring him or herself within the

---

47 [2001] 35 LS Gaz. 32

48 [2002] EWCA Civ. 522.

49 The parties to a credit agreement are described as the creditor and debtor and the parties to a hire agreement as the owner and hirer. Although the parties to a hire-purchase agreement are formally in a hire relationship, the Act treats such contracts as credit rather than hire contracts.

50 Section 8(2), CCA 1974.

protective scope of the CCA 1974, as only £20,000 credit will be borrowed. The less well-off consumer who can only put down a £3,000 deposit will not be protected as the credit advanced will be more than £25,000.

When calculating the amount of credit advanced, it is necessary to deduct any deposit and any element of the total charge for credit.[51] The Act plugs an obvious loophole that might have existed in relation to running-account credit. Creditors might have been tempted to fix a credit limit in excess of £25,000 (even though realistically that amount of credit would never be extended) in order to render the agreement unregulated. The credit limit is defined as the maximum debit balance allowed on an account, excluding any temporary arrangements.[52] Section 10(3), CCA 1974 prevents abuse by providing that running-account credit agreements will be regulated even if the credit limit exceeds £25,000, if:

(i)   the debtor cannot withdraw more that £25,000 at any one time; or
(ii) the total charge for credit increases or harsher terms come into force if more credit than a specified figure below £25,000 is withdrawn; or
(iii) it was not probable that more than £25,000 would be borrowed.

The CCA 1974 also applies to hire contracts. Consumer hire agreements will be regulated if they are capable of subsisting for three months and do not require payments in excess of £25,000.

The Government is proposing to remove the limit of £25,000 to include all consumer credit agreements.[53] This would bring the CCA 1974 in line with the Financial Services Authority's powers to regulate first charge mortgages with no financial limit. It would also be in accordance with anticipated proposals from the EC and reflect the reality that many consumer loans are for more than £25,000. Many such loans are often targeted at consumers with low credit ratings.

It was recognised that lifting the ceiling could be problematic for some business lending; for instance the CCA 1974 allows hire-purchase contracts to be terminated by paying half the total price and this could make traders reluctant to supply such goods on hire-purchase where they are of high value and possibly made to the special order of the customer. However, it was also appreciated that some businesses can be vulnerable.

---

51   The elements included as part of the total charge for credit are calculated on the basis of the Consumer Credit (Total Charge for Credit) Regulations 1980, S.I. 1980/51, but essentially consist of all interest and other necessary expenses connected with the loan.

52   Section 10(2), CCA 1974.

53   White Paper at p. 44 and pp. 66–67 and *Consultation Document on the Financial Limit and Exempt Agreements of the Consumer Credit Act 1974*.

A compromise was proposed under which business lending of up to £25,000 would be covered if borrowed by unincorporated bodies. This would cover sole traders, partnerships of up to three, and other unincorporated bodies not consisting entirely of bodies corporate. This clear distinction between business and consumer lending will probably require the CCA 1974 to be reformed to include a definition of consumer rather than merely refer to individual.

Of course agreements will not be regulated if they are exempt agreements. The categories of exempt agreements will be considered shortly, but before the exemptions can be understood, it is necessary to introduce some other terms which the Act uses. This terminology is also needed to understand the substantive provisions considered later in the chapter.

6.4.3 Terminology

Three sets of terms must be understood to make sense of the CCA 1974. These are important not only to be able to assess whether an agreement falls into one of the categories of exempt agreements, but also because they allow the Act to fine-tune the application of its principles to the different types of consumer credit. The three sets of terms are described below.

6.4.3.1 Fixed-Sum and Running-Account Credit[54]

Running-account credit is any facility under which a debtor is able to receive from the creditor or a third party cash, goods or services up to a credit limit. Any credit which is not running-account credit is treated as fixed-sum credit.

6.4.3.2 Restricted-Use and Unrestricted-Use Credit[55]

Restricted-use credit covers agreements:

(i) to finance a transaction between the debtor and creditor (for example, where a shopkeeper supplies goods under a conditional sale agreement);
(ii) to finance a transaction between the debtor and a supplier other than a creditor (for example, where a double glazing company introduces a

---

[54] Section 10, CCA 1974.
[55] Section 11, CCA 1974.

customer to a finance house and the finance company pays the money direct to the glazing company);[56]

(iii) to re-finance an existing indebtedness owed to the creditor or another person.

An agreement will not be a restricted-use agreement if the credit is provided in such a way that the debtor is free to choose how the money is spent, even if using it in certain ways would be a breach of the agreement. Any agreement which is not a restricted-use agreement is an unrestricted-use agreement.

6.4.3.3 Debtor-Creditor-Supplier and Debtor-Creditor Agreements[57]

This is perhaps the most important distinction in the Act, in that it seeks to differentiate pure money loans from loans explicitly connected to the purchase of goods and services. Debtor-creditor-supplier agreements would cover purchases made with a credit card and also those made with the assistance of a loan from a creditor associated with the seller. For example, a car might be purchased with the assistance of a hire-purchase agreement made with a company whose forms are provided by the car dealer. The CCA 1974 defines debtor-creditor-supplier agreements as:

(i)   restricted-use credit agreements financing a transaction between the debtor and creditor;[58]

(ii) restricted-use credit agreements financing a transaction between the debtor and a supplier other than the creditor, *if* the creditor has pre-existing relations with the supplier *or* enters into the agreement in contemplation of future arrangements;[59]

---

56   Since the identity of the supplier need not be known in advance, agreements entered into using a credit card are covered.

57   Sections 12–13, CCA 1974.

58   Note this means that there can be only two parties to a debtor-creditor-supplier agreement with the creditor and supplier being the same person.

59   Section 187(2), CCA 1974 provides that 'A consumer credit agreement shall be treated as entered into in contemplation of future arrangements between a creditor and supplier if it is entered into in the expectation that arrangements will subsequently be made between... [them] ...for the supply of cash, goods and services (or any of them) to be financed by the consumer credit agreement'. Goode suggests that this is narrower than might first be thought since the future transactions referred to must be financed by *the* (meaning *that*) agreement. Thus whilst a credit card used with a supplier who is not yet formally within the card scheme might be covered, it would not, it is suggested, apply where creditor or supplier come together for a trial

(iii) unrestricted-use credit agreements, but only *if* the agreement is made under pre-existing arrangements between the creditor and supplier *and* there is knowledge that the credit is to be used to finance a transaction between the debtor and supplier. This is an anti-avoidance device. It prevents money being given to the debtor (so that technically it is not restricted-use credit as the debtor can apply it for any purpose) when in reality the creditor knows it is being used to finance a transaction with a supplier with whom the creditor has pre-existing relations.[60]

Debtor-creditor-supplier agreements falling under category (i) are known as two party debtor-creditor-supplier agreements since the creditor and the supplier are the same person. Agreements which come within categories (ii) and (iii) are called three party debtor-creditor-supplier agreements since three distinct parties are involved.

Agreements which are not debtor-creditor-supplier agreements are debtor-creditor agreements. Rather than leave this as a residual category, the Act spells out which agreements are debtor-creditor, namely:

(i) restricted-use credit agreements financing transactions with a supplier other than the creditor, not made under pre-existing arrangements or in contemplation of future arrangements;
(ii) unrestricted-use credit agreements not made under pre-existing arrangements with the knowledge that the credit is to be used to finance a transaction between the debtor and supplier;
(iii) any refinancing agreements.

6.4.4 Exempt Agreements[61]

Certain categories of consumer credit agreements are exempted from the provisions of the CCA 1974, save for the extortionate credit bargain

---

transaction with a view to making the arrangement permanent (R. Goode (1989), *op. cit.*, at p. 147). The point about credit cards being covered (despite the identity of the supplier not being known at the time the credit agreement is made) is dealt with in s. 11(3), CCA 1974. This provides that an agreement can be of the restricted-use credit type (and therefore potentially a debtor-creditor-supplier credit agreement) even if the identity of the supplier is not known at the time the agreement is made. This might support s. 187(2) being given a broader interpretation, since the object of the narrow interpretation is provided for elsewhere in the Act.

[60] Note it is not sufficient when the credit is for unrestricted-use that future arrangements be contemplated, there must be pre-existing arrangements.

[61] See s. 16, CCA 1974 and Consumer Credit (Exempt Agreements) Order 1989, S.I. 1989/869 (as amended).

provisions. These can be divided into three groups based on (i) the nature of the creditor, (ii) the number of repayments and (iii) the charge for credit. It is likely that if the EC Consumer Credit Directive is reformed some of these exemptions will have to be removed. Whilst industry is keen to retain the exemptions, the Government is still considering its position and will report shortly.[62]

6.4.4.1 Nature of the Creditor

The exemptions based on the nature of the creditor involve contracts relating to the purchase of land or agreements secured on land and certain ancillary transactions. In essence land mortgages by local authorities, housing authorities, banks, building societies and certain other lenders are exempted where land or property is being purchased. Consolidation loans or loans to buy, say, a car secured by a mortgage would not be exempt. As the Financial Services Authority is to regulate first mortgages there is pressure to remove this exemption.

Also exempt are consumer hire agreements entered into by statutory gas, electricity and water undertakings for the hire of metering equipment.

6.4.4.2 Number of Repayments

The two most important types of agreement exempted on the basis of the number of instalments are (i) debtor-creditor-supplier agreements for fixed-sum credit (which require no more than four repayments payable within 12 months of the agreement being made) and (ii) running-account debtor-creditor-supplier agreements where the balance has to be paid in one instalment when it falls due.[63]

Exemption (i) covers everyday credit such as the newspaper or milk bill which is settled periodically. Such arrangements are not usually viewed as credit since individuals simply pay at set intervals for goods which are regularly supplied and where payment on delivery would be inconvenient to both parties. In the wake of *Dimond v Lovell*[64] this exemption has been used by accident repair companies to make their agreement fall outside the CCA 1974 and therefore be enforceable notwithstanding that the

---

62   White Paper, *op cit.*, at p. 67 and a *Consultation Document on the Financial Limit and Exempt Agreements of the Consumer Credit Act 1974.*

63   NB: These exemptions do not apply to agreements financing the purchase of land, most pledges or, most importantly, to conditional sale and hire-purchase agreements.

64   See Section 6.4.1.1.

formalities of the CCA 1974 are not complied with.[65] There is some concern that insurance companies are using this exemption when they allow premiums to be paid in four instalments and thereby avoiding the need to disclose the APR.[66] Where premiums are paid by 12 instalments the APR does have to be shown and although the four-instalment option may be more expensive this would not be apparent. Possibly the Government will propose reducing the number of repayments that warrant the exemption or restricting it to situations where interest is not charged.

Exemption (ii) draws attention to the difference between a charge card, which falls within the exemption, and a credit card that does not. Charge cards, such as American Express, fall within the exemption since the monthly bill must be paid in full, whereas credit cards such as Access and Visa, give the customer the option of repaying in full or paying a sum equal to or greater than the minimum repayment (which is typically five per cent of the outstanding balance) and carrying the balance on to the next month.

There is also an exemption relating to finance to purchase land that is included to ease conveyancing.

6.4.4.3 Charge for Credit

Debtor-creditor agreements are exempt on the basis of their low charge for credit if the annual percentage rate charged does not exceed one per cent above the highest rate published by specified banks in operation during the 28 days prior to the agreement being made. Crowther considered that much of the rationale for protection disappeared when the charge for credit is low, but astutely pointed out that this exemption cannot extend to low cost debtor-creditor-supplier agreements for the seller could then hide interest charges by inflating the cash price.[67] However, the exemptions only covers loans made to particular classes of consumers, such as students or employees. It does not apply to loans generally available. However all credit union loans are exempt so long as the interest is no more than 12.7 per cent.

---

65   In practice these debts may exist for longer than twelve months. There has been no litigation on this point, but, whilst it would seem open to a company not to enforce its debt, if this was stated at the outset as the company's practice the exemption might be threatened. Some very technical decisions have shown that it is important to draft the exemptions carefully so that the agreement cannot last for even one day longer than twelve months from its being made: see *Zoan v Rouamba*, [2000] 2 All ER 620.

66   *Consultation Document on the Financial Limit and Exempt Agreements of the Consumer Credit Act 1974*, at 13.

67   *Crowther, op. cit.*, at pp. 244–5.

6.4.4.4 Overseas Element

Consumer credit agreements are exempt when they relate to trade credit with respect to the supply of goods or services from the United Kingdom to outside or within a country of between countries outside the United Kingdom. Also certain loans made by US creditors to US armed forces are exempt.

6.4.4.5 Limited Exemptions

'Non-commercial agreements'[68] and 'small agreements'[69] provide a half-way house between regulated and exempt agreements. They are exempt from various provisions, notably those relating to formalities and the cancellation provisions. Non-commercial agreements are also exempt from the connected lender provisions contained in s. 75, CCA 1974.[70]

A 'non-commercial agreement' is a consumer credit or consumer hire agreement which is not made by the creditor or owner in the course of a business carried on by themselves. Business does not refer to only consumer credit businesses. Thus a loan made by an employer, for instance, would not be classed as a non-commercial agreement as it would be made in the course of a business.

Small agreements are consumer credit agreements (other than hire-purchase and conditional sale agreements) for credit not exceeding £50 and consumer hire-agreements not requiring payments of more than £50.[71] The Act tries to prevent creditors from gaining the exemptions that apply to small agreements by simply breaking a larger transaction down into a series of smaller transactions. It seeks to achieve this by disapplying the small agreement exemptions to agreements made at or about the same time between the same parties or their associates where it appears probable that there would have been a single agreement but for the desire to avoid the operation of provisions of the Act.

---

68 Section 189(1), CCA 1974.
69 Section 17(1), CCA 1974.
70 These would in any event probably not apply to small agreements as s. 75 only applies where the cash price exceeds £100.
71 It has been proposed to raise this limit to £150; see *Consumer Credit Deregulation, op. cit.*, at p. 112.

6.4.5 Multiple Agreements

Of course, consumer credit contracts may contain more than one type of credit agreement. The Act makes provision for multiple agreements and provides that the different parts of an agreement will be treated as separate agreements for the purposes of the Act. The Act should apply to each agreement in the appropriate manner.[72] This causes many problems, especially where increasingly complex financial products combine several different types of credit product. There are likely to be many technical breaches of the rules in relation to such agreements rendering the contracts unenforceable. To date the courts seem willing to try to look at the essence of what was agreed and not break agreements down into artificial separate agreements merely to assist a debtor seeking to avoid his or her responsibilities by claiming the agreement was unenforceable.[73] Reform of these rules has been discussed. It is understood however, that the government will not reform this area, which is regrettable as it is too complex at the moment.

6.4.6 Credit-Tokens[74]

Cards, checks, vouchers, coupons, stamps, forms, booklets or other documents are credit-tokens if given to an individual by a person carrying on a consumer credit business, if that person undertakes on production of the card etc. to supply cash, goods or services or to pay a third party for these things in return for payment to him by the individual. Thus credit cards are, in the language of the CCA 1974, credit-tokens. A credit-token agreement is a regulated agreement for the provision of credit in connection with the use of the token.

Credit cards were just emerging at the time of the Crowther report and it is in relation to them that the CCA 1974 provisions have sometimes proven to be difficult to apply, particularly in relation to connected lender liability.[75] This illustrates the law's difficulty in keeping pace with technological developments and changing commercial practices.

---

[72] Section 18, CCA 1974.

[73] *National Westminster Bank v Story* [1999] Lloyd's Rep Bank 26 and *National Home Loans v Hannah* [1997] CCLR 7 (Cty Ct).

[74] Section 14, CCA 1974

[75] See Chapter 6.11.

6.4.7 APR

The 'APR' or annual percentage rate is required to be disclosed in agreement documents, quotations and most advertisements for credit. Whereas the use of 'flat' interest rates can be misleading, the APR seeks to give a fairer basis of comparison, by taking into account the length of the loan period and the size and rate of repayments. Calculation of the rate is complicated and subject to debate surrounding the fairness of the formula as between different types of loan. Overdrafts have been treated preferentially and one of the main issues in the recent White Paper has been to make the assumptions used for credit card APR's fairer so better comparisons can be made. In fact the Consumer Credit (Total Charge for Credit) Regulations 1980[76] provide various methods of calculating the APR and the Government has produced volumes of tables to assist in the calculation of the APR.

In the past it has been suggested that it should not be necessary to disclose the APR for loans of less than £150, because it is inappropriate to require disclosure of the APR for small loans as the fixed administrative costs leading to high APRs on such loans give a misleading indication of the value of such credit.[77] However, the APR still indicates the true cost of such loans, even if the value of the loan to the individual might better be judged by the total interest payable or the size of the repayments. There seems little justification for not providing the APR as well as the other information so the consumer can make an informed choice. Studies show that the majority of consumers have an awareness of APRs, but that even where they consider it they take other factors into account as well when deciding from whom to borrow.[78] This indicates that the APR can be a useful comparator, although more consumer education is still needed, for it really to serve as a means of promoting competition in the market place.

6.5 FORMALITIES AND COPY PROVISIONS

An important policy of the CCA 1974 is to make consumers better informed so that they enter into prudent credit contracts suited to their needs and circumstances. This policy partly explains the regulation of advertisements and quotations discussed in Chapter 9. There is some scepticism about the value of disclosure provisions as a means of assisting consumer behaviour; indeed some commentators believe that the duties to

---

[76]   S.I. 1980/51.
[77]   *Consumer Credit Deregulation* (OFT, 1994)
[78]   I. Crow, G. Howells and M. Moroney, *op. cit.*, and *Consumers' Appreciation of Annual Percentage Rates* (OFT, 1994).

supply copies of the contract and information are of more significance on default. Ramsay considers these provide 'a "contract synopsis" – a comprehensible summary of the central aspects of the contract which may be referred to during performance and in the event of dispute'.[79] Copy provisions therefore have two functions: warning the consumer of the full extent of the commitments being entered into and providing a permanent record of the agreement by reference to which any disputes can be adjudicated.

6.5.1 Pre-contract Controls

The CCA 1974 provides for controls over pre-contractual documentation. Thus s. 55 permits regulations to be made prescribing pre-contractual information that must be disclosed. No such regulations have been made.

Section 58, CCA 1974 provides that where an agreement is secured on land[80] a copy of the unexecuted agreement indicating the debtor or hirer's right to withdraw, together with copies of other documents referred to, should be given[81] to the debtor or hirer seven days before the actual unexecuted agreement is sent. These seven days, together with the shorter of either seven days from the sending of the actual unexecuted agreement or the date on which the unexecuted agreement is returned signed, are known as the 'consideration period'. The creditor or owner must refrain from approaching the debtor or hirer during this period, except in response to a specific request to do so which was made after the commencement of the consideration period. The rationale for this extra protection for agreements secured on land is partly that they are not cancellable. The section also seems to take note of the particular need for consumers to reflect on the risks they undertake when entering into contracts secured by property.[82]

---

79 I. Ramsay, *Consumer Protection* (Weidenfeld and Nicolson, 1989) at p. 332. Note ss. 77–79, CCA 1974 also impose obligations on creditors and hirers to provide information during the course of agreements, other than non-commercial agreements. On making a written request and payment of a fee (currently 50p) the debtor or hirer is entitled to a copy of the executed agreement and a statement of account, provided that a month has passed since any previous request relating to the same agreement. Also in relation to running account agreements (other than small or non-commercial agreements), the creditor must send the debtor a periodic statement.

80 Other than remortgages and bridging loans.

81 In the CCA 1974 'given' means delivered (although not necessarily personally) or sent by post; see s. 189(1).

82 One criticism of this provision is that it can lead to the consumer being given three copies of the agreement (one prior to the commencement of the consideration period,

6.5.2 Form of the Agreement

Section 61, CCA 1974 provides that regulated agreements must be in the prescribed form,[83] contain all the prescribed terms and be signed by the debtor or hirer[84] and by or on behalf of the creditor or owner; must contain all the terms of the agreement other than implied terms and be readily legible.[85] Failing to make the agreement in the prescribed form and containing the prescribed terms can have serious consequences. In *Wilson v First County Trust (No.2)*[86] the House of Lords confirmed such agreements were unenforceable, even where the error was due to an understandable mistake.

All the information relating to financial and related particulars should be gathered together at one point in the document and not be interspersed throughout it, thus reducing the chance of the consumer being misled by devious presentation of the figures. The APR must be given no less prominence than other financial information. Where the Regulations place some prescribed information in capitals, this must also be given prominence in the document either by using capitals, underlining or by large or bold print. The print must be readily distinguishable against the colour of the paper. A signature box must be provided for the debtor or hirer, with the creditor or owner signing outside the box.

The Government intends to revise the format of agreements to make them clearer and more transparent.[87] Key information will have to be provided together as a whole with appropriate prominence. More information will be required to be given about consumer rights and a wealth warning will be included stating 'Missing payments will have severe consequences and may make obtaining credit more difficult in the future'. It has, however, stopped short of requiring a 'Schumer' summary

---

another on signing the unexecuted agreement and a further copy of the executed agreement). In such cases the Director-General has proposed that there is no need for the consumer to receive the second copy of the unexecuted agreement; see *Consumer Credit Deregulation, op. cit.*, at p. 58.

[83]   Meaning that it must comply with the Consumer Credit (Agreements) Regulations 1983, S.I. 1983/1553.

[84]   Note the debtor or hirer must sign personally. It would not be sufficient to sign a blank form and allow the details to be filled in later; see *Eastern Distributors Ltd v Goldring (Murphy, Third Party)* [1957] 2 QB 600.

[85]   Note that there is no requirement that the language be easily comprehensible although see Regulation 7, Unfair Terms in Consumer Contract Regulations 1999, S.I. 1999/2083. See Chapter 5.6.1.2.

[86]   [2003] 3 WLR 568

[87]   White Paper, *op cit.*, at 2.25–29 and *Establishing a Transparent Market, op cit.*

box,[88] although credit card issues have announced they will introduce such summaries.[89]

6.5.3 Copy Provisions

The debtor or hirer must always receive one copy of the agreement and all documents referred to in it. Whether the debtor or hirer should receive an additional copy depends upon whether the agreement becomes executed upon their signature.[90] If the debtor or hirer's signature executes the agreement, only one copy need be supplied. This will not usually be the case for creditors and owners do not normally sign the agreement before the debtor or hirer. Where the debtor or hirer's signature does not execute the agreement, the debtor or hirer must be given a copy of the agreement when it is either presented for signature or sent to them. A copy of the executed agreement, after signature by the creditor or owner, must then be given to the debtor or hirer within seven days of the agreement being concluded.[91]

Special provisions relate to cancellable agreements.[92] These require that where a second copy is needed this must be sent by post. Where no second copy is required, a notice of cancellation must be sent by post within seven days of the conclusion of the agreement. The Act attempts to alert consumers to the right of cancellation by the copies of the agreement and notices having to contain a box with information on the right of cancellation, how and when that right is exercisable and the name and address of a person on whom notice of cancellation may be served. In addition, the second copy or notice of cancellation rights must contain a cancellation form which the debtor or hirer can use to facilitate cancelling the agreement. The provision of a form can be seen as a useful facilitative technique to assist consumers and it is perhaps surprising such a requirement is not found in all cancellation provisions beyond the credit context.

---

88   Named after the US Senator who instigated their use in US Truth and Lending legislation.

89   See www.apacs.org.uk, Press Release 8 October 2003.

90   The copy provisions are to be found in ss. 62–64 of the CCA 1974 and Consumer Credit (Cancellation Notices and Copies of Documents) Regulations 1983, S.I. 1983/1557.

91   Section 189(1), CCA 1974 provides that 'give' means to deliver or send by post.

92   See Chapter 7.8.

6.5.4 Form Requirements and Contracting on the Internet

Several of the formal requirements pose problems for consumer credit contracting on the Internet. For instance, whilst English law is usually very flexible as to what constitutes a signature, the Agreements Regulations 1983 is very specific by requiring the signature be within a specified signature box. Moreover, where notices have to be posted this can clearly not be effected electronically. The government is proposing to liberalise the laws to make it possible to contract for consumer credit electronically, although it is likely that old-fashioned paper communication will still be needed for cancellation and default notices.[93]

6.5.5 Enforcement of Improperly Executed Agreements

If the form and content of an agreement or notice are incorrect or the copy or notice provisions have not been complied with, then the agreement is said to be 'improperly executed'. This means that it is only enforceable against the debtor or hirer by order of the court.[94] Enforcement includes retaking goods or land to which a regulated agreement relates.[95]

A general weakness of the enforcement powers of the CCA 1974 is evident in the rule contained in s. 170(1) that a breach of any requirement made by or under the Act shall incur no civil or criminal sanction, except to the extent (if any) expressly provided for by or under the Act.[96] Thus save for exceptional cases, such as protected goods under hire-purchase contracts,[97] if a contract is enforced without a court order, there is no effective sanction save for reporting the matter to the licensing authorities. This is unless some breach of the debtor or hirer's legal rights can be established, such as an action for breach of the implied warranty of quiet possession[98] or an action in trespass or conversion. Equally it is possible to use other criminal laws where prosecution does not depend upon a breach

---

[93] *A Consultation Document on Enabling and Facilitating the Conclusion of Credit and Hire Agreements Electronically Under the Consumer Credit Act 1974* (DTI, 2002) and Establishing a Transparent Market, at pp. 26–29 (DTI, 2003).

[94] Section 65, CCA 1974. Note the agreement is not void or illegal – merely not enforceable. Thus the consumer can still sue on the agreement if goods or services supplied are defective.

[95] Section 65 (2), CCA 1974.

[96] This is perhaps a reaction against some of the technical defences which were raised by debtors under the previous laws: see *Crowther, op. cit.,* at pp. 310–13.

[97] See Chapter 7.13.3.

[98] E.g. s. 12(2)(b), Sale of Goods Act 1979.

of the Act.[99] Where the only illegality is the enforcement of the contract in breach of the Act, the suggestion has been made that a mandatory injunction could be applied for to restore the status quo.[100] Nevertheless, the sanctions for infringing the Act's provisions remain weak and at best obscure.

A further weakness in the regulatory regime established by the CCA 1974 is that the requirement to obtain a court order (or where appropriate an order by the Director-General) before taking certain steps is waved if the debtor or hirer consents at the time the action is taken. The consent must be at the time the action is taken and so a clause giving consent in advance could not, for instance, be included in the credit agreement.[101]

However, assuming reputable creditors would only enforce the agreement after obtaining a court order, it is important to consider the court's powers. The court can dismiss an application to enforce the agreement, but only if it considers it just to do so. In making this assessment, the court must take into account the degree of culpability, the prejudice caused and its own powers to do justice.[102] These include both the specific power to make an enforcement order which reduces or discharges a sum payable by the debtor, hirer or their surety in order to compensate for the prejudice suffered,[103] and the court's general powers to impose conditions on or suspend the operation of orders, or its powers to amend agreements.[104]

There are three circumstances in which the court cannot make an enforcement order:

1. Where a document in the prescribed form containing the prescribed terms has not been signed by both parties. Where a debtor or hirer signed a document containing all the prescribed terms, even if it was not in the prescribed form, then the court has the discretion to allow the agreement to be enforced, but can direct that it is to have effect as

---

[99]   See, *R v Kettering Magistrates' Court, ex parte MRB Insurance Brokers Ltd*, 2000 Lawtel, where a wrongly stated APR was upheld as a misleading price indication, under s. 20 Consumer Protection Act 1987 as the offence did not depend on the agreement being regulated or failure to comply with the statutory requirements.

[100] R. Lowe and G. Woodroffe, *Consumer Law and Practice*, (3rd ed.) (Sweet & Maxwell, 1991) at p. 323. Indeed s. 170(3), CCA 1974 expressly states that s. 170(1) does not prevent the grant of an injunction or the making of an order of certiorari, mandamus or prohibition.

[101] Section 173(3), CCA 1974.

[102] Section 127, CCA 1974.

[103] Section 127(2), CCA 1974.

[104] Sections 135–6, CCA 1974.

if it did not include a term omitted from the document signed by the debtor or hirer.[105]

2. If any of the copy provisions have not been complied with and the creditor or owner has not given the debtor or hirer a copy of the executed agreement and any documents referred to in it prior to the commencement of proceedings.[106] This is not very protective, however, since a creditor or owner only has to provide the relevant documents at any time prior to the commencement of proceedings and an enforcement order can be made.

3. Where a notice of cancellation rights has not been provided.[107] This is the most significant of the restrictions on the court's powers to enforce improperly executed agreements and emphasises the importance of the cancellation provisions.

Circumstance 1, above, has been the subject of much recent litigation. It was the subject of a particularly audacious, but unsuccessful, attempt to render an agreement unenforceable on the grounds that the creditor had failed to put down as one of its terms the fact it was willing to compromise its enforcement of the agreement.[108] It also led to a declaration of incompatability with the Human Rights Act 1998 by the Court of Appeal,[109] when Mrs Wilson borrowed £5,000 at an APR of 94.7 per cent pawning her BMW car as security. She was charged a £250 'documents fee'. This was added to her loan by the finance company, which treated the loan as being for £5,250. This was found to be wrong under the Regulations with the consequence that one of the prescribed terms, the credit, was wrongly stated. This meant the agreement was unenforceable. Mrs Wilson could get her car back, keep the £5,000 and did not have to make any repayments. The Court of Appeal were understandably disturbed that the Act gave them no discretion to intervene to do justice and found the credit company's rights had been infringed under the European Convention for the Protection of Human Rights and Fundamental Freedoms Art. 6 (right to a fair trial) and Art. 1 of First Protocol (peaceful enjoyment of possessions). The House of Lords took a more robust approach and was unwilling to intervene with Parliament's chosen way of dealing with a social policy issue.[110] This is a good example of the trend

---

105   Sections 127(3)(5), CCA 1974. The prescribed terms are to be found in Schedule 6 of the Consumer Credit (Agreements) Regulations 1983, S.I. 1983/1553.

106   Section 127(4)(a), CCA 1974.

107   Section 127(4)(b), CCA 1974.

108   *Broadwick Financial Services Ltd v Spencer* [2002] EWCA Civ. 35.

109   [2001] 3 WLR 42.

110   It also found the rules on unjust enrichment could not assist the finance company as this would contradict the statutory intention.

we identified in Chapter 1[111] of the Courts being resistant to attempts to use Human Rights legislation to challenge legislation designed to address a particular social ill. Nevertheless, the case served the useful function of focussing attention on whether the enforcement regime established continued to be appropriate. Indeed their Lordships noted that it might not be once the £25,000 ceiling was lifted. That point is perhaps a little misguided as the impact on credit companies can be very severe, even for loans less than £25,000. The company could have – and most probably has – made the same mistake in many of its contracts and thus rendered them all unenforceable. In any event, in the White Paper Government says it is looking to find a more proportionate approach to enforcement once the financial limit is removed.

A final comment should perhaps be made on the emphasis placed by the CCA 1974 on the duties to supply copy documents and cancellation notices.[112] It is estimated that 39 per cent of borrowers only read the main information on the front page of agreements.[113] 56 per cent of consumers do not understand the terms used on credit agreements.[114] Criticisms have been also been made that such rules do not really help lower-income groups and ethnic minorities, who are more likely not to comprehend the document. This does not mean that information rules should not be available to protect consumers. It may mean though that the limits of protection through information provisions need to be recognised and seen as merely part of a package of protective measures, alongside licensing provisions, controls over terms and creditor remedies and the creation of alternative forms of social credit.

Techniques such as bringing all the financial information together in one place and the use of a cancellation form attempt to make the provisions as consumer friendly as practicable. Of course, being given a copy of the agreement does not help to improve its terms (except to the limited extent that creditors may be too embarrassed to put unconscionable terms down on paper), which is why it is important that consumers be given time to reflect on the commitments they have entered into. However, the cancellation provisions do not apply to all credit contracts.

6.6 WITHDRAWAL

Consumers frequently enter into credit agreements which they later regret. It is worth remembering that, on ordinary contract principles, a consumer

---

[111] See Chapter 1.9.3.
[112] Cf. discussion of information provisions at 1.8.3.
[113] White Paper, *op. cit.*, at p. 33.
[114] *Ibid.*, at p. 19.

can revoke an offer at any time until it has been accepted by the other party. Thus, as in most instances it is the consumer who fills in the application form and waits to hear if the creditor accepts the offer, the consumer is free to revoke his or her offer until the time of acceptance. It is as well to remember that the basic common law rules provide that acceptance is completed when posted (assuming the post to be an acceptable means of communication) so that any revocation would have to reach the other party before that time.

The CCA 1974 improves the position of the consumer who wishes to withdraw his or her offer to enter into a regulated consumer credit or consumer hire agreement[115] by extending the range of persons on whom notice of withdrawal can be served. In addition to the creditor or owner, notice can also be given to those persons deemed to be their agent. This can be either a credit broker or supplier who was a negotiator in antecedent negotiations or, most importantly, any person who, in the course of a business, acted on behalf of the debtor or hirer in any negotiations for the agreement. Thus, if a solicitor arranges a loan, it is sufficient to communicate notice of withdrawal to him or her. Notice of withdrawal, must in accordance with general contract principles, be communicated to the other party and if posted only becomes effective on receipt. The notice can be oral or written and need not state that it is a notice of withdrawal, so long as it indicates an intention to withdraw from a prospective regulated agreement.

Withdrawal from a regulated agreement will have the same effects as if the agreement had been cancelled. Consumers are further protected by the provision, in s. 59, CCA 1974, which makes agreements void to the extent that they seek to bind a person to enter into a prospective regulated agreement.

6.7 RESCISSION AND REPUDIATION

Where a debtor or hirer is no longer able to withdraw from a contract, they may wish to consider whether there are any circumstances, such as misrepresentation, which might allow them to rescind the contract, or if there has been any breach of contract which would allow them to repudiate it. The Act again extends consumer protection by allowing notice of rescission to be given to the extended category of persons on whom notice of withdrawal could be given.[116]

---

[115] Section 57, CCA 1974.
[116] Section 102, CCA 1974.

6.8 CANCELLATION

Some of the most significant consumer protection measures relate to cancellation rights. The CCA 1974 gives consumers who enter into certain credit contracts a period of time in which to reflect on the agreement and to cancel it if they do not want to proceed. Typically this will apply to debtor-creditor-supplier agreements entered into in the consumer's home. Cooling-off periods of this type attempt to protect individuals against high-pressure sales techniques and also to provide consumers with information and time to consider whether the product or service suits their needs. Doorstep sales are concluded in circumstances where it was not possible to compare the product or service against those offered by competitors.

Concern to protect consumers, who enter into contracts on the doorstep, is also evidenced by the Consumer Protection (Cancellation of Contracts Concluded away from Business Premises) Regulations.[117] To avoid confusion between those Regulations and the cancellation rules for credit contracts, the former do not apply to contracts which are cancellable under the CCA 1974.[118]

Confusion continues to exist between the seven day cooling-off period from the date of the conclusion of the contract in doorstep sales and the cooling-off period in consumer credit contracts. For the latter, the period can range between six and 12 days, or even longer depending upon when the formalities were carried out and the efficiency of the postal service. Now the Distance Selling of Financial Services Directive has introduced a 14 day cooling off period. It has been suggested that this might become a common cooling-off period of 14 days and that this be extended to all consumer credit contracts as has been proposed by the EC.[119] However, such a blanket right to cancel would have to be subject to some exceptions. Traders might react by not supplying goods until the cancellation period has expired and so one might think of circumstances where consumers should be able to waive their right to cancel in return for immediate access to goods or services.[120]

---

[117] S.I. 1987/2117: see Chapter 7.2.

[118] *Ibid.*, Regulation 4(2).

[119] *A Consultation Document on Enabling and Facilitating the Conclusion of Credit and Hire Agreements Electronically Under the Consumer Credit Act 1974* (DTI, 2002).

[120] A similar compromise had been proposed by the DTI in its 1991 consultation document, *Revised Proposals for Legislation on Credit Marketing* (DTI, 1991) at pp. 3–4. It suggested that debtor-creditor-supplier agreements and hire agreements signed on trade premises following face-to-face negotiations should be cancellable. To counter objections that this would harm the consumer interest (as consumers would probably not be allowed to take goods home with them straight away), it was proposed to give consumers the right to contract out of the cancellation rights, although the

Terry Ison has made the provocative suggestion that some type of doorstep selling should be banned altogether, rather than simply be made subject to a cooling-off period.[121] He considers that cooling-off periods, with the requirement for the consumer to give notice of cancellation, can only protect fairly sophisticated consumers. Yet, many of the problems involving doorstep selling result from the targeting of low-income consumers who are unlikely to enforce their rights.[122] Ison therefore suggests a prohibition on itinerant salesmen who sell one type of item on credit terms or who require part-payment in advance.[123] This is radical, but we shall see there is already outright prohibition on unsolicited marketing of debtor-credit agreements off trade premises.[124] One problem with prohibitions is that they do not necessarily curb the practice, but simply force them underground. Ison's choice of contracts to be banned resulted from an empirical study of credit practices, which discovered that the incidence of problems experienced varied depending upon the nature of the seller. Nevertheless, it may be particularly difficult to enforce a prohibition that only applies to a class of sellers, because of definitional problems. For instance, an itinerant salesman selling only one product could easily circumvent the prohibition by giving the appearance of selling more than one type of item. On the other hand, selective prohibition might go some way to meet the objection that a blanket prohibition would simply disadvantage low-income consumers by reducing their choice or by forcing them to seek help on the black market. Possibly a more acceptable way of removing creditors who indulge in bad practices would be to strengthen the licensing system.[125] Making the licensing system more proactive would allow the authorities to stamp out bad traders, whilst allowing reputable traders to continue trading and thereby increasing consumer choice and allowing competition on a level playing field.

---

waiver of such rights would not be allowed as a condition of sale. The cancellation rights would be forfeited if the goods were not returned or were returned in a significantly worse condition.

[121] T. Ison, *Credit Marketing and Consumer Protection* (Croom Helm, 1979) at pp. 119–120.

[122] It might be objected that this is too paternalist an attitude and underestimates the ability of low-income consumers to look after their own interests. Whilst it is true that many low-income consumers are very astute purchasers, nevertheless they do seem less aware and/or willing to enforce their legal rights.

[123] Ison, *op. cit.*

[124] Section 49, CCA 1974: see Chapter 11.2.3.

[125] See Chapter 9.2. This may also be a function of a general duty to trade fairly: see Chapter 13.9.

6.8.1 Cancellable Agreements

For an agreement to be cancellable under the CCA 1974:

(i)   it must be a regulated agreement;
(ii) oral representations must have been made in the presence of the debtor or hirer by a person acting as, or on behalf of, the negotiator. The representations must be oral, not written, and must be made in the presence of the debtor or hirer, so that a telephone conversation would not be sufficient. There is no restriction as to where the oral representations were made – they need not have been made in the consumer's home and could, for instance, be made at the creditor's office so long as the agreement was subsequently signed by the debtor off trade premises. Nor is there any restriction on when they were made – they need not be made at the same time as the contract was signed;
(iii) the unexecuted agreement must be signed by the debtor or hirer off trade premises. This means not at the permanent or temporary business premises of the creditor or owner, or of any party to a linked transaction or of the negotiator in antecedent negotiations. A cancellable agreement could be even signed at the debtor or hirer's business premises or in the street, but normally would be signed at the debtor or hirer's home.[126]

Certain agreements are exempted from the cancellation provisions notably, (i) non-commercial agreements, (ii) 'small' debtor-creditor-supplier agreements for restricted-use credit, (iii) certain agreements relating to land, (iv) overdraft agreements and (v) debtor-creditor agreements relating to payments to be made in connection with, or arising on, the death of a person.

6.8.2 How and When Can an Agreement be Cancelled?

The debtor or hirer can cancel the agreement at any time after the unexecuted agreement is signed by them up until the end of the fifth day following receipt of the second copy of the agreement or the notice of cancellation.[127] The cancellation period therefore expires five days after the second copy or notice was received and not five days after it was sent.

What then is the position if the notice is lost in the post? Can the cancellation period continue indefinitely? This would appear absurd, but

---

[126]   Section 67, CCA 1974.
[127]   Section 68(a), CCA 1974.

could be the case if the Act were applied strictly. If the creditor or owner is unable to post a replacement copy within the prescribed seven-day period, then the replacement cannot properly be said to have been posted 'under' the Act. The courts are unlikely to see any advantage in penalising the genuine creditor or owner in this way, especially as the Act mandates use of the post; rather, they are likely to find that the cancellation period expired at the end of the fifth day following receipt of the replacement copy.

Another interesting scenario would arise if the second notice were posted outside the prescribed seven-day period. The courts could be equally sympathetic and treat the cancellation period as starting from receipt of the late copy or notice, since it could be argued that the consumer has not been disadvantaged in any way. They may, however, wish to be less lenient in such circumstances for the creditor or owner can be considered in some sense blameworthy. Moreover, since the agreement has not been properly executed, it is unenforceable: as stated previously, failure to comply with the cancellation notice provisions is one of the situations in which the courts are absolutely barred from making an enforcement order. There may also be sound policy grounds for not permitting late copies to be sent. Once the agreement has been running for some time, consumers may find it psychologically harder to cancel an agreement and feel morally bound to honour agreements if they have enjoyed substantial use of the product.

Cancellation can be effected by serving a written notice. This notice can be the form included in the second copy or notice sent to the debtor or hirer; but, equally, it can be in any form so long as it indicates the intention to cancel the agreement. The written notice must be served on any of the following:

(i)   the creditor or owner,
(ii)   any person named in the notice of cancellation rights as being a person on whom such notice can be served,
(iii) the agent of the creditor or owner, who, as with the right of withdrawal, is given an extended definition.[128]

The notice must be served on the other party. It need not be posted, but there is a decided advantage to posting it, for the notice is deemed to have been served at the time of posting. Therefore a notice of cancellation posted one minute before the expiry of a cooling-off period will be

---

[128] Section 69(6), CCA 1974: see Chapter 6.6 for a discussion of those who are deemed to be the agent of the creditor or owner. Note this includes those who are the debtor or hirer's agent, but this category of deemed agent cannot be used for all subsequent functions.

effective, even though it could not possibly have been received within the permitted time. Indeed, it would seem to be effective even if never received. Equally, it would not appear possible to withdraw a notice of cancellation once posted.

6.8.3 Effects of Cancellation

Cancellation has the effect that the agreement and most linked transactions[129] are treated as if they had never been entered into. Moreover, any offer by the debtor/hirer or their relative to enter into a linked transaction is withdrawn. Any sums paid are to be repaid on cancellation and any sums which would have become payable cease to be payable.[130] Normally the sums are repayable by the person to whom the money was paid, except in the case of debtor-creditor-supplier agreements for restricted-use credit where the creditor and supplier are jointly liable. The debtor or hirer or (where relevant) their relative, has a lien over goods in their possession supplied under the cancelled agreement, in respect of sums which are repayable.

Where there is a debtor-creditor-supplier agreement for restricted-use credit, a consumer hire agreement or a linked transaction (so that a supply contract is also cancelled), the debtor or hirer is under a duty to return the goods subject to any lien he or she may have over them.[131] The debtor or hirer has a duty to retain possession of the goods and take reasonable care of them for a 21 day period from the date of cancellation. However, this period is extended if a request to deliver the goods was received, which the debtor or hirer has either unreasonably refused or unreasonably failed to comply with. However, the duty is only to deliver the goods at the possessor's own premises; there must have been a written signed request served either before or at the time the goods were collected. The duty to take care of the goods can be brought to an end at any time by delivering them to a person on whom notice of cancellation could have been served (other than to a person who was the deemed agent of the debtor or hirer) or by sending the goods at the debtor or hirer's own expense to such a person. If the goods are sent to the other party, reasonable care must be taken to ensure that they are received by the other party and are not damaged in transit. This presumably requires the use of a reputable carrier under conditions of carriage appropriate for the type of goods involved.

---

129 Some are saved by the Consumer Credit (Linked Transactions) (Exemptions) Regulations 1983, S.I 1983/1560.

130 Section 70, CCA 1974.

131 Section 72, CCA 1974.

Breach of the duty to return the goods is actionable as a breach of statutory duty. However, in the following four circumstances the duty to return the goods does not apply. Special rules apply both to goods supplied in emergencies and to goods incorporated into land or some other thing prior to cancellation. Imposing the full effects of cancellation would be particularly unfair on a supplier who had supplied goods in an emergency or where the goods had been incorporated into something else. In such cases it is provided that, where the goods were supplied under a debtor-creditor-supplier agreement for restricted-use credit, only the credit part of the agreement is cancelled, with the debtor having a continued liability to pay for the goods supplied. Also, for obvious reasons, there is no duty to return perishable goods or goods which by their nature are consumed and which were so consumed before cancellation. Although understandable, these provisions could allow consumers a rare opportunity to have their cake and eat it without paying for it. Cautious sellers will not supply such goods until the cancellation period has expired.

Where a negotiator[132] agreed to take goods in part-exchange under a regulated agreement and the goods have been delivered to him or her, then, unless the goods are returned within ten days of cancellation, in substantially the same condition as when delivered, the debtor or hirer is entitled to a sum equal to the part exchange allowance.[133] The sum will be either that agreed or, if no figure were agreed, then an amount it would have been reasonable to allow. Until repaid, the debtor or hirer has a lien on goods supplied under the cancelled agreement.

Unless the effects of cancellation are modified, possible injustices could arise where credit has been advanced under the agreement before cancellation occurs. Debtors might seek to hide behind the rule that any sums payable cease to be payable in order to avoid returning any advance. The Act has special provisions to deal with this situation.[134] If an agreement (other than a debtor-credit-supplier agreement for restricted-use credit)[135] is cancelled the agreement shall continue in force so far as it relates to repayment of credit and payment of interest. No interest is payable on amounts repaid within one month of the service of the notice of cancellation or, in the case of credit repayable by instalments, on amounts repaid before the date on which the first instalment is due. The debtor has the option of repaying the whole amount or just a portion without attracting

---

132 Section 56(1), CCA 1974 provides that this includes the creditor, owner, credit-broker and suppliers in three-party debtor-creditor-supplier agreements who conduct negotiations with the debtor or hirer.

133 Section 73, CCA 1974.

134 Section 71, CCA 1974.

135 The problem does not arise in debtor-creditor-supplier for restricted-use credit as the money would have been paid to the supplier rather than directly to the debtor.

interest on the amount repaid. Repayment can be made to any person on whom notice of cancellation could have been served, except those who had acted on behalf of the debtor. In the case of credit repayable by instalments the debtor, who has not repaid the whole amount outstanding, is still not liable to repay any credit until a written request stating the amount of the remaining instalments is received. The instalments should only include sums in respect of the principal and interest. The creditor must recalculate the instalments as nearly as possible in accordance with the agreement without extending the repayment period.

The rules restricting the manner of rescheduling give rise to some difficult questions of interpretation. For instance, does the repayment period, which must not be extended, refer to a fixed date or to a period of time? If the former, then the instalments may be larger than under the original agreement. Furthermore, should the creditor try to make the instalments as close as possible in size to those under the original agreement, or should the objective be to provide that the APR of the rescheduled agreement is equivalent to that of the original?

No notice need be sent where the credit is repayable otherwise than by instalment. Such agreements continue in force in so far as they relate to the duty to repay the principal and interest.

6.9 TERMINATION

The CCA 1974 gives debtors the right to terminate hire-purchase or conditional-sale agreements[136] and hirers the right to terminate hire agreements.[137] Termination can be effected by giving written notice to anyone entitled or authorised to receive payments. This may be a useful option when the consumer cannot continue to meet his obligations. The effects of termination, however, are only prospective, with the effect that arrears and any contractual liabilities are not affected by it. In addition, unless the contract provides for a lesser amount, on termination of a hire-purchase or conditional sale agreement, the amount paid under the agreement must be made up to half of the total price. Where the total price includes an installation charge, then the amount to be paid is that charge plus one-half of the remainder. The court can order payment of a lesser amount if it considers that it would adequately compensate the creditor for the loss caused by the termination. Thus in some cases the debtor may be well advised to tender a figure below half the total price, if the goods still retain sufficient value so that the creditor would be adequately compensated by their return and the amount tendered. The amount payable

---

[136] Sections 99–100.
[137] Section 101.

by the debtor can be increased by the court to take account of loss caused to the creditor resulting from the debtor's breach of the obligation to take reasonable care of the goods. If the debtor wrongfully retains goods after the agreement has been terminated the court must order the goods to be returned, unless it considers that, in the circumstances, it would not be just to do so. The court also has powers to make return and transfer orders.[138]

Consumer hire agreements cannot be terminated until 18 months of the agreement have elapsed; the court has no discretion to reduce this period. Notice must be given. The notice period will usually be equal to the shortest payment period under the agreement, unless the agreement provides for a shorter period. In any event the notice period cannot be longer than three months. The right to terminate does not apply if, *inter alia*, (i) the agreement requires payments in excess of £1,500 each year, or (ii) the agreement relates to goods hired for the hirer's business, which have been selected by the hirer and acquired by the owner at the hirer's request, from a person other than an associate of the owner, or (iii) the goods are let for the purpose of releasing in the course of the hirer's business.

6.10 EARLY SETTLEMENT AND REBATE

Where the debtor has paid a large portion of the total price and the goods still retain some value, then, rather than terminate the agreement, the debtor may find it more beneficial to exercise the right to complete payments ahead of time, take advantage of the statutory rebate for early settlement and then resell the goods or alternatively find a cheaper source of finance.[139] To exercise the statutory right of early repayment,[140] the debtor must give the creditor written notice and tender all amounts payable under the agreement, less the statutory rebate. The debtor can make a written request for the creditor to inform him of the amount which must be paid to discharge his indebtedness.[141]

The rebate is calculated in accordance with Consumer Credit (Rebate on Early Settlement) Regulations.[142] These Regulations are excessively complex, containing five different formulae to calculate the rebate depending upon the repayment provisions and the settlement arrangements. For instance, where credit is repaid by equal instalments the 'rule of 78'

---

[138] See Chapter 7.14.2.
[139] Sections 94–7, CCA 1974.
[140] There is a common law right to pay debts ahead of time, but this does not carry with it the advantage of a rebate.
[141] See Consumer Credit (Settlement Information) Regulations 1983, S.I. 1983/1564.
[142] S.I. 1983/1562.00

applies. This rule derives from the fact that a loan for a year with 12 equal instalments can be analysed as a series of 12 reducing monthly loans: its name results from the fact that the sum of 12 months is 78 (i.e. 1+2+3+4+5+6+7+8+9+10+11+12=78). Although the formulae are complicated, the policy underlying them is to provide a fair balance between creditor and debtor and, in particular, to recognise that the creditor incurs set-up costs and the bulk of administrative expenses at the start of the loan.

In the recent reviews of consumer credit the early settlement rules were seen as one aspect of the consumer credit laws that impacted unfairly on consumers.[143] It is estimated that a remarkable 70 per cent of unsecured loans will be repaid early. It is proposed to make the rules fairer by replacing the Rule of 78 with a new fairer actuarial formula. The Rule of 78 was favoured in pre-computer days as it was relatively easy to work out, but increasing computing power has made more sophisticated models practical. Lenders will be allowed to postpone the settlement date for 28 days to allow processing of the final payment and to recover one months interest over and above the settlement figure for loans of more than one year as a contribution towards their costs. Information will also play a role, as lenders will be required to provide examples of early settlement figures as part of the agreement package to be considered before signing.

6.11 CONNECTED LENDER LIABILITY

6.11.1 Policy

Section 75, CCA 1974 introduced an important consumer protection measure in the form of connected lender liability. This involves making the creditor jointly liable with the supplier for the quality of goods and services. Crowther had set out the rationales for imposing this liability on financiers.[144] Lenders, who offer suppliers business and financial inducements to make misrepresentations about goods or to supply defective goods, should not be able to simply walk away from the problems the consumer is left with. Equally a customer in dispute would find it easier if the credit commitments relating to the goods were removed, especially if such goods were sold as a means to help the person produce income, as for example was the case with knitting machines. Connected lender liability also removes the need for consumers to have to mobilise

---

[143] *A consultation document on the early settlement of credit agreements under the Consumer Credit Act 1974* (DTI, 2002), *White Paper, op cit.*, at pp. 39–40, and *Establishing a Transparent Market 6–10.*

[144] *Op. cit.*, at paras. 6.6.24–31.

their resources and energies to mount a legal action: they can simply default on the loan, wait to be sued and raise s. 75 as a defence.

6.11.2 Credit Cards

The connected lender liability provisions highlight the fact that Crowther and the subsequent CCA 1974 were a response to the needs of the time and dealt with market conditions as they existed some three decades ago when credit cards were just beginning to be marketed. The connected lender liability rules were principally aimed at the bad marketing practices current at that time. Central heating installations were a particular problem since some suppliers went insolvent before installation, leaving consumers with no heating but large debts. In more recent times one could draw parallels with the double-glazing or timeshare industries. In addition to the large number of consumer complaints, the common feature is that the supplier and creditor have close business relations. Indeed s. 75 seems to require that there be a close relationship before the connected lender liability bites: thus it only applies to three party debtor-creditor-supplier agreements.

Credit card agreements can fall within the scope of s. 75[145] and yet there is not the same intimate connection between most credit card companies and the businesses they offer their facilities to.[146] The link between card issuer and supplier has become even more attenuated with the growth in overseas use of cards and with competition rules which require card issuers to honour purchases made by any supplier bearing their card's logo – i.e. Mastercard or Visa – even if that supplier was recruited by a different merchant acquirer.[147] There is no doubt that many

---

[145] Although note that charge cards, where the balance has to be paid off in one instalment (such as American Express and Diners Club) are not covered as they are exempt agreements. Also note that debit cards, which electronically transfer funds from a current account in a bank, are now also expressly excluded: see s. 187(3A), CCA 1974.

[146] Both *Crowther, op. cit.*, at paras. 6.12.1–12 and the White Paper *Reform of the Law on Consumer Credit, op. cit.*, at para. 75 recognised that credit cards would be caught by the provisions, but considered that the same basic conditions applied as when a trader offered hire-purchase or personal loan facilities. Note that s. 75 would not apply to hire-purchase agreements since there the goods are first sold to the finance company who then acts as creditor and supplier of the goods.

[147] Typically, when a credit card purchase is made, the supplier sends the voucher to a merchant acquirer who pays him the amount less a Merchant Service Charge (typically 1.6 per cent). The merchant acquirer is in turn reimbursed by the card issuer minus an Interchange fee (typically 1 per cent) and the issuer then sends a statement to the consumer for payment. For a legal analysis of the relationships created by a credit

consumers have benefited from the protection they derive from having purchased their defective goods or services with the use of a credit card. This has been particularly noticeable in the case of holiday company and airline collapses.[148] But the question remains, whether credit card companies should be forced to act as insurer in this way? It certainly seems to be a rather *ad hoc* response. Compensation depends upon the chance of whether a credit card was used to effect the purchase. It also forces the cost of individual consumer's purchasing choices to be borne by all users of the credit facility. One might guess that the benefits of connected lender liability are more likely to be known of and used by better educated and prosperous credit card holders. Indeed many poorer consumers will not have access to credit card facilities at all. It might be better to ensure proper compensation is received from suppliers or, where they have become insolvent, from compensation funds. For instance bonding schemes such as that operated in the holiday industry by ABTA and the proposals contained in the EC distant selling Recommendation[149] might provide a fairer way forward. Absent such reforms, one might be tempted to view connected lender liability for credit card companies as a second best solution.

Even if it is considered unfair to impose connected lender liability on all credit card companies, there would be difficulty in differentiating between those lenders who do have a special relationship with the supplier and can therefore legitimately be expected to have responsibility for the quality of goods, and credit supplied by credit card companies with less close connections. Simply excluding debtor-creditor-supplier agreements which involve a credit-token would not work, for one can easily imagine a proliferation of finance companies issuing cards, as indeed many already

---

card, see *Re Charge Card Services Ltd* [1988] 3 All ER 702 (although note that that scheme did not involve a merchant acquirer). *Re Charge Services Ltd* involved a credit card for fuel and the litigation arose when the credit card company went into liquidation. The litigation was between the garages and the company to whom the credit card company had factored its debts. The court found that three separate bilateral contracts were created – between the credit company and supplier, the credit company and cardholder and the cardholder and supplier. The garage's acceptance of payment by the card was an unconditional acceptance of payment of the price; the cardholder was therefore only obliged to repay the credit company, regardless of whether the supplier had been reimbursed.

148 Although it should be noted that some credit card companies are questioning whether they always have liability for travel firm collapses. If the contract was with the travel agent and the agent performed its part of the bargain (for example, by delivering the tickets) it is argued that the supplier has not breached its contract even if the travel company supplying the service subsequently goes out of business.

149 OJ 1992 L156/21.

do. It may be possible to exclude agreements where the token is capable of obtaining both cash and goods and can be used when purchasing from more than a prescribed number of firms, but this number would have to be sufficiently large so as to exclude retail group cards. It has been suggested that a similar result is achieved by Art. 11(2)(b) of the EC Directive on consumer credit. This article requires that, in order for connected lender liability to apply, 'the grantor of the credit and the supplier of the goods or services have a pre-existing agreement whereunder credit is made available exclusively by that grantor of credit to customers of that supplier for the acquisition of goods and services from that supplier'. It is argued that the word *exclusively* precludes the provision applying to credit cards. Indeed if the provision were given a very literal interpretation, it would require that the creditor only supplied financial services to that particular supplier and no one else. What is clear is that Art. 11 is badly drafted and, perhaps, this supports the view that making such a distinction will inevitably be very difficult. In any event the OFT favours retaining the liability of credit card companies, arguing that they should have some incentive to control those who join their networks and that they are in practice exposed to very little liability due to their right to join suppliers as defendants and claim an indemnity.[150] The claim-back procedures of the various international networks should allow the claim to be traced back to the merchant acquirer and eventually to the responsible trader through accounting procedures.[151] The OFT is currently bringing a declaratory action to try to clarify whether s. 75 apples to credit card transactions, particularly when they are used overseas.[152] The outcome of this litigation is awaited with interest, for although there are complex issues in relating the provisions to credit cards, equally, the right to look to your credit card for compensation is well known and well liked by consumers and provides an effective and practical means of consumer redress.

In its *Connected Lender Liability* report the OFT promised to consider whether the liability of credit card issuers should be 'second in line liability' i.e. only arising when the supplier could not satisfy the claim (which is the basis of connected lender liability under the EC Directive).

---

[150] Sections 75(2) and (5), CCA 1974. It does not apply to debit cards which simply arrange for the electronic transfer of funds from a bank current account: s. 187(3A), CCA 1974.

[151] *Connected Lender Liability*, (OFT, 1994).

[152] In *Jarrett v Barclays Bank* (1997) 2 All ER 484 the Court of Appeal had no problems in finding it had jurisdiction to hear claims brought under s. 75 with respect to timeshares situated in Spain and Portugal. The claim was based on s. 75 and not the interest in the property and so Art. 16 of the Brussels Convention giving jurisdiction to the courts of the place where the land is situated did not apply.

After consultation this approach was rejected.[153] The OFT did, however, propose to help credit card issuers by limiting their liability to the amount of credit loaned and giving them subrogation rights against insurers or bond administrators.[154] Once the principle of liability is accepted the limitation of the amount seems no more justifiable for card issuers than any other creditor. On the other hand the right of subrogation against, for instance, travel industry bonding schemes, does seem fair since it places the burden of default on the industry responsible for the loss. It is perhaps surprising that connected lender liability has not featured in the recent discussions concerning reform of the CCA 1974.

6.11.3 Section 75

Section 75 applies to three-party debtor-creditor-supplier agreements. In common language loans to purchase goods where the creditor and supplier are different persons.[155] The effect of the section is to give the debtor who has any claim against the supplier in respect of a misrepresentation or breach of contract a like claim against the creditor.[156] This section applies even if the transaction may have breached an agreement with the creditor, for example, by exceeding a credit limit.[157]

The importance of s. 75 is that it makes creditors liable for breach of implied terms, such as those relating to satisfactory quality and fitness for purpose. The use of the phrase 'like claim' has caused some uncertainty: why was the term 'like' used and not 'identical'? In the Scottish case of

---

[153] This was a correct conclusion for second in line liability would reduce the consumer's bargaining position, for it would be uncertain when the consumer had taken sufficient steps against a supplier and could legitimately turn to the creditor. This is particularly true of overseas transactions. Would a consumer have had to have attempted to bring a legal claim in an overseas jurisdiction?

[154] See *Connected Lender Liability* (OFT, 1995).

[155] Some credit card companies claim that liability does not attach to them for cards issued prior to the section coming into force on 1 July 1977, and the OFT seems to accept this point (*ibid.*, at p. 30). Therefore the companies are only willing to make *ex gratia* payments up to the amount charged to the account. However, this seems to miss the point that a debtor-creditor-supplier agreement can only come into place when the supplier is identified, namely when the purchase is made – which will be post 1 July 1977. There is clearly a need to distinguish the credit-token agreement from the agreements entered into using the credit-token.

[156] Unless the parties have agreed otherwise, the creditor has the right to be indemnified by the supplier.

[157] Section 75(4), CCA 1974.

United Dominions Trust Ltd v Taylor,[158] like claim was very broadly construed. Section 75 was used to allow a debtor to rescind a credit contract because of a breach of a term of the supply contract. This seems wrong since at the very least a like claim would appear to refer to a claim under the same contract.[159] The claim would, however, cover consequential damages, such as physical damage caused by dangerous products. To do justice credit charges incurred when buying defective goods and services ought to be recoverable as consequential damages, at least when goods are rejected.[160] A like claim has been said not to be an identical claim as remedies, such as injunctions and specific performance that might be available against the supplier, but would not be possible against a creditor.[161]

The claim would appear to cover the full extent of the debtor's loss even if only part of the agreement was financed by the debtor-creditor-supplier agreement. This point has become a real issue in the context of timeshares where perhaps only the deposit was paid using debtor-creditor-supplier finance.

Section 75 does not apply to all regulated agreements. In particular it does not apply to non-commercial agreements or to claims relating to a single item to which the supplier has attached a cash price that does not exceed £100 or which is more than £30,000. These monetary restrictions were introduced in the White Paper which preceded the Act, but their rationale was not explained.[162] The lower limit would seem to serve as a filter. For the sake of efficiency the policy appears to be not to make the creditor liable for minor losses. This may be reasonable, but as some products, such as hi-fi's, can be broken down into component parts to which a price of less than £100 could be attached, there is scope for

---

[158] 1980 SLT 28.

[159] A misrepresentation concerning the supply contract intended to induce a credit contract could however lead to rescission of the credit contract by virtue of s. 56: see Chapter 7.11.4

[160] Of course, the claim would then be a restitutionary claim and although not literally a claim for misrepresentation or breach of contract one suspects the courts would view it as covered by s. 75 since it arose out of a breach of contract. Other problems arise with respect to situations where only damages are being claimed for then, if the buyer is awarded damages to put him in the position he or she would have been in had the contract been properly performed, there would seem to be no need to upset the credit part of the transaction. Consumers may well feel aggrieved by this. Other solutions to this problem are discussed by P. Dobson, 'Consumer Credit – a Connected Lender Conundrum' [1981] *JBL* 179. The authors would like to thank Rob Bradgate for helpful discussions on this point.

[161] *Jarrett v Barclays Bank*, (1997) 2 All ER 484.

[162] *Reform of the Law on Consumer Credit, op. cit.*, at para. 78.

circumvention of the rules. Also goods of low value can give rise to large claims for consequential damages, if for instance they cause personal injury or death. The upper limit presumably reflects the fact that consumers, who purchase goods and services of significant value can be expected to make their own inquiries about the provider and not rely on any implicit approval of a creditor. Sensibly, and in contrast to the situation when determining whether an agreement is regulated, the exemption refers to the cash price and not the amount of finance. It has not been proposed to remove these limit.

6.11.4 Section 56

Where an agreement is excluded from s. 75, for instance, because the price of the goods falls outside the relevant financial limits (£100–£30,000), the debtor may still be able to make the creditor responsible for the goods or services supplied based on comments made during the negotiations. Section 56(2), CCA 1974 provides that certain negotiations with a debtor shall be deemed to be conducted by the negotiator as an agent of the creditor, as well as in his or her actual capacity. At common law a dealer is not held to be the agent of the hire-purchase company.[163] This provision can, of course, also be used in addition to s. 75.

The negotiator is the person who conducts 'antecedent negotiations' with the debtor or hirer.[164] This includes conduct of the creditor or owner or a credit broker conducting negotiations with a consumer prior to the broker selling the goods to a creditor, who then makes a two-party debtor-creditor-supplier agreement. An example is a car dealer who makes comments about a car before the car forms the basis of a hire-purchase deal between a finance company and the consumer. This provision is restricted to negotiations 'in relation to goods sold'. Cases have arisen where dealers have taken a car in part-exchange promising to pay off the outstanding credit, but have failed to do so. The credit company for the purchase of the new car tried to resist being liable for the outstanding finance, by claiming that they were only liable for the product sold i.e. the new car. However, the Court of Appeal has decided that the part-exchange and the purchase of

---

163 *Branwhite v Worcester Works Finance* [1968] 3 All ER 104. This was applied in the context of s. 56 in *Mynshul Asset Finance v Clarke (T/A Peacock Hotel)*, unreported, (although it is not clear that it was relevant since s. 56 is concerned with someone being deemed an agent, rather than actually being an agent), but was distinguished in *Woodchester Leasing Equipment v Clayton and Clayton* [1994] CL 72 as the thrust of the representations were to persuade the purchaser to lease rather than to buy outright.

164 Section 56(1), CCA 1974.

the new car should be viewed as one transaction to which s. 56 applies.[165] The negotiator as agent provision also covers antecedent negotiations made by suppliers who are party to a three-party debtor-creditor-supplier agreement.

The antecedent negotiations are taken to commence when the negotiator and the debtor or hirer first enter into communication and include any representations or other dealings between the parties. The breadth of this provision is indicated by the inclusion of advertisements as being an instance when the parties first enter into communication.[166]

Depending on the circumstances, statements made by the negotiator could either be actionable misrepresentations or form part of the terms of the contract. Section 56(2) is thus broader in the scope of contracts it covers than s. 75, which places financial limits on the price of the goods it relates to. Section 56(2) also covers statements made by credit-brokers prior to the consumer entering into a two-party debtor-creditor-supplier agreement. Significantly, however, s. 56, unlike s. 75, does not extend to imposing liability for breach of the implied terms.

Section 56(3) renders void agreements which seek to circumvent the provision of the section by making the negotiator the agent of the debtor or hirer or relieving the creditor of liability for the actions of his negotiator.

6.12 EXTORTIONATE CREDIT BARGAINS

6.12.1 Policy

One of the most controversial aspects of credit regulation is the question of whether there should be direct controls over interest rates. This debate is not about the regulation of high street credit, where the mass of the population might feel that the financial institutions could have more competitive interests rates. Equally we are not talking about illegal moneylenders who operate in an unlicensed manner and often use threatening tactics. This has been recognised as a separate, specific if as yet unquantified problem.[167] Rather the present debate centres on those marginal lenders who lend to low-income, and therefore generally high-risk, borrowers. Many such loans are entered into with doorstep collectors and can often have APRs of 100–500 per cent. Regulating such transactions gives rise to a moral quandary. The lenders may be able to show that they do not make excessive profits, when the high default rate and high collection costs (often door-to-door collections) are taken into

---

[165] *Forthright Finance v Ingate* (1997) 4 ALL ER 90.
[166] Section 56(4), CCA 1974.
[167] See Section 9.2.2.

account. Yet frequently such loans force debtors into a spiral of default as they are persuaded to take on roll-over loans to meet their commitments.[168] However, because the regulation of interest rates may have exclusionary or degenerative effects,[169] leaving the poor even worse off, policy formulations in this area need to be carefully thought through.[170] It is particularly important that reforms that might lead to a reduction in the amount of private sector finance available to poorer sectors of the community should take into account the need to develop social lending[171] and self-help schemes such as credit unions[172] to replace the private sector.

Most legal systems have some form of control on credit rates charged. The debate has largely centred on how stringent the controls should be and on whether the technique of control should involve an unconscionability standard (perhaps backed up by a presumption that loans above a certain level are unconscionable) or whether there should be a statutory ceiling on interest rates.[173] Commonwealth countries have tended to follow the unconscionability approach, whilst interest rate ceilings have been a feature of US credit laws and are to be found in France and Germany and other European countries. The Government has recognised the current controls are not working very effectively, but the White Paper stated it was as yet unconvinced by the case for interest rate ceilings.[174] There is some ambivalence on the part of policymakers as to whether they simply want to protect weak consumers from sharp practices or whether they want the law to have wider redistributive effects by challenging market-determined outcomes. Whilst there are signs the Government wants to get tougher with extortionate credit bargains, it is hesitant to bite the bullet and challenge market outcomes, preferring to fasten onto sharp practices as indications of market failure.

In the UK, the Moneylenders Act 1927 allowed the courts to re-open transactions which were harsh and unconscionable. There had been a *prima facie* presumption that interest rates in excess of 48 per cent were excessive and the transaction was therefore harsh and unconscionable. Crowther supported controls on credit costs saying that 'there is a level of

---

168 For a description of money-lending to low income consumers, see K. Rowlingson, *Moneylenders and their Customers, op. cit.*

169 See D. Cayne and M. Trebilcock, *op. cit.*

170 See G. Howells, 'Controlling Unjust Credit Transactions: Lessons from a Comparative Analysis' in G. Howells *et al., op. cit.*

171 See G. Howells, 'Social Fund Budgeting Loans – Social and Civil Justice?' (1990) *CJQ* 9.

172 See reference in note 20.

173 See G. Howells, 'Controlling Unjust Credit Transactions: Lessons from a Comparative Analysis' in G. Howells *et al., op. cit.*

174 *White Paper, op cit.,* at pp. 62–64.

cost above which it becomes socially harmful to make loans available at all'.[175] Yet, because of a fear that the maximum would become the norm and the problem of setting a maximum figure for loans of differing sizes and durations, Crowther preferred extending the provisions of the Moneylenders Act and imposing strict licensing controls rather than the introduction of ceilings. In the White Paper which followed, the Government came out in favour of extending the powers to re-open harsh and unconscionable agreements to all credit agreements, but did not favour the use of a presumption because of the wide variety of agreements involved.[176]

6.12.2 Present Controls

The present controls on extortionate credit bargains are to be found in ss. 137–140, CCA 1974.[177] The Act gives the courts the power to re-open extortionate credit bargains. These are agreements requiring the debtor or hirer to make payments which are 'grossly exorbitant' or 'otherwise contravene principles of fair dealing'. These provisions apply to all credit agreements and not just regulated agreements.

There is no level above which the interest rate is presumed to be exorbitant. The court is, however, directed to have regard to relevant circumstances and in particular to:

(i)   interest rates prevailing at the time the agreement was made;
(ii) the debtor's age, experience, business capacity and state of health and the degree and nature of any financial pressure he was under when making the credit bargain;
(iii) the degree of risk the creditor accepted having regard to any security, the creditor's relationship to the debtor and any colourable cash price quoted in relation to goods or services included in the credit bargain.

It is generally accepted that the extortionate credit bargain provisions have proved to be rather ineffectual and are in need of reform. There are only about 30 reported instances of the provisions being invoked and ten instances of the courts re-opening credit agreements.[178] This may

---

175   *Op. cit.*, at p. 275.
176   *Op. cit.*, at pp. 19–20.
177   It should not be forgotten than common law doctrines such as unconscionability, undue influence and economic duress may also be relevant.
178   Examples of the courts use of the power include: *Barcabe v Edwards* [1983] CCLR 11 (100 per cent reduced to 40 per cent); *Shahabini v Gyachi*, unreported, 1988 (156 per cent reduced to 15 per cent, increased on appeal to 30 per cent) concerning

underestimate the impact of the provisions. Creditors may have modified their charges so as not to fall foul of the provisions, while the threat of invoking the provisions may help in negotiations with creditors. There are, however, several reasons to suspect that empirical observations would not reveal the provisions having a strong influence on the conduct of creditors.

The drafting of the provisions indicates a greater concern for procedural than substantive justice. Thus the charging of 'grossly exorbitant' interest is simply viewed as one way of contravening the principles of fair dealing. However, procedural unfairness might not be enough by itself. In *Woodstead Finance v Petrou*[179] it was not held to be sufficient that the principles of fair dealing had been breached: there must also be a 'manifest disadvantage'. This seemed erroneously to import a requirement of the doctrine of undue influence into the statutory provisions.

The courts have declined to use the extortionate credit bargain provisions to challenge the market and have accepted its fragmentation into different sectors.[180] The courts have analysed the credit market as consisting of a number of markets for different categories of loan which tend to reflect different levels of risk. Therefore, the interest rates charged to high-risk or 'marginal' debtors are only compared to similar rates charged to equally high-risk or 'marginal' debtors.

Moreover, the courts have tended to accept the creditor's assessment of risk involved. Despite being directed to consider the value of security, the risk in *Ketley v Scott*[181] was described as 'considerable' and that in *Davies v Directloans*[182] to be of a 'high degree', despite the fact that the loans amounted to only 85 per cent and 83 per cent of the value of the respective securities. The courts have also been unsympathetic to the plight of debtors. Thus in *Wills v Wood*[183] the fact that the borrower was an old lady was not considered relevant as she was not an 'unworldly recluse' and in *Ketley v Scott*[184] a protected tenant, who was trying to purchase a house

---

unsecured loans and the following involving secured loans: *Devogate v Jarvis*, unreported, 1987 (39 per cent reduced to 30 per cent); *Prestonwell Ltd v Capon*, unreported, 1988 (42 per cent reduced to 21 per cent) and *Castle Phillips & Co v Wilkinson* [1992] CCLR 83 (four per cent per month reduced to 20 per cent per annum).

[179] *The Times*, 23 January 1986.

[180] See *Davies v Directloans* [1986] 1 WLR 823 where Nugee QC divided the market into banks, building societies, finance houses and secondary finance associations and accepted evidence of the interest charged in each.

[181] (1981) ICR 241.

[182] [1986] 1 WLR 823.

[183] *The Times*, 24 March 1984.

[184] (1981) ICR 241.

was not said to be under 'real' pressure as the transaction was of a speculative nature and there was no question of him being left homeless.

Perhaps, the biggest weakness of the extortionate credit bargain provisions is that the sanctions lack teeth. The interest rates charged must be grossly exorbitant to justify re-opening agreements; the court then has power to reduce the amount to that which is 'fairly due and reasonable'. In such cases, the courts have not been particularly harsh in their treatment of creditors, usually allowing interest to be charged at the top end of the range of what would be reasonable.[185] Even if the courts were tougher in their interpretation of what is fairly due and reasonable, simply to allow creditors to charge what would have been appropriate in the first place remains a weak sanction.

Finally, the courts have the discretion whether or not to re-open an extortionate credit bargain. According to some judicial utterances the courts would not have been prepared to re-open agreements, even if the bargain had been found to be extortionate, because of some fraud on the debtor's part. Again one sees the impact of equitable doctrines – such as 'he who comes to equity must come with clean hands' – on the statutory provision. Although there is some justification for the basic principle, it needs to be applied carefully and the naïve must not be confused with the truly fraudulent. For instance, one case involved a couple who stated 'we thought it was very funny to buy a house without having money'.[186] Although the debtors had some commercial motivation in entering the agreement, they also seem to be just the sort of people the law needs to protect from creditors and themselves.

Cases have come to court recently where it was attempted to argue that agreements were extortionate because of the way creditors had used their power to vary interest rates. However, it was held such post-contractual decisions could not be brought into the assessment of whether an agreement was extortionate. However, the case law more generally on variable interest rates has moved on from *Lombard Finance Ltd v Paton*[187] where the discretion of the lender was said to be unfettered. *Paragon Finance Plc v Nash*[188] is more debtor friendly to the extent that it was willing to imply a term that the power to vary interest rates should not be used capriciously, but on the facts it was found that it had not been since it was passing costs on to customers to relieve its serious financial

---

185 See cases cited in note 179.
186 *First National Securities v Bertrand* (1980) CCLR 5.
187 [1989] 1 All ER 918.
188 [2001] 2 All ER (Comm.) 1025.

difficulties.[189] Similarly in *Broadwick Financial Services v Spencer*[190] the court seemed to be willing to envisage a failure to disclose that the lender's policy was not to change interest rates with market conditions to be a breach of fair dealing, but then gave few reasons for finding it not to be such a breach in the instant case, save possibly that it would not have affected the lender's decision to proceed. There seem to be few current controls on the powers to vary interest rates and certainly none within the extortionate credit bargain provisions.

6.12.3 Possible Reforms

In 1991, in a report entitled *Unjust Credit Transactions*,[191] Sir Gordon Borrie, the then Director-General, singled out secured loans made to 'non-status borrowers' and unsecured roll-over or top-up loans as the forms of credit whose cost gave most cause for concern. The report proposed changes to the extortionate credit bargain provisions, recommending that the concept of 'extortionate credit bargain' be replaced by that of 'unjust credit transaction'. Reference to 'grossly exorbitant' payments would be changed to 'excessive' payments. The test of whether an agreement contravened ordinary principles of fair dealing would be replaced by one similar to that used for determining credit licence applications, namely whether the transaction involved business activity which was deceitful or oppressive or otherwise unfair or improper (whether unlawful or not). Also it was proposed that a new factor to be taken into account would be 'the lender's care and responsibility in making the loan, including steps taken to find out and check the borrower's credit-worthiness and ability to meet the full terms of the agreement'.

A couple of influential reports encouraged the Government to keep reform of extortionate credit bargains on the agenda.[192] The general thrust of the 1991 Report can be found reflected in the latest White Paper, *Fair, Clear and Competitive*.[193] This would seek to lower the threshold when

---

189 This has been said to only impose negative constraints on the exercise of discretion and not impose positive obligations to reduce interest rates: *Steling Credit v Rahman*, Lawtel.

190 [2002] 1 All ER (Comm.) 446.

191 (OFT, 1991).

192 E. Kempson and C. Whyley, *Extortionate Credit in the UK* (Personal Finance Research Centre, 1999) and *Daylight Robbery – The CAB case for effective regulation of extortionate credit* (CAB, 2001).

193 *Op cit.*, at pp. 52–61, see also *A consultation document on making the extortionate credit bargain provisions within the Consumer Credit Act 1974 more effective* (DTI, 2003).

agreements could be re-opened by introducing the concept of an 'unfair' rather than an extortionate credit bargain. The focus would be on both unfair credit practices (product mis-selling, unacceptably high pressure selling techniques, churning credit agreements and aggressive debt-collection practices) and where credit payments excessively exceeded market levels.

As regards the unfair credit practices, it is clear that churning is a major concern and has been ever since the 1991 Report talked about the problems associated with roll-over and top-up loans. Debts can spiral as salesmen persuade debtors to take out new loans incurring charges along the way. Concerning credit payments, the focus would not just be on the interest charged, but also the total due. Particular concern had been focussed on a term of credit agreements that keeps interest accruing even when debtors are repaying the outstanding debts, because of a challenge to such a term brought by the Director-General against First National Bank. Not unsurprisingly debtors were shocked to be confronted with a hefty bill for accrued interest, when having paid the agreed instalments to deal with arrears they mistakenly believed their debts had been cleared. This element of surprise persuaded the Court of Appeal to hold the term to be unfair.[194] Although not happy with the practice as they accepted consumers might be surprised, the House of Lords was not prepared to use the Unfair Terms in Consumer Contracts Regulations to counter it. It was less persuaded than the Court of Appeal had been by the fact that debtors would not in practice use the remedies available to them under the CCA 1974. It was willing to accept the creditors had the right to include such a term and had brought it adequately to the attention of the debtor.[195]

In the future it is likely that the assessment of the contract will not be limited to the terms of the agreement when it was entered into. In *Paragon Finance PLC v Bash & Staunton*[196] and *Broadwick Financial Services Ltd v Spencer*[197] the lenders had been given a discretion to vary the interest rate and the Court of Appeal had decided that variations in interest rate were not to be taken into account when determining whether the agreement was extortionate. This may well change in the future.

It had been mooted that courts be allowed to re-open extortionate agreements on their own motion. The judiciary was uneasy about this. In any event it might be doubted how often such a power would be used. The Government is looking at whether a form of ADR system can be introduced to encourage debtors to invoke the extortionate credit bargain

---

[194]   [2000] QB 672.
[195]   [2002] 1 AC 484.
[196]   [2001] 2 All ER (Comm.) 1025
[197]   [2002] 1 All ER (Comm.) 446.

provisions (or whether ever they become called). However, the thinking about such an alternative is currently embryonic.

The Government also talks about the principle of responsible lending, which is mentioned in the EC Directive. This is concerned with making sure the creditor has done appropriate checks on the debtor. The problem is not normally that creditors to not make such checks; rather once they have made them they might sometimes be criticised for being over ambitious in their assessment of the debtor's ability to repay, especially if their interest is protected by a mortgage. It will be difficult to call instances of irresponsible lending without interfering seriously in the free market order, which is something the Government and courts seems reluctant to do.

An important debate may have to take place concerning the relationship between the extortionate credit bargain provisions (or whatever they are called in future) and the proposed Unfair Commercial Practices Directive. Can the proposed Directive assist in controlling malpractice and/or will it restrict national laws that provide more stringent controls?

The link between the extortionate credit bargain provisions, time orders and the power under s. 136, CCA 1974 to amend the agreement, by for instance, reducing interest rates is discussed below.[198]

6.13 CREDITOR REMEDIES

Lending is a risky business and creditors are obviously keen to have contractual rights they can enforce to secure their position should the agreement go wrong. The law has an interest in ensuring that these rights are not used unfairly or oppressively against debtors in straightened circumstances. Terry Ison has suggested that, in debtor-creditor-supplier type situations, the sanction for non-payment should be limited to repossession of the goods and an adverse credit report.[199] Ison thought such an approach to be justified, since as the court system was not able to handle claims by consumers effectively, then it should not be given over to the enforcement of retailer claims. Several beneficial side effects were seen as flowing from the abolition of debt recovery. Creditors would have a greater interest in viewing the goods supplied as security, which would provide an incentive not to sell shoddy goods. Lenders would be more careful in their lending policy and would, for instance, obtain credit reports and require significant down payments. There would most likely be a switch from sales-financing to loan-financing where the consumer was a marginal credit risk. This would make the cost of credit more transparent

---

[198] See Section 6.14.1.

[199] T. Ison, *op. cit.*, at pp. 284–90.

and also provide a space for consumers to contemplate the wisdom of the transaction as they went to another place to negotiate a loan. Similar views had been put to the Crowther Committee by Ison. Whilst the Committee appreciated his reasoning, it nevertheless felt unable to go along with such drastic restrictions on creditors' remedies.[200]

6.13.1 Requirement of Notice

6.13.1.1 Non-Breach Situations

The policy of the CCA 1974 is to require the debtor or hirer to give at least seven days notice before terminating the agreement or enforcing terms with serious consequences for the debtor or hirer. Section 76, CCA 1974 requires the creditor or owner to give notice before seeking to enforce a term which allows him to:

(i)   demand early repayment of a sum;
(ii)   recover possession of goods or land; or
(iii) treat any right conferred on the debtor or hirer as terminated, restricted or deferred.

Section 76 does not apply where there has been a breach of the agreement. Section 98, CCA 1974 provides for a notice requirement where the debtor or hirer wishes to terminate the agreement otherwise than by reason of breach of the agreement. In practice the most significant provisions are those on default notices contained in s. 87, CCA 1974. However, ss. 76 and 98 are needed to prevent contracts from being drafted in such a way that events that might normally be considered breaches of contract are in fact not construed as such, but nevertheless cause similar consequences to flow. A useful comparison can be drawn with the common law rule which will strike down penalty clauses resulting from a breach,[201] but is seemingly powerless when similar results arise in non breach situations. Thus a minimum payments clause under a hire-purchase contract has been upheld when a hirer exercised his right to terminate the agreement, rather than place himself in breach and permit the owner to terminate for breach.[202]

---

[200] *Op. cit.*, at pp. 30–5.

[201] *Dunlop Pneumatic Tyres Co Ltd v New Garages Motor Co* [1915] AC 79.

[202] *Associated Distributors v Hall* [1938] 2 KB 83. This was followed by the Court of Appeal in *Campbell Discount Co Ltd v Bridge* [1961] 2 All ER 97. However, the House of Lords (*Bridge v Campbell Discounts Co Ltd* [1962] 1 ALL ER 385) avoided having to follow *Hall* by finding that a letter, written by the defaulter (in which he said he was sorry that he could not keep up repayments) was not an exercise of his

6.13.1.2 Default Notices

Section 87 requires a default notice to be served on the debtor or hirer before the creditor or owner can, by reason of any breach by the debtor or hirer:

(i)   terminate the agreement,
(ii)   demand earlier payment,
(iii) recover possession of any goods or land,
(iv)   treat any right conferred on the debtor or hirer as terminated, restricted or deferred, or
(v)   enforce any security.

The default notice must be in the prescribed form.[203] The rules must be strictly complied with. Overstating the amount of arrears, for example, would invalidate the notice.[204]

The default notice is in fact one of the most useful consumer information provisions as it provides consumers with relevant and timely information. Two particularly useful statements that must be contained in default notices are:

IF YOU ARE NOT SURE WHAT TO DO, YOU SHOULD GET HELP AS SOON AS POSSIBLE, FOR EXAMPLE YOU SHOULD CONTACT A SOLICITOR, YOUR LOCAL TRADING STANDARDS DEPARTMENT OR YOUR NEAREST CITIZENS' ADVICE BUREAU.

IF YOU HAVE DIFFICULTY IN PAYING ANY SUM OWING UNDER THE AGREEMENT YOU CAN APPLY TO THE COURT WHICH MAY MAKE AN ORDER ALLOWING YOU OR YOUR SURETY MORE TIME.[205]

---

right to terminate the agreement, but rather a breach of the agreement. The minimum payments clause was then held to be a penalty clause. Lord Denning (at 399) would have been prepared to go further and grant relief whatever the reason for terminating the hiring in order to avoid equity committing itself to the absurd paradox that 'It will grant relief to a man who breaks his contract but will penalise the man who keeps it'. Note that the amounts involved took the contract outside the controls in the Hire-Purchase Act 1938.

[203] See Consumer Credit (Enforcement, Default and Termination Notices) Regulations 1983, S.I. 1983/1561.
[204] *Woodchester Lease Management Services Ltd v Swain & Co*, 1998, Lawtel.
[205] This refers to the possibility that the court will make a time order, a subject considered at Chapter 6.14.1.

The default notice must state the nature of the alleged breach. If the breach is capable of remedy, it must specify what action is required to remedy it; if the breach is irremediable, it must specify the compensation demanded for the breach. It must also state the consequences of failing to comply with the notice. The debtor must be informed of a date (at least seven days after service of the notice) by which time the necessary actions must be taken or the compensation paid. Within this period the creditor or owner can take no action which requires the service of a default notice.[206] If the breach is remedied or the compensation paid, then the breach is treated as if it had not occurred. It is only in relation to s. 87 notice that the debtor or hirer has the right to rectify matters. There is no corresponding right where the creditor or owner seeks to enforce a right or terminate an agreement in a non-breach situation, and yet, as we have seen, whether an action of the debtor or hirer amounts to a breach can often depend on how the contract was worded. For instance, a debtor who defaults may be in breach or, alternatively, the agreement could state that non-payment makes the whole of the outstanding balance payable.

A general weakness with the enforcement powers of the CCA 1974 is the provision, in s. 170(1), that there is no sanction for breach of requirements laid down in the Act, except to the extent expressly provided for. This weakness is well illustrated by the fact that no such sanctions are provided for failing to comply with the default notice procedure (or indeed the procedures required by ss. 76 and 98). Is there then no redress when the notice procedures are not followed? The answer is often no, unless relief can be found in common law provisions. Any redress available to the consumer is therefore the result of accident rather than planning. In *Eshun v Moorgate Mercantile Co Ltd*[207] where goods were recovered without a notice being served (as required under the former Hire-Purchase Act 1965) an action for wrongful retaking of possession was successful. What is the position if, instead of the goods being repossessed, the creditor invokes an accelerated payments clause and the debtor has paid money to the creditor? A. Hill-Smith has suggested that this may be recoverable on the basis that the money was had and received by the creditor on the basis of a mistake

---

206 Sections 76, 87 and 98 of the CCA 1974 do not prevent a creditor from treating the right to draw upon credit as being restricted or deferred and taking steps to that end (e.g. placing a stop on a credit card or bank account).

207 [1971] 1 WLR 722: this seems to have been on the basis of conversion, although it has been suggested that an alternative basis could be that the goods were returned under a mistake of law. The courts have taken the view that all back payments are recoverable, but it may be doubted whether this approach would be followed where the debtor had benefited from considerable enjoyment from the goods for a substantial period of time.

of law.[208] It is unfortunate that the CCA 1974 did not contain more explicit sanctions for non-compliance, which could have reflected consumer protection values rather than rely on the *ad hoc* solutions provided by the common law.

There are some instances where the CCA 1974 does provide for severe sanctions for creditors who do not comply with the proper procedures for enforcing their rights. These are considered in the next paragraphs.

6.13.2 Breach of Statutory Duty

Section 92, CCA 1974 provides for an action for breach of statutory duty in two situations when goods or land are recovered without a court order. This action arises when either (i) a creditor or owner enters premises to take possession of goods under a regulated hire-purchase, conditional sale or consumer hire agreement, or (ii) a creditor under a conditional sale agreement seeks to recover possession of land from the debtor. It is important to remember the general rule, to be found in s. 173(3), CCA 1974, that the need for a court order can be ignored if the debtor or owner gives consent to the doing of such actions at the time they are actually undertaken.

6.13.3 Protected Goods

There are very severe sanctions laid down in ss. 90–91, CCA 1974 if a creditor under a hire-purchase or conditional sale agreement seeks to recover possession of 'protected goods' without a court order.[209] Goods are protected if:

(i)   the debtor is in breach of a regulated hire-purchase or conditional sale agreement, and
(ii) the property in the goods remains with the creditor, and
(iii) the debtor has paid one third of the total price of the goods.

Where the creditor was required to install the goods and the agreement provided for a specified installation charge, then goods are only protected once that charge and a third of the remaining total price have been paid. As an anti-avoidance measure, once a third of the total price of any goods has

---

[208]   *Consumer Credit: Law and Practice* (Sweet & Maxwell, 1985) at pp. 179–80.
[209]   Although once again it is sufficient that the debtor consents to the taking of the goods at the time they are repossessed.

been paid then that condition is held to be satisfied as regards any subsequent agreement which relates to the same goods.

There are severe consequences if protected goods are wrongfully repossessed. The agreement is terminated[210] (if it was not already) and the debtor is released from all liabilities under the agreement and can recover all sums paid under the agreement. These consequences are intended to deter creditors from repossessing 'protected goods', for the debtor is in effect given free use of the goods up until the time of termination and the creditor risks being left with goods which have deteriorated in value. However, in practice some creditors may continue to 'snatch back' goods if their residual value is greater than the amount to be refunded. The debtor cannot require that the goods be returned,[211] nor for that matter can the creditor bring the agreement back to life by restoring the goods.[212]

The prohibition only relates to recovering possession of goods *from* the debtor. It does not apply if the goods have been abandoned[213] or are recovered from a third party to whom they have been wrongfully sold. However, the section would seem to prevent the creditor recovering goods from a third party to whom the debtor had entrusted the goods; for example, a mechanic repairing protected goods.[214]

6.13.4 Consumer Hire

Section 132, CCA 1974 provides relief to hirers where the owner has repossessed goods forming the subject matter of a regulated consumer hire-agreement without having obtained a court order. The provisions aim to prevent hirers from being forced to maintain payments even after the goods have been repossessed. It seeks to do justice where the repossessor would otherwise receive a substantial windfall profit in circumstances where significant payments had already been received.

---

210 Note that the whole of the agreement is terminated even if the protected goods only formed part of the subject matter of the agreement.

211 Cf. *Carr v James Broderick & Co Ltd* [1942] 2 KB 275 where it was held that the property was and always had been with the hire-purchase company. The hirer was not given a right of possession. The Act merely provided that a hirer could only properly be deprived of possession by an action brought in the courts.

212 Cf. *Capital Finance Co Ltd v Bray* [1964] 1 WLR 323 where it was held that there would have to be a new agreement to reinstate the hire-purchase agreement. The mere fact that the hirer had used the car was not sufficient to demonstrate such agreement.

213 *Bentinck Ltd v Cromwell Engineering* [1971] 1 QB 324 (decided under Hire-Purchase Act 1965).

214 *F C Finance Ltd v Francis* (1970) 114 SJ 568 (decided under Hire-Purchase Act 1965).

Where goods have been wrongfully recovered the hirer can apply to court for an order that the whole or part of any sum paid under the agreement should be repaid and that obligations to pay further sums in respect of the goods should cease. Such applications can be granted in full or in part, according to what the court considers to be just, having regard to the extent of the enjoyment of the goods by the hirer. The court may make similar provisions whenever it makes an order for the delivery of goods back to the owner.

6.14 POWERS OF THE COURT

The CCA 1974 gives the court some very important powers to assist it to do justice between the parties. It should be mentioned at the outset that these are additional to the court's inherent equitable power to grant relief against forfeiture. This equitable relief has been widely invoked with regard to mortgages to prevent mortgagees from unfairly exercising their equity of redemption. The courts have been circumspect about extending such relief to agreements relating to personal property, though the application of the principle to such cases does appear to have been accepted.[215]

6.14.1 Time Orders

If it appears just to do so, s. 129, CCA 1974 gives a court the power to make a time order in the following circumstances:

(i) on application for an enforcement order;
(ii) on an application by the debtor or hirer after he or she has been served with a default notice or a notice under Ss. 76 and 98, CCA 1974; and
(iii) in any action brought by a creditor or owner to enforce a regulated agreement or any security, or to recover possession of any goods or land relating to a regulated agreement.

Thus the power arises not only on application by the debtor or hirer, but also with respect to actions brought by the creditor or owner. Although the provision seems to be worded permissively, in *Southern and District*

---

215 *Stockloser v Johnson* [1954] 1 QB 376: the scope of the court's jurisdiction remains uncertain. Does the creditor have to have acted unconscionably? Does it apply to hire contracts? Is the court only able to give the debtor more time, or can it order payment to be returned and future payments to be ignored?

Finance v Barnes[216] Leggatt LJ spoke in terms of the court having to consider whether it was just to make a time order whenever a lender was seeking possession of property.

Under a time order the court can reschedule the payments under the agreement and, in order to do justice, provide for the payment of such instalments at such times as it considers reasonable. Time orders allow for instalments to be reduced and the repayment period extended. They are, however, only intended to deal with temporary financial difficulties where there is a prospect of the payments being resumed to at least the contractual rate.[217] However, as Lord Bingham observed in *Director-General of Fair Trading v First National* Bank[218] the Court of Appeal in one of the cases heard alongside *Southern and District Finance v Barnes* was prepared to allow rescheduling over 15 years and the general feeling is that the courts should be left a great deal of discretion to deal with cases as they see fit. Where a time order relates to the repayment of money then it can only cover 'sums owed', meaning sums due and owing under the agreement and not the full amount of the loan. However, where possession proceedings are brought the full amount owed will usually be demanded and therefore all sums under the agreement can be subject to the time order.[219] As part of the time order interest rates can be varied using the power under s. 136 CCA 1974 'to amend any agreement or security in consequence of a term of the order'. Although the Court of Appeal has noted that the variation must have been a consequence of the time order, and there is not a more general power to vary interest rates, other than for extortionate credit bargains, it also appreciated that where the sum owed is the whole of the outstanding balance then the courts have recognised there will inevitably be consequences for either the term of the loan or the interest rate or both.[220] Time orders can be used to reduce the interest rate payable under the agreement.[221] Courts will strive to strike a balance between the creditor's loss in having repayment over a longer period and the debtor who might be faced with paying additional interest if the order requires payments less than the contractual amount. In striking this balance the court is aware that lenders rates do make some allowance for the risk of repayment difficulties. When deciding the size and rate of repayments, the

---

[216] [1995] CCLR 62.
[217] *Ibid.*, at 68.
[218] [2002] 1AC 484.
[219] *Southern and District Finance v Barnes,* [1995] CCLR 62.
[220] *Ibid.*
[221] In *Southern and District Finance v Barnes,* [1995] CCLR 62 Leggatt LJ held that the interest rate could be varied where it was just to do so. See also *Cedar Holdings Ltd v Jenkins* [1988] CCLR 34 and *Cedar Holdings Ltd v Thompson* [1993] CCLR 7, but these had not been followed in *J & J Securities v Lee* [1994] CCLR 44.

court must have regard to the means of the debtor or hirer. However, a time order was held to be inappropriate if the debtor's offer did not even meet the accruing interest charges and if there was no realistic prospect of the debtor's financial position improving.[222]

With respect to non-monetary defaults, such as a failure to take reasonable care of goods, the court can specify a period of time for the debtor to put matters right; if the breach is remedied, it is treated as if it had never occurred. This period of time is known as the 'protective period' during which the creditor or owner cannot take any action which requires the serving of a default notice or invoke any secondary provision which becomes operative on the breach. The protective period has effect without prejudice to anything done by the creditor or owner prior to its commencement, so that goods that have been repossessed cannot be ordered to be returned.

This protective period only applies to non-monetary breaches. Thus, although instalments might have been rescheduled, there is nothing to prevent the creditor or owner invoking other rights, such as the right to repossess goods. The debtor or hirer would then have to ask the court to use its general powers to suspend orders or impose conditions under s. 135, CCA 1974.

6.14.2 Return and Transfer Orders

Section 133, CCA 1974 gives the court the power to make 'return' or 'transfer' orders during proceedings relating to hire-purchase or conditional sale agreements for an enforcement or time order or in any action brought by the creditor to recover possession of the goods.

A return order, as its name suggests, requires the goods be returned to the creditor. Such an order is usually suspended and can be made conditional on the creditor returning any surplus on sale to the debtor.[223] An order could be for the immediate return of the goods, but this would be of little practical significance since, on payment of the total price of the goods at any time before they enter the possession of the creditor, the debtor can claim the goods.[224]

A transfer order provides for title in part of the goods to be transferred to the debtor, with the remainder of the goods being returned to the creditor. Limits are placed on the value of goods that can be transferred to the debtor. These limits are intended to compensate the creditor for having to accept the goods back. The maximum value of goods that can be

---

[222] *First National Bank v Syed* [1991] 2 All ER 250.

[223] The court would use its powers under s. 135, CCA 1974.

[224] Section 133(4), CCA 1974.

transferred to the debtor equals the amounts which have been paid under the agreement less one-third of the unpaid balance. Where the agreement does not specify the value of individual goods forming part of the agreement, then the court determines which portion of the total price it is reasonable to allocate to the goods being transferred.

6.14.3 Conditional and Suspended Orders

In any order relating to a regulated agreement, s. 135, CCA 1974 allows the court (i) to make the operation of any term of the order conditional on the doing of specified acts by any of the parties, or (ii) to suspend the operation of any term, either until such time as the court subsequently directs or until the occurrence of a specified act or omission. There are some limits to these powers. For instance, a court cannot suspend the operation of a term requiring a person to deliver up goods, unless it is satisfied that they are in that person's possession. Also the power to suspend a term of the order cannot be used to extend the period for which a hirer is entitled to possess goods under a hire agreement.

6.15 APPROPRIATION OF PAYMENTS

Where a debtor or hirer has more than one regulated agreement with a creditor or owner, it can be important to know how payments have been appropriated between the agreements. On this question may hang determinations such as which goods are 'protected', whether a transfer order can be made (or how much can be transferred) and how much refund, if any, is appropriate under consumer hire agreements where the owner has repossessed the goods. Section 81, CCA 1974 gives the debtor the right to appropriate sums between agreements as he or she sees fit. However, where the debtor fails to specify how the sums are to be appropriated, the Act provides a default procedure where one of the agreements is a hire-purchase, conditional sale or consumer hire agreement or an agreement for which security is provided. This default procedure provides that sums should be appropriated to the agreements proportionately to the sums due under them. However, if the default procedure does not apply, then the matter is covered by the common law, which leaves it to the creditor to decide how to appropriate payments.

6.16 LOST, STOLEN OR MISUSED CREDIT CARDS

The advent of the plastic revolution has brought many benefits to consumers, but has also introduced new dangers of financial risk through the unauthorised use of cards. The CCA 1974 contains some protection against such risks. First, a debtor is not liable under a credit-token agreement for the use made of the credit-token unless he or she has accepted it.[225] Acceptance occurs on signing the token or a receipt for it or when the token is first used. Second, even after acceptance, liability for misuse of the token can be avoided by giving oral or written notice to the creditor that it is liable to be misused. Indeed, there will be no liability at all if the credit-token agreement failed to specify the name, address and telephone number of a person on whom such notice can be served.[226] If the credit-token is misused by someone who acquired it with the debtor's consent, then there is unlimited liability until such time as the creditor is notified of the possibility of misuse, even if the person has used the card in an unauthorised manner. In other cases, such as where a card is lost or stolen, the maximum liability a debtor can incur for misuse of the card will be £50 (or the credit limit if lower). Charge cards, being exempt from the Act, are excluded from this protection. It is a matter of some concern that debit cards too are not subject to such a limitation of liability, although a similar limit is contained in the Banking Code of Practice.

6.17 CONCLUSION

There is no doubting the complexity of consumer credit law. Although with hindsight some features of the CCA 1974 could be simplified, the law in this area will inevitably be complex, given the need to make rules watertight so that businesses cannot evade regulation simply by adopting new trading forms. The CCA 1974 was a brave attempt to regulate the substance rather than the form of credit agreements. Even with the recent crop of reform proposals the basic structure and philosophy behind the CCA 1974 will remain in place. Nevertheless the Act's limitations are illustrated by the problems it experiences in handling the issues raised by credit cards and EFTPOS cards. Consumer law has once again been shown to be one step behind commercial practice.

There is a general consensus, even amongst the credit industry, about the need to regulate consumer credit. Credit is a product whose value consumers find difficult to understand and which they can easily use to excess. Respectable industry members appreciate the value of laws which

---

[225] Section 66, CCA 1974.
[226] Sections 83–84, CCA 1974.

deal with rogues, who may not be removed by market forces alone. The industry's acceptance of the CCA 1974 may also be due to the fact that the Act controls the form of the agreement and restricts some remedies, but leaves the parties largely free to determine its core terms, such as interest rates, security and guarantees. Thus it seeks to ensure fairness in market transactions without questioning whether the market mechanism is appropriate. The extent to which consumer law can bring about redistributive effects is clearly a theme readers need to consider.

The recent White Paper and proposed reforms seek at the same time to simplify the rules where possible; focus on real consumer needs as far as information provisions are concerned; and, remedy some aspects of the law that had proven to be unfair to consumers. On the whole these proposals seem well balanced. Where the impact of policy becomes more difficult to assess is in relation to the reforms to extortionate credit bargains and unlicensed dealers. The Government clearly wants to have a greater impact on how markets operate, but seems unwilling to take measures which challenge its belief in free markets. On the other hand it is useful that links are made between consumer law, general financial literacy policy and other policy initiatives dealing with over-indebtedness.

Consumer credit law is complex. Few consumers will be able to know the way the law applies to them in detail. This need not, prevent the law assisting them. Several steps can be taken to allow consumers to enjoy the benefits of laws. First, it is important to draw consumers' attention to their rights in ways that are easily comprehensible. Statements in agreement documentation explaining consumer rights in simple prescribed language are an easy way to achieve this. Some of the proposed reforms should help simplify the information being presented to consumers and make it more digestible. Second, consumer education should not be neglected. What is the point of informing consumers of the APR if they do not know what that means? Third, consumers should be able to invoke their rights with the minimum of formality. The provision of a form to facilitate cancellation is an example of how legal remedies can be made accessible to consumers. Fourth, it is important that there are properly trained and funded advisers to whom consumers can turn once they recognise they have a problem which the law might be able to assist them with. Fifth, the market cannot be regulated by simple reliance on the initiative of consumers to invoke their private law rights. This emphasises the necessity for private law rights to be complemented by the public law controls on the credit market which are considered in Chapter 9 and injunction style procedures dealt with in Chapter 13.

Chapter 7

Regulation of Trade Practices from Doorstep to Internet

7.1 DOORSTEP AND DISTANT SELLING – POLICY REASONS FOR INTERVENTION

Many, if not most, consumer transactions take place between a consumer and trader in a retail outlet. In such cases the consumer will have had the opportunity to see the product and to compare it with other products on sale. Typically the product will be taken away immediately the purchase is complete or arrangements will be made for its delivery. The consumer will have met the supplier and visited the trading premises and will therefore be in a position to make some assessment of the character of the supplier and of the goods or service. Of course there are always risks even when buying in this traditional manner, but two methods of selling – doorstep and distance selling – do not fit the typical consumer sale model described above and give rise to particular consumer protection issues. Both have been the subject of scrutiny by the European Community legislators.

Doorstep selling was the subject of one of the first EC Directives dealing with consumer protection.[1] At first blush the intervention of the European legislator to something as close to home as doorstep selling may seem paradoxical,[2] but as some such firms use European wide strategies for selling at consumer's home the adoption of a Directive is defensible. Nevertheless, it is strange that it was one of the first consumer issues tackled by the EC. It has been implemented in the UK by the Consumer Protection (Cancellation of Contracts Concluded away from Business Premises) Regulations 1987[3] and has subsequently been amended to close some loopholes.[4]

Distance selling potentially raises more complex issues. At the European level it was first the subject of a non-binding Recommendation.[5]

---

[1] Council Directive of 20 December 1985 to protect the consumer in respect of contracts negotiated away from business premises: 85/577/EEC, OJ 1985 L372/31.

[2] See Editorial, (2000) 37 *CMLRev* 1301.

[3] S.I. 1987/2117.

[4] See Consumer Protection (Cancellation of Contracts Concluded away from Business Premises) (Amendment) Regulations 1998, S.I. 1998/3050.

[5] Commission Recommendation of 7 April 1992, OJ 1992 L156/21.

Subsequently there has been a directive covering distance selling in general[6] followed by a specific directive dealing with the distance marketing of consumer financial services that had been excluded from the general directive.[7] The former has been implemented into UK law by the Consumer Protection (Distance Selling) Regulations 2000,[8] whilst implementation of the distance selling of consumer financial services directive is still awaited. One difference between the general distance selling and the financial service directive is that the former provided for minimal harmonisation allowing member states to retain or introduce stricter provisions. The latter seeks to create maximum rules, in order to facilitate cross-border trade. However, it does not achieve this fully and has, for example, had to accept that pending further harmonisation member states may have additional information obligations to those provided for in the Directive.

Although many laws seek to protect the consumer from unfair selling and marketing practices, there are particular reasons for singling out doorstep and distant selling for special treatment. These two selling techniques are at different ends of the marketing spectrum. Doorstep sales often depend on cold selling of a highly personalised form to consumers in the comfort of their own home. Distant selling on the other hand can be highly depersonalised relying on mailshots, faxes, junk spam e-mails, catalogues and even television, although it can also be more personalised, when, for example, it is undertaken by telephone. Since the original distance selling directive was enacted e-commerce in the business to consumer ('B2C') sector has become more prominent due to the growth in access to the internet. The internet also throws up some very specific issues. Indeed one of the problems with the Distance Selling Directive might be that it was developed when internet trading was in its infancy. A number of legislative rules specific to the internet have been enacted. For this reason we will devote a specific section to the problems of regulating the internet. Although it should be remembered that other forms of distance selling continue to be important.

First, we will review the reasons which justify special legislative intervention for doorstep and distance selling. Some apply to both, but many apply to only one form of selling. Although, for instance, cancellation rights are used as methods of protection in both situations the reasons for granting them are different. Also in the distance selling legislation emphasis is also placed on providing the consumer with

---

6   Directive 97/7 on the protection of consumers in respect of distance contracts: OJ 1997 L 144/19.
7   Directive 2002/65/EC concerning the distance marketing of consumer financial services: OJ 2002 L271/16.
8   S.I. 2000/2334.

information, which is less obvious in the doorstep contracts where only the right to cancel has to be informed.

7.1.1 Restriction on Consumer Choice

One justification for intervention, common to both doorstep and distant selling, is their potential to restrict consumer choice. This is particularly so in the context of doorstep selling. A salesperson may knock on the door and persuade a consumer to buy a product that he had never thought he needed, or even possibly even knew existed, before the trader called. In these circumstances the consumer has no time to compare the product offered with those of its competitors. The problem of the consumer's restricted opportunity to compare products and services also applies to some forms of distance selling (e.g. television selling where offers are only available for a short time), but not to others. For instance, goods viewed at leisure in catalogues can often be compared with High Street equivalents. Difficulties arise when the goods are not available in the High Street, for then a consumer at a distance is always faced with uncertainty as to the quality of the goods. Even if there is a description, photograph or television display of the goods this cannot be equated with actually being able to see and handle the goods.

7.1.2 Lack of Knowledge About the Supplier

In both doorstep and distant selling there can be a problem arising from the consumer's lack of knowledge of the character of the seller. This is most acute in distant selling where at its most extreme the order (and money) could be posted off to an anonymous postal box number or sent to a server situated anywhere in the world-wide-web. The problem also exists in relation to doorstep selling for, although the consumer will have met a representative of the supplier, he or she is unlikely to have seen the supplier's trading premises.

7.1.3 Coercion

Another reason for intervening in doorstep selling, which does not usually apply to distance selling, is that consumers often feel coerced to sign contracts for goods they do not really want simply because they are in their own home. This may be because the salesperson harangues them to such an extent that it seems easier to sign than to argue, or possibly because when 'entertaining' in their own home, people find it difficult to be discourteous and insist that they do not want the product or service. One might suggest that consumers should not be so weak and gullible, but it is surprising how many normally sensible people have regretted entering contracts signed in their home on the spur of the moment. The problem is even more acute with vulnerable consumers, such as the elderly. There may be some similarities with instances of distance selling when customers are solicited over the phone, but people tend to be more willing to put the phone down.

7.1.4 Privacy

Some of the marketing techniques adopted by distance selling companies give rise to issues of privacy. Data protection is relevant since they use databases to target their marketing. We shall see that the internet raises many novel privacy concerns. The consumer's privacy is also affected in doorstep selling, perhaps in an even more direct way, but (short of banning such selling techniques)[9] there is little that can be done to prevent this traditional way of selling. Also with doorstep selling there is less incidence of data being used to target particular individuals; more commonly, areas having a certain social structure will be canvassed.

7.1.5 A Comment on the Methods of Protection Chosen

We will notice that an important technique of protection discussed below relates to information provision. The role of information in protecting consumers is an important contemporary theme and one which the reader may find useful material about in this chapter. Questions about how useful information is, the extent to which it can replace the need for more interventionist rules and how best information can be conveyed to the consumer arise particularly in relation to distance selling (including the internet). Cancellation rights can be seen as an extension of the information policy. They allow the consumer to take advantage of goods and service and then have a period to withdraw if that experience makes them feel the contract is not to their liking. Cancellation rights challenge traditional views of contract. They may also make traders nervous about the possibility that consumers may take advantage of such rights simply to obtain goods free of charge for the short period they need them. Equally from a consumer protection standpoint one may question whether all

---

9   As is the case with debtor-creditor credit agreements: see s. 49, Consumer Credit Act 1974 discussed at 9.3.3. There is currently a proposed Private Members' Bill that would ban doorstep selling, but it is unlikely to be enacted and rather serves to focus attention on rogue practices, especially in the building trade.

consumers will have the confidence to cancel contracts. There may be psychological barriers to such action. Consumers may not want to confront the trader and indeed will usually look to reinforce the belief they made a good bargain by playing down any negative signals. Indeed the relatively short cancellation periods will increase the likelihood that they are not widely invoked. Again the reader will find examples of cancellation rights in this chapter which can be used to reflect on how effective is the protection they afford and whether this can be enhanced.[10]

7.2 DOORSTEP SELLING[11]

Doorstep selling has a trade association, the Direct Selling Association, which has a Code of Practice, but has also been subject to statutory regulation for a long time. The Consumer Protection (Cancellation of Contracts Concluded Away from Business Premises) Regulations 1987[12] came into force on 1 July 1988. These provide consumers with a seven-day cooling-off period within which they can cancel contracts governed by the Regulations. This period allows consumers to compare the bargain they have struck with other possibilities. It also gives them the chance to withdraw from agreements they have entered into as the result of undue pressure. Despite this legislation, dangers still exist when contracting with doorstep traders about whom little is known. For instance, there is no compensation fund to protect pre-payments or to underwrite guarantees about the quality of such goods.

7.2.1 Scope of the Regulations

The Regulations apply to contracts made for the supply of goods and services by a trader to a consumer in four circumstances:[13]

(i)   During an unsolicited visit by a trader to the consumer's home, the home of another person or the consumer's place of work. A visit is

---

10   See P. Rekaiti and R. van den Bergh, 'Cooling-Off Periods in the Consumer Laws of the EC Member States. A Comparative Law and Economics Approach' (2000) 23 *Journal of Consumer Policy* 371.

11   A. Hill-Smith (1988) 85, 21, *LSGaz* 37–38, 41. Just as the final touches were being made to this manuscript the OFT issued a market study on *Doorstep Selling* (May 2004) and the DTI issued a consultation paper *Doorstep Selling and Cold Calling* (July 2004).

12   S.I. 1987/2117.

13   Regulation 3(1).

unsolicited unless it takes place at the express request of the consumer. A previous loophole was closed by excluding requests made after a trader, or someone acting in his name or on his behalf, indicated they would be willing to visit the consumer during a phone call or visit.[14] It is perhaps surprising that the Directive and Regulations limit the places where the rules apply to the home or workplace of the consumer. What about the workplace of the consumer's friend or even in the street? Indeed an important case of *Faccini Dori v Recreb*[15] went to the European Court of Justice concerning an English language correspondence course concluded near Milan Central Station. The Advocate-General was not sure whether this was within the scope, but the Court was convinced it was on the basis of the fifth recital that noted 'this surprise element generally exists not only in contracts made at the doorstep but also in other forms of contract concluded by the trader away from trade premises'. Dori lost her case, however, as the Court refused to accept the Directive had horizontal direct effects. Does English law have to be given a similarly purposeful interpretation as regards the places where the Regulations apply?

(ii) In the circumstances mentioned in (i), even if the consumer had requested the visit, so long as the goods or services concerned are different from those to which the request related and provided that, when the visit was requested, the consumer did not and could not reasonably have known that the supply of those other goods or services formed part of the trader's business activities. This is to catch 'bait and switch' tactics where a trader claims to be selling one commodity, but is really more interested in catching the consumer's attention to sell other products and services.

(iii) Excursions organised by traders away from their permanent or temporary business premises. Thus excursions to a conference centre or hotel would be caught, whereas those organised to a factory shop would not be covered.

(iv) Contracts are also covered if they are not made by the consumer in the above circumstances, but an offer was made on such occasions. This is included to plug a possible loophole that could exist if offers were accepted by the trader on business premises and therefore the contracts were concluded on business premises, but only in a strictly formal sense.

There are various 'excepted contracts':[16]

---

14   Regulation 3(3), amended by S.I. 1998/3050.
15   Case C–91/92 [1994] ECR I–3325.
16   Regulation 3(2)–(5).

(a) Various contracts for the sale of land, construction or extension of buildings and related finance. Contracts for the supply of goods to be incorporated into land and for the repair or improvement of property are included so long as they are not financed by a loan secured on land.

(b) Contracts for food, drink and other goods intended for current consumption by use in the household and supplied by regular roundsmen (e.g. the milk or newspaper delivered to the home).

(c) Contracts entered into by a trader with whom a continuity of contracting is expected and whose terms are contained in a catalogue. Prior to the contract being concluded, the trader's catalogue must have been readily available for the consumer to read in the absence of the trader or his representative. It must have contained or been accompanied by a prominent notice giving the consumer the right to return the goods supplied within seven days of receipt or otherwise cancel the contract within that period without incurring liability. Consumers remain responsible for damage due to their failure to take reasonable care of the goods in their possession.

(d) Contracts of insurance.

(e) Investment agreements.

(f) Credit agreements (other than hire-purchase or conditional sale agreements) for credit not exceeding £35.

(g) Any other contract under which the consumer makes total payments not exceeding £35.

The Regulations define consumer as 'a person, other than a body corporate, who, in making a contract... is acting for purposes which can be regarded as outside his business'. Attempts before the European Court of Justice to widen the similar definition found in the Directive to include businesses when not acting in their usual line of business have failed as the European Court of Justice has been keen to limit protection to consumers in the traditional sense of private individuals.[17] Although as a minimal Directive it would be permissible for the UK courts to interpret our provision more broadly, it is more likely that the European Court of Justice's interpretation will be followed. Equally the European Court of Justice has not been prepared to allow the Directive to assist guarantors who are acting outside their normal business, when the main contract was used for business purposes.[18]

---

[17] *Criminal Proceedings against Patrice di Pinto*, Case C–361/89 [1991] I–1189.

[18] *Bayerische Hypotheken und Wechselbank Ag v Dietzinger*, [1998] ECR I–1199 and *Berliner Kindl Brauerei v Siepert*, C208/98 [2000] ECR I–1741.

7.2.2 Notice

The Regulations provide that the contract shall be unenforceable unless the consumer is given a written notice of his or her right to cancel the contract within seven days.[19] The notice should contain information about the trader, a statement of the right to cancel (and that the cancellation form provided can be used) and the name and address of a person on whom notice of cancellation can be served.[20] The notice should be legible and, if incorporated into the document, be given no less prominence than other information except the heading, names of the contract parties and anything inserted in handwriting.[21] The notice must be dated and delivered when the contract is made or when the consumer makes an offer (if the contract would have been cancellable had it been concluded at the time the offer was made).[22] The Regulations were strengthened in 1998 by making it a criminal offence to fail to provide a cancellation notice in the proper form.[23]

7.2.3 Cancellation

The consumer can cancel the contract within seven days from when it was made.[24] Notice of cancellation can be served on the trader or anyone specified in the cancellation notice as a person on whom notice can be served.[25] The cancellation notice can be used to effect the cancellation, but any written notice will suffice so long as it indicates the consumer's intention to cancel the contract. A notice of cancellation sent by post is deemed to have been served at the time of posting, regardless of whether it is actually received.[26] This is similar to the position regarding cancellation of consumer credit contracts under the Consumer Credit Act 1974; the consequences of cancellation are also provided for in a similar manner.[27]

In relation to four categories of goods, there is no duty to return goods. These are perishable goods; consumable goods which have been consumed prior to cancellation; goods supplied in an emergency; and, goods which have been incorporated in land or other things. The Consumer Credit Act

---

[19]   Regulation 4.
[20]   See Schedule 1.
[21]   Regulation 4(3).
[22]   Regulation 4(4).
[23]   Regulation 4A.
[24]   Regulation 4(1).
[25]   Regulation 4(5).
[26]   Regulation 4(7).
[27]   See Chapter 6.8.

1974 has similar exemptions and plugs the possible loophole created in respect of goods supplied in an emergency and goods incorporated in land or other things by cancelling the credit element, but continuing the obligation to pay. However, it allows the consumer to have perishable and consumable goods without paying for them. The Doorstep Regulations are stricter requiring the consumer to pay for all four categories of goods and for services provided in connection with their supply.[28] This weakens the protection for these types of goods, although other elements of such contracts, such as credit, may be cancellable.

The cooling-off period is a technique familiar to UK consumer law from the context of consumer credit.[29] As the rules are slightly different under both sets of legislation, there was a need to decide which legislation should cover a cancellable contract caught by both provisions. The approach adopted was to withdraw from the scope of the Doorstep Regulations those contracts which are also cancellable under the Consumer Credit Act 1974. There was a problem, however, since the cancellation provisions under the Consumer Credit Act 1974 do not apply to agreements for less than £50. This threshold was too high for the Doorstep Regulations which had a threshold of £35, as dictated by the EC Directive. Therefore the Consumer Credit Act 1974 was amended so that, for agreements cancellable under the Consumer Credit Act 1974 and to which the Doorstep Regulations also apply, the threshold is £35 and not £50.[30]

Problems may still arise because the cancellation period is calculated differently under the Consumer Credit Act 1974 than under the Doorstep Regulations. Under the latter the consumer must have not less than seven days from the making of the contract to cancel it. However, under the Consumer Credit Act 1974 the cancellation period runs out at the end of the fifth day following the day on which the consumer received the second statutory copy of the contract or notice of cancellation. This second copy or notice must always be posted within seven days of the contract being made. Thus a more generous cancellation period is possible than that provided for under the Doorstep Regulations. This need not be a problem, though the period could be for less than seven days if the notice is posted on the day of contracting, in which case there is a question mark over whether this correctly implements the Directive which requires a seven day cooling-off period from receipt of the notice of cancellation rights. As the second copy or notice must be posted, the earliest it will arrive at the consumer's address is the day after the contract was made. The consumer then has until the end of the fifth day following receipt of the notice to cancel the contract.

---

[28] Regulation 7(2).
[29] See Chapter 6.8.
[30] Section 74(2A), Consumer Credit Act 1974.

The DTI's view appears to be that the cooling-off period for regulated credit agreements signed off trade premises amounts in all normal circumstances to at least the seven days specified in the Directive. There is perhaps an understandable desire not to have to amend legislation unnecessarily or to have too many conflicting systems, especially when any consumer injustice is likely to be minimal and when, in most cases, consumers will be better off under the UK law than under the protection demanded by the Directive. There have been proposals to bring the consumer credit cancellation period laws into line with those contained in the EC Doorstep Directive and EC Distance Selling – namely seven days from the signing of the agreement. [31] If this were to occur, the net result would be to reduce consumer protection since many consumers currently benefit from a longer cooling-off period where there is a credit element to a cancellable contract. This may have been a price worth paying to simplify the law. Fortunately it seems more likely that European laws will be harmonised to provide a common minimum of 14 days which is a feature of more advanced consumer protection laws.

7.3 DISTANCE SELLING

Europe first addressed distance selling by adopting Commission Recommendation of 7 April 1992 on distance selling.[32] It seeks to promote codes of practice for the protection of consumers in respect of contracts negotiated at a distance. In relation to such contracts, the Codes should have provisions relating to the dissemination of solicitations for custom; the presentation of solicitations; sales promotion; financial security; the right of withdrawal and promoting knowledge of the Code. Subsequently it adopted a Directive in 1997.[33] The focus of what follows is on the Consumer Protection (Distance Selling) Regulations 2000, which implement that Directive it. Nevertheless, it should not be forgotten that a number of Codes of Practice do in fact operate in this area, notably those

---

[31]   Office of Fair Trading, *Consumer Credit Deregulation* (OFT, 1994) at pp. 62–3.

[32]   OJ 1992 L 156/21.

[33]   Directive 97/7 on the protection of consumers in respect of distance contracts: OJ 1997 L 144/19. On the draft directive see generally R. Bradgate, 'Distant Selling in the United Kingdom and the Proposed E.C. Directive' (1993) 1 *ConsumLJ* 19: G. Howells, 'A Consideration of European Proposals to Regulate Distant Selling' in *Enhancing the Legal Position of the European Consumer,* J. Lonbay (ed.), (IEL/BIICL, forthcoming) and for a view in French by the official responsible for European legislation in this area see J. Allix, 'La protection du consommateur en matière de contrats à distance' [1993] *REDC* 95.

of the Direct Marketing Association (DMA)[34] and the Mail Order Traders Association (MOTA).[35] The DMA Code certainly reflects the influence of the Directive. We shall also see that prior to the 2000 Regulations there were some specific legal controls affecting distance selling and certain general laws like the Data Protection Act 1998 have a major impact on marketing practices.

7.3.1 What is Distance Selling?

Distance selling covers a wide range of trading activities. Some forms are fairly traditional, such as mail order catalogues, mail order advertisements in newspapers, personalised direct mailing and door-to-door distribution of leaflets. Others are of more recent origin. One particularly prevalent practice in recent times has been telephone selling. This has caused a great deal of concern as it can be intrusive to receive unwanted telephone calls that have to be answered. As long ago as 1983 the OFT found that 21 per cent of consumers surveyed who owned a telephone had received an unsolicited call, with 17 per cent of these having received five or more calls.[36] One suspects today the figures would be far higher. More recently, videotex systems allow the customer to view information about products on the television screen and order using a television key-pad. Satellite and cable television have introduced shopping channels on which goods are advertised and consumers phone through their orders. The growth of the internet as a selling medium has threatened to revolutionise the way we shop and is dealt with separately below. It is easy to dismiss some of the more esoteric forms of distant selling as belonging to the world of science fiction. However, by the end of the century we are just as likely to sign an electronic cheque on a computer terminal in our homes as we are today to write a cheque or give our credit card details over the phone.[37] That the last example is now commonplace shows just how quickly new technology has allowed distance selling to become a regular feature for many consumers.

Distance contracts are defined in the Distance Selling Regulations 2000 as:

> any contract concerning goods or services concluded between a supplier and a consumer under an organised distance sales or service provision

---

[34] See http://www.dma.org.uk. It also offers Best Practice Guidelines.

[35] Surprisingly it does not have a web page.

[36] *Selling by Telephone* (OFT, 1984).

[37] On e-money see Directive 2000/46/EC on the taking up, pursuit of and prudential supervision of the business of electronic money institutions: OJ 2000 L275/39.

> scheme run by the supplier who, for the purposes of the contract, makes exclusive use of one or more means of distance communication up to and including the moment at which the contract is concluded.

This definition only covers organised schemes. The fact my local florist as a favour sometimes takes an order over the phone and delivers flowers to my wife does not make the contract a distance contract. In contrast Interflora is set up to take orders over the phone and would result in a distance contract if a means of distance communication were used to place the order. Also there must be exclusive use of distance communication until the contract is concluded. If at any stage in the pre-contractual process there is face-to-face contact the Regulations cease to apply. Schedule 1 of the Regulations gives an indicative list of means of distance communications. This illustrates the breadth of application of the Regulations is as broad as our description of distance selling set out above. It ranges from printed matter to teleshopping. Mention is made of e-mail, but interestingly not websites. This evidences that when the Directive was first proposed in the early 1990's internet selling was just being speculated about and even by the time of the Directive's adoption in 1997 internet selling was not as prominent as it is today.

There are various exceptions for contracts to which the Regulations do not apply.[38] These cover contracts:

(i)   for the sale or disposition of land and such contracts that also include the construction of buildings, except for rental agreements;
(ii)   concluded by means of an automated vending machine or automated commercial premises;
(iii) concluded with a telecommunications operator through a public pay-phone;
(iv)   concluded at an auction (thus telephone auctions and eBay would be excluded);
(v)   relating to financial services. Schedule 2 gives a non-exhaustive list of financial services including investment services, insurance and re-insurance operations, banking services and services relating to dealings in futures or options. Financial services have been the subject of a separate Directive that is awaiting implementation.

7.3.2 Restrictions on Marketing

The Unsolicited Goods and Services Acts 1971 and 1975 had provided that in certain circumstances a person who receives unsolicited goods could

---

[38]   Regulation 5.

treat them as an unconditional gift. This arose either (i) when six months had elapsed from when the goods were received or (ii) when 30 days had elapsed from when the recipient sent the sender of the goods notice that they are unsolicited. This has been replaced by rules on inertia selling in the Distance Selling Regulations 2000.[39] These allow the recipient of unsolicited goods to treat them as an unconditional gift. There is no longer any need to keep the goods for a period of time. The only limitations are where the recipient has agreed to acquire or return the goods, or has reasonable cause to believe they were sent with a view to being acquired for business purposes. A person who (i) demands payment for unsolicited goods and services, or (ii) threatens to bring legal proceedings for such payment, (iii) threatens or places the consumer on a defaulters' list, or (iv) threatens or invokes a collection service, is guilty of an offence.

Some of the rules in the Unsolicited Goods and Services Acts remain in place. In fact they contain very similar offences relating to demanding payment.[40] There are also rules prohibiting demanding payment for entry into directories[41] and for sending unsolicited publications describing or illustrating human sexual techniques.[42] The Consumer Credit Act 1974 makes the sending of circulars to minors an offence[43] and prohibits the sending of unsolicited credit tokens.[44] The Financial Services Authorities Conduct of Business standards also have some restrictions that apply to financial services, such as those on unsolicited promotions and on the use of the internet.[45]

The Data Protection Act 1998 has a significant impact on distant selling practice. Registered users have to comply with the eight Data Protection Principles set out in Schedule 1 of the Act. The First Principle is the most significant in the present context, requiring that personal data be obtained and processed fairly and lawfully. Unless consent has been given any processing must be necessary to permit a contract to be made or performed, to fulfil legal obligations, to protect the vital interests of the data subject or to facilitate the administration of justice or work of other officials.

The Second Principle requires data to be obtained for specified and lawful purposes and not to be used or disclosed in a manner incompatible with such specified purposes. Further principles requires, *inter alia*, that personal data be adequate, relevant and not excessive; accurate and up-to-

---

[39] Regulation 24.
[40] Section 2.
[41] Regulation 3.
[42] Regulation 4.
[43] Section 50.
[44] Section 51.
[45] See FSA Handbook available at http://www.fsa.gov.uk.

date; not kept for longer than necessary; and processed in accordance with the data subject's rights. Measures should be put in place to prevent unauthorised or unlawful processing and against accidental loss, destruction or damage to personal data. Data should not be transferred outside the EEA unless to a country ensuring adequate protection. This has caused some problems with transferring data to the US, where data protection laws are less strict and has resulted in the so-called safe harbour principle where equivalent protection is ensured through US firms registering with the US Department of Commerce that they are willing to agree to certain data protection principles.

The Data Protection Act 1984 had provided a limited exemption for mailing lists held only for the purpose of distributing articles or information. There are some transitional provisions in the 1998 Act for processing that was already underway in 1998, but in any event this exemption is likely to have been little used since it required prior consent, gave the data subject the right to have his or her name removed and only afforded limited rights to trade in the data. As most mailers wish to trade their lists they will register under the Act.

The Mailing Preference Service is a voluntary scheme run by the DMA. Its Suppression List includes names and addresses of those individuals who have indicated that they wish to receive less promotional material. Each quarter a Consumer File is sent to mailers who are members of the scheme and they are meant to ensure the current Suppression List is applied to their mailing list. The preferred method is to leave the name on the list, but to apply a suppression marker so that it is not inadvertently added to the list again at a later date. The DMA also runs similar lists for telephones, faxes and e-mail as well as one for people who have miscarried or suffered an infant death and do not wish to receive information on baby products. The Data Protection Act 1998 also gives individuals the right to prevent processing for direct marketing purposes by giving written notice to individual data controllers.[46]

These matters are also addressed in the British Codes of Advertising Practice and Sales Promotion,[47] which provide guidance on list and database practice. The Advertising Association has produced a Code of Practice Covering the use of Personal Data for Advertising and Direct Marketing Purposes. As mentioned the Direct Marketing Association (DMA) and the Mail Order Traders' Association (MOTA) have Codes of Practice which cover these matters. There is also a National Newspapers Mail Order Protection Scheme (MOPS) Code of Practice, which controls who can advertise mail order goods in national newspapers.[48]

---

[46]   Section 11.
[47]   See Section 10.6.
[48]   On Codes of Practice see Section 13.9.5.6.

7.3.3 Controls on Contents of Marketing

Distance sellers are subject to the general rules on misleading trade descriptions,[49] but also to some specific supplementary provisions. Thus the Mail Order Transactions (Information) Order 1976[50] requires that in all written advertisements, circulars or leaflets which invite postal orders requiring payment in advance, there should be a legible description of the name and full business address of the person inviting the order. The Business Advertisements (Disclosure) Order 1977[51] provides that anyone seeking to sell goods in the course of a business shall not publish or cause to be published an advertisement unless it is reasonably clear from it that the goods are to be sold in the course of a business.

The content of marketing relating to distance sales is also covered by the self-regulatory codes. Indeed the British Codes of Advertising and Sales Promotion have a special section on distance selling. The DMA Code contains rules on solicitations; for example, it requires that any advertisement which could result in the entry into a contractual commitment for goods and services should include a short, simple statement of the essential points of the offer, clearly displayed for the customer to keep. The matter is also covered in the MOTA Code. The Independent Television Commission had a Code of Practice containing provisions related specifically to distant selling advertisements and home shopping features. Its functions have been transferred to OFCOM.

Certain of the information requirements in the Distance Selling Regulations 2000 will be complied with in advertisements.

7.3.4 Information Requirements

One of the major impacts of the Distance Selling Regulations 2000 has been the increase in information requirements. These divide broadly into two types: pre-contractual disclosure and written disclosure at or soon after the conclusion of the contract.

Pre-contractual information must be given in good time prior to the conclusion of the contract.[52] Although this does not mandate the information be in an advertisement, this will often be the easiest way of complying. So long as it is clear and comprehensible the information can be given in any manner appropriate to the means of distance communication. This gives a certain flexibility which is especially

---

49 See Chapter 8.
50 S.I. 1976/1812.
51 S.I. 1977/1918.
52 Regulation 7(1).

important in relation to internet selling. Regulation 7(1) then goes on to list 11 pieces of information that the trader might have to provide. These cover (i) identity of the supplier; (ii) description of the main characteristics of the goods and services; (iii) price; (iv) delivery costs; (v) arrangements for payment, delivery and performance; (vi) existence of a right of cancellation; (vii) cost of means of communication, if other than basic rate, (viii) period of validity of offer or price, (ix) where appropriate the minimum duration, (x) information as to whether the supplier wishes to supply substitute products if the product ordered is unavailable, (xi) information that the cost of returning substitute product would be met by supplier.

Some of the problems with information requirements as consumer protection mechanisms have already been discussed.[53] This list of information requirements highlights the problem of information overload. The number of pieces of information can overwhelm consumers, for whom it is said 'less is more'.[54] Indeed on average it has been suggested that consumers can only process seven 'chunks' of information.[55] The problem is even greater in the Directive on Consumer Financial Services, which has 21 information obligations relating to the supplier, the financial service, the distance contract and redress. There is an obvious conflict here between the consumer's desire to have as much information as possible and yet be able to discern the wheat from the chaff so that his attention is directed to the matters that really affect him when making decisions. In fact there could be incentives for suppliers to over-provide information in an unstructured manner so that consumers fail to pick up on important information. Indeed research on credit has shown that lots of small print can give consumers the misleading impression that the product must be well regulated. What may be needed is some prioritisation as to which information has to be given particular prominence. Comparisons might be made with some of the techniques used in consumer credit contracts to draw attention to particular terms, such as the use of boxes or requirements as to prominence of certain terms.

A second set of information requirements can be complied with either prior to the conclusion of the contract or thereafter in good time, which means in the case of services during the performance of the contract or in

---

[53]   See Section 1.8.3.

[54]   B. Wendlandt, 'EC Directives on Time-Sharing and for self-employed commercial agents – Apples, Oranges and the Core of the Information Overload Problem' in *Information Rights and Obligations: A Challenge for Party Autonomy and Transactional Fairness,* G. Howells, A Janssen and R. Schulze (eds.) (Ashgate, forthcoming) quoting a German thesis by Kind.

[55]   G. Miller, 'The Magical Number Seven, Plus or Minus Two: Some Limits on Our Capacity for Processing Information' (1956) 63 *The Psychological Review* 81.

the case of goods (unless being delivered to a third party) at the time of delivery. As they can be complied with post contractually, the function of these disclosures is less to influence contracting behaviour and more to serve as a record of what has been achieved.

It is possible for these disclosures to be made at the same time as the pre-contractual disclosures, but as the requirements do not wholly overlap some additional information will have to be supplied. Also these disclosure requirements must be provided in writing or any durable medium. This restriction is discussed below in the context of the electronic contracting. However, at this point it should be noted that in one respect the Distance Selling Regulations 2000 have failed properly to implement the Directive, for whilst the Directive gives a choice of writing and durable medium for most aspects, it states the right to cancel must be given in writing. This special requirement for writing regarding cancellation is not found in the Regulations. This may have little impact since the requirement for writing in the UK is being viewed as easier to satisfy than providing information in a durable medium. This example, may in fact suggest the generous English approach to writing may be misplaced. This is discussed below in relation to the internet.[56]

This second set of information requirements apply with respect to items (i)-(vi) of the pre-contractual information obligations listed above and in addition information relating to the right to cancel (including notice of whether the consumer must return the goods and at whose expense); a geographical address of the supplier's business to which complaints can be addressed; information about after-sales service and guarantees; conditions for exercising the right to cancel where the contract exceeds one year or is of unspecified duration; and, the fact that unless agreed otherwise contracts for services cannot be cancelled once performance has begun.

7.3.5 Cancellation

The motives for allowing a right of cancellation in the context of distance selling are more complex than in relation to doorstep selling, where the desire is clearly to allow parties a chance for quiet reflection on a contract struck in the heat of the moment. Removing the danger of rash decision-making certainly plays a part in relation to distant selling, especially where the solicitation is by telephone (which may perhaps be equated to a personal visit) or by an enticing television home shopping feature. This motivation would not explain why the right is extended to mail order sales (for instance, in response to newspaper advertisements) or catalogue sales. Here the policy is far more influenced by a desire to give the consumer an

---

[56]   See Section 7.4.3.

opportunity to assure themselves of the quality of the goods. Thus the right of cancellation can be seen as an extension of the policy of ensuring that the consumer makes a fully informed choice.

Mail order companies have traditionally allowed consumers to keep goods for a trial period or have offered money-back guarantees. Indeed the MOTA Code recommends that goods should be supplied on not less than 14 days approval. The DMA Code has similar rules. Prior to recent reforms English law knew of some instances of cancellation rights. We have already seen how such a right was introduced for doorstep selling under the influence of EC law. Similarly a right of cancellation was included in the Timeshare Act 1992. Certain financial service contacts are subject to cooling-off periods under the rules of the Financial Services Authority. Some consumer credit contracts have of course been subject to cooling-off periods, but in the case of consumer credit agreements 'pure' distance sales would be excluded as there is a requirement that there be oral representations made in the presence of the debtor. Now thanks to the impact of the Distance Selling Regulations there is a general seven day cancellation right for most distance selling contracts not concerning financial services. When the Directive on the Distance Selling of Consumer Financial Services is adopted then, subject to some exceptions, there will be an even longer cancellation period of 14 days for services covered, extending to 30 days for life and personal pensions.

We will concentrate on the right to cancel as set out in the Distance Selling Regulations 2000.[57] This provides for a cancellation period of seven working days, but there are exclusions for contracts for services where the consumer has been informed that the contract may not be cancellable and performance has begun; goods and services subject to fluctuations in the financial market; goods made to the consumer's specification or clearly personalised that by their nature cannot be returned or are liable to deteriorate; audio or video recordings or computer software that have been unsealed; newspapers, periodicals or magazines; or gaming, betting or lottery services.

Cancellation can be effected by the consumer giving notice of cancellation to the supplier or any person previously notified as someone to whom notice of cancellation can be given. The consumer is assisted by the fact that notice is treated as being properly given if it is left at the last known address of the supplier or posted, faxed of e-mailed to the last known address. It is taken to be given on the day the notice was left or sent. Notice must be in writing or in another durable medium available and accessible to the supplier. It can be expressed in any manner so long as it indicates the intention to cancel the contract. Interestingly, and perhaps disappointingly, the practice from consumer credit of requiring the

---

57   Regulations 10–18.

consumer to be provided with a cancellation form which they can use has not been adopted.

Assuming the supplier has complied with his information obligations, the cancellation period starts on the day the contract was concluded and expires seven working days[58] from the day after the day on which the consumer (or a third party) receives the goods or is provided with the required information.[59] Similar rules apply to services, save that the period will run from the day on which the contract was concluded, so long as the information provisions have been complied with.[60] However, where necessary information has not been provided the seven day period begins to run three months after the contract was concluded. This rule is found in the Directive and seeks to prevent the contract being cancellable indefinitely if the information provisions have not been complied with. However, the policy runs counter to that of the European Court of Justice in *Heininger v Bayerische Hypo-und Vereinsbank AG*,[61] when it struck down a German law implementing the Doorstep Selling Directive. That Directive had included no outer limit for cancellation where information obligations had not been complied with. Germany introduced a limit of one year, but the Court was concerned the right to cancel could in practice be avoided if the consumer was simply not informed of the right and the supplier trusted in general consumer ignorance of their rights. Of course such a long term right to cancel could be abused. That possibility has to be taken into account when considering whether a three month and seven day cancellation period offers sufficient protection. Nevertheless, one might think of a scheme under which the use and enjoyment of the goods could be taken into account when the contract was cancelled, say, after more than three months.

---

[58] Working days are defined to mean all days other than Saturdays, Sundays and public holiday, Regulation 3(1). In doorstep selling simply 'days' are referred to rather than 'working days'.

[59] Regulation 11.

[60] Regulation 12.

[61] Case C–481/99 [2001] 1 ECR 1–9945. The Heiningers had been pressed into buying property in East Germany by the sales pitch that it was the last chance to benefit from Government tax breaks: see G.P. Calliess, 'The Limits of Eclecticism in Consumer Law: National Struggles and the Hope for a Coherent European Contract Law. A Comment on the ECJ's and FCJ's 'Heininger'-decisions' (2002) 3 German Law Journal available at http://www.germanlawjournal.com/article.php?id=175. Calliess notes that the impact of the German law was that the Heiningers received back interest payments, but had to pay something for the value of the credit and so would only gain if the agreement rate were higher than the market rate at the time the contract was concluded. The underlying problem of being sold a flat at double its market value was not addressed.

Cancellation has the effect of treating the contract as if it had not been made.[62] The consequences are similar to those for cancelled consumer credit agreements.[63] On cancellation any sums paid by or on behalf of the consumer should be reimbursed and any returned.[64] The reimbursement should be made as soon as possible and in any event within 30 days. The supplier can keep some money back if the contract provided that the consumer should return the goods and he either has not done so or has done so at the supplier's expense.

The consumer is also under a duty to take reasonable care of the goods prior to cancellation and to restore the goods on cancellation subject to any security being returned.[65] Unless there is a term requiring the consumer to return the goods to the supplier, his only obligation is to deliver them up at his own premises, pursuant to a request in writing or other durable medium. The consumer can however discharge his obligations by delivering them to a person on whom notice of cancellation could be served or sending them so long as he has taken reasonable care to ensure they are received by the supplier and are not damaged in transit. If the consumer receives, but fails to comply with, a request to return the goods within 21 days of cancellation the duty to take reasonable care continues until he delivers or sends the goods. If no request is forthcoming within 21 days the duty to take reasonable care ceases. This period is extended to six months where a term of the contract requires the consumer to return the goods. If any goods were given by the consumer in part-exchange, he will be entitled to receive a sum equal to the part-exchange allowance, unless they are returned to him in a substantially similar condition.[66]

There is also automatic cancellation of related credit agreements.[67] No interest will be payable on amounts repaid within one month or in the case of instalment credit before the date on which the first instalment is due. Otherwise the consumer remains liable to repay the balance of principal and interest (excluding all other sums) once he has received a written request[68] recalculating the remaining instalments as nearly as may be in accordance with the agreement and without extending the period.

---

[62] Regulation 10(2).
[63] See Section 6.8.3.
[64] Regulation 14.
[65] Regulation 17.
[66] Regulation 18.
[67] Regulation 15.
[68] Note a request by an alternative durable medium is not sufficient.

7.3.6 Performance

Regulation 19 requires that the supplier performs the contract within 30 days starting from the day after the day on which the consumer sent his order. This could of course be quite difficult if the order is lost in the post! But the policy is clearly not to keep the consumer hanging on where a trader simply is not able to perform promptly. Where the supplier knows he is unable to perform within that period he should inform the consumer and reimburse any sums paid by or on behalf of the consumer.[69] The money should be reimbursed within 30 days from the day following the expiration of the period for performance. Suppliers may supply goods or services of equivalent price and quality provided this possibility was provided for in the contract and the consumer had been informed that the cost of returning substitute goods would be met by the supplier.

7.3.7 Payment by Card

The Distance Selling Directive required the consumer to be protected against fraudulent use of his payment card. Certain protection already existed under the Consumer Credit Act 1974. Section 83 protected debtors under a regulated consumer credit agreement against misuse of the credit facility. As regards credit-tokens, such as credit and debit cards, s. 84 allows for liability for misuse up to £50 before the creditor has been notified of the loss. These are supplemented by the Distance Selling Regulations 2000 to cover situations not covered by s. 83 of the 1974, perhaps because the credit agreement was not regulated (such as charge cards). Also the £50 liability does not apply to contracts covered by the Regulations.

The Regulations cover fraudulent use of a payment card in relation to a contract to which they apply.[70] Payment card is said to include credit cards, charge cards, debit cards and store cards. Where such payments are unauthorised the consumer can cancel it and be recredited or have sums returned by the card issuer.

One slight complication is that this protection both under the Consumer Credit Act 1974 and the Distance Selling Regulations 2000 applies when the person making the fraudulent use of the card was not acting, or was not to be treated as acting, as the consumer's agent. It is fair to exclude cases of agency, but in which situations will someone be treated

---

[69] The parties can agree to no reimbursement in the case of outdoor leisure events which by their nature cannot be rescheduled.

[70] Regulation 21.

as acting as an agent and will this undermine the Directive's requirement to protect consumers against all fraudulent use?

7.3.8 Protection of Advance Payments

There is no protection of advance payments, but there is a very real danger to consumers' money in distant selling contracts where pre-payment is required. The danger may consist of fraud, with rogue traders advertising non-existent goods or services. The greatest danger, however, is the risk of insolvency. This risk is inherent in every transaction requiring a pre-payment, but is exacerbated where consumers are not familiar with the nature of the business they are dealing with, as is frequently the case in distance selling. Companies may be able to reduce the risks to their customers in the event of an insolvency if pre-payments are paid into a separate account and held on trust for the customer.[71]

This problem is tackled by Codes of Practice, most stringently by the MOPS Code of Practice. This Code prohibits 'forward trading' which is the practice under which customer payments are used to purchase goods to satisfy orders. The Code also provides for additional safeguards to be put in place when there is uncertainty about the ability of the advertiser to meet his potential commitments. For instance, this might include (i) where goods advertised are of high value, or (ii) where a large-scale advertising programme is envisaged, or (iii) where there is doubt about an advertiser's solvency. The advertiser might then be required to furnish an indemnity This may take the form of a bank guarantee or even the requirement to open a stakeholder account so that the funds are placed in the hands of a trusted third party until the goods are despatched.

7.3.9 Risk

The rules as to when property passes had frequently resulted in goods supplied under distance sales contracts being at the consumer's risk, at least once they are despatched. This harsh rule had been alleviated somewhat by Codes of Practice. Thus the MOTA Code allows the consumer to return goods damaged in transit and obtain a replacement; if no replacement is available the supplier should offer a full refund together with any carriage costs paid. The legal position has now been improved as a result of a general reform of sales law, which provides that in consumer

---

[71] See, *Re Kayford Ltd* [1974] 1 WLR 279. Such schemes may run into technical legal problems, however, as there is a requirement to show a sufficient intention to create a trust.

sales the goods remain at the seller's risk until they are delivered to the consumer.[72]

7.3.10 Enforcement

The Regulations contain injunction procedures that can be used where a person is in breach of his or her obligations.[73] These are similar to the general powers contained in the Enterprise Act 2002, but some of the requirements of the 2002 Act do not apply such as the need for collective harm and also the parties that can bring actions are limited to enforcement authorities i.e. the OFT and trading standards departments.[74] Consumer groups do not have standing in respect of domestic infringements of the Regulations, although cross-border disputes would be subject to the community infringement procedure under the Enterprise Act 2002.

7.4 ELECTRONIC COMMERCE

7.4.1 Growth of Electronic Commerce

The internet has been viewed as one of the major engines for growth and innovation in the economy. However, few, if any, traders are running profitable web trading businesses. Some of the more fanciful estimates of the growth of this sector have proven to be hopelessly optimistic. Yet it remains the case that the www has had a significant impact on retailing. More and more consumers are using the internet to shop or at least view products. This has been most marked in areas such as travel, where buying flights and hotel rooms over the internet, is a familiar feature. Also sales of books and CDs, because of their ease of shipping and the fact people usually know what they are buying, have been important sectors for internet trading. Equally software, which can be downloaded, has been predictably another important area, although it raises some particular legal issues as the product is delivered on-line.[75] Even some larger appliances, such as white kitchen goods, are being sold over the internet and delivered

---

[72] See, now, s. 20(4), Sale of Goods Act 1979.

[73] Regulation 27.

[74] For discussion of procedure under Enterprise Act 2002, see Section 13.9.5.3.

[75] For instance the right of cancellation under the Distance Selling Regulations does not apply where software is unsealed by the consumer, but what about where it does not have to be unsealed as it is simply delivered to his computer terminal? Can information obligations be complied with in such cases? Should different rules of private international law apply where the whole transaction is electronic?

direct to the consumer from warehouses missing out the retailer. Internet auction rooms like eBay are also now familiar features of the marketplace.

The full impact of the internet on how we buy and sell is still being worked out. For instance, intelligent agents are being developed to match consumer preferences to the market offerings. In theory the internet offers great potential for small companies to start up without having to pay for High Street premises. However, the tendency remains for internet shopping to be dominated by established High Street names or companies that have built up a strong brand, such as Amazon. This is because consumers are still nervous about this new medium. They are aware of the advantages of shopping from home and the greater choice and often lower prices the internet brings, but they also ask themselves questions such as: will the goods arrive? Is there a danger of credit card fraud? How will my data be used? What do I do if the goods are not satisfactory? One typical reaction is to shop on the internet, but only with brands that they can trust, or to use the internet as a shop window and then buy through more traditional means. If the internet is to be a place where small businesses prosper it probably needs the legal protection to be strong so that consumers can have confidence in shopping on-line. One problem with establishing this confidence is the ephemeral nature of the internet. It is hard to track down where suppliers are. Scam merchants often target consumers in other jurisdictions in order to use national borders as a shield against enforcement[76] and often disperse the proceeds through a complex trail. Regulators face a major challenge in overcoming the widely held belief that the internet is an ungovernable environment. Not only do they need robust laws, but also mechanisms for co-operation with regulators in other countries.[77]

7.4.2 Regulation of the Internet Shopping

The Distant Selling Regulations are a significant source of protection for consumers shopping on the internet. However, this topic merits special attention as a suite of laws have been developed to regulate the internet and these also impact on consumer protection. A feature of e-commerce regulation is that many legislators rushed to enact legislation, hoping to be at the forefront of initiatives so as to mark their jurisdiction out as being 'e-commerce friendly'. It was in this vein that the EC adopted its Directive on

---

[76] Recent there was publicity surrounding Canadian scammers targeting British consumers with hoax e-mails suggesting they have won the Canadian lottery.

[77] On which see Chapter 13.8.

Electronic Commerce.[78] This is implemented by Electronic Commerce (EC Directive) Regulations 2002,[79] but some matters had already been addressed in the UK by Electronic Communications Act 2000. This also deals with Digital Signatures that are also subject to European legislation.[80] There is also specialist data protection legislation for electronic commerce deriving from EC law.[81] There have also been attempts to ensure that regulation of the internet and consumer protection is developed in line with sound principles at a global level. Notable amongst these initiatives are the UNCITRAL Model Law on Electronic Commerce[82] and digital signatures and the OECD Guidelines for Consumer Protection in the Context of Electronic Commerce. Reforms of private international law have also taken account of e-commerce.

7.4.3 Formation

At the time the Distance Selling Directive was being established the internet was in its infancy. Annex I mentions electronic mail as one of the means of distance communication. However, using electronic mail is only one way in which consumers might contract over the internet. Another method that is increasingly popular is through web pages where a link between the server and client machines is in place during data exchanges.[83]

The legal consequences of the two methods of contracting via the internet may be different and be affected by the fact the web involves a continuously open link, whereas e-mail involves sending packets of information over the internet though various servers and is not instantaneous, even if it sometimes seems as if it is. A web advertisement

---

78 Directive 2000/31/EC on certain aspects of information society services: OJ 2000 L 178/1. See R. Brownsword and G. Howells, 'Europe's E-Commerce Directive – A Too Hasty Rush to Judgment?' (2000/1) 11 *Journal of Law and Information Science* 77.

79 S.I. 2002/2013. Financial services are dealt with in the Electronic Commerce Directive (Financial Services and Markets) Regulations 2002, S.I. 2002/1775.

80 Directive 1999/93 on a Community Framework for electronic signatures: OJ 2000 L 13/12.

81 Directive 2002/58/EC concerning the processing of personal data and the protection of privacy in the electronic communications sector (Directive on privacy and electronic communications): OJ 2002 L 201/37. Implemented by the Privacy and Electronic Communications (EC Directive) Regulations 2003 S.I. 2003/2426.

82 This is said not to override any consumer protection rules.

83 A. Murray, 'Entering into Contracts Electronically: The Real W.W.W. ' in *Law & the Internet* L. Edwards and C. Waelde (Hart, 2000).

or e-mail can be either an offer capable of acceptance by the consumer or a mere invitation to treat. This will depend upon construction of the terms, just as in the off-line environment. The courts are likely to be unwilling to find web advertisers liable to sell when the price has been mistakenly placed far too low or where demand far outstrips supply. Nevertheless at some stage one of the parties will make an offer and the other party will accept. It will be important to know whether the acceptance is made when the consumer clicks on an icon saying submit in the case of a web-contract, or, when an e-mail is sent or only when the other party receives the message of acceptance, or possibly when it is received by his server so that he could access it. This may affect both the time and place of contract.

Normally acceptance would only be effective when received. There is a well-known exception for acceptances that have been posted.[84] The courts have treated telexes[85] as instantaneous means of communication and therefore subject to the normal rule rather than the postal rule. One might expect faxes to be treated similarly. There is no ruling so far on the status of internet contracts, but a possible distinction might be drawn between web and e-mail contracts. Communication over the web might be considered instantaneous, as either party will know whether the link has been broken. In contrast e-mails might be viewed as more on a par with posting a letter. The sender entrusts his message to a service provider which breaks it down into packets of information that are sent down the wire through various often different routes before they are eventually reassembled frequently after they have passed through a complex maze of servers.

On the whole e-commerce seems simply to require the application of traditional legal rules to the new context of internet selling.[86] However, as the justifications for the postal rule and its application to e-commerce are fairly ambiguous, this might justify legislation setting down the consequences of various contractual steps. Indeed the draft E-Commerce Directive had attempted to resolve the question of the moment of conclusion of contracts. For consumers this would have been when they had received a receipt of acceptance and had confirmed receipt of the same. The adopted E-Commerce Directive as implemented in the Electronic Commerce (EC Directive) Regulations[87] simply requires the service provider to provide information on the different technical steps to

---

84   *Adams v Lindsell* (1818) 1 B & Ald. 681.

85   *Entores Ltd v Miles Far East Corp* [1955] 2 QB 327 and *Brinkibon Ltd v Stahag Stahl und Stalhwarenhandelsgesellschaf mbh* [1983] 2 AC 34.

86   R. Brownsword and G. Howells, 'When Surfers Start to Shop: Internet Commerce and Contract Law' (1999) 19 *Legal Studies* 287.

87   S.I. 2002/2013.

follow to conclude the contract.[88] In any event that obligation does not apply to contracts concluded exclusively by electronic mail.[89]

7.4.4 Formalities

The E-Commerce Directive requires that legal systems allow contracts to be concluded by electronic means. The English common law is in fact very flexible as to the means by which contracts can be concluded and there are no inherent obstacles to contracting electronically. However, there are numerous formalities set down in specific legislation. Section 8 of the Electronic Communications Act 2000 contains enabling powers to modify legislation so as to authorise or facilitate electronic communication.

Some of the present consumer protection rules clearly could not be complied with electronically. For instance, the Consumer Credit Act 1974 requires that certain notices be actually posted.[90] Amidst this rush to promote e-commerce one might wonder whether some traditional rules do not serve a purpose, since consumers may react differently to a letter through the post than to an e-mail and in sensitive areas like consumer credit one should perhaps be slow to interfere with established rules. The Government seems to have come to a sensible compromise by suggesting that whilst there is general facilitation of online consumer credit contracting, at least cancellation and default notices should continue to be required to be posted. It recognises that the consequences of failing to read the notices could be particularly severe and that postal communications were more difficult to overlook or destroy than electronic communications.

Generally the extent of reform needed will depend upon whether existing writing requirements can be satisfied electronically and if the requirements for signatures can be met by electronic signatures. The Interpretation Act 1978 states:

> Writing includes typing, printing, lithography and other forms of representing or reproducing words in a visible form, and expressions referring to writing are construed accordingly.[91]

In its Advice *Electronic Commerce: Formal Requirements in Commercial Transactions*,[92] the Law Commission believes that e-mail and websites satisfy the test for writing as they are another form of representing or

---

[88]   Regulation 9(1)(a).
[89]   Regulation 9(4).
[90]   See Chapter 6.5.4 for discussion of reforms.
[91]   Schedule 1.
[92]   2001.

reproducing words in a visible form. They rejected the alternative view that the digital information was not itself visible until a coding convention had been applied to it.[93]

Of course where the requirements for writing derive from EC legislation it is entirely possible that European law might be more demanding as regards the requirement for writing. However, when Commission officials speak about the requirement, their views seem as liberal as those of the Law Commission.

Analysis of the Directives might not entirely support this view. The Distance Selling Directive requires certain information to be provided in writing or another durable medium, but singles out information on the right of withdrawal[94] to be given in writing. This suggests writing was seen as a more demanding requirement than durable medium. In fact the UK implementation singularly fails to take account of the special treatment of information about cancellation.[95]

Durable medium is not defined in the Distance Selling Directive/Regulations but in subsequent directives, such as the Distance Selling of Consumer Financial Services Directive it is said to mean:

> any instrument which enables the consumer to store information addressed personally to him in a way accessible for future reference for a period of time adequate for the purposes of the information and which allows unchanged reproduction of the information stored.

As Recital 20 explains this includes information on floppy discs, DVD's and the hard drive of the consumer's computer on which electronic mail is stored, but not websites unless they satisfy the criteria of durable medium, which is unlikely as their content can be changed. This is admirably clear, but one might wonder if in all circumstances it is safe to rely on the consumer taking the initiative to store the e-mail with this vital information. What might suit a contract for a music CD, might not be adequate for a major financial services contract. Indeed it is interesting that, although the UK government has proposed a very flexible regime to facilitate the selling of consumer credit over the internet, it will still require cancellation and default notices to be sent by traditional rather than

---

[93] See C. Reed, *Digital Information Law – Electronic Documents and Requirements of Form* (Centre for Commercial Law Studies, 1996).

[94] The Directive uses the phrase withdrawal, but this is synonymous with cancellation.

[95] Consumer Protection (Distance Selling) Regulations 2000, Regulation 8.

electronic means.[96] It might be necessary to have different regimes for different types of product or service.

English law has long held a flexible approach to what amounts to a signature. In principle it can easily accommodate digital signatures. The most common form of digital signature is public key crypotography, whereby a signer would use their private key to sign a document that would be decrypted using their public key.[97] The EC Digital Signatures Directive requires certain signatures, known as 'advanced electronic signatures', to satisfy the legal requirements of a signature when based on qualified certificates created by a secure-signature-creation device.[98] Section 7 of the Electronic Communications Act 2000 seems to stop short of that by simply stating electronic signatures and certificates relating to them will be admissible in evidence. The 2000 Act also seems deficient in how it deals with cryptography services. It establishes a voluntary approval regime for such providers, but does not impose any statutory liability on such providers as required by the Directive.[99] The statement that the Government is relying on existing law and contractual arrangements does not seem adequate.[100] Such signatures backed by certificates are in fact not commonly used by private consumers because of their cost. However, electronic signatures in a general sense are used widely by consumers on the internet, for instance whenever they write their name at the end of an e-mail or use a PIN when submitting a web form.

7.4.5 Extra Information Obligations

The main information obligations are found in the rules applying to distance selling contracts with consumers.[101] However, the Electronic Commerce (EC Directive) Regulations 2002 provide for some additional rules that apply to consumer contracts, but are not restricted to the consumer context. Anyone operating an 'information society service' must make certain details available about themselves in a form and manner that is easily, directly and permanently accessible.[102] There are also rules regarding commercial communications, requiring them to be identifiable as

---

[96] *Establishing a Transparent Market* (DTI, 2003) at 27. See also *Consultation Document on Enabling and Facilitating the Conclusion of Credit and Hire Agreements Electronically Under the Consumer Credit Act 1974*, (DTI, 2002).

[97] See M. Hogg 'Secrecy and Signatures' in Edwards and Waelde (eds.), *op. cit.*

[98] Article 5(1).

[99] Article 6.

[100] *Promoting Electronic Commerce*, (Cm. 4417) at 2.

[101] See Section 7.3.4.

[102] Regulation 6.

such, identifying on whose behalf they are made and controlling promotional offers, competitions and games.[103]

Certain specific information must also be communicated in a clear, comprehensible and unambiguous manner prior to any order being received.[104] These relate to the technical steps needed to conclude the contract, whether it will be filed and accessible, the technical means for identifying and correcting input errors prior to the placing of the order. As regards consumers, codes of conduct should always be mentioned and information provided on how they can be consulted electronically. Terms and conditions should be made available in a way that allows them to be stored and reproduced. It certainly complicates the position to have information obligations scattered around so many different texts.[105]

7.4.6 Contract Terms Incorporation

An important issue for consumers is the extent to which they can be bound by standard terms. This has long been an important concern for consumers as evidenced by many of the old 'ticket' cases in contract law, where traders tried to bind consumers to their general trading terms and conditions by statements on tickets and receipts. This has been problematic in the e-commerce context, because of the ease with which terms and conditions can be imposed on consumers.[106] A similar debate has centred on 'shrink-wrap' agreements: typically digitalised products are sold with a wrapping and it is indicated that by opening the product the consumer accepts the terms and conditions. The problem is that the consumer often cannot see those conditions before he or she unwraps the product and loads the disc into the computer.[107]

In the e-commerce context similar issues are raised by 'click-wrap' agreements where consumers have to assent to terms in order to use a service or proceed with a purchase and there are dangers that they become bound without really being aware of the terms. This is even more problematic in the case of so-called 'browse-wrap' agreements where

---

[103] Regulation 7.

[104] Regulation 9.

[105] G. Howells and A. Nordhausen, 'Information Obligations in EC E-Commerce Law' in *EU Electronic Commerce Law*, R. Nielsen, S.S. Jacobsen and J. Trzaskowski (eds.), (DJØF, 2004).

[106] For a comprehensive survey of case law on this topic see C. Coteanu, *Cyber Consumer Law and Fair Trading* (Ashgate, forthcoming).

[107] *Beta Computers (Europe) Ltd v Adobe Systems (Europe Ltd)* 1996 SLT 604: see S. Robertson, 'The Validity of Shrink-wrap licences in Scots Law' (1998) 2 *JILT* available at http://elj.warwick.ac.uk/jilt/cases/982rob/.

consumers are not even asked to assent, but are simply informed of hyperlinks to where terms and conditions can be found. The courts are likely to judge click-wrap agreements on the basis of how much effort was made to draw the terms to the consumer's attention and is likely to be sceptical of binding consumers to terms found in browse-wrap agreements. However, given the increased controls on the fairness of consumer contracts in the UK, this is less of a problem than in the US where unfair and expensive arbitration clauses in particular have been a cause of concern.[108]

7.4.7 Privacy – Controls on Marketing

Privacy and the internet is one of those issues many consumers claim to be very concerned about, but frequently they will invest very few resources to protect their privacy.[109] Indeed often consumers confuse the issue of privacy with credit card security. As we have seen in Europe, there is legal protection against fraudulent use of credit cards on the internet.[110]

True privacy issues concern the way companies have the ability to monitor our preferences and life-style, for instance through technology like 'cookies' that track which websites we visit. Also there are fears about how the many footprints we leave when using the internet can be brought together and used for ever more sophisticated data analysis and potentially combined with Government records or data held offline.[111] There have been instances when personalised marketing has caused severe problems for consumers. For example, an on-line book retailer may embarrass a customer by e-mailing recommendations for gay books based on the customer's previous buying pattern.

On the whole, the EC Data Protection Directive as implemented by the Data Protection Act 1998 should protect against most abuses. Problems may arise in that the internet may lead to data being held in countries with less rigorous laws or where enforcement is less effective. Even with respect to US companies there have been some difficulties in establishing the mechanism by which safe harbours can be established to allow data to

---

[108] See F.L. Miller, Arbitration Clauses in Consumer Contracts: Building Barriers to Consumer Protection (1999) 78 *Mich. B.J.* 302.

[109] L. Edwards and G. Howells, 'Anonymity, Consumers and the Internet: Where Everyone Knows You're a Dog' in *Digital Anonymity and the Law* C. Nicholl, J. Prins and M. van Dellen (ed.), (TMC Asser Press, 2003) at 226–7.

[110] See Section 7.3.7.

[111] The merger in the US of DoubleClick (which provides on-line ads) and Abacus (which held the largest conventional direct marketing database) was greeted with concern and this led to denials that the databases were to be merged.

be transferred from Europe. It is sometimes suggested that technical solutions rather than legal solutions are more appropriate to the internet context.[112] In the privacy context schemes like 'P3P' give consumers the opportunity to match their privacy preferences against those of suppliers, but one of the problems is that most consumers are not technologically confident enough to take advantage of such schemes even if they could afford the time and expense of using them.[113]

A major annoyance to many consumers is spam – the bulk mailings of unsolicited commercial communications. Few legitimate businesses use this technique. Best practice is moving towards 'permission based marketing'. Spam e-mails almost certainly would involve breaches of EC data protection law.[114] The European legislator was hesitant to prohibit spam e-mails and for a long time only imposed the requirement for prior consent on automated calling machines and faxes.[115] Recently unsolicited e-mails have been added to this list of prohibitions. This is implemented by Regulation 22 of the Privacy and Electronic Communications (EC Directive) Regulations 2003.[116] However, whether this will have any impact is debateable and well highlights the problem of governing the internet. Spammers know that there is little chance that they will be caught, tracked down and prosecuted. Enforcement authorities have limited resources and more pressing concerns. Also the spammers may be working from outside the jurisdiction and in regimes where what they are doing may not even be illegal. Spam is – perhaps surprisingly given the low quality of many offers using that medium – often a highly profitable business and this has caused some internet service providers and states to turn to private law as a way of tackling these annoying e-mailers.[117] However, such attempts to use private law are still unproven, but do illustrate how private law is sometimes turned to out of frustration when public regulation is seen as being ineffective.

---

[112] L. Lessig, *Code and Other Laws of Cyberspace* (Basic Books, 1999).

[113] Edwards and Howells, *op. cit.*

[114] S. Gauthronet and E. Drouard, *Unsolicited Commercial Communications and Data Protection*, summary available at:
http://europa.eu.int/comm/internal_market/privacy/docs/studies/spamsum_en.pdf.

[115] See for example Art. 10 of the Distance Selling Directive.

[116] S.I. 2003/2426.

[117] L. Edwards, 'Canning the Spam: Is there a Case for Legal Control of Junk Electronic Mail?' in Edwards and Waelde, *op. cit.* In the US there are constitutional challenges based on free speech or states interference with commerce to such laws.

7.4.8 Country of Establishment Principle

The impetus for the E-Commerce Directive was clearly to promote e-commerce within the internal market. A clear recognition of this is Art. 3 of the Directive which places an obligation on Member States to ensure that within their 'co-ordinated field' information society service providers comply with national law. Significantly, however, it cannot restrict the freedom to provide services of providers based in another member state for reasons within the co-ordinated field. The principle is that minimum European standards are guaranteed by the Directive and adequate protection for all Europe's consumers is assured by effective regulatory supervision in the state the trader is established in. This is a familiar and increasingly important aspect of European trade law deriving its inspiration from the country of origin principle set down long ago in *Cassis de Dijon*.[118] It is being supported by some important reforms of regulatory structures so that regulatory agencies in the member states can better co-operate with one another in exchanging information and enforcement. This is discussed in Chapter 13.

The country of establishment principle is difficult to apply fully in practice. States welcome the principle, but do not always accept that the EC framework is sufficiently robust to provide the protection their citizens require. The E-Commerce Directive meets these concerns by limiting the harmonised field to the co-ordinated field, which although quite broad expressly excludes requirements relating to the goods, delivery of goods or services not provided by electronic means.[119] Also Member States retain their freedom to act in certain areas, including crucially for our purposes 'the protection of consumers, including investors' so long as there is a serious and grave risk and the measures are proportionate.[120] Nevertheless, the principle of country of establishment is business friendly.

7.4.9 Private International Law

By contrast recent reforms to EC private international law have been viewed as consumer-friendly. These are considered generally in Chapter 14. Traditionally the rules of jurisdiction and applicable law did not provide much assistance to consumers who contracted on their own

---

[118] *Rewe-Zentrale AG v Bundesmonopolverwaltung Für Branntwein*, Case 120/78 [1979] ECR 649.

[119] Article 2(h) and Regulation 2(1) of Electronic Commerce (EC Directive) Regulations 2002.

[120] Article 3(4(a)(i) and Regulation 5(1)(d) of Electronic Commerce (EC Directive) Regulations 2002.

initiative with traders in other states. Such *active* consumers were not seen as deserving of protective rules allowing them to sue in their home jurisdiction and to be assured of national protective laws. Such protection was reserved for *passive* consumers who were lured by traders outside the state to contract with them. This active/passive distinction breaks down on the internet for it is hard to tell who is seeking whom when a traders posts an advertisement on a website and arranges for it to be prominent in search engine searches and the consumer trawls the internet looking for offers.

Business is afraid of being faced with suits in many countries which it cannot afford to defend. In fact this is probably unrealistic given that consumers only litigate as a last resort. Equally most consumers plainly cannot afford to sue across borders. In fact for most purchases on the internet some kind of online dispute resolution is probably the only practical solution.[121]

Nevertheless the private international law issue raised by the internet have been a political hot potato. The Brussels Regulation 44/2001 on Jurisdiction and Enforcement of Judgments on Civil and Commercial Matters[122] seems consumer friendly as it gives jurisdiction to the courts of the consumer's jurisdiction if the trader directs commercial or professional activities to the consumer's state. Yet there are still many debates to be had as to whether a trader is directing activities at a particular state. For instance, use of Greek on a website, might suggest a trader is targeting consumers in Greece, but does that mean he is not also directing such activities at Greeks in London? What exactly does directing activities mean? If it was flights to Athens then Greeks in London might well be the target audience. What relevance is the language? Are all sites in English targeting British Consumers? To what extent can traders limit their exposure by stating they will only contract with consumers from specific states? These issues are still to be worked out, but the general approach of consumer friendly jurisdiction rules for internet contracts is in line with the main US approach. Of course, even once jurisdiction is established, issues of choice of law will remain.

---

[121]   See, E-confidence forum at http://econfidence.jrc.it. See J. Hörnle, 'Online Dispute Resolution in Business to Consumer E-commerce Transactions', *The Journal of Information, Law and Technology (JILT)* 2002 (2) http://elj.warwick.ac.uk/jilt/02–2/hornle.html and S. Kierkegaard, 'Online Alternative Dispute Resolution' in Nielsen *et al, op. cit*; also see Section 14.7.9.

[122]   OJ 2001 L12/1, Arts. 15–17. See in more detail Section 14.9.2.

7.5 CONCLUSION – THE BALANCING OF INTERESTS

This chapter has looked at two forms of marketing – doorstep and distance selling (and in particular the internet variant of the latter). In principle there is no reason why consumers should be threatened by either selling technique. Indeed they can be seen as bringing extra choice to consumers, especially those who, for one reason or another (perhaps because of disabilities or family circumstances) do not have easy access to the normal shops. Both techniques, however, have been shown to involve risks of consumers being exploited by disreputable traders. In addition, many forms of distance selling rely on electronic communication techniques and electronic payment systems which carry inherent risks even when run by reputable traders. Few people would wish to prohibit doorstep and distance selling,[123] but the consumer's right to safeguards must be recognised. In the long term these safeguards are also essential to traders in these sectors, as they will only flourish if consumers have confidence to buy goods through these mediums. The internet exemplifies this well. Its success as a selling medium is dependent upon consumers feeling secure. This involves technological and logistical issues, but also legal security is an important factor. Moreover, unless a legal framework is put in place that inspires confidence the internet will simply bolster the position of established brand names rather than being a vehicle through which small independent traders can benefit from lower entry costs to the market place to provide more choice and better value to the consumer. Not all consumers need initially to be persuaded to use the internet, but sufficient numbers have to have confidence in it that they can spread news of its advantages so that ultimately it becomes a familiar part of the retail environment that most consumers are happy to use.

---

[123] Cf. the views of T. Ison discussed at Section 6.6.

Chapter 8

Trade Descriptions, Advertising and Unfair Commercial Practices

8.1 THE POLICY OF THE LAW

The suppression of misleading trade practices possesses a long history in the United Kingdom. Hallmarking law has a pedigree going back centuries. The first more general statute in the field was the Merchandise Marks Act 1862, replaced by the Merchandise Marks Act 1887. Several statutes of that name followed, the last in 1953. Pressure grew for broader and more sophisticated protection. A Royal Commission was established, yielding the Molony Committee Report on Consumer Protection in 1962.[1] This prepared the ground for what became the Trade Descriptions Act 1968, the centrepiece of the current law and the principal object of investigation in this chapter.

Part of the rationale for such laws lies in the endemic lack of information available to the consumer in the modern market-place. The perception that the consumer cannot grasp a full awareness of products, especially those that are technologically advanced, has spawned a range of laws requiring labelling and other forms of information disclosure. This technique and some of its manifestations are examined in Chapter 1.[2]

The law studied in this chapter concerns practices that mislead the consumer. The attachment of a false description to a product distorts the operation of the market, damaging the consumer and the fair trader. In fact, the rationale of protecting fair traders is at least as strong as that of protecting the consumer; the Trade Descriptions Act is firmly part of the wider field of trade practices law. There are limits on the capacity of the market to 'punish' misleading practices. Consumers may decline to revisit dishonest traders, but, for that consumer, the damage may already be done and, given the limited scope for transmission of information, the only way for other consumers to learn is by making the same mistake. The private law has a role to play, but it cannot plug all the gaps. In some cases making a false trade description will be both a crime and a breach of contract and, occasionally, even a tort. However, this will not invariably be so. Some misleading practices may not constitute violations of private law rights.

---

[1] Cmnd. 1781.
[2] Section 1.8.3 above.

False advertising may be insufficiently precise or formal to generate contractual liability. Even where capable of contractual force, the rules of privity will frequently preclude a consumer bringing an action against an advertiser unless the item has been bought from him or her.[3] The EC's Sales Directive, implemented in the UK in 2002, has caused consumer-friendly adjustment in this position,[4] but has by no means plugged all the gaps. Tort law has a limited role to play in these instances of economic loss.[5] Practical problems of securing effective consumer access to justice add to the inadequacy of private law as a means of deterring misleading trade descriptions.[6] In combination, these factors make the case for public intervention.

The central statute in this area is the Trade Descriptions Act 1968.[7] At stake are also advertising controls, control of misleading prices and misdescriptions of land, found in other enactments and examined below. The 1968 Act is wide-ranging. A Chief Trading Standards Officer, drawing on practical experience, has written that it is the motor trade and the holiday industry which have been especially affected.[8] More recent statistics indicate that the motor trade remains plagued by malfeasance, that the holiday industry has improved its standards and that the home improvements sector is a growing source of concern.[9] However, despite the pattern of problems arising unevenly in particular sectors, the application of the Act is in principle broad.

The 1968 Act created three main offences. The 'Section 1' offence catches the application of a false trade description to any goods or supplying or offering to supply any goods to which a false trade description is applied. This is examined in 8.2 below.

The 'Section 14' offence concerns provision of services. It catches the making of a statement concerning the provision of services, knowing it to be false or being reckless in that regard. This offence requires inquiry into the state of mind of the perpetrator, unlike the s. 1 offence which concentrates exclusively on the act. Section 14 is examined in 8.3 below.

---

3   Chapter 1.3 above.

4   Chapter 3.2, 3.7.

5   Chapter 1.4.

6   This is mentioned in Chapter 1.6 and examined more fully in Chapter 14.

7   The most comprehensive modern treatment is found in R. Bragg, *Trade Descriptions* (OUP, 1991).

8   D. Roberts, '25 Years of the Trade Descriptions Act 1968' (1994) 13/3 *Trading Law* 193.

9   Annual Report of the Office of Fair Trading, 2001 HC 773 2001–2002; 2002–March 2003 HC 906 2002–2003. These reports are available electronically via http://www.oft.gov.uk.

The 'Section 11' offence originally caught offers to supply goods that involved a false indication of price, but proved inadequate for that purpose. This area of law is now covered by Part III of the Consumer Protection Act 1987, studied in 8.5 below.

A key current question asks how far the control of marketing practices should stretch beyond criminal statutes of this nature. The imposition of criminal sanctions is attractive as a contribution to securing effective deterrence and punishment of practices deemed unacceptable in the market. The use of criminal controls is by no means without disadvantages. For good reasons rooted in the preservation of legal certainty criminal offences are subject to tightly-drawn definitions. It may be that marketing practices which are – loosely – undesirable escape the reach of the criminal law. Attention has increasingly been paid to the development of methods of scrutinising marketing practices which are not apt for control under the criminal law and yet which should not be left wholly unsupervised. The advertising sector provides a good example of an industry which may generate indecent or otherwise objectionable practices that are inapt for control under criminal law or *via* the law of tort or contract, and yet which should not be left to the market alone. The pattern, examined in Section 8.6 below, is a mix of public control and self-regulation. More broadly still, the European Commission has proposed the adoption of an EC measure forbidding unfair commercial practices. This is introduced in Section 8.7 below. Such a regime is appealing for its breadth and its disassociation from the more technical rules of orthodox criminal law. The other side of this coin is that such control may be vague, erratically enforced and damaging to commercial certainty.

The collection of regulatory devices surveyed in this chapter, both existing and proposed, comprises a core of criminal sanctions surrounded by a penumbra of softer forms of governance. One question that will deserve attention is whether this a coherent concoction. Another is whether consumer protection is better secured through a retreat from orthodox criminal law towards methods of regulation that are directed more sensitively at education and encouraging co-operative solutions. The particular context of misleading trade practices is illuminating and the matter is addressed more fully in Chapter 11.

8.2 FALSE OR MISLEADING DESCRIPTIONS OF GOODS

8.2.1 The Offences

The heartland of the law governing misleading trade practices is occupied by the Trade Descriptions Act, which creates criminal offences. Section 1(1) of the Trade Descriptions Act 1968 provides that;

> Any person who, in the course of a trade or business –
> (a) applies a false trade description to any goods; or
> (b) supplies or offers to supply any goods to which a false trade
>   description is applied;
> shall, subject to the provisions of this Act, be guilty of an offence.

There are three offences created, one under s. 1(1)(a), the core offence of application of a false trade description to goods, and two offences under s. 1(1)(b), which catch the supply or offer to supply goods to which a false trade description is applied – not necessarily by the defendant. Contrary to the norm in English criminal law, the prosecution is not required to prove *mens rea* – the guilty mind of the defendant. The absence of any *mens rea* requirement means that, once a false trade description has been applied to an item and continues to be applied, resellers and resuppliers may be guilty of an offence under s. 1(1)(b).[10] Usually, but not invariably, s. 1(1)(a) catches dishonest traders, s. 1(1)(b) careless traders.[11] Formally, however, these are strict liability offences and proof of *mens rea* need not be presented.[12] Nonetheless, the due diligence defence common to a number of consumer protection offences may permit the exoneration of the careful trader.[13] It should also be appreciated that the defendant's mental state will typically affect enforcement practice[14] and, were the matter to proceed to formal conviction, would also be relevant to sentence.[15]

The scope of s. 1(1)(b) is widened by s. 6, according to which 'A person exposing goods for supply or having goods in his possession for supply shall be deemed to offer to supply them'. This provision is important in taking the scope of the law beyond the rather limited notion of 'offer' in the law of contract formation.[16] The display of goods in shop windows or on shelves falls within the control of the Trade Descriptions Act, even though such displays are not normally viewed as constituting an 'offer' which can be 'accepted' by a customer in a way effective to conclude a contract. This also implies that it is not a necessary element of the offence that a consumer be shown to have been misled, nor indeed that

---

10 The defendant must, however, know of the application of the trade description; *Cottee v Douglas Seaton Ltd* [1972] 1 WLR 1408, [1972] 3 All ER 750, discussed in Chapter 8.2.3 below.

11 Cf. Lord Lane CJ in *R v Southwood* [1987] 3 All ER 556, 561g.

12 For a clear statement in this regard, *Alec Norman Garages Ltd v Phillips* [1985] RTR 164.

13 Chapter 11.2 below.

14 Chapter 11.3, esp. 11.3.5 below.

15 Chapter 11.3.4 below.

16 Cf. *Pharmaceutical Society v Boots* [1952] 2 QB 795.

a purchase has occurred.[17] This wider reach is important to the effective application of the law in correcting the imperfections of the market. The Act is motivated by policies quite distinct from the law of contract formation. The two systems are therefore properly kept separate, though statutory clarification was probably necessary to ensure that this point was taken by the judiciary.[18]

8.2.2 Course of a Trade or Business

The offence is committed only by a person[19] acting 'in the course of a trade or business...'.[20] The House of Lords adopted a perhaps surprisingly narrow notion of dealing in the course of a trade or business in *Davies v Sumner*.[21] Davies was a self-employed courier who transported films and other related material around Wales for the Harlech television company. He owned a car, which he traded in with a misleading odometer reading, thereby obtaining a price far higher than the market value.

Davies was not a car dealer, but the sale of the car was incidental to his work as a courier. The House of Lords was asked to address the question of whether, for the purposes of the statute, Davies was acting in the course of a trade or business when he applied the description. He was not. Lord Keith, delivering the only fully reasoned speech, took the view that a defendant must pursue the trade with some degree of regularity to fall within the scope of the Act. 'Sporadic selling off of pieces of equipment which were no longer required for the purposes of a business' is not caught.[22] Davies had no normal practice of selling cars.[23] Misdescription in the context of one-off sales of used items, or even occasional disposal of items to be replaced, may engage contractual or, less likely, tortious

---

[17]   *Chidwick v Beer* [1974] RTR 415; *Stainthorpe v Bailey* [1980] RTR 7.

[18]   Cf. on the notion of dealing in the course of a business, Chapter 8.2.2 below, where the courts, perhaps unhelpfully, have felt it necessary to align comparably worded criminal and civil law statutory provisions.

[19]   Normal rules of interpretation dictate that this covers a limited company. Section 20 permits prosecution of both a body corporate and, in defined circumstances, an officer thereof. Cf. Chapter 11.2.

[20]   Except for those prosecuted under the by-pass provision, s. 23; Chapter 11.2.5 below.

[21]   [1984] 3 All ER 831.

[22]   At 834a.

[23]   Contrast *Havering LB v Stevenson* [1970] 3 All ER 609, where there was sufficient regularity. Cf. Bragg note 7 above Chapter 2.

liability, but does not attract criminal liability as a regulatory offence.[24] This decision restricts the scope of the Act, although it does not mean that misdescription in a one-off sale will never be caught. A one-off sale could be caught if that transaction itself constitutes a trade.

Davies v Sumner was followed in *R and B Customs Brokers Co Ltd v UDT*.[25] That case involved the demarcation under the Unfair Contract Terms Act 1977 ('UCTA') between transactions involving those who deal as consumers and other commercial deals. The latter are still capable of being affected by the Act, but the controls are distinct and, loosely, less intrusive.[26] Dillon LJ took the point that the Trade Descriptions Act is penal whereas UCTA is not; notwithstanding arguments that analogies between the two were therefore inappropriate, he felt driven to a common interpretation of the notion of 'course of business' which appears in both statutes.[27] The Court of Appeal therefore drew on *Davies v Sumner* for a narrow approach to 'course of a business.'[28] A shipping broker and freight forwarding company which had acquired a car on credit terms for only the second or third time lacked the requisite regularity and was therefore not operating in the course of a business (and could accordingly use the Act to invalidate an exclusion clause).[29]

8.2.3 Application of a Trade Description

The notion of 'application' receives elaboration in s. 4. According to s. 4(1), a person applies a trade description to goods if he;

(a)　affixes or annexes it to or in any manner marks it on or incorporates it with – (i) the goods themselves, or (ii) anything in, on or with which the goods are supplied; or

(b)　places the goods in, on or with anything which the trade description has been affixed or annexed to, marked on or incorporated with, or places any such thing with the goods; or

---

24　Although extreme cases may involve offences of obtaining property by deception under the Theft Acts; cf. D. Roberts, 'The Use of the Theft Act in Trading Standards Cases' (1992) 9 *Trading Law* 205.

25　[1988] 1 All ER 847.

26　Chapter 5.

27　At 853. Also Neill LJ at 859.

28　For criticism, see D. Parry, 'Business or Consumer: a Trap for the Unwary' (1988) 6 *Trading Law* 270. Cf. comment by D. Price (1989) 52 *MLR* 245.

29　Had the transaction been within the course of a business, the clause would have stood if reasonable; Chapter 5.5 above.

(c)   uses the trade description in any manner likely to be taken as referring to the goods.

Section 4(2) provides that 'an oral statement may amount to the use of a trade description'.

This seems reasonably broad. In *Roberts v Severn Petroleum*[30] a large pole sign outside a garage displayed the Esso logo and a smaller version of the sign hung over the workshop. The site was in Esso livery. However, no sign appeared on the pumps, which referred only to the star grading of the petrol. The garage was not selling Esso petrol. The High Court ruled that the garage should properly have been convicted of an offence of applying a false trade description.

Repairs effected to a car may amount to the application of a trade description. In *Cottee v Douglas Seaton Ltd*[31] repairs done to a car had subsequently been so carefully covered up that it appeared that the car was completely free from repair work. The High Court considered that a trade description had been applied. Lord Widgery stated that 'an alteration of the goods which causes them to tell a lie about themselves may be a false trade description'. Thus the seller of such a repaired car risks criminal liability, though in fact the case ended in acquittal. The case turned on the sale by a subsequent owner who had not been involved in covering up the repair work and who, moreover, was completely unaware that repairs had been done. An essential ingredient of the offence was missing. Knowledge of the falsity of the trade description is not required for conviction, but knowledge that a trade description is applied to the goods is essential. That was missing in the case.

Buyers as well as sellers may commit the offence. In *Fletcher v Budgen*[32] a car dealer told the owner of a Fiat car brought in for inspection that it was fit for scrap. The dealer knew this was untrue, but the owner, discouraged, sold it to the dealer for £2. After repairs costing about £56, the dealer offered the car for sale at £135. The High Court decided that it was possible to convict a buyer under the Act, not simply a seller. Lord Widgery CJ took account of the normal restrictive approach taken towards criminal statutes; he confessed that, subconsciously, he had always assumed that sellers alone were caught. However he thought that protection was needed against misleading descriptions applied by buyers acting in the course of a trade or business just as much as those applied by sellers. He interpreted the Act accordingly.

---

30   [1981] RTR 312.
31   Note 10 above.
32   [1974] 2 All ER 1243.

In *Fletcher v Sledmore*[33] a car dealer and potential customer visited the defendant, a seller of old cars. The customer asked the defendant about a particular car and was told that it was 'a good little engine'. This was far from the truth. The defendant dealer sold the car to the visiting dealer who then sold it to the customer. The defendant was convicted of applying a false trade description. This decision simply, but clearly, demonstrates that the Act reaches beyond the limitations of contractual relationships.

It is important to be aware that, to a significant extent, the true impact of the Trade Descriptions Act 1968 is not best judged by reading the tiny number of cases that reach the appellate courts, nor even the larger number of decisions on points of fact decided by magistrates. Take *Fletcher v Budgen*.[34] The consumer was unwise, even naive. Why rely on the dealer's comments? It is unlikely that there was no competition in the market; he could have shopped around. Why should resources be devoted to public intervention designed to help consumers so unprepared to look after themselves? – *a fortiori* where private law remedies for misrepresentation would have been available. *Tesco v Nattrass*, examined at length in Chapter 11,[35] was fought all the way to the House of Lords to establish whether Tesco should have been convicted for displaying packs of washing powder on the shelves at a price one shilling above that advertised on posters.[36] Was such lengthy and expensive litigation justified? Views may differ.[37] However, the real test of the benefit of the Act lies, not in individual cases, but in the more general improvement to the operation of the market resultant on the widespread basis of fair trading instilled by the Act. Its purpose is not to secure a clutch of convictions, but to raise standards.[38]

The trade description must be applied at the time of or before the sale or supply. Typically it is the time of sale that is relevant. The cases mentioned above follow this straightforward model. By contrast in *Hall v Wickens Motors Ltd*[39] dealers who had sold a car received a complaint about the steering several weeks later. They informed the buyer that 'there is nothing wrong with the car'. This was far from the truth, but it was held

---

33 [1973] Crim LR 195.

34 Note 32 above.

35 Chapter 11.2.4 below.

36 They should not have been convicted because they had taken adequate precautions – 11.2.4 below.

37 See further Chapter 11, esp. Sections 11.3.4, 11.3.5, discussing *inter alia., Smedleys Ltd v Breed* [1974] AC 839, in which a caterpillar in a tin of peas made its way to the House of Lords, a progress of admittedly questionable benefit to the consumer interest.

38 Further on enforcement practice, Chapter 11.3.

39 [1972] 1 WLR 1418.

that they had committed no offence. The application of the false description amounts to an offence only where it is associated with the sale or supply of goods and not where it occurs subsequently. This part of the statute is concerned to eliminate deceptive practices that distort consumer buying decisions. The untruth in *Hall v Wickens Motors Ltd* was not of this type and the customer's apparently ill-judged purchase was thus properly left to the private law. A different approach is taken in relation to the misdescription of services, where the supply is not simply a 'one-off' transaction.[40] However, *Walker v Simon Dudley Ltd*[41] demonstrates that even under s. 1 an offence may be committed where a trade description is applied after sale but before supply. The defendant firm had made a successful bid for a contract to supply a fire engine to Shropshire County Council. Subsequently modifications to the specifications were agreed between the parties. The vehicle that was delivered complied with neither the original nor the agreed amended specifications. This was plainly a breach of contract but the High Court felt able to rule that the representation that the goods would conform to the purchaser's specifications was still in force at the time of supply. In these circumstances criminal liability under s. 1 exists alongside but independently of the possibility of an action for breach of contract. This is a surprisingly (and probably unhelpfully) broad reading of the statutory offence. Phillips LJ recognised this, felt unable to avoid it under the prevailing statutory language but referred to the discretion of trading standards officers in deciding whether or not to prosecute in circumstances where a civil claim was the only action appropriate. This, in his opinion, was just such a case.

8.2.4 Meaning of a Trade Description

Section 2(1) of the 1968 Act provides the following definition of a trade description;

> A trade description is an indication, direct or indirect, and by whatever means given, of any of the following matters with respect to any goods or parts of goods, that is to say –
> (a)   quantity,[42] size or gauge;
> (b)   method of manufacture, production, processing or reconditioning;

---

40   Section 8.3.3 below.

41   [1997] *Trading Law* 69.

42   Defined in S. 2(3) to include length, width, height, area, volume, capacity, weight and number. Note also the concern for quantity accuracy in the Weights and Measures Act 1985.

(c)   composition;

(d)   fitness for purpose, strength, performance, behaviour or accuracy;

(e)   any physical characteristics not included in the preceding paragraphs;

(f)   testing by any person and results thereof;

(g)   approval by any person or conformity with a type approved by any person;

(h)   place or date of manufacture, production, processing or reconditioning;

(i)   person by whom manufactured, produced, processed or reconditioned;

(j)   other history, including previous ownership or use.

The list's scope is a great deal more extensive than that of the pre-1968 law.[43] However, the use of this exhaustive, albeit extensive, list (rather than a general, broadly-phrased test) still creates the risk of loopholes through which objectionable practices of a type that ought to be caught by the law might fall. The preference for such a list was motivated by the perceived need for precision in drafting criminal offences. However, more recent trends have introduced some generally worded offences into the law of consumer protection as part of a policy of securing flexibility.[44] Proposed European initiatives to prohibit unfair commercial practices suggest a similar, albeit not necessarily identical, trend towards rather more broadly phrased controls.[45] Were the Trade Descriptions Act to be redrafted from scratch today, this type of specific list would probably not be employed.[46]

8.2.5 Is the Trade Description False?

According to s. 3(1) of the Trade Descriptions Act, 'A false trade description is a trade description which is false to a material degree'.

The scope of the offence is extended by the rest of s. 3. Section 3(2) provides that 'A trade description which, though not false, is misleading, that is to say, likely to be taken for such an indication of any of the matters specified in s. 2 of this Act as would be false to a material degree, shall be deemed to be a false trade description'. Section 3(3) adds to the scope of the 'trade description' by providing that 'Anything which, though not a

---

[43]   At length, Bragg note 7 above pp. 22–42.

[44]   Chapter 1.8.1.

[45]   Section 8.8 below.

[46]   Chapter 11 discusses more generally whether the use of the criminal law in circumstances of market failure is helpful.

trade description, is likely to be taken for an indication of any of those matters and, as such an indication, would be false to a material degree, shall be deemed to be a false trade description'.

Section 3 of the Act allows half-truths or economy with the truth to be caught. It would be fruitless for a trader to deny the falsity of a description that a car has done 50,000 miles by pointing out that it had indeed done 50,000 miles – but also several tens of thousand more miles left unmentioned.[47]

Exhaustive analysis of case law would do little to elucidate what is at heart a question of fact – the falsity of the description. However, illustrations may help.[48] In *Holloway v Cross*[49] a dealer sold a car that had actually done 73,000 miles. The dealer did not know how many miles it had done, but, when asked by the customer, estimated 45,000. The dealer argued that this was no more than an expression of opinion for which he had been asked and not a false trade description. This submission was not successful. It was held that this might fall within s. 2, but that that point need not be decided because the comments made were plainly a false trade description within s. 3(3).

An example of a more trader-friendly decision is provided by *R v Ford Motor Co Ltd*.[50] A car was sold described as 'new'; in fact it had undergone £50 repairs as a result of an accident suffered in transit. Bridge J held that;

> if the damage which a new car after leaving the factory has sustained is, although perhaps extensive, either superficial in character or limited to certain defined parts of the vehicle which can be simply replaced by new parts, then provided that such damage is in practical terms perfectly repaired so that it can in truth be said after repairs have been effected that the vehicle is as good as new, in our judgment it would not be a false trade description to describe such a vehicle as new.

The jury had been given a less flexible direction and the conviction was accordingly quashed. By contrast, in *Robertson v Diciccoa* description of a car as 'beautiful' when, beneath a gleaming exterior it was badly corroded, resulted in conviction.[51] There is a grey area in which what are close to throwaway comments may attract criminal liability. This suits regulatory policy. The message for the trader is to be cautious in what he or she

---

47 Cf. D. Roberts, 'Trade Descriptions: False by Reason of what it omits' (1988) 6 *Trading Law* 145.

48 More fully, Bragg note 7 above, pp. 42–8.

49 [1981] 1 All ER 1012.

50 [1974] 3 All ER 489, [1974] 1 WLR 1220.

51 [1972] RTR 431.

chooses to throw away. In fact, the different results in *Ford* and *Robertson v Dicicco* are explicable by reference to s. 3's avowedly fact-based, non-theoretical standard of falsity 'to a material degree'. The statute makes no attempt to elaborate any sophisticated notion of the level of consumer gullibility in respect of which it seeks to provide protection.

8.2.6 Disclaimers, Odometers and 'Clocking'

Trade descriptions law has been applied to second-hand car dealing with extraordinary frequency. The statistics alone should be enough to act as an amber light to the informed car-buying consumer.[52] The main points have arisen in relation to odometers, which show the mileage a car has done, and which are therefore also commonly and less technically known as mileometers. All too often they are found to have been altered, to display a lower figure than is accurate. The OFT has made it clear that such practices may prejudice a trader's application for a consumer credit licence,[53] but it may also involve a criminal offence under the Trade Descriptions Act. The torrent of case law that has swept through the courts justifies a special section in this chapter devoted to this particular sector, although the overwhelming impression of such investigation is that it is high time that odometers were made 100 per cent tamper-proof[54] or, at least, that more effective methods were found for making information about a car's history readily available.[55]

The odometer is taken by the courts to amount to a 'trade description', within the Act. The reading is an indication of the car's previous use within s. 2(1)(j).[56] If it is false, an offence has *prima facie* been committed. This has commonly arisen because of the practice of dishonest dealers of 'clocking'; reducing the mileage figures shown on the odometer, thereby allowing the dealer to charge a price inflated above the car's real market value.

---

[52]   OFT Annual Reports, note 9 above.

[53]   *Secondhand car dealers warned about unfair trading practices*, 5 February 2003, OFT PN 13/03. See Chapter 9 for the detail of this regime.

[54]   Cf. Donaldson LJ's weary opening sentence in *Holloway v Cross* [1981] 1 All ER 1012: 'This is another of the odometer cases'. The writing on the subject too is extensive; for a comprehensive collection of examples from case law and further references to writing, see Bragg note 7 above, Chapter 3.

[55]   The White Paper, *Modern Markets: Confident Consumers* Cm 4410 (1999), para. 3.21, envisages improved supply of information about mileage, using *inter alia* electronic media.

[56]   *R v Hammertons Cars Ltd* [1976] 1 WLR 1243, [1976] 3 All ER 758.

Naturally most car dealers are honest and are as keen to see such practices stamped out as the consumer.[57] However, all dealers are affected by clocking because, once the car is clocked, it may pass through a number of hands and it will be difficult to discover whether the odometer reading remains accurate. Dealers make the trade description when they put a car on display and may unwittingly commit the s. 1(1)(b) offence of supplying or offering to supply goods to which a false trade description is applied. This has no *mens rea* requirement.

A dealer might opt to do nothing, hoping there has been no clocking; then, if it emerges that there has been clocking, seek to rely on the due diligence defence to defeat a prosecution.[58] This is unlikely to succeed in the face of consistent judicial insistence that the defence requires that at least *some* steps be taken.[59] Therefore traders commonly try to avoid potential criminal liability by disclaiming the truth of the reading. This may be an effective means of defeating a prosecution, but the courts have been wary. They have identified the risk that traders may use disclaimers that are deliberately half-hearted and therefore will not effectively prevent the consumer from being misled. Accordingly the message of the case law, broadly summarised, is that a disclaimer must effectively prevent market failure if the trader is to avoid criminal liability under s. 1.[60]

There is no magic in the type of disclaimer that may be used. In *Norman v Bennett*[61] Lord Widgery CJ accepted that the effect of a false trade description can be neutralised by a contradictory disclaimer. But to be effective the disclaimer must be 'as bold, precise and compelling as the trade description itself'.[62] In *R v Hammertons Cars*[63] Lawton LJ commented that the trader '...must take positive and effective steps to ensure that the customer understands that the mileometer reading is meaningless...'. In essence the trader must ensure that the false statement is disregarded. In *Farrand v Lazarus*[64] the High Court took the view that where a dealer knows the true mileage of a vehicle and that this is materially understated by the odometer reading, the law requires disclosure of the true mileage. Anything less would not meet the requirement of an

---

[57] Although, alarmingly, Roberts note 8 above writes that before the Act came into force in 1968, clocking 'was practised by even the highest class of motor dealers'.

[58] See Chapter 11.2 on this defence.

[59] Cf. Chapter 11.2.3.

[60] Although if market failure occurs despite the trader having taken real and effective steps to prevent it, then the due diligence defence may still be available; 11.2 below.

[61] [1974] 1 WLR 1229, [1974] 3 All ER 351.

[62] Precisely these words are used in relation to disclaimers in the Motor Industry's own Code of Practice.

[63] [1976] 1 WLR 1243, [1976] 3 All ER 758.

[64] [2002] 3 All ER 175.

emphatic contradiction of the incorrect message communicated by the odometer. In *Waltham Forest LBC v TG Wheatley Ltd*[65] a notice in a dealer's office was held ineffective even though it clearly stated that cars were sold subject to an understanding that mileage could not be guaranteed. Lord Widgery explained that[66] 'the purpose of the disclaimer is for it to sit beside, as it were, the false trade description and cancel the other out as soon as its first impression can be made on the purchaser'. The notice in the office was insufficiently proximate to the false descriptions on the cars. A favourite case is *Corfield v Starr.*[67] The trader was convicted despite having displayed alongside a clocked car a notice declaring that 'With deep regret due to the Customer's Protection Act we can no longer verify that the mileage shown on this vehicle is correct'. Doubtless conviction would still have followed even if the trader had cited a statute that actually existed! In law an oral disclaimer may suffice, but it would be imprudent for a trader to rely on this method. Aside from evidential difficulties, the oral disclaimer would often lack the required boldness to overcome the reading on the clock. Worse, the trader planning an oral disclaimer might find that the s. 1(1)(b) offence of offering to supply goods to which a false trade description is applied has already been committed before any opportunity orally to disclaim occurs.

In *R v Hammertons Cars*[68] Lawton LJ was conscious of the practical value of avoiding overly-refined discussion of whether the disclaimer is a type of defence, a means of denying the falsity of the description, or a means of preventing the description being 'applied' in the first place. The evidence, he thought, should be looked at as a whole, with the decision lying with the trial court. Ultimately, for Lawton LJ, the question is as follows: 'Has the prosecution proved that the defendant supplied goods to which a false trade description was applied?'

There is much to be said in support of Lawton LJ's emphasis on practicality, but it seems regrettable that the precise legal effect of a disclaimer has not been pinned down. It was held by the Court of Appeal in *R v Southwood* that the disclaimer is not relevant to the offence under s. 1(1)(a).[69] The clocker would be unable to evade criminal liability for the application of the false trade description by the use of a disclaimer. Perhaps this seems desirable as an overall policy choice. However, if a disclaimer can prevent a description being applied under s. 1, then it is

---

[65]   [1978] RTR 333.

[66]   At p. 339.

[67]   [1981] RTR 380.

[68]   Note 63 above.

[69]   [1987] 3 All ER 556, applying *Newman v Hackney LBC* [1982] RTR 296. Followed in *Southend BC v White* [1992] 11 Trading LR 65; *R v Shrewsbury Crown Court ex p Venables* [1994] Crim LR 61.

hard to see any strict logic in distinguishing s. 1(1)(a) from s. 1(1)(b) in this fashion; after all, the neutralising effect of a sufficiently prominent disclaimer is quite unaffected by the history of the clocking that has occurred.[70] Subsequently the Court of Appeal in *R v Bull*[71] appeared to accept this more coldly logical analysis, but *Bull* goes unmentioned in the High Court's decision in *Farrand v Lazarus* which assumes that a disclaimer cannot be effective in a s. 1(1)(a) case. *Farrand v Lazarus* stands with *Southwood* in placing emphasis on the relevance of the disclaimer to the s. 24(1) defence, not the scope of the s. 1(1)(a) offence itself.

It is submitted that the logical route through this regrettably dense thicket of case law lies in acceptance that in principle a disclaimer may be used to prevent either a s. 1(1)(a) or a s. 1(1)(b) offence occurring in the first place. The key question is whether, taking all the circumstances into account, a false trade description has been applied. If the disclaimer is ineffective to defeat that element of the offence, it seems it may still be advanced as a defence to the charge via s. 24.

The Court of Appeal in *Southwood* added that a trader who returns the odometer to zero applies a false trade description. This rejects the argument that 'zeroing' makes it plain that no description is being applied because no one could possibly think that a used car had done no miles. Lord Lane CJ commented that:

> The fact that no one was misled or was likely to be misled [by a zeroed odometer] is an irrelevant consideration.

The trader would have to make more strenuous efforts to alert the customer to the falsity, such as use of a disclaimer, and then (it seems) seek to invoke s. 24(1) as a defence to the s. 1(1)(b) charge.

8.2.7 Defences and Enforcement

In common with other consumer protection statutes, the Trade Descriptions Act contains defences which mitigate the apparent severity of the main offences which impose strict liability. These may permit exoneration of the careful trader. Given the availability of these defences in several areas of the law (not simply trade descriptions), it is appropriate to consider their nature and purpose separately. This forms part of the subject matter of Chapter 11.

---

[70] Cf. Lord Lane CJ in *Wandsworth LBC v Bentley* [1980] RTR 429, *obiter dicta* that the disclaimer prevents a representation being made.

[71] [1997] RTR 123, [1996] Crim LR 438. See similarly *R v Gregory* 1998 WL 1670525.

Sections 26–29 of the Trade Descriptions Act 1968 place enforcement responsibilities in the hands of Trading Standards Authorities, operating at local level. In this book, the practice of enforcement of trade descriptions law is also examined separately in Chapters 11 and 13, because it has much in common with general practice in consumer protection law.

No civil remedy is created by the Act. According to s. 35, a contract for the supply of goods is not void or unenforceable by reason only of the fact that it breaches the Act. In some instances, of course, precisely the same event will be capable of giving rise not only to criminal, but also civil, liability. Misdescription could involve a breach of contract; liability in tort may arise. A trader may have to face both criminal and civil consequences. However, the Act criminalises conduct that is not in breach of private law. The objectives are quite distinct: the existence of the Act is based on the assumptions of the inadequacy of the private law in curing market failure.[72]

8.3 FALSE OR MISLEADING DESCRIPTIONS OF SERVICES

8.3.1 The Offence

Section 14(1) of the Trade Descriptions Act 1968 provides that:

> It shall be an offence for any person in the course of any trade or business –
>
> (a)   to make a statement which he knows to be false; or
> (b)   recklessly to make a statement which is false;
>   as to any of the following matters, that is to say, –
>   (i)   the provision in the course of any trade or business of any services, accommodation or facilities;
>   (ii)   the nature of any services, accommodation or facilities provided in the course of any trade or business;
>   (iii) the time at which, the manner in which or persons by whom any services, accommodation or facilities are so provided;
>   (iv)   the examination, approval or evaluation by any person of any services, accommodation or facilities so provided; or
>   (v)   the location or amenities of any accommodation so provided.

Several of the elements of s. 14 run in parallel to s. 1. Both have in common the limitation of liability to the course of trade or business,

---

[72]   In depth, see Chapter 1.

already examined above in Part 8.2.2.[73] The breadth of s. 3 has a (not quite exact) counterpart in s. 14(2)(a). 'False' means false to a material degree – s. 14(4) echoes s. 3(1).

The most striking difference between the s. 14 offence and the s. 1 offence lies in the mental element required. Section 14 is *not* an offence of strict liability. This represented a deliberate choice in 1968. Control of misdescription in the services sector was covered by neither the old Merchandise Marks Acts nor by the Molony Report. Section 14 was an innovation, which explains the rather more tentative approach it takes to *mens rea* in contrast to the s. 1 strict liability offence applicable to misdescription of goods.[74]

8.3.2 *Mens Rea*

The presence of a *mens rea* requirement under s. 14 leads inevitably to the need for some sophisticated and complex legal reasoning. *Wings Ltd v Ellis*[75] concerned the s. 14(1)(a) offence of making a statement known to be false. The case, which reached the House of Lords, arose out of the publication of a holiday brochure including a false statement about the availability of air conditioning in a hotel in Sri Lanka. The company found out the statement was false after it issued the brochure and tried to ensure that corrections were made by all those in receipt of it. However, at least 250,000 brochures had been distributed, so it was scarcely feasible that the company could mount a completely effective campaign. A consumer subsequently read an unamended brochure, booked a holiday and, on returning, complained of the application of a false trade description relating to the accommodation available.

A consumer had been misled; there was a false statement. The House of Lords confirmed the Court of Appeal's decision in *R v Thompson Holidays*[76] that a new statement is made on each occasion that a customer reads a brochure.[77] The defendants knew the statement was false. The problem was that the trader did not know of the falsity when publishing the brochure; but did know when the consumer read it. Furthermore, there was no intent to make a false statement to that particular consumer at that

---

[73] Section 1 refers to a trade or business; s. 14 to any trade or business. No practical differences seem to have followed.

[74] For an explanation in Parliament, see 759 HC Debs 683 (22 February 1968).

[75] [1984] 3 All ER 577, [1984] 3 WLR 965. Cf. *Yugotours v Wadsley* [1988] Crim LR 623.

[76] [1974] 1 All ER 823; not all aspects of that decision were confirmed.

[77] Lord Brandon preferred to see a continuing false statement as long as the brochures remained in circulation.

particular time; quite the reverse, in fact. Was the requisite mental element for conviction present?

The House of Lords took the view that conviction was proper, although there are shades of differing emphasis in the speeches. Conviction, Lord Scarman felt, 'advances the legislative purpose embodied in the Act, in that it strikes directly against the false statement irrespective of the reason for, or explanation of its falsity'.[78] Lord Scarman was not deterred by the submission that this leads to a situation where liability may be imposed, as in this case, without knowledge of the making of the particular statement. He declared that the Trade Descriptions Act 1968 'is not truly a criminal statute. Its purpose is not the enforcement of the criminal law but the maintenance of trading standards. Trading standards, not criminal behaviour, are its concern'.[79]

To this extent, the *mens rea* requirement of s. 14 has been interpreted as a lower threshold to conviction than would be the norm in 'proper' criminal statutes.[80] To the submission that this may criminalize the innocent, the answer is that statutory defences are available where a defendant has done everything possible to avoid commission of the defence.[81] Wings Ltd was ill-advised in not advancing such a defence.

Section 14(1)(b) creates an offence of recklessly making a statement which is false. According to s. 14(2)(b) a statement made regardless of whether it is true or false shall be deemed to be made recklessly, whether or not the person making it had reasons for believing that it might be false.

MFI Warehouses Ltd v Nattrass[82] shows a judicial readiness to follow the rather flexible approach to recklessness intimated by s. 14(2)(b). Lord Widgery referred to the distinctive consumer protection flavour of the Trade Descriptions Act and concluded that 'Parliament was minded to place on the advertiser a positive obligation to have regard to whether his advertisement was true or false'.[83] Absence of regard to truth or falsity will suffice; neither dishonesty nor even deliberately closing one's eyes to the truth are required ingredients of the offence.

Both *Wings Ltd v Ellis*, under s. 14(1)(a), and *MFI Warehouses Ltd v Nattrass*, under s. 14(1)(b), stand as statements of the separation of the regulatory offence from the normal sweep of English criminal law. The nature of the Regulatory Offence is examined more fully in Chapter 11.

---

[78]   At 589j.

[79]   *Wings Ltd v Ellis* [1984] 3 All ER 577, 587. See further Chapter 11.1 on the policy of the regulatory offence.

[80]   Chapter 11.1.

[81]   Chapter 11.2.

[82]   [1973] 1 All ER 762.

[83]   At 768b.

8.3.3 Statements about the Future

It will be recalled that under s. 1 of the Act a statement made after and unassociated with the sale or supply of goods cannot constitute the application of a misleading trade description. The position is different under s. 14, in reflection of the typically ongoing nature of the provision of services in contrast with the 'one-off' sale or supply of goods. In *Breed v Cluett*[84] contracts were exchanged between the defendant builder, Cluett, and buyers of a bungalow which the defendant was still in the process of completing. Three weeks after the exchange of contracts, Cluett told the buyers that the bungalow was covered by the national House-Builders Registration Council 10-year guarantee. Had this been true, it would have meant that the builders bore continuing obligations throughout the guarantee period. However, the claim was untrue and the defendant was found reckless in making the statement. Dorset justices considered s. 14 to be limited to statements inducing entry into a contract, which had not occurred here. However, Lord Parker CJ thought it wrong to confine the scope of s. 14 in this way and returned the case to the justices with a direction to convict.[85]

As opposed to *Hall v Wickens Motors Ltd*,[86] where it was held that no s. 1 offence was committed where a statement was made several weeks after both sale and supply were complete, *Breed v Cluett* was distinguished as a s. 14 case where descriptions are caught if applied *in the course* of providing services.

A distinct question arises where a statement relates to the provision of services in the future. In *Beckett v Cohen*[87] a builder, Cohen, agreed to build a garage for a customer within ten days. The garage would be like the customer's neighbour's. The builder ran out of money and did not complete in time. Nor was the garage identical with the neighbour's. Lord Widgery did not decide conclusively that this was the provision of a service, but indicated that he would be surprised if it were not. However, he began his judgment by declaring that 'this is another case in which prosecuting authorities appear to me to be pressing the ambit of the Trade Descriptions Act 1968 to a wholly unacceptable degree'. Lord Widgery stated that s. 14 'has no application to statements which amount to a promise in regard to the future, and which therefore at the time when they are made cannot have the character of being either true or false'. Section 14 does not catch a promise as to what a provider will do before the

---

[84]   [1970] 2 QB 459.
[85]   Applied in *R v Bevelectric Ltd* (1993) 157 JP 323, discussed by G. Holgate and C. Clayson (1994) 13 Trading Law 55.
[86]   Note 3 above.
[87]   [1973] 1 All ER 120.

contract is completed, where the promise does not relate to an existing fact. This was, he felt, a case correctly belonging in contract law, not criminal law.

There is some force in the submission that the limits of criminality would be overstretched were the criminal law employed in cases of over-optimistic forecasts. Yet it is possible in part to unpick the claim that a promise as to the future cannot be true or false at the time it is made. If X promises to do Y within ten days, then the fact of whether Y will be done is true or false at the moment the promise is made; it is simply that for ten days we will not know which. The core of the offence, as explained in *Beckett v Cohen*, seems to rest on the need for an existing and presently discoverable fact that is being misrepresented.[88]

If X makes the promise and intends to carry it through, then there is no offence if he fails. By contrast, as was famously observed by Bowen LJ in *Edgington v Fitzmaurice*,[89] 'the state of a man's mind is as much a fact as the state of his digestion'. So to say that one will do Y, when at the time one has no intention of doing Y, could be a crime, whereas there is no crime if one hopes to do Y but simply fails. In *British Airways Board v Taylor*[90] a passenger was told that he had a definite booking on a flight from London to Bermuda. He did not get the promised seat because the airline operated a deliberate commercial policy of overbooking. The House of Lords held that this was a false statement within the scope of s. 14 of the Act, not simply a promise as to future conduct.[91] The confirmation of the booking expressed an intention that the airline did not in fact have, for its real intention was to overbook and to jeopardise the passenger's chances of getting a seat.

Although the law does not criminalize over-optimistic forecasts, its application to statements of existing fact may indirectly allow the projection of the law into the future. In *R v Clarksons Holidays*[92] the defendant had made statements about the quality of services available at a hotel in Benidorm. An artist's impression was printed in the brochure. It was not mentioned on that page that construction was still underway. In fact, the hotel had not yet been built and holidaymakers arrived to find it still unfinished and dirty. The conviction of the firm under s. 14 was upheld by the Court of Appeal. This was considered to be a statement about existing fact – that the hotel was a going concern – that was untrue. That a representation of existing fact was at stake was sufficient to ground

---

[88] Cf. A. White, *Misleading Cases* (OUP, 1991), Chapter 9.

[89] (1885) 29 Chapter D 459, 483.

[90] [1976] 1 All ER 65.

[91] An acquittal followed for technical reasons associated with transfer of ownership of the airline.

[92] (1972) 116 Sol Jo 728.

liability.[93] One might presume that had it been stated clearly that the hotel 'will be ready', this would not have been an offence, but rather a matter of breach of contract. But an argument by analogy with the s. 1 case of *Walker* v *Simon Dudley Ltd*[94] would suggest that even this would fall within the reach of the criminal law.

8.4 MISDESCRIPTIONS AND INTERESTS IN LAND

The word 'accommodation' within s. 14 of the Trade Descriptions Act 1968 seems capable of bringing misdescription of premises let for a short period within the scope of the regulatory offence. However, it does not seem possible to employ the Act more broadly to catch misdescription connected to sale of interests in land. The estate agent who misled was beyond the scope of the regulatory offence. It is difficult to justify protecting the consumer from market failure when he or she buys washing powder,[95] but not when he or she buys a house. This was altered in 1991 with the entry into force of the Property Misdescriptions Act.[96]

Although the Act has been newsworthy predominantly for its impact on estate agency, it is apt to catch other parties involved in sales of interests in land. Section 1(1) provides that:

> Where a false or misleading statement about a prescribed matter is made in the course of an estate agency business or a property development business, otherwise than in providing conveyancing services, the person by whom the business is carried on shall be guilty of an offence under this section.

The 'prescribed matter' is 'any matter relating to land which is specified in an order made by the Secretary of State',[97] the relevant order being the Property Misdescriptions (Specified Matters) Order 1992.[98] The list of 33 matters in the Schedule to the Order is fairly broad, covering obvious issues such as location and address, view and proximity to services, but

---

[93] Contrast *R v Sunair Holidays Ltd* [1973] 2 All ER 1233.

[94] Note 41 above.

[95] *Tesco v Nattrass* 8.2.3 above.

[96] For a valuable survey of the law prior to the Act and a critique of the Act, see R. Bragg, 'Regulation of Estate Agents: A Series of Half-hearted Measures?' (1992) 55 *MLR* 368.

[97] Section 1(5)(d).

[98] SI No 2834. For comment, see A. Samuels, 'Property Misdescriptions Act 1991' (1993) 10 Trading Law 138.

extending much further, for example to easements and to the existence of public or private rights of way.

False means 'false to a material degree'. Misleading, though not false, statements may be caught.[99] The core of the statute is directed at curtailing the reputation for extravagantly imaginative description long enjoyed by (some) estate agents. It would be an offence to publicise a 'charming cottage with views of the sea' if the sea would be visible only to a resident ten-foot tall and willing to stand on the roof. Liability is strict, but the normal due diligence defence applies.[100] This defence, common to several statutes creating regulatory offences, is not readily made out.[101] Agents should be cautious about describing property in accordance with clients' instructions without carrying out their own checks, although in one of the earliest reported decisions under the Act it was held that on the facts an agent who had relied on both his own local knowledge and experience as well assurances by the seller was properly acquitted despite having misdescribed the property.[102]

The enforcement of the Act is yet another responsibility for local trading standards authorities. The multiplicity of regulatory offences enforced at local level justifies separate treatment of enforcement powers and practice. This is provided in Chapter 11. Estate agents are potentially subject to other legal controls that may bear incidentally on the consumer interest. Their conduct in the market may affect the treatment of an application for a consumer credit licence.[103] Moreover, the Estate Agents Act 1979 lays down certain standards of proper conduct, relating for example to disclosure of personal interest in a transaction. It also includes a power to ban individuals from acting as agents, although there is no requirement of prior licensing. In 2004 the OFT published a report which concluded that the costs of introducing such a licensing scheme would outweigh the benefits.[104]

The Property Misdescriptions Act 1991 is a valuable measure, but it does not provide the comprehensive coverage of the Trade Descriptions Act 1968 'proper'. There is a strong case for extending its scope to run in parallel to the general offence, as well as a strong case for achieving this as part of a general consolidation of the scattered law of trade descriptions.[105]

---

[99]   Section 1(5); cf. 8.2.5 above under the Trade Descriptions Act.

[100] Section 2.

[101] Further on the defence, Chapter 11.2.

[102] *London Borough of Enfield v Castles Estate Agents Ltd* [1996] 36 E.G. 145.

[103] Chapter 9.x.

[104] *Estate Agency Market in England and Wales*, OFT 693 (March 2004). See Chapter 1.8.2.2.

[105] See further Chapter 8.7 below.

8.5 MISLEADING PRICE INDICATIONS

The Trade Descriptions Act 1968 introduced provisions designed to control aspects of practices likely to mislead consumers about prices. These provisions, contained in s. 11 of the 1968 Act, were a step forward at the time, but it became apparent that their scope was unduly limited.[106] Traders were able to evade them while still employing practices that were, as a matter of policy, equally objectionable. For example, pricing of services, rather than goods, was excluded. Ingenious attempts by enforcement authorities to stretch s. 14 to plug this loophole largely came to grief in the face of a judicial policy of unwillingness to extend the meaning of a statute imposing criminal liability.[107] *Newell v Hicks*[108] involved an advertisement offering a video cassette recorder absolutely free with the purchase of a Renault car. The offer was misleading. The trade-in value of an old car was reduced to take account of the cost of the recorder, so in fact it was not free at all. This was held not to involve potential criminal liability under s. 14, since it was not a question of the provision of services, but rather the terms on which the services were provided.[109]

The area of misleading pricing indications is now covered by Part III of the Consumer Protection Act 1987,[110] a prohibition supported by a Code of Practice which fleshes out its scope. In policy terms, Part III of the 1987 Act represents a significant shift in regulatory philosophy. It supplies a good example of the modern trend in legislative consumer protection regulation towards flexible, generally expressed requirements.[111] A general duty allows essential flexibility to enforcement agencies who, in the exercise of control, are constantly 'firing at a moving target'.[112]

Section 20(1) of the Consumer Protection Act 1987 creates an offence in the following terms:

---

[106] For a full account, Bragg note 7 above Chapter 4.

[107] But to address market failure effectively, an active judicial role is important; cf. Chapter 11.1 on the possible value of abandoning the use of the criminal law in this area.

[108] (1983) 128 Sol Jo 63.

[109] Cf. the narrow interpretation of s. 14 in *Westminster City Council v Ray Alan (Manshops) Ltd* [1982] 1 WLR 383, [1982] 1 All ER 771. Cf. discussion by P. Cartwright (1992) 9 Trading Law 2.

[110] At length, Bragg note 7 above Chapter 5.

[111] Cf. Chapter 1.8.1.

[112] Sir Gordon Borrie, *The Development of Consumer Law and Policy* (Hamlyn Lectures, Stevens and Sons, 1984) p. 64.

> Subject to the following provisions of this Part, a person shall be guilty of an offence if, in the course of any business of his, he gives (by any means whatever) to any consumers[113] an indication which is misleading as to the price at which any goods, services, accommodation or facilities are available (whether generally or from particular persons).[114]

Plainly this offence may be committed by traders engaging in sharp practice which is damaging to the consumer interest but unlikely to generate liability in tort or contract. For example, in *DSG Retail Ltd v Oxfordshire CC*[115] Dixons in the Clarendon Centre in Oxford displayed a notice declaring sweepingly that 'We guarantee to match any local price'. But staff refused to lower the stated price for a CD-player even though it was available more cheaply elsewhere in the city. The High Court confirmed that conviction was proper, and that it was not an essential ingredient of the offence that identified specific goods or a specific price be displayed.

Section 20(2) widens the scope of liability. Giving an indication which later becomes misleading within meaning of s. 20(1) is an offence where 'some or all of those consumers might reasonably be expected to rely on the indication at a time after it has become misleading and [the trader has failed] to take all such steps as are reasonable to prevent those consumers from relying on the indication'.

Section 21 elaborates the meaning of misleading for the purposes of s. 20. An indication given to any consumers is misleading as to a price if what is conveyed by the indication, or what those consumers might reasonably be expected to infer from the indication or any omission from it, includes any of the following, that is to say:

(a) that the price is less than in fact it is;

(b) that the applicability of the price does not depend on facts or circumstances on which its applicability does in fact depend;

(c) that the price covers matters in respect of which an additional charge is in fact made;

(d) that a person who in fact has no such expectation –
   (i) expects the price to be increased or reduced (whether or not at a particular time or by a particular amount); or
   (ii) expects the price, or the price as increased or reduced, to be maintained (whether or not for a particular period); or

---

113 Defined in s. 20(6).

114 The scope of provision of 'services and facilities' and provision of 'accommodation' are amplified by ss. 22 and 23. Probably the law would now catch the practice in the *Ray Alan* case, note 109 above.

115 [2001] 1 *WLR* 1765.

(e) that the facts or circumstances by reference to which the consumers might reasonably be expected to judge the validity of any relevant comparison made or implied by the indication are not what in fact they are.

Section 21(2) offers a parallel list of indications that are misleading to consumers as to a method of determining a price.

The scope of s. 21 is broad. It covers the straightforward instance of goods priced on the shelves at £50 for which £60 is charged at the till (point (a) in the list). It also includes cases of goods priced at £50 which, it is stated, will soon rise to £60 where there is no such expectation (point (d) in the list). It also covers subtler cases where goods are priced at £50 which, it is falsely stated, were once priced at £60 or are priced at £60 at a nearby shop (point (e) in the list). Where *The People* newspaper ran an advertisement offering a £50 watch for £4.99, a conviction was secured pursuant to s. 20(1) given that such watches were nowhere available at a price as high as £50.[116] Section 21(3) is directed specifically at defining relevant comparisons for the purposes of point (e). It should be noted that accurate price comparisons are not suppressed.[117]

The style of the regime established by Part III of the Consumer Protection Act 1987 is significantly affected by the role of Codes of Practice envisaged in s. 25. Section 25(1) provides that:

> The Secretary of State may, after consulting the Director-General of Fair Trading and such other persons as the Secretary of State considers it appropriate to consult, by order approve any code of practice issued (whether by the Secretary of State or another person) for the purpose of –
>
> (a) giving practical guidance with respect to any of the requirements of S. 20 above; and
>
> (b) promoting what appear to the Secretary of State to be desirable practices as to the circumstances and manner in which any person gives an indication as to the price at which any goods, services, accommodation or facilities are available or indicates any other matter in respect of which any such indication may be misleading.

---

[116] *MGN Ltd v Ritters, The Times* 30 July 1997.

[117] German law of unfair competition has traditionally been much more interventionist and has controlled even accurate comparisons. Such perceived over-regulation of the market has brought German law into frequent collision with EC law of free movement when applied to restrict the development of integrated, cross-border advertising campaigns. The matter is now subject to a harmonisation measure governing the permitted scope of comparative advertising, Directive 97/55 OJ 1997 L290/18. See e.g. Case C–44/01 *Pippig Augenoptik v Hartlauer* [2003] ECR I–3095 and, more broadly, Chapter 2.

The legal aspects of Codes of Practice are examined in Chapter 13.9. Section 25(2) declares that contravention of an approved Code 'shall not of itself give rise to any criminal or civil liability'. Nevertheless, it is permissible for contravention of, or compliance with, codes to be taken into account in proceedings for an offence under ss. 20(1) and (2).

Some of the policy considerations that underpin the use of Codes of Practice are elaborated more fully in Chapter 13.[118] One of several benefits lies in the ability of the Code to provide some specific illustrations of the way in which the law is intended to operate. In a statute, such factual precision runs the risk of rendering the law too rigid or even of offering hostages to fortune but, in a Code, the illustration simply becomes part of the interpretative climate.

In November 1988 the key Code of Practice was approved by the Secretary of State – the *Code of Practice for Traders on Price Indications*.[119] Naturally the Code is influential and has become typically the starting point for both commercial planning and enforcement practice in the pricing field. The Code is especially helpful in its amplification of the scope of legitimate price comparison (both with the same goods or services previously offered or competing goods or services).[120] In 2003 – not before time – the OFT initiated a consultation process designed to lead to the adoption of a renovated version of the Code.[121] Among other changes, it is envisaged that the spread of EC-derived obligations, relating for example to distance contracts, will be reflected in the text. The increasing prominence of e-commerce will also be taken into account.

Section 26 confers a power on the Secretary of State to make regulations. Section 26 is a counterpart to s. 25, but offers the opportunity to make 'harder' law than the soft law Codes of Practice envisaged by s. 25. However, the current policy preference for flexible regulatory regimes dictates a subsidiary role for specific regulations. The same is true of consumer safety law under Part II of the Act, where the same power to make specific regulations may be observed in conjunction with a policy preference to exercise that power sparingly.[122]

Section 24 contains specific defences relevant to Part III. The general due diligence defence in the Consumer Protection Act 1987 is available in relation to s. 20(1) offences, which are offences of strict liability. The general defence is examined in Chapter 11.

---

[118] Chapter 13.9; see also Chapter 1.8.4.

[119] SI 1988 No 2078.

[120] Cf. G. Holgate, 'Consumer Protection: Comparisons with other Traders' Prices' (1993) 10 *Trading Law* 22.

[121] Progress may be tracked via http://www.dti.gov.uk/ccp/consultations.htm.

[122] Chapter 10.2.

The above account concerns control of misleading price descriptions. The obligation to disclose prices constitutes a regulatory technique with a separate rationale. It aims to cure a basic imbalance in information flowing from the conditions of the modern market, rather than to address any specific misleading practice.[123] The Price Marking Order 1999 imposes such obligations,[124] being a measure of particular relevance to shaping a legal framework for 'unit pricing' – prices expressed by reference to units of measurement.

8.6 ADVERTISING

8.6.1 The Regulatory and Constitutional Challenge of Advertising

Assessment of the role of information in achieving effective consumer protection occupies a central place in this book.[125] Advertising is part of this theme. In the government White Paper, *Modern Markets: Confident Consumers*,[126] it is stated that 'Advertising is important to the effectiveness of markets. It is the most visible way that companies promote their products and services. But consumer confidence depends on advertising claims being true'.[127]

An advertisement that is misleading is perfectly capable of falling within the control of the Trade Descriptions Act 1968. In s. 39 advertising is broadly defined to cover catalogues, circulars and price lists. This provision is designed simply to confirm the breadth of the Act's scope. Other standard types of advertising are also perfectly capable of falling foul of the Trade Descriptions Act. If the ingredients explained in 8.2 above are all present, then an advertiser has committed an offence. Advertisements in which a trade description is used in relation to a class of goods are the subject of special treatment in s. 5 of the Trade Descriptions Act. An innocent party whose business is publishing advertisements has a special defence under s. 25. Misleading pricing in advertisements may fall within the offence created under Part III of the Consumer Protection Act 1987, examined in 8.5 above.

The law operates beyond the Trade Descriptions Act, since it is widely perceived that advertisements require a more general type of control. Advertisements may not mislead within the confines of the Act, yet there may still be grounds for public concern. Advertisements have an

---

123 See further Chapter 1.8.3.

124 SI 1999 No 3042, replacing earlier versions. This implements relevant EC Directives.

125 See Chapter 1.8.3.

126 Cm 4410 (1999).

127 Para. 3.14. See Chapter 1.9.2.3 for fuller discussion of the White Paper.

extraordinary prominence in contemporary culture. In some jurisdictions, advertising regulation has developed into a hotly contested area of public activity.[128] It has been attacked as an intrusion into constitutional rights of (commercial) free expression and as an infringement on the ability of the individual to make his or her own choices free of State intervention. This in turn has prompted spirited defences of the role of the State in correcting market failures and protecting the consumer from the perceived baneful influence of advertising as preference-distorting.[129] Such issues are capable of forming the basis for litigation about the constitutionality of controls over advertising. Some of these issues, which have arisen with particular pertinence in connection with tobacco but which are by no means confined to that sector, are explored more fully in Chapter 1 in connection with the broader issue of the extent to which market regulatory laws may be subject to constitutional review.[130]

8.6.2 Self-regulation of Advertising

For all the occasional furore in the UK about 'shock' advertising techniques,[131] there has not yet been experience of legal or political debate at such a level of intensity. Self-regulation has a long-standing tradition in the UK. The Advertising Standards Authority is non-statutory and is established by the industry. It has its own Codes of Practice. The British Code of Advertising Practice and the British Code of Sales Promotion Practice were consolidated in 1995 into a single document, the British Code of Advertising and Sales Promotion. The current version, the eleventh edition, is now entitled the British Code of Advertising, Sales Promotion and Direct Marketing. It was released in March 2003. Complaints may be lodged with the Authority,[132] which may ask advertisers to withdraw or to amend advertisements that infringe a Code. Reports are published; advertisers are expected to abide by decisions. The core of the Code requires that advertisements be decent, honest and

---

[128]   Cf. D. Harland, 'The Control of Advertising – a Comparative Overview' (1993) 1 *Competition and Consumer Law Journal* 95. For investigation of several different jurisdictions see also W. Skouris (ed.), *Advertising and Constitutional Rights in Europe* (Nomos, 1994); J. Maxeiner and P. Schotthöfer (eds.), *Advertising Law in Europe and North America* (Kluwer, 1999).

[129]   E.g. I. Ramsay, *Advertising, Culture and the Law* (Sweet and Maxwell, 1996); cf. R. Shiner, *Freedom of Commercial Expression* (Oxford, 2003).

[130]   Chapter 1.9.3; see also 8.6.4 below.

[131]   For good or ill, Benetton, in particular, has attracted attention in this way.

[132]   ASA, Brook House, 2–16 Torrington Place, London WC1E 7HN. Its website is at http://www.asa.org.uk/index.asp.

truthful. It will be appreciated that it is the element of decency, in particular, that takes the scope of the Code far beyond the control of the Trade Descriptions Act 1968.[133] A special regime operates in the financial services sector – complaints should be made to the Financial Services Authority (FSA). And the Independent Television Commission deals with commercial television, including satellite and cable television.

Self-regulation is notoriously vulnerable to the allegation that honest traders conscientiously comply while the minority of real rogues are able to ignore it without incurring any formal legal sanction. Tougher sanctions against repeat offenders, perhaps including fines and/or obligations to print corrective advertising, have therefore been proposed.[134] The advantages of self-regulation lie in the speed, low cost and co-operative spirit of a well-functioning system. It is fair to state that, within the inevitable constraints that attach to any self-regulatory regime, the ASA has a generally good reputation as a body able to deal effectively and fairly with complaints about advertising.[135] For example, when Ryanair used the slogan 'Expensive BA ... DS' as part of an advertising campaign in which it compared British Airways' prices unfavourably with its own, the ASA concluded that the public would interpret 'BA ... DS' to mean 'BASTARDS' and found the campaign likely to cause serious or widespread offence. Ryanair terminated use of the slogan. They instead pursued a campaign using the less aggressive slogan 'Expensive BA' within the context of the same quest to persuade consumers of the price advantages offered by Ryanair when compared to British Airways. Litigation followed in which BA unsuccessfully tried to show that its rival had committed torts against it in this campaign.[136] Adverse publicity is the most potent sanction available to the ASA, and the strength of this method of inducing compliance with ASA findings by advertisers should not be underestimated. Nor should one underestimate its advantages compared with the arduous formality of adversarial litigation.

8.6.3 Public Regulation of Advertising

As a result of EC intervention, self-regulation is no longer the exclusive method of control of advertising in the UK. The EC Directive on Misleading Advertising was adopted in 1984 after stiff debate among

---

[133] Cf. S. Locke, 'Self-Regulation in Advertising' (1994) 4 *Consumer Policy Review* 111.

[134] B. Middleton and D. Rodwell, 'Regulating advertising – time to get tough?' (1998) 8 *Consumer Policy Review* 88.

[135] For a balanced view of the case for and against, see D. Parry, 'The future of voluntary regulation of advertising' (2000) 8 *Consumer Law J* 137.

[136] *British Airways v Ryanair* [2001] FSR 541.

Member States with different traditions in the field.[137] The variations in practice prevented agreement on a wider role for EC legislation in the regulation of advertising. The original draft Commission proposal in the field covered misleading, unfair and comparative advertising.[138] The Directive as finally adopted excluded provisions concerning both unfair and comparative advertising, although State regulation of both phenomena has fallen foul of primary Community law.[139] In part as a result of the incentives created by the unfeasibility of excluding national rules from judicial scrutiny under EC trade law, a legislative response to comparative advertising was subsequently also agreed at EC level. This is Directive 97/55.[140] It amends the Misleading Advertising Directive and sets out the conditions under which comparative advertising is to be permitted. The Treaty legal base of both Directives is that governing harmonisation of laws as a tool of market integration.[141]

The UK implemented the Misleading Advertising Directive by Statutory Instrument in the Control of Misleading Advertisements Regulations 1988.[142] These were amended by the Control of Misleading Advertisements (Amendment) Regulations 2000[143] in order to implement the Comparative Advertising Directive.

The substance of the control required by EC law which addresses misleading advertising[144] requires its suppression by the Member States. The definition of 'misleading' for these purposes is found in Regulation 2(2) of the 1988 Statutory Instrument, which reflects Arts. 2(2) and 3 of the EC Directive. It is the deceptive nature of the advertising that is the key element. It is provided in Regulation 2(2) that:

> ... an advertisement is misleading if in any way, including its presentation, it deceives or is likely to deceive the persons to whom it is addressed or whom it reaches and if, by reason of its deceptive nature, it is likely to

---

137   Directive 84/450 OJ 1984 L250/17. For an insight into the flavour of the debate at the time, see P. Thomson, then Director-General of the Advertising Standards Authority, 'Self-Regulation in Advertising – Some Observations from the Advertising Standards Authority', Chapter IV in G. Woodroffe (ed.), *Consumer Law in the EEC* (Sweet and Maxwell/CCLR, 1984).

138   OJ 1978 C70/4, amended proposal OJ 1979 C194/3.

139   See Chapter 2, esp. 2.2.5.

140   Note 117 above. See P. Spink and R. Petty, 'Comparative Advertising in the European Union' (1998) 47 *ICLQ* 855.

141   Chapter 2.3.3.

142   SI 1988 No 915.

143   SI 2000 No 914.

144   Cf. Case C–373/90 *Procureur de la République v X* [1992] ECR I–131 for the interpretative assistance of the European Court.

affect their economic behaviour or, for those reasons, injures or is likely to injure a competitor of the person whose interests the advertisement seeks to promote.

The practical impact of the regime naturally depends on the institutional structures set up to police it. Member States have very different traditions. Most of those possessing established control mechanisms employ a more formal system than the UK. This gave rise to difficult debate about the proper structure of the EC Directive. The agreed objective is contained in Art. 4(1) of the EC Directive, a provision which obliges Member States to:

ensure that adequate and effective means exist for the control of misleading advertising in the interests of consumers as well as competitors and the general public.

Legal provisions shall enable persons or organisations regarded under national law as having a legitimate interest in prohibiting misleading advertising to pursue one or both of two stipulated routes: first, the taking of legal action against such advertising and, second, the bringing of such advertising before an administrative authority competent either to decide on complaints or to initiate appropriate legal proceedings. Article 4(2) of the Directive requires courts and administrative authorities to be empowered to take stipulated forms of action, including the making of cessation orders, in the event of offending advertising.

The policy was to permit States the option of retaining administrative structures as adequate regulation in the area. The UK, in particular, was concerned to avoid the imposition of a judicial structure since the Government viewed self-regulation as satisfactory. Article 4(3) of the Directive requires that, where the administrative option is taken, the authorities shall be, *inter alia*, impartial – not dominated by advertisers; also, where the powers are the exclusive preserve of the administrative authority, decisions shall be reasoned and shall be subject to judicial review in the event of impropriety or unreasonableness.

Article 5 of the Directive further illustrates the receptivity of the EC structure to extra-legal enforcement. Article 5 makes it clear that voluntary control of misleading advertising by self-regulatory bodies is not excluded, although proceedings of this nature must be additional to, not in substitution for, the court or administrative route established by Art. 4.

The UK initially chose to implement the Directive at the institutional level by empowering the Director-General of Fair Trading, to whom complaints were to be made under Regulation 4 of the 1988 Regulations. The Director-General's office was abolished by the Enterprise Act 2002, and the functions of the Director were transferred to the OFT. Regulation 5 provided a power, now held by the OFT, to apply to a court for an injunction against any person involved in the publication of a misleading advertisement. In essence, the system is self-regulation endowed with statutory backing and it represents an interesting method for securing administrative supervision of the market, beyond the private law, but separate from the criminal law.[145] Subsequently it was agreed that enforcement powers would also be placed in the hands of other bodies, including trading standards officers and designated consumer organisations. This system of multiple collective enforcement is now contained in the Enterprise Act 2002 within the context of a wider reform of the enforcement of consumer protection laws originating both from domestic sources and from the EC. The relevant procedures are set out in Part 8 of the Enterprise Act 2002 and they are designed to pave the way for a more effective system for combating commercial practices that harm the collective interests of consumers, while also seeking to avoid the imposition of unnecessary regulatory burdens on business. They are examined in depth in Chapter 13.9.

There has been little formal action taken against misleading advertising under these procedures in the UK. Most matters have normally been dealt with by the ASA and go no further. Matters that progress beyond the ASA to reach the OFT normally go no further than the OFT. Litigation is very uncommon. This is in part attributable to the judicial attitude on the few occasions that disputes have spilled over into the courts. Judicial review of ASA rulings is possible, but the courts are willing to allow the authority a margin of discretion. For example, in *R v ASA, ex parte SmithKline Beecham plc*[146] review was sought of an ASA ruling that an advertisement for Ribena ToothKind was misleading in its claim that the soft drink did not encourage tooth decay. It was held that although the ASA had taken advice from an individual whose negative views on the health aspects of the product were already known, the decision-making process had been kept separate from that advice. There was no real danger of bias. Moreover the ASA was entitled to find the health claims in the advertisement to have been advanced in an unjustifiably unconditional manner.[147] Litigation in *Director-General of Fair Trading v Tobyward Ltd* permitted Hoffmann J (as he then was) to discuss the role of the procedure once an ASA ruling is placed in the hands of the OFT.[148] Complaints about advertisements for a

---

[145] For general policy discussion, T. Wilhelmsson, 'Administrative Procedures for the Control of Marketing Practices – Theoretical Rationale and Perspectives' (1992) 15 *JCP* 159.

[146] [2001] EMLR 23.

[147] For a similarly limited approach to the role of judicial review of ASA decisions, cf. *R v ASA, ex parte Vernons* [1992] 1 WLR 1289; *R v ASA, ex parte Charles Robertson (Developments) Ltd, The Times* 26 November 1999.

[148] [1989] 2 All ER 266.

slimming aid marketed by Tobyward were upheld by the ASA, but the advertisements were not discontinued. The ASA referred the matter to the Director-General, who sought an injunction. Hoffmann J granted it, feeling it proper to 'support the principle of self-regulation'[149] by granting an injunction that would effectively give legal backing to the ASA's finding. He also felt that the interests of consumers demanded the protection of an injunction. The decision is important in instilling respect for ASA rulings and in discouraging advertisers from contesting the decisions of the ASA through litigation.

8.6.4 The Future of Public Control of Advertising Regulation

It remains to be seen to what extent the expansion in opportunities to initiate formal legal proceedings now enshrined in the Enterprise Act 2002 will generate an increase in practice. Since 2000 the OFT has remarked on a noticeable increase in the number of complaints it has received about advertisements.[150] Those targeted at vulnerable consumers – 'miracle cure' products aimed at the ill, for example – generate particular anxiety. The OFT will act promptly if persuaded detriment is imminent, notwithstanding the availability of the industry's own procedures. Statistics bear out the impression of increasing activity. In 2000 the OFT set up a dedicated team to deal with advertisements and it quickly reported that 'many more cases than before' were reaching it.[151] One might wonder the establishment of the team was itself a factor in generating a higher workload but the published statistics bear out the assertion. 87 cases were raised in 2000, which led to five undertakings by traders to cease publishing offending advertisements. This rose to 159 cases in 2001 (although only one undertaking was secured). In the fifteen-month period from the beginning of 2002 to the end of March 2003 the figure shot up to 437 cases, involving 38 undertakings and 11 formal orders.[152] One may anticipate that trading standards officers and designated consumer organisations will be offered similar opportunities to take on a heavy caseload. On the other hand, one may predict a readiness among advertisers to resort to the language of human rights to seek to rebuff such intervention. Freedom of expression, propelled by the combined legal force of the European Convention on

---

[149] 270g.

[150] E.g. *Fair Trading* September 2002, pp. 10–11.

[151] Annual Report of the Office of Fair Trading, 2001 HC 773 2001–2002.

[152] The figures are slightly misleading in that one incident may generate multiple responses, e.g. if natural and legal persons are involved. See Annual Report of the Office of Fair Trading, 2001 HC 773 2001–2002; 2002–March 2003 HC 906 2002–2003. These reports are available electronically via http://www.oft.gov.uk.

Human Rights and the Human Rights Act 1998, will doubtless come to play a more prominent role in judicial discourse in this area.[153] This combination is likely to herald a rise in the 'legalisation' of advertising regulation in the UK. Much the same is likely at EU level. The well-known decision of the European Court in 2000 upholding a German challenge to the validity of regulation of advertising of tobacco products was dealt with as a matter of legal competence,[154] but one cannot in principle exclude the possibility that a measure of advertising regulation for which the EC is legally competent – which was not the case in *Tobacco Advertising* – could be successfully impugned for interference with constitutionally protected rights held by the advertiser.[155] These trends invite comparative inquiry into the experience of legal systems that have already taken this path.[156]

8.7 REFORM OF THE LAW

8.7.1 Consolidation of the Law of Trade Descriptions

Why not a consolidated trade descriptions law regime? There is no adequate answer to the question. Consolidation would be welcome.

The motivation in 1968 for confining liability for the newly created offence of misdescription of services to those possessing a (defined and admittedly limited) guilty mind was understandable.[157] More than 35 years later, however, the justification for distinguishing between ss.1 and 14 in this way has been completely eroded. The cause of coherent consumer protection designed to correct market failure would be served by converting s. 14 offences into strict liability offences (like those under s. 1) in preference to the current 'semi-strict' liability. The argument has been aired[158] and subsequently it was apparently accepted in the 1999 White

---

[153] For an early hint see *R v Advertising Standards Authority, ex parte Mattias Rath BV*, *The Times*, 6 December 2000. See also C. Munro, 'The Value of Commercial Speech' (2003) 62 *Cambridge Law Journal* 134.

[154] Case C–376–98 *Germany v Parliament and Council* [2000] ECR I–8419. See Chapter 2.3.5.

[155] This was discussed by A.G. Fennelly in his Opinion in Case C–376/98 note 154 above, but the Court, having annulled the Directive for want of competence, did not need to address the issue and did not do so.

[156] See note 128 above.

[157] Chapter 8.3.1 above.

[158] A DTI Communication in 1991 made such a suggestion. In this direction, see P. Cartwright, 'Reforming the Trade Descriptions Act 1968' (1993) 3 *Consumer Policy Review* 34.

Paper, *Modern Markets: Confident Consumers*.[159] Legislation has not yet been forthcoming.

Moreover, the law controlling price indications and the description of land could profitably be consolidated into a single, overall regime. This general reform would provide the opportunity to eliminate oddities such as the liability of private individuals under s. 23 TDA, exposed in *Olgeirsson v Kitching*.[160] Another example of an inconsistency that could usefully be ironed out concerns the oddities connected with the timing of a statement constituting an offence which were exposed in *Walker v Simon Dudley Ltd*, discussed in 8.2.3 and 8.3.3 above. Consolidation of the law into a general control over misleading trade descriptions, based on the normal pattern of the regulatory offence examined in Chapter 11, would reduce compliance costs for business, enhance effective enforcement and make the law more transparent for consumers.

8.7.2 Unfair Commercial Practices under UK Law

A further and more radical step would be to advocate a general control outlawing misleading or unfair trade practices. English law, of course, traditionally fights shy of such general clauses. Such legal intervention as currently exists is typically narrower in its focus and intent. An unfair commercial practice may constitute a breach of contract in appropriate cases, but actions for breach of contract are not properly seen as part of any general policy commitment to rooting out unfair commercial practices which harm the collective interests of consumers. Equally the use of deception or illegitimate pressure to lure a party into a contract may have the effect that the victim is entitled to escape from the contract, but this would be regarded as a matter falling within relatively well-defined rules governing misrepresentation and duress rather than as a general protection against unfair commercial practice. A number of torts and related causes of action are potentially relevant. One may mention misrepresentation, defamation, inducement to breach a contract, conspiracy and breach of confidence. But there is no general common law rule against unfair competition. Torts typically generate legal actions by individuals suffering harm, and each tort is marked and limited by its own (frequently rather eccentric) governing criteria, and the law of torts cannot convincingly be presented or conceived as a general framework principle outlawing unfair commercial practices.[161] Indeed the English judiciary steadfastly avoids any such rationalisation, either rhetorically or in substance. Public

---

[159] Cm 4410 (1999), para. 3.19.

[160] See Chapter 11.2.5.

[161] Cf. H. Carty, *An Analysis of the Economic Torts* (OUP, 2001).

regulation has been considered in this chapter and in several others in this book. Specific criminal statutes such as the Trade Descriptions Act and the Property Misdescriptions Act combine with broader measures such as the Competition Act and the Enterprise Act[162] to establish a complex network of regulatory offences and administrative control. But broad notions of fairness are not the overt concern of these statutes. It may be true that once one collects together the several strands of statutory and common law control over commercial practices found in the English legal system, one will have a well-filled bag that may be thought to constitute something that is in practice not so very far removed from a general legal control over the fairness of commercial practices. But this is not how English law is currently structured. And it is not how orthodox commercial and consumer lawyers working in the English legal system would typically think. They would necessarily focus on the search for a specific common law or statutory basis for challenging a particular commercial practice. Moreover, many such lawyers would be highly suspicious of the introduction of a regime based on such an open-ended notion as fairness. They might recognise its value as a flexible tool of regulation but they would be anxious about its potentially unpredictable application. Even the report of the National Audit Office published in 1999 under the suggestive title *The Office of Fair Trading Protecting the Consumer from Unfair Trading Practices*[163] tends to mislead. Though certainly important for its proposals for reform of the structure and delivery of consumer protection in the UK, the paper does *not* advocate any general rule against unfair trading practices.

8.7.3 The Proposals of the European Commission

The European Commission has now advanced the debate by adopting relevant proposals. A Green Paper on Consumer Protection was published in October 2001.[164] It tracked the heap of diverse national laws that are relevant to the regulation of marketing practices.[165] It describes the sheer number of legal obligations that arise in the Member States as 'off-putting' to 'nearly all businesses but those who can afford to establish in all Member States', and, in addition, a brake on consumer confidence.[166] A

---

[162] Chapter 12 covers competition law.

[163] HC 57 1999–2000, 8 December 1999. Available via:
http://www.nao.gov.uk/publications/nao_reports/990057.pdf.

[164] COM (2001) 531, 2 October 2001.

[165] See H.-W. Micklitz and J. Kessler, *Marketing Practices Regulation and Consumer Protection in the EC Member States and the US* (Nomos, 2002).

[166] Para. 3.1.

follow-up document in 2002 reported that consultation had showed strong support for the adoption of a framework Directive in the field.[167] This was followed by a Draft Directive published by the Commission in June 2003.[168] This proposes a prohibition against unfair business-to-consumer commercial practices. In accordance with the orthodox impact of harmonisation of laws, the adoption of a common EU-wide regime would be designed *both* to eliminate barriers to trade caused by diverse national approaches to the regulation of unfair practices *and* to achieve a high level of consumer protection. It would be incumbent on Member States to secure the suppression of all practices falling within the scope of the Directive's prohibition, but it would be excluded that Member States could prevent the commission of practices judged fair under the standard of control envisaged by the Directive in so far as such action restricted cross-border trade in goods and services.

From the perspective of both trader and advocate of consumer protection the vital question is what is envisaged by an 'unfair' commercial practice. The Commission's draft Directive sets out two general conditions to apply in determining whether a practice is unfair. First, that the practice is contrary to the requirements of professional diligence; second, that the practice materially distorts consumers' behaviour.

Two particular categories of unfairness are envisaged: *misleading* and *aggressive* practices. A commercial practice may mislead either through action or omission. No attempt is made to define a comprehensive list of information to be positively disclosed in all circumstances. The duty imposed on businesses is not to omit 'material' information which the average consumer needs to make an informed decision. Core items of information are listed (non-exhaustively). These include the main characteristics of the product, the price (inclusive of taxes) and, where appropriate, delivery charges and the existence of a right of withdrawal where one exists. The measure would incorporate the current provisions of the misleading advertising Directive but would, of course, go far beyond the phenomenon of advertising. The draft identifies three ways in which a commercial practice may be regarded as aggressive. These are harassment, coercion and undue influence.

The draft Directive's vulnerability to criticism for lack of precision is qualified by the inclusion of an Annex listing (non-exhaustively) specific types of banned commercial practice. In the bag of misleading practices one finds *inter alia* a false claim that a trader is a signatory to a code of conduct or a false claim that a code of conduct has an endorsement from a public body; use of the expression 'liquidation sale' or equivalent when the

---

[167] COM (2002) 289, 11 June 2002.

[168] COM (2003) 356, available via:
    http://europa.eu.int/comm/consumers/cons_int/safe_shop/fair_bus_pract/index_en.htm

trader is not about to cease trading; an inaccurate statement that a product can be legally sold; paying for the publication of an advertisement without making clear the item is in fact an advertisement; and establishing, operating, or promoting a pyramid scheme. Aggressive practices include creating the impression that the consumer cannot leave the premises until the contract is signed or the payment made; making extended and/or repeated visits to the consumer's home and making persistent and unwanted solicitations by media including telephone, fax, and e-mail; targeting consumers who have recently suffered a family bereavement or serious illness as a strategy to sell a product directly related to the ill-fortune; demanding payment for products supplied by the trader but not solicited by the consumer. This proposes a non-exhaustive black list of unacceptable clauses.

Notwithstanding the attempts made in the draft to put flesh on the skeletal concept of an unfair commercial practice, a major question asks whether one can realistically imagine that such a regime could be enforced in a uniform manner across the territory of the 25 Member States of the European Union. With this in mind the Commission's package also includes a proposal for a Regulation on consumer protection co-operation.[169] Enforcement agencies in each Member State are required to direct their activities at offending traders based in their jurisdiction irrespective of the location of the consumers targeted for unfair exploitation. In this sense British enforcement is designed to protect the interests of not only British consumers but also French and German and all other EU consumers. Equally British consumers should be able to expect that their interests will be relevant to enforcement practice in other Member States, where the UK market is the target of exported unfair practices. The draft Regulation envisages the creation of a network of mutual assistance between enforcement authorities in different Member States which will give practical force to the quest to achieve effective supervision of cross-border commercial practices.

8.7.4 The Developing Debate in the UK

Some of the proposal's specific listed unfair practices have long been condemned as unlawful in the United Kingdom. There is an obvious congruence with much of the thrust of the Trade Descriptions Act and of Part III of the Consumer Protection Act, which have been examined at length in this chapter. Other more specific existing measures such as the Unsolicited Goods and Services Act would seem similarly to forbid the sort of practices that are the target of the draft Directive. The UK would be

---

[169]   COM (2003) 443.

able simply to maintain such statutes alongside a more general implementation of the Directive (were it to be adopted). The UK might prefer to take the opportunity to launch a comprehensive overhaul of the law, but, crucially, it would be permitted to maintain criminal sanctions to condemn such well-established ill-favoured unfair practices, while using less severe administrative means of controlling other matters falling within the Directive's scope.

In some respects the draft suggests control over commercial practices not readily tamed under existing English law. One example would lie in reluctance to make pre-contractual disclosure of material information; another would be provided by product imitation in circumstances in which the protection afforded by the law of passing-off would not currently reach. So the draft, if adopted, may lead to an upgrade in the quality of consumer protection in the UK.

What of the other side of the coin? It is submitted that it is hard to imagine anything the United Kingdom currently refuses to tolerate that would be foisted on it pursuant to this proposed regime. So the adoption of this proposal should not lead to a diminution in consumer protection in the UK. However, this positive assessment may conceivably prove to be a shade complacent. Much would depend on the interpretation of the precise material scope of the measure – the extent of its effect 'pre-empting' national autonomy.[170] The Commission does not intend that it will affect contract law, though precise demarcation might be difficult to achieve. Moreover, in so far as the control of unfair practices would become a matter of EC law, it could not be ruled out that future interpretation of the control test would promote preferences hostile to orthodox readings of consumer protection in the United Kingdom (and in other Member States). It is also hard to see how such an EU-wide system, founded on the desire to establish a common regulatory framework that allows business to treat the EU market as integrated, can permit scope for local autonomy to choose to offer extra protection to particular vulnerable groups of consumers. This exposes the project to criticism for its suppression of regulatory diversity and learning opportunities. Admittedly it should be appreciated that EC law is currently committed to the achievement of a high standard of consumer protection.[171] However, much will depend on precisely how this is approached, and in particular on how the image of the 'consumer' is reflected in a regime based on a general duty.

The issue of broadest interest lies in the nature of the general clause which prohibits unfair commercial practices. This gives the appearance of a qualitatively different legal regime from that to which most lawyers in the UK are accustomed. Should this draft Directive secure a safe passage

---

[170] Chapter 2.3.7.

[171] Arts. 3, 95(3), 153(2) EC, Chapter 2.3.4.

through the legislative process, it will present a challenge to orthodoxy in the UK. How troubling is this likely to prove? The objection frequently raised by English lawyers that the notion of unfair commercial practices is worryingly vague and therefore conducive to commercial uncertainty may be countered by the observation that a number of key aspects of the existing law are themselves already vague. One may cite the open-ended notion of 'reasonableness', which has been a key feature of the control of some types of contractual term since the entry into force of the Unfair Contract Terms Act in 1977 and, moreover, the 'reasonableness' of an individual's action has long played a central part in determining the imposition of liability under the tort of negligence. So it would be false to say that the very idea of a Framework Directive governing unfair commercial practices would represent a wholly alien intrusion into English law. Some of the tools are there already. But it must nonetheless be conceded that such a Framework Directive would, as a minimum, introduce a basis for intervention in the market that would appear different, and broader, than is currently permitted in the UK. It would appear conceptually distinct from the current approach of control exercised through a range of relatively detailed common law and statutory rules.

A consultation process was initiated by the DTI.[172] It is widely thought that the UK had no particular initial enthusiasm for the Commission's proposal. The consultation accepts that the draft is more conducive to commercial certainty in an integrated market than earlier versions and particularly welcomes its focus on tackling unfair practices rather than seeking to establish prescriptive rules governing fair practices. In short, UK thinking is less troubled by rules suppressing unfairness than it would be by rules requiring fairness. The DTI also commissioned and published an important report by a team of Sheffield-based academics[173] which accepted that the doctrinal form favoured by the Commission's proposal – a general clause rather than specific provisions – challenges traditional English law assumptions, but reached the conclusion that English law was unlikely to be found deficient in its readiness to address the key questions arising out of the embrace of a test of substantive unfairness.[174] Put another way, they believed that the draft, stripped down to the core of its nature and purpose, has more in common with the trends in English consumer law of contract than might be supposed at first glance. And they

---

[172]   Available via http://www.dti.gov.uk/ccp/consultations.htm

[173]   'The Impact of Adopting a Duty to Trade Fairly', authored by R. Bradgate, R. Brownsword and C. Twigg-Flesner (July 2003), available via http://www.dti.gov.uk/ccp/topics1/pdf1/unfairreport.pdf.

[174]   Cf. R. Zimmermann and S. Whittaker, *Good Faith in European Contract Law* (Cambridge, 2000), reviewed in this vein by R. Brownsword, 'Individualism, Cooperativism and an Ethic for European Contract Law' (2001) 64 *MLR* 628.

saw no compelling reason why its relatively interventionist flavour should serve to contaminate the wide realms of commercial contract law, which have long been imbued with a spirit of rugged self-reliance.[175] English law, they observed, has become perfectly at home with the notion of ring-fencing consumer contract law and even though judicial practice might lead to a degree of leakage from the consumer to the non-consumer sphere there would be no risk of the basic notion of broadly separate treatment at law becoming lost. The team did however express anxiety about the choice of an EC model which precluded Member States setting standards above that fixed by the EC. This, they warned, would stifle the evolutionary potential of national law. However, as a general observation, this reasoned report left little scope for policy-makers in the UK to argue that the proposed Directive forbidding unfair business-to-consumer commercial practices is in any fundamental sense alien to the English legal tradition. And in October 2003 the DTI published its *Comparative Report on Consumer Policy Régimes*[176] which accepted that international comparisons revealed the virtue of a general duty to trade fairly both as a backstop to piecemeal legislation and as a simply worded reassurance to the public. The UK's lack of such a provision placed it 'behind the best' in global terms.[177] It is therefore probable that the UK will be supportive of the Commission's draft proposal to outlaw unfair commercial practices as it wends its way through the EC legislative process.

---

[175] Chapter 1.3, especially 1.3.4.

[176] http://www.dti.gov.uk/ccp/topics1/pdf1/benchmain.pdf.

[177] Page 33.

Chapter 9

Public Regulation of
Consumer Credit

9.1 INTRODUCTION

The complexities of the Consumer Credit Act 1974 were introduced in
Chapter 6 when we discussed how the Act seeks to protect individual
consumers through private law mechanisms. In this chapter we focus on
the public law regulation of the credit market provided for by the
Consumer Credit Act 1974, namely the licensing, advertising and
marketing controls and also the controls regulating information held by
credit reference agencies. In 1994 the OFT's report on *Consumer Credit
Deregulation*[1] had concluded that the system worked fairly well and was
supported by the credit industry. While it proposed some changes it
basically found that the system worked satisfactorily. Industry even
welcomed licensing as being 'neither particularly onerous nor costly, yet
provid[ing] a measure of reassurance that all those operating in the field of
credit and hire have met at least some basic requirements of fitness'.[2]

However, there were clearly some themes that have continued to
emerge as problematic. The consultation paper *Tackling loan sharks – and
more*[3] focussed on the need to reform the licensing regime to better target
rogue traders and reduce burdens on legitimate business as well as
simplifying the advertisement regulations. Reform proposals in these areas
have been further developed in subsequent consultation papers and the
White Paper.[4]

9.2 LICENSING

9.2.1 Current Position

Credit is a product about which consumers are very easily confused. It is a
product which consumers often seek when they are at their most

---

1   (OFT, 1994).
2   See *Consumer Credit Deregulation, op. cit.* p. 104.
3   (DTI, 2001).
4   See Chapter 6.1.

vulnerable. It is also an industry that in the past has had a bad reputation with regard to its enforcement practices. Hence it is sensible to restrict entry into the industry to those who satisfy certain basic requirements of good character and probity. A licensing system was adopted. A useful by-product of this system is that it provides a fall back mechanism through which the Director-General of Fair Trading (hereafter Director-General) can ensure that the substantive rights given to consumers are honoured and traders satisfy their obligations. A licence is required to carry on a consumer credit, consumer hire or ancillary credit business.[5] Ancillary credit businesses include credit brokerage, debt adjusting, debt counselling, debt collecting or operating a credit reference agency.[6] In fact licences are issued to cover various categories – lending money (category A), consumer hire (category B), credit brokerage (category C), debt adjusting and debt counselling (category D), debt collecting (category E) and credit reference agencies (category F).

At present a licence applicant must determine which categories he or she wishes to be licensed for. In practice many applicants apply for all categories just in case they should wish to undertake some business falling outside their mainstream work. The definitions of consumer credit and consumer hire businesses relate to those entering into 'regulated agreements'.[7] Thus, if such a business only ever made unregulated or exempt agreements, then no licence is needed. However, the same is not true of ancillary credit businesses; these must always be licensed regardless of the type of agreements they are involved with. It should be noted that the Act has a general provision that provides that a person should not be treated as carrying on a business of a particular type merely because he or she occasionally enters into transactions of that type.[8] This would remove the need to obtain a licence for marginal activity. Nevertheless, the fact that a trader does not need to be licensed does not mean that other provisions of the Consumer Credit Act 1974 do not apply.

Most consumer credit licences are standard licences issued to named persons, though some group licences have been granted, for example to the Law Society for ancillary credit business carried on by solicitors. The period for which the licence is granted has varied dramatically over the years; initially fixed at three years, it was subsequently increased to ten years in 1979 and to 15 years in 1986. The aim was to reduce the administrative workload of the OFT and to lessen the burden on businesses. It was soon realised, however, that the licence period was too

---

5   Sections 21 and 147, Consumer Credit Act 1974.

6   Section 146, Consumer Credit Act 1974.

7   Section 189(1), Consumer Credit Act 1974 and see Chapter 6.4.2.

8   Section 189(2), Consumer Credit Act 1974. See *Roy Marshall* (1990) 90 Cr App Rep 73; *Hare v Schurek* [1993] CCLR 47.

long for the regulators to be able to exercise effective monitoring and control of businesses[9] and in 1991 it was reduced to five years, at which period it currently remains.

There are estimated to be around 215,000 active consumer credit licences. Over half a million licences have been issued since 1976 with 15,855 new standard licences issued in 2002. 15 group licences are in existence.[10] The application fee in 2004 was £100 for a sole trader and £275 for a partnership or limited company The licence application procedure is a positive one, which means that the onus is on the applicant to satisfy the Director-General that he or she is a fit person to engage in the activities covered by the licence and that the name under which he or she applies is not misleading or otherwise undesirable.[11] When determining a licence application, the Director-General can take any relevant circumstances into account, but is particularly directed to consider whether the applicant or his or her past or present employees, agents or associates (or where the applicant is a corporation, the controller of the body corporate or associates) have committed offences of fraud, dishonesty or violence; contravened the Consumer Credit Act 1974 or regulations made under it, or similar provisions in EEA states; carried on discriminatory practices, or engaged in deceitful, oppressive or otherwise improper business practices (whether unlawful or not).[12] The breadth of these powers is quite significant, especially the fact that behaviour can be taken into account even if it is not unlawful. The Financial Services Authority can also notify the OFT where it thinks an application should be refused.[13] In practice the OFT receives much of its information from trading standards officers.

It is perhaps not an overstatement to suggest that the threat of refusal or withdrawal of a credit licence is the most important weapon in the Director-General's fair trading armoury, since almost every trading business needs to obtain a consumer credit licence. Directors-General have shown themselves willing to use the threat of withdrawing licences to

---

[9] This is particularly true since the Director-General has no powers to seek information from a licensee other than when he or she makes an application under the Act. In *Consumer Credit Deregulation, op. cit.*, p. 102 the Director-General proposed that he should be given such powers.

[10] *A Consultation Document on the Licensing Regime under the Consumer Credit Act 1974* (DTI 2003) at 3.

[11] Section 25, Consumer Credit Act 1974; cf. the negative procedure under s. 3, Estate Agents Act 1979 under which the Director-General can make an order prohibiting an unfit person from carrying on estate agency work, but there is no requirement to first obtain a licence.

[12] Section 25(2).

[13] Section 25(1).

promote general business standards, not necessarily just those related to the credit aspects of the business.[14] It was very noticeable in the *Consumer Credit Deregulation* report (as on other occasions) that the then Director-General frequently drew attention to practices which caused him concern and requested the industry to put its own house in order, with the none too veiled threat that he would invoke his licensing powers should they fail to do so. In one sense licensing is a severe form of regulation, for without it entry to a market is precluded. Nevertheless the Director-General made the point that licensing allows him to exert informal pressures which help avoid the need for excessive regulation of particular practices and also prevent the imposition of sanctions where the problem is incompetence or bad management rather than dishonesty.[15] In fact the Director-General has also issued Guidance on a number of matters. The DTI has power to issue conduct of business rules on licenses, but has used this power sparingly.

On application for a credit licence, the Director-General can grant the licence, grant it subject to conditions, or refuse the application.[16] During its currency he can vary the licence either on application by the licensee[17] or compulsorily if he would subsequently be minded to grant the licence on different conditions.[18] He also has similar powers to suspend or revoke a licence.[19] Where the Director-General is minded to refuse an application, to grant it in different terms from the application, or to vary, suspend or revoke a licence he must inform the applicant of his reasons for that decision and give him or her the opportunity to submit representations in support of his or her application. However, this procedure is not unproblematic for the Director-General. As a former Director-General has pointed out, the most difficult 'minded to refuse' notices are those based solely on complaints. By their very nature such complaints are based on only one version of events given to the enforcement authorities by discontented consumers. The specific case may have been less memorable to the trader concerned, who deals with a large number of such matters each day and may be unable to remember clearly the incident complained of, and yet still be able to raise sufficient questions and doubts about the complaints to make it impossible for the OFT to make a finding of fact on the issue raised.[20]

---

14   See for example the action taken against photocopier leasing firms engaged in unfair
      selling practices, *Bee Line*, 91/4 at p. 12.
15   *Consumer Credit Deregulation, op. cit.* at pp. 98–9.
16   Section 27, Consumer Credit Act 1974.
17   Section 30, Consumer Credit Act 1974.
18   Section 31, Consumer Credit Act 1974.
19   Section 32, Consumer Credit Act 1974.
20   G. Borrie, 'Licensing Practice under the Consumer Credit Act' [1982] JBL 91.

In the early 1990s it was estimated around 19,000 licence applications were made each year, with the OFT questioning the fitness of around 900 traders (including existing licensees). Of these 900 cases, 200 would be formally put to adjudicating officers acting on behalf of the Director-General to consider whether their licence should be refused, varied or revoked. For the five years 1989–93, the average number of decisions going against the applicant or licensee was 106.[21] In 2001–2002 the OFT refused 27 applications, 20 renewal applications and revoked 19 active licenses.[22] Between January and September 2002 39 licences were refused or revoked (18 involving the motor trade and 9 financial services). The sanction of revoking a licence is only rarely invoked because the consequences are so severe. One high profile exception revocation involved the television rental company Colorvision, which ceased trading once they lost their credit licence.[23]

Unlicensed traders who undertake activities for which a licence is required commit an offence punishable by a fine if tried summarily or a fine or up to two years imprisonment if convicted on indictment.[24] The more serious sanction, however, is the unenforceabilty of such agreements without an order from the Director-General. This sanction applies to all regulated agreements entered into by unlicensed creditors or owners, other than non-commercial agreements.[25] An incentive is also placed on creditors and owners to monitor their brokers, for any agreements entered into as a result of introductions effected by unlicensed brokers will be unenforceable, even if the creditor or owner is licensed.[26] Contracts for the services of ancillary credit businesses will also be unenforceable if the business does not have a licence.[27] When determining whether to make a validating order, the Director-General is directed to take all relevant circumstances into account. In the case of an unlicensed trader entering into a regulated agreement[28] or an agreement for the services of an ancillary credit business,[29] the Director-General is particularly directed to consider the prejudice caused by the trader's conduct, whether it was likely that a licence would have been granted if one had been applied for and the

---

21 *Consumer Credit Deregulation, op. cit.*, p. 94.

22 *A Consultation Document on the Licensing Regime under the Consumer Credit Act 1974* (DTI, 2003) at 324

23 However, the OFT was found guilty of maladministration by the Parliamentary Ombudsman and paid nearly £5 million in compensation.

24 Section 39, Consumer Credit Act 1974.

25 Section 40(1), Consumer Credit Act 1974.

26 Section 149, Consumer Credit Act 1974.

27 Section 148, Consumer Credit Act 1974.

28 Section 40, Consumer Credit Act 1974.

29 Section 148, Consumer Credit Act 1974.

degree of culpability for the failure to obtain the licence. Where the order is being applied for by a creditor or owner following an introduction by an unlicensed credit-broker, the Director-General is again directed to consider the prejudice caused by the broker's conduct and the degree of culpability on the part of the applicant in facilitating the continuance of an unlicensed business by the credit broker.[30] The Director-General has pointed out that a validating order is only needed if the agreement has to be enforced through the courts; it is not needed to request or take payments under the terms of the agreement or to accept the *voluntary* surrender of goods.[31] Although intended to counter charges that the law places too great a burden on businesses, this statement also serves to illustrate the ease with which the legal protection afforded to consumers can be circumvented by the trader who takes advantage of the consumer's ignorance of his or her legal rights. This underlines the point that the unenforceability sanction in the Consumer Credit Act 1974 is not very effective.[32]

9.2.2 Reform

The White Paper *Fair, Clear and Competitive – The Consumer Credit Market in the 21ˢᵗ Century*[33] has made a number of suggestions for significantly reforming the licensing system with the aim of both streamlining the system by moving towards indefinite licences and at the same time making the system more rigorous. In the consultation document much was made of the comparison with the more detailed approach of the Financial Services Authority and it is likely that inspiration will be drawn from their practice.[34] Lomnicka makes some unflattering comparisons between the consumer credit licensing regime and the well-resourced and rigorous Financial Services Authority ('FSA') with its modern regime providing strong investigative powers, rule-making ability and flexible enforcement powers.[35] She wonders whether it would not be better to bring consumer credit within the ambit of the FSA, but ultimately believes that more will be gained by having regulatory competition between the two agencies.

---

30   Section 49, Consumer Credit Act 1974.
31   *Consumer Credit Deregulation, op. cit.*, p. 100.
32   These weaknesses have already been considered in relation to the situations where agreements should only be enforceable by court order, see Chapter 7.5.4.
33   Cm 6040 (DTI, 2003).
34   Consultation Document, *op cit.*, at 15–20.
35   E. Lomnicka, 'The Future of Consumer Credit regulation' *Contemporary Issues in Law* (forthcoming).

The current fitness test will be strengthened so that the OFT can not only look back at past conduct, but also forward at the general preparedness of the applicant to run a credit business. The OFT will produce guidance. There has for a long time been a debate as to whether there should be one class of credit license or different categories with different levels of regulation. This part of the White Paper is not very specific, but one suspects there will be differentiation between types of lender and the activities they undertake. This would fit it with the general policy of providing indefinite license with merely an obligation to pay maintenance fees, so that unproblematic creditors need not be troubled unduly. This will be coupled with greater investigative powers. The appeal procedure will also be reformed with appeals being dealt with by a tribunal rather than by the Secretary of State.

Also a wider range of enforcement powers will be introduced so that creditors can impose special conditions on or take undertakings from license holders. Financial penalties will be introduced for breach. This might be seen as a move towards a middle law[36] and away from reliance on traditional criminal law. Interestingly the OFT reports that it was notified of 70 successful CCA prosecutions in 2001 resulting in fines of £83,350 and only 18 in 2002 with fines totalling £55,100; similarly 469 credit cases were referred by trading standards departments in 1995–6 and only 77 in 2001–2. The feeling that their information was not leading to positive outcomes is suggested as one reason why less information is being passed on.[37] In combination with the new powers to deal with breaches of the CCA detrimental to the collective harm of consumers contained in the Enterprise Act 2002[38] these reforms should give the regulators a better chance of intervening to stop consumers suffering harm. Previously, even if a license had eventually been revoked many consumers would have been harmed in the meantime.

Of course there is still the problem of creditors who operate without a license. Illegal money-lending is something the White Paper seeks to address, whist recognising that enforcement in that area is difficult.[39] It quotes a Strathclyde study which found 60 illegal money-lending rings each with an annual income of £100,000. The Government is to commission research into the scale of the problem in order to assist in developing a strategy to tackle the problem.

---

[36] See Chapter 11.1 citing the work of Tench.
[37] Consultation Document, *op cit.*, at 6 and 27.
[38] See Chapter 13.9.5.3.
[39] *Op cit.*, paras. 5.55–5.60.

9.3 SEEKING BUSINESS

The Consumer Credit Act 1974 has some specific controls on how credit businesses solicit their customers.

9.3.1 Unsolicited Credit Tokens

Certain forms of seeking business are prohibited by the Consumer Credit Act 1974. Thus s. 51 makes it an offence to give a credit token to a person who has not asked for it. Credit tokens include such things as trading checks and credit cards. This provision was a response to the marketing practices of some credit card companies who, when credit cards were first launched in the early 1970's, promoted this form of credit by sending unsolicited cards to prospective customers. It has had a more modern relevance when certain store cards have converted to credit cards and been sent to existing account holders without seeking their express permission.

9.3.2 Minors

It is also an offence, with a view to financial gain, to send a circular to a minor inviting him or her to borrow money, hire goods, obtain goods or services on credit or apply for advice or information on borrowing money, obtaining credit or hiring goods.[40] In *Alliance & Leicester Building Society v Babbs*[41] there was found to be no intention to obtain financial gain from minors as (i) the circular stated, albeit in regrettable small print, that credit was not available to under 18s, (ii) it was the Society's policy not to lend to minors and (iii) their computers were programmed to prevent money being lent to minors. There is a defence for a person who can prove that he or she did not know and had no reasonable cause to suspect that the person was a minor, but this defence does not apply where the circular is sent to a school or educational establishment for minors.[42] The DTI's Consultative document *Revised Proposals for Legislation on Credit Marketing*[43] proposed removing this defence, on the basis that the costs it imposed on creditors having to check mailing lists was too high. Instead a new defence was proposed requiring that 'appropriate' precautions be taken to minimise the risk of sending credit circulars to minors and that all 'reasonable' precautions are taken to ensure that any credit circular inadvertently sent to

---

[40]   Section 50(1), Consumer Credit Act 1974.
[41]   [1993] CCLR 277.
[42]   Section 50(2), Consumer Credit Act 1974.
[43]   DTI (1991).

a minor clearly states that the credit is not available to minors. This reform has not, however, been implemented.

9.3.3 Canvassing Debtor-Creditor Agreements Off Trade Premises

One of the most restrictive controls on methods of seeking business is that which makes it an offence to canvass off trade premises for debtor-creditor agreements[44] or credit brokerage, debt adjusting or debt counselling services.[45] The aim of these provisions is to protect consumers from being pressured into entering into such contracts in their own home or at social gatherings. Such agreements can only be canvassed if there has been a written request signed by or on behalf of the person making the request. This does not contain the additional safeguards now found in the Consumer Protection (Cancellation of Contracts etc.) Regulations 1987 to prevent traders using the phone or another visit as the excuse to obtain an invitation; but the need for a written request should help prevent the rules being circumvented too casually.

The definition of 'trade premises' is crucial to the offence. For debtor-creditor agreements this prohibition does not extend to a place where a business is carried on (whether on a permanent or temporary basis) by the creditor, owner, supplier, canvasser or his employer or principal, or the consumer.[46] Where the offence relates to the ancillary credit businesses, then the prohibition does not apply to the permanent or temporary place of business of the ancillary credit business, the canvasser or his employer or principal, or the consumer.[47] Thus the offence can be committed in the consumer's home, unless the consumer runs a business from there; in a public house, unless the landlord is the canvasser; or on the public highway, for instance, by approaching customers outside the work's gate or post office.

The offence requires an individual to solicit entry into the relevant agreements by making oral representations during a visit to a place other than a trade premise. Since the oral representations must be made during the course of the visit, telephone canvassing is not caught. For there to be an offence, the visit must have been carried out for the purpose of making such oral representations. Therefore no offence would be committed if such representations were made during a conversation incidental to a social occasion or during the course of collecting repayments under existing loans – unless offering the loan facility was the underlying reason for the visit.

---

44   Section 49, Consumer Credit Act 1974.
45   Section 154, Consumer Credit Act 1974.
46   Section 48, Consumer Credit Act 1974.
47   Section 153, Consumer Credit Act 1974.

The prohibition does not apply to debtor-creditor-supplier agreements. A common ruse is for a company to sell a service to a family through doorstep selling (family portraits are a common example) and then sell on the account to moneylenders, who offer their money-lending services when collecting the payment. This is an attempt to circumvent the prohibition on canvassing debtor-creditor agreements. It might be argued that the purpose of the visit was not to make the oral representations, but rather to collect the payment and any offer of a loan was incidental. However, if it can be shown that there was a policy of offering such loans then there should still be an offence committed as making those oral representations would be one purpose of the visit. It should be noted that the soliciting of an overdraft is excluded from the prohibitions.

No offence will be committed if the visit is carried out in response to a request made on a previous occasion. Thus a company can canvass by mail, advertisements or telephone and make appointments to discuss such agreements in the consumer's home. However, if on that visit an individual is solicited to enter into a debtor-creditor agreement, a separate offence will have been committed unless the request was in writing and signed by or on behalf of the person making it.[48]

9.4 CONDUCT OF BUSINESS

Section 26, Consumer Credit Act 1974 also contains wide powers to make regulations governing the conduct of business, though the only regulations issued to date cover credit reference agencies[49] and pawn records.[50] There are also powers to issue regulations governing the seeking of business by licensees and to require businesses to display prescribed information, but no such regulations have been enacted.[51]

9.5 ADVERTISING AND QUOTATIONS

Our study of its private law provisions demonstrated that the Consumer Credit Act 1974 is less concerned with controlling the content of the

---

[48]   Section 49 (2), Consumer Credit Act 1974: there would appear to be no such offence in relation to soliciting ancillary credit business, where a previous request for a visit, in any form, would appear to be a sufficient defence.

[49]   Consumer Credit (Conduct of Business) (Credit References) Regulations 1977, S.I. 1977/330.as amended by S.I. 2000/291.

[50]   Consumer Credit (Conduct of Business) (Pawn Records) Regulations 1983, S.I. 1983/1565.

[51]   Sections 53–54, Consumer Credit Act 1974.

agreement than with ensuring that it is transparent and entered into without undue pressure being exerted on the consumer. The requirement to provide copies of the agreement and the prescription of the information that it must contain support this policy. Yet, frequently, once the consumer has reached the stage of signing an agreement, he or she will be psychologically, if not legally, tied into taking credit from that source. Thus it is important that, prior to this stage, the consumer has access to reliable information on alternative credit sources available.

9.5.1 Advertisements

In addition to the law's general controls on advertising,[52] there is a specific prohibition in s. 46, Consumer Credit Act 1974 on the conveying of information concerning credit which is in a material respect false or misleading. There is also a prohibition on advertising restricted-use credit agreements where the person is not holding him or herself out as willing to sell the goods or provide the service for cash, presumably because it is then impossible to calculate the true cost of credit.[53] In addition, there are powers to make regulations governing the form and content of advertisements, breach of which is an offence.[54]

'Advertisement' is defined very broadly by the Act and covers all forms of advertising, from circulars to television and radio broadcasts. These rules apply to those who indicate that they are willing to provide credit or bail goods, and thus catch a wider category of persons than many of the provisions in the Act: even non-regulated agreements may be caught if they are secured on land. Nor are all of the 'exempt agreements' excluded from the effect of these provisions. However, the provisions do not apply to advertisements for credit which are clearly restricted to corporations or where the credit must exceed £25,000 and there is no requirement that there be security involving land.

The content of the advertisement regulations has been controversial. It took until 1980 for the first set of regulations to be agreed upon. Those regulations established a tripartite structure where the requirements depended upon whether the advertisement was deemed to be a simple, intermediate or full credit advertisement. This structure has proven to be complex. In particular the distinction between full and intermediate advertisements has been difficult to discern. Many technical breaches have occurred, even by reputable traders who wished to comply. The present regulations of 1989 amended the original ones and, whilst clarifying their

---

52 See Chapter 8.
53 Section 45, Consumer Credit Act 1974.
54 Sections 44 and 167(2), Consumer Credit Act 1974.

application to brokers and making some simplifications, nevertheless retain the same basic structure, but also introduce the requirement for warnings about the risks associated with secure loans and foreign currency mortgages.[55] With the use of warnings very much in vogue, the DTI's 1991 *Revised Proposals for Legislation on Credit Marketing* proposed a whole raft of new warnings to be included in credit advertisements.

In the *Consumer Credit Deregulation* report the Director-General took a more robust approach. The Director-General accepted the retention of warnings about the consequences of failing to keep up mortgage repayments, but in printed advertisements only. Though promising to undertake further discussions on the question of the use of warnings, he appears to have been lukewarm, at best, concerning their effectiveness. This would fit in with his general antipathy to the 'generation... of small print purely to meet regulatory requirements'.[56]

He proposed that a general requirement be retained that all information given should be clear and easily legible. Beyond this, traders should be free simply to advertise in general terms the services they offer. However, where an interest rate or other figure relating to the cost of credit is specified he suggested the APR should also be shown and given the same degree of prominence as any given interest rate.[57] Equally where a particular credit product or specific examples of terms are given then information should be supplied about the amount of credit offered (lump sum or credit limit), the number, timing and amount of repayments, the interest rate and the APR, and any other charges and fees.[58] Similar proposals were made in relation to consumer hire advertisements.

The general thrust of simplifying advertisements is carried forward in the White Paper[59] and accompanying consultation paper *Establishing a Transparent Market*.[60] However, the use of warnings is back in favour. This is despite the DTI quoting research that found small print in advertisements by its very presence suggests to consumers that a product is closely regulated.[61]

---

55   Consumer Credit (Advertisements) Regulations 1989, S.I. 1989/1125.
56   *Consumer Credit Deregulation, op. cit.*, p. 38.
57   The present Regulations require that it be given greater prominence, which has given rise to some difficult problems of interpretation; for instance, is it satisfied by merely underlining the APR?
58   For variable interest rates where this is an initial discounted rate, the APR should also be stated based on the current variable rate, with less prominence and with a brief statement as to its applicability, for the period subsequent to the initial rate period.
59   Pages 30–33.
60   Pages 11–19
61   White Paper at p. 31.

The DTI proposes abolishing the Simple, Intermediate and Full distinction. All advertisements will have to include the name of the lender, but need only otherwise comply with general requirements, unless their name makes a subjective claim; www.cheapest-loans.com is given as an example of a name making an implicit claim. Such claims would require the APR to be quoted. Otherwise there will be some situations where the APR will have to be quoted – where any interest rate is shown, or the amount or range of credit is shown; loans targeted to those who find it difficult to obtain credit elsewhere i.e. 'CCJ's – no problem'; or where there is any descriptive or subjective reference i.e. 'low interest'.

There will be occasions where it will be sufficient to simply display the APR, but where other financial information is provided the APR must be located with it, be more prominent than it and be twice the size of any other financial information. However if one of a list of indicators are shown then they must all be mentioned and the APR stated as well. These indicators are the amount of credit (but this can be shown alone with APR); any deposit: any advance payment; the frequency, amount and number of payments; total amount payable; notification of other charges and fees; the cash price of goods and in the case of foreign currency mortgages a warning about the risk of exchange rate fluctuations. Similar rules will apply to hire contracts.

One particular problem has been the advertising of APR rates for credit cards and the Total Charge for Credit Regulations will be amended so that better comparisons between running account credit offers can be made. The APR will usually have to reflect the best rate available to 66 per cent of customers. Creditors can still advertise APRs starting from a certain per cent, but this must be based on ten per cent of the business written and be accompanied by a figure typical for 90 per cent of the business written.

9.5.2 Quotations

Similar problems of complexity characterised the Regulations which prescribe the form and content of quotations.[62] In *Consumer Credit Deregulation*, the OFT took the view that the Regulations were too burdensome, especially as consumers rarely expressly requested a full quotation, but tended instead to inquire about specific terms. The Regulations have been revoked. It was proposed to amend s. 46, Consumer Credit Act 1974 to make it an offence to provide quotations which are materially false or misleading. This reform proposal has not been followed

---

[62] Consumer Credit (Quotations) Regulations 1989, S.I. 1989/1126.

through. Certain warnings do have to be provided where quotations involve mortgages or foreign currency loans.[63]

9.6 CREDIT REFERENCE AGENCIES

At the time the Consumer Credit Act 1974 was enacted, the computer age was just dawning. Since then the amount of information stored on computers concerning consumers and in particular their credit record has expanded as has the ability of the credit companies to make use of the data when reaching credit-granting decisions. The ethical and policy issues surrounding the collection, storage and use of computer-stored information led to the enactment of the Data Protection Act 1984 and the creation of the Office of the Data Protection Registrar. This is now the Data Protection Act 1998 and the Registrar is now the Information Commissioner. The Registrar can ensure that the so-called 'data protection principles' contained in Schedule 1 of the Act are complied with. These have already caused some debate between the regulator and the credit industry mainly about the practices of credit reference agencies.

The Data Protection Act 1998 gives the data subject (the consumer) the right to access data held about him or her[64] on payment of a £2 fee and where appropriate to have it rectified, blocked, erased or destroyed.[65] Also the data subject can object to his data being use for direct marketing purposes[66] or decisions being made about him solely on the basis of automated decision-taking.[67] The data subject requesting information must also be informed of his rights under the Act and of his right to correct information under s. 159 of the Consumer Credit Act 1974. A request to a credit reference agency is rebuttably presumed to only be a request about the data subject's financial standing.

The Consumer Credit Act 1974 also gives the debtor or hirer the right, within 28 days of the termination of negotiations, to make a written request that the creditor, owner or any negotiator inform him or her of any credit reference agency consulted.[68] It is an offence to fail to comply with such a request within seven days. On payment of a £2 fee the consumer can then apply to the credit reference agency for a copy of his or her file. Within seven working days the agency must provide him or her with a copy or

---

[63]   The Consumer Credit (Content of Quotations) and Consumer Credit (Advertisements) (Amendment) Regulations 1999, S.I. 1999/2725.

[64]   Section 7.

[65]   Section 14.

[66]   Section 11.

[67]   Section 12.

[68]   Section 157.

give notice that no file is held. The agency must also inform the consumer of his or her right to give it notice to remove or amend any information which is incorrect and likely to be prejudicial if not amended.[69] Within 28 days of receiving such a notice, the agency must inform the consumer of what steps, if any, it has decided to take.[70] Unless the entry has been removed, the consumer then has 28 days from receiving the notice (56 days from sending the first notice in cases where the agency has failed to respond) to send a further notice requiring that a notice of correction be added to the file. The agency should inform the consumer within a further 28 days if it intends to comply with this request. If the consumer receives no such notice, or if the agency considers it improper to issue the notice of correction, then either party can apply to the Director-General, who will make such order as he thinks fit. There is some evidence that more consumers are becoming aware of their right to inspect credit reference agency files and seek corrections of inaccurate information, though many more probably remain ignorant of these rights. The increased numbers making applications to see their files have caused the credit reference agencies to seek to raise the application fee (which does not cover their costs). Any increase in this fee should be resisted, however, as otherwise consumers will be deterred from invoking this right.

9.7 DEFENCES

Breach of many of the public regulation provisions of the Consumer Credit Act 1974 lead to the commission of offences. Section 168 provides a defence to such charges where the person charged can prove:

(i) that his act or omission was due to a mistake, or to reliance on information supplied to him, or to an act or omission by another person, or to an accident or some other cause beyond his control, and;
(ii) that he took all reasonable precautions and exercised all due diligence to avoid such an act or omission by himself or any person under his control.[71]

9.8 PRIVATE VS PUBLIC CONTROLS

The public law controls are intended to prevent problems from arising and to allow authorities to ensure that problems that have arisen are not

---

[69] Section 158
[70] Section 159.
[71] For a detailed discussion of the general principles of the defence, see Chapter 11.2.

repeated. Though the relevance of the public law controls may seem rather tenuous to the individual facing a consumer credit problem, many consumers will have benefited from them. The problem is that nobody can quantify the number of individuals who have escaped exploitation by traders refused a credit licence or avoided being deceived by misleading advertisements that might have appeared but for the regulatory controls. Both private and public law controls have their role to play in this sensitive area of consumer protection. However, the lack of consumer education and inadequate access to legal services suggest that the private law cannot by itself assure the consumer of adequate protection against unfair credit practices. On the other hand the low reported rates of prosecutions is indicative of the meagre resources available to enforce consumer law. If the licensing regime is reformed to provide more flexible enforcement powers and trading standards departments and the OFT co-operate more closely some improvement might be made. However, the problem of controlling unlicensed money-lending remains a real problem that will be difficult to deal with within the budgets of trading standards departments. Such illegal activity probably needs to be dealt with by specialist enforcement agencies, possibly within the police. A distinction can be seen between 'real' consumer crime, which could be appropriately dealt with by the normal law enforcement agencies and 'regulatory' failures which perhaps need something more subtle than traditional criminal sanctions.

Chapter 10

Consumer Safety

10.1 RATIONALES FOR CONSUMER SAFETY REGULATION

It is probably the instinctive reaction of a consumer living in a modern Western economy that the State must 'do something' about the risk of unsafe and dangerous goods appearing on the market. The instinctive reaction of the consumer lawyer and policy-maker should be to focus much more closely on just why the State should intervene and what form that intervention should take. This reflects the theme, familiar throughout this book, of insisting on convincing rationales for the introduction of laws of consumer protection.

Why should there be laws governing consumer safety? After all, it is presumably not in the interest of any trader wishing to build up a customer base to sell unsafe goods any more than it is in the interest of any consumer to buy them. The mechanism of the market ought to dictate supply of safe goods. Even where an unsafe product slips through the net and causes injury, the private law ought to offer a remedy to the consumer without the need for any regulatory intervention. It is a breach of contract to supply a dangerous product and, even if the required contractual link is missing, the law of tort should fill the gap in consumer protection. Since *Donoghue v Stevenson*[1] it has been plain that manufacturers and other traders in the distribution chain may be liable to pay compensation where harm is suffered by consumers as a result of the supply of an unsafe product. This form of consumer protection has been strengthened by the removal of fault from the test of liability in Part I of the Consumer Protection Act 1987.[2]

Accordingly, the market should serve the consumer interest by dissuading the supply of dangerous products. The private law should complement that dissuasive effect by providing the consumer with a remedy against the trader where the market system breaks down and allows a dangerous product to come into circulation. The rationales for intervening in the market by setting safety standards have been discussed at length in Chapter 1. The modern market operates in a manner which greatly distorts the message about product preference which, on a simplistic analysis, may be communicated from consumer to trader. The

---

[1]   [1932] AC 562, Ch. 4.2.4.2.
[2]   For closer examination of the nuances of Part 1, see Chapter 4.2.4.3.

consumer is frequently under-informed about the nature of goods on offer
and will not be able to distinguish between varying levels of safety in
products. For these reasons and others,[3] the market is not a perfect
mechanism. Nor does the private law plug all these gaps. Consumer rights
arising in contract are limited by the doctrine of privity to a claim against
the party from which the item was purchased.[4] Accordingly, the consumer
typically has no direct contractual link with the manufacturer; a recipient
of a gift typically has no contractual link with anyone at all. This leaves the
law of tort as the only means of securing compensation in the event that a
consumer suffers injury from a dangerous product, but tort law, negligence
in particular, has its own inherent limitations. In claims which fall outside
the scope of the Consumer Protection Act 1987, the consumer must show
fault on the part of the defendant supplier.[5] Even under the 1987 Act,
where liability is in principle triggered by the condition of the product, not
the conduct of the trader, there remain hurdles for the consumer to cross,
such as the complexity in identifying a defect and the possible availability
of defences.[6] Moreover, the consumer is obliged to establish the chain of
causation whether the basis of the claim lies in negligence or the 1987 Act.
Causation is itself a significant barrier to successful consumer redress.[7]
Allied to these weaknesses of the law on paper are weaknesses of the law
in practice, which in many ways are even more significant. The time and
trouble that must be invested in taking a claim means that most instances of
consumer dissatisfaction provoke no complaint at all, and certainly no
formal legal proceedings.[8] In isolation, individual consumer loss is
typically small and absorbed by the individual, which may mean that a
trader 'gets away' with causing a large loss in aggregate. This is especially
the case where the loss relates to the quality of the product, but it may also
apply in relation to safety. This further weakens the 'message' sent by
consumer to trader about real preferences.

In many respects, the use of individual litigation is quite out of line
with the realities of mass production and collective consumption. The net
result is that market plus the private law emphasis on individual redress do
not necessarily prevent the supply of unsafe goods which consumers may
not want to buy. The market will operate inefficiently. Consumers may call

---

3   See more broadly Ch. 1. See also G. Howells, *ConsumerProduct Safety* (Dartmouth,
     1998), Ch. 1; P. Cartwright, *Consumer Protection and the Criminal Law: Law,
     Theory and Policy in the UK* (Cambridge UP, 2001), Ch. 5; P. Asch, *Consumer Safety
     Regulation: Putting a Price on Life and Limb* (OUP, 1988).
4   Chapter 3.
5   Chapter 4.
6   Chapter 4.2.4.3.
7   Chapter 4.2.4.3.
8   More broadly, Chapter 14.

for protection; honest traders too may call for protection from unscrupulous rivals. Generally the public interest in improving the performance of an imperfect market may call for public intervention to achieve higher standards of safety.

The question then turns to the appropriate type of intervention. Immediately it should be recalled that regulation cannot be cost-free. It is always necessary to examine both the benefits of regulating – safer goods – and the costs of regulating – reduction in consumer choice and higher prices where stringent minimum production standards are imposed. Where costs outweigh benefits, regulation need not automatically be excluded, but rationales more sophisticated than a simple cost/benefit calculation will need to be deployed. Chapter 1 explores these issues in more depth.

Chapter 1 also examines choices between forms of regulation.[9] An obvious regulatory response to the problem of unsafe goods lies in the establishment of minimum safety standards. Traders who fall below the minimum by supplying goods which fail to conform commit an offence. Current policy preferences dictate that the standards in question shall be flexible and broadly expressed. The standard expected by law is a rather broad notion of reasonable safety.[10] This regime benefits the consumer by providing a minimum guarantee of safety; however, it costs the consumer by removing the choice to buy less safe goods which, in theory, ought to be cheaper, provided the market is functioning with adequate transparency. It is also a persisting theme that, although honest traders may welcome regulatory intervention to secure protection from unscrupulous rivals, what may seem unscrupulous to an existing operator on the market may from another perspective amount to no more than the onset of fresh competition. Traders already in the market may consciously or unconsciously seek to maintain or even to raise regulatory standards in order to protect their investment from newcomers. From this point of view, minimum standards may serve to reduce competition and consumer choice in the market.

Regulating for a basic safety minimum amounts to the State choosing what can and cannot be bought on behalf of the consumer, rather than allowing the market to make that choice through the supplier/consumer relationship. As explored above, weaknesses in that supplier/consumer relationship provide rationales for State intervention, but this does not remove the intrinsic difficulty in shaping an appropriate minimum safety level chosen by regulatory intervention instead of the market. Rather than setting a minimum standard enforced by a ban on non-conforming products, an alternative method lies in regulation designed to reduce the information gap. Instead of banning less safe goods, it might be possible to require that such goods be labelled in order to display their characteristics.

---

9   Chapter 1.8.
10   Chapters 10.2. 10.3.3, 10.5.3 below.

The consumer then retains the choice denied by a minimum standard coupled to a ban, but is able to exercise that choice in a more informed fashion than is normal in the modern, increasingly complex, market. The case of tobacco products might be evaluated from this perspective.[11] Some very strong tobacco products are banned. Advertising too is allowed only through certain media. Relevant controls have been made steadily tighter in recent years in Europe, in part under the influence of EU rule-making – although the EU has no general competence to legislate in the field[12] – and in part as a result of domestic choices, which have been evidently hostile to tobacco advertising. The UK rules are contained in the Tobacco Advertising and Promotion Act 2002, which leaves very little scope for advertising of tobacco products other than at point-of-sale, and which also brings to an end the long-standing practice of tobacco-related sponsorship of sporting events. However, for most tobacco products there is no ban but rather a requirement that the product's packaging carry a health warning. In the UK, these warnings were for many years attached as a result of a voluntary arrangement between producers and government, but there has been a growth in formal legal rules in recent years. Once again this has been the result of the legislative activity at both the EU[13] and the State level: and once again the relevant rules have become increasingly stringent as warnings have been made ever more eye-catching. It might be noted in passing that the choice between quasi self-regulation and legislative rules is yet a further nuance of the choice between regulatory techniques.[14]

The regulator who chooses informational intervention over a ban must be satisfied that the consumer is capable of absorbing the information. A policy of 'protecting by informing' would go awry if the consumer were unable to identify and act upon the message. Where the consumer cannot readily process the information, the choice between regulatory instruments may swing back towards the minimum standard and the ban on non-complying products. That question remains difficult to resolve in practice. The case of tobacco products again deserves consideration. Some would argue that the risk is such that information cannot be properly absorbed by the consumer and that further restriction on availability is therefore

---

[11] Cf. e.g. R. Rabin and S. Sugarman, *Regulating Tobacco* (OUP, 2001).

[12] This was firmly established in the 'Tobacco Advertising' case, Case C–376–98 *Germany v Parliament and Council* [2000] ECR I–8419, in which Directive 98/43 was annulled. See Ch. 2.3.5. The relevant EC control is now found in Directive 2003/33 OJ 2003 L152/16.

[13] See Directive 2001/37 OJ 2001 L194/26, which was unsuccessfully challenged in Case C–491/01 *ex parte British American Tobacco* [2002] ECR I–11543.

[14] Chapter 1.8.

justified.[15] A further complication is provided by the argument that the deterioration in health caused by smoking acts as a burden on the health care system and that, accordingly, controls over consumption are justified. This aspect has tended to be used as a basis for the employment of a further regulatory technique: the imposition on tobacco products of heavy fiscal burdens.

An effective consumer safety policy cannot be confined to rules that dictate what shall be marketed, and under what conditions. 'Post-market' controls must be put in place that will allow action to be taken if unsafe products are released and pose a threat to consumers. This dimension of the legal regime has traditionally been much less elaborate than the basic task of standard-setting, but more recently both UK and EU practice has become much more actively concerned to assert the responsibilities of both public authorities and private commercial actors *after* a product has reached the market. This will be addressed in particular in Chapter 10.5.5 below.

This provides only a flavour of the debate concerning regulatory techniques. Chapter 1 contains an extended account of the debate about how best to regulate upholstered furniture, where the conflicting pressures for minimum standard plus ban and for informational intervention, preserving choice, resulted in a regime that incorporated both techniques.[16]

10.2 THE DEVELOPMENT OF CONSUMER SAFETY LEGISLATION IN THE UK

Prior to 1961 safety regulation in the UK comprised a patchwork of product-specific laws. Individual measures regulated goods such as medicines and fireworks, but there was no single statute capable of imposing obligations relating to safety on producers generally. Severe safety problems could be dealt with only by securing the adoption of new primary legislation, a laborious and cumbersome process. Typically, harm had to occur in order to stimulate a legal response.

These shortcomings were partially addressed in the Consumer Protection Act 1961, the first general statute in the field of consumer safety in the UK. This was innovative in the sense that it was enabling legislation. The Act provided the power for delegated legislation to be made to govern particular product areas which were identified from time to time as requiring specific regulation. Standards could be set to improve the safety of products, backed by criminal sanctions. The flexibility of recourse to

---

15 Cf. J. Hanson and D. Kysar, 'Taking Behavioralism Seriously' (1999) 112 *Harvard LR* 1420.

16 Chapter 1.8.3.3.

secondary rather than primary legislation made it much easier to act once a risk to consumer safety was identified. There was no longer a need to rely on primary legislation.

The structure of enabling legislation was maintained in the Consumer Safety Act 1978. Under this rather more sophisticated statute, four specific types of regulatory instrument were made available: the safety regulation, the prohibition order, the prohibition notice and the notice to warn.

The safety regulation, which was then and still remains (in adjusted form) the most important of these measures, is directed at particular products seen to require specific detailed control. So, for example, safety regulations made under the 1978 Act included measures which established standards, often very specific, which had to be met in the manufacture of products as diverse as gas catalytic heaters, children's hood cords and babies' dummies. Supply of non-complying goods constituted a criminal offence. Supply could also give rise to civil liability under the statute, although this has proved unimportant in practice.[17]

The three new measures introduced in the 1978 Act improved the capacity of the law to deal quickly with newly discovered hazards. The prohibition order involved a general ban on the supply of a particular product. The prohibition notice was served on an individual trader to prevent supply of a particular product. The notice to warn required a supplier to publish a warning about unsafe goods. The suspension notice was added by the Consumer Safety (Amendment) Act 1986. It prohibited the addressee from supplying the goods for a period of up to six months. Powers of seizure were also conferred on trading standards officers, although compensation provisions were attached for the protection of traders. It was also made possible to make an application to a magistrate's court for a forfeiture order against goods. The 1986 Act targeted enforcement more closely at point of first supplier or importer and away from the retail level in order to improve efficient use of scarce resources.[18]

Both the 1961 and the 1978 Acts had the great advantage over the pre-1961 system of allowing rapid action to be taken via secondary legislation on the discovery of a newly identified hazard. Moreover, the enforcement mechanisms were steadily improved through the 1961, 1978 and, particularly, the 1986 Amendment Act. However, the supply of an unsafe product was not of itself an offence in the absence of pre-existing rules governing that product. That was a serious deficiency. The legislation had no impact on producers and suppliers in sectors left uncovered by measures already in place. The only legal constraint on such traders supplying unsafe

---

17   This provision is now found in s. 41 Consumer Protection Act 1987.
18   Chapter 13 provides a general account of enforcement practice. See also Howells note 3 above, pp. 270–278.

goods lay in the private law, the inadequacies of which have already been discussed.

A 1984 White Paper on the Safety of Goods[19] commented that a general statutory duty on suppliers to supply safe consumer goods, backed by criminal sanctions;

> would induce a greater sense of responsibility on the part of those suppliers who currently regard themselves as unaffected by the legislation [and] would provide wider scope for swift remedial action by enforcement authorities in the case of newly identified dangerous products.

This perception underlies the Consumer Protection Act 1987, which made an important advance in consumer protection by introducing a general duty to supply only safe goods. This is the principal statute which now governs this field in the UK, although the implementation by Statutory Instrument of the EC Directive on general product safety has significantly altered the pattern of legal control (Chapters 10.3.3, 10.4 below). The relevant provisions are contained in Part II of the 1987 Act.[20] The innovation for consumer safety regulation introduced by this Act is a 'General Safety Requirement'. Section 10 imposes a duty to supply only safe goods. It is accordingly a criminal offence to supply unsafe goods even in the absence of pre-existing specific regulations applicable to the product category in question. The 1987 Act retains the structure of the 1961 and 1978 Acts whereby delegated legislation may be made to amplify requirements in particular product categories as appropriate, but shifts the emphasis of control towards the new flexible general duty.

Before making a safety regulation, the Minister is under a duty to consult 'such organisations as appear to him to be representative of interests substantially affected by the proposal' and such other persons as he considers appropriate.[21] The 1987 Act abolished the Prohibition Order which existed under the 1978 Act. The need to have the capacity to act quickly by making an interim order is covered in the 1987 Act by the 'Expedited Safety Regulation', which is rather wider in scope than the Prohibition Order. Such expedited measures may be made without consultation, but remain in force for no more than twelve months. Typically an emergency may be addressed by a measure made immediately, followed by consultation and a twelve-month period within

---

[19] Cmnd. 9302.

[20] Part I covers product liability and is examined in Ch. 4; Part III covers misleading price indications and is examined in Ch. 8.5.

[21] The duty was the subject of successful litigation to quash regulations in *R v Secretary of State for Health, ex parte United States Tobacco* [1992] 1 All ER 212, criticised by B. Schwehr and P. Brown [1991] *Public Law* 163.

which occurs calmer reflection on how to tackle the problem for the future. Both the Prohibition Notice and the Notice to Warn remain in place. They are not commonly used, though their availability is an important element in the overall strategy for enforcement. In April 2003 the first Prohibition Notice for over ten years was issued. This was directed at 'Yo-balls', a product made of a jelly-like material capable of being stretched into a band that had been shown to pose a risk of strangulation. Under the Notice named suppliers were prohibited from supplying the toy in the UK.[22]

Consumer Safety regulation has thus reached a position where all producers of consumer goods are subject to the regulatory regime's centrepiece, the General Safety Requirement, while specific areas may still be regulated more tightly and precisely than the general duty through safety regulations. These currently cover products such as upholstered furniture, which is subject to a system of control mapped out by safety regulations adopted in 1988.[23] These impose mandatory rules governing labelling that are designed to alert consumers to fire risks, and they are examined from the perspective of choice of regulatory technique in Chapter 1.8.3.3. Prams, pushchairs, hood cords and bunk beds are the subject of specific safety regulations. The Fireworks (Safety) Regulations 1997[24] prohibit supply of particular types of powerful fireworks, impose controls on retail outlets and ban the supply of fireworks to persons apparently under the age of eighteen. A small number of products notorious for their capacity to cause injury or distress, yet judged sufficiently popular or worthwhile to survive an outright ban, are subject to a separate specific statutory regime that goes beyond the area of safety alone. For example, fireworks are subject not only to the safety regulations adopted pursuant to the Consumer Protection Act mentioned above, but also to the Fireworks Act 2003 which goes beyond the field of product safety to empower the making of orders governing wider matters such as the anti-social use of the use of fireworks. However, from the perspective of product safety regulation, the crucial impact of the General Safety Requirement introduced by the Consumer Protection 1987 is that all traders are subject to legal regulation, not simply those operating in areas subject to sector-specific regulation.

The developed system of product safety regulation is treated as apt to exclude resort by enforcement authorities to techniques not formally envisaged by the statutory regime. In *R v Liverpool City Council, ex parte Baby Products Association*[25] judicial review was sought of a local authority's decision to issue a press release declaring a particular model of

---

22   P/2003/261, 24 April 2003, available via http://www.gnn.gov.uk.
23   The Furniture and Furnishings (Fire) (Safety) Regulations 1988, S.I. No.1324.
24   S.I. No. 2294.
25   [2000] *BLGR* 171.

baby-walker to be unsafe and calling for its recall. Lord Bingham CJ granted a declaration in favour of the applicant trade association. He observed that the statute offered the enforcement authorities a choice among several orders when confronted by an apparently unsafe product, and that this 'detailed and carefully crafted code' secured a balance between the objective of promoting public safety and allowing procedural protection to affected businesses, who are able to challenge decisions taken under the statutory regime and, in appropriate cases, to secure compensation. The local authority's action had deprived traders of those safeguards which Parliament had intended to confer on them. It lacked a statutory basis and it could not stand. Lord Bingham conceded that in exceptional cases of emergency one might conclude that the statutory regime could prove cumbersome and deficient, but this was a matter for Parliament to remedy.

Although the Court in *ex parte Baby Products Association* was unreceptive to initiatives designed to make enforcement practice more flexible (albeit more procedurally opaque), the law does not stand still. Recall procedures are of real practical significance in product safety cases. In contrast to several jurisdictions around the world, the UK, in developing its statutory framework for dealing with consumer safety, chose not to introduce provisions requiring recall of products. This was left to practice, underpinned by the incentives of traders to secure withdrawal of unsafe goods lest they be liable to compensate injured consumers. Consequently the common sight of recall notices in newspapers has been the result of decisions taken by private traders, not governmental compulsion. The DTI published a guide to best practice in order to spread knowledge about how effectively to manage a recall procedure.[26] Moreover, the Trading Standards Institute makes information about recalls available electronically.[27] In both instances, given the absence of any formal statutory backing, the problem is doubtless that reputable traders take seriously the need to consider a recall of suspect products, whereas shady operators prefer to hope to defy the risk of actions brought in tort or contract. The position has now been altered by the legislative input of the EC. Directive 2001/95 will adjust the pattern of the law governing recall in the UK. This is considered more fully below (Chapter 10.5.5).

---

[26] Available via http://www.dti.gov.uk/ccp/topics1/safety.htm. The publication is endorsed by the Confederation of British Industry and the British Retail Consortium.

[27] Available via http://www.tradingstandards.gov.uk/.

10.3 EUROPEAN COMMUNITY PRODUCT SAFETY LAW

10.3.1 The Growth of EC Product Safety Law

The law of consumer safety has been described earlier in this chapter as a response to the inadequacies of the market. This book has consistently emphasised that the market is increasingly European; as a reflection of this, the law of consumer safety comprises a combination of domestic and Community provisions.

One aspect of this process is that national consumer safety laws must be applied with regard to the integration of the market. Accordingly, national rules of consumer protection which are capable of impeding trade between Member States must be justified. For example, an insistence that goods comply with *British* standards and an unwillingness to accept imported goods meeting equivalent standards would violate Community law's insistence on mutual recognition of goods. The Court has gone so far as to insist that it is in breach of Art. 28 EC to adopt a national rule 'without including in it a mutual recognition clause for products coming from a Member State and complying with the rules laid down by that State'.[28] Modern British practice under the legislation mentioned above, in conformity with Community law, is to require compliance with British standards or their equivalent, and accordingly it respects the demands of EC trade law.[29] More positively and directly, Community legislative measures are implemented in the domestic system and become part of the fabric of domestic law. The substance of the law involves a mix of domestic and Community-inspired rules, although the mix may not always be smooth. As well as this substantive mix, the enforcement of the rules involves the creation of an institutional network throughout the European market.[30]

European Community consumer safety law has developed out of a rather different perspective from the market failure analysis presented above. As is examined at greater length in Chapter 2, the bulk of EC consumer policy finds its constitutional basis in Arts. 94 and 95 (ex 100

---

[28] Case C–184/96 *Commission v France* ('Foie Gras') [1998] ECR I–6197; Case C–59/00 *Vestergaard* [2001] ECR I–9505.

[29] S. Weatherill, 'Consumer Safety Legislation in the United Kingdom and Article 30 EEC' (1988) 13 *ELRev* 87.

[30] For empirical work and critical analysis, cf. H-W. Micklitz, *Post Market Control of Consumer Goods* (Nomos, 1990); H-W. Micklitz, T. Roethe and S. Weatherill (eds.), *Federalism and Responsibility: a Study on Product Safety Law and Practice in the European Community* (Graham and Trotman, 1994). See also E. Vos, *Institutional Frameworks of Community Health and Safety Regulation: Committees, Agencies and Private Bodies* (Hart Publishing, 1999).

and 100a) of the Treaty, which are directed at the process of market integration. Where national laws differ, they obstruct trade and require harmonisation in order to liberalise the wider market. Accordingly Community consumer laws have developed as part of the quest to create an integrated market founded on a bedrock of common rules. But the Community legislature is also constitutionally required to take account of the *quality* of the regulatory regime established at European level. Articles 95(3) and 153(2) of the EC Treaty assert a necessary linkage between market-making and the demands of consumer protection. In this sense the effect, if not the dominant formal constitutional intent, of such harmonised laws is to establish a common set of Community consumer safety laws which in turn affect the laws and markets of all the Member States.

The content of European Community product safety regulation is in many respects comparable to domestic UK laws in the area. At the level of general regulatory philosophy, this is an area where the absorption of Community law into the British system is relatively unproblematic.[31]

10.3.2 Toy Safety

The EC's legislative track-record contains a number of sector-specific measures which establish rules relevant to the safety of products. These include Directives dealing with medical devices[32] and lifts[33] and a vast pile of legislative paperwork dealing with cosmetics.[34] These measures cannot be examined in depth in this book. Instead attention is devoted to one helpfully illustrative measure that is firmly within the sphere of consumer law – toys.

The Toy Safety Directive[35] harmonises laws regulating toy safety throughout the Community. There are Community rules requiring a basic safety level. Only safe toys may be sold; States must admit to their markets toys which are safe. In this sense, the Community rule contributes to both the integration and the regulation of the market. This is a typical legislative model.

The Directive provides that toys subject to the regime 'shall satisfy the essential safety requirements', which are performance levels expressed in general terms and amplified in Schedule 2. Safety must be assessed with regard to the use of toys in an intended or in a foreseeable way, bearing in mind the normal behaviour of children. Plainly, a toy may be unsafe if

---

31 Contrast, for example, the examination of control of unfair terms in Ch. 5.
32 Directive 93/42 OJ 1993 L169/1, as subsequently amended.
33 Directive 95/16 OJ 1995 L213/1.
34 Directive 76/768 OJ 1976 L292/169, as subsequently amended.
35 Directive 88/378 OJ 1988 L187.

misused where that misuse is foreseeable. The formal legal requirement is conformity with the 'essential safety requirements', but there are two alternative routes open to the manufacturer wishing to show such conformity. One is to produce in accordance with standards – European standards produced by CEN which are adopted as national standards.[36] The other is to conform to an approved model. The manufacturer who does not wish to adhere to the standards may apply for a type approval certificate from an authorised body. The key is that the manufacturer has a choice of how to conform to the legal requirements, which permits a degree of flexibility and innovation.[37]

The manufacturer must show conformity by attaching a mark originally referred to as the EC mark but now known as the 'CE Marking' as a result of the amendments of Directive 93/68.[38] Because the marking is affixed by the trader and is not pre-checked, it is a statement of conformity and not a guarantee of safety. If toys are found on the market which are CE marked but which do not meet the essential safety requirements, then enforcement action should be taken against them. Such action affects the whole European market and must be managed through Community procedures, considered further below.

The Directive was implemented in the UK as a Statutory Instrument made under the Consumer Protection Act 1987 and the European Communities Act 1972 – initially under Regulations made in 1989, but the measure which currently governs the sector is the Toys (Safety) Regulations 1995.[39] The Toy Safety Regulations 'shall be treated for all purposes as if they were safety regulations within the meaning of the 1987 Act', subject only to a minor qualification relating to a penalty.[40] The Regulations require that '[t]oys to which these Regulations apply shall satisfy the essential safety requirements'.[41] In accordance with the Directive, provision is also made for the use of the CE marking.[42] It is an

---

[36] Relevant standards are available electronically:
      http://europa.eu.int/comm/enterprise/newapproach/standardization/harmstds/reflist/toy
      s.html.

[37] See Chapter 1.8.1, on the EC's New Approach to technical harmonisation; see also M.
      Egan, *Constructing a European Market: Standards, Regulation and Governance*
      (Oxford: OUP, 2001); K. Armstrong and S. Bulmer, *The Governance of the Single
      European Market* (Manchester UP, 1998), Ch. 6; and, with specific reference to issues
      of safety, Howells note 3 above, Ch. 2.

[38] OJ 1993 L220/1.

[39] SI 1995 No 204. The need to implement Directive 93/68 was the principal reason for
      the adoption of the replacement Regulations.

[40] Regulation 16.

[41] Regulation 4.

[42] Regulation 5.

offence to supply toys which do not satisfy the essential safety requirements or which do not bear the CE marking. Should a particularly serious case arise in which action is required to prevent supply, rather than simply to prosecute traders after the fact, a Prohibition Notice pursuant to the Consumer Protection Act 1987 could be issued. This occurred in the case of the perilously stretchy 'Yo-Balls', mentioned above.[43]

Digestion of this regime into the English system poses no fundamental difficulty,[44] since, before Community intervention, the safety of toys had already been the subject of regulatory attention in the UK. In fact, regulations governing toy safety were first made under the Consumer Protection Act 1961. The implementation of the Directive has been firmly rooted in this existing structure of control. The Directive required only a relatively technical adjustment to existing rules and, more significantly, the addition of institutional mechanisms to reflect its objective of market integration. Action taken by enforcement authorities can no longer be regarded as a purely domestic matter.[45]

10.3.3 General Product Safety

The parallel development of domestic and European rules continued with the adoption in 1992 of the first version of the General Directive on Product Safety.[46] The Directive largely followed the policy and the substantive pattern of Part II of the Consumer Protection Act 1987. It has now been replaced by Directive 2001/95 on general product safety,[47] which is the subject of closer examination below. Directive 2001/95, adopted after a process of review of previous practice,[48] makes some adjustments to the EC's regulation of product safety, but the basic convergence between the EC approach and the UK's choices manifest in the Consumer Protection Act remains striking. Like Part II of that Act, the Directive establishes control over all forms of supply of consumer goods

---

[43] Note 22 above.

[44] Cf. S. Weatherill, 'Toy Safety' in T. Daintith (ed.), *Implementing EC Law in the United Kingdom: Structures for Indirect Rule* (Wiley Chancery Law, 1995).

[45] Further below, Chapter 10.6.

[46] Directive 92/59/EEC on general product safety OJ 1992 L228/24. For an early discussion of the importance of developments in this field, cf. H-W. Micklitz, 'Perspectives on a European Directive on the Safety of Technical Consumer Goods' (1986) 23 *CMLRev* 617. On diverse national practice, see Howells note 3 above.

[47] OJ 2002 L11/4. See C. Hodges, 'A New EC Directive on the Safety of Consumer Products' [2001] *Euro Bus Law Rev* 274.

[48] COM (2000) 140, Commission report to the Parliament and Council on the experience acquired in the application of Directive 92/59.

irrespective of product sector,[49] but again it is a flexible notion of control to be elaborated through private standard-making. Whereas Community initiatives were the stimulus for domestic reform of product liability,[50] the reverse influence may be identified in relation to product safety regulation. The General Directive, modelled in significant respects on the UK's domestic regime,[51] requires no significant policy shift in the UK system. In this respect it is in direct contrast to the Product Liability Directive which marks a radical shift in direction for English law.[52] Article 17 of Directive 2001/95 asserts that the General Directive applies without prejudice to the Product Liability Directive.

According to Art. 1 of the Directive, 'The purpose of this Directive is to ensure that products placed on the market are safe'. Article 3(1) provides that 'Producers shall be obliged to place only safe products on the market'.[53] The similarity to the flexible control exercised by Part II of the Consumer Protection Act 1987 is plain; implementing the Directive accordingly presents no fundamental problems of principle for the UK. Practical problems could have been largely avoided too, had the Government chosen to implement the Directive in a statute consolidating the law drawn from the Directive with that already found in Part II of the Consumer Protection Act 1987. The creation of such a single regime would have done much for transparency and predictability. Regrettably, this course was not chosen. The first version of the EC Directive was implemented in the UK by the General Product Safety Regulations 1994.[54] The EC's 2001 replacement Directive was due for implementation by 15 January 2004. Frustratingly the deadline was not met. At the time of writing it seems unlikely that the UK will adopt Regulations to implement Directive 2001/95 until late 2004 at the earliest. This is out of tune with the UK's frequent claim that it is a tough negotiator but scrupulous in

---

49   Existing sector-specific Community rules governing product safety apply in preference to the general duty: Art. 1(2) Directive. But if particular aspects of the safety of a product are not covered by existing rules, those aspects fall under the general Directive. In *Caerphilly County BC v Stripp* [2001] 2 *CMLR* 5 it was held that the Road Traffic Act 1998 did not implement a sector-specific Community rule and that therefore prosecution under the 1994 regulations implementing the 1992 version of the Directive was appropriate in the case of supply of a dangerous second-hand car.

50   Chapter 4.

51   Cf. discussion in this vein on the 1992 version of the EC Directive by S. Weatherill, 'A General Duty to supply only safe goods in the Community: some remarks from a British perspective' (1990) 13 *JCP* 79.

52   Chapter 4.

53   Article 5 imposes additional obligations on producers and on distributors.

54   SI No 2328.

complying with EC obligations once undertaken.[55] The UK is in breach of EC law and could be brought before the European Court by the Commission pursuant to the Art. 226 EC infringement procedure and it is also possible, albeit unlikely in practice, that it may find itself liable in damages to a party suffering loss as a result of its default.[56] Of more direct pertinence to this chapter it makes depiction of the law extremely awkward. Consumer safety regulation in the UK is drawn from two sources: first, the Consumer Protection Act 1987 and, second, the Regulations which implement the Directive and which must be interpreted so as to conform to it.[57] But in the latter case there is, at time of writing, a gap between the General Product Safety Regulations 1994 and the provisions of Directive 2001/95 which will eventually be implemented by Regulations that will replace the 1994 Regulations. Apologies are due to the perplexed reader – but it is the fault of the UK government! It will be explained below where the 1994 Regulations will require overhaul because of the broader coverage foreseen by Directive 2001/95.

10.3.4 The Safety of Services

Article 2(a) of Directive 2001/95 makes plain that the regime catches a product supplied in the context of providing a service, but it does not touch the supply of services *per se*. In a manner comparable to a similar debate about the scope of liability rules,[58] one may readily advance the policy prescription that effective modern consumer protection requires that the

---

55   In fact Commission statistics reveal that the UK is better than some Member States and worse than others in the matter of implementing internal market Directives; a 'Scoreboard' is available via:

http:// europa.eu.int/comm/internal_market/en/update/score/index.htm.

56   Directive 2001/95 stipulates that implementing provisions should be effective from 15 January 2004. Were a person to have been injured by an unsafe product in the period during which the UK has not met this deadline and to be able to show that the injury would probably not have occurred had the Directive been implemented, then he or she might be able to claim damages from the State under EC law for failure to implement, as well as from the supplier in contract or tort. Probably this is rather fanciful, not least because the changes effected by Directive 2001/95 in comparison with Directive 92/59 are not major – but the implications of the *Francovich* ruling, examined at Chapter 2.4.2, are so extensive that any slippage in the implementation of Directives should alert the lawyer to the possibilities of a claim against the State. Sad to relate, the UK was also late in implementing Directive 92/59. No litigation ensued.

57   The *Marleasing* principle of interpretation drawn from Art. 10 EC, discussed in Chapter 2.4.2.

58   See Chapter 4.3.

law should address the potential harm done by supply of unsafe services as actively as it tackles the harmful potential of unsafe goods. However, in the EU this argument has not been won. In 2002 the Commission published a discussion document entitled *Safety of Services for Consumers* which aired the possibility of several responses, ranging from information exchange and sharing best practice to binding legal rules built around a general safety requirement for services accompanied by obligations on private parties and public authorities to identify and control risks.[59] This was followed by a Commission report to the Council and Parliament in June 2003. In December 2003 a Council Resolution on safety of services for consumers was adopted.[60] This accepts the value of acquiring greater information about problems associated with the safety of services against a background of diverse national practice. It invites the Commission to co-operate with the Member States in improving the knowledge base on the safety of services, while balancing the benefit of improved knowledge against the burdens associated with data collection. The Commission is invited to 'reflect' on the contribution that European standards could make to improving safety. This rather bland Council Resolution gives no indication that formal legislative developments should be expected imminently in the services sector.

10.4 THE PATTERN OF UK PRODUCT SAFETY LAW: DUAL SOURCES

The existence of two sources of product safety law in the UK raises questions of a constitutional nature that are equally of great commercial significance. The two regimes of control are not coextensive. In some respects Part II of the 1987 Act is broader than Directive 2001/95; in other respects the opposite is true. In such circumstances the implementation of the Directive demonstrably extends the scope of legal regulation in the UK.

The criteria for control under both systems is plainly comparable: both are concerned with safety, yet their precise equivalence cannot be guaranteed. The desirable route of consolidation of both regimes into a single statute remains as yet wishful thinking in the face of the pressures of the Parliamentary timetable.

The constitutional relationship between the two systems is as follows.[61] Within areas covered by the Directive, the Directive applies

---

59   Documentation is available via http:// europa.eu.int/comm/consumers/index_en.htm.
60   OJ 2003 C299/1.
61   These issues also have to be tackled in relation to Unfair Terms where again there is dual control – see Chapter 5. However, the pattern examined here is distinct. The Directive on Unfair Terms, as a minimum measure, permits stricter national rules in

alongside the Act and, to some extent, meshes with it, especially with regard to enforcement. But as a matter of EC law, the Regulations implementing the Directive have precedence over the Act in this sense: goods that are safe within the meaning of the Directive are entitled to be marketed in the UK; the 1987 Act may not be used to block their access. Goods that are unsafe in the sense of not conforming with the Directive must be controlled but, in some circumstances, that will not simply be a national matter, but will require the machinery of the Directive to be engaged. The core point is that the Directive is based on Art. 95 EC and is therefore formally an instrument of market integration. Its philosophy is that there shall be a common Community rule requiring the marketing of only safe goods; such safe goods, wherever made, shall then be freely marketable anywhere on Community territory. This central objective explains why national rules may not be used to control goods that are safe within the meaning of the Community rules. It also explains why, where national action against allegedly unsafe goods *is* taken, that action is not a purely national matter, but must instead be managed within a Community framework.

It is therefore required of national law that it should ensure removal from its market of products that fall below the stipulated safety level; also that it should allow on to its market goods that meet that stipulated safety level. The State may not cut across this basic structure. The 1994 General Product Safety Regulations that implemented the EC's 1992 Directive in the UK faithfully reflect this pattern. Regulation 7 contains the general safety requirement:

> No producer shall place a product on the market unless the product is a safe product.

Regulation 5 is designed to prevent the 1987 Act from cutting across the Directive's requirement that safe goods (within the meaning of the Directive) shall have access to the market. It disables the 1987 Act in areas covered by the Regulations implementing the Directive:

> For the purposes of these Regulations the provisions of section 10 of the 1987 Act are hereby disapplied to the extent that they impose general safety requirements which must be complied with if products are to be (i) placed on the market, offered or agreed to be placed on the market or exposed or possessed to be placed on the market by producers; or (ii)

---

the field whereas, subject to the authoritative ruling of the European Court, the General-Directive does not appear to be minimum in character; accordingly, it pre-empts stricter national controls within its scope of application.

supplied, offered or agreed to be supplied or exposed or possessed to be supplied by distributors.[62]

Thus the Act and the Regulations are designed not to overlap. Supply of an unsafe product engages one regime or the other, but not both. This is probably the next best solution after the option of consolidating both sources of law into a single statute was rejected. It is probable that this neat solution will be retained once the UK government meets its obligation to implement Directive 2001/95 in Regulations that will replace those made in 1994 – but this will not become clear until concrete proposals are made by the government (Chapter 10.3.3 above).

Assuming that Community rules on safety are at least as high as existing domestic rules, no concerns of policy arise consequent to the addition of the Community layer of safety regulation. True, there are certain practical problems to resolve in aligning the administration of the two regimes, but these are soluble. It is the possibility that the Community standard may be *lower* than the national regime that has stimulated concern. *If* this is the case, then goods that were previously excluded from the British market can no longer be excluded. This possibility has fed fears that Community market integration might be achieved at the expense of national standards of protection.[63] The charge cannot at this stage conclusively be admitted nor rejected, but the reader should bear this underlying policy issue in mind. It is a lurking concern for the development of consumer protection in the internal market.

What follows is a more detailed elaboration of the pattern of consumer safety law. Necessarily it draws on both relevant sources, the 1987 Act and the 2001 Directive, although it should be borne in mind that the UK's 1994 Regulations envisage that one or other of the regimes will apply, never both. It also must be borne in mind that comment may not be directed at the UK's implementation of Directive 2001/95 because this has not yet occurred (Chapter 10.3.3 above).

10.5 DETAILED ASPECTS OF THE LAW

10.5.1 What Types of Product are Covered?

For the Directive, 'product' means 'any product – including in the context of providing a service – which is intended for consumers or likely, under reasonably foreseeable conditions, to be used by consumers even if not

---

62 In the Regulations the words 'are hereby disapplied' appear at the very end of Regulation 5; we have changed their placement to assist clarity.

63 Chapter 2, esp. 2.3.4.

intended for them, and is supplied or made available, whether for consideration or not, in the course of a commercial activity, and whether new, used or reconditioned.' For the purposes of UK implementation the definition of a product is found in Regulation 2 of the 1994 Statutory Instrument, where it is additionally stated that 'a product which is used exclusively in the context of a commercial activity even if it is used for or by a consumer shall not be regarded as a product for the purposes of these Regulations provided always and for the avoidance of doubt this exception shall not extend to the supply of such a product to a consumer'.[64]

Under the Consumer Protection Act 1987, consumer goods are defined as 'any goods which are ordinarily intended for private use or consumption'. There is a range of excluded products:[65]

(a) growing crops or things comprised in land by virtue of being attached to it;
(b) water, food, feeding stuff or fertiliser;
(c) gas which is, is to be or has been supplied by a person authorised to supply it or under section 6, 7 or 8 of the Gas Act 1986 (authorisation of supply of gas through pipes);
(d) aircraft (other than hang-gliders) or motor vehicles;
(e) controlled drugs or licensed medicinal products;
(f) tobacco.

The Directive is inapplicable to second-hand products where they are supplied as antiques; also where they are supplied as products to be repaired or reconditioned prior to being used, provided that the supplier clearly informs the person to whom he supplies the product to that effect. These exclusions are implemented in Regulations 3(a) and 3(b). The exclusion of second-hand products from the 1987 Act is considerably wider in scope than that in the Directive. Section 10(4)(c) Consumer Protection Act 1987 provides a defence against a charge of violation of the general safety requirement where it is shown that the terms 'indicated that the goods were not supplied or to be supplied as new goods' where the recipient would acquire an interest in the goods.

10.5.2 Unsafe Products: Offences Committed

For the Directive, Art. 2(b) provides that 'Safe product' means any product which 'under normal or reasonably foreseeable conditions of use including

---

[64] Note that beyond the scope of consumer safety regulation may lie the Health and Safety at Work Act 1974.

[65] Section 10(7).

duration and, where applicable, putting into service, installation and maintenance requirements, does not present any risk or only the minimum risks compatible with the product's use, considered to be acceptable and consistent with a high level of protection for the safety and health of persons'. Matters to be taken into account according to Art. 2(b) include the characteristics of the product, its presentation, including labelling and warnings, and the categories of consumers at serious risk when using the product, in particular children and the elderly. These provisions are carried over into Regulation 2 of the UK's 1994 Statutory Instrument.

According to s. 19 Consumer Protection Act 1987, 'safe', in relation to any goods, means that there is no risk, or no risk apart from one reduced to a minimum, that the goods (or specified activities in relation to them) will (whether immediately or after a definite or indefinite period) cause the death of, or any personal injury to, any person whatsoever.

An offence is committed under s. 10 of the Act where a person, acting in the course of a business of his or hers, supplies or offers or agrees to supply or exposes or possesses for supply, any consumer goods which fail to comply with the general safety requirement.[66] Section 11(1) empowers the Secretary of State to make safety regulations for the purpose of securing that goods to which the section applies[67] are safe. The same s. 19 definition applies and it is an offence to supply in violation of a safety regulation.

Under the Directive it is for Member States to put in place laws which shall ensure that producers and distributors comply with their obligations under the Directive in such a way that products placed on the market are safe. It is also incumbent on Member States to establish authorities competent to monitor the compliance of products with the general safety requirements and to arrange for such authorities to have and use the necessary powers to take appropriate measures.[68] The UK achieved that in the 1994 Regulations by absorbing the requirements into the regulatory pattern already available under the Consumer Protection Act 1987. Regulations 12 and 13 create offences connected with the supply and/or distribution of goods that fall below the required safety standard. Regulation 11 places enforcement in the hands of local authorities. In practical terms, this means trading standards departments. This follows the same model as is found in the 1987 Act. The powers available to such officers and their practical application are examined in Chapter 13, although issues specific to product safety law and practice in the

---

66   It is provided in s. 46(5) that '... it shall be immaterial whether the business is a business of dealing in the goods'. 'Supplies' is defined in s. 46.

67   Section 11(7); the scope of goods which may be subject to safety regulations is rather broader than those subject to the general requirement.

68   Article 6.

integrating European market are discussed below in this Chapter at 10.6. The meshing of the Regulations implementing the Directive with the pattern familiar under the 1987 Act is further confirmed by the inclusion in the 1994 Regulations of the 'due diligence' defence that also appears in the Consumer Protection Act and other consumer protection statutes.[69] The inclusion of provision for the liability of persons other than the principal offender is also a common feature of consumer protection regulation.[70] These are normal aspects of the family of regulatory offences to which the General Product Safety Regulations were admitted in 1994. They are examined in more depth in Chapter 11.

However, as explained above, even though the two systems share a common regulatory framework, the 1987 Act and the 1994 Regulations implementing the 1992 Directive are kept separate in their substantive scope of application. As explained above (10.3.3) the UK is late in adopting Regulations to implement Directive 2001/95 and it remains to be seen whether it will persist with a model that separates the scope of application of the 1987 Act and the Regulations implementing the Directive, while drawing on the enforcement model of the 1987 Act to underpin the Regulations.

10.5.3 The Notion of Safety

The notions of 'safe' under the Act and the Directive, as implemented, run in parallel. It is possible that, in future, interpretations given by the European Court will diverge from British judicial practice, a perennial problem where laws deriving from different sources operate in the same field.[71] However, problems seem unlikely or at least likely to be technical only, in contrast to some other areas examined in this book where potentially ideologically different controls are envisaged under EC law on the one hand and existing domestic law on the other.[72]

For both regimes, potentially dangerous products may still be 'safe' within the legal definition. A hacksaw is plainly capable of inflicting injury, but if designed in a way which minimises the risk in using it, it will be 'safe'. The careful manufacturer will design a product in order to reduce the risk of mishap and will market it with an eye to safe usage, if necessary by attaching appropriate labels and warnings. It seems that products must be safe even if misused where that misuse is reasonably foreseeable. Many

---

69   Regulation 14.
70   Regulation 15.
71   Examined in Chapter 2.
72   Cf. particularly the problems of unfair terms, Chapter 5.

similar considerations apply in relation to avoiding civil liability for supplying unsafe products.[73]

The control systems envisage a band of safety which is permissible. In fact, what is at stake here is first of all risk assessment – what level of danger does a product pose? Then, once this calculation is made, there arises a distinct question – usually treated as one of risk management – which asks what level of danger society is willing to tolerate in pursuit of freedom and choice.[74] The former question demands expertise in calculation. The latter question, by contrast, is not in any sense narrowly technical. It engages potentially controversial judgements about what level of risk should be treated as acceptable in society. Politicians and specialist agencies may be confronted by these choices;[75] but so too, under the legal framework governing product safety, may courts. That absolute protection from harm is not at stake is reflected in the Directive's provision that 'The feasibility of obtaining higher levels of safety or the availability of other products presenting a lesser degree of risk shall not constitute grounds for considering a product to be dangerous'. This is implemented in Regulation 2 of the 1994 Statutory Instrument. Products can be less safe than competing items yet still be safe within the legal definition, a manifestation of the concern to maintain consumer choice between varying types of product.

Accordingly there is embedded within these definitions of 'safe' a cost/benefit analysis. A product which is moderately risky may be safe where its virtues to society are obvious and significant, yet unsafe if it is equally risky yet of trivial value. Section 10(2)(c) of the 1987 Act explicitly directs consideration to 'the existence of any means by which it would have been reasonable (taking into account the cost, likelihood and extent of any improvement) for the goods to have been made safer'. A floor level of safety must plainly exist below which it is not open to a manufacturer to claim that it would be unreasonable to expect the goods to be made safer. However, above that floor there is scope for development of judicial notions of reasonableness and proportionality in the pursuit of safety.

The practical application of the rules relies heavily on the use of standards set by private standardisation bodies. Section 10(2) of the

---

73   Chapter 4.

74   On how calculations may be made, cf. M. Jones-Lee, *The Economics of Safety and Physical Risk* (Blackwell, 1989); Asch, note 3 above. Exploring the nature of governance based on 'risk' has become an increasingly fertile field of academic inquiry; see e.g. C. Hood, H. Rothstein and R. Baldwin, *The Government of Risk: Understanding Risk Regulation Regimes* (OUP, 2001).

75   Vos note 30 above; R. Baldwin and M. Cave *Understanding Regulation: Theory, Strategy and Practice* (Oxford: OUP, 1999), Ch. 11.

Consumer Protection Act 1987 provides that 'any standards of safety published by any person' may be taken into account in assessing whether a product complies with the general safety requirement. Section 10(3)(b) affords an absolute defence where a product meets defined existing legal requirements. According to Art. 3 of Directive 2001/95 a product is 'deemed' safe if it conforms to the specific health and safety requirements of national law in the Member State in which it is marketed. A product is 'presumed' safe if it conforms to voluntary national standards transposing European standards, the references of which have been published by the Commission in the EC's *Official Journal*. The Directive includes provisions governing the making of European standards, which involve the Commission granting a mandate to the private standardisation bodies based in Belgium, CEN and CENELEC.[76] Pursuant to Art. 3(3) of the Directive standards other than those falling within this privileged category that creates a presumption of safety are capable of forming part of the assessment of whether a product is safe. So a trade association's own standards could be taken into account as a factor in deciding whether a product is safe. This system will doubtless be taken over into the UK's Regulations implementing Directive 2001/95 once they are adopted (Chapter 10.3.3).

It is accordingly clear that a product that conforms to a standard but is shown to be dangerous should be the subject of control exercised by national authorities.[77] Such action requires managing in the context of the quest to construct a border-free European market and so the Directive provides that the Commission should be informed of any such measures: this management procedure is considered below.[78] In this sense the core of the EC-derived product safety regime is to require compliance with the general safety requirement, and meeting a standard is merely an important method of demonstrating such compliance; indeed, as explained, in the case of conformity with national standards transposing European standards, a presumption in favour of the safety of the product is created. But compliance is not a guarantee of legal compliance. A trader could in principle be convicted of supplying an unsafe product even where it complies with a standard. In the UK the more credible the standard, the more confident he or she could be in successfully escaping conviction by

---

[76] Cf. Howells note. 3 above, pp. 87–100. Use of standards is firmly in line with the EC's 'New Approach', note 37 above.

[77] Article 3(4) Directive 2001/95. This point is taken by the House of Lords in a case concerning a dangerous imported product used at work, and the subject of proceedings pursuant to the Health and Safety at Work Act 1974: *R v Bristol Magistrates Court, ex parte Junttan Oy* [2003] ICR 1475.

[78] Chapter 10.5.2 above; and more generally see Chapter 11.2.

reliance on the statutory 'due diligence' defence,[79] although conviction was not evaded in such circumstances in *Balding v Lew-Ways Ltd*[80] where the court chose to make a careful distinction between the binding nature of the statutory standard of safety and the purely private character of a British standard. The trader had met the latter, but not the former, and was denied reliance on the statutory defence of due diligence.[81] Nonetheless it is plain that, in practice, the profile of European standards, which are implemented as national standards, is very high under this regulatory regime.

10.5.4 Accident Data

The accumulation of statistical data about accidents plays an important role in the development of any coherent consumer safety policy. Empirical evidence about where accidents occur should be part of the decision-making process on how to target scarce resources to rule making and to enforcement. Such data may also reveal the desirability of public information campaigns in relation to particular types of risk.

The UK began to operate a system for collecting information from hospitals in 1976 called HASS, the Home Accident Surveillance System. This was supplemented by LASS, the Leisure Accident Surveillance System. However, in 2003 it was announced that the DTI would no longer fund the collection or publication of the statistical data.

The United States has a uniquely well-developed system for collecting such data in the Consumer Product Safety Commission.[82] It gathers data primarily from hospital emergency departments, selected from all over the country in order to provide a representative profile. The Commission uses the information gathered to determine priorities as part of a conscious attempt to make objective assessments about risk.

The European Community has moved more slowly into the field of accumulating statistical data about accidents arising from the use of consumer goods. This is in part attributable to the constitutional inhibitions from which it suffers in developing an active consumer policy.[83] The Council established a pilot scheme for an accident information system in

---

[79]   This appears in the 1994 Regulations (Regulation 14) and seems likely to be retained in Regulations implementing Directive 2001/95.

[80]   *The Times*, 9 March 1995; [1995] *Crim LRev* 878.

[81]   It appears that the defence is less readily made out in cases involving threats to consumers' safety, rather than their economic, interests. Cf. Chapter 11.2.3.

[82]   At length, G. Howells, *Consumer Product Safety* (Dartmouth, 1998), Ch. 4.

[83]   Chapter 2.3.

1981,[84] but Member States were able to decide how they would participate and not all chose to become involved.

In 1986 a European Home and Leisure Accident Surveillance System (EHLASS) was established,[85] with data collected over a five-year period from casualty departments of selected hospitals throughout the Community. The data covered all accidents in the home, whether arising from products or behaviour. Evaluation followed as part of a process of establishing priorities for accident prevention. In this instance Member States were obliged to participate. There was resistance among some Member States to the continuation of the EHLASS project. In 1993, the Council agreed to its continuation for one year only.[86] The Commission pushed with determination to have the scheme placed on a firmer footing, and its pressure proved successful. A continuation of the scheme was agreed by the Council in 1994 to last until the end of 1997.[87] The monitoring of injuries by means of collection of data and the exchange of information on injuries is now conducted within the framework of the Community's more general policy in the field of public health. Decision 372/99 adopted a programme on injury prevention to cover 1999 to 2003.[88] The matter was then subsumed within Decision 1786/2002 adopting a general programme of Community action in the field of public health for 2003-2008, which is committed *inter alia* to improving data collection and data analysis.[89]

10.5.5 The Impact of the Regulations Implementing the Directive

In practical terms what difference have the Regulations made to the scope of consumer safety regulation in the UK since they were introduced in their first version in 1994? *Assuming* that the core safety standard will be applied in the same way as under the 1987 Act,[90] the major impact of the Regulations appears to be as follows.

First and as mentioned above,[91] the EC-inspired regime has extended the substantive scope of the control, for the Regulations catch second-hand goods. Moreover, a broader range of product sectors are caught. Medicines

---

84   Decision 81/623 OJ 1981 L229/1.
85   Decision 86/138 OJ 1986 L109/23, subsequently amended, OJ 1990 L296/64.
86   Decision 93/683 OJ 1993 L319/40.
87   Decision 3092/94 OJ 1994 L331/1 amended by Decision 95/184 OJ 1995 L120/36. For a Commission report see COM (98) 488.
88   OJ 1999 L46/1.
89   OJ 2003 L271/1.
90   Chapter 10.4 above.
91   Chapter 10.5.1 above.

and food, for example, largely excluded from the 1987 Act, are now in principle subject to the Regulations.[92] Regulation 11(c) of the 1994 Statutory Instrument makes appropriate provision for placing enforcement in relation to such products in the hands of the agencies normally responsible in such fields.

Second, Regulations 8 and 9 of the 1994 Regulations, reflecting the EC's 1992 Directive, impose more specific obligations on producers and distributors respectively than under the 1987 Act. The original General Safety Directive, Directive 92/59, envisaged a degree of obligatory vigilance exercised by private parties even after a product has been marketed, including a requirement that a producer provide information to consumers and adopt measures to inform him or herself of risks a product might present, and that a distributor[93] shall act with due care in order to help ensure compliance with the requirements of the general requirement. Post-market control is clearly envisaged and this is highly commercially significant.[94] Breach of the basic general safety requirement in Regulation 7 is converted into a regulatory offence by Regulation 12, but the obligations imposed on producers and distributors seem sanctionless within the Regulations themselves. However, the intention is that they are capable of enforcement by trading standards officers using their conventional powers of issuing a suspension notice prohibiting supply of goods or seeking forfeiture.[95] More specifically, Regulation 12 converts into an offence the supply by a distributor of 'products to any person which he knows, or should have presumed, on the basis of the information in his possession and as a professional, are dangerous products'.

As a result of Directive 2001/95 these 'post-market' rules have been significantly strengthened.[96] It is envisaged that producers and distributors will be required to inform the public authorities if they reach the conclusion that a product is dangerous, and thereafter they must co-operate in the quest to trace and, if necessary, withdraw the offending goods. Article 5 of Directive 2001/95 provides that:

1. Within the limits of their respective activities, producers shall provide consumers with the relevant information to enable them to assess the risks inherent in a product throughout the normal or reasonably

---

92   Though not in so far as sector-specific rules exist: cf. note 49 above.
93   Defined in Regulation 2 as 'any professional in the supply chain whose activity does not affect the safety properties of a product'.
94   Such action may already be part of business practice as a result of the indirect influence of the private law, especially the concern to avoid liability for supply of defective products; cf. Ch. 4.
95   Regulation 11(b). For more detail on enforcement powers, see Ch. 13.
96   Cf. Hodges note 47 above, pp. 278–9.

foreseeable period of its use, where such risks are not immediately obvious without adequate warnings, and to take precautions against those risks. The presence of warnings does not exempt any person from compliance with the other requirements laid down in this Directive. Within the limits of their respective activities, producers shall adopt measures commensurate with the characteristics of the products which they supply, enabling them to:

(a) be informed of risks which these products might pose;

(b) choose to take appropriate action including, if necessary to avoid these risks, withdrawal from the market, adequately and effectively warning consumers or recall from consumers.

The measures referred to in the third subparagraph shall include, for example:

(a) an indication, by means of the product or its packaging, of the identity and details of the producer and the product reference or, where applicable, the batch of products to which it belongs, except where not to give such indication is justified and

(b) in all cases where appropriate, the carrying out of sample testing of marketed products, investigating and, if necessary, keeping a register of complaints and keeping distributors informed of such monitoring. Action such as that referred to in (b) of the third subparagraph shall be undertaken on a voluntary basis or at the request of the competent authorities in accordance with Art. 8(1)(f). Recall shall take place as a last resort, where other measures would not suffice to prevent the risks involved, in instances where the producers consider it necessary or where they are obliged to do so further to a measure taken by the competent authority. It may be effected within the framework of codes of good practice on the matter in the Member State concerned, where such codes exist.

2. Distributors shall be required to act with due care to help to ensure compliance with the applicable safety requirements, in particular by not supplying products which they know or should have presumed, on the basis of the information in their possession and as professionals, do not comply with those requirements. Moreover, within the limits of their respective activities, they shall participate in monitoring the safety of products placed on the market, especially by passing on information on product risks, keeping and providing the documentation necessary for tracing the origin of products, and cooperating in the action taken by producers and competent authorities to avoid the risks. Within the limits of their respective activities they shall take measures enabling them to cooperate efficiently.

3.   Where producers and distributors know or ought to know, on the basis of the information in their possession and as professionals, that a product that they have placed on the market poses risks to the consumer that are incompatible with the general safety requirement, they shall immediately inform the competent authorities of the Member States thereof under the conditions laid down in Annex I, giving details, in particular, of action taken to prevent risk to the consumer.

      The Commission shall, in accordance with the procedure referred to in Art. 15(3), adapt the specific requirements relating to the obligation to provide information laid down in Annex I.

4.   Producers and distributors shall, within the limits of their respective activities, co-operate with the competent authorities, at the request of the latter, on action taken to avoid the risks posed by products which they supply or have supplied. The procedures for such co-operation, including procedures for dialogue with the producers and distributors concerned on issues related to product safety, shall be established by the competent authorities.

Article 6(1) of Directive 2001/95 provides that 'Member States shall ensure that producers and distributors comply with their obligations under this Directive in such a way that products placed on the market are safe'. As explained (10.3.3) the UK is late in meeting this obligation. One must therefore await the pattern chosen by the UK to implement Directive 2001/95 but it seems plausible that a model involving recourse to the existing enforcement powers under the Consumer Protection Act 1987 to back up the provisions governing the conduct of producers and distributors will be chosen, following the lead set by the 1994 Regulations.

      Third, the provisions governing recall are likely to shift UK practice away from the long-standing assumption that recalling products is a choice available to traders, and not a remedy imposed by the law. Article 8 of Directive 2001/95 provides that the competent authorities of the Member States shall be entitled to select from a (non-exhaustive) menu of measures:

(a)   for any product:
      (i)   to organise, even after its being placed on the market as being safe, appropriate checks on its safety properties, on an adequate scale, up to the final stage of use or consumption;
      (ii)   to require all necessary information from the parties concerned;
      (iii) to take samples of products and subject them to safety checks;
(b)   for any product that could pose risks in certain conditions:
      (i)   to require that it be marked with suitable, clearly worded and easily comprehensible warnings, in the official languages of the

Member State in which the product is marketed, on the risks it may present;

    (ii) to make its marketing subject to prior conditions so as to make it safe;

(c) for any product that could pose risks for certain persons:
to order that they be given warning of the risk in good time and in an appropriate form, including the publication of special warnings;

(d) for any product that could be dangerous:
for the period needed for the various safety evaluations, checks and controls, temporarily to ban its supply, the offer to supply it or its display;

(e) for any dangerous product:
to ban its marketing and introduce the accompanying measures required to ensure the ban is complied with;

(f) for any dangerous product already on the market:

    (i) to order or organise its actual and immediate withdrawal, and alert consumers to the risks it presents;

    (ii) to order or coordinate or, if appropriate, to organise together with producers and distributors its recall from consumers and its destruction in suitable conditions.

2.   When the competent authorities of the Member States take measures such as those provided for in paragraph 1, in particular those referred to in (d) to (f), they shall act in accordance with the Treaty, and in particular Arts. 28 and 30 thereof, in such a way as to implement the measures in a manner proportional to the seriousness of the risk, and taking due account of the precautionary principle.

In this context, they shall encourage and promote voluntary action by producers and distributors, in accordance with the obligations incumbent on them under this Directive, and in particular Chapter III thereof, including where applicable by the development of codes of good practice.

If necessary, they shall organise or order the measures provided for in paragraph 1(f) if the action undertaken by the producers and distributors in fulfilment of their obligations is unsatisfactory or insufficient. Recall shall take place as a last resort. It may be effected within the framework of codes of good practice on the matter in the Member State concerned, where such codes exist.

3.   In particular, the competent authorities shall have the power to take the necessary action to apply with due dispatch appropriate measures such as those mentioned in paragraph 1, (b) to (f), in the case of products posing a serious risk. These circumstances shall be determined by the Member States, assessing each individual case on its merits, taking into account the guidelines referred to in point 8 of Annex II.

4. The measures to be taken by the competent authorities under this
    Article shall be addressed, as appropriate, to:
    (a) the producer;
    (b) within the limits of their respective activities, distributors and in
         particular the party responsible for the first stage of distribution
         on the national market;
    (c) any other person, where necessary, with a view to co-operation in
         action taken to avoid risks arising from a product.

It seems that a major reason for the UK's tardiness in implementing
Directive 2001/95 lies in the difficulty of determining precisely how far the
law should move in the direction of a formal legal procedure covering the
mandatory recall of unsafe products. Therefore the shape of the
implementing Regulations that are eventually adopted will be particularly
intriguing to inspect from this perspective.

Fourth – and again an innovation consequent on Directive 2001/95 –
the public has a right to know. Article 16 of the Directive provides that:

1. Information available to the authorities of the Member States or the
    Commission relating to risks to consumer health and safety posed by
    products shall in general be available to the public, in accordance with
    the requirements of transparency and without prejudice to the
    restrictions required for monitoring and investigation activities. In
    particular the public shall have access to information on product
    identification, the nature of the risk and the measures taken.

    However, Member States and the Commission shall take the steps
    necessary to ensure that their officials and agents are required not to
    disclose information obtained for the purposes of this Directive
    which, by its nature, is covered by professional secrecy in duly
    justified cases, except for information relating to the safety properties
    of products which must be made public if circumstances so require, in
    order to protect the health and safety of consumers.
2. Protection of professional secrecy shall not prevent the dissemination
    to the competent authorities of information relevant for ensuring the
    effectiveness of market monitoring and surveillance activities. The
    authorities receiving information covered by professional secrecy
    shall ensure its protection.

It remains to be seen what the UK will make of this provision.

Fifth, the connection with the process of European market integration
and regulation means that administrative machinery has been set up to link
action taken against unsafe goods at local level with the broader framework
of the EC. This is examined further below.

As mentioned, all these comments assume that the safety standard under the Directive, once implemented, is no weaker than that under the 1987 Act. *If* the former turns out to be lower than that previously expected under the latter, then there will indeed be cause for concern about an influx of dangerous goods overwhelming national laws on the tide of market integration. However, this alarming perspective presently seems theoretical only. Of more practical concern may be the point that, even though the standard of safety may be unchanged despite the EC intervention, the establishment of a border-free market may make it more difficult to enforce the law and, particularly, to monitor dangerous goods that are in free circulation within the Community market. This raises issues of enforcement co-ordination, examined below.

10.6 ENFORCEMENT

Both the 1987 Act and the 1994 Regulations are enforced at local level by, in practice, trading standards officers. The formal powers of the trading standards officer have been mentioned above and are examined in more depth in Chapters 11 and 13, being relevant beyond the specific area of consumer safety. Although formal action may be taken against both trader and product, informal enforcement is the norm. Trading standards officers typically regard a prosecution as time-consuming, costly and risky. The outcome may not be clear, especially under the general duty where, in marginal cases, much will depend on the court's own reading of safety expectations. The practical result has tended to be a predominance of informal controls, including guidance to traders. This policy has many benefits for both sides in terms of saved time and money. Only a minority of operators need be dealt with by prosecution and by formal action against their goods. The modern statutory framework confers valuable flexibility on trading standards officers. However, in the majority of cases a co-operative relationship is mutually beneficial to enforcer and trader.

It is explained in Chapters 11 and 13 that administrative co-ordination has developed in order to minimise the peculiarities which can arise from local enforcement. The Home Authority principle has been developed by collaboration among local authorities confronted by the need to work together as trade patterns have become increasingly national and international. It is now under the auspices of LACORS, the Local Authorities Co-ordinators of Regulatory Services. The principle holds that the trader's home authority will normally act as the source of legal interpretation.

The problem becomes all the more acute at European level, where there is a tension between Europe-wide marketing and local or even national enforcement. This is especially problematic where unsafe products, rather than deceptive marketing practices, are at stake, because of the capacity of goods to cause immediate and serious harm to consumers. Therefore, an account of the development of a strategy for co-ordinating enforcement of product safety law at European level belongs here rather than in Chapters 11 and 13 (which deal with more generally applicable issues of enforcement practice).

Disparate interpretations of safety are capable of fragmenting the market where a product is lawfully marketed in one State but prohibited in another. Conversely, if a State allows a product on to its market, expecting it to conform to its own level of safety and then discovering that it does not, consumer safety may be put at risk. In either case, confidence in the viability of the internal market is undermined. Such problems may arise where national laws vary; also where harmonised Community rules have been put in place which are nevertheless subjected to differing interpretations in different Member States.

Increasingly, it is perceived that substantive Community law 'on paper' will not create an internal market without institutional mechanisms being put in place to secure effective and even enforcement of laws throughout the Community. It is precisely this issue which is at the heart of modern strategies for enforcing consumer protection law, national and European, in a market which is also both national and European.

Specific institutional recognition of the application of laws in the wider market may be found in the two Directives considered above, the Toy Safety Directive[97] and the General Directive.[98] Both merit further consideration as illustrations of the way in which the law operates in an integrated market, where traders are encouraged to treat the market as border-free and in which enforcement authorities too must adopt a strategy which recognises the decline in relevance of the national frontier.

For toys, the 'Safeguard Procedure' envisages the management of situations where toys pose a threat to health or safety, even where they bear the CE marking.[99] Action may be taken at national level against such goods (in the UK, by trading standards officers empowered by the Consumer Protection Act 1987). It is critically important to realise that EC law does not stop action being taken against goods that national agencies believe fail to meet safety standards, even where the toy in question bears the CE marking; quite the contrary, EC law *requires* that unsafe goods be removed from the market.[100] However, since the local or national action taken against CE-marked toys that are believed to be unsafe occurs within a framework of Community market integration, the Commission must be

---

[97]   Chapter 10.3.2 above.
[98]   Chapter 10.3.3 above.
[99]   Chapter 10.3.2 above.
[100]   Article 3 of the Directive, Chapter 10.3.2 above.

alerted and informed. So, for example, where a suspension notice is issued, the trading standards authority informs the DTI,[101] which in turn informs the Commission. In this fashion, local and national enforcement is managed within a Community framework.[102]

A similar pattern is established under the General Directive. Where action is taken to restrict the marketing of a product, or to require withdrawal or recall, Member States are to inform the Commission.[103] The only exception covers situations without cross-border implications which, in an integrating market, ought to be few and far between. The UK's 1994 Regulations reflect the need to put in place a channel for information transmission. Action taken at local level to prohibit or restrict the supply of any product or to have it forfeit under the Regulations triggers an obligation to notify the DTI,[104] which then passes on relevant information to the Commission in Brussels.[105] This will presumably be absorbed into the UK's Regulations implementing Directive 2001/95, once they are adopted (10.3.3). The Commission has conferred upon it specified management functions involving consultation and notification. This management system works better on paper than on the ground. The report into the operation of the original General Directive, which prepared the ground for the adoption of Directive 2001/95, was forced to concede that national authorities are 'uncertain' about how this procedure functions and that the Commission carries a heavy administrative burden which causes the procedure to operate slowly.[106]

In emergencies the Commission itself may adopt measures through specified procedures. The threshold criteria found in the original General Directive, 92/59, were restrictive and evidently rarely likely to be fulfilled.[107] The power was invoked just once by the Commission, when it intervened in the market to ban soft PVC toys intended to be put in the mouths of children under three years of age – teething rings and dummies

---

[101] This obligation is imposed explicitly by Regulation 14 of the Toys (Safety) Regulations 1995, Chapter 10.3.2 above.

[102] See further Weatherill note 43 above.

[103] Article 11 Directive

[104] Regulation 18 General Product Safety Regulations 1994, Chapter 10.3.3 above; Regulation 18(2) excludes action in respect of any second-hand product.

[105] An administrative matter not specifically included in the Regulations.

[106] COM (2000) 140, note 47 above.

[107] Despite their restrictive nature they were challenged – unsuccessfully – by Germany before the European Court, Case C–359/92 *Germany v Commission* [1994] ECR I–3681.

suspected of containing toxic materials.[108] The imposition of such high hurdles was difficult to reconcile with the perceived need for prompt action in emergencies.[109] The procedure now envisaged by Directive 2001/95 is designed to offer greater scope to the Commission to act in cases of emergency.[110] In particular, the Commission is no longer able to act only after at least one Member State has already adopted restrictive measures. However, even now that intervention by the Commission on its own-initiative is permitted, it still seems improbable that this procedure's invocation will be common.

The Rapid Exchange System (RAPEX) provides for the transmission of information about urgent measures taken at national level because of a 'serious' risk which a product presents for the safety of consumers.[111] The State informs the Commission, which then transmits details to other Member States; they in turn indicate to the Commission any measures they have taken. The Commission then circulates that information. In the UK the DTI acts as contact point. The System was first set up in 1984[112] and was duly consolidated in the General Directive. It has always had two branches, covering food products and non-food industrial products, but the system governing food is now governed by Regulation 178/2002,[113] leaving Directive 2001/95 to deal with alerts concerning other products.

The Safeguard procedures under the Toy Safety Directive (and many others) and the RAPEX system have suffered setbacks. They operate erratically. Under RAPEX, for example, levels of notification vary widely State-by-State, doubtless in part attributable to differing national interpretations of the threshold criteria. Moreover, the theory of a to-and-fro of information is not matched fully by practice. A 1993 Commission Report revealed that on average only seven out of (then) 12 Member States comply with their obligation to reply under RAPEX, with 89 days the average time for a reply.[114] The Commission has devoted energy to improving the practical operation of the system, emphasising the need for improved awareness among the public authorities in the Member States of

---

[108] Decision 1999/815 OJ 1999 L315/46. The ban can be temporary only (see now Art. 13(2) Directive 2001/95) but it has been maintained by subsequent Commission Decisions.

[109] Cf. Howells note 3 above, pp. 148–154.

[110] Articles 13–15.

[111] Article 12 Directive 2001/95. The threshold was a 'serious and immediate' risk under Directive 92/59 note 45 above.

[112] Decision 84/133 OJ 1984 L70/16.

[113] OJ 2002 L31/1.

[114] Commission communication on the handling of urgent situations in the context of implementation of Community rules, COM (93)430.

the importance of effective information-sharing.[115] In 2000 a Commission survey allowed it to conclude that the Member States are 'in general satisfied' with the operation of RAPEX, although it was admitted that variation among States in readiness to notify coupled to lack of precision in notifications made remained features of the system that could usefully be improved.[116] In January 2004, to coincide with the deadline for the implementation of Directive 2001/95, the Commission initiated an attempt to improve the transparency of the system by publishing weekly summaries of information received from the Member States pursuant to RAPEX.[117] The annual number of notifications ranged from 143 to 168 to 139 in 2001, 2002 and 2003 respectively and this pattern appears to be enduring into 2004, as a typical week yields two or three notifications. Toys and electrical appliances are the products that are most commonly involved.

The relatively slow and erratic progress of a system such as RAPEX is only to be expected as the EC attempts to secure the development of transnational systems of information-sharing and co-ordination against a background dominated by long-established State practices which are unreceptive to cross-border law enforcement and administrative co-operation. This demonstrates the difficulties in achieving workable integration and a reliable bridging of the gap between the law of product safety on paper and its reality in practice. In fact the significance of this issue extends far beyond product safety. The Commission regularly and vigorously cites the need to generate confidence in the viability of the internal market and correctly identifies visibly effective law enforcement as a key component in delivering that trust. 'Late transposition, bad transposition and weak enforcement all contribute to the public impression of a Union which is not delivering.'[118] And its Internal Market Strategy document, setting out priorities for 2003-2006, the Commission asserted that:

> Free movement of goods (and services) in the Internal Market is above all based on confidence. Confidence of businesses that they can sell their products on the basis of a clear and predictable regulatory framework. Confidence of Member States' administrations that the rules are respected in practice throughout the EU and that the competent authorities in other Member States will take appropriate action when this is not the case. And,

---

[115] Howells note 3 above, pp. 139–148.

[116] COM (2000) 140, note 47 above.

[117] IP/04/183, 9 February 2004. Documentation is available via http: //europa.eu.int/comm/consumers/cons_safe/prod_safe/gpsd/rapex_en.htm.

[118] Commission's White Paper on Governance, July 2001, COM (01) 428 p. 25.

> of course, consumers' confidence in their rights and that the products they buy are safe and respect the environment.[119]

As part of the quest to achieve these objectives in the particular context of product safety, Art. 10 of Directive 2001/95 envisages the establishment of a network of co-operation between product safety agencies in Europe. However, the task of making this real is Herculean, and the enlargement of the Union into Central and Eastern Europe adds to its daunting size.

In tandem with these attempts to manage the market within a framework of structures established by Community rules, there are also 'bottom-up' initiatives to develop cross-border enforcement. Trading standards officers in the UK began to develop links with counterparts in other Member States in the late 1980's, as the project to complete the internal market took shape.[120] The Institute of Trading Standards Administration, the trading standards officers' professional body, established 'PRODLINK', a database which contains information *inter alia* about dangerous products which are found on the market. Subscribers include British trading standards authorities, but also agencies in Sweden, Norway, the Netherlands and the Republic of Ireland. LACORS (the Local Authorities' Co-ordinators of Regulatory Services) has pursued several routes for enhancing knowledge on how to co-operate across borders. It is however realistic to conclude that contributing towards the solution of European transborder consumer problems and complaints seems likely to be a long haul.

---

[119] Commission Communication of May 2003, Internal Market Strategy, Priorities 2003–2006, COM (2003) 238.

[120] Cf. S. Weatherill 'Reinvigorating the Development of Community Product Safety Policy' (1991) 14 JCP 171–194.

Chapter 11

The Regulatory Offence

11.1 THE NATURE AND PURPOSE OF STRICT LIABILITY UNDER THE REGULATORY OFFENCE

The prevalence of offences of 'strict liability' in the consumer protection field runs through preceding chapters. Several offences created in the sphere of consumer protection law impose criminal liability on traders who are responsible for the commission of stipulated acts, without the need for any demonstration that the trader was at fault. The application of a false trade description to goods or the supply or offer for supply of goods to which a false trade description is applied[1] and the supply of an unsafe product[2] attract criminal liability even where the trader has neither deliberately, recklessly nor even negligently caused this to happen.

This characteristic concern with the act not the mind distances consumer protection law from the general sweep of English criminal law. Criminal liability is typically not incurred unless not only the perpetration of stipulated acts is established ('*actus reus*'), but also the requisite mental element is proved ('*mens rea*'). Doing an act is not normally deemed a criminal offence independently of inquiry into the actor's state of mind.[3]

The case for and against imposing strict criminal liability is complex and has been investigated elsewhere at a depth that cannot be replicated here.[4] Broadly, the normal insistence that conviction for crime demands a guilty mind rests on the perception that the imposition of criminal liability by the State on an individual is a very serious matter, involving a degree of moral turpitude. It may lead to the infliction of significant penalties,

---

[1]   Chapter 8.

[2]   Chapter 10.

[3]   A. Ashworth, *Principles of Criminal Law* (OUP, 2003), Ch. 5; J.C. Smith and B. Hogan, *Criminal Law* (Butterworths, 2002), pp. 69–95, 119–121.

[4]   For classic treatment pertaining to the rise of the 'regulatory offence' see B. Wootton, *Crime and the Criminal Law – Reflections of a Magistrate and Social Scientist* (Stevens, 1963); L. Leigh, *Strict and Vicarious Liability: A Study in Administrative Criminal Law* (Sweet and Maxwell, 1982). For a modern survey see P. Cartwright, *Consumer Protection and the Criminal Law: Law, Theory and Policy in the UK* (Cambridge U.P., 2001); also J. Horder, 'Strict Liability, Statutory Construction, and the Spirit of Liberty' (2002) 118 *LQR* 458.

including the individual's loss of liberty. Accordingly, only those guilty in both mind and deed should be punished.

It seems to be assumed that the same objections to the imposition of strict liability do not apply in the law of consumer protection. Several elements combine to lead to this conclusion.[5] The circumstances of the offence are different. Consumer protection offences are not victimless crimes, but the distance between offender and consumer is typically wider than that in crimes of violence or theft. The stigma of conviction under consumer protection laws is not so significant. This seems to form part of a loose notion that infringements of, for example, trade descriptions legislation lie far from the heartland of 'real' criminal law. This is recognised by the customary term used in this field, the 'regulatory offence'.[6]

In *Wings Ltd v Ellis*, a leading case concerning the Trade Descriptions Act,[7] Lord Scarman declared that the Act 'is not truly a criminal statute. Its purpose is not the enforcement of the criminal law but the maintenance of trading standards. Trading standards, not criminal behaviour, are its concern'.[8] This is rather under explained; the dictum assumes a sharp distinction between infractions of trading standards and crime, without elaborating why the two are mutually exclusive. However it must be taken as an important judicial expression of scepticism about the role of the 'true' criminal law in this area. Lord Scarman drew on *Sherras v De Rutzen*[9] for Wright J's well-known dictum that certain statutes (of which, in Lord Scarman's view, the Trade Descriptions Act is one) prohibit acts which 'are not criminal in any real sense, but are acts which in the public interest are prohibited under a penalty'. Therefore, given the subject matter of the 1968 Act, it does not attract 'the presumption recognised by Lord Reid in *Sweet v Parsley*[10] ...as applicable to truly criminal statutes that Parliament did not intend to make criminals of persons who were in no way blameworthy in what they did'.[11]

Apart from justification for strict liability based on the lower level of stigma attached to the (on occasion blameless) offender, the overturning of

---

5   Cf. Ashworth note 3 above, pp. 164–173; Smith and Hogan note 3 above, Ch. 7.

6   Cf. A.I. Ogus, *Regulation* (OUP, 1994), Ch. 5; R. Baldwin and M. Cave, *Understanding Regulation* (OUP, 1999), Chs. 4, 8; Cartwright note 4 above, esp. Chs. 3, 4.

7   [1984] 3 All ER 577, see Ch. 8.3.

8   [1984] 3 All ER 577, 587.

9   [1895] 1 QB 918.

10   [1970] AC 132 at 148, [1969] 1 All ER 347 at 349.

11   For a recent confirmation by the House of Lords that it is normally presumed that criminal offences require *mens rea* see *R v D.P.P.* [2000] 2 AC 428, [2001] 1 All ER 833, a sexual offences case.

the normal requirement of *mens rea* is also capable of justification with reference to the effective application of the law. The rationales for public intervention in areas such as trade descriptions and product safety lie in the need to achieve results that would not be produced by the market operating without regulation – the suppression of misleading trade descriptions and unsafe goods. This objective would be jeopardised by extended refined argument about guilt. At issue is correcting the unsafe or deceptive market.[12] This dictates a preference for addressing (and deterring) the fact of the occurrence of the prohibited act or omission, not the mind of the supplier.

More than 20 years ago it was famously and cogently suggested that the pattern of the regulatory offence could be developed much more coherently and with more awareness of its specific functions in curing market failure and achieving consumer protection were it to be formally disconnected from the 'criminal law'.[13] After all, if the justification for employing the regulatory offence is that traders are not really being accused of 'proper crime', but rather of (perhaps unwitting) participation in market failure, then why stigmatise them at all with the label of criminal activity? This analysis has much force and, it is submitted, would do much to align form with practice and perception. But no such reforming steps have been taken.

The imposition of strict liability affects and is affected by two further principal characteristics of the regulatory offence. The first is the due diligence defence, which in practical terms mitigates the severity of the basic strict liability offence. The second is the pattern of enforcement, which tends to emphasise co-operation and negotiation in preference to the imposition of formal penalties. These two aspects are considered below.

11.2 THE 'DUE DILIGENCE' DEFENCE

11.2.1 Nature and Purpose of the Defence

Prosecutions for breach of relevant provisions of a number of Acts examined in this book may be met by the defence that the accused has taken, loosely, all reasonable precautions and exercised all due diligence to avoid the commission of the offence; and/or that the commission of the

---

12 Chapter 1.

13 An important contribution is D. Tench, *Towards a Middle System of Law* (Consumers Association, 1981). Cf., with some sympathy for the Tench view but also some for the deterrent effect of the criminal law, Sir Gordon Borrie, *The Development of Consumer Law and Policy – Bold Spirits and Timorous Souls* (Hamlyn Lectures, Stevens and Sons, 1974), Parts III, VI.

offence is the fault of another. This type of defence is a long-standing feature of trade practices law and may be traced back to the 19th-century Merchandise Marks Acts.[14]

In *Wings Ltd v Ellis* the House of Lords was unmoved by claims that its interpretation of the relevant offence under the Trade Descriptions Act 1968[15] would criminalize the innocent precisely because of the availability of statutory defences. For example, Lord Templeman saw no need to require carelessness as an ingredient of the offence because s. 24 permits a defence to the careful trader.[16]

The availability of this defence goes some way to meet the objection to the concept of the strict liability offence that it criminalizes the non-blameworthy. It does not wholly meet that objection, for the ingredients of the offence are still committed by an 'innocent' trader who must then seek to bring him- or herself within the scope of the statutory defence. In practical terms this is significant; in the normal run of criminal cases, the prosecution has to prove *mens rea*, whereas, under the strict liability-plus-defence hybrid system, the defendant bears the burden of self-exculpation. Nonetheless the defence provides a practical means for the innocent trader to seek to avoid incurring criminal penalties. The availability of the defence also recognises that the rationale of inducing traders to take rigorous precautions to avoid committing prohibited acts does not suggest a need to impose criminal liability where the trader shows that he or she has in fact taken all such precautions. Indeed, were criminal liability unavoidable, firms might have a diminished incentive to improve their systems beyond the minimum needed to avoid easily preventable infractions.[17] The 'rational and moral justification' for imposing criminal liability in such circumstances is undermined.[18]

11.2.2 The Defences in Detail

For trade descriptions, the relevant provision is found in s. 24 of the Trade Descriptions Act 1968. This provides that:

---

14 Discussed by A. Painter, 'The Evolution of Statutory Defences' (1982) 1 *Trading Law* 181.

15 Section 14, effectively an offence of 'semi-strict' liability; see Ch. 8.2.3.

16 [1984] 3 All ER 577, 593a.

17 But cf. Chapter 11.2.3 below on the general impact of the defence on the climate for enforcement.

18 Cf. Lord Diplock in *Tesco Supermarkets Ltd v Nattrass* [1971] 2 All ER 127, 151e, 151h.

(1) In any proceedings for an offence under this Act it shall, subject to subsection (2) of this section, be a defence for the person charged to prove –
  (a) that the commission of the offence was due to a mistake or to reliance on information supplied to him or to the act or default of another person, an accident or some other cause beyond his control; and
  (b) that he took all reasonable precautions and exercised all due diligence to avoid the commission of such an offence by himself or any person under his control.

(2) If in any case the defence provided by the last foregoing subsection involves the allegation that the commission of the offence was due to the act or default of another person or to reliance on information supplied by another person, the person charged shall not, without leave of the court, be entitled to rely on that defence unless, within a period ending seven clear days before the hearing, he has served on the prosecutor a notice in writing giving such information identifying or assisting in the identification of that other person as was then in his possession.

(3) In any proceedings for an offence under this Act of supplying or offering to supply goods to which a false trade description is applied it shall be a defence for the person charged to prove that he did not know, and could not with reasonable diligence have ascertained, that the goods did not conform to the description or that the description had been applied to the goods.

In relation to specified offences in the field of consumer safety under Part II of the Consumer Protection Act 1987 and in relation to Part III of that Act's offence of misleading pricing, s. 39 of the Consumer Protection Act 1987 provides that:

(1) Subject to the following provisions of this section, in proceedings against any person for an offence to which this section applies it shall be a defence for that person to show that he took all reasonable steps and exercised all due diligence to avoid committing the offence.

(2) Where in any proceedings against any person for such an offence the defence provided by subsection (1) above involves an allegation that the commission of the offence was due –
  (a) to the act or default of another; or
  (b) to reliance on information given by another, that person shall not, without the leave of the court, be entitled to rely on the defence unless, not less than seven clear days before the hearing of the proceedings, he has served a notice under subsection (3) below on the person bringing the proceedings.

(3)   A notice under this subsection shall give such information identifying or assisting in the identification of the person who committed the act or default or gave the information as is in the possession of the person serving the notice at the time he serves it.

(4)   It is hereby declared that a person shall not be entitled to rely on the defence provided by subsection (1) above by reason of his reliance on information supplied by another, unless he shows that it was reasonable in all the circumstances for him to have relied on the information, having regard in particular –

(a)   to the steps which he took, and those which might reasonably have been taken, for the purpose of verifying the information; and

(b)   to whether he had any reason to disbelieve the information.

A number of other statutes within the scope of this book include analogous provisions. The Property Misdescriptions Act 1991 provides an example,[19] and the defence also appears in the Consumer Credit Act 1974 which creates offences out of a number of objectionable practices in that field.[20] The Timeshare Act 1992 offers a further example. In the realm of trade practices law beyond consumer protection as normally conceived, the due diligence defence has a role to play. For example, it appears in the Sunday Trading Act 1994.

These provisions are not replicas of each other. The Consumer Protection Act 1987 has pared down the defence from the more elaborate requirements of the Trade Descriptions Act 1968 to focus on due diligence. Nevertheless the defences share the broad policy of offering the careful trader a defined protection from conviction. Despite the textual differences, their practical application is doubtless similar.[21] Blaming another person is possible, although ss. 39(3) and (4) and s. 24(2) attach procedural requirements to such tactics.

11.2.3 The Practical Application of the Defences

A major argument in favour of strict liability is the flexibility conferred on enforcement agencies by the elimination of arguments that no offence has been committed where unsafe goods or misleading trade descriptions reach the market. Yet the due diligence defence undermines this objective. By protecting the innocent trader, it alters the regulatory climate and is liable to impede vigorous enforcement. It may create the risk that unmeritorious

---

[19]   Chapter 8.4.

[20]   Chapter 9.6.

[21]   Cf. Woolf LJ in *Rotherham MBC v Raysun* [1988] BTLC 292, [1989] CCLR 1.

defences will be advanced, even encouraged. This is especially important when account is taken of the primacy of informal enforcement and the reluctance of trading standards officers to pursue a path of formal prosecution. Although, as suggested above, it seems unjust and even pointless to impose criminal liability on traders who have truly done all they possibly could to avert the occurrence of the prohibited act, practice is rarely so clear-cut. The defence may muddy the waters sufficiently for effective enforcement to be impaired.[22]

Practice suggests a judicial awareness of the central importance of securing that the defence acts as a protection for the genuinely honest trader and not as a loophole through which the reckless, careless or even indifferent trader may escape. Admittedly much will depend on the facts of individual cases before individual courts.[23] Precedent has little formal role to play here. However the observations made by higher courts have confirmed the impression that the defence is not lightly to be accepted. This is demonstrated by the cases that follow, first in the area of consumer safety, then in the area of trade descriptions.

In *Taylor v Lawrence Fraser (Bristol) Ltd*[24] a company sought to rely on guarantees provided by its supplier. It carried out no tests of its own. It was held that this did not suffice to provide a defence to a charge of contravention of the Toy Safety Regulations, made under the precursor to the Consumer Protection Act 1987. Lord Widgery CJ commented that:

> Although every case depends on its own facts, I should think there are very few cases of this kind where reliance on certificates by itself is to be treated as sufficient when there is a possibility of professional sampling and that possibility has been deliberately rejected by the policy of the company.

The message from this case and others is that a defendant will be able successfully to invoke the defence only where it has taken active steps to look into the safety of the items unless, very exceptionally, a small firm is prosecuted and it has done as much as can reasonably be expected. Lord Lane CJ commented in *Garrett v Boots the Chemist Ltd*[25] that '[w]hat might be reasonable for the large retailer might not be reasonable for the village shop'.

---

22 Considered further below, Chapter 11.3.
23 For interesting empirical work, H. Croall, 'Mistakes, Accidents and Someone Else's Fault: the Trading Offender in Court' (1988) 15 *Jnl Law and Society* 293.
24 (1977) 121 Sol Jo 157.
25 1980, unreported, quotation from LEXIS.

In *Riley v Webb*[26] a dangerous level of chemicals was found in pencils and a small wholesaler was prosecuted. The defence was not made out in circumstances where the traders had sought to be diligent 'on paper' alone. The defendant's order form stated:

> This order is placed on condition that the goods will conform with all the requirements imposed by a statute or statutory regulations or orders in force and the date of delivery of the goods and particularly of the Toys (Safety) Regulations.

The suppliers also declared in writing that they had instructed their manufacturers and suppliers that all goods were to conform to statutory requirements. It was held that this was not enough to satisfy the requirements of the defence of due diligence. The size of the business was acknowledged as relevant, but doubt was expressed whether such 'paper' checking could ever be sufficient. Sampling would normally be required.

In *Rotherham MBC v Raysun*[27] toxic material was found in wax crayons made in Hong Kong. Checks had been performed by agents of the importers in Hong Kong. However, it was apparent that the agents' practice was to supply details only of adverse results. Specific information about the numbers of checks actually undertaken was not to hand. The importer also had the goods checked in Manchester, but in 1986 this involved no more than one packet from a batch of 10,800 dozen packets. Woolf LJ wryly described this as 'modest'; the defence was not made out and the importer was convicted.

The theme which emerges is an expectation of sampling – and effective sampling. Yet these are not rules. Small levels of sampling may suffice where, for example, it is shown that the goods are highly likely to be homogenous and that one packet could indeed be considered representative of a large batch. Moreover, sampling may not be required where the firm is small and has reliable and transparent sources.[28] However the due diligence defence is not readily made out and, in order to ensure that the law is capable of effective enforcement,[29] this rigour seems entirely appropriate.

---

[26] [1987] BTLC 65, [1987] CCLR 65.

[27] [1988] BTLC 292, [1989] CCLR 1. The case is examined by S. Weatherill at [1990] JBL 36.

[28] Cf. acquittal in *Hurley v Martinez and Co* [1990] TLR 189, a case under the Trade Descriptions Act 1968. The decision suggests a special respect for the reliability of German sources!

[29] Further below, Chapter 11.3; effectiveness does not refer simply to prosecution.

A similar impression of a predominantly rigorous judicial approach to the defence is obtained from case law concerning offences under the trade descriptions legislation.

Naish v Gore[30] was a case of a clocked odometer.[31] The defendant dealer was not the clocker. He had looked over the car and judged that it had in fact done only the mileage shown. He was wrong in this assessment. He had not consulted the log-book before selling the car, for it had latterly passed through the hands of a number of dealers and the log-book had not yet reached him. When the consumer buyer received the log-book, it was discovered that the mileage shown was inaccurate. Lord Widgery commented that '[i]t is for the defendant to prove that he took all reasonable precautions, and if he has taken none, that means he must prove that none could reasonably have been taken'. So failure to check excludes the defence where checking is possible.[32] Lord Widgery thought that, on the facts of the case, the magistrates' acquittal of the dealer should not be disturbed. However, he concluded by inviting courts before which such defences are presented 'to be meticulous in their consideration of all the courses which the seller might have adopted'.

In *Wandsworth LBC v Bentley*[33] a car dealer acquired a car at auction. He sold the car, whereupon it was discovered to have been 'clocked' in the past and the dealer was charged. The sale document stated that the previous owner was Shell UK and the dealer claimed he was entitled to assume that such a reputable firm would not be involved with clocked cars. The defence failed. He had not contacted Shell to check the car's mileage when the company had got rid of the car, nor had he even checked that it was actually Shell that was selling the car at auction. Lord Lane CJ would not entertain the argument that due diligence had been taken 'in the absence of that simple precaution'.

In *Texas Homecare Ltd v Stockport MBC* the High Court held that the Crown Court had been right to reject the defence where no system had been set up to check conformity of goods delivered to description.[34] The High Court also ruled that s. 24(3) demanded no lower standard of care than that required under s. 24(1).[35]

For all the impression conveyed by this case law that the defence will rarely be made out, it is nonetheless not to be regarded as a dead letter. As a general observation one may suppose that less tough demands are made

---

[30]   [1971] 3 All ER 737.

[31]   Cf. Ch. 8.2.6.

[32]   Cf. *Sherratt v Geralds Jewellers* (1970) 114 Sol Jo 147.

[33]   [1980] RTR 429.

[34]   [1987] TLC 331.

[35]   This is criticised at [1987] Crim LR 709 for overlooking distinctions between the two provisions explained in *Barker v Hargreaves* (1980) 125 Sol Jo 165.

of traders charged with offences associated with economic interests rather than consumer safety.[36] The version found in the Property Misdescriptions Act 1991 protected the defendant in *Enfield LBC v Castles Estate Agents*.[37] The estate agents had incorrectly described property to possess planning permission, but were acquitted because they had relied on assurances to that effect from the seller in circumstances in which an experienced estate agent would have had no reason to doubt the accuracy of the assurance. Concern not to expect expensive and exhaustive inquiry underpins the judicial attitude in this case to the scope of the defence, but the court did not write traders a blank cheque. Relying on sellers' promises even where they appear less than convincing is unlikely to permit successful invocation of the defence – *a fortiori* where safety is at stake. In *Popely v Scott*[38] the defence succeeded in unusual circumstances. The defence was that appearing in the Timeshare Act 1992, which also has much in common with the defence in the Trade Descriptions Act at stake in the cases discussed above. The defendants had taken legal advice to the effect that the commercial scheme they promoted was not covered by the regulatory requirements of the Act. They therefore ignored those requirements – wrongly, as it turned out, because the scheme was found to fall within the material scope of the Act. But, having secured legal advice, albeit of an incorrect nature, they successfully relied on the 'due diligence' defence to secure acquittal. This was not a case of trying to meet the statutory requirements, but failing. Instead it was a case of wrongly assuming they did not apply. But, in the light of the statutory wording, the court felt that the defence was in principle available and that on the facts it was made out. This seems generous.

11.2.4 Companies and their Employees

The invocation of the defence by a legal person, a company, charged with an offence is especially sensitive when the defendant seeks to defeat the charge by blaming not a third party, as in the cases mentioned above, but instead one of its own employees. This will be uncommon in product safety cases, but has arisen with some frequency in the realm of misdescription. On the one hand, it may indeed be true that the problem has arisen because of an individual employee's foolish or even wicked conduct, in which case the stigma, however small, of violation of the criminal law should not fairly be attached to the company. On the other hand, the company might be induced to escape liability by blaming

---

36 Cf. D. Parry, 'Judicial approaches to due diligence' [1995] *Crim LR* 695.
37 [1996] 160 J.P. 618.
38 [2001] *Crim LR* 417.

employees if permitted such a defence. It may be tempted to loosen supervision and to devolve more responsibility to lower level employees than it might otherwise prefer, simply to minimise its own chances of liability. More fundamentally, it might be pointed out that the company hires employees as part of its commercial, profit-making activities; by way of balance, it should therefore be equally subject to any detrimental effects flowing from its hiring policies.

These conflicting policy questions were addressed by the House of Lords in *Tesco Supermarkets Ltd v Nattrass*.[39] The decision offers scope for protection from conviction to the company, but on condition that serious efforts are made to ensure an effective supervisory system. The case arose out of misdescription of the price of 'Radiant' washing powder in Tesco's Northwich store. Although displayed as 2s 11d, the price marked on all packs on the shelves was 3s 11d.[40] Tesco was fined £25 with costs.

A shop assistant had put out packs marked with the higher price. The shop manager had not been told of this by the assistant, though he should have been. Nor had he checked the special offers, though he should have done. Tesco invoked the due diligence defence and blamed the manager, Mr Clement. Tesco was convicted by the local magistrates. Concern to protect its corporate image induced Tesco to pursue the matter to the House of Lords, where it was held that the firm had established the statutory defence.

The House of Lords confirmed that companies may commit regulatory offences through their employees. The key question was whether the company took all reasonable precautions and exercised all due diligence in order to bring itself within the defence. This took their Lordships into the metaphysics of how 'a company' acts. They insisted that a company has a 'directing mind'. For the purposes of this defence, it is required only that the company's directing mind establish an effective system designed to prevent the commission of offences. This it had done. Mr Clement's (in)activities were not part of the directing mind of the company. In fact his personal fault was what prevented the company's system from successfully forestalling the false price indication. The failings of a 'cog in the machine'[41] could not deprive the company of the statutory defence, provided it is shown that it (the company) diligently put in place an effective supervisory system.

It is a question of fact whether a company's system is indeed adequate. The courts appear aware of the peril for the effective application of the law that would result from an over-hasty acceptance that enough has been

---

39   [1971] 2 All ER 128.
40   Just under 15p; just under 20p.
41   Lord Morris 140f.

done. The invocation of the defence is typically scrutinised with rigour. Reliance on it failed in *DSG Retail Ltd v Oxfordshire CC*[42] where there was no evidence of active supervision of the conduct of staff in the retail outlet in which pricing offences contrary to the Consumer Protection Act had been committed.[43] Moreover, in *McGuire v Sittingbourne Co-operative Society Ltd*[44] the importance of pinning down precisely what has led to the breach was emphasised. The defendant firm simply named all the assistants working in the shop at the time of the offence and alleged that one or more was at fault. There was no evidence of what steps had been taken to investigate how the offence had occurred or who was responsible. This was not enough to justify an acquittal.

Is the law too generous to firms in Tesco's position? The company was allowed to separate the failings of its own manager from the assessment of the operation of its overall system. It was able to convert its own employee into 'another person' for the purposes of the statutory defence. One may wryly observe that the profits made as a result of the employee's misconduct are certainly not disowned by the company. Yet it seems that the courts view such opportunity for exculpation based on a genuinely effective overall system as the essence of the statutory defence. In other areas of the law, Tesco has been distinguished precisely because of the availability there of the statutory defence. For example, in *National Rivers Authority v Alfred McAlpine Homes East Ltd*[45] the company was prosecuted for pollution of controlled waters contrary to the Water Resources Act 1991. The site agent and site manager accepted responsibility. The justices considered that these employees were too lowly within the company structure to fix the company with criminal liability. Simon Brown LJ disagreed. He found that the justices had misinterpreted Tesco. In connection with the commission of the offence, they had wrongly used an analysis that had been presented in Tesco in relation to the statutory defence. The company had committed the offence of pollution through its employees. The separation of individual employees from the company's overall supervisory scheme could arise only in relation to the due diligence defence, as in Tesco. However, since the 1991 Act contains no equivalent defence to that in S. 24 Trade Descriptions Act 1968, conviction was proper. This seems to suggest that it is perfectly possible under English law to develop regulatory systems without the addition of the due diligence defence. Be that as it may, in the consumer protection

---

42   [2001] 1 WLR 1765.

43   Cf. *Denard v Smith and Dixons Ltd* [1991] Crim LR 63, where Dixons had similarly not done enough. See also discussion of *Robert Gale v Dixon Stores Group Ltd* by D. Roberts at (1994) 13 *Trading Law* 50.

44   [1976] Crim LR 268.

45   [1994] 4 All ER 286.

field, the defence has become a well-entrenched feature. One may conclude that its interpretation in *Tesco v Nattrass* allows companies to defend themselves from conviction by, in effect, showing that blame lies within the organisation but at a low level. This generous approach has not found favour in, for example, the field of corporate responsibility for violation of rules governing health and safety.[46] But for the time being in the consumer field *Tesco v Nattrass* reigns.

11.2.5 Liability of Persons Other than Principal Offender – 'Bypass'

The statutory defences envisage the possibility of acquittal where, loosely summarised, the real responsibility for the offence lies with another.[47] Whether or not the principal offender is charged, it is explicitly provided that action may be taken against that other person. This 'by-pass' procedure assists flexibility in enforcement practice.

Section 23 of the Trade Descriptions Act provides that:

> Where the commission by any person of an offence under this Act is due to the act or default of some other person that other person shall be guilty of the offence, and a person may be charged with and convicted of the offence by virtue of this section whether or not proceedings are taken against the first-mentioned person.

Section 40 of the Consumer Protection Act 1987 provides that:

> Where the commission by any person of an offence to which section 39 above applies is due to an act or default committed by some other person in the course of any business of his, the other person shall be guilty of the offence and may be proceeded against and punished by virtue of this subsection whether or not proceedings are taken against the first-mentioned person.

And, it can be added, he can be convicted even where proceedings taken against the first-mentioned person have ended in acquittal because of the successful invocation of a statutory defence.[48]

Special rules also provide that where an offence committed by a body corporate is proved 'to have been committed with the consent and

---

46 Cf. *R v British Steel plc* [1995] 1 WLR 1356; see Cartwright note 4 above, pp. 96–111.

47 Cf. D. Roberts, 'The Act or Default of Some Other Person' (1991) 8 *Trading Law* 145.

48 This robust interpretation was adopted in *Coupe v Guyett* [1973] 1 WLR 669.

connivance of, or to be attributable to any neglect on the part of, any director, manager, secretary or other similar officer of the body corporate, or any person who was purporting to act in any such capacity, he as well as the body corporate' shall be liable to be proceeded against and punished accordingly.[49] So had Mr Clement been higher up in Tesco's organisation, he could have been liable under this section; Tesco, too, would presumably have lost the protection of the defence.

The criminal liability of Mr Clement was not in issue in *Tesco v Nattrass*.[50] By virtue of s. 23 of the Trade Descriptions Act (above), presumably he could have been prosecuted;[51] the defence of due diligence available to him would very probably not have been made out given his failure to check the shelves. However, the allocation of scarce enforcement resources to the formal prosecution of an individual employee will be relatively rare.[52]

Nonetheless, in *Warwickshire County Council v Johnson*[53] the manager of Dixons electrical goods shop in Stratford-upon-Avon was prosecuted for supplying a misleading price indication contrary to s. 20(1) Consumer Protection Act 1987.[54] Since the offence is committed only by a person acting 'in the course of a business of his', the House of Lords was asked to rule on whether this could catch a defendant employee. It was held that the section was aimed at defendants who were either the owner or holder of a controlling interest in the business. Broadly, employers are caught, but employees are not.[55] Probably, then, the authority should have charged Dixons. But Dixons would have been able to try to show due diligence and doubtless 'the ghost of *Tesco v Nattrass* still stalks the [Warwickshire] offices'.[56]

---

[49]   Section 20(1) TDA; s. 40(2) CPA; s. 169 Consumer Credit Act 1974.

[50]   Note 39 above. Obiter, 'he was liable to prosecution' per Lord Reid at 135g; undecided, per Viscount Dilhorne at 143c; 'no opinion' per Lord Pearson at 147j.

[51]   Cf. *Birkenhead and District Co-operative Society Ltd v Roberts* [1970] 3 All ER 391, 393.

[52]   Chapter 11.3 below.

[53]   [1993] 1 All ER 299.

[54]   Chapter 8.5.

[55]   The case was of constitutional interest for their Lordships' reference to Parliamentary debates on the Bill that became the relevant Act; this was one of the first instances of the relaxation of the rule excluding such material accepted in *Pepper v Hart* [1992] 3 WLR 1032. The Minister had explicitly commented that the words '... of his' were designed to ensure that individual employees would not be prosecuted (All ER 305f).

[56]   C. Wells, 'Corporate Liability and Consumer Protection: *Tesco v Nattrass* Revisited' (1994) 57 *MLR* 817, 820. The case provoked a correspondence between drafter and enforcement officer in the pages of the *New Law Journal* that was marked by extraordinary belligerence (especially by the former); (1993) 143 NLJ 8, 228, 356.

The decision in *Warwickshire CC v Johnson* seems to confirm the impression gained from a careful reading of the provisions that s. 20(1) and s. 40 of the CPA are distinct from s. 23 TDA. Section 23 TDA (above) does not contain the proviso that by-pass proceedings may be brought only against a person acting 'in the course of any business of his' – or even a person acting 'in the course of any business'. It refers to simply 'some other person'. It therefore allows by-pass proceedings to be brought even against private individuals – and, in line with the pattern of the Act, even in the absence of *mens rea*. Such by-passing occurred in *Olgeirsson v Kitching*.[57] The defendant, acting as a private individual, misdescribed the mileage when he sold his car to a dealer. The dealer then resold the car under this misdescription. Section 23 proceedings against the private seller were initiated and the High Court upheld a conviction.

On policy grounds, this is indefensible. There could be no s. 1 liability because of its restriction to action in the course of a trade or business; it is irrational that s. 23 liability could arise. This is a *fortiori* the case where other statutes creating regulatory offences completely exclude private liability. However, the plain words of s. 23 of the 1968 Act obstruct the achievement of consistency across similar statutes. Its explicit wording supports the interpretation adopted in *Olgeirsson*, as McNeill J observed in concluding his judgment upholding conviction of the private individual in that case.[58] It is submitted that the law of theft, not the regulatory offence, is the proper place for scrutinising the conduct of the likes of Olgeirsson, but it now lies with Parliament to amend the 1968 Act to achieve that result.[59] In the meantime one would not anticipate that prosecutions would be brought against private individuals with any frequency, especially in the absence of dishonesty.[60] Enforcement practice is discussed further below at 11.3.

11.2.6 Crime and Market Failure

That cases as trivial as *Tesco v Nattrass* and *Warwickshire CC v Johnson* should find their way from Magistrates Court all the way to the House of Lords serves to demonstrate a sensitivity of commercial firms to the

---

[57] [1986] 1 WLR 304.

[58] At 311b-d. However, the defendant was dishonest in *Olgeirsson*; perhaps MacNeill J might have tried harder to avoid conviction had the defendant been innocent in mind, even though the absence of *mens rea* requirement means that, strictly, such issues are irrelevant.

[59] Cf. comment by P. Cartwright, 'Reforming the Trade Descriptions Act 1968' (1993) 3 *Consumer Policy Review* 34. See also Ch. 8.7.

[60] As noted above, the defendant in *Olgeirsson* was dishonest.

imposition of criminal responsibility. Plainly Tesco, as a 'repeat player' in such litigation,[61] was eager to invest resources in order to establish a favourable precedent. It succeeded in that objective. Perhaps such expensive litigation acts as a further demonstration of the advantages of formal decriminalisation of such law.[62] After all, what is at stake is repairing the market failure of deceptive marketing practices and, if that can be more readily and more cheaply achieved by other types of law, then the application of a criminal statute, generating such litigation, is simply inefficient.[63] There is a case to be made in favour of a system that allows immediate preventive action to be taken by enforcement officers, with costs incurred to be borne by the trader. This would include provision for the trader to secure compensation in the event of abusive conduct by enforcement officers.[64]

This is not to propose the evacuation of criminal responsibility from the arena of consumer protection. Some 'regulatory offences' of the type at stake in this book form part of what would, for most, instinctively count as 'proper' criminal law. For example, a deliberate decision to make profits quickly by selling a batch of goods known to be thoroughly dangerous is no mere administrative infraction. Nevertheless, a reduction in formal criminal laws in favour of, for example, rigorously policed licensing requirements,[65] would permit the full weight of the criminal law to be reserved for the occasional scandal.

11.2.7 The Compatibility of the Due Diligence Defence with EC Law

The use of the due diligence defence is not explicitly authorised by any EC Directive, but nor is it excluded; the UK has chosen to implement several Directives by including this defence. Supply of toys that are not safe is to be prevented by Member States under the provisions of the Toy Safety Directive. More broadly, within the scope of the Directive on General Product Safety, supply of goods that are not safe is to be suppressed by Member States. The UK has implemented these Directives: the supply of offending items *prima facie* constitutes a regulatory offence. However, a

---

61   Cf. M. Galanter, 'Why the "Haves" come out ahead: Speculation on the Limits of Legal Change' (1974) 9 *Law and Society Review* 95.

62   Cf. Tench note 13 above.

63   It is interesting to note that from the criminal (rather than the consumer) law perspective, such offences of differing *mens rea* also cause problems for commentators seeking to impose coherence; cf. C. Wells, *Corporations and Criminal Responsibility* (OUP, 2001).

64   For the *current* law governing this matter see Chapter 11.3.3 below.

65   Cf. Chapter 1.8.2.

trader will escape conviction if able to bring him or herself within the due diligence defence, which is absent from the Directive but inserted into the UK's implementing regulations in accordance with the normal practice of the regulatory offence in the consumer protection field.[66]

Yet EC rules must be 'effectively' implemented at national level. It is arguable that the shelter of the due diligence defence – allied to the risk of incurring an obligation to pay compensation[67] – may inhibit British enforcement agencies from pursuing suspected violations of EC-derived rules. This would imperil the viability of the due diligence defence where EC rules are at issue; were the defence to be invalidated in that sphere, its continued application in other areas of domestic consumer protection law would begin to appear inconsistent.

It is submitted that this argument lacks sufficient weight to overturn the British predilection for inserting the due diligence defence into implementing regulations, even where this is not expressly foreseen in the EC Directive. Litigation would nonetheless be of interest, if only to clarify the EC notion of 'effectiveness' in this context. The EC has declared that Art. 10 (ex 5) EC requires Member States to take all measures necessary to guarantee the application and effectiveness of Community law and that penalties, where left to national law, must be effective and dissuasive.[68] Implementation choices rest with the national system, but within a required Community framework of 'effectiveness'. The insertion of a due diligence defence is probably a permissible subtlety within a domestic enforcement regime which generally permits effective control of suspect traders and suspect goods, especially at point of first supply.[69] This approach was taken by Lord Millett in *R v Bristol Magistrates Court, ex parte Junttan Oy*,[70] not a case concerning a consumer but instead arising out of a fatal accident in the workplace caused by an imported piling rig in circumstances falling within the scope of the EC's Machinery Directive.[71] He pointed out that the Directive does not require the imposition of criminal penalties, and added that in his view if a Member State chose to attach such penalties to domestic implementing measures 'the scope of the offence and the nature of the defences which they may allow... are matters for national law'. One might wish to add that national law is here qualified by the demands of 'effectiveness' rooted in Art. 10 EC, but it is submitted

---

[66] Chapter 11.2.1. above.

[67] Chapter 11.3.3 below.

[68] E.g., Case 68/88 *Commission v Greece* [1989] ECR 2965; Case C–213/99 *De Andrade* [2000] ECR I–11083; Case C–354/99 *Commission v Ireland* [2001] ECR I–7657.

[69] Chapter 11.3 below and see also Chapter 10.2.

[70] [2003] ICR 1475.

[71] Directive 98/37 OJ 1998 L207/1.

that the same result should obtain under consumer protection law as Lord Millett reached in *ex parte Junttan Oy*. The UK's orthodox due diligence defence should be treated as compatible with its EC obligations.

11.2.8 The Compatibility of the Due Diligence Defence with Human Rights Law

From the perspective of human rights the objection to the defence is that it requires the defendant to demonstrate that circumstances arise that justify acquittal, rather than placing the burden of proof fully on the prosecution. That, indeed, is the structure of the regulatory offence. So – the argument runs – imposing a legal burden of proof on the defence conflicts with the presumption of innocence protected as a convention right by the Human Rights Act.[72]

It is submitted that the argument should fail, but it is not trivial. *R v Lambert* is a decision of the House of Lords which demonstrates its potential vitality.[73] The defendant was convicted of possession of a controlled drug with intent to supply, contrary to the Misuse of Drugs Act 1971. He had been arrested in possession of a bag containing a quantity of drugs and sought to rely on a statutory defence under the 1971 Act that he neither knew nor suspected the bag to contain illegal drugs. Their Lordships treated this as a legal burden imposed on the defence. It should be interpreted in an evidential manner. Acquittal should follow if the jury felt he was probably not entitled to the benefit of the defence but entertained a reasonable doubt about his guilt. In this way the House of Lords absorbed the statutory defence into the core of the offence, instead of treating these as separate stages in the inquiry. *Lambert* has inevitably provoked further litigation by optimistic defendants. In *R v Carass*[74] a defence under the Insolvency Act allowing a defendant to prove that he had no intent to defraud was similarly treated by the Court of Appeal.

For regulatory offences in the consumer field a defence-friendly argument inspired by this case law would hold that the prosecution would succeed only if it shows, in short, that the trader has not taken enough care. The due diligence defence would in effect become part of the assessment of whether the regulatory offence has been committed, and not a specific means for the trader to show that enough care has been taken to justify acquittal.

This would be tantamount to eliminating the strict liability characteristic of the regulatory offence. It would severely damage effective

---

[72]   On the Act see Chapter 1.9.3.1.

[73]   [2001] 3 WLR 206.

[74]   [2001] EWCA Crim 2845.

enforcement. Rightly so, *if* an infraction of a defendant's human rights is truly at stake. However, it is submitted that this is not so. *Attorney-General's Reference (No 4 of 2002)*[75] concerned the treatment of a suspected member of Hamas under the Terrorism Act 2000. It is an offence to belong or profess to belong to a proscribed organisation. It is a defence to prove the organisation was not proscribed on the last occasion on which the defendant became a member or began to profess to be a member, and that the defendant has not participated in activities while the organisation is proscribed. Here the Court of Appeal found no breach of Convention rights. It tried to pick its way through the case law by focussing on discovery of the true nature of the offence. It thought that in *Lambert* the House of Lords treated the true nature of the offence as including knowledge of possession of the drugs. So the defence was, in reality if not in form, part of the shape of the offence. By contrast in the *A-G's Reference* the Court of Appeal treated the offence as capable of tight definition as belonging or professing to belong to the organisation. The defence was carefully limited and did not form part of the true nature of the offence. The demands it placed on the defence were compatible with Convention rights.

One would protect the structure of the regulatory offence from accusations that it is incompatible with the presumption of innocence by regarding the true nature of the offence to lie in the misdescription of goods or the supply of unsafe goods. The due diligence defence would on this model serve only as a separate and limited defence targeted at the particular issue of taking adequate precautions. A distinct argument would hold that the wrongdoing at stake under the consumer protection statutes cannot be equated with 'real' criminal law and that therefore a lower level of individual protection is apt. But this again raises the troubling point that this *is* criminal law and its violation may generate significant penalties. Litigation on the point would plainly be helpful and, given the commercial incentive to seek the shelter of human rights, it may be confidently expected to arrive sooner rather than later.

11.3 ENFORCEMENT

11.3.1 The Pattern of Local Enforcement in National and International Markets

Enforcement of the rules pertaining to the regulatory offence belongs in the hands of officers of local authorities. In practice, enforcement lies with the authority's Trading Standards Department, which holds responsibility for a

---

[75]   [2004] 1 All ER 1.

wide range of consumer protection and general trade practices law. The formerly common label 'weights and measures' is far too narrow to describe modern practice and is more or less redundant.

A feature of the British system has always been local enforcement: each trading standards authority has jurisdiction within its locality. The institutional pattern of consumer protection in the UK is surveyed at length in Chapter 13, but features of particular relevance to the nature and practice of the 'regulatory offence' are summarised here. Enforcement practice is not directed by central government and is liable to vary from town to town. This may create confusing divergence and impose costs on traders. Administrative co-ordination has developed in order to minimise the peculiarities which can arise from local enforcement. The Home Authority principle was developed by LACOTS, the Local Authorities' Co-ordinating Body on Food and Trading Standards, a non-statutory entity established by the authorities themselves, which has been superseded by LACORS, the Local Authorities' Co-ordinators of Regulatory Services.[76] That new name, LACORS, was assumed in 2002 to reflect the wider responsibilities cast upon local authorities. The Home Authority principle holds that it is normally the trader's home authority which will act as the source of legal interpretation, wherever in the country the firm may be active. This is not a formally binding rule, but its advantages are such that in practice it is largely adhered to. Accordingly traders are normally able to rely on a single source of interpretation of the law.

Local enforcement is capable of displaying beneficial sensitivity to particular local concerns. On the other hand its fragmented impact may prove inefficient. Governmental efforts over the last decade and more have been directed at striking an appropriate balance. A review into the organisation of enforcement functions of local authorities generated a report published in September 1994 in which great play was made of the benefit for business of consistency in enforcement practice.[77] But no radical change was forthcoming. The matter was duly taken on by the Labour government which took office in 1997. It has sought to maintain the traditional emphasis on local enforcement while attempting to promote consistency in practice and effective co-operation between enforcement bodies located in different geographical regions. This is tracked in Chapter 13 of this book.

The perceived problem with local enforcement is that much commercial activity is more geographically extensive – not simply national but increasingly international. It is essential to put in place strategies for even and effective law enforcement in Europe. This is a long-standing

---

[76] See http://www.lacors.gov.uk/pages/trade/lacors.asp.
[77] Report of DTI Review of Local Government Enforcement.

perception. It was a major theme in the Sutherland Report of 1992 into the future management of the internal market:

> Each authority responsible for applying and enforcing Community legislation at national and local level should accept a duty to co-operate with other such bodies, both through direct contact and via central contact points. This requires them to recognise and respond to their Community-wide responsibilities which arise from the fact that their official functions directly affect citizens of all other Member States. Their officials have Community-wide responsibilities.

Developments of this nature have been most marked in the co-ordination of practice in the product safety field although, even there, an enormous range of tasks remains to be completed.[78] Probably the immediate and direct threat of the unsafe product stimulated a degree of willingness to act in the field which was initially lacking elsewhere. Less has thus far been achieved in developing cross-border control of trading malpractice causing prejudice to the economic interests of consumers. However, more active recent initiatives have pursued the quest to establish practical co-operation between concerned enforcement agencies in different Member States. The Commission too has prepared formal proposals for co-operation in the enforcement of its proposed general control over unfair marketing practices.[79]

11.3.2 Specific Enforcement Powers

The Trade Descriptions Act 1968 and the Consumer Protection Act 1987 invest trading standards authorities with powers of enforcement that are distinct in detail, but nevertheless share sufficient points of similarity to permit a common broad description.[80]

Section 27 of the Trade Descriptions Act 1968 and s. 28 of the Consumer Protection Act 1987 empower the making of test purchases.

Section 28 of the Trade Descriptions Act 1968 and s. 29 of the Consumer Protection Act 1987 contain powers of entry, search and related powers. These are available to a duly authorised officer of an enforcement authority at any reasonable hour. They encompass powers of inspection of goods and entry to premises (other than those occupied solely as a person's residence).

---

[78] See Chapter 10.6.

[79] Chapter 8.7.3.

[80] For more depth than is here possible, see C. Andrews, *The Enforcement of Regulatory Offences* (Sweet and Maxwell, 1998).

Further powers are triggered only where the officer has reasonable grounds for suspecting that an offence has been committed. Such powers cover requirements to produce records and to have them copied, and the seizure and detention of goods.[81] Officers have the opportunity to seek court orders to secure entry;[82] the statutes create offences of obstruction of an authorised officer.[83]

Under the Consumer Protection Act 1987, special powers are available in respect of goods suspected not to have been supplied in the UK since they were manufactured or imported.[84] This provision reflects a policy of targeting enforcement at point of first supply where action can be taken most efficiently, rather than waiting until batches have been split up and distributed throughout the country.[85]

11.3.3 Compensating Traders

A number of statutes contain provisions that envisage the compensation of traders affected by the exercise of enforcement powers. We focus here on the Trade Descriptions Act 1968 and the Consumer Protection Act 1987.[86] Section 33 of the former provides that where an officer in the exercise of powers under s. 28 seizes and detains goods and the owner

> suffers loss by reason thereof or by reason that the goods, during the detention, are lost or damaged or deteriorate, then, unless the owner is convicted of an offence under this Act committed in relation to the goods, the authority or department shall be liable to compensate him for the loss so suffered.

Section 34 of the Consumer Protection Act 1987 provides that, in cases of the exercise of powers of seizure and detention under s. 29;

> the enforcement authority shall be liable to pay compensation to any person having an interest in the goods in respect of any loss or damage

---

81 Sections 29(5), (6) CPA 1987; s. 28(1) TDA. The wording is similar but not identical.
82 Section 30 CPA; s. 28(3) TDA.
83 Section 32 CPA; s. 29 TDA.
84 Section 29(4) CPA 1987.
85 This policy was first introduced by the Consumer Safety (Amendment) Act 1986. Cf. the similarly motivated s. 31 on detention by customs officers. For discussion, S. Weatherill, 'Consumer safety legislation in the United Kingdom' [1987/2] *E Consum LJ* 81.
86 Cf. generally K. Cardwell and P. Kay, 'The Consumer Protection Act 1987: Liability of the Enforcement Authorities' (1988) 6 *Trading Law* 212.

caused by reason of the exercise of the power if – (a) there has been no contravention in relation to the goods of any safety provision or any provision made by or under Part III of this Act; and (b) the exercise of the power is not attributable to any neglect or default by that person.

The provisions may helpfully induce traders and officers to co-operate to minimise risks of loss caused through misunderstanding. In so far as such provisions spur officers to act swiftly, they seem valuable. Sums involved are usually relatively small, especially since it is frequently possible to restore goods unaltered, so the trader may suffer no loss at all. Admittedly, perishable goods will cause more problems.[87] It might also be added that protection of the innocent trader appears a justifiable objective.[88] However, such compensation provisions might deter active enforcement, especially in times of budgetary constraint at local level. For these reasons, the compensation provisions have always been controversial.[89] Parliamentary debate on what became the 1987 Act focused on the problem of striking a balance between the interests of the individual trader and tackling the broader issues of market failure.[90] This, of course, constitutes an endemic theme in the shaping of consumer policy.[91]

11.3.4 Prosecution

Ultimately formal prosecution is possible, although atypical, for reasons elaborated below. That trading standards officers are able to bring prosecutions in respect of most regulatory offences[92] explains the naming of many of the cases considered above. For example, *Kitching* in *Olgeirsson v Kitching*[93] was the prosecutor acting for Humberside County Council Trading Standards Department. Private prosecutions are possible but rare.[94]

---

[87] Consider also the hypothetical seizure 24 hours before kick-off of a large batch of specially-made souvenir items designed to be sold before Hull City played in the FA Cup Final (SW)/FA Vase Final (GH). Release of the goods only 24 hours later after the team's glorious victory would not prevent a dramatic depreciation in value.

[88] For *obiter dicta* on their back-up role, cf. Taylor LJ in *R v Birmingham City Council, ex p Ferrero Ltd* [1993] 1 All ER 530, esp. 537.

[89] Cf. comment by K. Cardwell, 'Consumer Protection Act 1987' (1987) 50 *MLR* 625.

[90] E.g. 116 HC Debs 347–9 (13 May 1987); 485 HL Debs 919–922 (12 March 1987).

[91] Cf. Chapter 1.9.

[92] Cf. ss. 222, 223 Local Government Act 1972.

[93] Note 59 above.

[94] Cf. policy discussion by C. Harlow and R. Rawlings, *Pressure through Law* (Routledge, 1992) Ch. 5.

R v Haesler[95] is authority for the proposition that a prison sentence is inappropriate save in cases of dishonesty. This case arose in relation to trade descriptions, but the commission of a regulatory offence will generally attract a custodial sentence only in exceptional circumstances. The imposition of a fine is typical.[96] In *R v Docklands Estates Ltd*[97] the Court of Appeal took the opportunity to insist on the need for fines to be realistic in order to be effective. The defendant, an estate agency business, had been convicted of three offences of misdescription of services contrary to the Trade Descriptions Act 1968. It had erected 'Sold' boards outside properties in order to suggest – incorrectly – that it had acted as the estate agent in the sale, thereby to impress and attract potential customers. Fined £7500 on each count, it appealed, arguing that fines of only £100 were normal practice for similar offences. Lord Woolf CJ thought that a fine as small as £100 was 'wholly inappropriate for a commercial crime'. The Court of Appeal reduced the fine from £7,500, but still required the defendant company to pay £2,000 per offence.

In addition to the imposition of a fine, a compensation order made under Part VI of the Powers of Criminal Courts Sentencing Act 2000, in favour of a consumer is possible. The compensation order is a potentially valuable device, which offers courts the opportunity of requiring a defendant to pay compensation to a victim independently of any private suit that may be initiated by the latter. Compensation orders are made only in clear and simple cases; where complex legal issues arise they are inappropriate, and a private action should be brought by the victim wishing to obtain compensation. Although compensation orders are particularly suited to cases of assault and property damage, where both the identity of the victim and the quantification of loss suffered are frequently relatively unproblematic, orders have been made in a gradually increasing number of cases arising under consumer protection legislation.

The High Court's decision in *R v Milton Keynes' Magistrates' Court, ex parte Roberts*[98] provides an interesting glimpse into enforcement practice and resulting judicial attitudes. Buckinghamshire trading standards officers investigated suspected violations of the Trade Descriptions Act 1968 and trademark legislation. After searching Roberts' premises, they brought criminal charges. In the background, however, was the Ford Motor Company which was concerned that widespread counterfeiting of its goods was at stake. Ford had requested the trading standards officers to act; Ford had had representatives present at the searches who were able to identify the suspect items; Ford had indemnified the authority for any

---

95   [1973] Crim LR 586.
96   D. Roberts, 'Sentencing under the Trade Descriptions Act' (1991) 8 *Trading Law* 36.
97   [2001] 1 *Cr. App. R.* (s) 78; (2000) 164 J.P. 505.
98   *The Independent* 26 October 1994.

compensation claims that might arise. The applicant submitted that Ford had effectively bought the authority's support in its pursuit of a civil trade mark dispute and that this amounted to an abuse of the process of the court. The application was rejected. Trading standards officers have wide discretion to enlist support for their statutory functions and, in the circumstances, they had not acted improperly.

The prosecution strategy appropriate for the regulatory offence has attracted occasional comment in the appellate courts. The prosecution in *Smedleys Ltd v Breed*[99] related to the discovery of a dead caterpillar in a tin of peas. The intruder was virtually indistinguishable from the peas and was quite harmless. The House of Lords upheld a conviction under food legislation in force at the time, but their Lordships commented on what they saw as the absence of utility in the pursuit of the prosecution in light of the manufacturer's real efforts to avoid committing the offence. In *Wings Ltd v Ellis*[100] Lord Hailsham, in common with other members of the House, explicitly declared that he did not wish to criticise the authorities who had brought the case. However, he added the observation that 'there is room for caution by prosecuting authorities in mounting proceedings against innocent defendants'.[101] Without offering any criticism of these dicta, it is submitted that there is also room for caution by appellate judges in making comments about enforcement practice. Prosecutions for regulatory offences typically form part of a nuanced strategy, attuned to particular sectors and localities, and have implications beyond the specific case at issue. Appellate courts do not see a representative diet of cases.

11.3.5 Informal Enforcement

Section 26 Trade Descriptions Act 1968 and s. 27 Consumer Protection Act 1987 establish that enforcement by local authorities is a duty.[102] However, a duty to enforce is not a duty to prosecute. In practice a great deal of enforcement work is informal; there is typically no desire to adopt a policy of regular prosecution.[103] Many trading standards officers regard prosecution as a last resort, and as ineffective in many instances. Some

---

[99] [1974] AC 839.

[100] Note 8 above and examined at more length in Ch. 8.3.

[101] Note 8 above at 585e.

[102] Chapter 11.3.3 above.

[103] For an important survey, R. Cranston, *Regulating Business – Law and Consumer Agencies* (Macmillan, 1979): the general issues have not altered radically since 1979. See also Cartwright note above, Ch. 7: G. Richardson, 'Strict Liability for Regulatory Crime: the Empirical Research' [1987] Crim LR 295; J. Rowan-Robinson *et al*, 'Crime and Regulation' [1988] Crim LR 211.

would even label over-rigorous prosecution policies as 'unprofessional'. Generalisations are perilous; naturally, attitudes and practices vary across the country and even among individual officers in the same department.

However, the overriding concern is typically to secure the objectives of the statute. If removal from the market is achievable by advice or gentle pressure, then that will commonly be the limits of action taken. Taking formal steps will be more costly and time-consuming – and will be no more effective than if the voluntary co-operation of the trader had been secured. Indeed, officers typically cite a co-operative relationship with 'their' traders as a cornerstone of effective enforcement practice. This would be jeopardised by formal prosecution. So if a trader is genuinely concerned to comply, prosecution will be wasteful. Enforcement in this sense involves a continuing process, not a 'one-shot' prosecution strategy. Prosecution is typically reserved for repeat offenders who exhibit high levels of careless disregard for the law and, a fortiori, for deliberate offenders.[104] The remarkably high number of cases involving 'clocked' cars that litter the law reports reveals much about the perception among trading standards officers of the practices of the second-hand car trade.[105]

In a sense, such practice reveals a *de facto* conversion of the offence into one requiring *mens rea*. Enforcement officers are naturally drawn to distinguish 'real' offenders from the unlucky or the slapdash.[106] However, the formal attachment of strict liability to the regulatory offence strengthens the power of enforcement officers. It permits a flexible approach; it allows guidance to be given with a strong back-up threat of recourse to law in the event of non-co-operation. It allows officers to judge the circumstances of individual cases in assessing how to achieve effective prevention.

The dilution of the practical impact of strict liability caused by the due diligence defence, examined above,[107] deserves attention. Permitting exculpation of traders able to show that responsibility for the mischief lies elsewhere brings with it the risk that the regulatory climate may change

---

[104] Cf. beyond consumer law I. Ayres and J. Braithwaite, *Responsive Regulation: Transcending the Deregulation Debate* (OUP, 1992); B. Hutter, *Regulation and Risk: Occupational Health and Safety on the Railways* (OUP, 2001); K. Hawkins, *Law as last resort: prosecution decision-making in a regulatory agency* (OUP, 2002); K. Hawkins, *Environment and Enforcement* (OUP, 1987); W. Carson, 'White Collar Crime and the Enforcement of Factory Legislation' (1970) 10 *Br J Criminology* 383. For an overview of the issues relevant to enforcement, cf. Ogus note 6 above pp. 89–97; Baldwin and Cave note 6 above Ch. 8.

[105] Chapter 8.2.6.

[106] Cf. similar findings in this vein in relation to the practices of Environmental Health Officers in B. Hutter, *The Reasonable Arm of the Law?* (OUP, 1988).

[107] Chapter 11.2.

because of the defence. Effective enforcement may be deterred. In practice, of course, trading standards officers will relatively rarely pursue a formal prosecution against a trader whom they believe is not blameworthy, whether the due diligence defence is expected to operate or not. The possibility that the defence may be raised in more serious cases, however, may make the enforcement agency pause to consider the value of investing significant resources in pursuing a formal prosecution when the outcome is less certain than it would be in a system of 'pure' strict liability. This is the price paid for including a defence designed to protect the innocent trader.

The recent UK and EC preference for regulation by generally expressed standards has contributed to the interest in avoiding formal proceedings. Under the general duty in Part II of the Consumer Protection Act 1987 or under the General Product Safety Regulations examined in Chapter 10 of this book, the outcome in marginal cases will depend on the court's own reading of safety expectations. The legal standard is imprecise. '[T]he fewer the uncertainties which attach to the law... the stronger is the [enforcement] agency's bargaining position'.[108] The practical result has tended to be the predominance of informal controls, including guidance to traders. Although this may diminish confidence in launching formal prosecutions, the policy of informal enforcement has many benefits for both sides in terms of saved time and money.

Resource constraints are a major factor affecting enforcement practice. Trading standards departments have seen their budgets cut in real terms over recent years. Cheaper practices hold strong attraction, militating against formal action. The provisions permitting compensation to be awarded to the trader play a part in this trend. The pattern of informal enforcement of the regulatory offence seems likely to endure.

---

[108] Richardson note 103 above.

Chapter 12

Competition Policy and the Consumer Interest

12.1 HOW COMPETITION POLICY FALLS WITHIN THE SCOPE OF CONSUMER LAW

12.1.1 Current Trends in Competition Policy as an Instrument of Consumer Protection

In August 2003 the OFT decided that ten businesses had been engaged in a network of agreements on the price that would be charged to consumers for replica football kit in 2000 and 2001. The companies concerned were manufacturers and retailers, and several were household names, including JJB Sports, Umbro, Manchester United, and the English Football Association.[1] Had there been competition between the traders concerned rather than cosy agreements, then prices of shirts ought to have been pushed downwards. This was not just theory. The OFT took the trouble to publicise its findings about trends in the market.[2] In 2000 and 2001, while the parties were in agreement about prices, most retailers charged just under £40 for adult England shirts and just under £30 for juniors. By 2003, when the OFT's inquiry had led to the abandonment of price-fixing and its replacement by market competition, an OFT study found a wide variety of prices for the newly-launched 2003 England shirt, ranging from £24 to £40 for the adult shirt and £18 to £30 for the junior version.

Nothing could more vividly capture the essential point that the vigorous application of laws against anti-competitive practices promotes consumer interests. One may be deeply sceptical that markets always work in the consumer interest. But one should accept that sometimes they do.[3] And laws that punish traders who try to make markets work for their own private gain at the expense of the consumer play a vital role in making the

---

[1] The 'Public Register' of decisions under the Competition Act 1998 is electronically available: see:
http://www.oft.gov.uk/Business/Competition+Act/default.htm.

[2] OFT Press Release, 'Large fines for replica football kit price fixers' PN/107/03, 1 August 2003.

[3] See generally Chapter 1.

best of consumer markets. The traders concerned had infringed the UK's Competition Act 1998 and they were fined a total of £18.6 million.[4]

An argument was made with sustained force in the first edition of this book that competition policy should be treated as an integral element in an effective strategy of consumer protection. We are pleased that the government now agrees. The 1999 White Paper entitled *Modern Markets: Confident Consumers*[5] insists on rooting out impediments to effective competition which flow from malfunctions on the supply-side of the market. Cartels and restrictive practices must be tackled, monopolies controlled, mergers scrutinised for potential anti-competitive implications. This is presented explicitly in the White Paper in terms of the consumer interest. And it forms the subject matter of this chapter.

Competition law has undergone a process of dynamic change in the last decade, both in the UK and in Europe. The first edition of this book, published in 1995, examined a UK regime that was badly out-dated and fundamentally ineffective. The White Paper *Modern Markets: Confident Consumers* accurately dismisses it as a 'soft touch'.[6] It was radically reformed by the Competition Act 1998, of which the football shirt price-fixers fell foul, which largely aligned UK law to the more sophisticated model found at EC level. This was only the Labour government's first step. The Enterprise Act 2002 added elements into UK law which exceed the vigour of the EC's control over anti-competitive practices, most notably the introduction of criminal sanctions for defined offences in the field of competition law. The EC system itself, rooted in Arts. 81 and 82 of the EC Treaty, has recently undergone significant changes at the procedural level. Regulation 1/2003 has adjusted the relationship between the European Commission and national competition courts and agencies in order to achieve a more effective working pattern that will make more efficient use of scarce enforcement resources. As a general observation, this chapter has demanded a great deal more re-writing than some in the preparation of the second edition of this book, but what is now under examination is a much more powerful framework of domestic and European competition law governing the operation of markets than was on offer a decade ago. This should be applauded as having advanced the consumer interest.

---

4   Four of the ten businesses have initiated appeals, two to challenge the finding of price-fixing and two to challenge the level of the fine imposed.

5   Cm 4410 (1999). Available via http://www.dti.gov.uk/consumer/whitepaper and considered more fully in Ch. 1.9.2.3.

6   Section 2.1 White Paper note 5 above.

12.1.2 How Producers and Suppliers may Evade the Invisible Hand

Chapter 1 of this book provides an overview of the theory of how markets could and should operate in order to benefit the consumer interest. The 'invisible hand' of the market system should ensure that producers behave in response to and in fulfilment of consumer preference. Private economic relations organise the market.

It was also noted in Chapter 1 that this model makes a number of assumptions about the market, some of which are unrealistic. Perception of this gap between theory and practice stimulates the debate about the role of law as a means of intervening in the market.

Chapters 3–6 examined aspects of the private law of consumer protection, where the State supplements the market by offering legal protection for the consumer interest. This occurs in respect of both machinery guaranteeing the legal enforceability of standards agreed between the parties and, of broader general importance, the imposition of minimum standards within transactions that apply independently of the consumer's ability to negotiate them. Chapters 7–11 examined the scope of public regulation of the market in the consumer interest. A range of practices are suppressed by law, partly as a result of the perception that the market system, supported by the private law, proves inadequate to yield efficient and/or fair outcomes.

This chapter, as already mentioned above, concentrates on the 'supply side' – on reasons why producers and suppliers may be immunised from the discipline of competition and the need to satisfy the consumer. As a general observation one may suppose that, in the absence of effective competition between producers and suppliers, the consumer interest will be damaged. The 'invisible hand' will be ill-directed where weakness in the competitive process renders the producer and supplier insensitive to consumer wishes.

Competition law is motivated by the objective of improving the functioning of the market as a whole. The consumer on the 'demand-side' should reap the benefits of an efficiently functioning 'supply-side'. Like laws forbidding the supply of unsafe products, competition policy is directed at the suppression of practices on the 'supply-side' that the market system, supported by private law, cannot root out unaided. However, because competition laws are addressed at commercial parties, their analysis has for too long been left out of account by consumer lawyers. Current UK governmental policy and practice challenges that, but it nonetheless remains true that in the main the competition laws of both the UK and the EC do not place an explicit textual emphasis on the consumer interest. Consumer policy is a concealed aspect of competition policy and vice versa!

12.1.3 Markets and their Weaknesses

It is a workable starting point that the consumer is potentially prejudiced by the restricted exposure of producers and suppliers to the full force of the competitive process. The obvious method of enhancing the consumer interest is to remove the muffle on the blast of competition. Thus competition law and policy should be directed at ensuring the market is reshaped into a competitive environment. The restraints which would be removed by such laws could be behavioural or they could be structural. Behavioural restrictions would include cartels agreed by producers and/or suppliers. Structural impediments would include monopolies where the pattern of the market is not competitive, irrespective of the behaviour of firms. The law could be used to prohibit cartels, to forestall the creation of monopolies (for example, by forbidding mergers) or to destroy existing monopolies (for example, by forcing large firms to sell off assets). The law would thus root out inhibitions on free competition.

Accepting that the purpose of this branch of the law is to foster 'perfect' competition is no more than a starting point, however. In some areas the purity of competition will not provide the best of all possible markets for the consumer. Limits on competition may rationally be recognised as desirable in the consumer interest. This compromise is often denoted by the comment that the law seeks 'workable' not 'perfect' competition. Desirable behavioural limitations on competition may include collaboration on research and development, where the pooling of resources may secure more effective research work carried out in common instead of duplication of superficial efforts. Desirable structural limitations may be observed in markets which are inappropriate for competition: 'natural monopolies' illustrate this phenomenon.[7] In these circumstances there is a place for competition law, but its function will not be to insist on competition. Instead, the law may be employed to permit beneficial agreements among firms. This implies a need for legal tests apt to distinguish between desirable and undesirable agreements and for institutions charged with the function of making the appropriate assessments. The law may also be used to acquiesce in monopolies, but to control their more pernicious effects.

In some circumstances the law may even be employed to provide a system which suppresses competition. If unconfined and unconfinable competition were the paramount rule of the market, there would be limited incentive for firms to invest in invention. Any new gadget would be promptly taken up by rivals who had not incurred expense in creating it. Profit would not follow investment. The long-standing response is the development of intellectual property law in the shape of rights such as

---

7   Further, Chapter 12.3.3 below.

copyright and patent. Such rights protect the inventor from competition by 'free-riding' rivals and, by conferring exclusive rights of exploitation, guarantee reward in the shape of profits for the duration of the right. Far from dedicating itself to foster competition, the law thus actually suppresses competition in pursuit of the greater good of innovation. 'Perfect' competition is set aside. Again, a nuanced approach will be needed to shape the detail of the law. For instance, just how long should the period of protection endure?

More generally still, the enhancement of innovation may not simply be regarded as involving the State acting to facilitate private efforts. The State may itself actively promote research and development, perhaps through its own agencies or through subsidy to private industry. The State may develop its own industrial policy, choosing to intervene in areas where the market is perceived to be performing unsatisfactorily. States themselves compete with each other and economic survival may rest on choices made about regulatory strategy.[8]

12.1.4 The Notion of Workable Competition

What emerges from this brief survey is a blend of many different policies and rationales for intervention in the market, ranging far from the notion of perfect competition. It is not simply doubtful whether perfect competition is attainable. More fundamentally, it is doubtful whether its pursuit is desirable. As already mentioned, this drift is frequently encapsulated in the phrase workable competition, a rather vague and flexible notion which accommodates a wide range of theory and practice in assessing the operation of markets. The phrase respects that variety; just because competition is not perfect need not mean that it is imperfect in any pejorative sense. The pursuit of the compromise of workable competition is entirely rational as a policy objective. Not all departures from the model of the perfect market can be corrected; not all should be. Competition is part of the structure of the economy, but its pursuit is not an objective which suppresses all other considerations. Accordingly, competition law and policy comprise a nuanced patchwork of intervention.[9]

---

[8] Cf. the influential work of M. Porter, *The Competitive Advantage of Nations* (Macmillan, 1998).

[9] The leading work on competition law and policy in the EC and UK is R. Whish, *Competition Law* (Butterworths, 2003). See also B. Rodger and A. MacCulloch, *Competition Law and Policy in the EC and UK* (Cavendish, 2001). Overview articles by influential figures which deserve attention despite their age include G. Borrie, 'The Regulation of Public and Private Power' [1989] *Public Law* 552 (the author was the Director-General of Fair Trading when he wrote the piece); C-D. Ehlermann, 'The

12.1.5 Defining Markets and Regulatory Authorities

The process of internationalisation of markets is not a recent phenomenon. Venice was the world's most powerful trading centre in the 13th-century; the British Empire was economically dominant six hundred years later. For the UK market integration has accelerated since joining the European Community at the start of 1973, a process that has intensified further following the completion of the internal market at the start of 1993.[10] The internal market is defined in the EC Treaty as 'an area without internal frontiers'.[11] It is designed to create conditions within which traders may treat the territory of the Community as a single marketplace. Such liberalisation should enhance competition, leading to those improvements in quality and reductions in price which in economic theory are associated with competitive markets. Consumers stand to gain from this process. From this perspective, national frontiers have in the past served as artificial impediments to the competitive process, now swept away on a tide of economic regeneration.

This process of economic integration has two major consequences for competition law in the UK. The first is that, as a system for the regulation of the market, it must be applied with an awareness that that market no longer stops at the frontiers of the country. The British market is not isolated behind national borders and the pattern of its regulation must be adjusted accordingly. The second consequence is that transnational agencies concerned to regulate the wider market have an impact on the UK. This invites consideration of, most prominently, the institutions of the European Union. The combination of these two influences dictates that appreciation of the sources of economic law in the UK, including the law of consumer protection, demands a broad focus. For competition law in particular this lesson has a vivid practical edge. Until the reforms instituted by the Labour government that came to power in 1997 there was a sharp divergence between the structure of UK competition law and its EC counterpart. The need to comply with two distinct regimes was costly for business and the problem was worsened by the general acceptance that the UK rules exerted a much weaker control over damaging anti-competitive practices than those applied from Brussels. This, in the view of the government, was bad for the economy and bad for the consumer.[12] The Competition Act 1998 was designed to bring UK law into broad alignment

---

Contribution of EC Competition Policy to the Single Market' (1992) 29 *CMLRev* 257 (author an influential official in Directorate-General IV [Competition] in the EC Commission).

10   Chapter 2.

11   Article 14 EC, formerly Art. 7a EC, and before that Art. 8a EEC.

12   White Paper note 5 above.

with EC law.[13] Although it did not do this in every detailed respect,[14] it is generally true to say that UK and EC competition law are today similarly motivated, similarly structured and will commonly produce similar outcomes. In fact, most domestic competition law systems in Europe today conform to the EC's model.[15] UK competition law has been brought out of its backwater into the European mainstream and at last it has become a force to be reckoned with in the attack on anti-competitive practices. Moreover, the elimination of the deep differences between domestic and EC competition law has reduced compliance costs imposed on business. Another winner is the law student. No longer does he or she have to grapple with the oddities of the old UK law as well as the quite differently shaped EC rules. Once the structure of EC law is grasped that know-how can be transplanted to UK law, which is very close to the EC law model in most respects. That structure is followed in this chapter: in relation to cartels, then monopolies and then mergers, the EC rules are set out first, and then the pattern of UK law is described against that background, drawing attention to the relatively small number of points on which the UK has chosen to take a different path from the EC.

12.2 CARTELS

12.2.1 Cartels and Economic Freedom

The theory of free and competitive markets tells us that consumer choice follows from rivalry among producers. Yet producers may prefer collusion to competition. As the example of replica football shirts reveals,[16] instead of trying to undercut each other's prices in order to increase sales, they may prefer to arrange a common selling price. This will make life altogether more comfortable for producers, but at a cost to the consumer: price competition will be suppressed. Such cartels appear antagonistic to the fundamental notion of the competitive market.

Legal intervention may be justified as a method of correcting the imperfection introduced by producer collusion. Producers must be free to

---

13   For a survey of the evolution of the debate, culminating in the 1998 Act, see R Whish, 'The Competition Act 1998 and the prior debate on reform', Ch. 1 in B. Rodger and A. MacCulloch, *The UK Competition Act* (Hart Publishing, 2000); D. Parker, 'The Competition Act 1998: Change and Continuity in UK Competition Policy' [2000] *JBL* 283.

14   See Chapter 12.2.4.3 below.

15   See G. Dannecker and O. Jansen (eds.), *Competition Law Sanctioning in the European Union* (Kluwer Law International, 2004).

16   Note 1 above.

compete, but they are not free under the law to surrender that freedom. The regulatory authority charged with the supervisory task must therefore devise a legal response to the damaging effects of cartels on free competition.

Suspicion of anticompetitive collusion has a lengthy pedigree. Legal control in several manifestations can be traced back several centuries. For example, the English common law doctrine of restraint of trade can be found in the 15th-century.[17] Public policy dictates that contracts in restraint of trade are not enforceable. The doctrine is flexible in scope and application, which to some extent renders it worryingly unpredictable. However, for all the recent increase in statutory control of restrictive practices, the doctrine is still a feature of English law and retains some modern significance.[18]

In the United States, the appreciation of the need for legislative control over anti-competitive practices came at an early stage in that country's remarkable acceleration in industrialisation. The Sherman Act of 1890 remains today a major plank of what is referred to in North America as 'antitrust law'. The deep belief in the potentially pernicious effect of co-ordination of conduct among producers is vividly portrayed in the following dictum from the decision of the Supreme Court in *United States v Topco Associates*:

> Antitrust laws in general... are the Magna Carta of free enterprise. They are as important to the preservation of economic freedom and our free-enterprise system as the Bill of Rights is to the protection of our fundamental personal freedoms.[19]

Such observations locate economic law and the pursuit of free markets in the sphere of discourse about democracy and the defence of individual rights. The linkage of the consumer in the economic sphere with the citizen in the political sphere is an aspect of the law which is examined further elsewhere in this book.[20]

In Europe competition law and policy have always held a high profile as part of the process of market integration and regulation. The first of the European Communities, the European Coal and Steel Community established in 1952 by the Treaty of Paris, included competition policy

---

[17]   The 'Dyer's Case' of 1414. See J.D. Heydon, *The Restraint of Trade Doctrine* (Butterworths, 1971); M. Trebilcock, *The Common Law of Restraint of Trade* (Carswell/Sweet and Maxwell, 1986).

[18]   Cf. discussion of *Schroeder v Macaulay* [1974] 3 All ER 616 and *Panayiotou* (better known as George Michael) *v Sony Ltd* in Ch. 1.3.6.

[19]   405 US 596 (1972) (Marshall J).

[20]   See especially Chapter 1.

provisions. The European Economic Community came into existence in 1958 as the creation of the Treaty of Rome and was of much broader scope than the Coal and Steel Community. That Treaty also included a chapter entitled 'Rules on Competition', comprising three sections, 'Rules applying to Undertakings', 'Dumping' and 'Aids Granted by States'. Enforcement powers were conferred on the Commission by Regulation. Some of the common policies of the Community emerged slowly over the later part of the 20th-century, with heavy reliance on the laborious development of secondary legislation; this is true of social policy and it is true of much of consumer policy.[21] In sharp contrast, however, the fundamental principles of competition policy have always been firmly embedded in the very fabric of the Treaty. The main pillars are Arts. 81 and 82 of the EC Treaty (ex 85 and 86),[22] governing cartels and monopolies respectively. The competition rules act as a cornerstone of the activities of the EU, prominent among which remain the establishment of 'a system ensuring that competition in the internal market is not distorted'.[23] The EC has gone so far as to describe Art. 81 EC as 'a fundamental provision which is essential for the accomplishment of the tasks entrusted to the Community and, in particular, for the functioning of the internal market'.[24]

12.2.2 Shaping a Legal Response to Cartels

As explained, for the consumer interest to be best served, legal supervision of cartels must be nuanced. In making an assessment of the appropriate scope of control over collaboration, it is helpful to distinguish horizontal from vertical agreements. Horizontal agreements are those concluded between parties at the same stage of the production or distribution process, for example, between two or more manufacturers or between two or more retailers. It is precisely these parties who, according to theory, should be competing against each other on price and quality in order to maximise consumer benefit. Accordingly the law generally tends to be hostile to horizontal agreements. Vertical deals tend to be far less pernicious and will often be ostensibly in the consumer interest. If manufacturer A agrees to supply retailer B, then a new outlet has been opened up and choice has been enhanced. Vertical agreements serve to create distribution chains, at

---

[21] See Chapter 2.

[22] Re-numbering is the result of the Treaty of Amsterdam, effective from 1999. See Chapter 2.1.4.

[23] Article 3(g) EC.

[24] Case C–126/97 *Eco Swiss China Time Ltd v Benetton International NV* [1999] ECR I–3055.

the end of which lies the expectant consumer. Even where the deal involves an exclusive arrangement between manufacturer and retailer, the consumer interest may stand to benefit. Suppose that a supplier agrees to provide ice-cream to a retailer and provides a freezer for the shop in which those ice-creams may be displayed. There is no obvious reason for legal intervention: goods are available and the consumer has a wider choice. Suppose, additionally, that the supplier imposes an obligation that only its brand of ice-creams are to be sold by the retailer, either from that freezer or even from that shop. The arrangement benefits the supplier by removing competitors from point of supply. In some respects the arrangement benefits the retailer who is able to concentrate streamlined efforts on one brand only. However, one might initially suppose that there is a rationale for intervention in such a practice, drawn from the reduction in choice to the consumer. Yet this need not be so. If there are plenty of other shops in which other brands are available, choice is maintained. Even if all the competing suppliers of ice-cream set up separate exclusive arrangements with their own tied retailers, there is no significant damage to competition where there are numerous suppliers and numerous shops. Competition to buy up retailers will develop. Consumer choice will be sustained.[25]

One might go so far as to argue that even price-fixing arrangements applied vertically, between manufacturer and retailer, do not call for legal control provided the market is competitive and consumers remain free to choose between different brands, the suppliers of which are not in collusion. One cannot be dogmatic in distinguishing between vertical and horizontal deals; each requires careful assessment against the background of the market in which they operate. However, as a framework for analysis it is useful to be aware that horizontal agreements may rationally generate more rigorous scrutiny than vertical agreements.

Such critiques require further investigation against the background of specific competition law regimes. This is provided below. However, observation regarding the function of competition and competition law should sharpen awareness of the intensely political nature of debate about legal intervention in markets. The more faith one has in markets, the more sceptical one will be about the need for and desirability of legal intervention.[26] The 'Chicago School' in the US has exerted much influence in recent decades in its preference for allowing markets to organise themselves, with a concomitant insistence that the application of antitrust

---

25   The ice-cream supply sector has attracted the interest of both EC and UK competition
      authorities; at EC level see e.g. Case T–65/98 *Van den Bergh Foods v Commission*
      [2003] ECR II–(not yet reported); in the UK, Competition Commission report on the
      Supply of Impulse Ice-Cream, Cm 4510 (2000), leading to undertakings as to future
      conduct by several major suppliers.

26   At length, Ch. 1, esp. 1.8 and 1.9.

law be reined in. It is in the Chicago School that one finds analysis which would leave even vertical price fixing outwith the range of legal prohibition.[27] That prescription has not been accepted by the courts in the US although other elements of Chicago analysis have affected the development of antitrust law.[28] In Europe and in the UK, policy remains noticeably less affected by such thinking. The functioning of unsupervised markets is viewed with rather less equanimity than in some North American quarters. For Europe, it should also be borne in mind that competition policy operates to regulate a market which is not integrated after the fashion of a national market. This lends to it a special, interventionist flavour not found in a national system.[29] This perspective is by no means exhausted. The enlargement of the EU, which has occurred in a series of steps over recent years, has tended to re-invigorate the importance of market integration as a characteristic guiding principle within the shaping of competition policy for Europe.

12.2.3 European Community Law of Cartels and Restrictive Practices

12.2.3.1 Consumer Choice in EC Trade Law

Consumer choice has played an important, though typically inexplicit, part in interpreting the application of the EC's competition rules. On occasion, however, the consumer interest in competitive markets has surfaced in explicit fashion. In *Co-operative vereniging Suiker Unie UA and others v Commission*[30] arrangements which led to the isolation of national markets from cross-border competition were condemned. The Court ruled such practices to be 'to the detriment of effective freedom of movement of the products in the common market and of the freedom of consumers to choose their suppliers'.[31] In *Zuchner v Bayerische Vereinsbank AG*,[32] concerning the market for banking services, the Court commented that Art. 81 (ex 85)

---

27   E.g. R. Bork, *'The Antitrust Paradox – a Policy at War with Itself'* (Basic Books, 1978).
28   For a flavour of the often ferocious debate, cf. R. Pitofsky, 'New Definitions of Relevant Market and the Assault on Antitrust' (1990) 90 *Columbia LR* 1806; A. Page, 'Ideological Conflict and the Origins of Antitrust Policy' (1991) 66 *Tulane Law Review* 1.
29   See especially Ehlermann note 9 above; also A. Albors-Llorens, 'Competition Policy and the shaping of the Single Market', Ch. 12 in C. Barnard and J. Scott (eds.), *The Law of the Single European Market* (Hart Publishing, 2002).
30   Cases 40–48, 50, 54–56, 111, 113 and 114/73 [1975] ECR 1663.
31   Paragraph 191 of the judgment.
32   Case 172/80 [1981] ECR 2021.

may apply where firms have abandoned their independence in favour of unlawful collusion which suppresses competition, '... thus depriving their customers of any genuine opportunity to take advantage of services on more favourable terms which would be offered to them under normal conditions of competition'.

Such statements are important because they locate competition policy in the general framework of European Community trade law which is designed to achieve an area in which national frontiers lose their economic relevance and in which consumer choice is broadened.[33] EC trade law controls State measures which fragment the European market along national lines; through competition rules, it also controls private measures which exert a similar effect. Most of the time, however, the virtue of EC competition law as a tool of consumer policy is left inexplicit. This is a poor reason to ignore or even underestimate its effect, and its influence will surface periodically in this book outside the confines of this chapter. For example, the enforcement of guarantees across a distribution network is promoted in a consumer-friendly manner by the requirements of Art. 81.[34]

12.2.3.2 The Pattern of Article 81 (ex 85) EC

EC restrictive practices law is based on the overall perception that supply side collaboration carries the potential to damage the operation of the market and, ultimately and typically inexplicitly, the consumer interest. Such practices are to be controlled, but with scope left for showing justification for beneficial collaboration.

Article 81 (ex 85) is the relevant provision of EC law, which reads as follows:

1. The following shall be prohibited as incompatible with the common market: all agreements between undertakings, decisions by associations of undertakings and concerted practices which may affect trade between Member States and which have as their object or effect the prevention, restriction or distortion of competition within the common market, and in particular those which:

     (a) directly or indirectly fix purchase or selling prices or any other trading conditions;

     (b) limit or control production, markets, technical development, or investment;

---

33   Chapter 2.

34   Chapter 3.3; see in particular Case C–376/98 *Metro ZSB-Grossmärkte GmbH and Co KG v Cartier SA* [1994] ECR I–15.

    (c)   share markets or sources of supply;

    (d)   apply dissimilar conditions to equivalent transactions with other trading parties, thereby placing them at a competitive disadvantage;

    (e)   make the conclusion of contracts subject to acceptance by the other parties of supplementary obligations which, by their nature or according to commercial usage, have no connection with the subject of such contracts.

2.   Any agreements or decisions prohibited pursuant to this Article shall be automatically void.

3.   The provisions of paragraph 1 may, however, be declared inapplicable in the case of any agreement or category of agreements between undertakings;

–   any decision or category of decisions by associations of undertakings;

–   any concerted practice or category of concerted practices;

–   which contributes to improving the production or distribution of goods or to promoting technical or economic progress, while allowing consumers a fair share of the resulting benefit, and which does not:

    (a)   impose on the undertakings concerned restrictions which are not indispensable to the attainment of these objectives;

    (b)   afford such undertakings the possibility of eliminating competition in respect of a substantial part of the products in question.

Article 81(1) contains the basic prohibition. The application of Art. 81(1) is based on the effects of an agreement. It does not matter what form the collaboration takes provided it has an effect which distorts trade (to summarise Art. 81(1)). Article 81(2) contains the sanction for violation of the prohibition, namely the nullity of the agreement (though, as mentioned below, the perpetrators may also be fined). Article 81(3) sets out the criteria for exemption of an agreement falling within Art. 81(1). It is here that the insight that not all collaboration is harmful is reflected. Article 81(3) is more precisely drafted than a simple cost/benefit analysis, but its broad purpose is to permit the pursuit of agreements that, though restrictive of competition, are nevertheless beneficial. In practice, since the application of Art. 81(3) solely through individualised decisions would be inefficient, the Commission has long found it prudent to issue Block Exemption Regulations. These govern particular categories of collaboration such as research and development[35] as well as providing a more general shelter for vertical agreements (between traders at different

---

[35]   Regulation 2659/2000 OJ 2000 L304/7.

levels in the distribution chain).[36] The content of the Block Exemptions is drawn from Art. 81(3); in relation to particular deals, they constitute the concrete clause-by-clause expression of the abstract requirements of the criteria for exemption in that Article.[37] Strictly, there is no obligation to adhere to a Block Exemption Regulation: firms may draft a novel agreement and seek to show it falls within Art. 81(3). However in practical terms, it is normal to choose the convenient route of compliance with the Block Exemption.

12.2.3.3 The Institutional Support for Article 81

At the institutional level within the EU, the administrative application of the prohibition on anticompetitive agreements affecting trade between Member States contained in Art. 81 rests with the European Commission, specifically with the Competition Directorate-General within the Commission. A supervisory jurisdiction is exercised, initially, by the Court of First Instance, with the possibility of an appeal to the European Court of Justice. The involvement of national bodies is also central to the practical administration of the rules. Both national courts and national competition authorities have responsibilities to apply the EC competition rules.

All three paragraphs of Art. 81 are susceptible to enforcement by both the Commission and national agencies. This has not always been so. Outside the sphere of Block Exemptions it used to be the case that the Commission enjoyed the exclusive right to decide whether or not to grant an exemption pursuant to Art. 81(3). This meant that commercial parties were required to notify practices to the Commission in search of the protection of exemption. This was burdensome for all concerned. It made a bottleneck of the Commission. It was changed by Regulation 1/2003.[38] Exemption is no longer dependent on a Commission decision. Firms do not notify agreements to the Commission in the hope of securing exemption. Instead they make their own assessment of what is allowed and what is not. Mistaken choices are tackled *ex post facto*, by an investigation initiated by the Commission and/or in proceedings before national courts or tribunals who, thanks to Regulation 1/2003, are equipped with the competence to apply Art. 81(3) which was denied them for the first 40 years of the lifetime of EC competition law. This system decentralises the application of EC competition law, and increases the number of responsible authorities.

---

[36] Regulation 2790/1999 OJ 1999 L336/21.
[37] For a detailed examination, see Whish note 9 above pp. 168–174, Chs. 15 and 16.
[38] OJ 2003 L1/1.

The Commission's main preoccupation in devising the modernised system of decentralised enforcement recently instituted by Regulation 1/2003 has been to improve efficient use of enforcement resources. Exemption is no longer its task alone. It is able to rely on national agencies to judge whether the Art. 81(3) criteria are satisfied. This allows the Commission to re-allocate the resources it previously spent on dealing with notification of practices by firms in search of exemption. These resources will be re-routed to the front-line of the attack on hard-core hidden cartels. Such cartels are particularly damaging to the consumer interest, and Commission successes in suppressing such practices will be beneficial to the consumer. Therefore, from the consumer perspective, much depends on the results achieved in practice under the regime introduced by Regulation 1/2003.[39] The Competition Directorate-General in the Commission is powerfully equipped to pursue this quest. Powers conferred initially by Regulation 17/62,[40] but now extended by and rooted in Regulation 1/2003, include powers to enter and to search premises and to seize documentation. Failure to co-operate may attract financial penalties which are independent of sanctions that may be imposed should a violation of the substantive rules come to light. The Commission also rules on whether a violation of Art. 81 has occurred and is empowered to impose fines on the participants up to a ceiling of ten per cent of the firm's world wide turnover. That has exceeded £50 million on occasion. The principle of proportionality ensures that most fines are much less severe, but the availability of such investigative powers combined with potential penalties of such magnitude mean that taking EC competition law lightly is not a practical option for business.

The principle of the direct effect of EC law has always meant that enforcement may be achieved through national courts in addition to activity by the Commission. This is blandly recited in Regulation 1/2003 which provides in Art. 6 that 'National courts shall have the power to apply Arts. 81 and 82 of the Treaty'. In principle the victim of a cartel incompatible with EC law could initiate proceedings at national level to secure an order that the practice should terminate. As a matter of Community law national courts must effectively protect Community law rights.[41] The landmark ruling in *Francovich v Italian State*[42] established that in appropriate circumstances this may include an obligation to order compensation in the event of loss suffered as a result of breach of EC law.

---

39 H. Gilliams, 'Modernisation: from policy to practice' (2003) 28 *ELRev* 451; J.S. Venit, 'Brave new world: The modernization and decentralization of enforcement under Articles 81 and 82 of the EC Treaty' (2003) 40 *CMLRev* 545.

40 1959–62 OJ Sp. Ed.

41 The source of this obligation is Art. 10 EC. See further Ch. 2.4.

42 Cases C–6, C–9/90 [1991] ECR I–5357, further examined in Ch. 2.4.2.

The case concerned liability incurred by the State. In *Courage v Crehan*[43] the EC applied this principle in the sphere of competition law in a case involving two private parties. It observed that the practical enforcement of Art. 81 would be promoted if it were accepted that an individual could claim damages for loss caused to him by a contract or by conduct liable to restrict or distort competition. The desire to maintain effective competition therefore prompted the Court to rule as a matter of EC law in favour of private actions for damages before national courts in the event of infringement of the Treaty competition rules.[44]

An action at national level may be initiated in parallel with a complaint to the Commission.[45] As part of that package the Commission has developed a policy of pursuing complaints only where there is a Community interest in doing so, leaving other matters to be pursued by the complainant at national level. This attempt to organise enforcement priorities and to promote decentralisation has secured judicial support.[46] The Commission is eager to rely ever more heavily on national-level enforcement.

Private enforcement of EC competition law before national courts is accordingly a practical feature of the system and although it used to be flawed by the inability of national courts to apply Art. 81(3), that obstacle was lifted by Regulation 1/2003. National courts are now expected to apply Art. 81 in its entirety. In this sense the ordinary courts of the Member States are also courts responsible for the application of EC competition law.

As explained, Regulation 1/2003 was directed at 'decentralising' enforcement of EC competition law, thereby to improve its effectiveness. Not only national courts but also national competition authorities are intended to form part of this scheme. National competition authorities are also enabled to apply Art. 81 in its entirety. In the UK this will be the province of the OFT.

The point of the pattern of enforcement crafted under Regulation 1/2003 is that it will be tough for firms to hide anti-competitive practices. There are many pairs of enforcement eyes and many places to challenge unlawful conduct. A solution had to be found for the risk of duplication of

---

43   Case C–453/99 [2001] ECR I–6297.

44   Cf. A. Komninos, 'New prospects for private enforcement of EC competition law' (2002) 39 *CMLRev* 457; G. Monti, 'Anticompetitive agreements: the innocent party's right to damages' (2002) 27 *ELRev* 282; and, more generally, C. Jones, *Private Enforcement of Antitrust Law in the EU, UK and USA* (OUP, 1999).

45   Article 7(2), Regulation 1/2003 confers standing for these purposes on 'natural or legal persons who can show a legitimate interest'. See Chapter 12.2.3.5 below on consumer complaints.

46   Case T–24/90 *Automec v Commission* [1992] ECR II–2223.

effort – or, worse, the risk that an agency in one Member State may go one way in enforcing the law, an agency elsewhere a different way and the Commission in a different direction again. The Commission, aware of these risks, has begun to establish a network of co-operation between responsible bodies pursuant to Chapter IV of Regulation 1/2003. It is also explicitly provided that where the Commission initiates proceedings this shall 'relieve the competition authorities of the Member States of their competence to apply Arts. 81 and 82'.[47] Moreover it is explicitly – and logically – stated that neither national courts nor competition authorities may take decisions which would run counter to a decision already adopted by the Commission.[48]

12.2.3.4 The Consumer Interest

In the application of the competition rules, the interest of the consumer normally remains inexplicit. Article 81 benefits the consumer in the broad sense that it forms part of the machinery for establishing the common market. A naked market-sharing agreement would violate Art. 81; it would suppress competition and consumer choice. A naked price-fixing cartel would act contrary to the consumer interest for similar reasons and would be incompatible with Art. 81. In this sense, consumers are envisaged as the ultimate beneficiaries of the application of the competition rules, as they are supposed to enjoy the fruits of the realisation of the internal market.[49]

However, in Art. 81(3) the consumer interest is explicitly injected into the structure of Community competition policy-making. Under Art. 81(3), an agreement may not be exempted from the prohibition in the first paragraph of Art. 81 unless it, *inter alia*, 'contributes to improving the production of goods or to promoting technical or economic progress, while allowing consumers a fair share of the resulting benefit...'. This requirement of consumer benefit must be satisfied as a precondition to a successful application to the Commission for individual exemption. The Block Exemption Regulations, which amount to formalised applications of the Art. 81(3) criteria to particular types of deal, also enshrine the consumer benefit requirement.

A textual point should be taken about the notion of 'consumer' under Art. 81(3). It does not simply refer to the end user, which is the normal connotation in English law. The choice in the French text of the word 'utilisateur' shows that any user is envisaged, not simply the ultimate consumer (which would normally be rendered as 'consommateur').

---

[47] Article 11(6), Regulation 1/2003.
[48] Article 16, Regulation 1/2003.
[49] Chapter 2.

In formal exemption decisions which approve a practice, the Commission is always obliged to provide an explanation of how it considers that the 'consumer benefit' criterion is satisfied. However, it is common for the Commission to identify an adequate consumer benefit in the economic advantages which flow from collaboration. Only infrequently is the requirement of consumer benefit given any sharp separate identity from the insistence in Art. 81(3) that the practice shall contribute to 'improving the production or distribution of goods or to promoting technical or economic progress'.

Typical is the exemption of the agreement between SOPELEM, a French company, and Rank, an English company.[50] The firms planned to collaborate on research and development, manufacture and distribution in the field of camera lenses. The Commission found that the agreement increased the range of products available to the consumer and that quality of both product and service was enhanced. It also came to the conclusion that these benefits would be maintained by virtue of the existence of efficient competition in the market. This was enough to cross the consumer benefit threshold. The Commission commonly seems prepared to assume that provided an agreement promotes efficient commercial structures and provided a sufficient level of competition endures, then the consumer will benefit in consequence.

One would not expect market sharing or price fixing to benefit the consumer and therefore such agreements should not be capable of exemption. They would, however, fail to satisfy other criteria under Art. 81(3), not simply that pertaining to consumer benefit.

In December 2003 the Commission announced an appointment to a new post which is designed to raise the profile of the consumer interest within the discharge of its task to administer the Treaty competition rules.[51] A 'Consumer Liaison Officer' will have the task of making active links between the Competition Directorate-General and consumer organisations at national and European level as well as between the Competition Directorate-General and other Directorates-General, most notably that dealing with Health and Consumer Protection. It remains to be seen whether this will inject a fresh and vigorous commitment to the consumer interest into competition policy-making. The appointee, Juan Riviere y Marti, has been a full-time official within the Competition Directorate-General since 1989 so at least on the surface this has the appearance of 'business as usual'.

---

50   Decision 75/76 OJ 1975 L29/20, [1975] 1 CMLR D72.
51   IP/03/1679, 9 December 2003.

12.2.3.5 Enforcement by Consumers

In theory, the consumer is able to enforce the EC competition rules as readily as any commercial party. The consumer may complain to the Commission and seek to persuade it to initiate an investigation.[52] The consumer can also rely on the direct effect of Art. 81 to challenge unlawful practices at national level.

As a practical matter, the obstacles to consumer access to justice are notorious.[53] The likelihood of a consumer making effective use of national courts or tribunals to challenge a cartel is slim. The institutional support of the Commission is potentially an important means of promoting the consumer interest in controlling anticompetitive practices; indeed, there are examples of consumer complaints acting as a spur to a Commission inquiry. In *Kawasaki*[54] a Commission inquiry prompted by the representations of a frustrated Belgian consumer led to a finding that an arrangement which prevented exportation of motorcycles to Belgium from Britain, where prices were relatively low, violated Art. 81.

However the Commission prioritises cases with a Community interest.[55] Where the Commission chooses not to act, it is up to the consumer to pursue the matter at national level, which is often rather unlikely in practice. However, the Court of First Instance's concern to provide support for the consumer interest in effective enforcement, at least where pursued collectively, is manifested in *BEUC v Commission*.[56] In that case BEUC, a consumer representative organisation (Bureau Européen des Unions de Consommateurs), had seen its complaint about the car market rejected by the Commission. The Court of First Instance reviewed the rejection decision, found it inadequately reasoned and annulled it. At the very least this demonstrates that the Commission is obliged to take consumer complaints seriously and to provide a response even though, ultimately, a principled and properly reasoned decision to take the matter no further is valid.[57] The Commission cannot be forced by a complainant to adopt a final decision on the lawfulness of the practice itself.[58]

Consumer groups may be permitted to intervene in proceedings before the Court in support of one of the parties.[59] In *Ford Werke AG and Ford of*

---

[52] Note 51 above.

[53] Chapter 14.

[54] Decision 79/68 OJ 1979 L16/9, [1979] 1 CMLR 448.

[55] 12.2.3.3 above.

[56] Case T–37/92 [1994] ECR II–285, welcomed from the consumer perspective by M. Goyens, 'A Key Ruling from the ECJ' (1994) 4 *Consumer Policy Review* 221.

[57] Cf. Case T–24/90 *Automec* note 46 above.

[58] Case 125/78 *GEMA v Commission* [1979] ECR 3173.

[59] Article 37 of the Protocol on the Statute of the Court of Justice.

Europe Inc v Commission[60] the President of the Court upheld the right of BEUC to intervene at the oral stage in support of the Commission's case. BEUC had complained to the Commission about Ford's practices, which involved suppression of imports into the UK. Naturally, the costs of intervention will dissuade frequent use being made of this possibility.

12.2.4 United Kingdom Law of Cartels and Restrictive Practices

12.2.4.1 Changing the Picture

In the UK, cartels and restrictive practices have been the subject of legal supervision since 1956, the year which saw the enactment of the first Restrictive Trade Practices Act. This was superseded by the Restrictive Trade Practices Act 1976. However, the whole framework of the law was radically overhauled by the Competition Act 1998. This consigned the Restrictive Trade Practices Act to history as an ineffective control, based on rigid legal rules instead of economic assessment and, moreover, barren of effective sanctions against cartels damaging to the economy in general and the consumer interest in particular. Sir Gordon Borrie, a former Director-General of Fair Trading, famously lamented that under that Act he had to 'fight cartels with one hand tied behind my back'.[61] For those with an interest in history the detail of the Restrictive Trade Practices Act is presented in the first edition of this book.[62] But it is not a pretty sight.

The core of the reform introduced by the Competition Act 1998 is the alignment of UK competition law with its EC counterpart. So for the purposes of controlling restrictive practices the model of Art. 81 is now found replicated in Chapter I of the Competition Act 1998. Sections 2(1)–(3) CA 1998 are textually similar to Art. 81(1) EC, although the prohibition applies only to practices that are, or are intended to be, implemented in the UK. Section 2(4) CA 1998 echoes Art. 81(2) EC. Section 4 CA 1998 and, setting out the relevant criteria, s. 9 CA 1998 deal with exemption in a manner that largely corresponds to Art. 81(3) EC. Collectively this has come to be termed the 'Chapter I prohibition', following s. 2(8) of the Act. It means that restrictive practices and cartels are treated in much the same way under UK law as they are under Art. 81 EC.

At EC level Block Exemptions are of great practical significance to commercial parties wishing to secure a reliable basis for navigating the

---

[60] Case 229 and 228/82R [1982] ECR 3091.
[61] (1988–89) HC 440 p. 19.
[62] First edition, Ch. 15.2.3.

pathway to legality.[63] This device has also been adopted under the UK system. Section 6 provides for a power to create Block Exemptions. Moreover, an explicit link between exemption under UK and under EC competition law is made by s. 10 of the CA 1998 which provides for a system of 'parallel exemption' whereby an agreement is treated under UK law as exempt from the prohibition in Chapter I CA 1998 if it is exempt at EC level from the prohibition contained in Art. 81(1) EC. Schedule 4 allowed for the exclusion of certain rules of professional bodies from the scope of the Chapter I prohibition, but this concession was repealed by the Enterprise Act 2002, with the result that the value to the consumer of such arrangements may fall to be assessed in a Chapter I investigation.[64]

The desire to secure faithful congruence between the application of the Competition Act 1998 and EC practice is reflected in s. 60. This provides that so far as is possible (having regard to any relevant differences between the provisions concerned), questions arising under the Act in relation to competition within the United Kingdom shall be 'dealt with in a manner which is consistent with the treatment of corresponding questions arising in Community law in relation to competition within the Community'. The obligation is imposed on courts in the UK and also on the OFT. It requires a search for consistency with 'the principles laid down by the Treaty and the EC, and any relevant decision of that Court, as applicable at that time in determining any corresponding question arising in Community law'; and also, less powerfully, courts and the OFT 'must, in addition, have regard to any relevant decision or statement of the [European] Commission'. Section 60, acting as a bridge voluntarily built by the UK between domestic matters and the path taken by the institutions of the EU, demonstrates the determination to minimise costs for business by making it unlikely that EC and UK competition law will make different regulatory demands. More is needed, of course. There is a risk that if EC practice changes, the UK may be left behind, and s. 60 will not suffice to deal with the gulf if the UK rules are locked into a statutory form which judges and competition officials cannot re-mould. Section 209 of the Enterprise Act 2002 adds to the policy of convergence. It permits the Minister to make regulations to modify the 1998 Act 'as he considers appropriate for the purpose of eliminating or reducing any differences between... the domestic provisions of the 1998 Act, and... European Community competition law, which result (or would otherwise result) from a relevant Community instrument made after the passing of this Act'.

---

63 See Chapter 12.2.3.2 above.
64 Chapter 1.8.2.3.

12.2.4.2 Enforcement of the Chapter I Prohibition

Enforcement is placed in the hands of the OFT. In fact, the 1998 Act refers throughout to the Director-General of Fair Trading in this context, but that office was abolished by the Enterprise Act 2002 and accordingly all references to the Director-General are today correctly read as referring to the OFT. Pursuant to s. 52 CA 1998 the OFT has issued a large quantity of guidelines designed to provide practical information elucidating how the system is applied. These may be inspected on the OFT's website;[65] they cover *inter alia* the Chapter I prohibition, the Chapter II prohibition (considered below), powers of investigation and enforcement. The consistent theme is cross-reference to EC practice. Close alignment is envisaged. The OFT, therefore, serves as the main focus of competition law enforcement in the UK, although the Act also empowers a number of sectoral regulators with responsibilities in specific areas.

The OFT is endowed with statutory powers which have much in common with those conferred on the European Commission by Regulation 1/2003. They are set out in Chapter III of the CA 1998.[66] They relate to investigation of suspected infringements of the prohibition contained in Chapters I and II as well as the power of formal decision on the existence of an infringement and the imposition of fines. A penalty shall not exceed ten per cent of the UK turnover of the undertaking, according to s. 36(8) of the 1998 Act. Guidelines have been issued by the OFT designed to elucidate the basis on which the scale of fines will be calculated.[67] These take into account, amongst other things, the gravity of the infringement, the need for deterrence and the turnover and degree of involvement of the parties concerned. They also offer leniency to firms that comply at an early stage. This device, also employed by the European Commission, is helpful in inducing 'whistle-blowing' from within, which is often the only way to crack really serious cartels. The first fine for violation of Chapter I was imposed in 2002 on *Arriva and First Group*[68] for market-sharing agreements that dampened competition on bus routes in Leeds. As mentioned above, the price-fixing subsequently uncovered in the market for football kit attracted fines totalling £18.6 million.[69] In both instances total or partial reductions in fines were allowed to participants in the cartel ready and willing to co-operate with the OFT.

---

[65] http://www.oft.gov.uk/Business/default.htm.

[66] I. MacNeil, 'Investigations under the Competition Act 1998', Ch. 4 in Rodger and MacCulloch note 13 above.

[67] Note 65 above.

[68] Available via:
http://www.oft.gov.uk/Business/Competition+Act/Decisions/index.htm.

[69] Note 1 above.

Judicial control is ensured. Under the 1998 Act the Competition Commission (CC) replaced the Monopolies and Mergers Commission. The CC's composition included an Appeals Tribunal whose function was *inter alia* to hear appeals against decisions of the OFT. This was altered by the Enterprise Act 2002 which created a free-standing Competition Appeal Tribunal (CAT) to assume the role of the Appeals Tribunal. The CAT hears appeals against OFT and sectoral regulators' decisions and it also reviews decisions of the OFT and of the CC exercising its more limited role in the fields of market investigations and merger control, mentioned below.[70] The CAT also enjoys a newly created power to hear damages claims, mentioned more fully below.

The powerful procedures for investigating suspected breaches of the Act and for imposing sanctions are likely candidates to provoke challenges from business parties inspired by the discourse of human rights.[71] In the High Court decision in *Office of Fair Trading v X*[72] Morison J decided that granting warrants to the OFT under the CA 98 to carry out an investigation did not infringe the Human Rights Act or the European Convention. He took the view that statutory safeguards, including the right of the court to scrutinise the evidence relied on, adequately protect the rights of defendants. This seems broadly convincing but if this view does not prevail, the recent radical reforms of the UK's competition policy will be in severe jeopardy. One may confidently anticipate further litigation in this vein. The 'bridge' built by s. 60 CA makes it highly probable that EC developments concerning rights protection will be directly influential before courts in the UK.[73]

In addition to enforcement by the OFT, it is also of course envisaged that the ordinary courts should refuse to enforce agreements that fall foul of the Chapter I prohibition. Such agreements are void according to s. 2(4) CA 1998. This follows the pattern whereby the ordinary courts should refuse to enforce agreements that fall foul of the prohibition contained in Art. 81(1) EC, for such agreements are also void according to Art. 81(2) EC.

No provision is made in the Competition Act 1998 for a right of private action against parties acting in violation of the Act, but nor is this possibility excluded. There are strong policy reasons rooted in securing effective policing of the regime in favour of finding such a private action. The s. 60 'bridge' between EC practice and the development of the law in

[70] Part 12.3.5.2, 12.4.3.
[71] See Ch. 1.9.3.1.
[72] [2003] EWCH 1042; case law is available electronically, see note 1 above.
[73] For discussion in this direction see P. Willis, 'Procedural Nuggets from the Klondike Clause: the application of section 60 of the Competition Act 1998 to the Procedures of the OFT' [1999] *ECLR* 314.

the UK has a role to play here. English courts should decide matters of interpretation left open by the Competition Act 1998 with an eye to what occurs and will occur at EC level. Although it is not stated whether a breach of the Competition Act 1998 should allow a third party that has suffered loss to sue the offender for compensation, this question, it was said in Parliament during debates on the Bill that became the 1998 Act, should be answered in the same way as EC law would answer the parallel question arising in case of violation of Arts. 81 and 82.[74] The EC's subsequent ruling on the point as a matter of EC law in *Courage v Crehan*[75] therefore exerts a significant spill-over effect on UK law. It seems to point firmly in favour of an interpretation of the CA 1998 that treats it as creating a private action, although at a detailed level there remain issues to resolve about precisely how to fit this into domestic practice.[76]

The Enterprise Act 2002 added a new power vested in the CAT to make a damages award.[77] Where the OFT or the European Commission has found an infringement, affected parties may seek damages before the CAT rather than the ordinary courts. This includes explicit recognition of the consumer interest. A claim may be brought before the CAT by a specified body on behalf of two or more consumers who have claims in respect of the same infringement. It remains to be seen how this brand of representative action will work, but it could allow the Consumers' Association, for example, to assemble evidence of loss to consumers caused by, for example, price-fixing and to pursue the offending firms in a claim for damages before the CAT. Quantification of loss would doubtless be awkward in so far as the gap between the fixed price and the (by definition suppressed) true market price would need to be calculated. But as a general observation it is firmly in line with government policy that more active private enforcement should flourish, *inter alia* in order to maximise the consumer benefit in competitive markets.

---

74   See e.g. House of Lords Hansard, 25 November 1997, col. 955; *ibid* 5 March 1998, col. 1325.

75   Case C–453/99, note 43 above.

76   Cf. B. Rodger, 'Private Enforcement and the Enterprise Act: an exemplary system of awarding damages?' [2003] *ECLR* 103; also K. Holmes, 'Public Enforcement or Private Enforcement? Enforcement of Competition Law in the EC and the UK' [2004] *ECLR* 25.

77   Section 47A CA 1998, as inserted by the EA 2002.

12.2.4.3 The Limits of Convergence Between the UK and the EC

The adoption of the Competition Act 1998 formed an important plank in the Labour government's policy of promoting open competitive markets. It was motivated by two connected assumptions. First, the pre-existing regime was judged frankly ineffective as a means of suppressing anti-competitive conduct. Second, the obligation of commercial parties to deal with two differently structured systems at UK and at EC level imposed wasteful costs. The Competition Act deals with the first concern by adopting a more vigorous basis for intervention and it addresses the second concern by aligning the UK with the EC so that although compliance with two regimes is still required, in most circumstances the demands will be the same. But this is not simply designed to improve the business environment. This is treated as consumer policy too. The White Paper *Modern Markets: Confident Consumers*[78] insists on the integration of an effective competition policy into the framework of a broadly conceived consumer protection programme. This conforms to the primacy given by the Labour government to open competitive markets in the service of consumers.

But UK competition law is not an identical (if younger) twin to the EC model. Section 60 CA 1998, mentioned above, provides that congruence shall be achieved 'so far as is possible (having regard to any relevant differences between the provisions concerned)'. This offers scope for divergent interpretation of similarly worded provisions in so far as a good reason exists. The most obvious issue that may generate disharmony is the emphasis in EC law on the promotion of market integration as a principle of interpretation. This is lacking in a purely domestic context and may cause the same words to mean different things in different contexts.[79] More generally one could take the view that the constitutionally fundamental nature of Art. 81, as perceived by the EC,[80] is absent in UK law and practice. This would tend to weaken the vigour of the transplant.

Some specific aspects of the EC system have not been accepted into the UK system without alteration. Section 50 CA 1998 allows the Secretary of State to make special provision by order (secondary legislation) for vertical agreements – that is, agreements between traders at different levels in the distribution chain, such as manufacturers to

---

[78]   Note 5 above.

[79]   Cf. K. Middleton, 'Harmonisation with Community Law: the Euro Clause', Ch. 2, in Rodger and MacCulloch, note 13 above, p. 45. See also P. Freeman and R. Whish, *A Guide to the Competition Act 1998* (London: Butterworths, 1999), pp. 88–94; S. Goodman, 'The Competition Act, section 60 – the Governing Principles Clause' [1999] *ECLR* 73.

[80]   Note 24 above.

wholesalers or wholesalers to retailers. This special provision was achieved in the Competition Act 1998 (Land and Vertical Agreements Exclusion) Order 2000.[81] Vertical agreements, as defined in paragraph 2 of the Order, are excluded from the scope of the Chapter I prohibition in the 1998 Act. There is no market share threshold above which the protection of the Order is lost, in contrast to the regime operative at EC level under Block Exemption Regulation 2790/1999,[82] so UK law allows vertical restraints even where the parties have considerable market power, which is more generous than the EC system.[83] Part of the explanation for the fact that the regime for vertical restraints under the CA 1998 seems unusually permissive lies in the appreciation that in the UK a market suffering from severe failure could be the subject of a separate investigation by the Competition Commission, pursuant to procedures now found in the Enterprise Act 2002.[84] But a broader reason lies in the different assumptions and motivations of EC and UK law. A major motivation for EC law's relatively sceptical attitude to vertical restraints lies in their capacity to perpetuate the fragmentation of the European market along national lines. Territorially-defined distribution networks may hurt the creation of an internal market. This anxiety has no place in a purely domestic competition law regime. Therefore the concern to promote market integration might explain why the EC's tough line on vertical restraints has been reflected only in a milder form in the UK.

But it seems possible that the distinctive treatment of vertical restraints under UK law may not survive. The government is considering repealing the Order and introducing a control of vertical restraints that will mimic the EC system precisely. This suggests there is a strong gravitational pull exercised by the EC model. Another example of this phenomenon is found in the system of notification and exemption of restrictive practices. The CA 1998 follows the structure which *then* prevailed at EC level. Firms are required to notify the OFT of agreements falling within s. 2 CA 1998. The OFT then considers whether to grant exemption. But the rug was pulled from under the UK's feet by the adoption of Regulation 1/2003, which completely abandons the model of exclusive Commission power to exempt at EC level.[85] The UK could maintain its divergent stance. But it seems very unlikely to choose to do so. It is expected to follow the EC's lead, once again confirming the strength of the pull towards the EC model.

---

81   S.I. 2000/ 310.

82   Note 36 above.

83   For discussion see B. Rodger and A. MacCulloch, 'The Chapter I Prohibition: Prohibiting Cartels, or Permitting Verticals? Or Both?', Ch. 8 in Rodger and MacCulloch, note 13 above.

84   Chapter 12.3.5.2 below.

85   Chapter 12.2.3.3 above.

Theoretical analysis emphasises that a rational divergence between UK and EC practice is plausible, chiefly because of the driving force of market integration, present at EC level but absent at UK level. However, given that a major reason for the UK to adopt an EC-inspired model was to reduce costs of compliance for business, it appears increasingly improbable that the concession to local preference in s. 60 where there are relevant differences will frequently be relied on to generate sustained divergent practice in the UK.

In any event Regulation 1/2003 precludes a *stricter* approach under national law than applies under Art. 81. An agreement that affects trade between Member States, but is compatible with Art. 81, is safe from challenge under domestic competition law.

12.2.4.4 Criminal Sanctions under the Enterprise Act 2002

The most remarkable difference between UK and EC practice is that the UK is prepared to impose criminal sanctions on those engaged in unlawful anti-competitive practices. This is the result not of the Competition Act 1998, but rather of the subsequent reforming statute, the Enterprise Act 2002. The only circumstances in which criminal sanctions are envisaged under the 1998 Act is in relation to defined types of obstruction of or non-compliance with enforcement authorities performing their investigation and enforcement duties under the Act,[86] but these are relatively minor matters normally attracting relatively minor sanctions. Following up the insistence on improved competition policy found in the 1999 White Paper *Modern Markets: Confident Consumers*[87] a further White Paper published in 2001, *Productivity and Enterprise: A World Class Competition Regime*[88] made a specific case for more vigorous criminal controls. The Enterprise Act 2002 adds a completely new dimension. Part 6 creates the 'Cartel Offence'. According to s. 188(1) EA 2002 an individual is guilty of an offence if he or she 'dishonestly agrees with one or more other persons to make or implement, or to cause to be made or implemented, arrangements' of a particular specified kind relating to at least two undertakings. Section 188(2) sets out the kind of practice that is targeted: the list comprises hard-core anti-competitive activities that would widely be regarded as inexcusable attacks on the normal conduct of a market economy, such as price-fixing, agreed restrictions on output and bid-rigging. Imprisonment for a term of up to five years is possible, in addition to a fine. In England and Wales and Northern Ireland, proceedings for an

---

[86] Sections 42–44, 55(8), 67 CA 1998.
[87] Note 5 above.
[88] Cm 5233 (2001).

offence may be instituted only by the Director of the Serious Fraud Office, or by or with the consent of the OFT. Powers of investigation are conferred on the OFT.

The criminal standard of placing guilt beyond reasonable doubt applies to the offence. One may speculate that it is unlikely that the requisite dishonesty will be proved with any frequency.[89] Prison sentences will probably be rarer still. However, as is true of much consumer protection law,[90] the real impact of the Act is best gauged in what it deters than what it penalises. One would hope and expect that companies would develop more active programmes designed to educate their staff to grasp what is not permitted when they deal with competitors; and one would hope and expect staff to take the matter seriously. The government was convinced that the introduction of criminal sanctions as an ultimate regulatory weapon would go a long way to embedding the competitive ethos deep into UK commercial practice. It faced down fierce opposition from the business community, which criticised the introduction of the criminal law as an undue burden.[91] And it was not swayed by the argument that the Enterprise Act's preference for criminal sanctions damaged the key ambition of the Competition Act 1998 to align UK practice with the EC. The government believed that the greater effectiveness generated by criminalizing cartels served as sufficient justification. It is probable, however, that the vast bulk of competition law enforcement will remain of a civil rather than a criminal nature.

12.3 MONOPOLY LAW

12.3.1 The Phenomenon of the Monopoly and Related Market Structures

Discussion of cartels is concerned with situations where the behaviour of producers and suppliers impedes the operation of the market. The structure of the market may also impede the operation of the invisible hand. Consumer choice in conditions of perfect competition assumes the availability of a sufficient number of suppliers to ensure genuine variety. Yet this may not always be the case. Where there are a few producers only, the invisible hand is weakened. Monopolies provide the most extreme example: where the supplier holds a monopoly, the consumer is no longer

---

[89]   Cf. I. MacNeil, 'Criminal Investigations in Competition Law' [2003] *ECLR* 151.
[90]   Cf. treatment of the 'regulatory offence' in Ch. 11.
[91]   E.g. 'CBI brands competition law changes Draconian', *Financial Times*, 18 October 2001, p. 11. See Ch. 1.9 generally on regulatory burdens.

sovereign. In consequence, the price and quality of what is produced are dictated by the choice of the producer, not the consumer.

Naturally, any control system must devote careful attention to the proper definition of a monopoly. Products may be interchangeable. The sole producer of widgets is not in a monopoly in economically meaningful terms if there are available sources of gizmos, a product that is readily interchangeable with widgets. If the widget producer hoists prices, consumers can switch to gizmos. There is no rationale for treating the market as a monopoly enjoyed by the widget producer. More subtly, even where a producer is the single source of widgets, for which there is no other interchangeable product, there is no monopoly if other producers are capable of altering their techniques in order to enter the market for widget production. In such circumstances, consumers have no immediate alternative supply source, but prices should nevertheless be held down to competitive levels because the sole active producer knows that price rises will attract new firms into the market, offering lower prices and consumer choice. Markets should therefore not be assessed as static. They should not be treated as monopolistic where they are in fact 'contestable'.[92] The need to define markets with care applies equally to geography as to product. The only British producer has no monopoly if the British market is open to external competition from sources of supply based in other countries. Monopoly law, like competition law generally, deals with the state of markets, so that where those markets change shape, the application of the law too must adjust.

These issues of market definition are critical in any policy of monopoly control. An underestimation of actual or potential competition will lead to an overestimation of market power. This in turn may prompt an intervention in the name of monopoly control where there is no monopoly. However, if a monopoly *is* identified, control may be judged appropriate in light of the potential damage caused by the absence of competition, ultimately to the detriment of the consumer.

12.3.2 Shaping a Legal Response to the Monopoly

The law may address the pernicious effects of monopolies in several ways. It may attempt to prevent them coming into being by exercising controls over mergers and acquisitions. It may be possible to preserve a competitive market by creating a regulatory agency for that market which is competent to forbid mergers between competitors where the result would be an undue diminution in the number of rival suppliers. The law of merger control is in

---

[92]   E.g. W. Baumol and R. Willig in D.J. Morris (ed.), *Strategic Behaviour and International Competition* (OUP, 1986).

this sense an aspect of both monopoly law and consumer law. Merger law is examined below.[93]

A related set of legal techniques concentrates on entry barriers which impede the creation of efficient competition. A theory based on the desirability of fostering markets which are contestable would direct legal instruments to the improvement of market flexibility, rather than treating markets as static and in need of regulation. So attention may be paid to removing legal or economic obstacles to firms which wish to enter markets or, stronger, to providing positive inducements to would-be new firms. Economic obstacles to entry may comprise the difficulty in obtaining the investment needed, especially (and on some views only)[94] where a new entrant will not obtain economies of scale already claimed by existing market participants. Legal obstacles may take the form of governmental regulation. Quality standards set by the State may have the benefit of preventing unsafe or unacceptable goods or services reaching the market; equally, they carry a cost in reducing choice by keeping out firms unwilling or unable to meet those standards. Chapter 1 provides an amplified discussion of these key issues in shaping regulation.[95] It is not unknown for firms already active in a market to arrange their own self-regulation and/or to seek public regulation which reflects their existing practices in order to protect themselves from the threat of being undercut by competitors. Whether competition is fair or unfair may be in the eye of the beholder: trader, would-be trader and consumer may have very different perspectives. In any event, the pursuit of market flexibility involves some difficult questions about the desirability of public intervention.

More radically still, the law may address the problem of existing monopolies by forcing the monopolistic firm to be broken up into constituent parts and sold off in order to (re)create competition. In practice this route is rarely chosen, although it was in vogue for a short period in the US in the early 20th-century. This technique should be sharply distinguished from a governmental policy of privatisation of monopolies. Privatisation connotes the transfer of assets from public to private sector and *of itself* it exerts a neutral effect on competition. A monopoly is a monopoly whoever owns it. It is a different matter where privatisation of monopolies is combined with an attempt to inject competition into the market by, for example, splitting up the monopoly into constituent, potentially rival, elements prior to selling it off.

---

93   Chapter 12.4 below.

94   Many of the issues are helpfully raised in the EC context by R. Baden Fuller, 'Article 86 EEC: Economic Analysis of the Existence of a Dominant Position' (1979) 4 *ELRev* 423; L. Gyselen and A. Kyriazis, 'Article 86: Monopoly Power Measurement Issue Revisited' (1986) 11 *ELRev* 134. In the US context, see Pitofsky note 28 above.

95   Especially Ch. 1.8.

There is a middle way between preventing monopoly power from coming into existence and destroying it once it has: to accept the existence of dominant economic power but to regulate the firm so that it cannot behave independently of the market and of consumer preference. This approach is the norm in the UK and the EC. For example, the firm may be subjected to price control or quality standards; it may be obliged to deal equitably with customers, existing or prospective. The essential point is that, once a firm has crossed a threshold of economic power which renders it in part immune from the pressure of competition, it becomes liable to act inefficiently and/or unfairly. There is then a rationale for exercising regulatory control which would not apply if it were economically weaker. So, whereas in a competitive market one might accept that ice-cream suppliers could install freezers from which their goods and no others could be sold, one might take a very different view of such activities by a firm which dominates a market.[96] A strong firm can tie up the market by exercising its economic clout to conclude deals with retailers. Such practices will reduce or even eliminate opportunities for smaller suppliers to compete in even a limited way. Consumer choice will shrink. The pursuit of exclusive ties in a market which is not fully competitive may be a cause for concern which would not arise in the presence of effective competition.

Decisions have to be made about the type of institution which should be established to wield regulatory power, including appropriate appeal and review machinery. Such controls in one sense mimic the results which would obtain were a competitive market in operation. In that case, an individual firm's prices would be controlled by reference to those set by rivals, but in a monopoly a regulatory authority may assume that function. The question of the precise level at which prices should be set (in the absence of guidance from the operation of the market) then becomes a point of detail, but one which is itself likely to be controversial.[97]

The need for regulatory agencies is very evident in the policy of privatisation of publicly owned monopolies which was actively pursued by Conservative governments in power in the UK from 1979 to 1997. The simple transfer of public assets into the unregulated private sector was not generally considered feasible where a monopoly was concerned, because of the power thereby handed to a private monopolist.[98] It was accordingly thought necessary to establish legal controls over the newly created private sector. This perception explains the rise of (a bewildering variety of) regulatory agencies charged with the task of overseeing the performance of

---

[96] Cf. Chapter 12.2.2 above.

[97] On capture theory and, still broader, public choice analysis, see Ch. 1.9.

[98] In some instances it was this perception that had prompted the State in the past to take the sector into public ownership; cf. A. Ogus, *Regulation* (OUP, 1994), Ch. 13.

nominally privatised industries. These have been largely retained since the Labour Party took power in 1997, although their shape and priorities have been tweaked. [99]

Looking briefly beyond competition policy as an economic instrument, it has been explained that price fixing by firms in a competitive market is almost invariably unlawful, whereas price fixing by a public authority in a non-competitive market can be justified for economic reasons. It might additionally be noted that price fixing by a public authority even in a competitive market may be justified, albeit not from the perspective of wealth maximisation. Legislation permitting the fixing of fair rents provides a good example, where the law may intervene to fix prices below the level at which the market would settle.[100] Political choices about wealth distribution and social justice may thus intrude into the shaping of economic law. In other sectors, the law may intervene to fix prices *above* the market price, typically to maintain capacity in the industry concerned. Such intervention has often been connected with a desire for national self-sufficiency, for example in food and energy, although where national markets are integrated into a wider market, such intervention can work only if undertaken at the transnational level.

12.3.3 Desirable Monopolies

In monopoly control, the wrinkle that should be taken into account is that monopolies are not always undesirable. In some sectors a monopoly may be the most effective and 'natural' method of structuring the market. For example, there are obvious limits to the potential for a competitive market for the supply of water from reservoirs or the operation of different train routes from London to Paris. There may conceivably be more than one supplier, but there is only one set of pipes or rails. The competitive market has its limits. The appropriate legal response to the true natural monopoly cannot be to forbid its coming into existence nor to break it up, but instead to regulate its operation. For the supply of water and energy there has been long-standing public concern to impose, for example, price controls and obligations of equitable supply to all consumers irrespective of geography.

However the term 'natural monopoly' demands careful attention, since it may cloak situations requiring more nuanced study. Transport markets are especially telling. Train travel seems to be a natural monopoly, yet the market may be competitive if defined to include a variety of forms of transport. There is only one train line between London and Birmingham,

---

[99]   See Chapter 12.3.5.3 below and discussion in Ch. 1.9.

[100] Further, Chapter 1.9.3, where it is explained that such policy preferences have been in flux in the UK in recent years.

but a train is not the only means of travelling between the two cities. Such questions of market definition are essential prerequisites to the choice of legal control.

In the UK, perceptions of the limits of natural monopolies have been sharpened in recent years. Attention has been paid to the possibility of paring down monopolies to a smaller core than had previously existed. Such activity has frequently accompanied decisions about the transfer of assets from public into private hands.[101] For example, the collection of water in reservoirs may be a natural monopoly, but retailing water may not. Competition may be injected into the retail sector. Similarly, a proliferation of railway track may not be desirable, but competition between operators wishing to use that track may be reckoned feasible.

12.3.4 European Community Monopoly Law

12.3.4.1 Article 82 (ex 86) EC

Article 82 (ex 86) acts as the EC monopoly control provision, although the terminology used is prohibition of 'abuse of a dominant position'.

> Any abuse by one or more undertakings of a dominant position within the common market or in a substantial part of it shall be prohibited as incompatible with the common market in so far as it may affect trade between Member States. Such abuse may, in particular, consist in:
> (a) directly or indirectly imposing unfair purchase or selling prices or unfair trading conditions:
> (b) limiting production, markets or technical development to the prejudice of consumers;
> (c) applying dissimilar conditions to equivalent transactions with other trading parties, thereby placing them at a competitive disadvantage;
> (d) making the conclusion of contracts subject to acceptance by the other parties of supplementary obligations which, by their nature or according to commercial usage, have no connection with the subject of such contracts.

Indirectly, Art. 82 is a consumer policy instrument in its capacity to suppress inefficient practices such as high prices which are not adequately controlled by the market in the absence of effective competition. It will be noted that (b) in the non-exhaustive list of abusive practices attached to Art. 82 contains one of the Treaty's rare explicit references to the position

---

[101] Cf. Chapter 1.9.3.

of the consumer.[102] Moreover, Art. 82 (ex 86)'s prohibition against
dominant firms strengthening their position by means other than recourse
to competition on the merits has been judicially described as motivated by
'the concern not to cause harm to consumers'.[103]

The chief relevant piece of evidence that a firm has sufficient
economic strength to render it subject to the Art. 82 obligation not to abuse
a dominant position is its ability to act in the market independently of
normal competitive pressures. Article 82 applies to firms able to ignore the
demands of 'competitors and customers and ultimately of consumers'.[104]
In this matter careful economic analysis of the state of the market is vital,
lest intervention be over-hasty or, at the other extreme, unduly reluctant. In
practice the Commission's Notice on market definition, published in 1997,
is helpful in explaining the factors which the Commission takes into
account in determining whether the structure of the market is tainted by
dominance and therefore properly subjected to public intervention in the
name of controlling abuse of market power.[105] The Notice offers as a
guideline a test based on inspection of consumer behaviour. If a five to ten
per cent non-transitory change in the price of a widget does not lead to
consumers switching to buying a gizmo instead, then the widget is not
regarded as forming part of the same market as the gizmo. They do not
compete with each other. So for example in *1998 Football World Cup*[106]
the Commission applied this test and found that consumers of tickets for
the Finals of the Football World Cup did not treat that product as
interchangeable with tickets for other football or sports events or other
forms of entertainment. This analysis led the Commission to the conclusion
that there was a separate market for the supply of World Cup tickets alone.
The competition organisers were free of effective competitive constraints
on that market. They enjoyed dominant market power.

It was explained above at 12.3.2 that monopoly law may be structured
to tolerate the existence of monopolies while regulating the exercise of
monopoly power. Article 82 bears precisely this stamp. Abuse is unlawful,
dominance *per se* is not. The firm that is assessed to possess dominant
market power is judged to fall under a 'special responsibility'[107] not to
abuse that power. The organisers of the *1998 Football World Cup* were

---

102   See Chapter 2.3.1.
103   E.g. Case T–65/98 *Van den Bergh Foods v Commission* [2003] ECR II–(not yet
       reported), para. 157.
104   Case 322/81 *Michelin v Commission* [1983] ECR 3461. See also Whish note 9 above,
       Chs. 1 & 5; W. Bishop and M. Walker, 'The Economics of EC Competition Law:
       Concepts, Application and Measurement' (2nd ed, 2002), esp. Chs. 3, 4.
105   Commission Notice on market definition OJ 1997 C 372/5, [1998] 4 CMLR 177.
106   Decision 2000/12/EC [2000] OJ. L5/55, noted by Weatherill [2000] *ECLR* 275.
107   Case 322/81 note 104 above.

fined for using their dominant market power to discriminate in favour of purchase by French consumers. Dominant firms may not set unfair prices or act to segregate the market. The most strikingly interventionist feature of Art. 82 is that it may be applied in order to require a reluctant dominant firm to respond to consumer demand. In this vein, the Commission found a violation of Art. 82 in *ITP, RTE, BBC*.[108] The three television companies printed separate guides to future programmes, using copyright which they held over their own listings to prevent the appearance of a single, integrated publication. A consumer of the information was thus forced to buy three separate guides. The Court of First Instance upheld the Commission finding that an abuse had occurred in *RTE, BBC, ITP v Commission*[109] and the EC subsequently dismissed appeals by two of the television companies.[110] The firms were obliged to make their listings available to third parties, subject to payment of a reasonable fee. The protection of the consumer interest is explicit in this decision, which imposes consumer choice on unwilling firms. Both courts observed that the companies had abused the economic power they enjoyed under their copyright by unjustifiably preventing the appearance of a new product for which there was potential consumer demand.

This decision, though plainly important, emphatically does not mean that Art. 82 is routinely used to strip exclusivity out of the hands of holders of intellectual property rights. That would severely inhibit commercial incentives to invest in innovation, which would not benefit consumers. In *Oscar Bronner GmbH v Mediaprint*[111] Oscar Bronner claimed that Mediaprint was acting in breach of Art. 82 by refusing to include Bronner's newspaper in its home-delivery delivery service (for which Bronner was prepared to pay). It failed. It had not been established that it was economically unviable to create a second home-delivery scheme for the distribution of daily newspapers with a circulation comparable to that of the daily newspapers distributed by the existing scheme. Mediaprint was entitled to keep Oscar Bronner out of the distribution network it had itself built up, even if that might diminish the consumer's opportunity of gaining ready access to Bronner's product. The exercise of an exclusive right may, in exceptional circumstances, involve an abuse condemned by Art. 82, but that had not occurred in *Oscar Bronner*. The Court took the opportunity to clarify the exceptional circumstances that had justified intervention in *RTE, BBC, ITP v Commission*:

---

108 Decision 89/205 OJ 1989 L78/43, [1989] 4 CMLR 757.

109 Cases T–69, T–70, T–76/89 [1991] ECR II–485, 535, 575.

110 Joined Cases C–241/91P and C–242/91P *RTE and ITP v Commission* [1995] ECR I–743.

111 Case C–7/97 [1998] ECR I–7791.

> [T]he refusal in question concerned a product (information on the weekly schedules of certain television channels) the supply of which was indispensable for carrying on the business in question (the publishing of a general television guide), in that, without that information, the person wishing to produce such a guide would find it impossible to publish it and offer it for sale ... , the fact that such refusal prevented the appearance of a new product for which there was a potential consumer demand ..., the fact that it was not justified by objective considerations..., and that it was likely to exclude all competition in the secondary market of television guides ....

These conditions will arise rather infrequently.[112]

Enforcement of Art. 82 lies in the hands of the Commission and national courts and tribunals. Much of the comment relating to Art. 81 may be applied *mutatis mutandis* to Art. 82.[113] It is directly effective and may consequently be enforced before national courts at the suit of private individuals.

12.3.4.2 Article 86 (ex 90) EC

State monopolies have been a common feature of the economies of most EC Member States. They are typically part of the patchwork of public and private participation in the modern mixed economy. One of the most high-profile developments in EC law in the last fifteen years is found in the increasing threat to State monopolies posed by the application of Art. 86 (ex 90) EC.

Article 82, examined above, controls existing monopolies. There are also trends in EC law directed at dismantling monopolies where the monopolistic market structure is created or sustained by State restrictions. In this vein, Art. 86(1) provides that:

> In the case of public undertakings and undertakings to which Member States grant special or exclusive rights, Member States shall neither enact nor maintain in force any measure contrary to the rules contained in this Treaty, in particular to those rules provided for in Article 12 and Articles 81 to 89.

Article 86(3) concerns enforcement. It provides that the Commission 'shall ensure the application of the provisions of this Article and shall, where

---

[112] Cf. B. Doherty, 'Just what are essential facilities?' (2001) 38 *CMLRev* 397; A. Bavasso, 'Essential Facilities in EC law' (2002) 21 *YEL* 63.

[113] Chapter 12.2.4 above.

necessary, address appropriate directives or decisions to Member States'. The fact that the Commission has become very vigorous in its determination to exercise these powers over the last 15 years is a major policy development. For many years, Art. 86 was regarded as relatively peripheral in practical terms. This perception has completely changed.

Read with Art. 82, Art. 86 has been used to forbid State measures which place an undertaking in a position where its isolation from competition will inevitably lead it to act abusively. For example, in *Höfner and Elsner v Macrotron*.[114] Höfner and Elsner had provided Macrotron with a candidate for the post of sales director. Despite his suitability, Macrotron did not appoint the person and refused to pay Höfner and Elsner. Since German law granted exclusive rights for employee recruitment to a public agency, the contract on which Höfner and Elsner sued Macrotron was void. Höfner and Elsner relied on Community law to challenge the German law which excluded them from the market for supplying staff. The Court ruled that Arts. 82 and 86 imposed an obligation on the State not to sustain a market which was uncompetitive. Here, the State prevented supply from meeting demand. This was incompatible with EC law. The decision amounts to a strong message in favour of liberalisation through which the structure of the market should be determined by private market decisions (supply and demand) and not by State regulation.

Article 86(2) provides an exception to the basic prohibition. It offers leeway to a State to pursue goals other than free competition:

> Undertakings entrusted with the operation of services of general economic interest or having the character of a revenue-producing monopoly shall be subject to the rules contained in this Treaty, in particular to the rules on competition, in so far as the application of such rules does not obstruct the performance, in law or in fact, of the particular tasks assigned to them. The development of trade must not be affected to such an extent as would be contrary to the interests of the Community.

Article 86(2) has been interpreted restrictively.[115] The EC has ruled against its application much more frequently than it has ruled in favour. This has tended to give primacy to the ethos of free competition in the first paragraph of Art. 86 over the receptivity to public service provision in its second paragraph.

---

[114] Case C–41/90 [1991] ECR I–1979. See similarly Case C–266/96 *Corsica Ferries France* [1998] ECR I–3949.

[115] E.g. Case 66/86 *Ahmed Saeed Flugreisen and Silver Line Reiseburo GmbH v Zentrale zur Bekampfung unlauteren Wettbewerbs e.V.* [1989] ECR 803.

However, Art. 86(2) remains potentially important as a forum in which development of a Community law notion of social and consumer policy provision within the free market could occur. Indeed, the wider the scope of Art. 86(1) in challenging State market regulation, the brighter the spotlight on the role Art. 86(2) may play in justifying intervention. Article 86(2) may be read as an invitation to elaborate a theory of the social market under EC law. *Paul Corbeau* concerned the State-conferred monopoly over postal services in Belgium.[116] The EC accepted that, if the core monopoly over letter delivery were lost, the social function of the service would be jeopardised. Private firms would have no interest in maintaining a national system; their preference would be to 'cherry-pick' profitable parts of the service, leaving rural consumers under provided. In *Corbeau* the Court recognised the role of cross-subsidy as a means of maintaining the viability of loss-making but socially worthwhile services. Article 86(2) is capable of justifying restrictions on competition in such circumstances. However, the Court *was* prepared to apply Art. 86 read with Art. 82 in order to lop off ancillary rights reserved to State monopolies and to open them up to competition. The case was an Art. 234 preliminary ruling, so the Court did not have the task of deciding the case, but merely of interpreting Community law. The ruling expresses an (as yet) undefined role for Art. 86(2) in insulating core elements of socially valuable State monopolies from the blast of free competition.

Deep political sensitivity attends this matter. It relates directly to not simply to the relationship between the State as supplier of services and the consumer, but to the responsibility of the State in providing for its citizens. Art. 16 (ex 7d) was an innovation of the Amsterdam Treaty. It provides that:

> Without prejudice to Articles 73, 86 and 87, and given the place occupied by services of general economic interest in the shared values of the Union as well as their role in promoting social and territorial cohesion, the Community and the Member States, each within their respective powers and within the scope of application of this Treaty, shall take care that such services operate on the basis of principles and conditions which enable them to fulfil their missions.

This provision does not appear to be intended to alter the law developed under Art. 86.[117] Its inclusion in the Treaty is attributable to a general

---

116   Case C–320/91 [1993] ECR I–2533.

117   A declaration on Art. 16 (ex 7d), annexed to the Amsterdam Treaty, states that its provisions 'shall be implemented with full respect for the jurisprudence of the Court of Justice, inter alia as regards the principles of equality of treatment, quality and continuity of such services'.

political sensitivity to the impact of Community law on public services, but its rather tame content reveals that no consensus could be assembled at Amsterdam to overturn the existing provisions which attempt uneasily to balance the interests of market liberalisation and public service reflected in Arts. 86(1) and (2).

It remains fiercely controversial whether EC practice takes sufficient account of the importance of maintaining social obligations to all consumers which is a characteristic feature of State monopolies. The benefit of increased competition for consumers may have to be weighed against the cost of diminished social justice flowing from the release of more orthodox direct forms of consumer protection such as universal service obligations. The Commission continues to engage in debate.[118] But no one pretends that the calculations involved are objective or straightforward.

12.3.5 United Kingdom Monopoly Law

12.3.5.1 The Chapter II Prohibition.

As with restrictive practices, so with monopoly control: the student can heave a deep sigh of relief because the reforms instigated by the Competition Act 1998 have aligned UK practice with the EC model found in Art. 82 and therefore the law today is a great deal easier to understand than it used to be. It is, moreover, a great deal more effective than it used to be. This is central to the Labour government's concern to sharpen up the application of competition law as part of its strategy for generating open and competitive markets that serve the consumer interest.[119]

The Competition Act 1998 enacts in s. 18 a prohibition which is textually closely comparable to that applied by Art. 82 EC. Section 18(4) provides that it shall be known as the 'Chapter II prohibition' and that has become orthodox terminology. It is enforced in the same way as the Chapter I prohibition examined in Part 12.2.4 above, according to the model of investigation and sanction by the Office of Fair Trading Act and, in some circumstances, including opportunity for private enforcement. The first fine imposed under the Competition Act 1998 related to a violation of Chapter II, rather than Chapter I – Napp Pharmaceuticals were fined £3.21 million for abusive practices in drug markets that involved excluding

---

[118] Green Paper on Services of General Interest, COM(2003) 270, available via http://europa.eu.int/eur-lex/en/com/gpr/2003/com2003_0270en01.pdf.

[119] Cf. Chapter 12.1.1. above, and more generally Chapter 1.9.2.3.

would-be market entrants and charging excessive prices. The fine was reduced on appeal to £2.2 million.[120]

It was remarked in relation to Chapter I that the OFT has issued important guidelines setting out its policy and the same is true in relation to Chapter II. For example, it has published guidelines on its approach to market definition,[121] a matter which is central to any coherent policy of monopoly control. These guidelines make frequent reference to the European Commission's 1997 Notice on market definition[122] in sketching the way in which the OFT proposes to define markets under the Competition Act 1998. The Guidelines promise that 'in general' they follow the same approach as the European Commission's Notice. So, for example, the test for market definition involving inquiry into how customers would react were prices raised by five to ten per cent above competitive levels appears in the OFT Guidelines as it appears in the Commission's 1997 notice.

12.3.5.2 Market Investigations under the Enterprise Act 2002

The Fair Trading Act 1973 and the Competition Act 1980 are the statutes that have been replaced by the Competition Act 1998's EC-inspired control of monopoly power. Those statutes applied a long-winded and complex system of control. Monopoly situations could be referred for investigation to the Monopolies and Mergers Commission. Its report, exploring the effect of the monopoly situation on the public interest, then turned the matter over for final decision on appropriate action by the Secretary of State of Trade and Industry. The contrast with the regime introduced by the Competition Act 1998, modelled on Art. 82 EC, is plain: there was no directly enforceable prohibition against abuse of monopoly power *per se*. The system was much more cumbersome. It is now much more penetrating and likely to exercise a much more serious deterrent effect.

However, the 1998 reforms chose to leave in place one feature of the pre-existing regime. This was the pattern for controlling complex and scale monopolies. This allowed investigation into markets that were perceived to be inefficiently structured, but in which the problem was not cartels or monopolies. The perception was this was a problem that is poorly addressed at EC level and that accordingly simply to absorb the EC model would be wilfully foolish.[123] The procedure was that used for the

---

120   *Napp Pharmaceutical Holdings Ltd v DGFT* [2002] 4 All ER 376.
121   OFT 403. Available via the OFT website, note 65 above.
122   Note 105 above.
123   See M. Furse, 'Monopolies, the Public Interest, the Fair Trading Act and the Chapter II Prohibition', Ch. 7 in Rodger and MacCulloch, note 13 above.

Competition Commission's high-profile inquiry into the UK *Supermarket* sector,[124] which in 2000 concluded that the market was broadly competitive, notwithstanding the presence of some local concerns, and that pricing and profits were therefore not excessive. This inquiry procedure has now been taken over into the Enterprise Act 2002. Part 4 of that Act is entitled 'Market Investigations'. On a reference from the OFT or from defined sectoral regulators, the Competition Commission may investigate markets which have features which may restrict competition in the UK. A competition-based test replaces the discarded vague public interest test found in the pre-existing statutes. Ministerial control over remedies is superseded by a dominant role conferred on the CC. The procedure is designed to allow a survey of markets that are perceived to be malfunctioning, but not in circumstances where any clear-cut violation of either the Chapter I or the Chapter II prohibition is at stake. An obvious candidate is markets of an oligopolistic nature – where there are only a few suppliers, who are not in agreement with each other within the meaning of Chapter I, nor is any single actor dominant within the meaning of Chapter II, but where because of the static market structure all players behave very similarly. This is the way critics viewed the UK supermarket sector, but the Competition Commission's investigation in 2000 left it unpersuaded. But if there *are* such structural malfunctions then the market will operate in a manner that is damaging to consumer choice. An investigation may give rise to recommendations for changes in the law or, at a softer level, changes in the rules of self-regulatory bodies. It may also, of course, propose no action.

The procedure for initiating market investigations of this type is not likely to be invoked regularly. The cutting-edge of UK competition law glitters in the pair of prohibitions found in Chapters I and II, examined above. However, it is possible that an additional alteration made by the Enterprise Act 2002 may provoke more frequent OFT investigations. Section 11 of the Act provides for super-complaints to the OFT. A designated consumer body is able to make a complaint to the OFT 'that any feature, or combination of features, of a market in the United Kingdom for goods or services is or appears to be significantly harming the interests of consumers'. The OFT has produced guidelines which set out how this complaint should be lodged.[125] The OFT then falls under a duty to respond within 90 days, setting out how it proposes to deal with the complaint. Designation of representative bodies is in the gift of the Secretary of State for Trade and Industry under the Act.

It is probable that matters will be resolved informally where possible and it is also possible that OFT will simply decline to proceed. However, a

---

124 Cm 4842 (2000).

125 *Super-complaints: Guidance for designated consumer bodies* (OFT 514, July 2003).

super-complaint may conceivably trigger an exploratory market study[126] and ultimately it may lead to the opening of a formal statutory market investigation. Two super-complaints were made to the OFT in 2003.[127] One concerned the mail consolidation business and following an initial inquiry the OFT decided not to investigate further. The other, concerning the care-homes market, was triggered by an informal super-complaint made by the Consumers Association. In this instance the OFT decided to proceed to a market study, expressing particular concern to assess the ability of consumers in the market to obtain clear and accurate information about fees and, in particular, whether the variability of fees over time is sufficiently transparent. The Consumers Association was not a designated super-complainant – its application is pending – but the OFT agreed to treat it as if it were. The super-complaint procedure has the potential to increase the active involvement of consumer bodies in the scrutiny of malfunctioning markets.

12.3.5.3 Privatisation and Monopolies

It was explained in Chapter 1 that UK policy for much of the last 25 years has pursued the path of privatisation in its several forms.[128] This is part of a process of withdrawal of State participation from the market, driven by a political choice in favour of the private ordering of the market as the preferred means of providing for the consumer interest, even in respect of 'public services' as traditionally conceived. But simply moving a monopoly from the public to the private sector has no effect on the structure of the market, which remains equally likely to operate inefficiently and unfairly. In some areas privatisation of monopolies was accompanied by an injection of competition. Where it was not, there was a perceived need to set up regulatory agencies. The loosening of direct State control over the supply of services of such vital importance to the consumer as gas, water and electricity has raised the profile of regulatory control of private monopolists. Several different regulators appeared – OFGEM, OFTEL, OFWAT and so on.[129]

Disputes between regulator and regulated industry about the appropriate level of control have become fairly common. Regulated industries have also looked beyond 'their' regulator to press the Government to lift, or at least relax, the control exercised. The regulated

---

[126] See s. 5 Enterprise Act 2002.
[127] Information is available via http://www.oft.gov.uk/Market+studies/Super-complaints/default.htm.
[128] Chapter 1.9.2 above.
[129] Chapters 1.9.2.2, 1.9.2.3.

industries typically demand that the shift in market structure be accompanied by a change in regulatory climate. Calls for the lifting of price caps, for example, have been heard with regularity. Where markets are becoming truly competitive, these requests are justified from the perspective of the theory of free markets, whereby prices ought to be controlled by the forces of competition. However, this is dependent on the markets assuming a genuinely competitive shape within which consumers are adequately informed about the nature of available choices, which some critics doubt is either feasible or desirable in sectors formerly viewed as 'public services'. The process remains dynamic and the to-and-fro between regulated industry, regulator and government continues. In some sectors initial reticence to alter the monopolistic structure when assets were transferred from the public to the private sphere has given way to a policy of trying to inject competition.[130] Direct input by the consumer seems rather neglected.

Over time attention has been paid to placing 'new' regulators of privatised monopolies/quasi-monopolies on a more standardised footing and aligning them more closely with the normal structure of regulatory control. Precise details vary sector by sector and regulator by regulator,[131] but the Competition Act 1998 is important for its grant to sectoral regulators of many of the enforcement powers that are conferred more generally on the OFT. Moreover, the Labour government has committed itself to improving the profile of the consumer interest in decisions taken by regulatory agencies,[132] although it remains to be seen whether this is more than mere rhetorical flourish.

12.4 MERGER LAW

12.4.1 Rationales for Merger Control

A merger or take-over occurs where two or more previously independent firms come under common control. For legal purposes the constituent elements of the merged entity may remain separate, but in economic terms what counts is the reduction in competition consequent on surrender of commercial independence.[133]

---

[130] Note also the role of Art. 82 EC, Chapter 12.3.4.2 above, in obliging the UK to take such a course.

[131] Cf. T. Prosser, *Law and the Regulators* (OUP, 1997); C. Graham, *Regulating Public Utilities* (Hart Publishing, 2000).

[132] Chapter 1.9.2.3.

[133] Reflected in UK law in s. 26 Enterprise Act 2002 and in EC law in Art. 3 Merger Regulation, in more detail below.

Mergers between firms may be seen as the expression of commercial free will. They can serve a valuable function of restructuring the market. Economic theory tells us that big firms should be able to produce goods and services more cheaply than small ones and that, in a competitive market, price savings should be passed on to consumers. Such mergers should serve the consumer interest. In Europe, mergers between firms in different countries can be especially important in the process of market integration. However, mergers may lead to a restriction of competition. The fewer the firms active or potentially active in a market, the more sceptical the law is likely to be about a 'horizontal' merger between rivals. Mergers may need to be controlled because they damage the competitive structure of the market by increasing concentration of economic power above acceptable levels. The ultimate loser in such circumstances is the consumer.

Economic considerations may not be the sole motivation for merger law. It may also seem important to subject mergers to control for social reasons. For example, they may rob a region of a firm and its associated jobs. It will be appreciated that a merger policy informed by such concerns will be rather interventionist. Whatever the political and economic motivations for merger control, the associated question arises of the appropriate institutional machinery. An agency of some type, accountable for its choices, must be established which will rule on the tricky economic and political aspects of merger control.

12.4.2 European Community Merger Law[134]

12.4.2.1 The Pattern of Control

In view of the significance of mergers in the economy, it is extraordinary to realise that the original Treaty of Rome, which entered into force in 1952, failed to put in place any specialist merger control machinery. The contrast with cartels and monopolies, tackled directly under the Treaty, was striking. Political disagreement at the time about the proper scope and structure of merger policy explains this gap. In the late 1980s a burst of merger activity, driven by firms preparing for the completion of the internal market at the end of 1992,[135] created a political environment

---

[134] See Whish note 9 above, Ch. 21; E. Navarro Varona, *Merger Control in the EU: law, economics and practice* (OUP, 2002); J. Cook and C. Kerse, *EC Merger Control* (Sweet and Maxwell, 2002). But *note* that subsequently to the publication of these works some of the detail, if not the broad picture, has been altered by the entry into force of Regulation 139/2004, considered below.

[135] See Ch. 2.1.7.

conducive to the adoption of secondary legislation to fill the gap. This was the Merger Regulation – more properly Regulation 4064/89[136] on the control of concentrations between undertakings, which was replaced with effect from 1 May 2004 by Regulation 139/2004[137] on the control of concentrations between undertakings. Since September 1990 mergers, or, in Community parlance, 'concentrations', have been controlled in the EC under the Merger Regulation by the Merger Task Force (MTF), a specialist unit within the European Commission's Competition Directorate-General. The heart of the control exercised under Regulation 139/2004 involves an assessment of the impact of the merger on competition within the EC. The Regulation also contains an attempt to demarcate the respective jurisdictions of national and EC authorities in a more clear-cut fashion than is available under Arts. 81 and 82 EC. It thus goes some way in helping business to cut costs by 'shopping' for rulings on their merger plans at one stop only.[138]

The Merger Regulation, Regulation 139/2004, controls mergers or concentrations, as defined.[139] There is an obligation to notify qualifying mergers to the Merger Task Force *in advance*. Procedures then impose tight time limits on the MTF. The basic structure provides that officials have one month to dispose of each case ('Phase I'), although they may take a further four months where serious issues are identified ('Phase II'). Exceptionally these deadlines may be exceeded,[140] but only in defined circumstances arising where there is a demonstrated need for the MTF and the parties to pursue extended negotiations with a view to allowing the deal to proceed subject to concessions such as undertakings as to future conduct or structural remedies such as post-merger divestment of assets. In the early years after 1990 most deals were scrutinised and cleared within the first month. More recently it has become more common for Phase II inquiries to be opened. Workload has steadily increased. There were 50 to 75 referrals annually in the Regulation's early years, but by the turn of the millennium this figure had eased upwards to an average of roughly 300

---

[136] OJ 1989 L395/1, corrected version published OJ 1990 L257/14. Amended with effect from 1 March 1998 by Regulation 1310/97 OJ 1997 L180/1, corrig. OJ 1997 L199/69.

[137] OJ 2004 L24/1.

[138] The Regulation provides that *only* the Commission will examine mergers with a 'Community dimension' within Art. 1; *only* national authorities will examine other mergers. However this jurisdictional demarcation is in part undermined by Arts. 9 and 21 Regulation where the merger has a Community dimension and by Art. 22(3)–(6) where there is no Community dimension.

[139] Article 3 Regulation.

[140] The insertion of these provisions was a principal feature of Regulation 139/2004 note 137 above.

notifications annually, peaking at 345 in 2000. Global economic downturn depressed the figure to 212 in 2003. As a general observation the MTF has gained a reasonably good reputation for speed and efficiency in coping with its workload. It has, however, been more recently buffeted by a degree of controversy about the substance of decisions it has taken: this is referred to in the next sub-section.

12.4.2.2 The Criterion of Control

The essence of the test is an inquiry into whether the proposed transaction will lead to a situation which is incompatible with the common market. Such deals will be blocked. More explicitly, the Regulation provides that:

> A concentration which would significantly impede effective competition, in the common market or in a substantial part of it, in particular as a result of the creation or strengthening of a dominant position, shall be declared incompatible with the common market.[141]

The emphasis of this test is firmly on competition in the market. Merger law assumes that the number of rivals in a market cannot be reduced below a level which permits adequate competition. This test therefore assumes the central importance of accurate market definition – the same is true of Art. 82 EC.[142] The typical case of a merger that rings regulatory alarm bells occurs when an economically dominant firm proposes to acquire control of a smaller rival, or where two competitors plan to merger and thereby create an economically dominant firm. However, as a careful reading of the text above makes clear, the scope of the Regulation is not limited to such circumstances. The test is also apt to catch a case where a merger will not result in the new entity extending or acquiring damaging market power, but where the merger will create a situation in which the new entity will be one of a small pool of players none of which is on its own economically dominant but in which all will be sheltered from effective competitive pressure by the 'oligopolistic' market structure. This might arise where the merger is not between the only two firms active in the market but between two of the five similarly-sized active firms. The new firm will not dominate the market but the merger will have eliminated a significant dose of competition in the market in question.[143] The regime

---

[141] Article 2(3) Regulation.

[142] The Commission's 1997 Notice, note 105 above, applies to mergers as well as to Art. 82, although it naturally emphasises the prospective nature of the inquiry into the impact of mergers, whereas Art. 82 cases involve retrospective assessment.

[143] Cf. the role of market investigations under the EA 2002, Part 12.3.5.2 above.

that applied prior to the entry into force of Regulation 139/2004 was ill-drafted to cope with this type of case. This deficiency caused severe problems in the effective regulation of mergers by the Commission.[144] But Regulation 139/2004 has broadened and improved the system of control.

In practice relatively few mergers are blocked. In the first four years of the application of the Regulation, only one merger was held incompatible with the test in the Regulation and blocked by the Commission, that contemplated by Aerospatiale Alenia, a French/Italian company, and De Havilland of Canada.[145] The merged group would have acquired a large slice of the market for short haul commuter aircraft and the Merger Task Force considered that the anticompetitive consequences took the deal beyond the realms of permissibility under the Regulation. This was confirmed in a formal Decision of the full Commission.

The list of blocked mergers has subsequently grown slowly, but still represents no more than one per cent of all notified transactions. A batch of other mergers have been permitted only after firms agreed to modify their plans.[146] Naturally it is mergers that are not permitted to proceed that attract the lion's share of interest. The Commission's decision to block the merger between *General Electric* and *Honeywell*[147] was based on the judgement that the merged firm would acquire a powerful position in the aerospace sector. There would have been a significant impediment to effective competition and prices would have risen in consequence. This created transatlantic friction because the authorities in the USA had concluded that the deal should be permitted to proceed. They believed by contrast that the merger would generate consumer-friendly efficiency savings in the sector and that the merged firm's conduct would be subject to competitive restraint because of the potential for future challenge by new entrants. This was a prospect viewed as inadequate to save the merger in Brussels. The MTF attracted some criticism for perceived over-interventionism consequent on mistrust of the market. The divergence of approach reveals a distinctively different assessment of the worth to consumers of public intervention in the market.[148] But the case is more exception than rule. Rarely do competition regulators around the world

---

144 Cf. Case T–342/99 *Airtours v Commission* [2002] ECR II–2585 (Commission Decision annulled). For comment see S. Bishop and D. Ridyard, 'Prometheus Unbound: Increasing the Scope for Intervention in EC Merger Control' [2003] *ECLR* 357.

145 OJ 1991 L334/42, [1992] 4 CMLR M2.

146 E.g. *Nestle/Perrier* OJ 1992 L356/1, [1993] 4 CMLR M17.

147 COMP/M2220, OJ 2004 L48/1.

148 Cf. M. Pflans and C. Caffarra, 'The Economics of GE/Honeywell' [2002] *ECLR* 115; E. Morgan and S. McGuire, 'Transatlantic divergence: GE-Honeywell and the EU's merger policy' (2004) 11 *Jnl Euro Pub Pol* 39.

differ radically in their assessment of the implications of mergers. Normally they co-operate amicably and constructively.[149] And in the overwhelming majority of cases in Europe, deals have been cleared, usually after the one-month 'Phase I' inquiry.

Commission merger decisions are subject to review by, initially, the Court of First Instance. This is no rubber stamp. In *Schneider/Legrand*[150] and in *Tetra Laval/Sidel*[151] the Commission had concluded that planned mergers were incompatible with test set out in the Regulation. The CFI annulled both negative decisions.[152] It found the Commission's analysis of the market to be founded on unconvincing reasoning. In both cases the Commission had, in short, failed to demonstrate to the required level of proof that sufficient damage to the competitive structure of the market would be caused by the mergers. In *Schneider* it had in addition failed to put all its concerns to the companies concerned in order to allow them to seek to rebut the Commission's case, thereby violating its rights of defence. The strong message of these decisions is that the Commission must be sure scrupulously to respect procedures and to produce tightly-reasoned analysis of market structures.[153] One aspect of the reforms made by Regulation 139/2004 is procedural renovation designed to improve the handling of such matters.

12.4.2.3 Social and Consumer Policy Under the Regulation

Consideration of the relevance of efficiencies is frequently critical in controversial cases dealt with under the Regulation. Here the classic problem arises where it is claimed that a merger will generate economic efficiencies, usually as a result of the release of economies of scale, but at a cost to competition in the relevant market. Horizontal mergers – between firms that are market rivals – are the most sensitive. The question is to select priorities and ultimately this is a question of what best serves the consumer interest. *GE/Honeywell*[154] provides a clear example of the

---

[149] This facilitated by the International Competition Network, which held its inaugural annual conference in Italy in 2002. See:
http://www.internationalcompetitionnetwork.org/

[150] COMP M2283.

[151] COMP/M2416, OJ 2004 L43/13.

[152] Case T–310/01 *Schneider Electric v Commission* [2002] ECR II–4071, Case T–5/02 *Tetra Laval v Commission* [2002] ECR II–4381.

[153] Cf. J. Temple Lang, 'Two important Merger Regulation judgments' (2003) 28 *ELRev* 259; H. Hofmann, 'Good Governance in European Merger Control: Due Process and Checks and Balances under Review' [2003] *ECLR* 114.

[154] Note 147 above.

possibility that different regulators may in good faith reach different conclusions on what reaction is appropriate. In the consultation period that preceded the preparation of the text that was ultimately adopted by the Council and Parliament as Regulation 139/2004 it was mooted whether the control test should be changed to provide a more focussed treatment of the relevance of economic efficiencies. The Commission concluded that changing the wording in the Regulation would not help. The issue is admittedly frequently tricky but it was concluded that it can be handled adequately under the existing wording of the Regulation. The Commission chose instead to elaborate what is at stake, *inter alia* from the consumer perspective, via a 'soft law' instrument. It duly adopted guidelines on its treatment of horizontal mergers.[155] These assert that for efficiency gains to be relevant to a finding that the merger is compatible with the common market they must 'benefit consumers, be merger-specific and be verifiable'; and they should be 'substantial and timely'.[156] The Commission makes plain that the greater the reduction in competition as a result of the merger the less likely it is to be persuaded that claimed efficiencies achieved by the deal will be substantial and/or likely to be passed on to consumers. This is clearly the core of the factual inquiry in individual cases and, as *GE/ Honeywell* illustrates, it is capable on occasion of causing disputes.[157]

Although the focus of the test in Art. 2 of the Regulation (above) appears to be on the competitive implications of a merger, there is a whiff of ambiguity in the Regulation. It is provided that the Commission shall take into account *inter alia* 'the interests of the intermediate and ultimate consumers, and the development of technical and economic progress provided that it is to consumers' advantage and does not form an obstacle to competition'.[158] On its face, it cannot be completely excluded that this could be interpreted as a window through which the Commission could introduce into merger policy an element of consumer and social policy making.[159]

---

[155] OJ 2004 C31/5. Also available via:
http://europa.eu.int/comm/competition/mergers/legislation/regulation/.

[156] Paras. 78, 79 respectively.

[157] Cf. C. Luescher, 'Efficiency Considerations in European Merger Control' [2004] *ECLR* 72.

[158] Article 2(1)(b) Regulation.

[159] Cf. F. Fine, 'The Appraisal Criteria of the EC Merger Control Regulation' [1991] 4 *ECLR* 148, esp. 150–151.

Sir Leon Brittan, Competition Commissioner in the early years of the Regulation, declared his view that this formulation does not deflect the Regulation from its paramount concern to secure a competitive market:[160]

> The technical and economic progress which a merger may bring about will certainly form part of the Commission's analysis of the reasons for a merger. However, this does not mean that such progress is a legitimate defence for a merger which creates a dominant position.[161]

This approach has not been altered by Commissioners who have assumed responsibility for the Competition portfolio since. Nor has the relevant wording in the Regulation been touched at any time, with the result that the debate remains alive.

The issues that are at stake can be illustrated with reference to the blocked merger mentioned above, that between Aerospatiale Alenia and De Havilland.[162] The negative Decision attracted two distinct levels of criticism from commentators who would have preferred the deal cleared. Some thought the MTF's market definition unduly narrow and that therefore the power of the merged firm was rather exaggerated by the exclusion of potential competitors in neighbouring markets. This turns on an essentially technical point of economic analysis of markets. The second criticism was broader. It was said that the MTF, led by Leon Brittan, had failed to use merger policy as an instrument of industrial policy. The deal, it was said, would have created a strong European firm capable of competing effectively in world markets and that this should have motivated support for the merger, even where there were anticompetitive implications internal to Europe. Such belief in the virtue of a policy of developing 'European Champions' has long been associated with France, though it is traditionally much less popular in Britain and Germany.[163] In any event, the Community regulatory authorities under Sir Leon Brittan declined to use the Regulation in this way and it remains a moot point whether the Regulation, as presently drafted, *could* be interpreted as an industrial policy instrument of this type. Shortly after the affair, the European

---

160 Sir Leon Brittan, 'The Law and Policy of Merger Control in the EEC' (1990) 15 *ELRev* 351 and, more fully, *Competition Policy and Merger Control in the Single European Market* (Grotius, 1991). See also C. Overbury (first head of the MTF), 'First Experiences of European Merger Control' (1990) *ELRev* Competition Law Checklist 79.

161 P.35 in *Competition Policy and Merger Control in the Single European Market*, note 160 above.

162 Note 145.

163 For discussion see J. Halverson, 'EC Merger Control: Competition Policy or Industrial Policy? Views of a US practitioner' [1992/2] *LIEI* 49.

Parliament adopted a resolution which proposed a revision of the Regulation to take account of industrial, social, regional and environmental factors. This has not been accepted, nor are such notions likely to find favour in the current political climate where Britain and Germany, in particular, are firmly wedded to using merger policy solely to protect competitive markets.

Echoes of this debate may be discerned in the *GE/Honeywell* flashpoint, mentioned above.[164] Here the criticism was, in a sense, applied in reverse. American interests complained that the deal, which was struck between two firms with most of their interests based in America, had been blocked in Brussels in order to protect smaller European interests who would have found it tough to compete with the new merged entity. The Commission vigorously rejected any such suggestion of protectionism.[165] It insisted that orthodox market analysis had brought it to the conclusion that the deal was anti-competitive within the meaning of Art. 2 of the Regulation. It argued strenuously that any such deal, irrespective of the parties' identity, would have been blocked and it denied it had any broader political motivation. It is endemic to merger control that it is difficult to make objective judgements on whether the allegation of 'politicisation' is justified or not. All one can conclude is that the Commission *says* that it applies the Merger Regulation in line with an assessment of the impact of the deal on the competitive structure of the market to the exclusion of wider concerns of industrial, social or consumer policy. And indeed, in an echo of the *Aerospatiale Alenia/De Havilland* wrangle a decade earlier, the Commission's (flawed)[166] decision to block the *Schneider/Legrand* merger itself attracted criticism from France precisely because it was seen to have damaged the capacity of European firms to grow through merger and thereby actively to compete in global markets.[167] Such criticism can be – and was – advanced from an economic perspective rooted in disputes about how to assess market power post-merger. And it can also be – and was – advanced from a more overtly political perspective that emphasises the need to protect and promote European industry under the cover of the merger control regime. So the Commission has been criticised from France for *not* acting in defence of European industry, while from America it was criticised in *GE/Honeywell* for doing precisely the opposite. In the meantime the Commission insists it simply applies the control test set out

---

[164] Note 147 above.

[165] E.g. 'EU defends legal case on takeovers', *Financial Times* 16 October 2001, p. 16. See also Commission Press Release 3 July 2001, IP/01/939.

[166] See the CFI rulings, note 152 above.

[167] E.g. 'France tries to overturn EU ban on merger', *Financial Times* October 5, 2001, p. 12; 'Fabius [Finance Minister of France] hits out at Commission over policy on competition', *Financial Times* February 14, 2002, p. 8.

in Art. 2 of the Merger Regulation, which is targeted on assessment of the implications of the merger for competition alone.

In common with most competition law, merger law assumes that consumers stand to benefit indirectly. Explicit reference to the consumer is relatively rare and participation of consumers in decision making rarer still. However, it might be noted that in *Comité Central d'Entreprise de la SA Vittel v Commission*[168] workers in a firm affected by a merger which the Commission had cleared were considered to have standing to challenge the Decision before the EC, although on the facts no interim measures were granted. It is possible that a consumer organisation could be sufficiently involved in a merger to have similar standing before the EC – now, initially, the Court of First Instance – in the event that a decision is taken which it considers contrary to the consumer interest. By analogy, the decision in *BEUC v Commission*[169] provides support for this view. But it will be rare.

12.4.3 United Kingdom Merger Law[170]

UK merger law, like UK law governing restrictive practices and monopolies, has been radically transformed by the Labour government that came to power in 1997. In common with the reform of those other spheres of competition law, the changes to merger law were motivated by the perception that the UK possessed a poorly-crafted legal regime that was out of step with that preferred by other developed economies and that UK business suffered in consequence. However, UK merger law has been reshaped into a pattern which has something in common with the model found at EC level but which is by no means the flattering imitation of Arts. 81 and 82 which has been adopted in order to tackle restrictive practices and monopolies. Accordingly UK merger law is usefully compared with EC merger law, and will probably normally generate similarly-motivated decisions, but it is not the same species.

The principal feature of merger control under the now-ousted regime under the Fair Trading Act 1973 was the centrality of political discretion.[171] There were three distinct steps. First, a discretion was vested in the Secretary of State for Trade and Industry to refer a merger to the Monopolies and Mergers Commission (MMC). Second, the MMC reported on the merger in the light of its judgement of its impact on the public interest, but its views were not necessarily conclusive. Stage three involved

---

168 Case T–12/93 R judgment of 6 July 1993.
169 Note 56 above.
170 Whish note 9 above, Ch. 22.
171 For a full account see the first edition of this book, Chapter 15.4.2.

final disposal of the case by the Minister, who could confirm the MMC's views, but who could give a green light even to a merger viewed unfavourably by the MMC. So MMC reports tried to expose the 'public interest', a notoriously nebulous concept, but even then the reports were not conclusive. Ministers issued periodic guidelines which set out their approach to the exercise of the discretion conferred on them by the statute. But these did not constitute binding statements of policy. At the heart of the regime lay a political discretion that was subject to only marginal judicial review.[172] From the perspective of firms considering commercial plans, this was potentially alarmingly unpredictable. Firms did not have to pre-notify merger plans. They had to proceed, hoping they would not be snared by the Fair Trading Act. On any measure this was worryingly badly designed regulation.

The perception grew that this scheme was unwieldy, intransparent and liable to generate excessive interventionism. It was also strikingly remote from the administrative style of review preferred in the EC. In fact there is little empirical evidence that UK merger control was unusually obstructive of business choices. In practice most deals were untouched. But one cannot exclude the possibility that plans were simply not pursued for fear that a politically-motivated intervention might scupper a carefully-planned deal.

The House of Commons Select Committee on Trade and Industry's report, *UK Policy on Monopolies*, was published in May 1995.[173] It made a strong case for streamlining the institutional structure and diminishing political discretion in favour of a more administrative model. The report is notable for an explicit recommendation that 'consideration of consumer interests be at the heart of competition policy'.[174] The Conservative government of the mid-1990's was unpersuaded by the value of the proposed changes, but the case was largely accepted by the Labour administration that assumed office in 1997. An August 1999 consultation document published by the DTI offered the promise to minimise the element of political discretion in the process. This has now been finally implemented.

Mergers were excluded from the statutory prohibitions introduced under the Competition Act 1998.[175] A more sophisticated regime was required. The 2001 White Paper *Productivity and Enterprise: A World Class Competition Regime* paved the way[176] and UK merger law is now governed by Part 3 of the Enterprise Act 2002. There is no obligation to

---

172   *R v Secretary of State for Trade and Industry, ex parte Lonrho* [1989] 2 All ER 609, [1989] 1 WLR 525.
173   HC Papers 249 1994–95.
174   Para. 72.
175   Schedule I Competition Act 1998.
176   Note 88 above.

pre-notify mergers. This distances the UK system from that which applies at European level. Mergers that meet the statutory definition may be referred for investigation by the OFT to the Competition Commission (CC). However, although this is neither procedurally nor institutionally a replica of the EC merger system the substantive test applied to judge the worth of mergers is much more readily comparable. The criteria governing the OFT's decision whether to refer the deal to the CC are directed at assessment of the perceived implications for competition in affected markets. The job of the CC is also to investigate the impact of the merger on competition – specifically, it is asked to determine whether the merger will lead to a substantial lessening of competition. This is a tighter test than the woolly public interest test previously employed under the Fair Trading Act 1973. As part of this inquiry it is explicitly provided that 'customer benefits', including reduced prices and innovation, shall be considered.[177] A negative finding by the Competition Commission will result in the merger being blocked, or, less severe, being allowed to proceed subject to conditions.

The leeway conceded to Ministerial involvement is confined to mergers in the defence and water industries; or, where a political claim to a more general public interest basis for intervention is raised, to circumstances where the Minister serves an intervention notice explaining the basis for his or her special concern. The intention is that this power, which contradicts the main thread of the reforms, shall be used rarely. Politicians are to leave the normal run of merger control well alone. A separate regime for the politically sensitive media sector, covering mergers involving newspapers or broadcasting activities, is established by the Communications Act 2003.

Probably one should not expect outcomes under the new system that are noticeably different from previous practice. For all the murk of political discretion, merger policy over the last two decades in the UK has normally in practice used a focus on the competitive implications for the market as the key basis for judging the desirability of a deal.[178] But the institutional pattern has been altered – and improved – by the Enterprise Act 2002. In the field of merger control, it is of course also provided that the UK authorities shall not examine mergers that fall under Community jurisdiction by virtue of Art. 1 of the Merger Regulation 139/2004, excepting only the possibility that the Commission might allow scrutiny at national level of a merger with a 'Community dimension' by virtue of Arts. 9 or 21 of the Merger Regulation.[179]

---

[177] Sections 30, 35, 41 EA 2002.

[178] S. Goodman, 'Steady as she goes: the Enterprise Act 2002 Charts a Familiar Course for UK Merger Control' [2003] *ECLR* 331; Whish note 9 above p. 908 *et seq.*

[179] Note 138 above.

Appeals are directed to the Competition Appeals Tribunal (CAT). It was widely supposed that a light touch would be adopted; these are not readily justiciable issues and involve the exercise of a broad discretion vested by the statute in the relevant administrative bodies, the OFT and the CC. This will probably prove to be the case, though mergers often involve high stakes and litigation may sometimes hold appeal as part of commercial strategy.

In its 2004 decision in *IBA Health v Office of Fair Trading*[180] the Court of Appeal overturned a decision of the CAT. A third party challenge by IBA Health to an OFT acceptance of a merger between its competitors Isoft and Torex had succeeded before the CAT. The CAT had taken the view that the OFT is required to pursue a two-stage analysis. It should consider whether there is a significant prospect of a lessening of competition and, if it thinks there is not, it should proceed to consider whether there is a significant prospect of the CC reaching a different view were it to be invited to conduct a full inquiry. The Court of Appeal held that as a matter of law the CAT demanded too much of the OFT. The statutory test under s. 33 EA refers to the OFT's belief that the merger may or may not be expected to result in a substantial lessening of competition. The extra element involving assessment of the CC's expected attitude, which the CAT envisaged to form part of the OFT's inquiry and which, if correctly stated by the CAT, would have led directly to a great increase in the size of the regulatory burden imposed by the regime, was rejected by the Court of Appeal.

12.5 COMPETITION POLICY AND THE CONSUMER INTEREST REASSERTED

Competition policy suffers from an obscurity born of the unavoidable imprecision of economic analysis and deepened by the (sometimes avoidable) confusion inflicted by institutional fragmentation. However, recent reforms in both the EC and, especially, in the UK have done much to improve the shape and vitality of the relevant legal provisions. Competition policy is a significant element in shaping the operation of the market in the consumer interest. Competition policy has, admittedly, typically been seen as an indirect expression of consumer policy. However, the deterrence of anticompetitive cartels, the control of abusive practices by monopolists and the supervision of firms proposing to merge are all elements in promoting free and fair market structures. The consumer stands to benefit from effective implementation of such policies. This perception has lately been driven much closer to the forefront of political rhetoric in

---

[180] [2004] EWCA Civ 142, *The Times* 25 February 2004.

the EC and, especially, in the UK. It is likely to remain true that the consumer has little tangible connection with the application of competition law. And there are – as, we hope, this book makes very clear – several features of market failure and injustice which require remedies in the consumer interest that are not the preserve of competition law. But the consumer, whether or not a collector of replica football kits,[181] is intended as a beneficiary of markets that are subjected to the discipline of an effective supervision of restrictive practices, cartels, monopolies or dominant positions, and mergers. Competition policy is (part of) consumer policy.

---

[181] Note 1 above.

Chapter 13

Consumer Law Enforcement in England and Wales

13.1 INTRODUCTION

So far this book has been principally concerned with the substantive rights consumers have. We have focussed on how the balance should be struck between protecting consumers and other objectives such as not placing excessive burdens on businesses or stifling innovation. We have also looked at techniques of protecting consumers and how the right mix of private law, regulation and self-regulation can be achieved. Increasingly it is being realised that, as well as having well drafted laws, it is vital that there be proper enforcement mechanisms. Indeed it is a criticism of consumer laws in many developing countries that whilst they frequently have state of the art substantive consumer protection rules, there are few viable enforcement mechanisms. Enforcement is, however, also a problem that taints consumer law is developed legal systems. This has been recognised and the need to focus on enforcement has been given a high priority at both the national[1] and European level.[2] In this chapter we look at enforcement of regulatory rules and in the final chapter we focus on individual access to justice.

13.2 DTI[3]

In the UK central government involvement on consumer protection is divided between the Department of Trade and Industry (DTI) and the Office of Fair Trading (OFT). The DTI is a central government department and the OFT relies upon the DTI to be its spokesperson within government.

The DTI's Consumer Safety Unit has some 'hands on' work in relation to consumer safety matters and even has some enforcement powers, although it uses them only sparingly.[4] For the most part though the DTI

---

1   See White Paper, *Modern Markets: Confident Consumers*, especially Ch. 7.
2   Effective enforcement of consumer protection rules is one of the Commissions three key objectives in its Consumer Protection Strategy 2002–6: OJ 2002 C 137/2.
3   See http://www.dti.gov.uk.
4   See Chapter 10.

acts as a policy-maker. For example, it is responsible for implementing the UK's consumer law obligations under EC law. Most significantly it has set the tone for consumer policy in its White Paper *Modern Markets: Confident Consumers.*[5]

The Ministry of Agriculture, Fisheries and Food (MAFF) was suspected of favouring farmers over consumers. This led to the establishment of the independent Food Standards Agency. Similarly it could be argued that there are potential dangers in the DTI being responsible for both promoting industry and protecting consumers. It is, however, noticeable that since the Labour Party came to government the DTI has given consumer protection a higher priority, although it is still cautious about the dangers of over-regulating.

The DTI has also organised several consumer awareness campaigns, such as that related to Safe Internet Shopping.[6] It has set up a Consumer Gateway providing a portal for consumer information.[7]

13.3 OFT[8]

The OFT is not a government department. Its structures were reformed in the Enterprise Act 2002 and are discussed below.[9] It has been the main government body responsible for protecting the consumer interest since it came into existence by the Fair Trading Act 1973. It is both a competition authority and a consumer protection authority. This has both advantages and disadvantages. As we have seen,[10] there are close connections between consumer and competition policy and the housing of both responsibilities under one roof should help consumer values be represented within competition policy. Equally, however, competition is by far the larger more high profile side of the OFT's work. This could leave consumer protection as the Cinderella operation. To date this has been avoided, but there is need for continued vigilance.

The OFT has a number of functions. For instance, it provides information to consumers to help them understand their rights and make better choices. It also acts as a co-ordinating body with other regulatory bodies at the national and international level. It is also a regulator of a number of pieces of legislation. By far the largest amount of time is spent on credit matters where its role as credit licensor gives it considerable

---

5   This is discussed in detail in Chapter 1.
6   http://www.consumer.gov.uk/consumer_web/e-shopping.htm.
7   http://www.consumer.gov.uk/consumer_web/index_v4.htm.
8   See http://www/dti.gov.uk.
9   See Chapter 13.9.5.3.
10   See Chapter 12.

influence on the market. Many consumer businesses need a credit license to operate. It also has functions as a regulator under numerous other laws: some that have been discussed in this book include the Control of Misleading Advertisement Regulations 1988, Consumer Protection (Distance Selling) Regulations 2000, and the Unfair Terms in Consumer Contracts Regulations 1999.

Later in this chapter we will look in detail at three other general functions the OFT has. These are all related to improving trading standards. First, the general function of keeping practices under review and possibly lobbying for law reform. Second, the encouragement of codes of practice. Finally there are the specific powers the OFT has to tackle rogue traders who breach consumer laws.

13.4 NCC[11]

Brief mention should be made of the NCC. This is a government sponsored body, which does not represent individual consumers, but seeks to ensure the consumer voice is heard in policy debates. It takes a particular brief to look after the interests of vulnerable consumers. This is important because whereas membership based organisations such as the Consumers' Association[12] and the organisations that make up the National Federation of Consumer Groups[13] provide an important voice for consumers, they tend to draw their support from the well-educated middle classes. Often the NCC and the Consumers' Association have similar objectives, but occasionally they differ because they do sometimes speak for different types of consumers. This is not to say Consumers' Association is not concerned for vulnerable consumers, simply that the NCC pays special attention to their needs.

13.5 SECTORAL REGULATORS[14]

It is a feature of modern consumer law that some areas have become so complex and specialised that they need to be treated as areas of law in their own right. That is why sectors like food and financial services are no longer possible to be treated fully within the confines of a generalist book on consumer protection. Similarly they have their own regulators, the Food

---

11   See http://www.ncc.org.uk/about.htm.
12   See http://www.which.net/corporate/contents.html.
13   See http://www.nfcg.org.uk/intro.htm.
14   These are also discussed at Chapter 1.9.2.2.

Standards Agency[15] and Financial Services Authority.[16] Privacy and freedom of information matters are dealt with by the Information Commissioner.[17]A number of sectors have their own regulators such as the Gas and Electricity Markets Authority ('Ofgem'),[18] Director-General of Water Services ('Ofwat'),[19] the Office of Communications ('Ofcom'),[20] the Rail Regulator[21] and the Civil Aviation Authority.[22]

13.6 LOCAL AUTHORITIES

It has been a tradition of UK consumer law for the bulk of enforcement to be carried out at a local level by Trading Standards Departments. Much of this work involves enforcement of criminal law and the particular issues that gives rise to have been discussed earlier.[23] However, increasingly Trading Standards is seeing its role as one of prevention and education. Examples of this include local fair trading schemes, where trading standards officers try to ensure traders and their staff are aware of consumer rights and will follow good practice in return for allowing then to use a fair trade logo.

Trading Standards Departments are found within local authorities. There is one in each unitary authority. Where two layers of local government exist this function will typically be carried on by the county council. In London it is the function of the boroughs. The growth of unitary authorities has meant that the number of trading standards departments has increased. This in turn has caused problems as smaller authorities have less resources and may be less able to perform the wide range of function required of them due both to the lack of resources and also shortage of expertise. Pooling resources may be advantageous so that, for instance, a one-off expensive testing of a product does not wipe out the entire technical budget of a department. There have been discussions about whether the system should be restructured on a regional basis and if regional assemblies became a reality this might be one model for the

---

15   See http://www.foodstandards.gov.uk.
16   See http://www.fsa.gov.uk.
17   See http://www.informationcommissioner.gov.uk.
18   See http://www.ofgem.gov.uk/ofgem/index.jsp.
19   See:
      http://www.ofwat.gov.uk/aptrix/ofwat/publish.nsf/content/navigation-homepage(ofwat).
20   See http://www.ofcom.org.uk.
21   See http://www.rail-reg.gov.uk.
22   See http://www.caa.co.uk/index.asp.
23   See Chapter 11.

development of trading standards services. In some respects the tradition of local enforcement stands out in stark contrast to the increasing national and transnational perspectives and organisational structures of business. Efforts to integrate and co-ordinate enforcement between local, national, European and International levels are complicated by different political traditions and priorities.

Local enforcement is considered effective because officers are aware of local circumstances and priorities. It also has some drawbacks. Local politicians may be sensitive to complaints by local businesses, which may be critical of what they view as excessive enforcement practices. There are also problems of inconsistency. These are sought to be addressed in a number of ways.

The Trading Standards Institute[24] tries to promote enforcement standards through training and the development of Codes of Professional Conduct. It also incidentally provides a Fair Trading Award as a qualification for key staff in the trading community. The Local Authorities Co-ordinators of Regulatory Services (LACORS)[25] provides an important co-ordinating role.

Two aspects of LACORS work are particularly noteworthy attempts to address the problem of inconsistent application of the law between Trading Standards Departments. Trading Standards Departments can seek advice on the interpretation of the law from LACORS.[26] Also the Home Authority Principle has been developed,[27] under which the Trading Standards Department where a company has its headquarters will advise and liase with that company and in particular act as the source for legal interpretation. Though it is not formally binding, the advantages of the Home Authority Principle are such that it is in practice largely, though not uniformly, adhered to. Nevertheless it does have some problems, especially as it puts significant stress on particular authorities. For example, the City of Westminster has a disproportionately large percentage of Head Offices within its boundaries. The Government has been keen to further reduce inconsistency and has sought to achieve this though measures aimed at better enforcement generally.

13.7 ENFORCEMENT CONCORDAT

Section 5 of the Deregulation and Contracting Out 1994 included powers that Government could use to make enforcement more effective and less

---

[24] http://www.tradingstandards.gov.uk.
[25] http://www.lacors.gov.uk.
[26] http://www.lacors.gov.uk/pages/trade/LACORSAdvice.asp.
[27] http://www.lacors.gov.uk.

burdensome on business. However, on coming to power the Labour Government preferred a more consensual approach to improving enforcement and has developed an Enforcement Concordat. Section 5 of the 1994 Act is replaced by a new power for the Secretary of State to make Codes of Practices relating to regulatory requirements;[28] but this is viewed as a 'light touch' reserve power.[29]

The Enforcement Concordat sets out principles of good enforcement.[30] These include setting annual published service standards against which performance will be judged; providing information in plain language and disseminating information widely; working on the basis that prevention is better than cure; having a well publicised, effective and timely complaints procedure; and, acting proportionately and consistently. Businesses will be told what is the law and what is just good advice. If possible there will be discussion before action is taken. If action is taken prompt explanations will be provided for why it was necessary. Advice on any appeal mechanisms will be provided when action is taken.

13.8 EUROPEAN AND INTERNATIONAL CO-OPERATION

The European single market has inevitable given rise to an increased number of cross-border regulatory issues. In the product safety chapter we noted that enforcement had been enhanced by the need for each state to establish an authority responsible for consumer safety matters that had to be vested with certain powers and through the introduction of mechanisms that exist for the exchange of information about unsafe products within Europe.[31] Europe is increasingly aware of the need for effective cross-border enforcement arrangements in other areas where the consumer's economic interests rather than his safety are at stake. Some disreputable businesses attempt to use national boundaries as shields against enforcement. This is possible because national enforcement officers may give a lower priority to unfair practices aimed at other member states' consumers[32] and sometimes national legislation only allows them to act when consumers in their domestic state are affected.

We shall see below that the Injunctions Directive seeks to allow 'qualified entities' (usually public consumer protection bodies or consumer

---

28   Section 9 Regulatory Reform Act 2001.
29   *Explanatory Notes to Regulatory Reform Act 2001*, para. 30.
30   Available at:
        http://www.cabinet-office.gov.uk/regulation/publicsector/enforcement/concordat.htm.
31   See Chapter 10.6.
32   This may violate EC law obligations to secure effective enforcement, but its occurrence in practice is doubtless not uncommon and hard to uncover.

organisations) in one member state to take action in another member state when traders of that other member state are harming their consumers.[33] The Commission is also proposing to go further in a proposed regulation on co-operation between national authorities responsible for the enforcement of consumer protection laws.[34] In many ways these are modelled on the product safety rules. Member states will have to designate competent authorities and a single liaison office and vest them with a range of powers to investigate and act against intra-community infringements. There will be obligations of mutual assistance when requests are made from authorities in other states to exchange information or take enforcement action. Where authorities become aware of intra-Community infringements posing serious risks there will be obligations to inform the Commission and other member states. Enforcement and surveillance activities will be co-ordinated, as will matters such as training and the collection of consumer complaints.

These developments are encouraging, but in the age of mass communications, and particularly given the impact of the internet, it is becoming increasingly meaningless to have effective protection only within the Community. One mechanism that gives slightly greater reach is the OECD that has long had a thriving Consumer Policy Committee. Ironically the development of consumer safety within OECD and in particular its procedures for the notification of product dangers was adversely affected by the impact of EC laws which became the main pre-occupation of member states. However, in the internet context the OECD has been to the fore developing model laws for consumer protection.[35] Also the International Consumer Enforcement and Protection Network (ICEPN)[36] (formerly known as the International Marketing Supervision Network) has been established and provides mechanisms for mutual assistance. It has been useful in reacting to scams like the Canadian fraudsters who claimed UK consumers had won the Canadian lottery but needed to pay sums to release the winnings. It is also conducts internet sweep days to target fraudulent and deceptive scams emerging on the Internet.

---

[33] See Chapter 13.9.5.3.

[34] COM(2003) 443.

[35] See *Guidelines for Consumer Protection in the Context of Electronic Commerce* (OECD, 1999).

[36] See http://www.imsnricc.org. It is comprised mainly of OECD members.

13.9 OFT – IN DETAIL

The remainder of this chapter will be devoted to the general powers the OFT has to bring about reforms in the law, promote Codes of Practice and deal with rogue traders. The problems surrounding the provisions of the Fair Trading Act 1973 will be considered before, the reform debates are considered and finally the product of that debate – the new provisions found in the Enterprise Act 2002.

13.9.1 Part II – Rule-making Powers[37]

When the Fair Trading Bill was passing through Parliament, pyramid-selling practices caused such concern that provisions to deal with them were included in the Act.[38] Part II of the Act was intended to be a mechanism through which the Director-General could propose amendments where the consumer's economic interests were threatened. It widely became recognised as a failure with one former Director-General describing it as 'an example of a bold idea smothered by an excess of nervous caution so that the resulting provisions have inevitably been a disappointment'.[39] In fact the Director-General only used the procedure for four matters. The first three references resulted in orders being made,[40] whilst the final reference on failures to indicate VAT in prices did not lead directly to a reform.

The Part II procedure involved the Director-General referring the matter to a Consumer Protection Advisory Committee. This committee was quite rigorous in its scrutiny of proposals and if the Committee rejected it the measure could not be adopted. If the Committee approved the proposal then the Secretary of State could either adopt the Director-General's proposals or those proposals as amended by the committee. He could not finesse the measure further. These restrictions meant that in the end the Director-General preferred to use other powers to amend the law or simply lobby ministers directly.

---

37 For more detail see first edition, pp. 502–507.
38 Sections 118–122, Fair Trading Act 1973 and Pyramid Selling Schemes Regulations 1989, S.I. 1989/2195 (as amended). The scope of the provisions was extended by the Trading Schemes Act 1986 to cover situations where people were paying to join schemes in the hope of making money from recruiting others: see now Trading Schemes Regulations 1997, S.I. 1997/30.
39 G.Borrie, The Development of Consumer Law and Policy, (Stevens, 1984) at p. 127
40 Consumer Transactions (Restrictions on Statements) Order 1976, S.I. 1976/1813, Mail Order Transactions (Information) Order 1976 S.I. 1976/1812 and Business Advertisements (Disclosure) Order 1977 S.I. /1918.

Although the procedures became ultimately moribund, the significance of these powers in the history of the OFT should not be underestimated. Now that it is an established institution, it is hard to imagine it as a fledgling organisation. However, in those early days the fact that it had a route to threaten legislative change was an important factor in causing businesses to take the OFT seriously.

13.9.2 Codes[41]

The decline of the Part II procedure led to the OFT placing increased emphasis on the development of Codes of Practice. Section 124(3), Fair Trading Act 1973, was something of a legislative after thought, that placed the Director-General under a duty 'to encourage trade associations to prepare and to disseminate to their members, codes of practice for guidance in safeguarding and promoting the interests of consumers in the United Kingdom'. The Director-General had a couple of levers to assist in promoting codes. He could threaten to refer the agreement to the Restrictive Practices Court for a determination that it was against the public interests and hence void. More positively he could lend his support to Code, typically by writing a preface. A good number of Codes were developed with the approval of the OFT.

At first the OFT would negotiate the detailed wording of Codes. In a study published in 1980, Pickering and Cousins were unable to ascertain whether the capture theory, whereby industries learned how to deal with government agencies, applied to the OFT and its development of Codes of Practice. Some traders argued the process had helped foster a greater understanding of each other's viewpoint. Another however, admitted that 'the trade quickly learned how to handle officials'.[42] In 1991 the OFT developed a new approach to Codes of Practice. Instead of looking at the detailed wording of codes, they would endorse those that met a series of 'best practice' criteria. However, during the 1990s the OFT became more sceptical both about the value of the content of some Codes and the effectiveness with which they were enforced.

---

[41] For more detail see first ed., pp. 507–511.

[42] J.F. Pickering and D.C. Cousins, *The Economic Implications of Codes of Practice* (UMIST, 1980).

13.9.3 Part III – Rogue Traders[43]

Part III of the Fair Trading Act 1973 was not concerned with general commercial standards, but rather with traders who failed persistently to comply with trading laws. It allowed the Director-General to seek assurances from rogue traders or as a last resort to go to court and obtain an undertaking or order. However the Director-General faced several problems when trying to use these powers, which eventually led to their repeal and replacement with a new regime under Part 8 of the Enterprise Act 2002.

The powers could only be exercised where there had been a breach of the criminal or civil law. This contrasts with his credit licensing powers where he could act against any conduct he considered to be 'unfair'.[44] We shall see this limitation also applies under the new regime. However, the problem was exacerbated in that the Director-General also had to show that the trader had 'persisted in a course of conduct'. It was very burdensome to collect proof of such breaches, Even when the procedure was streamlined it was still thought necessary to show evidence of six to ten complaints and possibly more if they related to a wide range of breaches.[45] Once sufficient evidence had been collected to make out a case the Director-General had first to use his best endeavours to obtain from the trader a written assurance that he would refrain from similar conduct. In one instance it took the Director-General 18 months to exhaust his best endeavours when a trader argued minor points on 44 complaints of breach of contract.[46] Court action could lead to either an undertaking being given to the court or an order requiring the trader to refrain from continuing similar conduct. The problem was that by the time the matter came to court the facts were often 'cold', because of all the delays built into the system.

13.9.4 Reform Debate

The OFT had long recognised that its powers to deal with rogue traders was inadequate. In the early the 1980s the idea of a fall-back power to deal with rogue traders more effectively has been mooted in the context of studies of the home improvements sector.[47] An ambitious discussion paper

---

43   For more detail see first edition, pp. 511–525.
44   See Chapter 9.2.
45   See *Part III Assurances – a New Approach* (Office of Fair Trading 1973).
46   See *Trading Malpractices* at p. 32.
47   *Home Improvements: a Discussion Paper* (Office of Fair Trading, 1982) and *Home Improvements: Report by the Director-General of Fair Trading* (Office of Fair Trading, 1983).

was put out in 1986 entitled A General Duty to Trade Fairly and this was followed by the more pragmatic Trading Malpractices report in 1990.

The 1986 Discussion Paper sought to use a general duty mechanism to raise trading standards, stamp out errant traders and improve consumer redress. Codes of practice would have been given an important role in fleshing out the content of the general duty. Enforcement would have been primarily by local trading standards officers with the OFT having the power to intervene in cases of general importance. Although informal approaches would have been used in the first instance, in the final resort court action could have been used to seek injunctions and redress.

Trading Malpractices dropped the idea of linking a general standard with redress. It focussed far more on streamlining the Part III procedure, for instance, by suggesting removing the requirement that a persistent course of conduct be shown and allowing cautions to be given rather than requiring that assurances be sought. We will see that the new Part 8 Enterprise Act 2002 regime reflects some of these features. However, there were also proposals to extend unfairness beyond conduct which breaches the criminal and civil law to also cover 'deceptive or misleading' or 'unconscionable' practices. This was said to mirror the Australian and Canadian fair trading laws. In a subsequent paper the OFT suggested replacing the reference to 'unconscionable' by 'oppressive' and sought to allay industry fears about trading standards having undue power by proposing the OFT should have exclusive enforcement powers.[48] However, the DTI were still cautious and in a 1994 consultation paper queried whether concepts like misleading, deceptive and oppressive were not unduly subjective and were clearly nervous about crossing the line between condemning unlawful and immoral practices.[49]

A general standard has yet to be introduced with reform debate focussing on making Codes of Practice more meaningful and reforms streamlining the Part III type procedure. The need to introduce a general unfairness standard may well arise under the influence of Europe and the need to implement the proposed Unfair Commercial Practices Directive.[50] The Government was initially hostile to this provision, but now supports it in part because it views a general duty as a means to lift regulation off businesses. The absence of general duty is also one of the weaknesses in UK legislation preventing it from being on a par with the best consumer protection regimes in the world.[51]

---

[48] *Revision of Part III, Fair Trading Act 1973* (Office of Fair Trading, 1993).

[49] For general discussion about balancing out regulatory benefits or burdens see Chapter 1.

[50] COM (2003) 356: see Chapter 8.7.3.

[51] *Comparative Report on Consumer Policy Regimes* (DTI, 2003).

In 1996 in Voluntary Codes of Practice[52] the OFT found that codes were not well respected by enforcement authorities and consumer advisers. It considered Codes had achieved 'real, though limited, successes'.[53] Indicators of success were identified as being: the availability of a strong sanction, a plausible threat of statutory regulation, a clear wish by the good players in the industry to distinguish themselves and obvious benefits to consumers, sufficient to affect their choice of trader. Reform was needed.

Subsequently, the OFT issued Raising Standards of Consumer Care.[54] Its subtitle Progressing beyond Codes of Practice indicated the thrust of the report which proposed that British Standards Institution (BSI) should develop a core standard and a suite of sectoral standards which businesses would sign up to in order to be able to display a 'better trader' logo. These standards would have to ensure an independent scheme for redress, perhaps under the auspices of an ombudsman. Policing would be undertaken by an independent approval body to avoid the difficulties that arise from trade associations having to discipline their own members. Firms would register to comply with the core standard and any relevant sectoral standard either by formal accreditation or annual public self-certification. A directory of registered firms would be published. Firms which generated either serious or numerous complaints could be deregistered by the approval body. This scheme was not favoured by the trade associations, who perhaps feared loss of influence over their members. Also the standardisation process, which has worked fairly well in the area of technical harmonisation, seems less well suited to marketing practices. Standards have been developed in relation to complaints handling, but the experience was not always an easy one.

The government stepped back from the standardisation approach and in its White Paper, *Modern Markets, Confident Consumers*[55] proposed that the OFT should have the role of developing core principles which the codes should comply with and awarding a seal of approval. We shall see that this is the scheme introduced by the Enterprise Act 2002.[56] It also proposed introducing a streamlined Part II procedure so that the Secretary of State could make an order against unfair commercial practices without having to refer to a Consumer Protection Advisory Committee, but no such provision is in the Enterprise Act 2002, which simply repealed Part II Fair

---

52   Office of Fair Trading.
53   *Ibid.*, at 15.
54   OFT (1998).
55   See Cm 4410..
56   A follow-up policy paper on Codes of Practice, http://ww.dti.gov.uk/consumer/law/2.htm, had suggested that the core principles be turned into directions given by the Secretary of State to the OFT which would then test Codes against them. This seemed a rather cumbersome procedure and has not been adopted.

Trading Act. The OFT will have to rely upon lobbying ministers for change and using other legislative powers.[57] As far as rogue traders are concerned the White Paper and follow-up report proposed a streamlined procedure for injunctions against specific practices where traders have breached laws.[58] This forms the basis of Part 8 of the Enterprise Act. It was also proposed to introduce banning orders prohibiting persons from carrying on business with consumers if they have proven themselves not to be fit to do so. This would have been a strong power, but it has not been included.

13.9.5 Enterprise Act 2002

The Enterprise Act 2002 contained a clutch of measures aimed at improving competitiveness and creating the conditions for enterprise. Reform of the traditional core of consumer protection law formed a small part of the total package, which also included important reforms to competition law and insolvency. However, as the 1999 White Paper, *Modern Markets: Confident Consumers*, asserted, competition policy is itself an under-recognised tool of consumer policy. This is examined in depth in Chapter 12. Outside the sphere of competition law, the measures explicitly targeted at the consumer included for the first time formally establishing the OFT; introducing a new approval schemes for Codes of Practice; and replacing Part III Fair Trading Act 1973 with a new injunction regime for traders breaking consumer laws.

13.9.5.1 Office of Fair Trading

The Fair Trading Act 1973 established the post of Director-General, but there is no mention in that statute of the OFT. However, the office supporting the Director-General became known as the OFT. The anomaly that the OFT was not officially established is remedied by the Enterprise Act 2002 which in Part I establishes the OFT[59] and simultaneously abolished the office of Director-General.[60] The functions of the Director-General are transferred to the OFT and references in legislation to the Director-General are to be treated as reference to the OFT. The OFT has a

---

[57]   See White Paper and follow up policy paper at:
       http://ww.dti.gov.uk/consumer/law/7.htm.
[58]   See White Paper and follow up policy paper at:
       http://ww.dti.gov.uk/consumer/law/8.htm.
[59]   Section 1.
[60]   Section 2.

board with a chairman, who in the first instance is John Vickers, the last Director-General. There is a separate Chief Executive.

The OFT has to produce an annual plan setting out its main objectives and priorities for the year.[61] It also has to publish an annual report.[62] Equally it can publish other reports relating to its functions. The OFT has to acquire information relating to its tasks.[63] It also has to make the public aware of how competition may benefit consumers and provide the public with information and advice on its functions, which of course includes consumer protection.

The rule-making procedures in part II of the Fair Trading Act 1973 are repealed. It is perhaps unfortunate that no new power to enact delegated legislation is put in place, but the position is simply the same as it was previously for the part II procedure was moribund. The Regulatory Reform Act 2001 has in any event given ministers greater powers to modernise laws. The OFT can make proposals or give information or advice to ministers or other public authorities, including about the law and proposed reforms. Ministers can ask the OFT for proposals, information or advice.

13.9.5.2 Codes

Section 8(1) of the Enterprise Act 2002 gives the OFT the function of promoting good consumer practice. As part of that function the OFT can make arrangements for approving consumer codes. As well as approving Codes it can also withdraw approval.[64] This arrangement is known as the Consumer Codes Approval Scheme. This is new as previously it was only possible to encourage codes, but there was no mechanism for officially granting or withdrawing approval. The OFT must specify the criteria to be applied by the OFT and guidance notes have been produced: see Core Criteria for Consumer Codes of Practice.[65] It can also provide for a symbol to be used to signify that a code is approved by the OFT and a logo has been developed and is being promoted.

The arrangements established by the OFT involves a two stage process. First, the code sponsor promises to meet the core criteria. In the second stage it must demonstrate, with evidence, that the Code meets the criteria in practice. Only at this second stage will approval be given and the use of the OFT-approved code logo be allowed.

---

[61]   Section 3.
[62]   Section 4.
[63]   Section 5.
[64]   Section 8(2).
[65]   OFT (2002).

In the first instance, code sponsors from seven 'priority sectors' were invited to apply for approval. These covered used cars, car repairs and servicing, credit, funerals, travel, estate agents and direct marketing. In December 2002 furniture and domestic appliance repair sectors were added to the list. Given increased resources the procedure has eventually been opened up to any interested sector. By the end of 2003 stage one had been reached by the Vehicle Builders and Repairers Association, the ombudsman for the Estate Agents Company Limited, the Direct Selling Association and the Association of British Travel Agents. A further 14 code sponsors are seeking approval. Interestingly some Trading Standards Departments have also expressed an interest in seeking approval for their local trader schemes. No organisation has yet reached stage two. What is interesting about stage two is that it requires demonstration of compliance and effective monitoring, which could involve mystery shopping and customer satisfaction surveys.

The OFT places emphasis on the code sponsors drafting their own codes to fit the needs of their sector, whilst taking the core criteria into account. It recommends code sponsors receive accreditation for plain English and they consider producing two versions of the code: one for consumers and a more detailed list of obligations for businesses. It lists seven core criteria, briefly these cover:

(i) Organisation
Code sponsors will typically be trade associations. The core criteria suggests that in practice the sponsor would normally have the majority of firms in a sector, but does not rule out approving niche progressive core sponsors. For some industries this may suggest that there needs to be some reorganisation of their trade representation. The funeral industry had five trade associations. Two of the largest have merged perhaps partly as a consequence if this criterion. Compliance with the Code must be mandatory on members. There must be independent disciplinary procedures dealing with non-compliance. A criticism of previous codes had been that trade associations were reluctant to sanction their members. The code sponsor must be adequately resourced.

(ii) Preparation of the code
It should be demonstrated that members will observe the Code, by for example obtaining written undertakings to that effect. Also it should be demonstrated that organisations representing consumers, enforcement bodies and advisory services have been adequately consulted both in the preparation of the Code and throughout the operation and monitoring of the Code.[66] These bodies do not have to be consulted on every provision or

---

66   See OFT's, *Consumer Code Approval Scheme.*

their views always taken into account, but it will be necessary to show that there has been real dialogue and their views considered.

(iii) Content
Naturally Codes should seek to remove or ease consumer concerns and address undesirable trade practices within a particular business sector. Importantly members must provide training and ensure relevant staff are aware of the Code. All too often trade associations adopted Codes and members advertised compliance, but the front line staff were not aware of their obligations under it. The following are marked out as areas Codes should address:

- clear and truthful marketing and advertising;
- clear pre-contractual information;
- clear terms and conditions of supply including fair contracts;
- delivery/completion dates;
- cancellation rights;
- guarantees and warranties;
- protection of deposit or prepayments;
- after-sales service provisions; and
- additional effort/help to be provided to vulnerable consumers.

In some of these areas the Codes may well simply support existing laws or existing self-regulatory institutions, like the Advertising Standards Authority. In some sectors rules such as cancellation rights might be extended into new areas. After-sales services is an area that legislators have steered clear off altogether.

Particularly interesting are the rules on vulnerable consumers. The guidance explains that vulnerable consumers are not just those having a bad day, nor merely those falling within the Disability Discrimination Act. Vulnerability might arise from poor literacy skills or lack of knowledge about a complex product or service. Equally consumers might be vulnerable when they purchase a funeral at times of distress. Such consumers are said to risk making an incorrect or inappropriate decision and responsible businesses should expend the necessary effort so that they understand all aspects of the transaction.

(iv) Complaints handling
There should be speedy, responsive, accessible and user friendly procedures for dealing with consumer complaints with reasonable agreed time limits for responding to complaints. The need for independence in such schemes is stressed. Conciliation services should be available and members should not be allowed to refuse to let matters go to the redress

scheme. Members should offer maximum co-operation with local consumer advisers or others consulted by consumers.

Traditionally Codes of Practice used low cost arbitration schemes, mainly run through the Chartered Institute of Arbitrators. Consumer arbitration in the UK has not the same bad press as in the US, where it is often used as an attempt to deny consumers justice by forcing them into expensive arbitration procedures.[67] Binding the consumer to arbitration in advance would not be allowed in UK law where the amount at stake is no more that £5,000 (the same as the current small claims limit).[68] Nevertheless in contrast to ombudsmen, which tend to be free to the consumer, can take good business practice into account and are only binding on the business, arbitration may appear less attractive. It often involves a fee, albeit subsidised. The decision is binding on the consumer, who enters a technical adjudicative process concerned with applying the law rather than best practice. There are, however some signs that arbitration is adapting and some schemes are taking on features of ombudsmen, i.e. free of charge to the consumer and non-binding.

(v) Monitoring

The monitoring obligations are novel and much of the success of the schemes will depend upon whether the benefits they provide traders, particularly through the use of the OFT logo are seen to justify the costs of implementing the monitoring obligations. Code sponsors need to develop performance indicators to measure the effectiveness of the Code. These might include mystery shopping and independent compliance audits. These results should be published. Annual reports should also be produced on the scheme including the number and type pf complaints referred to conciliation and independent redress schemes. Ideally these would be drawn up by an independent person or body. Copies should be provided to the OFT. The Code should be regularly reviewed and consumer satisfaction assessed to identify areas of the Code requiring amendment.

(vi) Enforcement

A procedure for handling non-compliance must be established. A range of sanctions should be set out, such as warning letters, fines, termination of membership. One of the problems has been that since trade associations are

---

67 See, F.L. Miller, Arbitration Clauses in Consumer Contracts: Building Barriers to Consumer Protection (1999) 78 *Mich. B.J.* 302.

68 Section 91 Arbitration Act 1996 and Unfair Arbitration Agreements (Specified Amount) Order 1999, S.I. 1999/2167. The Unfair Terms in Consumer Contract Regulations 1999 also apply to consumer arbitrations (s. 89 Arbitration Act 1996) and include as one of the indicatively unfair terms 'requiring the consumer to take disputes exclusively to arbitration not covered by legal provisions' (Schedule 2(1)(q)).

member based organisation it is hard for them to sanction their own members for fear of losing members and in turn income and influence. Only in certain sectors is membership of a trade association seen as important in order to trade effectively. ABTA and the travel industry springs to mind as one example where the public do look out for membership of the trade association. Indeed the sanction of expulsion is a difficult one to implement, since once a member is expelled there will be nothing the code sponsor can do to improve its behaviour. The OFT had earlier proposed that sanctions be dealt with by an independent body. The failure to require such an external supervision may yet prove to be an Achilles' heel in the new regime.

(vii) Publicity

Code sponsors and members must ensure consumers are aware of the Code. Adherence to the Code must be made clear in advertising and at point of sale. Copies must be available free of charge.[69] Code related publicity should be provided to the OFT. The logo should be used to signify OFT approval.

The OFT failed to introduce the far more independent scheme proposed in its Raising Standards of Consumer Care. Trade associations will be the ones responsible for drawing up and enforcing Codes. Nevertheless, the work of the OFT has forced many trade associations to recognise that their codes were not really bringing great benefits to consumers and convinced them of the need to embrace a more rigorous approach to self-regulation. The new procedures do seek to ensure Codes bring real benefits to consumers, although there is no explicit requirement that they go beyond the legal rules. There is also a new emphasis on proving that the scheme actually works to the consumer's advantage before approval is granted. It is still to be seen whether industry feels the benefits justify the efforts to seek approval. In the US a scheme for approving industry dispute settlement mechanisms has been unsuccessful because the standards were too rigorous.[70] The signs in the UK are that the relationship between the OFT and trade is such that there is some goodwill from industry to comply. This is a testament both to the efforts of the OFT and many trade associations. The test will be whether all industries can bear the additional costs.

Finally, it should be noted that there are still some legal issues surrounding the enforceability of Codes by consumers. Sometimes Codes may be expressly incorporated into contracts. Where this is not the case the

---

[69]   The writer applauds this, having had to pay for some Codes in the past!

[70]   Regulations under the Magnusson Moss Act 16 *Code of Federal Regulations* (CFR) 703.3–7; reproduced in I. Ramsay, *Consumer Protection* (Weidenfeld and Nicolson, 1989)) at 138–142.

consumer will have to rely on the courts implying a term that the Code will be followed. The courts have traditionally been reluctant to imply terms into consumer contracts unless they pass the business efficacy standard.[71] However, in *Bowerman v ABTA*[72] a consumer was able to enforce a Code of Practice on the basis of a notice of its terms in a travel agents. One might not be surprised if the courts increasing find means to hold traders to abide by Codes by using such traditional techniques as incorporation of the terms into the contract by notice. That said in most instances, non-compliance with Codes is in not an issue. Most traders are willing to abide by their voluntary commitments, but where they fail to do so and traders are willing to ignore their trade association, it would be useful if the consumer could have a contractual claim. Moreover, the wider availability in principle of a contractual claim is itself likely to induce ready compliance in practice, thereby furthering the ambition of the Codes to diminish the need for formal litigation.

The criminal law may be of some assistance. In *Re VG Vehicles (Telford) Limited*[73] a motor dealer was found to have breached s. 14, Trade Descriptions Act 1968 for falsely claiming he complied with the Motor Industry Code of Practice. Breaches of Codes can also be taken into account when the OFT exercises its the credit licensing function. Failures to comply with Codes were not however in themselves something which could form the basis of an action under Part III of the Fair Trading Act 1973 and the same would be true of Part 8 Enterprise Act 2002. Nevertheless, the requirement that a trader comply with Codes had been made a clause of assurances given by traders under Part III and the same would seem to be possible for undertakings under Part 8. The draft Unfair Commercial Practices Directive proposes that it should be treated as misleading for traders to fail to comply with firm and verifiable commitments in publicly accessible Codes.[74]

13.9.5.3 Part 8, Enterprise Act 2002

History

The reform of Part III of the Fair Trading Act was heavily influenced by the injunctions approach favoured by EC law. This injunctions approach

---

71 *Liverpool City Council v Irwin*, [1976] 2 All ER 39.
72 *The Times*, 24 November 1995.
73 (1981) 89 *ITSA Monthly Review* 91.
74 COM (2003) 356 Art. 6(2)(b).

first appeared in the Misleading Advertising Directive[75] when it was clearly for the national governments to decide whether to give this power to public authorities or consumer organisations. The Unfair Terms in Consumer Contracts Directive[76] was ambiguous on this point. At first the UK government restricted the power to challenge unfair terms to the Director-General,[77] but (under pressure from the Consumers' Association) when the Regulations were amended they included a wider range of public bodies able to seek injunctions as well as the Consumers' Association.[78]

This EC approach culminated in Directive 98/27/EC on injunctions for the protection of consumers' interests.[79] This extended the injunction procedure to a wider range of EC Directives. It also sought to tackle the problem of companies using the internal market as a means of evading enforcement by locating in one member state and directing unfair practices at consumers in a different state.[80] Bodies qualified in a member state to protect the consumer interest must be allowed to take action in the courts or before administrative authorities in other member states.[81] The Commission will draw up a definitive list of qualified bodies, which must be accepted by courts or administrative authorities. This was implemented in the United Kingdom by the Stop Now Orders (E.C. Directive) Regulations 2001.[82] These have now been repealed together with Part III of the Fair Trading Act 1973 and replaced by Part 8 of the Enterprise Act 2002. The OFT has produced substantial guidance notes, *Enforcement of Consumer Protection Legislation*[83] ('OFT Guidance').

Consumer
Part 8 introduces separate rules for breaches of domestic and Community law. Consumer is defined differently for domestic and Community infringements. Before any enforcement powers arise there must be harm caused to the collective interest of consumers.

---

[75]   OJ 1985 L250/17.
[76]   OJ 1993 L95/29.
[77]   S.I. 1994/3159.
[78]   S.I. 1999/2083 Art. 12 and Schedule 1: see Chapter 5.8.
[79]   OJ 1998 L 166/51.
[80]   See H.W. Micklitz, 'Cross-Border Consumer Conflicts – A French-German Experience' (1993) 16 *Journal of Consumer Policy* 411.
[81]   The OFT has used its cross-border powers for the first time in acting against a Belgium junk mailer: see Financial Times, 6 April 2004, p. 2.
[82]   S.I. 2001/1422.
[83]   Hereafter,'OFT Guidance'.

Consumer for Domestic Infringement

For domestic infringements the goods or services must have been supplied (or sought to be supplied) to an individual in the course of a business carried on by the person who supplied (or sought to supply them). The individual must have received (or sought to receive) them otherwise than in the course of a business carried on by him.[84] This is a fairly traditional approach to the definition of consumer in UK law, but it is extended also to cover individuals receiving goods or seeking to receive goods with a view to carrying on a business, but not in the course of a business carried on by him.[85] This rather cryptic wording covers persons setting up businesses and was intended to deal with scam home-working schemes and vanity publishers.

Consumer for Community infringement

Consumers for the purpose of Community infringements are persons within the definition of both the Injunctions Directive[86] and the directives (or parts thereof) listed in Schedule 13 of the Enterprise Act. Schedule 13 lists directives on misleading advertising, contracts negotiated away from business premises, consumer credit, package travel, unfair terms, timeshares, distance contracts, sale of consumer goods and e-commerce as well as some provisions in directives on television broadcasting and medicinal products for human use.

Collective harm

For the enforcement provisions to arise both sets of rules require the infringements to harm the 'collective interest of consumers'. Part 8 is not a means of dealing with individual cases. Although the collective harm is not defined in the Act, the OFT Guidance explains that it must affect, or have the potential to affect, consumers generally or a group of consumers.[87] This is a far more pragmatic approach than the French have taken to the concept of collective harm, where the jurisprudence has attempted to define collective harm as something distinct from simply the sum of individual harm, possibly involving loss in confidence in the market.[88] For the Community law infringements it will be necessary to be sensitive to the Community origin of the obligations and the possible ways in which the European Court of Justice will approach the matter. The UK approach is likely to be acceptable and even preferable to the philosophical French

---

84   Section 210(3)(4).

85   Section 210(4)(b).

86   OJ 1998 L 166/51.

87   Paragraph 3.8.

88   See G. Howells and R. James, 'Litigation in the Consumer Interest' (2002) *ILSA Journal of International and Comparative Law* 1 at 43.

approach, which has been difficult to apply in practice with many instances of only nominal damages being awarded.

The OFT Guidance talks of the need for evidence to support the collective harm and states that this might include an assessment of the importance of the practice or provision in question or of its prevalence and likely impact. This is problematic because establishing evidence is always costly and especially so when it involves showing what harm might occur rather than what harm has occurred. It also seems to suggest not only that the harm must be to the consumer collective, but also that the extent of harm has to pass a threshold of seriousness before action can be taken. Good enforcement practice may suggest a targeting of serious practices, but it is another matter to make this a pre-condition for action. These restrictions are not necessary implied by the legislation and should be treated as guidance for enforcement officers, rather than affecting the legal tests once an action is brought.

Domestic infringements[89]

Domestic infringements are acts of omissions done or made by a person in a course of a business that harm the collective interests of consumers in the United Kingdom. Note the limitation to consumers in the United Kingdom. National legislation restricting protection to their own state consumers has been one of the reasons why the EC has developed Community procedures such as the Injunctions Directive and proposed Enforcement Regulation. However, the trader need not have a place of business in the United Kingdom. So an overseas company selling in the UK or an internet trader, subject to country of origin rules within the EC,[90] could commit a domestic infringement.

The infringement must be of a provision specified by the Enterprise Act 2002 (Part 8 Domestic Infringements) Order 2003.[91] This currently lists 43 statutes affecting England and Wales. In addition the provision must relate to any of a number of types of measures listed in s. 211(2). These cover: (i) criminal contraventions; (ii) breaches of contract; (iii) breaches of non-contractual duties; any acts or omissions which (iv) give rise to a remedy or sanction enforceable in civil proceedings, or (v) which would render the agreement or security void or unenforceable to any extent, or (vi) where a person contrary to an enactment purports or attempts to exercise a right, or (vii) seeks to avoid liability where such avoidance is restricted or prevented under an enactment. These measures need not relate

---

[89]   Section 211.
[90]   See Chapter 7.4.8.
[91]   S.I. 2003/1593.

to consumers as such. It is immaterial whether there have been any proceedings, convictions or any waiver of breach of contract.[92]

When bringing or defending a Part 8 action the first stage is therefore to identify that the law in question has been specified by the Order, but then it will be necessary to go on and check that it fits within one of the seven headings summarised above. An attempt has been to draw the categories of potential infringement widely. The provisions will work well where there are specific clearly stated obligations that can easily be tested for compliance. Such examples might be rules relating to form of documents or information requirements. It will be relatively simple to show where there has been a breach.

The provisions may be less useful where defendants either deny there has been any breach on the specific facts or challenge the enforcer's interpretation of the law. Defendants might seek to argue that on the facts of the case the law has not been broken. For example, a trader might suggest that his goods, although easily recognisable as being of poor quality, were nevertheless satisfactory under the condition in which they were sold. We have seen how under Part III proceedings a trader once argued minor points on 44 breaches of contract.[93] Such defences are equally possible under the new procedure.

Although there is no need for there to have been legal action, it would be difficult to use Part 8 proceedings where the underlying issue was whether there had been on the facts an infringement. Given that individual circumstances are likely to vary greatly it will often be difficult to use Part 8 where factual assessments are necessary. This does not mean that Part 8 cannot be used whenever the outcome of the application of the law is uncertain. In *Director-General of Fair Trading v First National Bank*[94] the injunction procedure under the Unfair Terms in Consumer Contracts Regulation was used to challenge a term that required interest to be paid on outstanding balance even after agreed repayments for outstanding debt had been repaid. Although the clause was eventually found to be fair no-one doubted the correctness of using that procedure. A distinction should perhaps be drawn between practices aimed at the public generally, such as standard form contracts, documentation and advertising where an assessment can be made in the abstract and other rules where the question of infringement has to be judged on an individual basis. For instance, whether goods are unsatisfactory may depend upon what was said between the buyer and seller or the price of the goods. Equally, for example whether credit contracts are extortionate will depend upon the circumstances. Part 8

---

92 Section 211(4).
93 See 13.9.3.
94 (2001) 3 WLR 1297.

is probably inappropriate where individual assessments need to be made to determine breach.

A Part 8 action is also probably not the most appropriate mechanism to use where what is at issue is the interpretation of law, rather than its application. For example, there have been some high profile cases in consumer credit recently each determining whether wide-scale and long-standing practices breached the Consumer Credit Act 1974. *McGinn v Grangewood Securities*[95] concerned whether the discharge of a previous loan should count as credit or part of the total charge for credit and *Dimond v Lovell*[96] concerned whether contracts made to hire cars following road accidents were exempt from the Consumer Credit Act 1974 and hence recoverable as part of the claim for the road traffic accident. Both went to court as test cases and this seems clearly right given the uncertain state of the law. A Part 8 action would not have any advantage in similar circumstances. At alternative procedure that can be used where the facts are unlikely to be disputed is under another Part 8, this time Part 8 of the Civil Procedure Rules. The dispute between the OFT and some banks about the application of s. 75 of the Consumer Credit Act 1974 to overseas credit card transactions is being brought under this procedure. There seems little advantage in using the Enterprise Act 2002 procedure where what is desired is an authoritative determination of the law. Indeed it may be more complex to litigate under the Enterprise Act 2002 where the trader denies there has been any infringement on their understanding of the law.

Community infringement[97]

Community infringements are acts or omissions that contravene laws, regulations or administrative provisions of an EEA state giving effect to one of the listed Directives, mentioned above. A slight complication arises in that it also covers national measures providing additional permitted protections. Some EC directives provide very precise circumstances in which additional protection can be provided. The freedom to remove the development risks defence from laws implementing the Product Liability Directive would be one example. Many more directives include a general minimum harmonisation clause allowing additional national protective rules so far as they are compatible with the Treaty. The relevant national measures would seem to include those permitted either specifically or on the basis of a minimum harmonisation clause. This seems to be the UK's approach, for the OFT's Guidance refers to 'any provision which directly implements provisions in the Directives listed in the Injunctions Directive

---

[95]   [2002] EWCA Civ 522.
[96]   (2000) 2 WLR 1121.
[97]   Section 212.

or provides greater consumer protection of a related kind'.[98] The
Enterprise Act 2002 (Part 8 Community Infringements Specified UK
Laws) Order 2003[99] specifies those UK laws the Secretary of State
believes fall within the scope of the Community infringement provisions.
Generally measures classed as Community infringements are not also
treated as domestic infringements. There are some exceptions such as the
Consumer Credit Act 1974 where it was considered difficult to tell which
provisions implemented the Consumer Credit Directive, which provided
additional permitted protection and which fell outside the scope of the
Directive.[100]

Enforcers
Part 8 of the Enterprise Act 2002 provides for three categories of
enforcers: general enforcers, designated enforcers and community
enforcers.

General enforcers are the OFT, every local weights and measures
authority i.e. Trading Standards Departments and the Department of
Enterprise, Trade and Investment in Northern Ireland.[101] A general
enforcer may make an application for an enforcement order in respect of
any infringement.

Designated enforcers are those the Secretary of State determines have
as one of their purposes the protection of the collective interests of
consumers and has been so designated by order. They can be either public
or private bodies. Public bodies must be independent,[102] but their
designation is conclusive evidence that they are indeed public bodies.[103]
The Civil Aviation Authority, Director-General of Electricity Supply for
Northern Ireland, Director-General of Gas for Northern Ireland, Director-
General of Telecommunications, Director-General of Water Services, the
Gas and Electricity Markets Authority, Information Commissioner and Rail
Regulator have all been made designated public bodies.[104] They can make
applications in respect of any infringement to which their designation
relates, but in fact they have all been designated for all infringements.[105]

---

[98]   Paragraph 3.21.
[99]   S.I. 2003/1374.
[100]   OFT Guidance, para. 3.24.
[101]   Section 213(1).
[102]   Section 213(3).
[103]   Section 213(8).
[104]   The Enterprise Act 2002 (Part 8 Designated Enforces: criteria for Designation,
        Designation of Public Bodies as Designated Enforcers and Transitional Provisions)
        Order 2003, S.I. 2003/1399, Regulation 5 and Schedule.
[105]   *Ibid.*, Regulation 5.

Private bodies must satisfy criteria specified by the Secretary of State.[106] These relate to matters such as independence, impartiality, experience, competence, expertise, ability, capability, readiness to follow best practice and to co-operate with the OFT, other enforcers and regulators. The DTI has published guidance for private bodies seeking designation.[107] To-date no private bodies have been designated, but the Consumers' Association continues to have standing to seek injunctions under the Unfair Terms in Consumer Contracts Regulations 1999. The role of Consumers' Association in enforcing consumer laws is sometimes disputed, because since it has its own trading arm there could be a conflict of interest. However, the Regulations allow for this so long as the trading arm does not control the applicant and any profits are used to further the stated objectives of the applicant.

Community enforcers are qualified entities specified in the Official Journal.[108] However, this does not include general and designated enforcers and so will be restricted to qualified entities from other member states. Designated bodies can request to be notified as qualified entities so that they have standing in other member states.[109] Community enforcers can bring applications in respect of Community infringements. The Court can refuse the application if it thinks the purpose of the Community enforcer does not justify its making the application.[110]

Powers and Procedures

Information[111]
The OFT has the power to seek information to enable itself to exercise or consider exercising its functions and to enable private designated enforcers and Community enforcers to consider exercising any functions. Information can also be sought to help them consider whether undertakings or orders are being complied with. Other general enforcers and designated enforcers that are public bodies have their own powers to seek information. These can if necessary be supported by an application to court 65.

Consultation
Before applying for an enforcement order, the enforcer must consult with the person against whom the order would be made and with the OFT (if it

---

[106] *Ibid.*, Regulation 3.
[107] *Designation as an Enforcer for Part 8 of the Enterprise Act 2002* (DTI, 2003).
[108] Section 213 (5).
[109] Section 213(10).
[110] Section 215(7).
[111] Sections 224–7.

is not the enforcer).[112] The duty to consult can be waived if the OFT thinks an application for an enforcement order should be made without delay.[113] The obligation lasts for 14 days, seven if an interim order is being sought.

Application[114]

The application must name the person who has engaged in or is engaging in a domestic or Community infringement. In the case of a Community infringement only it is possible to bring an action when someone is merely likely to engage in action which constitutes a Community infringement. The OFT can direct that the enforcement application be brought by itself or such other enforcer as it directs.[115] In any event the OFT must be informed of the results of any applications.[116]

Undertakings[117]

An enforcer who could make an application can also accept an undertaking. This applies even where the OFT has directed that the application for an enforcement order should be made by someone other than that enforcer.[118] Any undertaking must by notified by the enforcer to the OFT. Undertakings can also be accepted by the court instead of making an enforcement order. The undertaking can require publication of the terms of the undertaking or a corrective statement.[119]

Enforcement orders[120]

When an infringement is found the Court has a discretion to make an enforcement order.[121] It must have regard to whether any undertaking was given and whether it was complied with. The order must indicate the nature of the infringement. A person complies with the order if he does not continue or repeat the conduct, engage in the conduct in his or any other business nor consent or connive in the carrying out of such conduct by a body corporate with which he has a special relationship.

The enforcement order can also require the order or corrective statement to be published. This duty to publish the order comes from the Injunctions Directive and is inspired by French traditions. It is unlikely to

---

112   Section 214.
113   Section 214(3).
114   Section 215.
115   Section 216.
116   Section 215(9).
117   Section 219.
118   Section 216(3)(a).
119   Section 217(9).
120   Section 217.
121   Where expedient it is possible for an interim order to be made: s. 218.

be widely used by British courts. It is more likely that publicity will be given to decisions by the OFT. Under Part III of the Fair Trading Act 1973 this had been problematic at times. In *R v Director-General of Fair Trading, ex parte FH Taylor & Co Limited*[122] the courts upheld the Director-General's freedom to publish an assurance, but made some comments that caused him to be cautious for a while. In due course he started again to issue press releases about court orders and assurances and the OFT Guidance indicates an intention to continue in this vein.[123] Indeed apart from press releases the intention is to place this information of the Consumer Regulations Website.

Follow-up[124]

If an undertaking is breached an application can be made to court, including asking for an enforcement order. Equally if an enforcement order is not complied with an application can be made to the court and the OFT has the same rights to apply as the enforcer that made the original application.

13.9.5.4 OFT Co-ordinating Role

During the discussions surrounding reform of Part III of the Fair Trading Act 1973 one of the issues was whether the power should be retained by the OFT or shared with trading standards. As trading standards are general enforcers the political decision seems to have been made that it is better to share out the power. Indeed the OFT Guidance states that when there is a local or sectoral problem it should be dealt with by the local or sectoral enforcer.[125] The OFT Guidance also makes it clear that it will expect the Home Authority Principle and Enforcement Concordat to be adhered to.[126]

However, the OFT has a number of mechanisms for controlling how the new powers are used. It must be consulted where enforcers believe an infringement has occurred and can direct which enforcer should make an application, taking over the case itself where it considers that appropriate. It is clear that it will favour referring matters to sectoral regulators, even self-regulatory bodies like the ASA.[127] It also provides guidance. We have referred to some of these documents, which will be brought together on a Consumer Regulations Website.

---

[122] [1981] ICR 292.
[123] Paragraph 3.85.
[124] Section 220.
[125] Paragraph 3.76.
[126] Paragraph 3.80.
[127] Paras. 3.77–78.

It also has powers to make the system run effectively. For instance, it can seek information, not only for itself but also for Community enforcers and private designated enforcers. It can step into monitor compliance with undertakings and orders, notwithstanding that another enforcer had previously been involved.

The OFT is also the co-ordinator at the international level.[128] Where UK consumers have complaints about businesses based in other member states it will seek to find a Community enforcer or if necessary bring an action itself. Equally if complaints are received from other member states about British companies it will investigate (unless the matter is more appropriately dealt with by another enforcer in which case it will be referred to them). Indeed Community enforcers are under an obligation to consult the OFT before taking action. If action is needed the OFT will take it, if not it will advise the Community enforcer accordingly. The OFT cannot, however, prevent a Community enforcer from taking action.[129]

13.10 CONCLUSIONS

Few sensible commentators would deny the need for there to be public enforcement of consumer laws. The individual harm caused by many breaches of consumer law will provide few incentives for individuals to bring claims, they may not have the resources to take action and in any event prevention is better than cure. Prevention requires supervisory structures. Nevertheless funding of public enforcement is always a major problem. Particularly as enforcement is mainly a local authority responsibility it can sometimes be seen as a 'Cinderella' service. Signs are that affairs are improving with more recognition from Government of the need to improve funding, but almost inevitably there is less evidence that the increases will be of the size needed to tackle the problems effectively. Also recent years have seen the establishment of new powerful national agencies dealing with food and financial services and a rationalisation of regulation of utilities and other services of a general interest.

One of the greatest challenges is to obtain the right blend of local, national, regional and international enforcement. The benefits of local knowledge needs to be balanced with resourcing of efficient units. Also structures must ensure consistent application of the law and the development of policy. The EC adds an extra dimension that has to be taken into account when establishing consumer enforcement structures. These need to be able to address the increased dangers from disreputable businesses that seek to take advantage of the internal market and yet hide

---

[128] Paras. 3.87–89.
[129] Section 216(6).

from enforcement behind national boundaries. The internet shows how transnational co-operation has to be at the international and not just the European level. Positive steps are being taken to allow the enforcement structures to match up to the challenges of the modern market place. Yet the resources of enforcement agencies are always likely to be inadequate. This perhaps is one reason why individual access to justice remains important. As well as assisting the individuals who have suffered personally, it also provides a means of controlling the behaviour of businesses especially if the litigation can reflect the total scale of the problem, as in class actions, and mechanisms are built in to allow practice to respond to the problems highlighted by litigation. It is to individual access to justice that we turn in the final chapter.

Chapter 14

Access to Justice

In the last chapter we focussed on public enforcement. Public enforcement helps to promote standards and thereby indirectly benefits consumers, though it can rarely provide the individual aggrieved consumer with a remedy. In this chapter we concentrate on ways in which individual consumers can seek redress. This should not blind us to the debate as to whether resources are best used to improve public enforcement of regulatory laws or to establish consumer rights in the court system. To a large extent this explains differences of approach between Europe, which retains a regulatory approach, and the US where private actions are seen as performing an important regulatory function.[1] Of course the picture is more complicated than that with features of both public and private enforcement existing in all systems. Indeed the recent trend within Europe has been to reduce the amount of state involvement in consumer protection, often by moving to more self-regulatory models. Also the state struggles to cope with the increased demands placed on it to regulate more complex and sophisticated products and services and this in turn can create pressures for the private law to be available to redress harm caused by market failures. This debate largely centres on one's belief in the effectiveness of public law regulation and regulatory agencies as opposed to the value in allowing the citizen the right to protect his own interests by litigation.

14.1 IS THERE AN ACCESS TO JUSTICE PROBLEM?

Consumer and money problems are some of the most frequently encountered problems by individuals.[2] At many points in this book lacunae in the protection afforded to consumers by the private law have been noted. However, the most damning criticisms of private law as a method of

---

[1]   G. Howells and T. Wilhelmsson, 'EC and US Approaches to Consumer Protection – Should the Gap be Bridged?' *Yearbook of European Law 1997* 207.

[2]   H. Genn *et al, Paths to Justice: What People Do and Think about Going to Law* (Hart, 1999) at 39–41 found they were the most common with 15 per cent of the sample having complaints about faulty goods and services. Also some of the 9 per cent reporting problems to do with money would raise consumer issues.

consumer protection relate to the inability of legal institutions to deal with consumer complaints. Critics claim that, even if the substantive law were framed in the most pro-consumer terms, the rights granted to consumers would not be effective because the amounts of money involved are generally too small to be worth litigating; because the legal system and lawyers appear alien to the average consumer and only the more educated consumers are aware of and can articulate their complaints in terms which allow them to take advantage of the law. These criticisms have been well made and have encouraged responses seeking to question the way legal services are delivered to consumers and to re-examine dispute resolution procedures.[3] Moreover, they should cause us to question the way we structure substantive rules if they rely on enforcement that is unlikely to be practical either by individuals or public agencies. Rules like cooling-off periods or rights against creditors for faulty goods may have some advantages as often the consumer can invoke the right and wait to see if the other party takes action to challenge it. In similar vein, Ramsay, who raises the issue of 'self-enforcing' laws for debate, gives the example of several North American jurisdictions where consumers automatically receive a free repair if they are not provided with the proper documentation.[4]

Many reforms have still been based on a paradigm which involves an individual consumer in dispute with an individual business. Attempts have been made to even up this relationship by providing or subsidising the advice costs of the consumer or making legal action less expensive, less intimidating, less risky and more convenient.[5] However, legal reforms which continue to view consumer problems as individual problems are going to lead to a continuation of many of the present difficulties. In fact many consumer disputes concern problems common to a large number of consumers (i.e. common product defects, unfair contract terms or selling practices).[6] In devising structures to litigate these group problems it is necessary to bear in mind that consumer cases can involve large sums (e.g. personal injury, some financial services) where individuals may still feel motivated to bring cases in traditional ways, or with some modifications, perhaps by allowing the cases to be grouped. For these cases traditional

---

3   See generally I. Ramsay, 'Consumer Redress Mechanisms for Poor Quality and Defective Products' (1981) 31 *UTLJ* 117.

4   I. Ramsay, 'Consumer redress and access to justice' in *International Perspectives on Consumers' Access to Justice*, Rickett and Telfer (eds.) (Cambridge University Press, 2003).

5   See W. Whitford, 'Structuring Consumer Protection Legislation to Maximise Effectiveness' [1981] *Wisc LR* 1018.

6   For a discussion of the characteristics of consumer disputes see, G. Howells and R. James, 'Litigation in the Consumer Interest' (2002) 9 *ILSA Journal of International and Comparative Law* 1 at 7.

remedies may be suitable. The more difficult challenge to private law is to deal with situations where the amount of harm to individual consumers is small. Few rational individuals will litigate such claims,[7] unless they suffer from super-spite.[8] Where the harm to the collective is great it is important that mechanisms are found to litigate such issues. Even where small amounts are involved these may be significant to the individuals concerned and procedures need to be in place to address their concerns. Unless the full range of consumer concerns are taken on board, consumer law will continue to be viewed as 'middle class' law, for it will only be worth litigating disputes involving high-cost goods and services (although many middle-class consumers will themselves be excluded by the high cost of lawyers). Equally, consumers should be allowed to claim the organisational advantages that are automatically available to all but the smallest businesses. One response is to recognise the collective dimension by increasing the public law protection of consumers. Alternatively, consumers can be permitted to aggregate individual claims in group or class actions, or consumer organisations can be allowed to invoke private law rights on behalf of consumers generally.

Sometimes it is suggested that too much is made of the problem of lack of consumer redress. Susan Silbey reminds us that consumers do not always expect their purchases to satisfy their expectations 100 per cent. She impliedly questions whether consumers benefit from attempts to remedy every minor harm:

> Are we engaged in an ever escalating cycle of increasing expectations, the major beneficiaries of which are those whose occupation it is to provide remedies and services for the victims of failed expectations?[9]

It should not be forgotten that litigation is in itself a cost to society.[10]

Whilst it is right that care should be taken to ensure that reforms benefit consumers and not merely their advisers, it would be wrong to suggest that society necessarily wastes its resources when it allows litigation to proceed over minor disputes. Admittedly, certain systems may at times look like they work more to the advantage of lawyers than harmed consumers. Where lawyer fees far outweigh the damages recovered, one might wonder whether this works in the collective consumer interest given that consumers have to pay for those services indirectly through the price of the product. Likewise some of the settlements in US consumer class

---

7   M. Olsen, *The Logic of Collective Action* (Harvard UP, 1965).
8   A.A. Leff, 'Injury, Ignorance and Spite' (1970) 80 Yale LJ 1 at 21.
9   S. Silbey, 'Who Speaks for the Consumer? [1984] *Am Bar Foundation RJ* 429.
10   A. Duggan, 'Consumer Access to Justice in Common Law Countries: a Survey of the Issues From a Law and Economics Perspective' in Rickett and Telfer (eds.), *op. cit.*

actions seem to offer the consumer little (typically a voucher or possible reduction in price of future services) and can seem more about business paying-off the lawyers who have found the infringement to leave them alone. However, it should be remembered that litigation has functions apart from direct redress. First, it gives the parties the opportunity to air their grievances in front of an impartial third party.[11] Second, society has a wider interest in the outcome of the dispute than the actual decision, for the rules established can affect supplier behaviour in the future. Laura Nader has made an impassioned plea for 'little injustices' to be taken seriously:

> Little injustices are the greater part of everyday living in a consumption society, and of course, people's attitudes towards the law are formed by their encounters with the law or by the absence of encounters when the need arises. If there is no access for those things that matter then the law becomes irrelevant to its citizens and, something else, alternatives to the law become all they have.

Of course it may be legitimate to argue that other forms of regulation and enforcement are more efficient than private law in achieving these objectives. Nevertheless allowing individuals to enforce their own rights corresponds to the notion of the rule of law. It is also an important safeguard, at times when public authorities are not able to enforce laws as effectively as they might wish (be that for reasons of lack of resources or political dictate).

However, it is true that lawyers can become blinkered into seeing legal means of redress as all important. It is salutary to recall that Genn's study found that while there was a high claiming rate for consumer problems compared to other justiciable issues, most consumers were able to handle their problems without the intervention of a third party.[12] Courts and ombudsmen played a secondary role in consumer dispute resolution and mediation, perhaps surprisingly, hardly figured at all. That is why this chapter starts by noting that most consumer disputes are settled by consumers complaints being dealt with by either negotiation or trader internal complaints procedures. We next discuss the availability of access to lawyers if matters need to be taken further. This includes discussion of

---

[11]   Although only a few high-income consumers are likely to be motivated solely by altruism in bringing complaints, nevertheless most complainants welcome the opportunity to get the grievance off their chest; see E. Steele, 'Fraud, Disputes and the Consumer; Responding to Consumer Complaints' (1975) 123 *UPaLR* 1107.

[12]   *Genn, op cit.*, at pp. 106–109 around six in ten consumers dealt with problems themselves, most commonly by contacting the other side directly. Even when advice was sought it was often to the effect of suggesting trying to contact the other party to get them to deal with the problem.

the availability of legal services for consumers, which inevitably involves the ability of lawyers to handle consumer disputes and alternative sources of advice as well as the funding of legal assistance. Most of the rest of the chapter is concerned with innovations whose object is to increase access to justice for consumers – small claims courts, Ombudsmen and arbitration schemes all seek to make it more practical for consumers to have their complaints heard by a third party by simplifying the procedures, stripping costs out and often encouraging the consumer to act without a lawyer. On the other hand class actions seek to make consumer claims viable by allowing the costs of litigation to be spread and reflecting that the sum total of harm might warrant litigation, even where individual harm might not. We then contemplate the European and international dimensions of the problem, especially as this age of global travel and increased access to the internet makes cross border disputes ever more likely.

When surveying trends in consumer access to justice a good starting point is Capelletti's work describing three waves.[13] The first wave was economic in nature, providing the consumer with the legal means to seek justice. We shall see that this has had to evolve from simply providing legal aid to more affordable forms of assistance. The second wave was organisational, granting standing to bodies that could act in the consumer interest and developing class actions. This is still an important and developing feature of consumer litigation. Especially the use of injunctions by consumer groups and public bodies has been an important feature in recent years. The third, developing ADR continues apace. It has been suggested to these one might add new waves which emphasise the regulatory role of litigation and the cross-border dimension.[14]

14.2 COMPLAINING

It is perhaps understandable that lawyers concentrate predominantly on formal legal rules and legal dispute resolution fora. In the consumer context, however, a broader view of dispute resolution is needed. Yet even some of the most liberal thinkers still view consumer redress mechanisms as involving third parties as negotiators, mediators, conciliators, arbitrators or adjudicators. The evidence suggests that this is not how most complaints are resolved. We have already noted this was the conclusion of Genn. Best and Andreasen's survey based on 2419 telephone calls with consumers in

---

13   M. Cappelletti and B. Garth, *Access to Justice* (Sijthoff and Noordhoff, 1978), M. Cappelletti, *Access to Justice and the Welfare State* (Sijthoff and Noordhoff, 1981) and M. Cappelletti, *Alternative Dispute Resolution Processes within the Framework of the Worldwide Access to Justice Movement* (1993) 56 MLR 282.

14   Howells and James, *op. cit.*

34 cities in the US found that only 1.2 per cent of consumers who perceived a complaint 'voiced' this to a third party.[15] This would seem to support the OFT's research which showed that less than 2 per cent of those taking some form of action threatened court action.[16]

Best and Andreasen found that only 39.7 per cent of consumers who perceived a problem took any action to obtain redress. This does not mean that the remaining consumers were inactive in an economic sense; they may simply have decided to 'exit' (that is not purchase that product in the future, at least not from that supplier). Interestingly, complaining to the supplier directly was found to be fairly effective, with a 'satisfactory' solution being reached in 56.5 per cent of cases.[17] The study found that complaints were more likely to be voiced if they involved high price items and if the complainant had a high socio-economic status. Interestingly voiced complaints over represented simple objective problems, such as where the product was broken or the wrong product supplied, whilst there was a reluctance to voice judgmental complaints. Judgmental matters clearly covers questions of product design or durability, but could also include complaints about dubious selling methods.

From their study of complaint-handling by a major store in Denver (Colorado), Ross and Littlefield also concluded that complaining directly to retailers was a cheap and effective means of consumer redress.[18] In fact they found retailers were prepared to go beyond their strict legal obligation under the Uniform Commercial Code, for example by accepting goods back where the decision to return them was quite arbitrary. Again, complaining was seen to be a greater advantage to the middle classes, who were more confident and better able to articulate their problem. It was suggested that the generous policy adopted may be explained by the fact the study was based on a large store for whom the complaints represented a small proportion of their turnover. It might be conjectured that small retailers faced with complaints about expensive goods would be less liberal in their complaints handling policy. Smaller retailers may also find it less

---

15   A. Best and A. Andreasen, 'Consumer Response to Unsatisfactory Products: A Survey of Perceiving Defects, Voicing Complaints and Obtaining Redress', (1976–7) 11 *Law and Soc R* 701.

16   Quoted in *Ordinary Justice*, (NCC, 1989) at p. 283.

17   This is in line with the results found in relation to the outcome of consumer complaints to UK insurance companies: in 39.6 per cent of cases the company gave the complainant everything asked for and in 25.4 per cent of cases the complainant was given something: see J. Birds and C. Graham. 'Complaints against Insurance Companies' (1993) 1 *Consum LJ* 92 at 104.

18   L. Ross and N. Littlefield, 'Complaint as a Problem Solving Mechanism' (1978) 12 *Law and Soc R* 199.

easy to return goods to suppliers as they have less bargaining power than large retailers.

A study by Ramsay and Enzle[19] confirmed that businesses usually allowed consumers rights which went beyond their strict legal entitlement. The reasons for doing so were to encourage repeat business and to engender good publicity. As the estimated cost of providing services to dissatisfied customers was less than one per cent, this could be viewed as money well spent. However, Ramsay 'obtained the impression that it might be easier for a consumer to obtain a refund or replacement where he was returning goods on arbitrary grounds for which their was no legal justification than if goods were being returned for judgmental problems... for which there might be legal justification'. Presumably this can partly be explained by the fact that goods returned for arbitrary reasons (the wrong colour) can be easily resold and the consumer can often be persuaded to take a substitute product, whereas a claim that the product is defective may involve the retailer incurring costs. Also suppliers may become more defensive when the quality of their product or service is being questioned.

The practical value of complaining should not be underestimated. Complaining can be encouraged by increasing consumer awareness of their rights. However, there are also warning signs, which should alert us to the limits of this approach to consumer protection. First, members of lower socio-economic groups appear less willing to complain. Of course they are also less likely to invoke the law. The difference is that, if the law is strengthened and made more accessible, they will benefit. If, however, lower status consumers are simply encouraged to complain and perhaps even given increased access to consumer advisers, they may still not improve their success rate. This is because much of the high success rate of complaining is due to retailers' goodwill, which is extended in the hope of retaining consumer loyalty. Retailers may be less concerned to retain the custom of low-income consumers. Second, retailers are less willing to accept complaints of a judgmental nature. Yet, matters such as the durability of goods, their quality, misrepresentations and bad selling practices are the very problems which consumer protection laws seek to redress. Third, there is a danger that voluntary settlement by traders may mask problems which continue to affect the sizeable number of consumers who take no action when confronted with a similar problem.

There is little research into the extent to which businesses monitor consumer complaints and use them to improve standards. Ross and Littlefield suggested that consumer complaints had an important role in quality control and that retailers passed on complaints to manufacturers.[20]

---

19   Described in Ramsay (1981), *op. cit.* at 126–130.
20   L. Ross and N. Littlefield, *op. cit.*

In their study of insurance companies, Birds and Graham[21] found that all except the smallest stressed the importance of learning from complaints. One suspects that that exception is quite significant and that the extent to which companies attempt to learn from complaints varies greatly and often correlates to size. Even if smaller companies want to learn from complaints, they may not have the expertise, resources or even volume of complaints to be able to put this aspiration into practice. In this respect it is significant that, in the Birds and Graham study, the large companies had well established processes for monitoring complaints, but smaller companies' practices were often less well organised.

Above we noted that substantive law should be drafted in such a way as to make enforcement easier for consumers, by, for instance, favouring techniques such as cancellation rights that are easier for consumers to invoke. Equally, in developing responses to the law it may be useful to look at ways of promoting informal dispute resolution between the parties. For example, promoting guarantees of goods and services might be effective in permitting consumers to recognise their rights and having a relatively simple means of addressing their concerns to the trader. This might in practice be even more fruitful than granting ever greater substantive rights, which consumers do not in practice invoke.

A form of complaining that obtains a lot of publicity is that involving the media. It is undoubtedly the case that television programmes like *Watchdog?* can have high profile impact and many will have heard it said that the best way to get a consumer problem resolved to write to newspaper advice columnists. Certainly they can have a big impact when they address problems, but they inevitably cherry-pick the cases they deal with and journalists have a notoriously short term interest in a problem. It is therefore doubtful as to how great their overall impact is. An admittedly dated US study of media action lines suggested that they tended to act as a passive referral service and were used infrequently by the disadvantaged.[22] Certainly the media cannot replace more traditional means of consumer advice.

14.3 CONSUMERS AND LAWYERS

14.3.1 Access to Legal Services

A lot of practical advice for consumers will in fact be given by public authorities. Trading standards officers are the state's frontline based in every local authority. Although they cannot take on individual cases they

---

21   *Op. cit.*

22   F. Palen. 'Media Ombudsmen: A Critical Review' (1979) 13 *Law & Soc Rev* 799.

will usually be happy to advise consumers of their rights. Members of the public usually have less occasion to come into contact with central government consumer officials, but the OFT publishes a number of useful leaflets and the DTI has established a Consumer Gateway website to steer consumers to information and advice.[23] The funding of legal services was sharply changed following the White Paper, *Modernising Justice*,[24] and the enactment of the Access to Justice Act 1999. Previously the system of civil legal aid had seen private practice solicitors funded by the state as the main source of advice for clients who satisfied a means and merits test. However, costs were burgeoning, with a few high profile cases costing staggering amounts with often little return. Particularly with regard to consumer cases not involving personal injury, lawyers had little interest and often little expertise.

Civil legal aid was replaced by a Community Legal Service run by the Legal Services Commission. It has established a Funding Code to determine how money should be allocated. The new approach is to target money more effectively. One element is to contract with organisations like the Citizens Advice Bureaux to provide advice to consumers. This is seen as more cost effective than paying solicitor rates and also can ensure that the advice given is of a consistent standard through the training in consumer matters given to advice workers. Debt advice is another sector which has expanded and become more professional about the quality of its work.

Public funding of cases would continue to be available for some cases on a more focussed basis. Many consumer cases would not usually qualify, however, as they fall within the small claims limit. Also funding can be refused if Ombudsmen or alternative dispute resolution schemes have not been used. Wherever possible (including nearly all cases involving personal injury) cases would be expected to be brought under a conditional fee arrangement (CFA). Cases brought under a CFA might be assisted by support funding to help with investigative support or litigation support to perhaps help with expensive disbursements, such as experts' fees, which it would be unrealistic to expect lawyers to meet on a CFA basis. For other claims public funding may be given for full representation or in the first instance for investigative help. There are strict financial rules, which apply for most, but not all cases, and a cost-benefit criteria to judge whether it is worth investing pubic money. Encouragement is also given to non-court based methods of dispute resolution such as mediation. Special rules apply to very expensive cases, such as group actions. For cases not provided for by the rules the intention is to encourage the development of legal expenses insurance.

---

23   See, http://www.consumer.gov.uk.
24   Cm 4155 (1998).

The effect of these rules is that, whilst consumers should have access to information and advice through the Consumer Gateway and the networks of CABx and debt advisers, they will usually be expected to act without legal assistance taking their cases to arbitration, ombudsmen or in person before the small claims courts. For personal injury claims it will usually be possible to bring cases on a CFA basis.[25] This means that the lawyers work on a 'no win no fee' basis and in return obtain an uplift, if successful, of up to 100 per cent depending on how much risk the case involved. The successful litigant normally has his fees, including now the success fee, paid by the defendant. If he loses he remains liable for the defendant's costs under the usual loser pays rule. These will normally be covered by a legal expenses insurance, whose premium is again recoverable should he win. So the consumer's maximum exposure is normally the cost of the insurance premium and possibly some expenses. However, the costs of this litigation do not disappear, they are simply shifted on to the defendants and increased to cover the lawyer's success fee and insurance premiums. This should mean these costs have to be borne by the consumer collective in higher prices.

Outside the field of personal injury there will be few areas where the lawyers will have an incentive to take CFAs. This is because consumer cases are usually one-off cases, where the lawyer will have to invest a lot of resources for only the chance of a modest return. One area where CFAs are being used is in relation to the misselling of endowments. In this area there are large numbers of claims for what can be substantial sums and the procedures can be standardised. The position can be contrasted with the US where lawyers are given economic incentives to take on consumer cases. They often work on contingent fees taking up to usually 30–40 per cent of the damages. This can seem objectionable, but it does give them a real incentive to seek out consumer harm, even small harm if it can be wrapped up in a group action. Other US statutes specifically permit reasonable attorney fees to be recovered.[26] Thus the US private practitioner is viewed as a policer of the market in a way his UK counterpart is not; the UK relies far more on administrative control of market practices. Few individuals can afford to employ lawyers for run-of-the-mill consumer case, perhaps concerning a defective car or double glazing. If a solicitor is involved in such cases it is most likely he is funded by a Legal Expenses Insurance.[27] This form of insurance is less common in the UK than on continental Europe. However, it is increasingly being

---

[25] Section 27 Access to Justice Act 1999, see: C. Hodges, *Multi-Party Actions* (Oxford, 2001), *op cit.*, Chapter 11.

[26] See for example 15 USC s. 1692 (Supp. IV 1980) (Fair Debt Collection Practices Act).

[27] On which see Hodges, *op. cit.*, Chapter 10.

included as an extension to car, household or building cover. One of the problems is that few people appreciate that they have such cover and indeed solicitors have been criticised for failing to check whether their clients are covered by such policies. These policies do have their limitations. The cover is usually for a set limit, there will usually be a merits test and often restrictions on which solicitors can be used. However, premiums are still rather low (perhaps because of low take up of services) and it can be a useful way forward for many consumers to access legal services to which more publicity could usefully be given.

14.3.2 How Good are Lawyers at Consumer Law?

However, do lawyers offer consumers a good service? Macaulay suggests that consumers may be given a raw deal by the legal profession.[28] His study found a wide degree of ignorance on consumer law matters amongst lawyers who do not come into contact with them on a regular basis. Lawyers are also less likely to empathise with consumers and the problems they face. Lawyers tend to be able to understand the consumer contracts they sign personally and may not appreciate the problems experienced by some consumers with legal technicalities. As small businessmen themselves, lawyers are likely to appreciate the position of the businesses involved and view consumers who complain as 'freaks'. Lawyers who acted aggressively to protect consumer rights were viewed as 'members of the "rag tag bar"'. The respectable role for the lawyer was seen merely as a mediator, putting the consumer in touch with the right person in the relevant organisation to deal with the complaint. Whilst there is clearly a role for conciliation, the danger is that consumer claims can be too easily compromised and that settlements fail to establish positive legal principles which other consumers can rely on in future cases. There is also a problem as most lawyers come across consumer problems infrequently. Whereas businesses will often get their advice from specialists, consumers will tend to access generalists who may have little knowledge or interest in consumer law or non-lawyers operating within the Community Legal Service framework.

14.3.3 Is a Different Type of Consumer Lawyer Needed?

The consumer's position in the legal system is structurally weak. In the terminology of Galanter, the consumer is a 'one-shotter' as opposed to

---

28   S. Macaulay, 'Lawyers and Consumer Protection Laws' (1979) 14 *Law and Soc R* 115.

business which is a 'repeat player'.[29] The problem is not merely that the repeat player may be a better lawyer, or at least one more conversant with consumer law. Rather business has the advantage of being only marginally concerned with the instant case and more interested in the development of the law. Thus repeat players have 'the ability to play for rules as well as for immediate gain. It pays a recurrent litigant to expend resources in influencing the making of the relevant rules and avoiding unfavourable outcomes through settlements'. Thus Ramsay astutely defines the disparity in legal services as being not so much between rich and poor, but rather as between individuals and organisations.[30]

Drawing on the work of Wexler[31] in the area of poverty law, Ramsay[32] argues that consumers may need a different type of lawyer from that traditionally found in High Street offices. Just as an army of poverty lawyers could not deal with all the legal problems of the poor which were recognised, yet alone those which remain unrecognised, so consumer problems are too numerous to be dealt with effectively through traditional lawyer/client relationships. Consumer lawyers may need to have skills such as the ability to mobilise consumers, teach consumers how to help themselves and act as lobbyists and strategists for the consumer movement. Indeed, often consumer law is responsive to the problems consumers present. These may or may not be the best cases to bring if one looks at the broader interest of consumers. The New South Wales Legal Aid Board in Australia developed a different strategy and with limited resources concentrated on finding cases which highlighted the significant problems consumers faced.

14.4 SMALL CLAIMS

In 1970 the now defunct Consumer Council published a document, *Justice Out of Reach: A Case for Small Claims Courts*, which showed that consumers were not using lawyers or the courts to settle their disputes. In fact the study did not reveal a single instance of a consumer suing a business. The county court system was castigated as little more than a debt collection agency for business. The Government's response was to introduce an arbitration procedure for small claims in the county court (the so-called small claims court), which aimed to be more informal and not apply the usual rule that costs follow the event. The small claims

---

29   M. Galanter, 'Why the "Haves" Come out Ahead: Speculations on the Limits of Legal Change' (1974) 9 *Law and Soc R* 95.

30   I. Ramsay, *op. cit.,* at p. 136.

31   S. Wexler, 'Practising Law for Poor People', (1970) 79 *Yale LJ* 1049.

32   Ramsay, *op. cit.,* at pp. 138–9.

arbitration procedure was established by the Administration of Justice Act 1973.[33] This procedure was refined over the years with a higher financial ceiling being introduced.[34] The term arbitration was always something of a misnomer as it was not arbitration in any real sense, but rather a simplified court procedure. The term arbitration has now been dropped in the Civil Procedure Rules, which instead refers to the small claims track.[35] The rules of the small claims court will first be summarised, then some evidence of its actual operation will be considered, before addressing some questions about its effectiveness.

14.4.1 Procedure

Small claims are commenced like all other claims by the issue of a claims form. The amount of the issue fee is a contentious subject as the court service now tries to recoup its running costs. High costs in small claims are certainly a disincentive to litigation. The minimum issue fee is currently £30 for claims of less than £300 rising to £120 for claims of just under £5,000. Claims with a financial value of less than £5,000 will usually be allocated to the small claims track. There are certain exceptions, notably where personal injury damages of more than £1000 are involved. Exceptionally, judges may allocate a case to another track, despite the amount falling within the small claims limit, for example because of the complexity of the case. Such cases will then usually be dealt with under the fast track procedures.

In practice the allocation decision is crucial where lawyers are involved. They will be keen to remove cases from the small claims track, where most costs are not recoverable, and bring them within the fast track where if successful their fees can be recovered from the other party. Usually lawyers will drop out if claims remain within the small claims, unless they are paid privately or though an insurance.

It is significant that the loser pays rule for costs does not usually apply

---

[33] For a good history of small claims procedures see C. Whelan, 'Small Claims in England and Wales: Redefining Justice' in C. Whelan (ed.), *Small Claims Court: A Comparative Study* (Clarendon Press, 1990). He is especially interesting on the independent small claims courts which were set up in Manchester in 1971 and in London in 1973. Both eventually failed due to funding problems, but the procedure of the London scheme in particular was markedly different from that of county court small claims, being far more informal and for the most part eschewing legal representation.

[34] There was an influential report by the National Consumer Council, *Simple Justice* (1979), see also *Civil Justice Review* (Cm 394, 1988).

[35] Part 27.

in small claims costs. Normally the loser is only liable for the court fees, travel and loss of earnings for a party or witness and expert fees (limited to £200). Lawyers' fees are not recoverable. This rule can be deviated from when a party has behaved unreasonably. Many district judges will no doubt employ this rule sympathetically, especially where the consumer is a litigant in person. Indeed practitioners sometimes feel frustrated when judges are lenient on parties, especially if the eventual outcome is fairly easy to predict and the result is merely to rack up costs, say where adjournments are allowed. Equally, however, the small claims track is still governed by the Civil Procedure Rules and it is easy for the inexperienced to transgress. The nature of district judges varies widely and unreasonable behaviour can at times be judged by the standards applied to lawyers' conduct of cases rather than lay litigants.

Originally a preliminary hearing was introduced into the procedure in the belief that this would help the parties resolve their disputes, or at least speed matters up and make the actual trial more effective. However, experience showed that these advantages did not accrue. Preliminary hearings are still possible, but are rarely used.

The court can adopt any method of proceeding it considers to be fair. Although in *Scarth v United Kingdom*[36] the European Court of Human Rights found that it breached the Human Rights Convention to hold the hearing in private. Hearings are informal and strict rules of evidence do not apply. Evidence need not be taken on oath and cross-examination can be limited. The court must give reasons for its decisions. The previous regime had attempted to have a similarly flexible regime, but in *Chilton v Saga Holidays Plc*[37] this was not held to go so far as challenging the adversarial system and the Court of Appeal overruled the registrar's[38] opinion that, where one party was unrepresented, he could prohibit cross-examination and require all questions to be put through the chair. Such an approach should be possible under the new procedures, if justified by the circumstances and considered fair.

14.4.2 Empirical Evidence

As part of the *Civil Justice Review* the Lord Chancellor's Department commissioned management consultants *Touche Ross* to undertake an empirical study of the operation of the small claims court.[39] Of the sample

---

[36]   (1998) 26 EHRR CD154.
[37]   [1986] 1 All ER 841.
[38]   Registrars are now known as district judges.
[39]   Touche Ross, *Civil Justice Review: Study of the Small Claims Procedure* (Touche Ross, 1986).

of 876 defended cases, the *Touche Ross* study found that private citizens were plaintiffs in 21 per cent of cases against small business or local professionals and in 20 per cent of cases against fellow private citizens; seven per cent of cases were brought by the combined force of small businesses, local professionals or private citizens against large defendants. Small litigants accounted for about 88 per cent of all defendants. Whilst it could be shown that in 20 per cent of cases private citizens were defending cases brought by fellow private citizens and 14 per cent were defended by private citizens against large litigants it is not possible to know how many cases involved private citizens defending cases against small businesses.

In a subsequent study, Bowles has shown that these figures give a misleading impression because they concentrate on defended cases. Private individuals are less likely to defend claims and more likely to have their claims defended. Thus, in Bowles' sample, individuals were defendants in 59 per cent of the cases but only entered a defence in 14 per cent; although individuals only brought 12 per cent of cases, they accounted for 29 per cent of those cases in which a defence was filed.

60 per cent of claims in the Touche Ross study involved claims for money owed for goods sold or work done; 13 per cent sought the refund of money for unsatisfactory goods or services or claims for related damages, and five per cent related to repayment of loans, overdrafts, hire-purchase instalments and the like. The study states that 67 per cent of cases were won by the plaintiff. Yet this fails to recognise that a paper victory for the plaintiff may well disguise an actual victory for the defendant if the plaintiff recovered or settled for less than the amount claimed.

The Touche Ross data on legal representation does not break the information down into detailed categories. Nevertheless in 39 per cent of cases one party was represented by a solicitor (12 per cent the plaintiff and 27 per cent the defendant) while in nine per cent both parties were represented. Bowles found that solicitors filed only 2 of the 12 cases brought by private individuals in his sample, whereas of the 59 claims filed against private individuals 21 were filed by solicitors. The likelihood of representation increased with the size of the claim and also the size of the litigant. Solicitors were by far and away the most likely source of advice. However, the study claimed that whether or not the parties were legally represented made little difference to the outcome.[40]

John Baldwin has undertaken a very thoughtful analysis of small claims based on empirical research.[41] He found that 'for the most part,

---

[40] Despite flaws in the study's methodology this finding mirrors the results of US studies: see J. Ruhnka and S. Weller, *Small Claims Courts*, (National Center for State Courts, 1978).

[41] *Small Claims in the County Courts in England and Wales: the Bargain Basement of Civil Justice* (OUP, 1997).

small claims hearings involve well-to-do people suing other well-to-do people'.[42] He poetically describes district judges as 'emperors in relatively small dominions'[43] meaning that they were free to handle cases as they saw fit. Significantly he noted the wide variation in styles between judges, even from one courtroom to another in the same building. For many district judges small claims consumer disputes that require dealing with litigants in person are clearly an unwelcome distraction from the more standard diet of work they undertake. Baldwin also makes the significant point that many users of the small claims system feel frustrated when, eventually even if they are successful, they are thwarted because of the impossibility of enforcing judgments. In practice it seems over a quarter of small claims judgements may not be complied with, with perhaps only around half being fully complied with.[44]

14.4.3 Perennial Questions

Certain perennial questions are raised about the role and functions of small claims courts.[45] At the root of these lie debates about the need for the civil justice system to balance two factors:

(i)   the desire to have a quick, cheap, accessible system of delivering justice which provides common sense solutions to consumers' problems, against;

(ii) the need to ensure that the parties are given an adequate opportunity to present their case and have it decided by an impartial adjudicator on the basis of established legal principles.

The 'smallness'[46] of consumer claims and the fact that consumers are not used to dealing with legal formalities have tended to militate in favour of the former considerations in recent years. However, there is an ongoing debate as to how the balance can best be struck.

---

42   *Ibid.*, at p. 166.
43   *Ibid.*, at p. 92.
44   *Ibid.*, at p.134.
45   The issues discussed here are dealt with more fully in Consumer Council, *Justice Out of Reach* (HMSO, 1970), *Civil Justice Review* (Cm 394, 1988), *Ordinary Justice, op. cit.*, and Whelan, *op. cit.*, which has a useful concluding chapter dealing with these issues entitled 'Small Claims Courts: Heritage and Adjustment'.
46   There is of course a debate as to what constitutes a small claim. Recent years have seen the small claims limit raised by more than the rate of inflation. In addition, claims of small monetary value may have a high symbolic or moral value and, to a low-income consumer, may be of considerable significance.

14.4.3.1 Business Plaintiffs

A frequently raised issue is whether businesses should be allowed to bring claims in small claims courts: in other words, should the court be a small claims court or simply a consumer court? The argument against allowing access to businesses is that their cases can clog up the system and also create an atmosphere of business values and formalism that may prevent the courts being viewed as 'people's courts'. The answer, however, may not be to ban businesses, but rather to make sure that the presence of business claimants is not allowed to tarnish the image and reality of the small claims courts as a consumer friendly forum for resolving disputes. To ban them from using this cheap form of justice may indeed have adverse effects on consumers. After all, it is consumers who normally have to pay for the enforcement costs of businesses – either directly by costs being added to debts or indirectly through the price of commodities.

14.4.3.2 Legal Representation

A further suggestion for making small claims courts more user-friendly is the prohibition of legal representation. Allowing legal representation may seem unfair to consumers since businesses are more likely to have access to lawyers. Even if a consumer employed a lawyer and won the case, he or she would be unable to recover their costs because of the no costs rule. Removing the right to legal representation is, however, a step not to be taken lightly in a society based on the rule of law. It is also doubtful whether to do so would assist consumers greatly. For instance, there is no way to prevent parties from taking legal advice prior to court action or from being coached for the trial. Also the result is likely to be that consumers will find themselves up against company officials more experienced in court proceedings than themselves. With evidence that legal representation has little impact on the outcome of cases, the emphasis should perhaps be placed on creating an atmosphere in which legal representation is not viewed as necessary in small claims cases.

14.4.3.3 Making the Courts More Consumer-Friendly

Much more can perhaps be done to make the prospect of taking or defending a case less formidable and thereby hopefully to increase the number of consumers who use the court system to resolve their consumer disputes.[47] Court staff can be encouraged to assist litigants in filling in the various forms and can advise the parties on the workings of the system. Advice agencies, like citizens' advice bureaux, can be given a clear role in advising parties of their legal position. The information available on the small claims system can be improved. Legal jargon can be avoided. Perhaps most importantly, the judge can be given a far more interventionist role in the process of establishing the facts. The judge should not simply rely on the parties to present salient evidence. In appropriate cases, judges should be allowed to seek their own expert evidence and, where reasonable, charge this to the business party to the litigation, or, alternatively, pay for it out of a contingent fund, perhaps financed by a levy on the summons fee. Courts could be encouraged to make access easier by dealing with some matters purely by way of written papers so that individuals do not need to take time off work. Experiments with evening sessions should be encouraged.

14.4.3.4 Law or Justice?

The judge in a small claims case is supposed to decide the case on the basis of the law and does not act as an arbitrator, mediator or conciliator.[48] Although doubtless all judges perform these tasks, as well as adjudication, to various degrees at various times. Indeed the Civil Procedure Rules place an increased emphasis on mediation and unreasonable refusal to mediate can lead to costs consequences.[49] However, as the small claims track procedure is a truncated procedure in any event there is perhaps, ironically, less room for mediation which may simply make the procedure disproportionately lengthy. This does not of course mean that many consumer disputes cannot be subject to ADR procedures , but simply that in the small claims track they play little role at a formal level.

However, whilst the judge should be a judge and not an arbitrator, mediator or conciliator, there is still a debate about what laws should be applied. Earlier chapters illustrated how many traditional legal concepts could be inappropriate in the consumer context and require modification. In small claims cases, an argument can be made for allowing cases to be

---

[47] It is not encouraging to note that a 1985 OFT survey found that less than two per cent of consumers who took further action in respect of a consumer dispute threatened court action, and that an even smaller number actually took their case to court: quoted in *Ordinary Justice, op. cit.*, at p. 283.

[48] The pre-hearing assessment provides a good opportunity for judges so inclined to attempt to mediate a solution.

[49] *Halsey v Milton Keynes General NHS Trust* [2004] EWCA Civ 576 Independent, May 21, 2004.

decided on their merits and for not allowing technical legal defences to be raised. Thus s. 15(4), New Zealand Small Claims Tribunals Act 1976 provides that:

> The Tribunal shall determine the dispute according to the substantial merits and justice of the case, and in doing so shall have regard to the law but shall not be bound to give effect to strict legal rights and obligations or to legal forms or technicalities.[50]

Indeed in *Hertz NZ Ltd v Disputes Tribunal*[51] a decision was upheld even though the court admitted the appellant was not and could not be liable at law.

Similar rules requiring fairness and equity to override strict legal concerns are to be found in Australia,[52] while in Scandinavia the Consumer Complaints Boards take an openly pro-consumer interpretation of the law.[53] Objections that such provisions undermine the certainty of the law can be countered by pointing out that the courts are unlikely to use this power extravagantly and that, since the amounts involved are small, so the effects will only be minor. Indeed Baldwin found that a majority of district judges were happy to depart from the law to achieve a just result despite being formally bound by the law.[54] Of course, as the small claims limit increases, so may the validity of the objections to judges departing from the law. Indeed, many of the issues relating to informality may have to be reconsidered if the system is asked to deal with more than truly 'small' claims.[55]

---

[50] See A. Frame, 'Fundamental Elements of the Small Claims Tribunal System in New Zealand' in C. Whelan, *op. cit.*

[51] 8 PRNZ 145 (1994).

[52] See C. Yin and R. Cranston, 'Small Claims Tribunals in Australia' in C. Whelan, *op. cit.*

[53] The decisions of the boards are not binding, but are persuasive on the ordinary courts. K. Vitaanen, 'Consumers Access to Justice in Finland' in *Consumer Protection in Czechoslovakia and Finland*, T. Wilhelmsson and J. Svestka (eds.), (Institute for Private Law, 1989).

[54] *Op. cit.* at p. 71.

[55] Kate Tokely makes this point in relation to the New Zealand system, where the financial limits have been significantly increased and yet the tribunals are free to depart from the law. This may not always assist consumers. A tribunal might, for example, find restrictions on freedom to include exclusion contracts to be unfair: 'Dispute Tribunals: Should the Monetary Limits Have Been Increased?' (1999) 5 *NZ Bus LQ* 13.

14.4.3.5 Appeals

In *Ordinary Justice* the National Consumer Council recommended that the right of appeal be extended, especially as the claims limit increases. In its opinion, simple justice need not be rough justice. This was not the position until the introduction of the Civil Procedure Rules. Previously, appeals in small claims were only allowed in restricted circumstances. This could be justified as in small claims, which have no or little precedent value, most people would be happy to accept the determination of an independent third party. In any event the right of appeal would probably be used far more by businesses than consumers. However, these restrictions have been removed and the same rules on appeals apply for small claims as for other cases, save that the documents required are less extensive and permission to appeal is required in all cases. However, as there will be potential liability for costs on an appeal they will still be rare and even more rarely invoked by consumers.

14.5 ADR

Small claims tribunals represent a step away from formal court-provided justice towards informal justice. Recent years have seen a growth in a number of institutions which represent a further stage in the 'delegalisation' of consumer disputes. Ombudsmen and arbitration are two classic examples of this studied below. We have already seen that as small claims courts have evolved there have been a number of debates as to the extent to which traditional safeguards of the legal system, such as legal representation, rules of evidence and strict application of substantive law can be sacrificed to make justice affordable. Access to justice has also raised issues about the costs of participating, including the need to remove the need for lawyers. However, as the small claims courts works within the overall safeguards of the legal system one can accept many of the compromises arrived at with a certain degree of equanimity. These issue become far more sensitive in ADR procedures, which have often been established by private bodies, where the very impartiality of the decision-maker is added to the concerns.

There have been some attempts to set down criteria by which ADR schemes should be judged. Some of the most important have been by the European Commission.[56] Although, their motivation was to ensure minimum guarantees could be offered throughout the Community,

---

[56]   Australia has adopted fairly similar *Benchmarks for Industry-Based Customer Dispute Resolution* (1997). They identify considerations of accessibility, independence, fairness, accountability, efficiency and effectiveness.

particularly in the case of cross-border disputes, the criteria can for the most part be usefully used to assess national schemes. In 1998 the Commission adopted a *Communication on the out-of-court settlement of consumer dispute*[57] which included the *Council Recommendation on the principles applicable to the bodies responsible for out-of-court settlement of consumer disputes* (98/257/EC) ('ADR Recommendation') and in 2001 the Commission adopted a *Recommendation on the principles for out-of-court bodies involved in the consensual resolution of consumer dispute*[58] ('Consensual Resolution Recommendation').

The ADR Recommendation recommends that bodies responsible for the out of court settlement of consumer disputes respect the following principles:

- independence,
- transparency,
- adversarial,
- effectiveness,
- legality,
- liberty,
- representation.

This Recommendation only applies to bodies that seek to settle disputes through the intervention of third parties. Schemes which merely seek to bring the parties together were excluded, but are now covered by the Consensual Resolution Recommendation, This invokes the principles of impartiality, transparency, effectiveness and fairness.

It is useful to bear these criteria in mind when assessing the ADR schemes described below. Although it should be noted that the concepts mentioned above are in fact complex concepts whose content can be debated and whose application can be difficult as principles need to be balanced to produce a system that is fair and yet affordable for the wide variety of consumer claims.

14.6 OMBUDSMEN

14.6.1 Background

The Scandinavian Ombudsman model, which allows the complaints of individuals against the state to be investigated by an independent person, was imported into the United Kingdom in 1967 by the establishment of a

---

57 COM (1998) 198.
58 OJ 2001 L109/56.

Parliamentary Commissioner for Administration. This was subsequently extended to local government and to other areas which were, at least at that time, the responsibility of Government, such as the health service. The Scandinavian countries also have a Consumer Ombudsman,[59] who has proved very successful; not so much in resolving individual disputes, but rather in monitoring market practices.[60] The UK has no equivalent public institution, although the OFT might be viewed as fulfilling some of the functions of the Scandinavian Consumer Ombudsmen.

There was, however, a trend in the UK to establish private sector Ombudsmen to deal with complaints from the public. This was most apparent in the financial service sector. The first was the insurance Ombudsman scheme established in 1981, and eventually eight financial services schemes were established.[61] These schemes were all voluntary save for the Building Societies Ombudsman, which was set up following the requirement in the Building Societies Act 1986 that all societies belong to an Ombudsman scheme. The Building Societies had failed to establish a voluntary scheme along the lines of the banks. All these eight schemes have now been amalgamated into the Financial Ombudsman Service (FOS).[62] We will discuss this in detail below and comment on the changes

---

59 Known as 'Ombud' in politically correct Norway.

60 See T. Wilhelmsson, 'Administrative Procedures for the Control of Marketing Practices – Theoretical Rationales and Perspectives' (1992) 15 *JCP* 159.

61 The others were the Banking Ombudsman, Building Societies Ombudsman, Investment Ombudsman, Insurance Ombudsman, Personal Insurance Arbitration Service, Personal Investment Authority Ombudsman, Securities and Futures Authority Complaints Bureau and Arbitration Service, Financial Services Authority Direct Regulation Unit and Independent Investigator. See J. Birds and C. Graham, *op. cit.* and 'Complaints against Insurance Companies' (1993) 1 *Consum LJ* 92; National Consumer Council, *Ombudsman Schemes in the Private Sector: A Comparison and Assessment*, (NCC, 1988) and *Ombudsmen Services* (NCC, 1993); P. Morris, 'The Banking Ombudsman' [1987] *JBL* 131 and 199 and 'The Banking Ombudsman – Five Years On' [1992] *LMCLQ* 227; R. James and M. Seneviratne, 'The Building Societies Ombudsman Scheme' (1992) 11 *CJQ* 157 and M. Seneviratne, R. James and C. Graham, 'The Banks, The Ombudsman and Complaints Procedures' (1994) 13 *CJQ* 253; P. Rawlings and C. Willett, 'Ombudsmen Schemes in the United Kingdom's Financial Sector: the Insurance Ombudsman, the Banking Ombudsman, and the Building Societies Ombudsman' (1994) 17 *Journal of Consumer Policy* 307; P. Morris and G. Little, 'The Ombudsmen and Consumer Protection' in *Consumer Protection in Financial Services*, P. Cartwright (ed.), (Kluwer, 1999); R. James and P. Morris 'The new Financial Ombudsman Service in the United Kingdom: has the second generation got it right?' in Rickett and Telfer (eds.), *op. cit.*

62 See James and Morris, *ibid.*, and R. James, 'The New Dispute Resolution System in the U.K. Financial Services Industry' [2002] *J.I.F.M.* 191.

made to the nature of the process given that the schemes are now all set up on a mandatory statutory basis.

Ombudsmen are clearly part of the government's wider agenda of providing solutions proportionate to the issues at stake.[63] In its discussion paper on *Alternative Dispute Resolution*[64] they were used as exemplars of decision-making bodies providing 'alternative adjudication'. Ombudsmen have spawned in other service sectors beyond financial services, covering such matters as estate agents, legal services and even complaints against newspapers. There was a funeral ombudsman, but this was abandoned by the industry due to cost concerns and the relatively low number of complaints. This proliferation of Ombudsmen, many of them set up on a private basis, has caused the Ombudsmen to come together under the auspices of the British and Irish Ombudsmen Association, to set down criteria which institutions should meet before being admitted to membership. There is no legal status to the term 'Ombudsman' unlike the position in New Zealand where only designated bodies can use the term. Such a designation has also been suggested by the European Commission in their Green Paper on Access to Justice.

From the industry perspective, Ombudsmen can be viewed as providing a dispute resolution machinery that promotes the reputation of the sector as they are perceived as offering their customers open and fair consumer redress mechanisms. Ombudsmen schemes also provide business with other advantages over the ordinary courts. These include their greater speed, lower costs and the decision-maker's specialist knowledge of the industry, which hopefully results in higher quality decisions. Another important advantage to industry is that the Ombudsman is a private grievance resolution mechanism, which prevents it from having to hang out its dirty washing in public. Cynics might argue that such systems are simply ways of reducing costs and keeping disputes out of the court system to be dealt with in a private and more manageable environment.[65] However, this might be an unfair assessment of a system which has made it far easier for dissatisfied customers to receive redress.

One of the great advantages of the ombudsman for consumers is that the service is free. It is also only binding on the industry. So it effectively gives consumers a free bite at the cherry. It is operated on the basis that legal representation is not necessary and ombudsmen staff will assist in explaining the process and helping complainants formulate their claim, without actually giving them any advice. The fact ombudsmen schemes are funded by the industry explains why they have tended to concentrate in

---

63   *Modernising Justice* (Lord Chancellor's Department, 1998).
64   Lord Chancellor's Department (1999).
65   R. Abel, 'The Contradictions of Informal Justice' in *The Politics of Informal Justice* (Academic Press, 1982).

service sectors, especially financial services. These are often relatively wealthy sectors that can afford to fund such schemes and the players are identifiable and usually sizeable. There have been calls for a broader ombudsmen covering all consumer disputes, but a problem would be finding a funding mechanism, particularly as regards goods where the number of producers and traders is enormous and range from multi-nationals to small traders.

14.6.2 FOS

Our attention will focus on the FOS as it is the most important of the ombudsmen institutions. It was established under the Financial Services and Marketing Act 2000 and sits alongside the Financial Services Authority (FSA), which has rule making and supervisory functions in relation to the financial service institutions. Previously the structures of the ombudsmen had been typically to have a board appointed by industry to ensure the financing of the scheme, but to ensure independence by having a majority of independent members on the Council that actually appointed the Ombudsman. Independence from the industry is now more easily assured because of the statutory basis of the FOS.

The FOS is still, however, financed by the industry. How it is funded varies between its compulsory jurisdiction (essentially covering regulated activities within the previous scope of the eight sectoral schemes) and its voluntary jurisdiction. The compulsory jurisdiction is financed by a standing charge based on activity related to a number of indicia and a case fee based on usage. Fees for the voluntary jurisdiction are based on standard terms binding on firms subscribing to the voluntary jurisdiction.

There are still some dangers that the FOS may not be sufficiently independent of FSA, which appoints the Chair and Board of the Ombudsman Company. These are partly addressed through a memorandum of understanding on the exchange of information agreed by the FOS and FSA. Also, the board comprises twelve 'public interest' members.

Walter Merricks was appointed the first Chief Ombudsmen. The notion of a 'one-stop shop' for ombudsmen has been widely applauded as the previous plethora of Ombudsmen was very confusing for consumers. Certainly it was confusing for the same product to be dealt with by different ombudsmen depending on the status of the provider. Mortgages, for instance, might be referred to the building society or banking ombudsman depending from whom the loan was taken out. The advantage of the old scheme was that each Ombudsman was familiar with the sector he was regulating. Originally the idea had been to retain the advantages of product knowledge by having a layer of specialist ombudsmen dealing with problems on a product, rather than provider, basis. This happened to some extent at first, but now there are three Principal Ombudsmen and 19 panel ombudsmen and whilst some have areas of expertise the emphasis is on multi-tasking. Although this may have some managerial advantages and possibly ensures a more consistent approach, this may come at the price of bureaucratisation and standardisation, which leaves the ombudsmen more remote from the problems they are handling. This routinisation may be inevitable given the service received 462,340 front line enquiries in the year to 31 March 2003 and opened 62,170 new cases in the same period, an increase from 43,330 in the previous period.[66] However, it might make some rue the demise of the smaller more manageable sectoral regulators, where an energetic Ombudsman could stamp his authority on a sector to improve standards. There may be a temptation to see success in terms of procedures and processing claims.

It has already been noted that the FOS has both a compulsory and voluntary jurisdiction. Jurisdiction is limited by a ceiling of £100,000 on the damages awardable. Also several of the limitations found in the sectoral schemes are maintained. Many of these seek to ensure that the FOS does not interfere with commercial freedom of firms and so matters relating to interest rate policy, calculation of bonuses, lending decisions and application of standards are excluded.

Some of the sectoral schemes had a test case provision whereby cases could be referred to courts for decisions of principle. The present Chief Ombudsman considers this power unnecessary given the power to terminate cases early where court resolution is most appropriate.[67] However, there is no guarantee that such cases will reach the courts and such a power could be a useful mechanism for developing the law under the new regime of financial services law. Some ADR schemes also allow class actions and it might be useful to have considered whether this would be possible in the FOS. Some consumer problems might benefit from this if it is possible to reflect the collective scale of the problem. One might, for example, anticipate that victims of endowment misselling might fare better if they were able to act collectively with expert advisers rather than have their cases picked off one by one.

As under the sectoral schemes, the complainant must still have exhausted internal complaints procedures before taking the case to the ombudsman. This clearly has advantages in terms of reducing costs and hopefully speeding up settlements and promoting the relationship between the provider and customer. However, reliance on complaints procedures can be problematic. Research has shown that in the past the commitment to such schemes has been more apparent at senior management level than at the branch level, with the result that customers may not be made aware of

---

[66] See, http://www.financial-ombudsman.org.uk/publications/ar03/ar03-keyfacts.htm.
[67] James and Morris, *op. cit.*, at 184.

the schemes or not encouraged to invoke them.[68] Also there is a well known phenomenon called 'clumping', which refers to the fact that even when people can be bothered to start a claim they often give up as the claim drags on and they contemplate the amount of effort needed to prosecute it. However, at least the new regime has taken steps to ensure the quality of the internal complaints procedures. FSA rules, for instance, require regard to be had to the BS standard on complaints systems;[69] the operation of the schemes is monitored by the FSA and there are extensive reporting requirements.

Once the complaint enters the Ombudsman system it will be screened for eligibility. The actual procedures are governed by due process giving each party the chance to make representations. Much of the work is undertaken by adjudicators reporting to Ombudsmen. A provisional assessment will be made and if either party disagrees a determination will be made. The ombudsman has a great deal of freedom to decide what evidence to consider. The procedure is predominantly paper-based, although telephone contact is possible and exceptionally a meeting might be held. In view of *Scarth v United Kingdom*[70] it might be thought these procedures might give rise to some art. 6 human rights issues, but the scheme has to work this way for economic efficiency arguments.

There might also be some human rights concerns that businesses no longer voluntarily acquiesce to the Ombudsman's jurisdiction and yet the Ombudsman can deviate from the law and decide the case on the basis of what is in his or her opinion 'fair and reasonable in all the circumstances'. Even one of the main advocates of such an approach in private sector voluntary schemes, Julian Farrand, has wondered whether this is going too far in a statutory scheme.[71] Lord Ackner had considered such a phrase to hold the industry a hostage to fortune and the subjective views of the Ombudsman.[72] Against that it can be argued that such a standard is not entirely arbitrary, but rather guided by equitable principle and informal persuasive precedent.[73] Similarly tensions can be seen in the debate the private sector schemes had about the reference to industry standards. Should this be restricted to applying industry determined standards of good practice or was the ombudsman's function to help establish good

---

[68] C. Graham, M. Seneviratne and R. James, 'Publicising the Bank and Building Societies Ombudsman Schemes' [1993] *Consumer Policy Review* 85.

[69] BS 8600.

[70] (1998) 26 EHRR CD154, see Chapter 14.4.1.

[71] J. Farrand, 'An Academic Ombudsman' Centenary Lecture Series, University of Sheffield, 16 November 2000.

[72] *Report on a Unified Complaints Procedure* (PIA, 1993) para. 93.

[73] James and Morris, *op. cit.*, at p. 185.

practice?[74] As James and Morris note the proliferation of sectoral codes and FSA guidance should render this debate less important The FOS rules do not expressly state that such codes and guidance should be given precedence over the law, but this must be assumed. The 'fair and reasonableness' test should allow this as well as permitting justice to be done taking account of individual circumstances. The courts have held that matters of interpretation of Codes are for them and the ombudsman will have erred if he has not interpreted them properly. However, this does not prevent him from developing his own standards of unfairness, which may be stricter, so long as they are rational and consistent when judged by public law standards.[75]

In most instances indications of a likely adverse determination by the ombudsman will cause the company to settle a dispute, before a determination was made. Where a decision is made, compensation is limited to an overall ceiling of £100,000.[76] Unlike some of the previous schemes, there is no limit on the non-pecuniary element within these awards. Ombudsmen can also issue an injunction style direction to order a firm to 'take such steps in relation to the complainant as [he] considers just and appropriate'. This gives the ombudsman a great deal of discretion to fashion a remedy to suit the circumstances and is not limited to what a court could order.

Under voluntary schemes members contracted to abide by the decisions. Under the statutory Building Societies scheme it was possible for a society to choose to ignore a decision if they published the fact of their non-compliance with reasons in a manner acceptable to the Ombudsman. This option was taken on one occasion by the Cheshunt Building Society and was clearly not consumer-friendly. The FOS, although also statutory, has not backed down from making its decisions binding. Indeed the new scheme has gone further and made the awards binding in the courts; although non-compliance will be rare and most likely due to insolvency when the complainant will have to seek redress from the Financial Services Compensation Scheme. By contrast the complainant remains free to drop his ombudsman claim and seek redress from the courts at any time up until formal acceptance of the offer. Some of the previous schemes had given a dissatisfied complainant an appeal, not on the merits of the decision, but rather as regards procedural matters. Such an appeal is not provided for under the FOS.

Making the scheme mandatory and with enforceable judgments marks

---

74 James and Morris, *op. cit.*, at p. 187
75 *R v Financial Services Ombudsman Service, ex parte Norwich and Peterborough Building Society, The Times* 13 Dec 2002.
76 Section 229, Financial Services and Marketing Act 2000. Higher compensation can be recommended, but this is not binding.

a change in policy away from the previous voluntarism. In effect, the business party is excluded from having their rights decided by the courts. The question has been raised whether this infringes art. 6 of the European Convention on Human Rights. This provides that:

> in the determination of his civil rights and obligations or of any criminal charge against him, everyone is entitled to a fair and public hearing within a reasonable time by an independent and impartial tribunal established by law. Judgment shall be pronounced publicly.

Other matters of concern might to the private nature of the process and the fact the case can be decided on a fairness criterion even if this goes against the law. Whilst *Scarth v United Kingdom* in relation to the private nature of small claims hearings shows how this provision can bite – and perhaps indicates how difficult it is to always reconcile grand principles with practical reality – by contrast the House of Lords in *R v Secretary of State for the Environment, Transport and Regions, ex parte Alconbury Developments Limited*[77] was reluctant to unsettle establish practices and saw the availability of judicial review as a sufficient protection. Ombudsmen whose functions arise out of consent on the part of the business and are not binding on consumers are unlikely to be subject to judicial review.[78] However, when they have a statutory basis that mandates firms to submit to its jurisdiction judicial review will be possible. The FOS is certainly subject to judicial review.[79] This means that questions like whether an Ombudsman was right to refuse an oral hearing or took too broad an interpretation of fairness will be judged by public law standards. This juridification of the ombudsman process may be undesirable, but is probably better than building lots of due process checks and balances into every proceeding before the Ombudsman.

Even when an adverse determination is made, no formal decision is published. Nor do the decisions of the Ombudsmen create binding precedents, although they are likely to be followed by the Ombudsman in the future. Although consumers individually may be satisfied with a system which resolves cheaply and expeditiously their particular dispute, in a broader perspective consumers need a grievance system which also promotes standards and encourages good practice. The FOS seeks to address this through various means such an annual reports and a monthly newsletter commenting on policy and providing case studies. Thus

---

[77] [2002] 2 WLR 1389.

[78] *R v Insurance Ombudsman Bureau, ex parte Aegon Life Assurance Ltd.*, *The Times*, 7 January 1994.

[79] *R v Financial Services Ombudsman Service, ex parte Norwich and Peterborough Building Society*, *The Times* 13 Dec 2002.

individual firms are not named and shamed, but best practice can be developed. Indeed it could be argued that because of its links with industry the ombudsmen have better means to influence practice than the indirect impact of court decisions. The close links between the FOS and FSA, although at times problematic in terms of the perceived independence of the FSO, can be useful if the FOS is able to flag up difficulties with individual firms or potential systemic problems to the regulators.[80] Yet there can be a sense in which the FOS could be viewed as a vehicle for diverting and diluting problems in the hope that they can be processed and their impact minimised without addressing the root problem. Endowment mortgages are a good example. Customers whose endowments are not going to meet their mortgage commitments are being directed to the FOS and asked to prove misselling; when the real problem of endemic overselling from an over-optimistic financial services market eager for commissions is left unaddressed. Some consumer problems may just be too difficult even for governments to handle.

14.7 ARBITRATION

14.7.1 Legal Status

Ombudsmen's decisions are not binding on the consumer and Ombudsmen are not bound by the strict letter of the law. By contrast, arbitration involves referring the complaint to an independent arbitrator who will hand down a binding decision in respect of the case according to strict legal rules. Arbitrations are governed by the Arbitration Acts 1996, which only permits limited rights of appeal from an arbitrator's decision to the ordinary courts on points of law. Arbitration is an alternative to the county court system and is viewed as beneficial to consumers because it is meant to be quicker, cheaper and more informal than the courts. However, in the US arbitrations are abused by traders who force consumers into arbitrations that are prohibitively expensive.[81] In the UK clauses which bind consumers in advance to arbitration agreements for sums less that £5,000 are not allowed.[82]

We have also already noted that the under s. 124(3), Fair Trading Act 1973 the Director-General was under a duty 'to encourage relevant trade associations to prepare, and to disseminate to their members, codes of practice for guidance in safeguarding and promoting the interests of

---

[80] James and Morris, *op. cit.*, at 192.

[81] F.L. Miller, 'Arbitration Clauses in Consumer Contracts: Building Barriers to Consumer Protection', (1999) 78 *Mich. B.J.* 302.

[82] See Chapter 13.9.5.2(iv).

consumers' and the Office of Fair Trading continues to be charged with approving Codes of Practice.[83] Most of the Codes of Practice contained low-cost arbitration schemes. In addition there are several other consumer arbitration schemes which are not part of an OFT sponsored code. The Chartered Institute of Arbitrators runs most of the consumer arbitration schemes.

The OFT has established model procedures for handling consumer complaints to which most trade association schemes roughly conform. Consumers first take up their complaint with the trader. If this fails the matter should be referred to the trade association, which will attempt conciliation. If this too is unsuccessful, the consumer can opt for arbitration; both sides will sign an arbitration agreement accepting to be bound by the arbitrator's decision. The consumer is then precluded from taking the matter to court, save for the instances where there are limited rights of appeal from the arbitrator's decision. Although, a recent trend has been to amend some arbitrations procedures, to make them more like ombdudsmen, so that the decision is only binding on the trader.

There is little recent empirical work on the functioning of consumer arbitration schemes. Much of the discussion below involves a useful study by the National Consumer Council, which provides some interesting discussion of consumer perceptions of arbitration as opposed to small claims courts. It is, however, now more than a decade old. In fact the challenge to arbitrations comes from ombudsmen rather than the courts. Ombudsmen have raised consumer expectations of ADR. They have become used to them being free and only binding on the trader. In contrast a scheme the consumer has to pay for (even if it is subsidised registration fee), that binds the consumer and is decided by an arbitrator, whom the consumer may not appreciate is independent of the trade association may not be too appealing. In fact there are signs that arbitration schemes are trying to respond and replicate the features of the ombudsmen schemes.

Where arbitration is binding on the consumer it is important that they should be informed about their choice as to the forum in which the case should proceed and also about the pros and cons of the two options. In its study of three low cost trade arbitration schemes (run by the Association of British Travel Agents (ABTA), the Glass and Glazing Federation (GGF) and British Telecom (BT)) the National Consumer Council preferred the fuller explanation of the alternatives which ABTA provided to its complainants.[84]

---

83   See Chapter 13.9.2 and 13.9.5.2.
84   *Out of Court*, (HMSO, 1991) at 62.

14.7.2 Procedure

Although arbitration prevents the consumer from having access to the courts it does not mean that he or she is barred from taking legal advice. In fact, the National Consumer Council found that only 15 per cent of complainants had legal advice in preparing their cases for arbitration.[85] The parties submit written evidence to the arbitrator. Most arbitrations are based simply on the written papers, although the GGF code does provide for arbitrators to make site visits where necessary. The consumer will pay a registration fee (usually at that time less that £40) which is returnable if he or she wins; there is no extra charge for a site visit under the GGF scheme. If the consumer loses, he or she is only liable for an amount up to the cost of the registration fee. The rest of the costs are borne either by the trader or trade association and also indirectly by the arbitrators, who seeing this work as a kind of social service, charge well below their normal rates. Some schemes also offer cheap testing facilities: thus for £36 the Footwear Testing Centre used to test shoes (but this facility has recently ceased) and for a £45 fee (which is refundable if the claim is wholly or partially successful) Qualitas will report on furniture faults. The arbitrator will give reasons for his decisions,[86] which can be enforced through the court system.

14.7.3 Conciliation

The controversial features of the arbitration procedure are the inclusion of a conciliation stage and the reliance on paper only hearings. In its *Out of Court* report, the National Consumer Council noted that little is known about the conciliation stage. However, many of the consumers who responded to its survey on arbitration felt that conciliation had been a waste of time.[87] Adding in a conciliation stage certainly prolongs proceedings and speed was not found to be one of the best features of the arbitration schemes. There were in fact allegations that traders deliberately delayed matters during the conciliation process. In its 1981 report, *Redress Procedures under Codes of Practice*, the OFT had recommended that trade bodies should set targets of not more than three months for the conclusion

---

[85] *Ibid.* at 33.

[86] This follows on from a recommendation to that effect contained in the OFT's report *Redress Procedures under Codes of Practice: Conclusions Following a Review by the OFT* (1981).

[87] *Out of Court op. cit.* at 26; but note the National Consumer Council's sample was biased as it only covered persons for whom conciliation had failed and who had proceeded to arbitration.

of the conciliation stage. In 1991 the Office was forced to concede that, where conciliation was used to any great extent, this target was often not met.[88] Consumerists tend to be wary of any attempt to conciliate, especially when undertaken by a trade association for, by definition, conciliation involves the two parties finding a compromise solution. If the consumer has a valid claim, this inevitably means that he or she recovers less than is due.

The National Consumer Council found that consumers mistrusted the evidence provided by traders and were concerned that, whilst their evidence was passed on to the trader, they did not receive copies of the trader's replies. The OFT has therefore recommended that trade bodies give serious consideration to having the conciliation process conducted by independent people.

14.7.4 Paper Only Proceedings

The National Consumer Council found that two-fifths of the consumers surveyed would have liked to have met the arbitrator face to face, and that complainants to the GGF were more likely to consider the result fair if a site visit had occurred. They also noted that arbitrators were reluctant to keep going back to the parties for further information as this meant postponing the decision. It was recommended that personal hearings ought to be allowed where the claim exceeded the small claims limit, with the additional cost (estimated to be £150) being paid by the consumer, but being returnable if the case was won. The National Consumer Council thought this could benefit complainants from lower socio-economic groups with whom personal hearings were particularly popular, although the requirement to pay a fee would obviously deter them. The OFT had recommended, in its 1981 report, that arbitrations be conducted on a documents only basis[89] and has continued to maintain this position, arguing that personal hearings, when available, have been little used and add to costs and delay. It points out that consumers who want their day in court can use the county courts which now have higher financial limits on the claims they hear. This would seem to go to the crux of the matter, for if arbitrations start to replicate court procedures, then the advantages of cost and speed which they ought to provide to the consumer are diminished.

---

88   *Consumer Redress Mechanisms* (OFT, 1991).

89   *Redress Procedures under Codes of Practice, op. cit.* This report followed some reported instances where consumers had been held liable for substantial legal costs incurred following the holding of personal hearings.

14.7.5 Awareness and Use of Arbitration

One of the most disturbing features of the arbitration schemes is the lack of use made of them. Most are hardly ever used. Indeed the National Consumer Council found that the funeral scheme had never been used, the photography scheme had been used only once and, whilst a referral had been made under the caravan scheme, no arbitrator had been appointed at the time its report was prepared. On the other hand, ABTA received 14,200 complaints in 1989, 756 (5.3 per cent) of which resulted in an arbitration application being submitted. One explanation for the lack of use of arbitration schemes is a lack of awareness of the existence of the codes. Whilst more people were aware of the ABTA scheme than knew of the existence of the small claims courts,[90] the lack of awareness of lower-profile codes is dramatic. Thus only 11 per cent of those buying furniture had heard of the furniture code and only four per cent recalled the symbol of the trade association.[91] There is a clear need for the schemes to be given increased publicity, both to the general public and more particularly to consumer advisers.

14.7.6 Comparison with the Small Claims Court

It is interesting to note the comparisons made in the National Consumer Council's *Out of Court* report[92] between their present survey and that made in their 1979 report *Simple Justice*[93] on small claims procedures in the county court. Respondents rated arbitration and the county courts on a scale of 1–4, with 4 being the highest rating.

	Court	Arbitration
Approachable	2.68	2.90
Simple forms	3.04	3.25
Fair decisions	3.15	2.55
Informal procedure	2.95	3.00
Low costs	2.68	3.20
Speedy settlement of claims	2.36	2.37
Easily enforceable judgments	2.34	3.00
Base (nos. of respondents)	248	127

---

90 *Consumer Redress Mechanisms, op. cit.* at 32.
91 OFT, *Furniture and Carpets: a Report by the Director General of Fair Trading* (OFT, 1990).
92 *Op. cit.* table 4.1 at 39.
93 *Op. cit.*

It will be seen that arbitration fares particularly well on cost and the ease with which judgements can be enforced, although rating of the latter varied between the different schemes. ABTA scored an impressive 3.19 on this count, but the GGF scored marginally less well than the county courts (2.33). The ABTA score may reflect the fact that failure to comply will lead to expulsion of the trader from ABTA and *de facto* from the UK travel industry. Concern must, however, be expressed at the low regard users of the arbitration schemes had for the fairness of the decisions. Most of the criticisms seemed to concern the size of the awards made. Earlier research by the Consumers' Association also suggested that arbitrators would award on average only between 58–64 per cent of the amount a registrar (as they were then called) in a county court would award.[94] It must also be disturbing to see that arbitration had not improved upon the speed at which cases are disposed of. Whilst the arbitration stage itself normally averages 20 weeks (compared to the 26 weeks which *Simple Justice* found it took for the county court to dispose of a case), when the conciliation stage is taken into account, the disposal time rises to 54 weeks for the GGF scheme and 45 weeks for ABTA.

14.7.7 Raising Standards by Publishing Information on Arbitration Practice

At present arbitration and conciliation are purely private affairs. Currently arbitrators meet informally to discuss the schemes. The National Consumer Council has recommended that this be formalised and that the Chartered Institute for Arbitrators be responsible for publishing annual reports giving statistical breakdowns of the cases heard, a summary of what the arbitrators perceive to be the main issues arising during the year and anonymous reports of cases. It has also proposed that there should be similar reports for the large conciliation schemes.[95] These reports would help publicise the schemes, raise awareness of the approach arbitrators are taking and enable industry to develop good practice. This public accountability is needed if arbitration is going to raise standards as well as efficiently resolve individual disputes.

---

[94] Consumers' Association, 'Package Holiday Disasters', *Holiday Which?* September 1986, p. 194.

[95] *Out of Court, op. cit.*, at 60—1. This approach is broadly followed by the OFT in *Consumer Redress Mechanisms, op. cit.* at 53.

14.7.8 Utilities[96]

Limitations of space prevent us from looking in detail at consumer protection and access to justice within the privatised utilities such as gas, electricity, water and telecommunications. These industries do have unique features and we would like to stress the need for proper control of these sectors and adequate redress for consumers, especially as the action of utilities can affect in a very real way the standard of living of the poorer sections of the community who rely on these basic services. The privatised utilities are regulated by regulators. Increasing these powers and providing a role for compensation to consumers who suffer unsatisfactory services had been central to John Major's Citizen's Charter initiative and were reflected in the strengthening of standards under the Competition and Services (Utilities) Act 1992.[97] The value of the Citizen's Charter programme and the real amount of influence the regulators have were and continue to be matters of contention. However, it seems that dealing with consumer complaints was never viewed as a high priority for regulators, which understandably focussed on broader concerns of industry regulation and competition. The modern trend seems to be for complaint and dispute resolution procedures to be dealt with by a body other than the regulators. Thus s. 2 of the Utilities Act 2002 sets up the Gas and Electricity Consumer Council. This is known as Energywatch.[98] In the water industry complaints are dealt with by Water Voice.[99] Under s. 52 of the Communications Act 2003, OFCOM has to approve bodies to handle complaints and disputes. Two schemes have been approved: the Office of the Telecommunications Ombudsman (Otelo)[100] and the Communication and Information Services Adjudication Scheme (CISAS).[101] Interestingly rail complaints are the responsibility of the individual companies, but the Rail Passenger Council and its network of companies helps mediate complaints that cannot be settled.

---

[96]   See Chapter 1.9.2.2.

[97]   See A. Barron and C. Scott, 'The Citizen's Charter Programme' (1992) 55 *MLR* 526 and P. Rawlings and C. Willett, 'Consumerism and the citizen's charter' (1994) 2 *Consum LJ* 3.

[98]   See, www.energywatch.org.uk.

[99]   See, http://www.ofwat.gov.uk.

[100]   See, http://www.otelo.org.uk.

[101]   See, www.cisas.org.uk.

14.7.9 ODR

An area in which arbitration is becoming more popular is in relation to online disputes, where it has its own label 'online dispute resolution' (ODR). There are various types of ODR. Some are simply automated settlement systems, designed to resolve monetary disputes often through blind bidding. Others are mediation schemes acting as a conduit for negotiations between the parties. Binding arbitration is often considered inappropriate for consumer disputes,[102] but the WebTrader scheme established by the Consumers' Association and the Chartered Institute of Arbitrators is of interest.[103] It is only binding on the trader and the consumer only has to pay a registration fee, which currently ranges from £11.75 for claims less than £200 to £58.75 for claims between £5001–£10,000.

The attraction of ODR is obvious.[104] With traders and consumers in different countries it is often impractical, especially where small amounts are at stake, to use traditional court procedures. ODR also avoids one side having the advantage by imposing its legal system on the other. However, ODR also brings with it certain dangers as consumers may be drawn into accepting a form of justice whose quality and independence they may be unsure about. This is an area that is likely to develop in the future and needs to be kept under surveillance. It underlines the need for there to be minimum standards adopted, preferably at the international level.

14.8 GROUP OR CLASS ACTIONS

Consumer complaints can either be viewed as isolated one-on-one disputes, or they can be considered as social problems calling for collective solutions. Clearly some consumer complaints affect only individuals, who have been unfortunate enough to buy a rogue product or have suffered poor service in a one-off situation. Frequently, however, consumers suffer collective grievances which affect all, or a large proportion, of the users of a certain product or service. Consumers may find particular difficulty in litigating such claims. The loss to the individual consumer may be so small that it is simply not viable for the consumer to litigate. Even if the loss is substantial, consumers may be deterred from going to court because the cost of litigating, and in particular the cost of losing, may be too high. The expense of producing the required scientific and technical evidence, in

---

[102] See Chapter 14.7.1.

[103] See, http://www.arbitrators.org/WebTrader/index.htm.

[104] See S. Kierkegaard, 'Online Alternative Dispute Resolution' in *EU Electronic CommerceLaw*, R. Nielsen, S. Jacobson and J. Trzaskowski (eds.) (Djøf, 2004).

product liability cases, for instance, can be enormous. Lawyers in the UK are now allowed to act on a 'no win, no fee' basis, but it is not clear whether this will assist consumers with non-personal injury claims. Moreover few claimants' lawyers are likely to be able to afford to fund complex litigation where the outcome is uncertain.[105] Even if claimants can afford to commence litigation, they may still be reluctant to do so, because of the rule in the UK that an unsuccessful claimant normally has to pay the defendant's costs and the insurance market to cover such costs liability is not well developed.[106]

One obvious potential solution is for a 'group or class' action to be brought on behalf of all affected consumers. This allows the consumers to have a better chance of access to resources with which to take on the defendants, who are frequently wealthy corporations. This type of collective approach is necessary for whilst it is unfair that traditional rules *de facto* bar consumers from taking legal action, equally the court system could not function if it had to adjudicate individually on all consumer claims. However, class action procedures do raise important issues about who has the right to act for the class and whether members of the class should be able to dissociate themselves from the action. Class actions may also call for novel remedies, if the individual members of the class cannot be identified or if individual damages are not appropriate. Also if one assumes that society has tailored its regulatory and liability rules with regard to their impact in terms of the present degree of enforcement, any increased enforcement may eventually require a re-evaluation of the impact of the substantive law of consumer protection.

Three ways of protecting the collective interests of consumers have been identified.[107] We shall call these:

(i) The *private initiative* model, where the case is brought by the individual consumers affected. This is what is traditionally thought of as a class or group action.

(ii) The *consumer organisation* model, where consumer organisations are given standing to represent consumers.

---

[105] See M. Mildred, 'Representing the Plaintiff in Drug Product Liability Cases' in *Product Liability, Insurance and the Pharmaceutical Industry*, G. Howells (ed.) (MUP, 1991).

[106] We have already noted that this does not usually apply where the claimant is legally aided or in the small claims court.

[107] See Th. Bourgoignie's Preface to his edited work *Group Actions and Consumer Protection* (Story Scienta, 1992). Here we are concerned with protection through some kind of court procedure: obviously it is possible to rely on stronger administrative regulation, but that is another debate taken up elsewhere: see Chapter 13.

(iii) The *public agency* model, where public bodies can act to protect the consumer interest.

Whilst we shall largely concentrate on the first of these models, readers should not underestimate the value of the other two, both of which have received detailed scrutiny in recent times and have been increasingly utilised. To some extent the choice of model depends upon the outcome to be achieved. Litigation led by individual consumers appears more appropriate where damages are sought, whereas organisation or agency involvement seems appropriate for claims for injunctive relief. Although one should not be too quick to restrict consumer organisations or public agencies to simply seeking injunctive relief; attention might be paid to whether actions by them should also lead to damage awards.

Class actions can have a considerable impact on the moulding of future behaviour, partly because of the large amounts of money at stake and partly because of the publicity that typically surrounds them. Class actions can also be a vehicle for promoting consumerism as part of a social action agenda.[108]

14.8.1 Private Initiative Model

A distinction could be (and has been in the literature) drawn between a group action involving a co-ordinated litigation strategy by a group of consumers with a common or similar grievance, but using traditional procedures, and class actions where consumers use a dedicated procedure for class litigation. In manner respects the English solution in the Civil Procedure Rules straddles both models. The Group Litigation Order (GLO) is a formal procedure, but simply provides the judge with extra flexibility to depart from standard procedures.

Certain perennial issues are always raised in debates surrounding class action as to the exact conditions under which they operate. At the heart of this lies a debate over the form of the procedural rules. Should there be a clearly set out procedure? This would have advantages in terms of certainty but also brings the drawbacks of reduced flexibility and satellite litigation around the entry requirements to access the procedure? This is typified by the US class action procedure. By contrast the GLO adopted by the UK's Civil Procedural Rules offers greater flexibility. It gives the judge more control to use it as a mechanism to improve case management, but equally engenders uncertainty as the parties have no firm rules to guide them as to how the judge will use the rules. Even more fundamental is perhaps the

---

[108] See I. Ramsay, 'Consumerism, Citizenship and Democratic Politics: Class and Group Actions' in Th. Bourgoignie (ed.), *op. cit.*

substantive debate as to whether the emphasis in class actions should be on the generic core aspects, with individual cases being settled in the wake of these common decisions or whether individual cases should be filtered before being added to the claim. Defendants fear that if the former approach is adopted they may be swamped by claims of dubious value that they will feel forced to settle. On the other hand claimants and their funders do not want to spend a lot of money screening cases if they are to fail on a matter of principle that could be determined at the outset.[109]

14.8.1.1 History

Although group/class actions are usually seen as a modern phenomenon, the history of the group/class action goes back to chancery procedures on the eve of the agricultural revolution when it was used as a means of establishing and modernising villager rights based on manorial or parochial relationships.[110] During the industrial revolution it was used to test the rights of parties in organisations which were not yet properly recognised in law, such as friendly societies and joint stock companies. It was only in the late twentieth century that the concept of group action was adopted by social activists fighting for the rights, *inter alia*, of tenants, the environment and, of course, consumers.

14.8.1.2 Overseas Experiences[111]

The US and Commonwealth inherited the English legal tradition, but have developed distinctive class action procedures. It is in the US that the class action has gained the most prominence – even noterity.[112] There are seven

---

[109] See Hodges, *op. cit.*, at 15–18.

[110] S. Yeazall, 'Group Litigation and Social Context: Towards a History of the Class Action.' (1977) 77 *Colum L Rev* 866.

[111] A good comparative survey is given in Scottish Law Commission, Discussion Paper 98, *Multi-Party Actions: Court Proceedings and Funding* (Scottish Law Commission, 1994). See also Hodges, *op cit.*, Chapters 13–15 and M. Mildred, 'Group Actions' in G. Howells, *The Law of Product Liability* (Butterworths, 2000) at pp. 379–395.

[112] For further reading see J. Fleming, *The American Tort Process* (Clarendon Press, 1988); Note, 'Developments in the Law: Class Actions' (1976) 89 *Harv L Rev* 1318; K. Dam, 'Class Actions: Efficiency, Compensation, Deterrence and Conflict of Interest' (1975) 4 *J Leg Stud* 47, P.H. Lindblom, 'Group Actions: A Study of the Anglo-American Class Action from a Swedish Perspective' in Th. Bourgoignie (ed.), *op. cit.*: L. Harbour, S. Croft and T. Sheehan, 'Class Actions: An American Perspective' in Hodges, *op. cit.*

pre-requisites which an action must satisfy before the courts will certificate it as suitable for the class action procedure:

(i)   there must be a class,
(ii)   the plaintiff must be a member of the class,
(iii) the number of members of the class must be numerous enough,
(iv)   there must be common questions of law or fact,
(v)   the claim must be representative of the group members' claims,
(vi)   the plaintiff and representative must be adequate to represent the class, and
(vii) the claim must fit into one of the three categories set out in Rule 23(b) of the Rules of the Federal Supreme Court.

These three categories are that:

(i)   separate actions would be likely to cause the defendant to face inconsistent standards or would as a practical matter dispose of the case with respect to other members of the class;
(ii)   the defendant has acted or refused to act on grounds generally applicable to the class which make injunctive or declaratory relief appropriate;
(iii) questions of law or fact common to members of the class *predominate* over any questions affecting only individual members and a class action is *superior* to other available methods for the fair and efficient adjudication of the controversy.

A great deal of litigation has taken place considering whether the common issues predominate and whether the class action is superior. By focusing on such technical points, defendants (who fear the potentially devastating impact of class actions, particularly in mass tort cases where punitive damages are claimed) have tried to fight a rearguard action against the advance of the class action.

In Australia, Victoria led the way by introducing class action procedures at the state level, though a Federal procedure has now been introduced.[113] In Canada, Ontario adopted a class action procedure in 1992.[114] The French law province of Quebec has known a class action procedure since 1979.[115] This is interesting for traditionally the class action has been viewed as a common law rather than a civil law mechanism. Admittedly this is changing. Class action procedures have

---

[113] See J. Kellam and S. Clark, 'Multi-Party Actions in Australia' in Hodges, *op. cit.*, Mildred (2000), *op cit.*, at pp. 389–395.
[114] I. Ramsay, 'Class Action: Class Proceedings Act 1992' (1993) 1 *Consum LJ* CS 39.
[115] N. L'Heureux, 'L'action Collective au Quebec' in Th. Bourgoignie (ed.), *op. cit.*

been introduced in Spain and Sweden.[116] In France the 'Commission de Refonte de Droit de la Consommation' proposed a class action procedure. Though not introduced, there has been established an 'action d'intérêt collectif' which is considered below under the consumer organisation model. Holland has recently established a representative action procedure but again it concerns the power of organisations to bring claims and there is no right to claim damages, but such cases can lay the basis for subsequent damage claims.[117] Class actions are also being discussed in a number of other European countries, but it remains at heart a common law phenomenon. The EC at one time showed an interest in class actions, but it is not currently at the heart of its agenda.

14.8.1.3 United Kingdom[118]

Until recently the English legal system knew of no specific class or group action procedure; although, of course, there have been many cases that can be described as class or group actions.[119] Instead, until recently, it muddled through in good common law fashion by using a test case strategy, perhaps combined with some sort of 'group action'.[120] This system worked well so long as the costs of the group/class action were borne either by a trade union or the legal aid fund. Whilst trade unions will continue to underwrite the costs of test cases, the tacit consensus over the use of the legal aid fund to finance group actions was smashed by the *Opren* case.[121]

---

[116] *Product Liability in the European Union* (Lovells, 2003), Appendix 4.

[117] See N. Frenk and E. Hondius, 'Collective Action in Consumer Affairs: Towards Law Reform in the Netherlands' [1991] *EConsum LJ* 17 and I. Giesen and M. Loos, 'Liability for Defective Projects and Services: The Netherlands' (2002) 6 *Electronic Journal of Comparative Law* available at http://www.ejcl.org/64-6.html.

[118] The following discussion draws on the paper by G. Howells 'Mass Tort Litigation in the English Legal System – Have the Lessons from Opren been Learned?' in *United Kingdom Law in the Mid-1990s* J. Bridge *et al.* (eds.) (UKNCCL, 1994).

[119] Hodges, *op. cit.*, Chapters 16–32 provides a number of case studies. Mildred (2000), *op cit.*, also provides a summary 398–409.

[120] But note that in *Horrocks v Ford Motor Company, The Times,* 15 February 1990, Lord Donaldson, the Master of the Rolls, said: 'Standard court procedures were designed for the determination of the general run of claims coming before the Courts. But, if the Courts were presented with large numbers of claims with special features in common they would devise new procedures specially adapted to such cases'. This represents a flexible attitude on the part of the judiciary towards group litigation. The major problem has been the financing of such litigation and the liability for costs.

[121] *Davies v Eli Lilley & Co* [1987] 1 WLR 1136.

Opren involved almost 1,500 plaintiffs who were suffering side-effects after having taken Opren, an anti-arthritis drug. Two-thirds were eligible for legal aid, which was granted to applicants who pass both a merits test and a means test judged against both income and capital. Of the 500 or so plaintiffs who failed to obtain legal aid, most failed on the capital means test as the majority of the victims were old people whose savings were above the permitted capital (£4,850). Prior to the *Opren* case, such plaintiffs had in effect been provided with a free ride on the back of legally aided plaintiffs, who were selected to be the test cases. Defendants had never seen fit to question this – perhaps fearing adverse publicity if they were seen to be intimidating hapless victims. In *Opren* the Government was joined as a defendant. The Treasury Solicitor, representing the Committee on Safety of Medicines and the Medicine Act Licensing Authority, was not shy of seeking guidance on the question of liability for costs. In the High Court, Mr Justice Hirst concluded that the 500 non-legally aided plaintiffs could not have a free ride on the back of the legal aid fund and that the costs should be borne equally by all plaintiffs. This decision was upheld by the Court of Appeal.[122] In the event the non-legally aided Opren victims were only able to continue with their claims because a millionaire benefactor, Mr Godfrey Bradman, underwrote their costs. The reason why the plaintiff lawyers were so keen to use legally aided plaintiffs for the test cases was because, if they lost, the normal rule that 'costs follow the event' did not apply. Making non-legally aided plaintiffs liable for a proportion of the costs was effectively pricing justice out of their reach. Even if they could have afforded to risk their money on a legal battle, this might not have been sensible given that the damages involved were relatively modest[123] and that, even if the case were won, costs could easily be incurred due to unsuccessful interlocutory or preliminary applications.

As a response to the *Opren* case the Supreme Court Procedure Committee issued a *Guide For Use in Group Actions* in May 1991 which sought to provide practical advice about how group actions could be brought under the then existing rules. As the law stood there were several forms of procedure a group action can rely on, which remain available today.

The Representative Action
The Rules of the Supreme Court provided a mechanism for a representative

---

[122]   *Ibid.*

[123]   It has been suggested that few of the claims were worth more than £10,000 with many worth only around £1,000, the reason for the low damage levels being the old age of many of the victims: see G. Dehn, 'Opren – Problems, Solutions, and More Problems' (1989) 12 *JCP* 397.

action to be brought 'where numerous persons have the same interest in any proceedings'.[124] There were, however, numerous hurdles to be overcome before this procedure can be invoked. For instance, there was some authority that claims for damages (or debt) could never involve parties with the same interest. Equally parties might not have the same interest if, in spite of some common ground, there were also peculiarities in the individual cases, for example defences or counterclaims not applicable to the class as a whole. The action also imposed the onerous procedural requirement that, in cases of doubt, the names of members of a class should be annexed to the writ. The tendency, however, was to be more generous in allowing the representative action. The consequences of a representative action could be quite draconian for Order 15, Rule 12(3) stated that the judgement or order is binding on all parties who are considered to have been present by representation, even if they had not been informed of the court action (although it can only be enforced against persons who were not party to the action by leave of the court). A defendant with a specific defence (or a plaintiff who did not want to be a party to the action) would have to apply to be excluded from the action under Order 15, Rule 12(1) 'by reason of facts and matters particular to his case'.[125]

Similar rules are now to be found in Civil Procedure Rule 19.6. These cover both situations where claims are begun as representative actions or are consolidated. This provision still talks about there being the need for the parties to have the same interest, but, instead of the requirement that there be numerous persons, it can be used whenever more than one person has the same interest. It still binds all parties represented, but can only be enforced against a person not party to the claim with the permission of the court.

The representative action is in the control of the representee. This means that the representee and not the represented parties is liable for costs. It also means that the representee has power to settle the case on such terms as he or she thinks fit. A party can apply to court for a direction that a person should not act as representative. If the parties cannot agree on who should be the representative then previously the court might determine that a representative action would not be possible. The new rules seem to read as if a representative has the right to act for one or more people. Anyone dissatisfied with that representation is presumably entitled to represent themselves or have a different representative if they are two or more.

---

124 RSC Order 15, Rule 12(1).
125 RSC Order 15, Rule 12 (5).

Joint Plaintiffs

The Court rules allowed one solicitor, who either represents a large number of plaintiffs or has powers delegated to him or her through a committee of instructed solicitors, to issue one writ covering all the actions.[126] It was estimated that serving one writ on behalf of 1001 plaintiffs instead of individual writs would save £70,000 in court fees for the writ alone and £10,000 for each interlocutory summons.[127] This is still possible under the Civil Procedure Rules.

Test Cases

The court also had power to select certain test cases or lead actions – a useful approach if all parties co-operate.[128] Once selected, plaintiffs in lead cases should pursue to judgment; equally, defendants should not seek to 'buy off' actions which have been selected as lead actions. This advice from the Supreme Court Procedure Committee reflected a serious problem with the test case strategy – defendants may try to settle the strongest cases in the hope of avoiding liability in weaker cases.

Multi-Party Action Arrangements

The Legal Aid Act 1988 allowed for the possibility of contracting out legal aid services. This was followed up in the context of 'multi-party actions' (actions with ten or more assisted persons) in personal injury cases by provisions being made for representation by means of contracts under procedures set out in the Legal Aid Board Multi-Party Action Arrangements 1992. The contracting out of legal aid services in multi-party actions was driven by two sets of considerations. First, experience shows that costs in such cases can soon escalate to the extent that they far exceed the sums being claimed; moreover, costs are often duplicated with different firms doing the same work. Second, there is concern over the quality of work in large-scale personal injury cases. Handling not only the legal aspects but also the public relations side of such litigation requires both expertise and also a large infrastructure which can only be found in a limited number of firms. There is an obvious danger that these rules, which are aimed at protecting the consumer, could instead end up benefiting the small circle of law firms which have been quick to develop experience in this type of work. To some extent this danger was recognised and explains why only the generic work was expected to be subject to the multi-party action arrangements, with clients being able to retain their own solicitors for matters such as assessment of damages. This also goes some way to strike a balance between the desire to allow clients their choice of

---

126   RSC Order 15, Rules 4, 5 and 6.
127   *Guide For Use in Group Actions*, at p. 18.
128   RSC Order 4, Rule 9(1).

representation and the need to ensure efficient and effective delivery of legal services. This basic model still influences current public funding arrangements for complex group actions.

Group Litigation Order
When Lord Woolf wrote the blueprint for the reform of English Civil procedure, *Access to Justice* he came out in favour of an extremely flexible approach to group actions, despite initially favouring a prescriptive approach. Instead of adopting a class action procedure with all the litigation surrounding certification, he proposed the concept of a multi-party situation giving flexibility to deal with cases 'which will or may require collective treatment to a greater or lesser degree'. In the end a formal mechanism was adopted, the Group Litigation Order (GLO), but it retains this flexible character.

The GLO is very flexible. CPR Rule 19.11 simply states such an order can be made when there are a number of claims giving rise to the GLO issues.[129] However, the judge must also obtain the consent of the Lord Chief Justice or Vice-Chancellor. Thus there are no minimum numbers required and it is possible to have a GLO for only certain aspects of the dispute. The GLO establishes a register that litigants have to sign up to (it might be questioned whether it is desirable to require all potential litigants to issue a claim). It must also specify what are the GLO issues and identify a management court to manage claims on the register. Further orders may be made to manage cases within the GLO, including publicising the GLO. Registering can be a voluntary matter, but equally the court has the power to require that all claims raising one or more of the GLO issues should be started in the management court and entered on the group register. Any judgment or order concerning a claim on the group register is binding on the parties to all the other claims, unless the court orders otherwise. Any party adversely affected can appeal an order or judgment, unless they joined the register after the order or judgment was made. There are a number of specific case management powers including providing for test cases and appointing solicitors for one of the parties to be lead solicitors. Rules are established for costs sharing, which allows the court to make parties liable proportionately for common costs without having to make individual orders.

The hallmark of the GLO is flexibility. In certain respects this is to be welcomed as very often these type of cases have unique features which require individualised treatment. The downside is that as the judge has a lot of discretion there will be a certain degree of uncertainty engendered as the parties will find it hard to predict how the judge handling the case will deal with it.

---

[129] See Mildred, (2000), *op. cit.* at 409–460.

More Radical Funding Reform?

Funding remains a problem for group actions. Public resources are stretched to try to assist with many such cases. Some more radical proposals to the funding problem have emerged. In 1982 the Scottish Consumer Council issued a report proposing a class action procedure for Scottish courts.[130] This suggested the establishment of an independently administered Class Action Fund to finance class actions. Successful litigants would be required to pay a percentage of any damages recovered to the Fund, so that, in time, it would be self-financing. Such a model has much to commend it, especially as its funds could be further enhanced by paying over to it the damages of any members of a class who cannot be traced. However, the need for an initial outlay of cash would seem to make this option politically unacceptable in the present climate.

Damages

Frequently it will be the case that in group actions damages should be assessed individually, even if liability is to be determined communally; in other cases a rough and ready apportionment of damages may be the only practicable course. In some instances damages may be more appropriately paid to collective organisations representing the interests of the victims than to individuals directly. Thus, in the *Agent Orange* case brought in the US courts by Vietnam veterans who claimed to have suffered injury as a result of a chemical defoliant used in the jungle war, a substantial proportion of the damages was paid to veterans' associations rather than to individuals.[131] Other cases may call for still more innovative remedies. For instance, in the *Yellow Cab*[132] case, when overcharging was proven in a class action, the company was ordered to reduce its costs until the damages suffered generally had been returned to the public. The car company Rover has agreed to pay the Consumers' Association £1M for breaches of competition law involving limiting the discounts available from dealers.[133] Since it would be impossible to trace the customers affected, it was thought best to provide money for the benefit of all British car buyers. Such innovation is to be commended.

---

[130]   Scottish Consumer Council, *Class Actions in the Scottish Court* (1982); this proposal has recently been placed back on the reform agenda by the Scottish Law Commission *op. cit.*

[131]   P. Schuck, *Agent Orange on Trial* (Harvard UP, 1987).

[132]   *Daar v Yellow Cab Co.*, 63 Cal Rptr 724 (Cal 1976).

[133]   See *The Independent*, 17 November 1993 at p. 2.

14.8.2 Consumer Organisation Model

The private initiative model essentially continues to see the complaint in terms of an aggregation of individual grievances, albeit having wider implications which justify modifying certain rules of procedure and remedies. Continued reliance on private initiative alone would mean that many consumer complaints would still not reach the courts, due to the remaining problems of funding litigation and/or a lack of motivation on the part of consumers to bring claims. Consumers may be uninterested in taking action if the damages are only minor; in some cases, there might also be difficulty in showing individual damage. One response is to allow consumer organisations to bring claims on behalf of consumers generally.[134] Usually this would be for injunctive relief. We have discussed this mechanism in Chapter 13, where the rights of consumer groups have been expanded under the influence of European law. It has also been the subject of a broader discussion in the Lord Chancellor's Department Consultation Paper *Representative Claims: Proposed New Procedures*.[135]

One might wish the court to be able to award damages to redress a wrong suffered by specific consumers. However, there is reluctance to go beyond injunctive relief, although the possibility was floated in the Consultation Paper on *Representative Claims*. The £1M payment by Rover to the Consumers' Association for breach of competition law illustrates the sort of order which could be possible even if individual losses cannot be traced.

The consumer organisation model is perhaps best developed in France where consumer organisations are allowed to bring actions representing the consumer interest where there has been a criminal infraction or an unfair contract term has been used. Furthermore, consumer organisations can participate in civil cases started by individuals and seek the cessation of illegal acts which damage the consumers' collective interest. There is also a class action procedure in France, which individuals cannot bring themselves, instead the action must be brought by a consumers' association.[136]

---

[134] There are of course important questions about the legitimacy of consumer groups representing the consumer interest. See G. Howells, 'Consumer Representation' (1993) 1 *Consum LJ* 17.

[135] (2001).

[136] See J. Calais-Auloy, 'Settlement of Disputes by Judicial Means: Situation in France' in *III European Conference on Consumer Access to Justice* (Instituto do Consumidor, 1992).

14.8.3 Public Agency

The Scandinavian consumer ombudsman model is perhaps the most developed public agency model. Although many countries have powerful public agencies to supervise consumer matters, notably the US which has a very powerful Federal Trade Commission and Food and Drug Administration. In the UK the most influential public agency for consumer affairs is the OFT.[137]

The powers of the OFT to intervene under the misleading advertisements regulations were scrutinised by the courts in *Director-General of Fair Trading v Tobyward*[138] where Hoffmann J, as he then was, endorsed the use of injunctive powers to support the self-regulatory controls on advertising.[139] Since then we have seen that the OFT's powers have broadened and strengthened, culminating in the powers found now in Part VIII of the Enterprise Act 2002.[140] It can also invoke its powers as a licensing authority for consumer credit.[141]

Public agencies are well placed to perform a policing role on behalf of consumers. Organisations such as the OFT build up a lot of experience of trading practices and are sufficiently aware of commercial reality to arrive at sensible judgements about what is reasonable business conduct.[142] The justification for public agencies taking on this role is self-evidently the inability of consumers to protect their diffuse interests. A distinction may perhaps be drawn between the desirability of public agencies seeking injunctive relief and litigating claims for damages. Questions may be raised as to whether litigation to help individual consumers obtain damages is a proper role for a public agency and the most effective way of using limited public resources. But this perhaps relates more to the question of how the powers should be exercised, not whether they should theoretically be available. Indeed in France the fact that civil damages can flow from a criminal prosecution means that consumer redress frequently obtains an indirect subsidy from public authorities. Our impression is that the power to award compensation under the Powers of Criminal Courts Sentencing Act 2000 is not used in a systematic way to award damages to consumers injured by breaches of the regulatory criminal law.

---

137 See Chapter 13.
138 [1989] 2 All ER 266.
139 See Chapter 8.6.2.
140 See Chapter 13.9.5.3.
141 See Chapter 9.2.
142 It should be noted that the business community is more concerned when such powers come into the hands of local trading standards officers, who they suspect lack consistency and feel can sometimes be too zealous.

14.9 THE EUROPEAN DIMENSION

14.9.1 The Nature of the Problem

The creation of a single market within Europe requires consumer law to take account of the European dimension of consumer problems. These problems are likely to increase as cross-border transactions become more frequent in the future as consumers become more mobile and by virtue of the internet.

There are several variants of cross-border problems which can affect consumers. UK consumers may be sold products and services in the United Kingdom by firms based in other Member States. These sales may be effected at a distance or be made through local retail outlets in the UK, which may, or may not, be branches of the foreign company. Traditionally the overseas firms have been manufacturers, but recently several foreign companies have entered the UK retail sector (e.g. Aldi, Ikea, Lidl, Netto). Foreign manufacturers may or may not have set up local branches or subsidiaries.

However, as business and tourist travel increases within the European Union, another dimension of the cross-border problem will increase in significance: namely, that of the consumer who purchases goods and services abroad. Consumers on holiday in Italy may well avail themselves of local services such as hairdressers and almost certainly will have to use hotels and restaurants. They may also want to take advantage of differential pricing within the Union to buy local bargains; for example, many Danish consumers buy televisions from Germany where they are a lot cheaper, while many UK consumers would be happy to pay the lower prices for cars enjoyed by consumers in many European countries. New technology and the increased use of distant selling mean that consumers can make purchases from overseas via the internet from the comfort of their own home. These cross-border transactions inevitably give rise to consumer complaints, which are even more difficult to resolve than domestic disputes.

14.9.2 Private International Law

There are several European Conventions and Regulations aimed at making litigating within Europe simpler and more effective. Although many of these have special provisions governing consumer transactions, frequently only certain types of consumer transactions are covered. More fundamentally the practical difficulties (language, travel etc.) and cost of cross-border litigation makes it impracticable for consumer complaints of relatively low monetary value to take advantage of traditional court procedures. It has been calculated that the average cost of suing across borders in the EU for a 2000 Euro claim is 2500 Euro and the proceedings will take between 12 and 64 months, depending on the country.[143]

Civil cross-border disputes give rise to two distinct sets of questions: the jurisdiction question of which courts should hear the case and the choice of law question of which laws should apply. Many lawyers fail to appreciate the distinction or wrongly assume that the applicable law is that of the state of the court hearing the case. In many cases this latter rule might be sensible, but will not always be the case. However, it is true that courts do tend to prefer to apply their own laws. In practice the costs escalate to such an extent whenever private international law is raised that it effectively prices most consumers out of justice and local lawyers may become fearful when faced with such complex issues. Certainly it is hard to imagine the economics of consumer litigation justifying running to trial many cases where foreign law has to be established in another state's courts.

14.9.2.1 Jurisdiction and Enforcement

Jurisdiction and enforcement used to be governed by the Brussels Convention on Jurisdiction and the Enforcement of Judgements in Civil and Commercial Matters 1968. The EC has since gained competencies to deal with matters concerning judicial co-operation in cross-border civil matters, including conflicts of law and jurisdiction. One of the first steps in fulfilling this mandate was to deal with jurisdiction and enforcement matters in Council Regulation 44/2001 on Jurisdiction and the Recognition and Enforcement of Judgments in Civil and Commercial Matters.[144] The rules of particular relevance to consumers allow actions to be taken:

(i) in matters relating to a contract, in the courts for the place of performance of the obligation in question.[145] It goes on to clarify that the place of performance of the obligation in the case of the sale of goods shall be where, under the contract, the goods were delivered or should have been delivered and for services the place where, under the contract, the services were provided or should have been provided.[146]

---

[143] Report by the European Consumer Law Group, *Jurisdiction and Applicable Law in Cross-Border Consumer Complaints – Socio-legal Remarks on an Ongoing Dilemma Concerning Effective Legal Protection for Consumer-Citizens in the European Union.*

[144] OJ [2000] L12/1.

[145] Regulation 5(1)(a).

[146] Regulation 5(1)(b).

(ii) in matters relating to tort, in the courts where the harmful event occurred or may occur.[147]

(iii) as regards claims for civil damages arising out of criminal acts the criminal courts will have jurisdiction to the extent that they can award civil damages.[148] This may be more relevant in countries such as France, where civil actions typically follow on from criminal prosecutions, but does mean the UK courts should be able to continue to make awards under the Powers of Criminal Courts Sentencing Act 2000.

(iv) as regards a dispute arising out of the operation of a branch, agency or other establishment, in the courts for the place in which the branch, agency or other establishment is situated.[149]

There is another set of provisions which are specifically consumer protectionist.[150] These permit a consumer to bring proceedings against the other party to a contract either in the courts of the Member State in which that party is domiciled or in the courts for the place where the consumer is domiciled.[151] Proceedings may be brought against a consumer by the other party to the contract only in the courts of the Member State in which the consumer is domiciled.[152] This applies if:

> (a) it is a contract for the sale of goods on instalment credit terms; or (b) it is a contract for a loan repayable by instalments, or for any other form of credit, made to finance the sale of goods; or (c) in all other cases, the contract has been concluded with a person who pursues commercial or professional activities in the Member State of the consumer's domicile or, by any means, directs such activities to that Member State or to several States including that Member State, and the contract falls within the scope of such activities.[153]

The last basis was the most controversial; in particular debate centred on the implications for contracts made by consumers on the internet. This provision seems rather consumer friendly seemingly favouring the state of destination, in contrast to the public law controls in the e-commerce

---

[147] Regulation 5(3).

[148] Regulation 5(4).

[149] Regulation 5(5).

[150] Section 4 (Regulations 15–17).

[151] Regulation 16(1).

[152] Regulation 16(2).

[153] Regulation 15(1). Transport contracts are excluded from this provision, other than contracts which for an inclusive price offer a combination of travel and accommodation.

directive, which favour country of origin controls. Previously the Brussels Convention had only included consumers generally where the contract had been preceded by a specific invitation addressed to them in their state of domicile and took in that state the steps necessary for the conclusion of the contract. The Convention approach is not easy to maintain in the internet context. It gave protection to the passive consumer who was sought out by the trader, but not the active consumer who found the trader in another country. Although apparently more consumer friendly the wording of the Regulation still needs to be interpreted to determine exactly which websites will be deemed to be directing their activities to a particular member state.

This issue has not unsurprisingly also been much debated in the US. One of the early leading cases was *Zippo Manufacturing. Company v Zippo Dot Com, Incorporated*[154] which tested jurisdiction on the basis of the degree of interactivity between the website and forum. On this basis passive websites which simply provided information would not be subject to jurisdiction. Integral websites where orders can be processed would be subject to jurisdiction. The middle category of interactive sites where contact could be made by toll-free numbers or e-mail depended upon the degree of interactivity and the commercial nature of the site. More recently courts have preferred also to invoke an effects based test, deriving from pre-internet cases, where the important question is whether the party intended there to be effects in the state seeking jurisdiction. It has been suggested that courts in the US will use a combination of the *Zippo* and effects test.[155] The effects test will no doubt vary depending upon the context. For instance, it may be relatively easy to show that defamation is intended to cause harm to someone in their state of domicile, even if posted on the world wide web. We shall be concerned to find out if the intended effect of the web page was that a contract will be entered into by consumers in that state. Does someone posting a web page in English direct activities to everyone in England simply because it was accessible from a computer in England? Can the activities be limited by disclaimers stating which countries' consumers the site is willing to contract with? What role does language or currency play in making this assessment?

The Hague Conference on Private International Law is also trying to draft a convention of jurisdiction and enforcement in civil and commercial matters. Issues surrounding the internet and consumer protection have again proven to be one of the most controversial issues.[156] One of the

---

[154] 952 F. Supp. 1119 (W.D. Pa. 1996).

[155] J. Gladstone, 'Determining Jurisdiction in Cyberspace: the "Zippo" test or the "Effects" test' *Informing Science* (2003) June 1.

[156] *Electronic Commerce and International Jurisdiction*, summary of discussions (Ottawa, 28 February-1 March 2000) by C. Kessedjian and *The Impact of the Internet*

issues raised there is the extent to which consumers could be allowed to make an informed choice to opt out of a regime that favours giving jurisdiction to the consumer's home state. This may not be very attractive in consumer protection terms, although if the choice was made to opt for ODR[157] then, subject to safeguards, there might be more support for it.

Yahoo! Inc., v La Ligue Contre Le Racisme Et L'Antisemitisme,[158] highlights some of the problems of asserting jurisdiction and also indicates that for all the sophisticated rules being developed within Europe to deal with internet problems there may still be the need for an international solution given the global nature of the internet. In this case a French court ordered Yahoo to filter out access to a site offering Nazi memorabilia. Despite the site only being accessible through the English Yahoo.com and not the French Yahoo.fr the French courts ordered that the site be filtered out for French users on pain on a substantial daily fine. The United States District Court of Northern California refused to recognise the judgment as it infringed US constitutional free speech requirements.

The consumer provisions in the Brussels Regulation can only be departed from by an agreement:

(i)   entered into after the dispute has arisen; or
(ii) which allows the consumer to bring proceedings in courts other than those indicated; or
(iii) entered into by the consumer and the other contacting, both of whom are domiciled or habitually resident in the same member state, and which confers jurisdiction on the courts of that state, provided that such an agreement is not contrary to the law of that state.[159]

There are also some rules which give exclusive jurisdiction to courts to a particular state. Of particular note is the rule that disputes about rights *in rem* in immovable property or tenancies of immovable property should be heard by the courts of the Member State in which the property is situated.[160] However, this did not prevent some victims of timeshare selling malpractices bringing a claim in the UK as they were relying on their action against the bank under s. 56 and 75 of the Consumer Credit Act 1974 rather than the property right.[161]

---

on the Judgments Project: Thoughts for the Future, by A Haines for the Permanent Bureau.

[157]   See Chapter 14.7.9.
[158]   169 F. Supp 2d 1181, (2001)
[159]   Regulation 17.
[160]   Regulation 22(1).
[161]   *Jarrett v Barclays Bank*, (1997) 3 WLR 654.

However, despite these provisions there may still be occasions when consumers are left to litigate in foreign legal systems – a daunting prospect for the average consumer![162] Regulation 33 requires that a judgment given in a Member State shall be recognised in the other Member States without any special procedure being required. There are certain exceptions to this, notably where it is irreconcilable with other judgments in cases between the parties in other states or where recognition would be against public policy. It has always been easier to set down the rules for recognition than to get courts to except them. Even the simplest legal action to enforce judgments adds an unwelcome layer of complication and cost in consumer disputes and underlines why such litigation will be rare in the consumer context.

14.9.2.2 Choice of Law

Contract
As well as the question of jurisdiction there is also the matter of which law applies. In contract, this matter is governed by the Rome Convention on the Law Applicable to Contractual Obligations 1980, which was implemented in the UK by the Contracts (Applicable Law) Act 1990. This convention sets out two basic principles. First, where the parties have made a choice of law, this will generally be respected (Art. 3(1)). Where no choice of law has been made, the contract will be governed by the country with which it is most closely connected (Art. 4(1)). Article 4(2) presumes that the contract is most closely connected:

> with the country where the party who is to effect the performance which is characteristic of the contract has, at the time of the conclusion of the contract, his habitual residence, or in the case of a body corporate or unincorporate, its central administration. However, if the contract is entered into in the course of that party's trade or profession, that country shall be the country in which the principal place of business is situated or, where under the terms of the contract the performance is to be effected through a place of business other than the principal place of business, the country in which that other place of business is situated.

As the characteristic of a consumer contract is the supply of goods and services then in most cases the governing law will be that of the supplier's country, unless the performance is effected through another place of

---

[162] Even despite efforts to make consumers better informed about courts in other states: Council Decision of 28 May 2001 establishing a European Judicial Network in civil and commercial matters, OJ 2001 L 174/00.

business, which may or may not be in the same jurisdiction as the consumer.

Article 5, however, gives some special protection to consumers, the problem being that this is limited to certain consumer contracts defined in a limited manner. The consumer contracts to which Art. 5 applies are 'contracts the object of which is the supply of goods or services to a person ('the consumer') for a purpose which can be regarded as being outside his trade or profession, or a contract for the provision of credit for that object' (Art. 5(1)). In addition one of the three conditions outlined in Art. 5(2) must be satisfied, namely:

(i) in the country of the consumer's habitual residence, the conclusion of the contract was preceded by a specific invitation or by advertising and the consumer had taken in that country all the steps necessary on his part for the conclusion of the contract (this parallels the exception provided under the Brussels Convention discussed above);

(ii) the other party or his agent received the consumer's order in the country where the consumer is habitually resident;

(iii) in the case of sale of goods contracts, the consumer travelled from the country of his habitual residence to another country and the consumer's journey was arranged by the seller for the purpose of inducing the consumer to buy (this will be more common on the continent, but could apply for instance to a trip specially arranged by a French retailer or vineyard for English consumers with the intention that they would buy wine in France).

For consumer contracts falling within this definition a choice of law clause in a consumer contract cannot deprive the consumer of 'mandatory rules'. These are defined as rules of law in the consumer's country which cannot be derogated from by contract (Art. 3(3)), such as the implied quality conditions in consumer sale of goods contracts. Also for this limited range of consumer contracts where there is no choice of law clause, the contract will be governed by the law of the country in which the consumer has his or her habitual residence.

The consumer protection rules can be viewed as not adequately protecting the mobile consumer. Especially when contrasted with the Brussels Regulation the position of the internet consumer seems less well protected. Also as the consumer choice of law rules only apply as regards mandatory provisions, this can give rise to a situation of different aspects of the contract being governed by different laws. These issues are now up for consideration as the Commission tries to enact applicable law Regulations under the Treaty powers in the same way as it enacted the Regulation on jurisdiction and enforcement. This debate has started with the *Green Paper on the Conversion of the Rome Convention 1980 on the law applicable to contractual obligations into a Community instrument and its modernisation.*[163] A preliminary draft has been circulated. This is known as Rome I.

Tort

There is no equivalent of the Rome Convention governing choice of law in tort law.[164] Although the Commission is envisaging a Rome II dealing with choice of law in non-contractual situations.[165] Instead each state has its own rules of private international law. In the UK the position used to be governed by the double actionability rule in *Phillips v Eyre.*[166] This required that the tort must be actionable both in the English legal system (*lex fori*) and in the foreign country in which it is alleged that the tort occurred (*lex loci delicti*). This rule was reformed by the Private International Law (Miscellaneous Provisions) Act 1995. As a general rule this makes the applicable law that of the country in which the events constituting the tort occurred, but this could be displaced where factors make the laws of another country substantially more appropriate. The EC has made a proposal for a Regulation of the European Parliament and the Council on the law applicable to non-contractual obligations (ROME II).[167]

14.9.3 Cross-Border Access to Justice for Consumers

In a Green Paper entitled *Access of Consumers to Justice and the Settlement of Consumer Disputes in the Single Market,*[168] the European Commission tried to encourage debate on consumers' access to justice. As early as 1975 the Council of Europe had recognised the right of consumers to proper redress by means of swift, effective and inexpensive procedures

---

[163] COM(2002) 654.

[164] There is the Hague Convention on the Law Applicable to Products Liability 1973, but this has only been signed or ratified by a small number of states, not including the United Kingdom.

[165] See, *Consultation on a Preliminary Draft Proposal for a Council Regulation on the Law Applicable to Non-Contractual Obligations* available at:
http://europa.eu.int/comm/justice_home/unit/civil/consultation/index_en.htm.

[166] (1870) LR 16 QB 1.

[167] COM(2003) 427.

[168] Com (93) 576: see discussion of the Green Paper in the special issue of the *Consumer Law Journal* devoted to Access to Justice in the light of the Green Paper (1995) 3 *Consum LJ* 1–39.

as one of five categories of fundamental rights.[169] The Green Paper saw access to justice as a way of ensuring that the rhetoric of a 'People's Europe' is made a reality for consumers. The Sutherland Committee on meeting the challenge of the internal market had also recommended that the effective protection of consumers' rights be given 'rapid consideration'.[170]

In fact the Community has made a determined attempt to improve the conditions for access to justice. This is no small task. We have already noted the Recommendations setting minimum standards for ADR bodies and conciliation services.[171] A complaints form has also been developed.[172] The form is available in all the official EC languages and the use of multiple choice questions clearly circumvents some of the language problem, although some text is still required. It was originally intended that this be used to help access to other member states courts, but this was abandoned. Instead it is useful in assisting negotiations and helping invoke ADR procedures. The Commission has set up two clearing houses for complaints to ADR bodies. These are the general European Extra-Judicial Network (EEJ-NET) and for financial services FIN-NET. Under these schemes national bodies will help consumers identify which ADR bodies in other states they can address their complaint to.

As the complaint form experience indicates it is harder to reform court systems. However, some steps have been taken. Council Decision of 28 May 2001 established a European Judicial Network in civil and commercial matters to facilitate co-operation between courts in different Member States and to inform the public.[173]

There is a directive establishing minimum access to legal aid for cross border disputes[174] and there is also proposal to promote ADR within court structures.[175] The Commission has flirted from time to time with notions such as introducing class action procedures, but these have not moved beyond the discussion stage.

---

[169] Council resolution of 14 April 1975 on a preliminary programme of the European Economic Community for a consumer protection and information policy: OJ 1975 C92/1.

[170] Recommendation No. 22.

[171] See Chapter 14.5.

[172] See S. Mitchell. 'Cross Border Disputes: To Sue or Not to Sue' (1999) *Consumer Policy Review* 97.

[173] Decision 2001/470/EC: OJ 2001 L174/25.

[174] Council Directive 2002/8/EC to improve access to justice in cross-border disputes by establishing minimum common rules relating to legal aid for such disputes: OJ 2003 L26/41.

[175] See, *Green Paper on alternative dispute resolution in civil and commercial law*, COM (2002) 196. A draft proposal is currently circulating.

It should also be remembered that the EC has introduced several measures to improve cross-border enforcement of laws. The Injunctions Directive is a prime example of this.[176] There is also a proposal for a Regulation on co-operation between national authorities responsible for the enforcement of consumer protection laws.[177] This would no doubt complement the work of the OECD International Marketing Supervision Network.

14.10 FINAL REMARKS ON ACCESS TO JUSTICE

Consumer rights are only as effective as their enforcement, be that through individual initiative as discussed in this chapter or by public authorities as discussed in Chapter 13. The greatest challenges are often in actually enforcing laws. Many less developed countries have wonderful laws on paper, but consumers have great difficulty in accessing them and governments do not have the resources to enforce them. Even in the UK enforcement is problematic. It is expensive to access lawyers or have effective enforcement regimes. Also businesses may well squeal if they feel the full force of the law being applied to them. An important shift in policy can, however, be detected as the significance of access to justice and effective enforcement has been appreciated and these issues have forced their way up the agenda. This should ideally not only mean that individual problems are resolved, but also business can use complaints positively to improve standards and law reformers can draw on them to inform debate about the future direction of the law.

14.11 SOME FINAL REMARKS TO THE READER

The reader who has stayed with us this far will know that consumer lawyers need a wide range of legal knowledge, covering, *inter alia*, competition law, common law, criminal law, administrative law, European law, soft law and procedural law. The list does not end there for they must also be conversant with economics, sociology and psychology. All these skills are needed because consumer problems are on the borderline of private/public and social/commercial problems. Consumer law forces one to consider the position of the individual in the complex modern world, a world which is becoming more complicated with the increased internationalisation of trade and the use of new technologies. The future offers great opportunities for consumers, but consumer law must ensure

---

[176]   See Chapter 13.9.5.3.
[177]   COM (2003) 443.

them the freedom to choose how to exploit these possibilities without danger to themselves, their fellow citizens or their environment. We hope the reader will feel better able to engage in these debates for having read or consulted this book.

Index